THE ENCYCLOPEDIA OF THE
ROMAN EMPIRE

THE ENCYCLOPEDIA OF THE ROMAN EMPIRE

GENERAL EDITOR:
CARLOS GÓMEZ

amber
BOOKS

Copyright © RBA Coleccionables, S.A.

English translation copyright © 2019 Amber Books Ltd.

Published by Amber Books Ltd
United House
North Road
London N7 9DP
United Kingdom
www.amberbooks.co.uk
Instagram: amberbooksltd
Facebook: www.facebook.com/amberbooks
Twitter: @amberbooks

All rights reserved. With the exception of quoting brief passages for the purpose of review no part of this publication may be reproduced without prior written permission from the publisher. The information in this book is true and complete to the best of our knowledge. All recommendations are made without any guarantee on the part of the author or publisher, who also disclaim any liability incurred in connection with the use of this data or specific details.

ISBN: 978-1-78274-761-1

Contributing Authors: Alison Howard, Claudia Martin and Alex Woolf
Project Editor: Sarah Uttridge
Design: Hart McLeod Ltd.

Printed in China

4 6 8 10 9 7 5 3

CONTENTS

PART I
THE ROMAN EMPIRE — 8

Introduction — 10

Octavian's rise to power — 14

Emperor Augustus — 32
Feature: Rome: The Capital of the Empire — *54*

Tiberius & Caligula — 62

A scholar on the throne — 86
Feature: The Legions of Rome — *102*

The monarchy of Nero — 110

Four Caesars in a single year — 128
Feature: Roman Villas and Imperial Palaces — *140*

THE ORIGINS OF ANCIENT GREECE

PART II
ROME DOMINATES THE WORLD   148

The Flavian dynasty   152
Feature: Pompeii: Precious Victim of Vesuvius   *174*

The reign of Domitian   182
Feature: Early Christianity   *200*

The 'good emperors'   204

The travelling emperor   222
Feature: Eastern Cults in Rome   *240*

The mature empire   244

The end of an era   262
Feature: 'Panem et circenses'   *278*

PART III
THE FALL OF ROME — 286

From the Severans to the Tetrarchy	290
Feature: The Nabataeans and the Palmyrenes	*312*
From Constantine to Theodosius	320
The fall of the empire	338
Society in the late empire	358
Feature: The Fayum Mummy Portraits	*372*
Philosophy and religion in the Late Empire	376
The Christianization of the empire	386
Feature: The Basilica, a model for Christian temples	*398*
The Germanic kingdoms	404

Appendices — 424

Index — 438

PART I

THE ROMAN EMPIRE

EMPEROR AUGUSTUS
A statue of Emperor Augustus in the Roman Theatre of Orange in Vaucluse, France.

INTRODUCTION

Ancient Rome grew from a small town on central Italy's Tiber River into an empire that at its peak encompassed most of continental Europe, Britain, much of western Asia, northern Africa and the Mediterranean islands. It is not just in the roads and ruins, however, that the empire's immense legacy can be found. We need only look at modern law, at philosophy, at how Latin words are still used in scientific classification, to see that the world today stands, in part, on the shoulders of Ancient Rome.

At its height, the Roman Empire had an estimated population of between 50 and 90 million people which was approximately 20 per cent of the global population of the time. And for 500 years, up until the early fifth century AD, the city of Rome was the largest in the world, superseded around 500 AD by the new capital in the Eastern Roman Empire – Constantinople.

From the rise of Octavian, who would become Rome's first emperor in the first century BC, to the fall of the Rome and the establishment of the Germanic Kingdoms, the book spans the 500-year history of the Roman Empire. But it is much more than just an account of emperors, dynasties and politics. It is also an exploration of the empire's art and architecture, literature, advances in medicine, sports and gladiatorial games, military might, mythology, society and everyday life. It is the story of religion, of paganism, of the persecution of Christianity before it finally became the empire's religion. It is the story of agriculture and trade, of the ancient Mediterranean and the peoples who lived on its shores – from Europe to Arabia to North Africa. It is the story of Pompeii, Petra and Palmyra.

And it is the story of how one of the world's largest empires can become so powerful, can dominate Europe, Asia Minor and North Africa, and yet still decline and fall.

THE ROMAN EMPIRE

Rome under the Julio-Claudian dynasty (first century)

OCTAVIAN'S RISE TO POWER

ACTIUM
This painting by Johann Georg Platzer (1704–1761) depicts the battle won by the man who was to become the first emperor of Rome, Octavian. It is housed in the Wellington Museum, London. On the next page we see the commemorative coffin of Actium (Accio) in which Octavian was carried in triumph across the waters (Kunsthistorisches Museum, Vienna).

OCTAVIAN'S RISE TO POWER

At just 20 years old, Octavian entered the political scene to avenge the murder of Julius Caesar. His ambition plunged the Roman people into five consecutive civil wars, which led to the deaths of thousands of knights and senators of the old republican oligarchy. He subjugated the people and the Senate, took the role of sole ruler of Rome, and introduced a new form of government: the Principate.

Gaius Octavio Cepia Turino, known first as Octavio, later as Octavian and later still by his Augustinian title Augustus, was the first leader of the Roman Empire. He was born on 23 September 63 BC into a Volscian family that originated from the Velitrae (Velletri) colony. It had been prophesied, according to Suetonius, that 'one day, a citizen of that city would take over the world'. His father, Gaius Octavio Turino, was a *homo novus*, the son of a freedman who had become a rope dealer in Turios, and the grandson of a wealthy banker whose fortune had come from the widely despised practice of usury. Family money funded Gaius Octavio Turino's entrance into Rome's political life, helping him build personal influence and patronage through his role in the magistrate's court, and ultimately paving his way to the governorship of Macedonia. He died shortly after bringing his family back to Rome in 59 BC when Octavian was almost four years old and

THE ROMAN EMPIRE

Milestones of Octavian's career

63 BC
On 23 September, Gaius Octavio was born to a *homo novus* from Turios and Atia, a niece of Julius Caesar.

44 BC
The young Octavian returns from the East to Italy and ratifies his testamentary adoption. He was renamed Gaius Julius Caesar Octavianus, *Divi lius*.

43 BC
Mark Antony is defeated in Modena (Mutina) by Octavian, who receives the title of consul. The second triumvirate is established.

42 BC
With an army of 200,000 soldiers, Mark Antony and Octavian gain victory over Brutus and Cassius in the Battle of Philippi.

31 BC
The Battle of Actium (Accio). Agrippa, Commander of Octavian's Navy, defeats the fleet of Mark Antony and Cleopatra.

27 BC
On 13 January, Octavian nominally restores the Republic, and the Senate gives him the honorary title of Augustus.

---

his sister Octavia was five. Their mother, Atia Balba Cesonia – niece of Julius Caesar and daughter of Senator Marcus Atius Balbus, a first cousin of Pompey the Great – decided to marry her brother-in-law, a widower.

Years later, following the precedent set by Alexander the Great, a myth to lend authority to the founder of the Principate was built around stories of omens and premonitory dreams that said Augustus was not the son of Gaius Octavio Turino at all; instead, the god Apollo was said to have taken the form of a serpent and fertilized Octavio's mother in his own temple. Before giving birth, said the storytellers, Atia had dreamt that her bowels were stretched to heaven and spread over all the Earth while her earthly husband had dreamt that sun rays issued from her womb; Cicero and Lutatius Catulus swore they had seen him in dreams descending from the sky to the Capitol, attached to a gold chain, or holding hands with Rome's chief deity, Jupiter. Anecdotes about Augustus's childhood were interpreted as predictions of his destiny. An eagle was said to have torn a piece of bread from the child Octavio's hands and then returned it to him; at the ceremony to mark his adulthood in 48 BC, his tunic had slipped from his shoulders and fallen at his feet. The future prince was said to have interpreted this as a sign of his monarchical power to come: 'I will be faithful to my senatorial duties,' he said.

The start of a public career

After his father's death, Octavian was sent to the house of his grandmother Julia, Caesar's sister; he lived with her until her death when he was 13 years old. Returning to his mother and stepfather's house, he was strictly educated in both Latin and Greek and in the skill essential to Roman political life: the art of oratory. This period shaped his love for words. Throughout his life, Augustus surrounded himself with the most brilliant minds of his time, including Maecenas, Horace and Virgil.

At the outbreak of the war between Caesar and Pompey in 49 BC, Octavian's mother decided to move her family to a house she had inherited in Velitrae, well away from Rome. She feared reprisals against any member of Julius Caesar's family and watched over her son obsessively. His excessive attachment to her, combined with his severe and moralistic education, formed the cold and rational character noted by observers of his rule.

Julius Caesar had no legitimate children. His only child, Caesarion, had been born of his adulterous relationship with Cleopatra and was not recognized by Roman law. Therefore, he focused on the public career of his great-nephew. In his role as Pontifex Maximus (chief high priest), he appointed Octavian a member of the pontifical school. This gave him the right to enter all the temples and sacred precincts of Rome and to participate in all its ceremonies. A year later, Octavian became a judge and was seen for the first time speaking publicly and dispensing justice in the Forum. According to Suetonius, there was much comment on

---

The altar of the domestic god Octavian

Upon becoming heir to Julius Caesar in 44 BC, Gaius Octavio Turino was renamed Gaius Julius Caesar Octavianus. He took advantage of the divinization of the father to proclaim himself *Divi lius* (son of the divine). In Roman society, the importance of family ties is reflected in the ancestral cult of the Lares, the domestic gods. In the tenth century BC, Augustus re-established the cult of the Lares Compitales. Each of the 265 *vici* (neighbourhoods) of Rome had its own altar, with the statuettes of the public Lares and the *Genius Augusti*, the spirit of the emperor, guarantor of the prosperity of the State. The vicomagistri (representatives of the neighbourhood for the cult) of the *vicus* Sandalarius, to which the image on the altar corresponds, directed the prayers to the Lares, according to Ovid, 'So that the house that guarantees that peace lasts forever' (Uffizi Gallery, Florence).

'his extraordinary beauty, full of charm' and his precocious competence in legal matters.

Marcus Vipsanius Agrippa arrives on the scene
Julius Caesar's regard for his great-nephew became even more evident when he invited Octavian to join him in his triumphal procession when he returned from his successful military campaign in Africa in 46 BC. Octavian judged this a good time to ask his great-uncle's forgiveness for his closest childhood friend, Marcus Vipsanius Agrippa; his brother had fought with Julius Caesar's opponents, led by Marcus Porcius Cato, known as Cato of Utica. The two young men became inseparable, sharing battles and military victories and political successes and failures. Their first military expedition, when both were 16, was to Hispania as Caesar launched his attack on the children of Pompey. In reality, it seems that they arrived in the western province seven months after the war was over: Octavian, often in poor health, had been detained in Rome to be cared for by the emperor's doctors. Even so, the two young men eventually joined Caesar's retinue as it passed through Carthago Nova (Cartagena) and Tarraco (Tarragona) and collaborated in the administrative reorganization of the entire province.

Shortly after their return to Rome, Octavian was appointed Chief of the Cavalry to command the Macedonian legions in the final planned infanticide, scheduled for 44 BC. Octavian set out with Agrippa and Gaius Cilnius Maecenas, also of royal descent, for Apollonia (near present-day Walloon, in Albania). The youths were accompanied by a tutor, Apollodorus of Pergamon.

Octavian's journey to the East
Apollonia was at that time one of the most flourishing centres of study in the eastern

THE ROMAN EMPIRE

Maecenas, mentor of the arts and collaborator of Octavian

Gaius Cilnio Maecenas, descendant of a royal lineage of Arretium (Arezzo), came into contact with Octavian during his trip to Apollonia. He accompanied Octavian in the campaigns of Modena, Philippi and Perugia, as Propertius attests in one of his elegies. Although his participation in Roman politics was important, Maecenas stood out for having placed the best poets of his time at the service of the imperial regime. Dio Cassius, in a fictitious discussion with Marcus Vipsanius Agrippa, presents Maecenas (whose portrait is identified with this bust, found in 1952 on Via Crispi in Rome) as an advocate of the establishment of a monarchical regime that relied on propaganda entrusted to artists in the service of the court. The poetry produced by Horace, Propertius and Virgil became an instrument for exalting the figure of the sovereign, linked to gods and heroes of the Greco-Roman mythical tradition, and for the dissemination of the ideological pillars of his government: peace, justice, piety and victory. Ovid, who had not lived through the turbulent years of the civil war, did not share the same admiration for Augustus expressed in the verses of contemporary poets, and celebrated the leader's power with flattering falsehood.

Mediterranean, as well as a city that favoured Caesar and had supported him during the civil war against Pompey. Caesar sent his great-nephew there to receive a prince's education; he planned to appoint Octavian as heir of his estate and political enterprises in due course. In Apollonia, Octavian was to be instructed in military tactics, in addition to perfecting his studies of Greek rhetoric and oratory under the guidance of Apollodorus of Pergamon, the founder of a rhetoric school, opposed at that time to the one founded by Theodorus of Gadara. Apollodorus of Pergamon's teachings were dominated by the precepts of Atticism in oratory speech. This emphasized simplicity and purity of style, in contrast to the bombast and sophistication of the Asian style that often characterized the speeches of Mark Antony, for example.

From the future heir of Caesar's brief stay in Apollonia, classic authors relate an anecdote that must be added to the list of prodigies and omens used in the propaganda of Roman leaders for the legitimation of the monarchical power of the first princeps. Agrippa and Octavian went one day to the observatory of the astrologer Theogenes so he could study their horoscopes. When he gave a consultation to Agrippa, the astrologer predicted 'extraordinary and almost incredible things'. Octavian, fearing a future inferior to Agrippa's, at first refused to give his date of birth. When at last he did, the astrologer observed the predictions, then prostrated himself at the young man's feet in adoration.

A few months after his arrival in Apollonia, Octavian received a letter from his mother informing him of his great-uncle's murder during the Ides of March and warning that Caesar's relatives were in danger in a city divided between the dictator's supporters and those who wanted a return to senatorial oligarchy. She feared for her son's life and urged him to return to Italy, without informing him that Caesar had adopted him and appointed him his legitimate heir in his will.

Octavian returns to Rome

Octavian discovered the contents of Caesar's will when he disembarked at Brundisium. From this date, his formal name was Caesar Octavian. He was also told that the conspirators were led by Marcus Junius Brutus and Gaius Cassius Longinus. An amnesty had been declared in the days after the assassination, but the crowd had been moved by Mark Antony's eulogy in the Forum during Caesar's funeral and had demanded revenge. Mark Antony, commissioned to act as administrator of Caesar's affairs, had ignored his will and appropriated money from both his personal estate and the State coffers. Mark Antony considered Caesar's chosen heir 'a young man inexperienced in politics'. Octavian's mother and stepfather tried to dissuade him from claiming an inheritance that would trigger the hatred, envy and criticism of many Romans. Octavian, however, decided to set out for Rome, gathering around him those veterans who remained faithful to the name of Caesar.

Dio Cassius recounts the young Octavian's entry to the capital, arriving as a private individual and without any pomp because he wanted to build popular support before seeking revenge for his great-uncle's murder. He promised the people a number of celebratory festivals that had already been announced shortly before Caesar's death for the inauguration of the Venus Genetrix temple in the newly built Forum. During one of these events, in July 44 BC, a comet was seen crossing the sky. Octavian declared that this was a divine sign that Caesar had ascended to Olympus in the form of a star.

The Battle of Modena

Julius Caesar had distributed the empire's provincial governments among his supporters. Decimus Junius Brutus Albinus, commander of the Roman fleet and an Ides of March conspirator, had been given the governorship of Gaul Cisalpina, while Mark Antony had been entrusted with Macedonia. Gaul was a richer province and closer to Italy, so Mark Antony tried to take it for himself. He took charge of the four Macedonian legions at Brundisium and declared war on the Senate, the assassins' leader Brutus, and Caesar's heir Octavian.

By now, Octavian had largely won the support of the people of Rome, who considered him a descendant of the divine Julius. He also had the backing of Campania's veteran troops, having secured their loyalty with generous payments, and the support of the Senate and Decimus Brutus. To pay for the war, the senators offered Octavian a levy for each tile in the roof of the houses they owned or rented in Rome.

The two armies met in the city of Mutina (Modena) in July 43 BC as Mark Antony marched towards Gaul. Dio Cassius's account of Octavian's first military victory records that the Battle of Modena '… had the same result for all: the destruction of democracy and the

TEMPLE OF VENUS GENETRIX

Julius Caesar had this temple built in the Forum of Caesar in 46 BC and dedicated it to the goddess Venus, who was portrayed as a direct ancestress (genetrix) of the Julian family, the mother of the Trojan hero Aeneas and grandmother of Julius. The temple, made of marble, had eight columns on the façade and, inside, a cult statue of Venus next to those of Julius Caesar and Cleopatra. It was rebuilt during Domitian's reign; the remaining three columns belong to that time.

THE ROMAN EMPIRE

The three generals: Octavian, Mark Antony and Lepidus

On 11 November 43 BC, Octavian, Mark Antony and Lepidus met on an island formed on the River Reno, near Bononia (Bologna), to establish a mutual collaboration commitment that would allow them to fight their enemies and submit the Roman Empire under their command. The *Lex Titia* ratified the agreement of the three generals (*trium virum*) on 27 November. The anonymous author of this engraving, entitled *The Triumvirate of the Island in Reno* (1842), depicts the scene of that meeting, described by Dio Cassius and Plutarch. For three days, the triumvirates discussed how to share authority. They determined which of their enemies would be eliminated, each trying to save their loved ones and 'exchanging deaths for deaths', according to Plutarch. Octavian left the murder of Cicero to Mark Antony; Mark Antony entrusted Octavian with the death of his uncle, Lucius Julius Caesar, and Lepidus agreed to kill his own brother, Aemilius Paullus. The agreement to establish the three as responsible for the reordering of the State for five years and to divide the territories of the empire was settled with an oath and with the promise of Octavian to marry Claudia, daughter of Fulvia, the wife of Mark Antony. This friendship pact cost the lives of 300 citizens.

creation of tyranny [...]. On both sides the State reached its ruin and each of the opposing groups acquired a diverse fame because of their diverse fortune. Some were considered lovers of the country, because they won. The others were cursed and called enemies of the fatherland, because they were defeated.'

Among the multitude of citizens who lost their lives in that confrontation were the two consuls of that year, Aulus Hircio and Gaius Vibius Pansa.

The Second Triumvirate

When news of Octavian's victory reached Rome, 60 days of festivities were decreed in gratitude to the gods. However, the measures taken in favour of Octavian's enemies did not meet the wishes of the Senate and the Roman people: Sextus Pompey obtained the command of the fleet; Marcus Junius Brutus, the governorship of Macedonia, and Gaius Cassius Longinus, that of Syria. Mark Antony and his supporters were declared public enemies and all their assets confiscated.

However, the situation remained uncertain and the Senate attempted to create conflict among Octavian's soldiers in order to deprive him of military support. In response, he marched on Rome to demand his appointment as consul. The Senate objected that he was not legally old enough – he was still not yet 20 years old. At this, one of his soldiers raised a sword and shouted: 'If you do not give the consulate to Octavian, you will get this sword!' Cicero replied: 'If you ask, you will have it.'

With his appointment as consul secure, Octavian decided to break the Senate's alliance with Decimus Brutus and make a secret pact with Mark Antony. He distributed money from the public treasury to soldiers and Romans to curry favour and did as he liked with the city's affairs. He also obtained the senators' permission to recruit militias and secured more power than any other consul.

Now Octavian prepared to avenge Julius Caesar. He proposed legal sanctions against anyone who could be considered a conspirator, even if they were not in Rome when Caesar was

assassinated. Then he set out for Greece, where Brutus and Cassius had taken refuge. On the way, he met Mark Antony and Marcus Aemilius Lepidus. The three made a collaboration pact, formally concluded on an island near the city of Bononia (Bologna) in November 43 BC. The *Lex Titia* pact obliged them to 'reorganize the Republic' without the need to explain their actions to the people or the Senate. To counter accusations that they were seeking absolute power, they divided provincial control between them: Octavian took Cyrenaica, Egypt, Sardinia and Sicily; Lepidus took Hispania and Gallia Narbonensis; and Mark Antony took Gaul Cisalpina and Gaul Comata. The *Lex Titia* was approved on 27 November and granted the three men consular authority for five years.

Revenge against the Caesaricides
Before the persecution of Caesar's assassins began, the triumvirate began a bloody campaign to fund their war. As soon as they returned to Rome, the city began to fill with corpses. Bodies were abandoned like dead animals and the heads of the murdered were displayed on pikes on the Rostra (platform) of the Forum. The assassins' estates were confiscated and informers were rewarded with honorary posts or exemption from military service for their children and grandchildren. Citizens responded to this violence with more violence, avenging private grievances. Political opponents of the triumvirate, the rich and anyone who attempted to save one of the condemned were targeted. To make it clear that no opposition would be tolerated, a decree was passed that ordered all Roman citizens, on pain of death, to be happy.

Having stockpiled money to fund their war, Octavian and Mark Antony set out for Greece with their armies while Lepidus remained in Rome to direct the affairs of the city. Gaius Norbanus Flaccus and Lucius Decidius Saxa, besieged near Philippi in the mountains of Pangeo by Cassius and Brutus, far superior to them in military strength, had begged for urgent help.

Octavian fought first in Calabria against Sextus Pompey, who was attacking Italy from Sicily. Realizing that Pompey could not quickly be defeated, he decided to join Mark Antony in

THE FORUM OF AUGUSTUS
Built by Octavian himself on his own land when he was emperor, construction of the Forum began around 20 BC and ended almost four decades later. The temple that presided over the Forum (see picture) was vowed by Octavian to honour Mars Ultor (Mars the Avenger) after his victory at Philippi. Generals set off for battle from this temple; young men received the toga virilis *here, and trophies and weapons stolen from the enemy were kept here.*

THE ROMAN EMPIRE

Philippi: the end of Caesar's assassins

In October 42 BC, Mark Antony and Octavian engaged in two decisive battles against Caesar's assassins, Marcus Junius Brutus and Gaius Cassius Longinus, on a plain west of the city of Philippi, in eastern Macedonia, along the Aegean Coast. The Caesarians were supported by 130 ships, commanded by Gnaeus Domitius Ahenobarbus. Cassius had recruited the two legions of Quintus Caecilius Bassus, who had been besieged for three years in Apamea, the six legions besieging them, and four more that were being driven from Egypt to Laodicea. In turn, Brutus (below, in a portrait at the National Roman Museum in the Palazzo Massimo, Rome) had eight legions, two of them from Macedonia. According to Appian, the army of Brutus and Cassius comprised 80,000 infantry and 17,000 knights. The two triumvirs had 19 legions, with an adjusted number of troops. Shown right, a tapestry at the Almudaina Palace in Palma de Mallorca portrays the Battle of Philippi.

Greece and leave part of his army on the peninsula. When he and Mark Antony engaged Cassius and Brutus's armies in battle, both sides' forces were evenly matched. However, Cassius was deprived of his camp and, afraid that Brutus had been defeated, he committed suicide. Brutus was then defeated in a second encounter. Abandoned by many of his soldiers, he too took his own life. Suetonius records that Octavian sent Brutus's head to Rome to be placed at the foot of Caesar's statue but that the ship carrying it sank in a storm in the Adriatic Sea.

Julius Caesar was declared divine, and a temple was erected on the site of his cremation in the Roman Forum. The place where he had been murdered was turned into a public latrine and replaced with a new Curia Julia (Senate House) next to the Comitium (meeting space). Rome's citizens were ordered to celebrate Caesar's birthday each year on 13 July, and the day of his assassination was declared sacred.

A strategic marriage

After the victory of Philippi, the 200,000 soldiers recruited to avenge Caesar's death had to be decommissioned. Octavian began to seize property from landowners, especially in the north, and hand it to his veterans. Only a few, including the poet Virgil, who had powerful friends in Assinuis Pollo and Gaius Cornelius Gallus, managed to keep their lands. The dispossessed, led by Lucius Antonius and Fulvia Flacca Bambula, brother and wife of Mark Antony, fled to the battle of Perusia (Perugia), where Agrippa and Octavian's loyal troops defeated the rebels in February 40 BC. Three hundred rebels were burned to death on an altar erected in honour of the divine Julius Caesar on the fourth anniversary of his murder.

OCTAVIAN'S RISE TO POWER

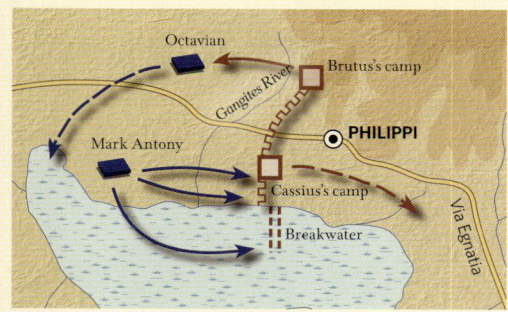

1 **Attack.** On 3 October 42 BC, Mark Antony attacks Cassius's fortifications.

2 **Assault.** The troops of Brutus, led by Messalla Corvino, attack Octavian, who flees.

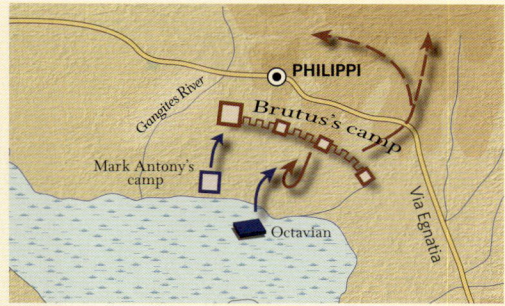

3 **Advance.** Mark Antony heads south, near the old camp of Cassius.

4 **Final combat.** On 23 October, Brutus is forced to attack. The soldiers flee.

Fulvia was then sent to her husband, who had remained in the East after the battle of Philippi and who was conducting an affair with Egypt's Queen Cleopatra. Mark Antony's mother took refuge with Sextus Pompey in Sicily. He had conquered the island in 42 BC with his huge fleet and was posing a serious threat to Rome's supply of grain. Octavian, who feared a military alliance between Mark Antony and Sextus Pompey, requested the hand in marriage of Scribonia, daughter of Cornelius Sulla and Lucius Scribonius Libo. She was the granddaughter of Pompey the Great and sister of Sextus Pompey. This matrimonial alliance between the Julians and that of Pompey and the Scribonians secured an armistice with Pompey, even though he was openly against their plans for government.

Octavian also had to strengthen relations with Mark Antony, badly damaged after the Battle of Perusia. As Mark Antony passed through Italy, the triumvirs signed a new pact in Brundisium in October 40 BC. Octavian was left in charge of the western provinces; Mark Antony took the eastern territories and Lepidus took the government of the African provinces. This agreement was sealed with the marriage of Mark Antony to Octavia, Octavian's sister. At that time, Octavia was 29 years old and had just been widowed after the death of her first husband, Gaius Claudius Marcellus, consul in 50 BC and opponent of Julius Caesar. At the time of her husband's death, Octavia was pregnant with Claudia Marcella the Younger, so the Senate had to give permission for her to marry. The three children she had with Claudius Marcellus joined the two of Mark Antony and Fulvia (Marcus Antonius Antyllus and Iullus Antonius) and the two Antonias who were born shortly after.

The poet Virgil and the divine origin of the Julian family

Publius Virgil Maron, represented between two Muses in this mosaic found in Hadrumetum (Bardo Museum, Tunisia), was born in 70 BC near Mantua. He was included in the literary circle of Maecenas after writing the ten eclogues that made up his first book, the *Bucolics*.

In the first one, a pastor named Meliboeus laments his sad situation, common to that of the numerous Italian peasants who had been banished from their lands as a result of the expropriations that Octavian carried out to settle his veteran legions. In contrast, Tityrus, the interlocuting pastor of Meliboeus in Eclogue I, lives in a privileged position, similar to how Virgil must have lived, thanks to the intervention of Gaius Asinius Pollio. Perhaps in gratitude for the favour granted, the poet wrote Eclogue IV, in which the Cumaean Sybil announces the beginning of a golden age, precisely during Pollio's consulate (40 BC), with the arrival of a saviour who would redeem the world from its miseries. With his second work, the *Georgics*, dedicated to Maecenas, Virgil celebrated the establishment of peace by Augustus and exalted a life dedicated to agricultural work in the fertile Italian soil. The teachings of the didactic poem emanated from the recent manual for farmers written by Varro, *De Re Rustica*. Virgil's masterpiece was the *Aeneid*, the epic poem that told of the weapons and the hero of Troy ('I sing of arms and the man who first from the shores of Troy ...'), Aeneas, making him the legendary ancestor of the Julian family and the symbol of filial piety, the main motto of Augustan propaganda.

Livia and the Claudian clan

In 39 BC, a general amnesty was declared to allow the return of all those who had fled from Rome because they were related to outlaws accused of conspiracy to assassinate Caesar. Among the returning republican nobility was the family of Tiberius Claudius Nero, who had supported the landowners' rebellion against Octavian and had sought refuge in Sicily with Sextus Pompey. With them came Tiberius's wife, Livia Drusilla, whom Paterculus described as 'the most beautiful woman in birth, virtue and beauty'.

The amnesty gave Octavian the opportunity to establish new relationships with the old nobility, whose support he needed in order to eliminate Mark Antony from the political scene. During a public banquet to mark his 24th birthday, Octavian met Livia Drusilla. Tacitus recorded that passion sparked Octavian's interest in her, but the alliance also had political potential: Livia was descended from two of the most illustrious lineages of republican Rome, those of Publius Claudius Pulcher and Marcus Livius Drusus. Octavian requested Livia Drusilla's hand in marriage. Tiberius Claudius, keenly aware that this alliance could protect him from his former enemy, accepted. Octavian rejected his wife Scribonia on the day she gave birth to his only daughter, Julia, and married Livia in January 38 BC. Livia gave birth to her son, Nero Claudius Drusus, just 12 weeks later. Romans joked that 'the lucky children are born in three months' rather than taking the usual nine to arrive.

Despite the marital break with her first husband, Livia remained faithful to the Claudian family for the rest of her life and pursued the main objective of making their son, Tiberius, Augustus's heir. To achieve this, she pursued a murderous campaign against the Julian family, disposing of Marcellus, the son of Octavia, and then Gaius and Lucius, the children of Octavian's daughter Julia.

The defeat of Sextus Pompey

Octavian's denial of his marriage to Scribonia ended his truce with Sextus Pompey that had

LIVIA DRUSILLA
In this beautiful cameo from the third century, Livia holds a bust of her husband Augustus with her right hand and in her left a sheaf of wheat ears, symbolizing the abundance of the earth and the goddess Ceres, with whom she liked to identify herself. The difference in size between the characters seems designed to highlight the importance of the future empress and underline her new affiliation after the death of her husband, who adopted her in his will. Livia and Augustus were married for 52 years. Although they had no children, she always enjoyed the respect of her husband and the privileged position of adviser to the emperor (Kunsthistorisches Museum, Vienna).

been signed in Misenum in 39 BC. Sextus Pompey had seized Sicily when the Senate had entrusted him with the State's coastal defence and had then infested the neighbouring waters with pirates who intercepted grain supplies arriving from Africa. His powerful legions and fleet made up of slaves, fugitives and outlaws were able to repel triumvirate attacks in the Strait of Messina. Octavian gave Agrippa, newly returned from victories in Gaul, the job of creating a new fleet trained for naval combat. Agrippa's ambitious two-year plan involved the creation of a new port where the entire Octavian fleet could be assembled and repaired. Two inland lakes, Avernus and Lucrinus, between Misenum (Miseno) and Puteoli (Pozzuoli) near Cumas in Campania, were chosen. The engineer Lucius Cocceius Auctus excavated an artificial channel of about 350m (1150ft) across the tongue of land between the two lakes to join them, and created an artificial outlet to the sea. The new harbour, named Portus Julius, connected Lake Avernus with the old port of Cumas. Agrippa gathered more than 40,000 freed slaves and trained them to become warship oarsmen during the winter of 36 BC.

The next spring, the new fleet, equipped with large ships laden with assault towers and trained soldiers, set out for Sicily, but at Cape Palinuro, south of Paestum, many of the ships were badly damaged in a storm. The fleet was repaired and regrouped and, later that year, Agrippa managed to defeat Sextus Pompey in two naval battles: one near Mylae (Milas) and the other in Naulochus on 3 September 36 BC. Appian of Alexandria describes how, during the battle of Naulochus, the sea was full of ships, the nearby coast teemed with armed men and the outcome was uncertain for a long time. When victory finally fell to Agrippa's fleet, the enemy ships sought refuge in Messina but only 17 managed to escape; 28 of Sextus Pompey's ships were sunk and the rest were burned or captured.

THE ROMAN EMPIRE

Euergetism as political propaganda in Roman society

Octavian set in place a system known as 'euergetism', used in the Hellenistic kingdoms to finance the construction of public works. Euergetism consisted of apparently disinterested donations of private capital for investment beneficial to the people. In exchange for delivering money, the benefactor obtained public prestige and the possibility of climbing the social ladder or of winning rulers' favour. A good part of the sums that a citizen gave to the State treasury to seek magistrate positions (*summae honorariae*) were invested in the construction of public works, on which the name of the benefactor that had paid for them was engraved. But even if the funds for the erection of a building were private, the design process for the manufacture of the construction had to adapt to the ideological programme of imperial policy and contribute to the official propaganda of the ruling family. Octavian and his most faithful collaborators, such as Marcus Vipsanius Agrippa (whose bust, below, is preserved in the Louvre Museum, Paris), were the first to put this system into practice. They paid for aqueducts, libraries, temples, basilicas and public buildings such as the theatre dedicated to Octavia's son, Marcellus (shown right). This was used for the first time in 17 BC for the celebration of secular games. In front of this rose the new temple of Apollo, whose restoration was carried out by Gaius Sosius.

Alexandria or Rome

Defeated, Sextus Pompey fled to Greece and then to the East, where he was captured and executed on the orders of Mark Antony. Meanwhile, Lepidus, the weakest of the triumvirs, tried to seize the island of Sicily for himself. Octavian accused him of treason and stripped him of all his titles and positions except for that of Pontifex Maximus, which he was allowed to keep until his death in 12 BC. Mark Antony and Octavian now held the monopoly of State power, the functions of State divided between then in an apparent alliance. But each hoped to wrest power from his adversary.

As the war against Sextus Pompey progressed, Mark Antony had attempted to conquer the eastern lands of the Parthians, a venture long planned by Julius Caesar. Although Mark Antony could claim some remarkable victories, largely thanks to the expertise of generals such as Publius Ventidius and Gaius Sosius, expeditions to these eastern territories proved expensive and were largely financed by Queen Cleopatra, with whom Mark Antony by now had three children.

Mark Antony's supporters in Rome attempted to conceal his military failures in the East, but he attracted more criticism for his relationship with his mistress. It was said that his three children with Cleopatra, twins Alexander Helios and Cleopatra Selene and their younger brother Ptolemy Philadelphus, had been honoured with lands conquered by the Romans, such as Arabia, Syria, Palestine, Crete, Cyrene and Cyprus. It was also said that he had rejected his wife Octavia when she arrived in Egypt at the head of two legions that Octavian had sent to help him in the war against the Parthians. There was also word that he had humiliated the king of Armenia and his

family, parading them triumphantly as spoils of war through the streets of Alexandria.

Meanwhile, the people of Rome had seen their city transformed by the private investments of Agrippa and Octavian. Octavian built the Portico and the Library of Octavia and resumed construction of the neighbouring theatre, later dedicated to Marcellus. Agrippa, at his own expense, repaired all of Rome's public buildings and streets, cleaned and sanitized the sewers, repaired the Aqua Marcia, the city's primary aqueduct, and offered free baths for men and women throughout the year. He also donated money, clothes and food to people during theatrical performances.

Mark Antony's will

These acts of public generosity, with the clear intent of self-promotion, did not take long to bear fruit. In the smear campaign undertaken by Octavian against Mark Antony and Cleopatra, he was careful to present himself as the foremost benefactor of the people, while offering an image of Mark Antony squandering his fortune on ostentatious festivals at the Alexandrian court, and being acclaimed there as a new Dionysus-Osiris.

To discredit his adversary, Octavian made known Mark Antony's secret plans to the Senate and the popular assembly. With help from the politicians Marcus Titius and Munatius Plancus, he had illegally obtained a copy of Mark Antony's will. He attended a senate session, where he was surrounded by soldiers and allies armed with daggers to defend themselves following accusations against him by the two consuls of 32 BC, Ahenobarbus and Sosius. He announced the presentation of documents that implicated Mark Antony, and a date for the will's reading was fixed.

THE ROMAN EMPIRE

MARK ANTONY AND CLEOPATRA: HISTORY AND MYTH

Cleopatra, hailed as 'queen of kings' by Mark Antony, has since antiquity been synonymous with seduction. But the proverbial beauty and charms of the lavish Hellenistic court, which seduced Julius Caesar, captivated Mark Antony and tried to subdue Octavian, were used as a weapon of power to recover the inherited throne of Cleopatra's father, Pharaoh Ptolemy XII Auletes, usurped by his brother Ptolemy with the help of his Pothorian adviser, and remain as the queen of Egypt against the conquering pressure of Rome. Mark Antony installed himself in Alexandria with Cleopatra as an Oriental king and identified himself with Dionysus, a god fond of wine, parties and women. He was defamed in Rome as the ultimate example of immorality.

CLEOPATRA
Here the legendary queen is portrayed by the British sculptor Henry Weekes (1807–1877).

A HISTORY OF PASSION

41 BC
Mark Antony requests the help of Cleopatra and summons the queen to Tarsus, Turkey. Cleopatra, dressed as the goddess Aphrodite, arrives via the River Cydnus aboard a ship decorated with purple sails, a golden stern and silver oars. Antony succumbs to her charms.

40 BC
Mark Antony returns to Italy and establishes with Octavian the Pact of Brundisium (Brindisi), which is sanctioned with the marriage of Mark Antony and Octavia. Meanwhile, his first two children with Cleopatra, the twins Alexander Helios and Cleopatra Selene, are born in Alexandria.

OCTAVIAN'S RISE TO POWER

MARK ANTONY

Mark Antony, whose bust is shown above (Capitoline Museums, Rome), tried to increase his power through marriage. After a brief relationship with Fadia, he married his cousin, Antonia Hybrid, who gave the couple an alliance with the senatorial class. She also bore him a daughter. Being the lover of the actress Citeride, he denounced his wife for adultery with Publius Cornelius Dolabella in order to inherit most of her enormous dowry. Cicero says that, before the divorce, he had begun an affair with Fulvia, who was still married to Publius Claudius Pulcher. When he met Cleopatra in Tarsus (here depicted in Lawrence Alma-Tadema's painting), he was captivated by her beauty and the possibility of creating with her an oriental kingdom more powerful than Rome.

EGYPT CAPTURED
'Egypt captured' is the inscription on this Roman *aureus* (gold coin), minted in 30 BC to commemorate the victory at Actium.

37 BC
Mark Antony denies his wife Octavia, who had been sent by her brother, Octavian, along with two legions of support, and marries Cleopatra in Antioch. Soon after, his third child with the Egyptian queen, a son, Ptolemy Philadelphus, is born.

34 BC
In Alexandria's gymnasium, on a golden throne, Mark Antony proclaims Cleopatra 'Queen of Kings', and appoints her son, Caesarion, sovereign of Egypt, Cyprus and Celesiria. He distributes among his three children the kingdoms of Armenia, Parthia, Cyrene, Phoenicia, Syria and Cilicia.

31 BC
Mark Antony and Cleopatra are defeated by Octavian in the naval battle of Actium, but manage to flee to Alexandria, where they create the society of 'those who must die together' (*Synapothanoumenes*).

30 BC
Octavian besieges Alexandria. Cleopatra pretends to commit suicide and locks herself in her mausoleum to make Mark Antony believe she has died. He, upon finding out the truth, kills himself. After failing to seduce Octavian, Cleopatra commits suicide by being bitten by an asp.

THE ROMAN EMPIRE

Actium: the key to the Roman domain

The last confrontation between Octavian and Mark Antony culminated in a naval battle on 2 September 31 BC on the coast of the Gulf of Ambracia. Virgil, in the *Aeneid*, turned the Battle of Actium into a struggle between Roman and Egyptian divinities: 'Gods of all traces and terrifying appearance and the "Barker" Anubis wield their spears against Neptune and Venus and the same Minerva'. The fleet of Mark Antony (depicted here in a bust preserved in the Vatican Museum, Rome) and Cleopatra principally comprised *quinquerremes*, large boats requiring 270 rowers; they were too heavy to move quickly, so the fleet was defeated by Gaius Vibius Pansa's boats.

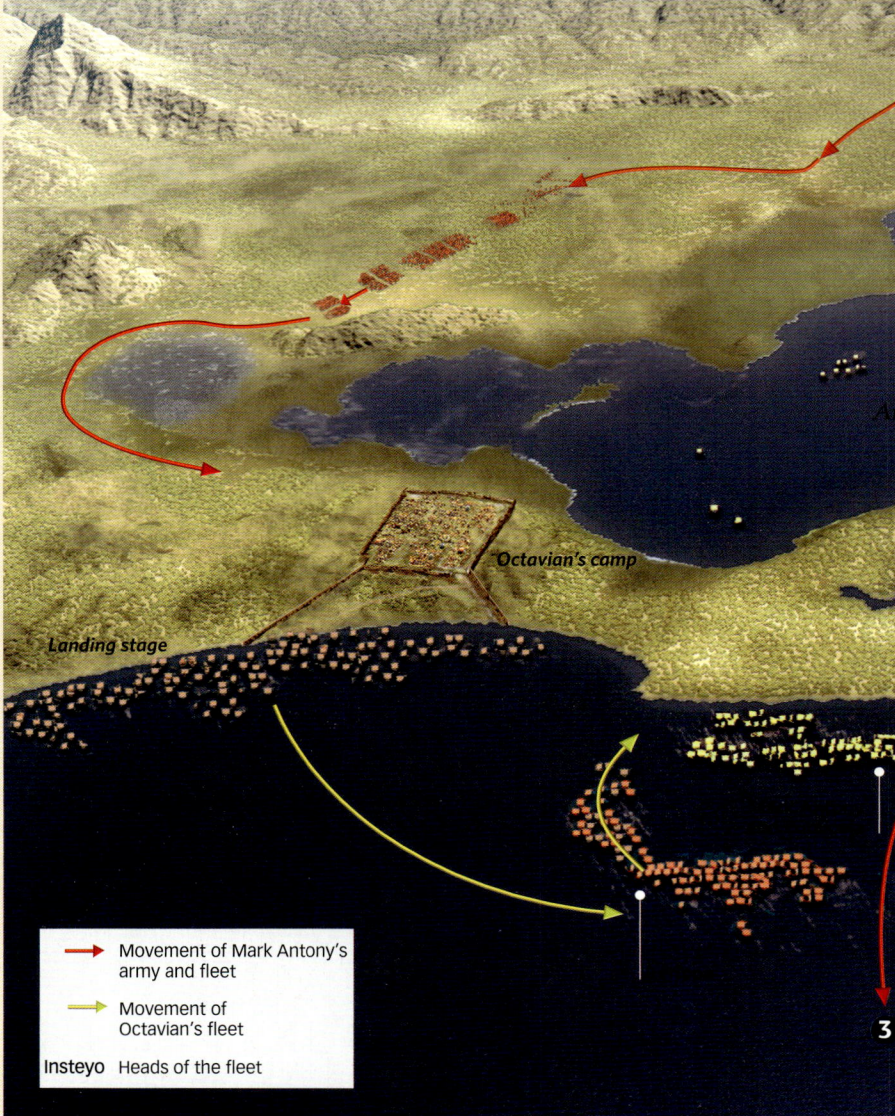

- → Movement of Mark Antony's army and fleet
- → Movement of Octavian's fleet
- **Insteyo** Heads of the fleet

When the date arrived, Octavian read out his rival's will. According to Dio Cassius, 'Mark Antony solemnly affirmed that Caesarion was truly the son of Caesar; [...] he had given splendid gifts to Cleopatra's children and wanted to be buried in Alexandria with that woman'. The historian affirms that all those present believed rumours that, 'should he be victorious, Mark Antony would give Rome as a gift to Cleopatra and transfer the seat of the empire to Egypt'. The Senate, now aware of Mark Antony's plans, deprived him of consular power. They declared war on Cleopatra, hoping that Mark Antony would come to her aid and therefore be declared as a belligerent for defending a foreigner against his own country.

Octavian's definitive triumph

The battle in which Mark Antony and Cleopatra were defeated took place near Actium, a city in Acarnania, east of Greece, in the entrance to the Actium Gulf, in September 31 BC. While Octavian was supported by the peoples of Italy, Gaul, Hispania, Illyria, Libya, Sardinia and Sicily, Mark Antony and Cleopatra had the support of the Eastern peoples of continental Asia, Thrace, Greece, Macedonia, Egypt and Cyrene; they also had a more powerful fleet, more soldiers and more military experience.

Agrippa, commanding the Caesarian fleet, led the attack against Mark Antony's tall ships, equipped with between four and ten orders of oarsmen. From a lower position, under the flanks of the enemy ships, Agrippa's ships were unlocking their oars, while their adversaries attacked them from above with war machines. After a long struggle with an uncertain outcome, Cleopatra, who had attended the battle from a ship anchored in the strait, retreated. Sailing with favourable winds, her boats gave the

OCTAVIAN'S RISE TO POWER

1 TERRESTRIAL ATTACK
In the spring of 31 BC, Mark Antony ordered an advance along the road that bordered the Gulf of Ambracia on the Greek coast of the Ionian Sea, with the purpose of capturing the springs of Octavian's camp. One of his generals, Statilius Taurus, managed to reject the order.

2 THE FIRST SHOCK
On the morning of 2 September, Mark Antony's fleet abandons the Gulf of Ambracia. The combat is fought until midday with a first advance by Sosius, followed by a circling manoeuvre by Agrippa. Cleopatra's fleet, which also holds the queen and Mark Antony's treasure chest and valuables, remains in the rear.

3 CLEOPATRA'S ESCAPE
Taking advantage of the movement of Octavian and Lucius Arruntius's fleets, Cleopatra, whose presence is rejected by many of Mark Antony's supporters, shuns the fight. Finally, she escapes with a squadron of 60 ships, crossing Agrippa's lines. Antony is not far behind, taking with him another 40 boats.

4 THE SURRENDER
Abandoned by their leaders, Mark Antony's depleted troops continue to fight well into the afternoon of 2 September. Surrender took place the next day. Agrippa, the victorious general, remains owner of about 140 vessels, which are incorporated into the fleet.

impression that she was running away terrified. Witnessing this, Mark Antony decided to follow her. Their soldiers, seeing their commander abandon them, threw their war machines overboard to lighten their load and set off in full sail. The ships that remained fought until Octavian resorted to fire to obtain the final victory. The supporters of Caesar began to throw burning coals and fish at their adversaries; according to Dio Cassius, 'the soldiers burned next to the ships as on a funeral pyre'.

With victory at Actium, Octavian became the sole ruler of Rome. He bestowed his allies with generous rewards and punished his opponents with the confiscation of all their property or execution. Queen Cleopatra returned to Egypt to prevent the insurrection of her people and chose to betray Mark Antony. She knew that if her lover learned of her death, he would not hesitate to follow her, so she spread the word of her suicide. Antony reacted as expected and threw himself on his sword. However, before dying, he realized that Cleopatra was still alive and asked to be led to her side so as to die in her arms. The Egyptian queen put an end to her life a few days later, when she was certain that Octavian would parade her as a war captive in his impending victory triumph. Caesarion was secretly executed by Octavian, and the annexation of Egypt to Rome was complete.

Indeed, as the Egyptian queen feared, the three orphans of Mark Antony and Cleopatra, Alexander Helios, Cleopatra Selene and Ptolemy Philadelphus, were taken to Italy as part of the spoils of war and paraded in chains in celebration of Octavian's triumph. After this, however, Octavia raised them and even had them educated together with her own children by Mark Antony.

APOTHEOSIS OF AUGUSTUS
Fragment of the frieze of San Vitale in which Antonia the Lesser (or Livia) and Augustus appear (National Museum, Ravenna). Shown opposite is an onyx seal of Emperor Augustus, decorated with a sphinx (Archaeological Museum, Florence).

EMPEROR AUGUSTUS

On 13 January 27 BC, Octavian restored the Republic. He formed a system of rule that, although based on the support of old republican customs, subjected them to his own authority. With a lifetime concession of the tribunician powers and the superior governorship and high command, Octavian, now called Augustus, assumed a power unrivalled by that of any other modern Roman.

As news of the conquest of Alexandria reached the city, honours were ordered to exalt the victor, now the ruler of Rome and its empire without rival. Two arches were built, one in Brundisium (Brindisi) and another in the Forum; spurs of enemy ships were placed in the Temple of Caesar; festivals were held in praise of the victory at Actium; details of Mark Antony were erased from monuments and his birthday was removed from the calendar. Reorganizing the Republic that the triumvirs had assumed was now assigned to Octavian, who created policies restoring peace to a city absorbed in social crisis and civil war. He began reform by reviewing State processes and public customs. The rise of the Principate was hidden by acts that showed a different course to those actioned. He accepted appointment as consul from 31 to 23 BC and was conferred with tribunician powers for life, granting him rights to convene the Senate and to veto magistrates, in addition to holding

THE ROMAN EMPIRE

AUGUSTUS WEARING A TOGA
This marble statue is preserved in the Louvre Museum. It was made by a contemporary of Augustus, one of those who initiated the tradition of representing the emperor not as a warrior, but as a member of the institutions of the Roman Republic, according to the new image of the princeps.

sacrosanct and inviolable civil status. With the power given to him by the *Lex Saenia* of 30 BC, he removed all who threatened his political agenda – supporters of Mark Antony and the Republic – and surrounded himself with conservative families to ensure their status. The powerful participated in the running of the State and contributed to the expansion of Rome. Rebellion was punished with exile or death. The varied governmental tasks and veiled ignorance of traditional institutions in the new political form separated Octavian rule from monarchies that had drawn parallels with tyrannies.

A new Romulus

In 27 BC, Octavian wrote in *Res Gestae*, a propaganda narrative, that the old triumvirate renounced their power, restoring 'the army, the laws and the provinces' to the Senate and the people of Rome. Before an audience of the senatorial class, pre-selected the previous year and in debt for their new social status, the young princeps was presented as a saviour of the homeland, focused on good rather than on personal gain. His speech, recounted by Dio Cassius, declared his disinterest in assuming the title of king that he de facto already held. 'I have placed myself at your disposal without limit to remedy all the risks that were incumbent upon you [...]. Of all this I have not obtained any personal benefit except to have safeguarded the country, while you benefit living in safety [...]. I am willing to die in order not to assume the monarchy.'

Some did not speak; others believed his words because they did not know his intentions. Everyone praised him 'calling for a monarchical government'. The re-establishment of the old Republic was now impossible.

A new position for Octavian meant a change of name too. Although he wanted to be named as the new Romulus of the empire because he considered himself the founder of a new Rome, that title openly hinted at his aspiration to monarchy. Plancus, a former supporter of Mark Antony, proposed the epithet of Augustus, which alluded to a status superior to human and, at the same time, brought to mind the

The gem of Augustus

Augustan propaganda used symbolism, via figurative arts, to express political ideas and values. The Gem of Augustus (pictured) is a cameo carved ca. 10–20 AD on Arabian onyx stone, credited to the gem cutter Dioscurides, and stored in the Kunsthistorisches Museum, Vienna. A popular interpretation of the scene in bas-relief shows the enthroned figure **(1) Augustus** as Jupiter, over whom **ecumene (2)**, the civilized world, holds the civic crown, which was given to the saviours of the fatherland. On the far right, the figures represent the **ocean (3)** and the land, **Gaia (4)**, over which the power of the princeps extended. Next to Augustus is the **goddess Roma (5)**, armed with spear and sword. A **Winged Victory (6)** rides in a chariot, perhaps to **Tiberius (7)**. The lower strip is disputed, but might be a war trophy depicting the Pannonian barbarian victory. **Trophy of war (8)** is believed to allude to the victory over the Barbarians of pannonia.

concept of *auctoritas* that had designated the authority of the ancient forefathers.

The image of a perfect princeps

Augustus's new name related to *augeo*, a verb that meant 'to make greater', and to *augurium*, the ritual act that determined the will of the gods through the omens told by the flight of birds. It was linked in turn with a radical change in public image that Octavian propagated through colossal portraits and demagogic statues. In opposition to Mark Antony, he resorted to the sculptural tradition of the representation of Ancient Greek kings, who crafted a public image of themselves as mythical heroes and venerable gods, minting coins to increase prestige. Augustus thus linked himself with a divine ancestry that began from the Divine Julius (Caesar deified) and descended back to Mars and Venus through the Trojan

Aeneas. The portraits of Octavian before 27 BC showed a young man eager for power. The new attitude of Augustus, respectful of republican institutions, could not have been further from the polemic image of the young triumvirate, overshadowed by civil war and tyrannical aspirations. His new portraits as princeps conveyed him with a serene expression resembling the image of Apollo, god of peace, avenger of human pride, purifier and healer, under whose protection the Augustan political programme could flourish. As a votive offering to the god of the Delphic Oracle, Augustus delivered numerous tripods of gold and silver, recast from old and arrogant-appearing statues, which he ordered to be removed from the porticos and streets of Rome. Furthermore, his supposed resemblance to Apollo served as a counterpoint to Mark Antony's promulgated semblance to Dionysus, the god who had travelled eastwards and subjugated his people but who, unlike Apollo, was related to lewdness and foreign immorality.

The Apollonian image was also in line with religious reform. Reclaiming the virtues lost in the preceding era began with restoring the prestige of the priesthood and renovating temples. Gaining the approval of the citizenry for the elevated status of the priesthood needed a significant amount of money (*summa honoraria*). Augustus also became a member of all the schools (pontiffs, augurs, decemviri and epulones), which brought him more power. He changed the system of appointing priests (until then elected by a committee formed from college members), with the exception of the flamines, the rex sacrorum and the vestals. From 12 BC, when Augustus became Pontifex Maximus, appointments were made directly by the emperor.

35

THE ROMAN EMPIRE

AUGUSTUS AS PONTIFEX MAXIMUS
With his head veiled like an augur (priest and official), this statue represents the emperor as the first of the priests of the Ancient College of Pontiffs of Rome. It was the most honourable Roman religion and had corresponding political authority (Roman National Museum).

THE VICTORIOUS GENERAL
This imperial portrait is a detail of the first-century statue known as Augustus of Prima Porta, the place where it was found. The emperor is wearing a breastplate, adorned with allegories of military triumphs (Vatican Museums, Rome).

The temples, damaged in the civil wars, were renovated with innovative designs in keeping with the new age. Archaic terracotta decorations were replaced by rich ornamentation carved in marble fit for a monarch.

With the power conferred to him upon becoming the Pontifex Maximus, Augustus manipulated the Roman festival calendar. Pageants, consecrated only to the gods or to the memory of significant historical events during the Republic, began to include festivals, which Varro defined as *hominum causae instituae* ('instituted because of men'). Private celebrations of the Julio-Claudian dynasty moved into the public sphere, as if it were a large family in which the father was the sovereign himself. Augustus made 30 new additions to the list of official pageants commemorating episodes in his life or in recent Roman history. The new festivals created a history of Rome dictated by Augustus.

The birthday of the princeps, for example, became a State festival, during which Augustus paid for events to entertain the people. As the supreme head of the empire could not finance all the festivals dedicated to him, donors funded some of them in exchange for prestige. This linked donors tightly to the Augustan regime. In Rome, after the death of Augustus, the organization of the commemorative games of his birth was carried out by the consuls.

In addition to the birth of the emperor, Rome also celebrated the main dates of his assumption of powers: on 16 January, the concession of the title of Augustus; on 6 March, his appointment as Pontifex Maximus; and on 5 February, his official appointment as father of the country, acquired in 2 BC.

Iron rule over the populace

Octavian became Augustus on 16 January 27 BC. His power increased and with it the greatness of Rome; the city symbolized the mirror that reflected the greatness of the princeps. The creation of a grandiose image of the capital and the growth of the rest of the empire was a fundamental purpose of the Augustan reforms. When Augustus assumed absolute power, the city of Rome had been totally neglected. It had expanded without urban planning; new neighbourhoods, with narrow alleys and high wooden houses, were a fire risk and were dangerous places for insurrection; the high tides of the Tiber flooded vast areas of the city, leaving no effective system to meet the needs of the people. Until then, control over public works and public security was the exclusive responsibility of the aediles (high-ranking officials).

Strabo, the acclaimed geographer and a contemporary of Augustus, in his *Geography* praises the intervention of the princeps, who 'took care of the problems of the city which were raised, as a measure against fires, a militia chosen among the freedmen and, for the damage caused by collapsed buildings, he interceded by reducing the height of new buildings to 70ft and prohibiting construction on public roads.' In effect, Augustus took responsibility for public services by establishing a system of curates and prefectures, which benefited the people, but also controlled them.

The first step was the appointment in 27 BC of a Praetorian prefect, who had under his orders 10,000 soldiers of the personal guard of the princeps. In 22 BC, Augustus created a fire brigade, seven cohorts of 1000 freedmen, controlled by a prefect of the equestrian order, elected by the emperor. Its mission was to put out fires and police the city. 6000 men guarded the city; they were split into four cohorts under the command of an urban prefect who was in charge of the public order of the city, its markets and the administration of justice.

With 23,000 men in the service of the emperor, the security of the Roman population was guaranteed.

Absolute government of the world

Strabo recounts the decision taken by Augustus, 'lord for life of war and of peace', in relation to the administration of all the territories conquered by the Romans and, therefore, territories obliged to pay taxes to Rome. According to him, Roman provinces were divided into two parts, one part assigned to the

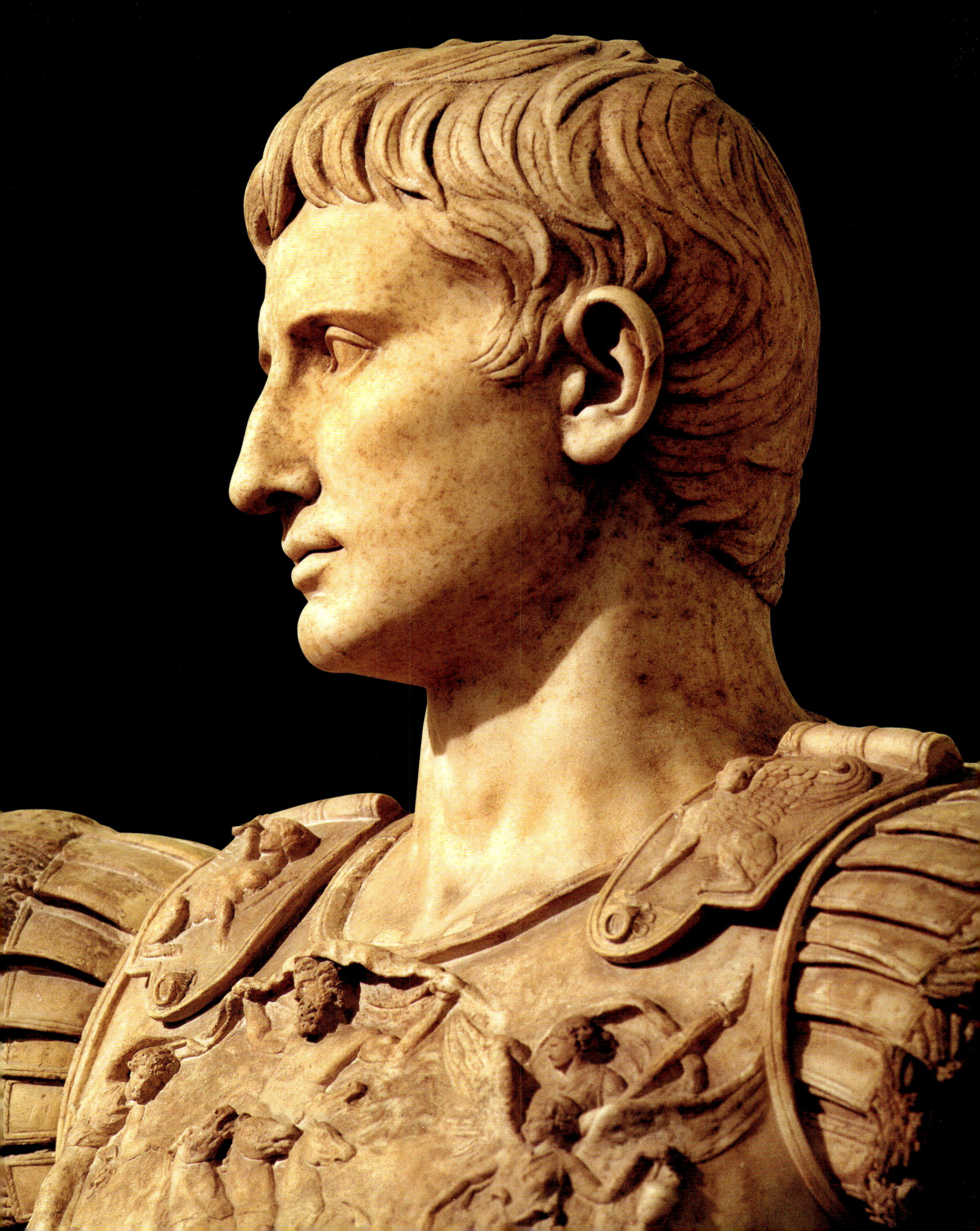

The praetorian Guard, Augustus's contribution to security

In 27 BC, Augustus had a total of nine units of 500 soldiers pledging security as escorts or urban control. Called the Praetorian Guard after the republican legions who escorted the praetors (magistrates) during battle, they intervened in the repression of conspiracies, coups d'etats and the acclamation of new emperors. Soldiers could serve 16 years in the imperial guard. In Augustus's time, only three cohorts remained stationed in Rome, while six were based in Italy. These were used as military reserves in battles in which the princeps intervened in combat, or as guard posts (*excubiae*) to avoid insurrections within the legion or violent clashes with the general public. Under the Principate of Tiberius, the nine cohorts set up base on the outskirts of Rome, in Castra Praetoria, where between 6000 and 9000 troops camped. The image above shows the funeral stele of Quintus Pomponius Proculus, a soldier of the IV Praetorian cohort, found in Scoppito (L'Aquila).

Senate and the other to the princeps. The Senate oversaw the weaker provinces, which did not need military detachments, such as Africa Proconsularis, Baetica, Gaul Narbonensis, Sicily, Macedonia, Cyrene, Bithynia and Asia. The rest, mostly frontier territories exposed to enemy attack, passed into the control of Augustus, who assumed rule of the legions.

The government of each province was assigned to a former magistrate. In senatorial provinces, elections were held annually with a Senate vote. The imperial provinces were managed by an ex-praetor or ex-consul elected by the emperor. One sent as governor to one of these provinces could remain in post for more than a year and had five magisterial attendants during tenure. The province of Egypt was an exception: there, Augustus appointed a prefect of equestrian rank, for fear that a senator would start to foster ambitions of greatness in the birthplace of the Ptolemies. No prefects were free from suspicion: Gaius Cornelius Galo, a friend of the emperor, was sent to Alexandria after falling from grace, and committed suicide for being seduced by ambition.

The halt to moral deprivation

Once in power, Augustus acted as a legislator without the intercession of any colleague – a circumstance that he used to initiate the restructuring of public morals.

The social situation in Rome at the beginning of his rule was alarming. The conquest of the East brought with it an economic boom and frivolous customs unfit for the masters of the world: the *pater familias* (male heads of families) had lost their moral authority; the traditional modesty of married women had gone out of style; motherhood was shunned; extravagance was rife and family deities were neglected. According to Sallust, 'greed overcame loyalty, honesty and other virtues, and in its place came arrogance, cruelty, and venality'.

As curator *legum et morum*, Augustus tried to resolve the situation with a moral code encouraging marriage and childbirth and punishing single adults, adultery and perverse sexual habits. The *Lex Julia* of *Maritandis Ordinibus* of 18 BC, together with the *Lex Julia* of *Adulteriis Coercendis* in the following year and the *Lex Julia Papia Poppea nuptialis* of 9 AD, sought to preserve the purity of the lineage of upper-class Romans, and marriage between a senator or his kin to a freedwoman or to actors or their kin was forbidden. Augustus punished adultery, incest, rape and prostitution with execution or exile to an island and the confiscation of property.

Legislative reforms prohibited the prostitution of freedwomen and paedophilia, awarded grants to families with more than three children, and barred single people or widowers without children from receiving inheritances, which forfeited to the public treasury.

A peace at the cost of blood
Augustus, as the head of the empire, ensured the success of his people by stamping out rebellion in the regions that were under his control. In 26 BC, the doors of the Temple of Janus in Rome opened again to symbolize a state of war.

The emperor went on campaign against the Vaccean, Canarian and Asturian peoples of Spain, while Marcus Terentius Varro, known for his literary skills but not military glory, tried to put an end to the insurrection in Gaul.

Augustus landed in Tarraco (Tarragona), accompanied by his stepson Tiberius, aged 16, and by his nephew Marcus Claudius Marcellus, aged 15. He remained in Hispania for two years in order to conquer resistance in the Iberian peninsula and establish routes extending into the province and the gold mines of Gallaecia. The princeps' ability to fight for long periods was restricted by severe cramps and high fevers, alleviated only by hydrotherapy from his doctor, Musa. A decision to abandon the battlefield came with a sign from Jupiter, when

HOUSE OF AUGUSTUS
The Domus Augustana (House of Augustus), located on the Palatine Hill, was begun in 36 BC, before the proclamation of Octavian as emperor. The Hall of Masks, which appears in this image, is one of the four rooms located in the east wing, and is decorated with colourful architectural elements. It was Octavian who determined that the Palatine Hill – where, according to tradition, Rome was first founded – be established as a place of residence for later rulers of the empire.

THE ROMAN EMPIRE

THE *ARA PACIS*, THE ALTAR OF AUGUSTUS

The *Pax Augusta*, a propaganda slogan of Augustus's regime, was honoured in the construction of a monumental altar consecrated on 30 January 9 BC. The *Ara Pacis* (Altar of Peace) next to the Via Lata, at the end of the Flaminia Road in the Field of Mars, was visited annually (coinciding with Livia's birthday) by the vestal virgins, the four flamines and the members of the four main priestly colleges (pontiffs, augurs, decemviri and epulones), led by Augustus as Pontifex Maximus. The ritual included placing incense on the altar before sacrificing a victim while praying aloud from Ovid's *Fasti*: 'And ask the gods who favour pious prayer that the house that brings peace, may so endure.' Staged annually on 30 March, this ritual paid homage to the deities of State conservation: Concordia, Health and Janus.

A SPECIAL ENVIRONMENT

The Altar of Peace (*Ara Pacis*) was originally beneath the Palazzo Peretti on the Roman road to Corso. In 1937, Mussolini moved it to the Mausoleum of Augustus. Today it is in the Richard Meier-designed Ara Pacis Museum.

1 AUGUSTUS
The princeps parades at the head of his court, surrounded by the consuls, like a good republican.

2 AGRIPPA
Son-in-law and right hand of Augustus, he parades with sacred clothing and his head covered like an augur.

3 GAIUS CAESAR
Son of Agrippa and Julia and grandson of Augustus. He was the designated successor, but died in 4 AD.

4 JULIA
The daughter of Augustus headed a line of successors opposed to Livia's, which was the one that would eventually prevail.

5 TIBERIUS
A son from Livia's first marriage, he succeeded Augustus, who adopted him after Julia's children died.

EMPEROR AUGUSTUS

6 ANTONIA THE YOUNGER
Daughter of Mark Antony and Octavia, wife of Drusus the Elder and mother of Germanicus and Claudius.

7 GERMANICUS
Nephew of Tiberius, married to Agrippina the Elder. His candidacy for succession was halted by his death.

8 DRUSUS THE ELDER
Son of Livia and brother of Tiberius, he had a glorious military career. He died in 9 AD.

9 ANTONIA THE ELDER
Wife of Lucius Domitius Ahenobarbus, she was a grandmother of the future Emperor Nero.

10 DOMITIA
Daughter of Antonia the Elder and Lucius Domitius Ahenobarbus, mother of Empress Valeria Messalina.

THE ROMAN EMPIRE

Augustus and Hispania: the provincial organization of the peninsula

In 16 BC, Augustus went to Hispania to administer Rome's control over Hispanic territory. Cantabrian war veterans also settled in colonies that were founded *ex novo* (from scratch) to focus Romanization and military power. The two provinces into which the Iberian peninsula had been divided in 197 BC now became three: Lusitania and Baetica, previously included in Hispania Ulterior, and Tarraconensis, corresponding to Hispania Citerior. Baetica was governed by the Senate; the other two by Augustus. Mining territories Sisapo (Almadén) and Cástulo (Linares) in the Baetica, the border route between the provinces, were modified and annexed to Tarraconensis, ensuring the Senate received operating profits. The Hercules Route, linking the Pyrenees with the port of Gades (Cádiz), was expanded by building more than 2000km (1240 miles) of roads connecting the interior, the north and the west of the peninsula.

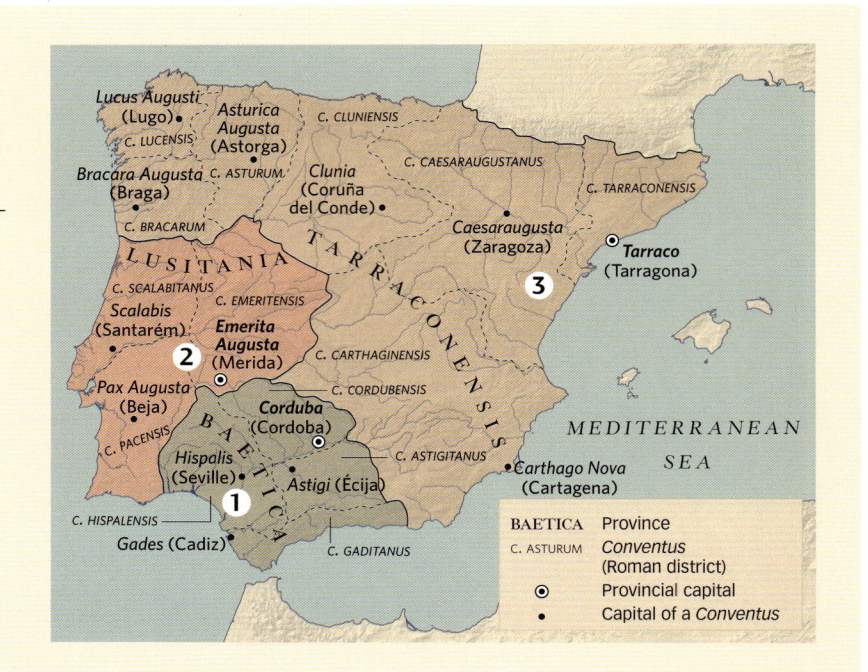

1 BAETICA
Colony Patricia Corduba (Córdoba) became the capital of the most Romanized province of Hispania, which was divided in four convents: Cordubense, Hispalense, Astigitano and Gaditano.

2 LUSITANIA
Emerita Augusta (Mérida), a colony founded from scratch to resettle the veterans of legions V *Alaudae* and X *Gemina*, became the territorial axis point of Lusitania, as well as its capital.

3 TARRACONENSIS
Colonia Iulia Triumphalis Tarraco (Tarragona) was elected provincial capital. Augustus founded Caesaraugusta (Zaragoza) with veterans of Legions VI and III *Macedonica* and X *Gemina*.

VOTIVE SHIELD
A marble copy of a golden votive shield awarded to Augustus by the Senate of Rome ca. 27 BC. Now preserved in the Musée Lapidaire of Arles (France), the shield was probably given to Augustus when he visited the colony of Arelate upon his return from the campaign in Hispania.

a bolt of lightning struck his carriage, killing one of his slaves.

Despite the Roman triumph in honour of Augustus's defeat of Hispania, the conflict in Citerior was not over. As the emperor left the province, a new rebellion rose against Governor Lucius Aelius Lamia, which was put down with reprisals: the indigenous villages were destroyed, the hands of captives amputated, and a majority of them were enslaved. In 22 BC, the native people again rebelled against the cruelty of Publius Carisus, legate of Lusitania, and Gaius Furnis, governor of the Roman province of Asia; upon defeat, the Cantabrians burned their homes down rather than submit to Roman rule.

In 25 BC, the praetor of Hispania Citerior, Lucius Piso, was assassinated by a peasant from Tiermes (Soria). According to Tacitus in his *Annals*, after his capture, the native was tortured in order to reveal accomplices but killed himself by hurling himself against a rock without revealing any names.

The famine of 22 BC

When the Cantabrians and Asturians revolted against the Spanish governors, Rome suffered an epidemic simultaneously. Storms caused the Tiber to flood the city, and a plague wilted crops. The previous year, Augustus had barred the appointment of Lucius Sextius as consul. People assumed this had angered the gods. To calm them, they demanded the emperor be made dictator and curator annonae (curator of grain supplies), under the threat of burning the Curia (the Senate house). The princeps rejected the role, but accepted that of commissar for the distribution of wheat. This required him to distribute free grain to the people, as the tribunate of Publius Clodius Pulcher had done.

In his *Res Gestae*, Augustus writes about

paying for wheat, abolishing public banquets and limiting gladiatorial games to two per year: 'In a time of extreme shortage, I did not refuse to take charge of the grain supply and freed the city from the terror'.

To avoid a future crisis, the princeps took charge of the grain supply, appointing equestrian-class prefects in place of their plebeian counterparts, who had been chosen by the Senate.

Rebellion at the borders

The famine removed focus from the Augustans for a time. No one spoke about the claims against Livia after the death of Marcus Claudius Marcellus, who was thought to have been poisoned to prevent Augustus, his uncle and father-in-law, from making him his successor.

Julia, the only daughter of Augustus, had married Marcellus when she was 15. She was widowed at 17, then married again to Agrippa, 23 years her senior, who had to divorce Claudia Marcella the Elder, the sister of the deceased. Agrippa, the loyal friend of the princeps, remained entitled to rule in place of the emperor when he was in the empire's provinces, while guaranteeing the offspring of the Julian family, which was still without male heirs. The son of Julia and Agrippa, Gaius Julius Caesar Vipsanius, was born in 20 BC.

When Augustus returned from Syria after reorganizing the management of the eastern provinces, Agrippa was sent to Gaul, the borders of which Germanic peoples were trying to invade. After resolving this situation, Agrippa left for Hispania, where the enslaved Cantabrians had rebelled again after killing their masters and returning to their villages. Agrippa struggled with the revolt in Hispania Citerior and with his own troops, exhausted by

ROMAN WALLS IN TARRAGONA
During Augustus's campaign to quell the Cantabrian rebellion and the Astures against provincial governors, the emperor resided in Tarraco (Tarragona) for two years. On his initiative, the city became the capital of the Tarraconensis province, and the most extensive in Hispania.

Augustus and the barbarians: conflicts on the borders of the empire

Consolatio ad Liviam's unknown author wrote verses on the death of Drusus: 'You, Germania, you no longer have the right to forgive. You, barbarian, will pay for your faults with death.' Tiberius, who succeeded his brother in the struggle, reached the Elbe in 8 BC, but withdrew his legions on the Rhine a year later. In 5 AD he returned to the border between Rome and the barbarians.

The submission of the Germanic peoples inspired this silverware from the Villa della Pisanella in Boscoreale near Pompeii. The 'Augustus cup' below shows the emperor, civil servants (lictors) and soldiers. German princes offer their sons in surrender as a globe-holding Augustus sitting on a throne receives a statue of Victory from Venus, his protective goddess. The piece personifies the virtue of the Roman people and provinces heralded by Mars (Louvre Museum, Paris).

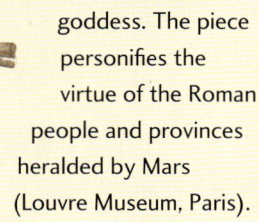

years of war. Despite this, he was victorious but did not want to celebrate in Rome. Instead, he sent soldiers as colonists to form two Hispanic cities that became the axis of territorial control of Lusitania and Tarraconensis: Emerita Augusta (Merida) and Caesaraugusta (Zaragoza).

The deeds of Tiberius and Drusus

Peace in Hispania did not end Rome's conflicts with the barbarian peoples besieging its borders. The year in which Augustus went to Hispania, accompanied by Livia's son Tiberius, with whom, since 26 BC, he had maintained a political alliance, the German peoples of Sicambri, Usipetes and Tencteri crossed the Rhine and invaded Gaul, and the Camunni, Vindelici and the Alpine tribes took up arms in Dalmatia, Pannonia and Thrace.

Augustus went to the German regions for a few months to agree a truce with the invading peoples. In order to resolve the Alpine conflict, Augustus sent Tiberius and his younger brother, Drusus, whose victories were commemorated by Horace in one of his Odes. 'With his soldiers, Drusus has subdued the Genoans, a restless tribe, and the swift Breunos with their forts raised threateningly high on the Alps, forceful on more than one occasion. The eldest of the Neros [Tiberius], known for his martial combat, undertook a tough campaign defeating ferocious challenges.'

These offensives followed the campaigns of Agrippa in Pannonia and, from 12 BC, the conquest of lands beyond the Rhine, in the still independent Germania led by Drusus. Augustus's dream of expanding the northern borders of the empire claimed the life of Livia's younger son in 9 BC, when Drusus was about to cross the Elbe after invading the lands of the Chatti, the Suebi and the Cherusci. Upon hearing the news of his brother accidentally falling off his horse, Tiberius went in search of him. Tiberius took charge of bringing his brother's corpse back to Rome, with the help of centurions, military tribunes and nobles of all the cities through which he passed. Two funeral prayers were said in Drusus's honour, one by Tiberius, alongside the deceased, and the other by Augustus, in the Circus Flaminius. Drusus was buried in the mausoleum of the Julii, where the remains of Marcellus and Agrippa were also laid to rest.

The death of Agrippa

Agrippa, Augustus's most faithful ally, whom the princeps had known since childhood and who shared his first battles and the most private affairs of the ruling house, died in 12 BC. He left as his descendants Gaius Caesar, the firstborn; Lucius Caesar; Agrippa, called Postumus, because he was born after his father had died, and two daughters, Agrippina the Elder and Julia the Younger. His young wife, Julia the Elder, was a widow for the second time and free to marry again.

At the time of his death, Agrippa was preparing to depart for Pannonia again, invested with the highest Roman authority – tribunician powers and the position of imperial proconsul, subject only to the authority of the princeps. Agrippa fell ill while in Campania when returning from the winter season. Augustus could not reach Agrippa before he passed away and took charge of bringing his body back to Rome, allowing his corpse to lie in state in the Forum, delivering the funeral speech, organizing festivals in his honour, which no other nobleman wanted to deal with, and burying his ashes in his mausoleum, despite the fact that the deceased already had a tomb in the Field of Mars.

Augustus was indebted to Agrippa for the victory at Actium over Mark Antony, the subjugation of the Hispanic Cantabrians, control of the Crimea, the conquest of the Upper Danube region and many other victories that Agrippa never wanted to celebrate with the triumphs that were granted; moreover, he had contributed his own fortune to the transformation and beautification of Rome. His aim was not to glorify his own family, but that of the Julians, with buildings such as the Pantheon and the Portico of Neptune or the arcaded precincts of the Saepta Julia where citizens voted at election times.

After the death of Agrippa, Augustus appointed his stepson Tiberius as a partner in his government. He forced him to divorce his wife Vipsania Agrippina, daughter of Agrippa, to marry Julia to ensure the continuity of the Julian family. This union proved tragic, for Julia's immoral life – totally at odds with Augustan moral precepts – ultimately caused her to be exiled on the island of Pandateria.

The succession issue

Augustus had not instituted a kingdom or a dictatorship with a system of family succession guaranteed by law, but, as Tacitus recounts, it

LA MAISON CARRÉE
Built on the orders of Agrippa in 16 BC in Nemausus (modern-day Nîmes), this temple was dedicated to his two sons, Lucius and Gaius, the grandchildren and adopted sons of Augustus. It is a typical Roman temple with a rectangular plan and a gable roof, surrounded by columns and with a staircase in its only entrance, which overlooked the city's forum.

THE PANTHEON, ROME (OVERLEAF)
Built by Agrippa, this is one of the most impressive buildings of the classical era; the dome, dating from Hadrian's time, rises to 43.2m (142ft) in height and was the largest in the ancient world.

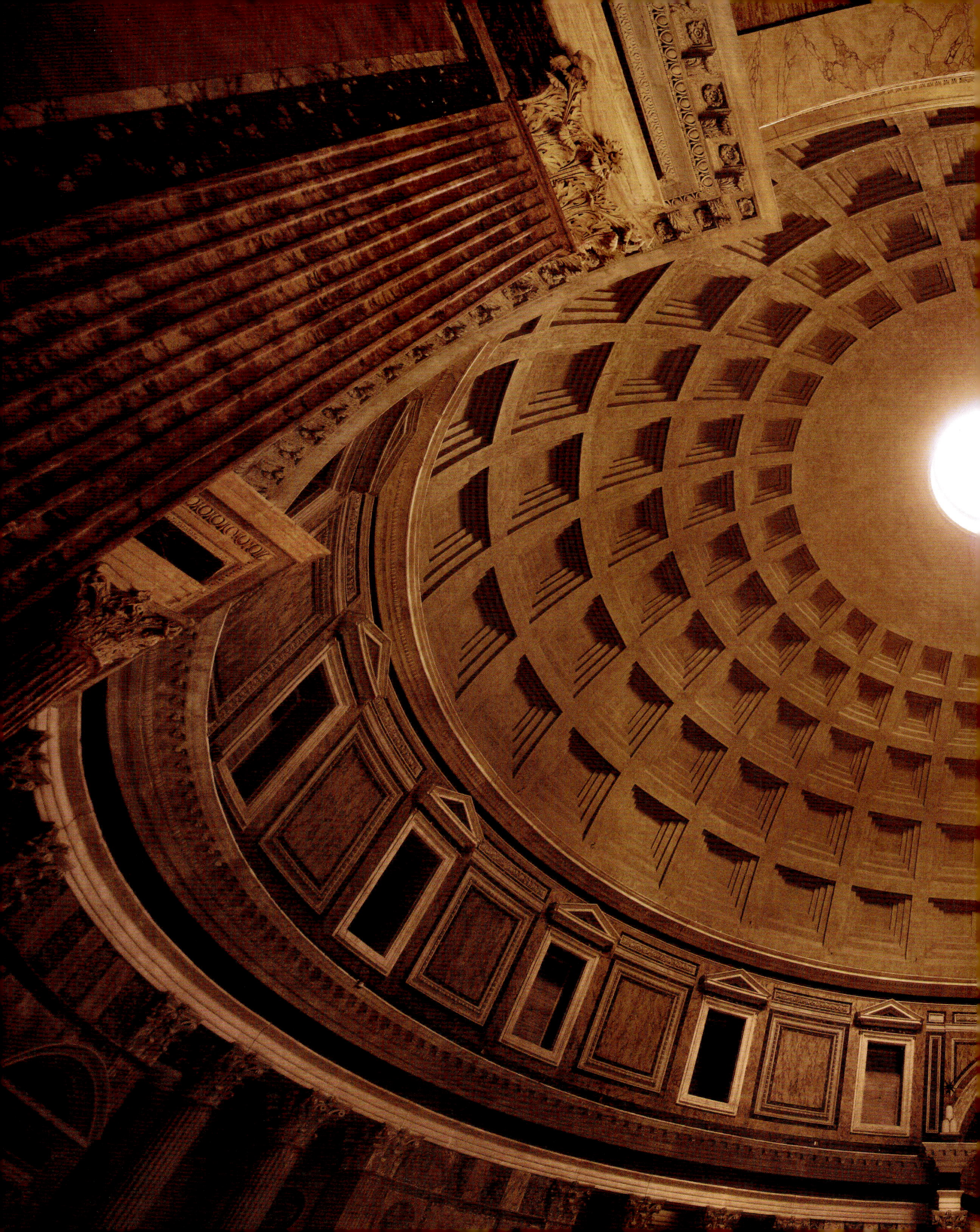

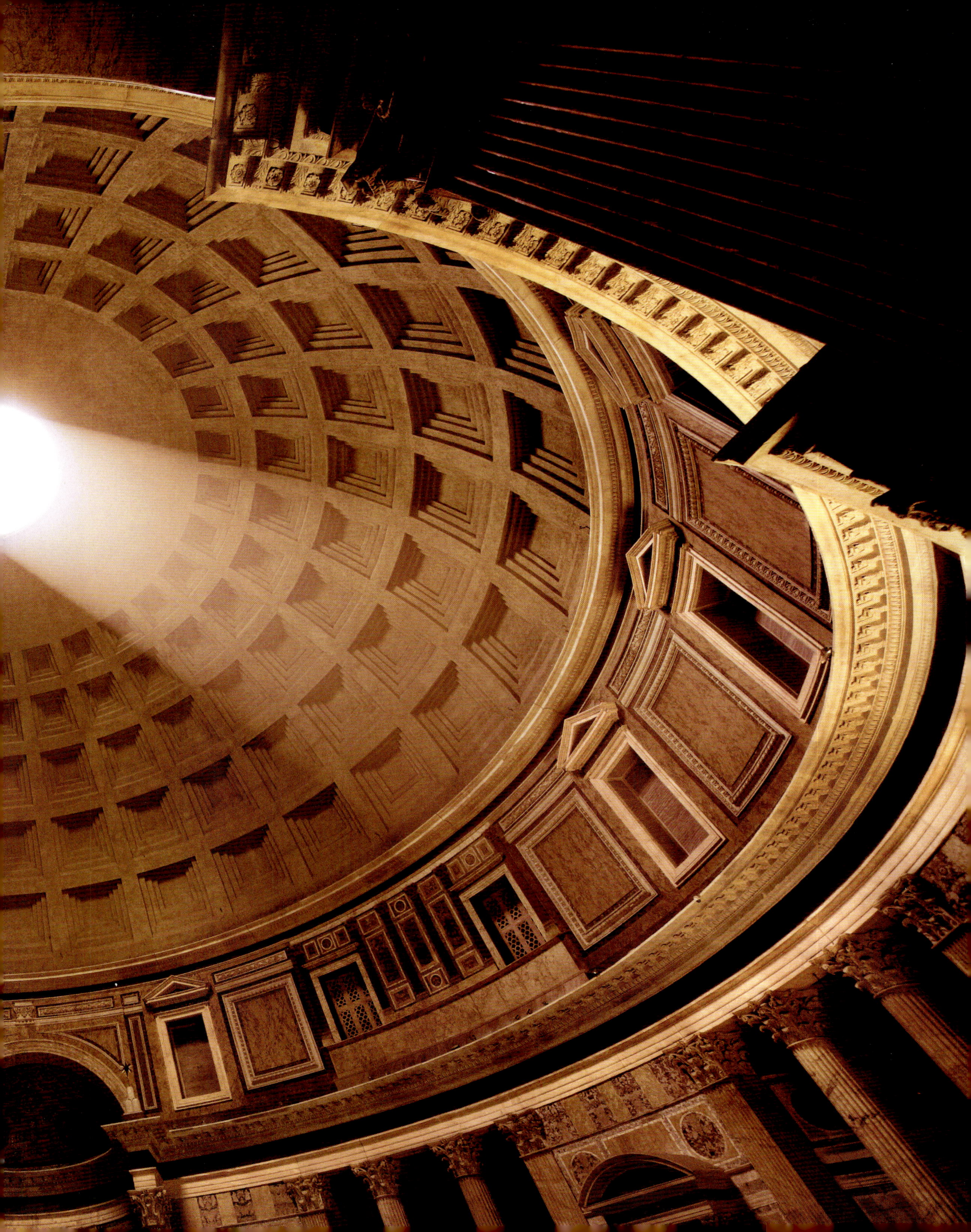

Augustus's succession: the destiny of the imperial family

After adoption via Julius Caesar's will, Augustus, of the Octavian family, joined the Julian family. Despite Augustus's attempts to infiltrate Julians into the principate, his son-in-law Marcellus, grandchildren Gaius and Lucius, wife Livia (here pictured with her son; Museum of Fine Arts, Boston), adopted son Tiberius and the Claudians' bloodline maintained sovereignty.

```
                                Gaius Octavian ———— Atia Balba
                                        |
Gaius Claudius Marcellus ———— Octavia the Younger
        |                       1      |   2                  1
                    Scribonia ——— Augustus ——— Livia Drusilla ——— Tiberius Claudius
        |              1                 2                            Nero
MARCUS CLAUDIUS MARCELLUS ——— Julia ——— Marcus Vipsanius Agrippa
First designated             the Elder
successor d. 23 BC
                     LUCIUS JULIUS CAESAR  GAIUS JULIUS CAESAR  Postumus        TIBERIUS
The numbers 1, 2 and 3  Second              Adopted by Augustus  Agrippa    3   Adopted by Augustus
correspond to 1st, 2nd and 3rd designated   as third designated  d. 14 BC       before his death in 14 AD
marriages.              successor, d. 2 BC  successor d. 4 BC
```

was a 'Republic constituted under the name of the Principate'. That is, it was a regime of complex domain, which had to respect, at least in appearance, republican institutions and, therefore, the 'free' choice of the heir of the supreme *auctoritas*. Even during the Republic there had been ways to transfer powers among the families of the senatorial nobility to ensure control of magistracies like the consulship in a small number of aristocratic lineages.

The main pitfall that Augustus faced was the fact that he did not have a direct male descendant. His first marriage to Scribonia gave him one daughter; his second marriage, to Livia, had been childless. Livia, however, had two sons, Tiberius and Drusus, with her former husband, Tiberius Claudius, and they were called upon to inherit their stepfather's government. But because of a passionate inclination towards the Julian family branch and an antipathy towards his older stepson, Tiberius, the emperor tried to secure succession via his daughter Julia, using adoption as a means to prevent the extinction of his family.

Marcellus was the first to rival Tiberius. Despite having the Claudian blood of his father, Gaius Claudius Marcellus, Marcellus was a Julian, first for being the son of Octavia and also for having married the emperor's daughter. His death marked the failure of Augustus's first attempt to find a successor. As Julia, Marcellus's young widow, had no offspring from this union, her father married her to his general, Agrippa. As soon as Julia's first two sons, Gaius and Lucius, were born, Augustus adopted them, granting them the title of Caesares. Augustus appointed Agrippa as future regent so that, should he die before his grandchildren reached the age of majority, no one could supplant them from the throne. No wonder that Tiberius resented the two 'princes of youth'. When Agrippa died, Livia's son had to accept being mentor to his vain, weak stepchildren, while he, with an unblemished career, was considered a subordinate mentor. The inclination of the princeps for his two grandchildren and the manifest contempt of his adulterous wife drove Tiberius to seek refuge in the island of Rhodes in 6 BC.

Neither he nor Augustus could have foreseen the premature deaths of Gaius and Lucius, in which Livia seemed implicated. In 4 AD, Gaius was in Syria when he was the victim of an attack that caused incurable wounds. He sought a solitary life and declined to return to Rome, despite Augustus's pleas. When he finally decided to return to Italy, Gaius was so weak that he died aboard a cargo ship in Limyra, on the Lycian coast. Two years earlier, Lucius had died in Massilia (Marseille) while leading an army to Hispania. The blame fell on Livia for the unexpected deaths of the two young men, because at the same time, Livia had called upon Tiberius to return from Rhodes.

Some Roman colonies held public mourning for the death of the two princes as a sign of allegiance to the emperor. In Pisa, for example, it was arranged that: 'given the gravity of such a great and unforeseen misfortune, that from the very day on which the death of Gaius was announced until the day his bones were transported and buried [...] everyone had to wear mourning dress, temples, public baths and taverns were closed [...] and mothers were obliged to mourn in public.'

The victory of the Claudians

Pressed by the urging of Livia and in need of a military leader, Augustus agreed to adopt Tiberius and bestowed upon him tribunician

AGRIPPA AND JULIA
On the side of the Ara Pacis, *forming part of the retinue led by Augustus, appear Agrippa and Julia, Augustus's daughter; with them is little Gaius, Agrippa's son, who, together with his brother Lucius, was adopted by Augustus with a view to his own succession. Agrippa married Julia, by then Marcellus's widow, after divorcing his second wife, Marcella, apparently through the intervention of Maecenas, who advised Augustus to link his family to the one he was already attached to.*

THE ROMAN EMPIRE

power for a decade. However, although the possibility of the Julians remaining in power was already remote, the princeps, for as long as he could, did not abandon support for the two remaining descendants with Julian blood who were still alive: the last son of Agrippa and Julia, Agrippa Postumus (although he was said by Suetonius to be 'brutal and bloodthirsty', while Velleius described him as 'depraved in soul and character'); and Tiberius's popular nephew, Nero Claudius Drusus, better known as Germanicus. He was the eldest son of Drusus the Elder and Antonia the Younger and brother of the future emperor Claudius. To groom these two for power without betraying his pledge to his wife, Augustus adopted Postumus, but kept him subordinate to Tiberius, and in turn forced his stepson to adopt Germanicus in the same ceremony, which took place in 4 AD.

The impositions that Augustus made increased Tiberius's resentment: he saw in Germanicus an adversary whom the legions and the people adored: he possessed, according to Suetonius, 'to a degree that no one has ever attained, all the virtues of the spirit and of the body', beauty and bravery, wisdom and talent to attract the sympathy of the people.

Augustus's preference for Germanicus became apparent again when he betrothed him to his granddaughter Agrippina the Elder, sister of the deceased Gaius and Lucius. Tacitus asserted that only Livia's tears prevented Augustus from publicly declaring Germanicus as his successor, a consequence that seemed unavoidable. It is possible that the fear of seeing her son Tiberius removed from power led Livia to call (without justification) for the banishment of Agrippa Postumus to the island of Planasia in 7 AD, and to plot the elimination of Germanicus – something she would achieve only a few years after the death of Augustus, in which she also had a hand.

In addition to the direct members of the two families of the House of Augustus, high-ranking figures of Rome were involved in this power struggle; this revolved around a plot in support of the princeps's daughter, Julia the Elder. Among these was Iullus Antonius, the son of Mark Antony; he was connected to the imperial family through marriage to his half-sister, Claudia Marcella the Elder, Augustus's niece, who had been divorced from Agrippa. After having boosted Iullus Antonius's career, the princeps granted him the consulship in 10 BC and made him proconsul of Asia four years later. However, Augustus accused Iullus Antonius of treason and sentenced him to death in 2 BC, when his incestuous relationship with Julia and his intention to gain power for himself were revealed.

Teutoburg

The same year that Tiberius was adopted by the Julian family, he was sent by Augustus to Germania to continue the pacification of the Rhine region, which he had occupied since the accidental death of his brother Drusus. Tiberius counted on the support of the three legions posted in Germania Inferior (Lower Germany) and of the two in Germania Superior (Upper Germany), and he captured the northern and central regions between the Rhine and the Elbe. He planned the occupation of the southern area, where the Marcomanni lived, led by Maroboduus, when a revolt broke out in Ilyria, and he was forced to postpone the plans.

Tiberius's return to Germania three years later, in 9 AD, occurred in one of the most dramatic circumstances that Augustus experienced in his reign. Tiberius had returned to Rome, victorious against Dalmatia, when a gift from Maroboduus arrived at the imperial palace. It was the scorched head of Publius Quinctilius Varus, the governor of Germania and a senator related to the princeps. With this 'gift', Maroboduus announced the terrible defeat at the Battle of the Teutoburg Forest (in present-day Osnabrück), with the loss of three legions, three contingents of cavalry and the suicides of the Roman officers in command, including that of Varus, the head of the army.

The Germanic tribes, facing pressure from the Roman governor, had rebelled. Arminius, leader of the Cherusci, at the head of the insurrection, lured Varus and his three legions

THE EAGLES OF THE LEGION
Since the reform undertaken by Marius in 104 BC, the eagle rose as pre-eminent among the other symbols of the republican legions, such as the bull, the wild boar, the wolf or the horse. The eagles were made of noble metals, silver and gold, or in bronze, and they were jealously guarded in the aedes signorum *(shrine of the standards). Losing the eagles, as happened to Crassus, to Mark Antony, and to Varus in Teuotoburg, was the greatest dishonour a legion could bear (Archaeology Museum of Catalonia, Barcelona).*

LIVIA, THE FIRST EMPRESS OF ROME

Livia Drusilla joined the Julian family in 39 BC. She was then 19 years old with one son, Tiberius, and was pregnant with her second, Drusus. Despite her wealth and social position, all authors praised her modesty in dress, her austerity and commitment to domestic chores. Ovid called her: 'the most vestal of our castes of Roman wives'. Octavian not only married her but included her in his struggle for power and granted her privileges hitherto not given to Roman women, such as the right to administer family assets and inviolability (civil immunity). However, some historians, including Tacitus and Dio Cassius, accused Livia of heinous crimes such as poisoning, ambition and an intense infatuation with guaranteeing the political future of the Claudian family. This beautiful marble bust of Livia is today preserved in the Capitoline Museums (Rome).

LIVIA PORTRAYED AS CERES

Livia was often portrayed with a crown surmounted with spikes to link her with the iconographic attributes of Ceres, goddess of the harvest, fertility and agriculture, as shown in this third-century mosaic (Bardo National Museum, Tunisia).

THE ROMAN EMPIRE

The Mausoleum of Augustus

Strabo described the Mausoleum of Augustus as 'a large riverside tumulus rising above a white marble base, covered by perennial trees'. The tumulus, inspired by Etruscan funeral shrines, was topped with a bronze statue of Augustus. As well as being the emperor's burial place, it housed the ashes of relatives and friends of the princeps. The first to be buried there was Marcellus, in 23 BC. He was followed by Agrippa, Drusus the Elder, Lucius and Gaius, Augustus, Drusus the Younger, Livia, Tiberius, and perhaps Claudius and Vespasian. Built as a symbol of Augustus's power and faithfulness to Rome, dual obelisks flank the entrance, which is open to the south (now in the squares of the Quirinal Fountain and the Esquiline). Two pillars mounted with bronze plaques summarize the *Res Gestae*, the successes carried out by the princeps. They are also preserved on the walls of the temple erected in honour of Rome and Augustus in Ankara.

to a territory believed to be loyal to Rome, but the Roman troops were attacked as they passed through the forest of Teutoburg, with the wind and the rain working in favour of the rebels. The surviving soldiers were captured by the enemy, while Varus and his officers committed suicide. The general's head was sent as a war trophy to Maroboduus, king of the Marcomanni, who, fearing the wrath of Rome, sent it on to the emperor.

Augustus, upon hearing the news of the disaster, assembled an improvised army of gladiators, slaves, legionaries and veterans and sent them with Tiberius and Germanicus to the front, for fear that the Germanic barbarians would invade Gaul and then enter Italy. Augustus had died by the time Germanicus, in 16 AD, succeeded in defeating Arminius and recovered two of the lost eagles, symbols of the annihilated legions.

The old age and death of the dictator

The death of those close to him in whom Augustus had placed hopes of perpetuating his dynasty, the betrayal of relatives who were involved in plots against him, and the political instability unleashed in several provinces of the empire overshadowed the final years of the life of the princeps. When he no longer had a strong enough voice to read out documents in the Curia, he decided to retire from public life. He died in Nola, in Campania, on 19 August 14 AD. He was 75 years, ten months and 26 days old, just 13 days shy of marking the 45th anniversary of his imperial government, after 'facing with integrity the farce that is my life', according to his own words.

Livia kept Augustus's death hidden until Tiberius had returned to Rome. The corpse was transported by the notables of each city through which the funeral procession passed.

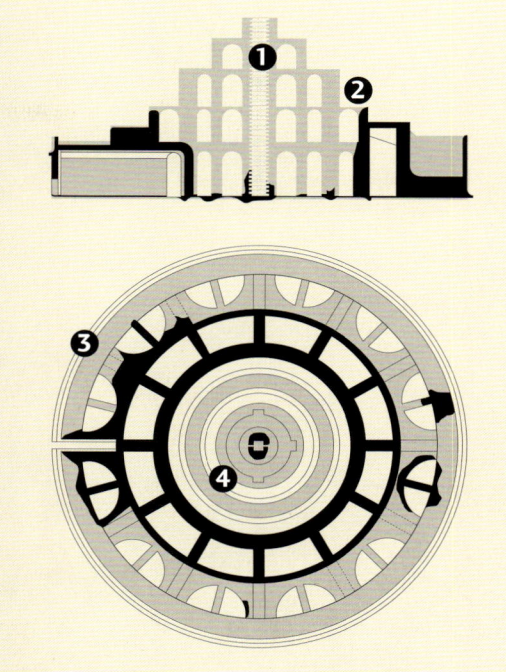

1 THE TOMB
This was in a rectangular chamber located inside the central pillar.

2 THE BASEMENT
The circular base, 87m (285ft) in diameter, was covered in travertine marble.

3 THE INTERIOR
This was formed by concentric tufa walls, joined together by radial walls.

4 THE CELA
In the centre of the tumulus a circular *cela* was set with three niches in which to place cinerary urns.

Near the city, the knights took over the procession to the Palatine Hill during the night. The following day, the funeral arrangements that Augustus had made were read to the Senate, as well as the *Res Gestae*, which were inscribed on two bronze columns that marked the entrance of his mausoleum.

The lifeless body of the emperor was driven to the Field of Mars inside a coffin of marble and gold. Above the body stood a wax representation of Augustus in triumphal dress; masked actors followed the cortege representing the ancestors of the Julian family, both human and divine, since the time of Romulus. Drusus the Younger, the son of Tiberius, read a funeral eulogy from the Rostra, while his father read another from the rostrum of the temple of Divine Julius. Then the body was taken to the pyre; while it burned, the junior senator Numerius Atticus, bribed by Livia with a million sesterces, proclaimed that he had seen the soul of the deceased ascending to the heavens.

According to Dio Cassius, the people showed no signs of suffering until many years later, when the tyrannical excesses of his successors made people recall the tenure of Augustus as a regime of moderate freedom, of a non-oppressive monarchy, free of the civil discord of the past.

Livia, who on the death of the princeps was declared the heir of a third of the family estates and adopted as a daughter of Augustus, became the official priestess of the cult of the deified princeps. It was established that the consuls would arrange the celebration of his date of birth every year and the name of Augustus was given to the month in which he had died, to which one more day was added, taken from the month of February.

■ THE ROMAN EMPIRE

Rome: The capital of the empire

Located along the banks of the Tiber River, Rome arose on the seven hills found on the great curve of this waterway. From what was once a mere village developed the mightiest city in the world.

During Octavian's youth, generals had fought to end the inept Republic by placing power in the hands of the emperor. Rome was a growing city that was poorly designed and managed. People crowded into the capital from the countryside and the regions of Italy, forming chaotic, deprived districts such as the Subura and the Aventine.

Meanwhile, controlling aristocrats lived in luxury. The Palatine, Quirinal and Esquiline hills reflected Hellenistic tradition, with marble houses and fine paintings. Public monuments relied on donations from rich families in exchange for political favours.

Rome showed some architectural grandeur designed by artists of the eastern Mediterranean in the Capitol, the Field of Mars and the Forum. According to Cicero, Julius Caesar wanted to build a new Hellenistic city, *ex novo*, by demolishing the old one, which he thought past repair, for which he promulgated the *Lex de urbe augenda* (law for the expansion of the city). Caesar's assassination in 44 BC ended the plans for urban renewal, including altering the course of the Tiber to connect the Field of Mars with the Ager Vaticanus. Although his plans were not realized, concepts such as the construction of the Forum Iulium, presided over by the Temple of Venus Genetrix; and the new Curia and Basilica Julia, monuments promoting leaders of the Republic, shaped the change of the city, based on the glorification of its first princeps.

THE HEART OF IMPERIAL ROME.
The Roman Forum, the heart of civic life. In the background is the Colosseum, built in the first century.

The foundation and development of Rome

XIV–VIII centuries BC
An agricultural town is established on the Capitoline Hill; it will join other small settled villages on the hills of future Rome. Tradition specifies the date of the mythical foundation of the city by Romulus as 21 April 753 BC.

XII century BC
During the government of Ancus Marcius, fourth king of Ancient Rome, the first bridge is made over the Tiber and the port at the mouth of the river is built in Ostia. Under Servius Tullius, the first walls are erected, enclosing 426 hectares (1050 acres) of urban space.

IV century BC
The Capitoline and the Palatine are constructed. Appius Claudius the Censor orders the construction of the Via Appia (Appian Way) and the first aqueduct in Rome. From the second century BC, buildings and squares are filled with works by Greek artists.

I century BC
With the beginning of the Principate, the magnificence of the capital of the empire increases and the largest administrative centres are created: the imperial Forums. Rome transforms from a city of brick to a city of marble.

THE CAPITOLINE WOLF
A bronze sculpture of the she-wolf, breast-feeding Romulus and Remus (Capitoline Museums, Rome).

Augustus continued Caesar's urban development policy in a less radical way, focusing on the Field of Mars, whose functions Caesar had sought to transfer to the Vatican area. He transformed it into a space designed to exalt himself and the Julian family. His efforts to beautify Rome, which he thought 'lacked the grandeur that the empire demanded', included other projects in the Forum, on the Esquiline and in the Trastevere, so the princeps 'could boast of having found a city of clay, and left one of marble', in the words of Suetonius.

Augustus spent his own wealth on new and old monuments, asking friends to commission works for public enjoyment. Transforming the city gave Augustus an opportunity for self-promotion and inspired public demonstrations of support for the dominant political regime.

Augustus praised his own work in his *Res Gestae*, including building temples to Apollo on the Palatine; Jupiter Feretrius and Jupiter Tonans on the Capitoline; Minerva, Juno Regina and Jupiter on the Aventine; Lares at the top of the Via Sacra; the Penates gods on the Velian Hill; Youth and the Magna Mater on the Palatine; Mars the Avenger in his own Forum; and that of Divine Julius in the republican Forum. Augustus also oversaw the completion of the Forum Iulium and the Basilica Julia, the restoration of the Capitol, the theatre of Pompey and the Via Flaminia, the cleaning of the Tiber's banks, the expansion of the Aqua Marcia and a theatre dedicated to his nephew and son-in-law, Marcus Claudius Marcellus.

THE ROMAN EMPIRE

Augustus complemented these construction projects with administrative reform, which remained in force throughout the imperial era: in 7 BC, he divided the city into 14 districts, incorporating the urban perimeter, Trastevere. His most symbolic architectural projects were the Forum devoted to Mars the Avenger (Forum of Augustus) and the monuments in the Field of Mars. The Forum of Augustus was invested in 2 BC, funded by the spoils of war and built on property that the princeps had seized in the Argiletum quarter. Its construction realized a vow from the Battle of Philippi (42 BC), in which Caesar's assassins were killed. The temple built in the square was consecrated to Mars the Avenger; the entire complex was conceived as a military trophy exalting the Julian family and as a site cultivating the State's new mythology.

The iconographic motif of the Forum of Augustus combined two myths that symbolized the dual origins of Rome and, simultaneously, legitimized the government of the Julio-Claudian dynasty: the myth of Troy, through the figure of Aeneas, son of Venus and Anchises, and the father of Ascanius, the legendary ascendant of the Julian family; and the legend of Romulus, son of Mars and Rhea Silvia. The myths were represented in two sculptural groupings, located in two exedras (semicircular recesses) expanding the porticoes that closed off the plaza lengthways. On one side was the hero Aeneas, who fled from the flames of Troy, saving his father, his son, and the Penates gods, protectors of the home; on the other was Romulus, who, carrying the oak trunk bearing the arms of the defeated Caeninenses, completed the first triumphal parade. The two scenes centring on these

Marble Rome

As the Roman Empire declined, the fifth-century Gaelic poet Claudius Rutilius Namatianus praised the city in verse: 'most beautiful in the world, received among the sidereal stars', 'mother of men and gods'. The splendour of the city is saluted in Horace's poem *Carmen Saeculare*: 'With your shining chariot herald then hide the day, born again new yet the same, you never see anything greater than Rome.' The brick Rome that, according to Suetonius, had first received Augustus, was transformed into a city protected by gods guarded in marble temples that made the Roman way of life the envy of the rest of the world.

EMPEROR AUGUSTUS

1	Tiberine Island	14	Forum of Trajan	27	Ludus Magnus
2	Aemilius Bridge	15	Forum of Augustus	28	Temple of the Divine Claudius
3	Theatre of Marcellus	16	Basilica Aemilia	29	Aqua Claudia Aqueduct
4	Forum Boarium	17	Forum of Nerva	30	Septizodium
5	Arch of Janus	18	Forum of Vespasian	31	Palace of Septimius Severus
6	Temple of Jupiter Optimus Maximus	19	Basilica of Maxentius	32	Domus Flavia
7	Tabularium	20	Temple of Venus and Rome	33	Domus Augustana
8	Temple of Trajan	21	Temple of Caesar	34	Palatine
9	Arch of Septimius Severus	22	Colossus of Nero	35	Circus Maximus
10	Basilica Julia	23	Arch of Constantine	36	Temple of Apollo
11	Senate House	24	Flavian Amphitheatre/Colosseum	37	Temple of Cybele
12	Roman Forum	25	Baths of Titus	38	Aqua Marcia Aqueduct
13	Forum of Caesar	26	Baths of Trajan		

THE ROMAN EMPIRE

The imperial Forums

Julius Caesar moved administration from the republican Forum to a new Forum signifying his power. The Forum of Caesar, built on a site of the Argiletum bought by Cicero, joined the Forums of Augustus, Vespasian, Nerva and Trajan, modifying Rome's landscape. Part of the city map appears in the *Forma Urbis* (below, a fragment), in the Museum of Roman Civilization in Rome.

1 FORUM OF TRAJAN
Designed by Apollodorus of Damascus in 107 AD. The hill that linked the Capitol with the Quirinal was paved in order to build it.

2 FORUM OF AUGUSTUS
Presided over by a temple dedicated to Mars Ultor (Mars the Avenger), dedicated in 2 BC, and separated from the Subura area by a 33m-high (108-ft) wall.

3 FORUM OF CAESAR
Built between 54 and 46 BC at the start of the Clivo Argentario. Behind it was the Temple of Venus Genetrix, full of artworks.

4 FORUM OF NERVA
Mandated by Domitian and inaugurated by Nerva, this included a temple dedicated to Minerva and a pseudo-portico that ran along both sides.

5 FORUM OF VESPASIAN
Also called the Peace Forum, this was built between 71 and 75 AD. It was the seat of the urban prefect.

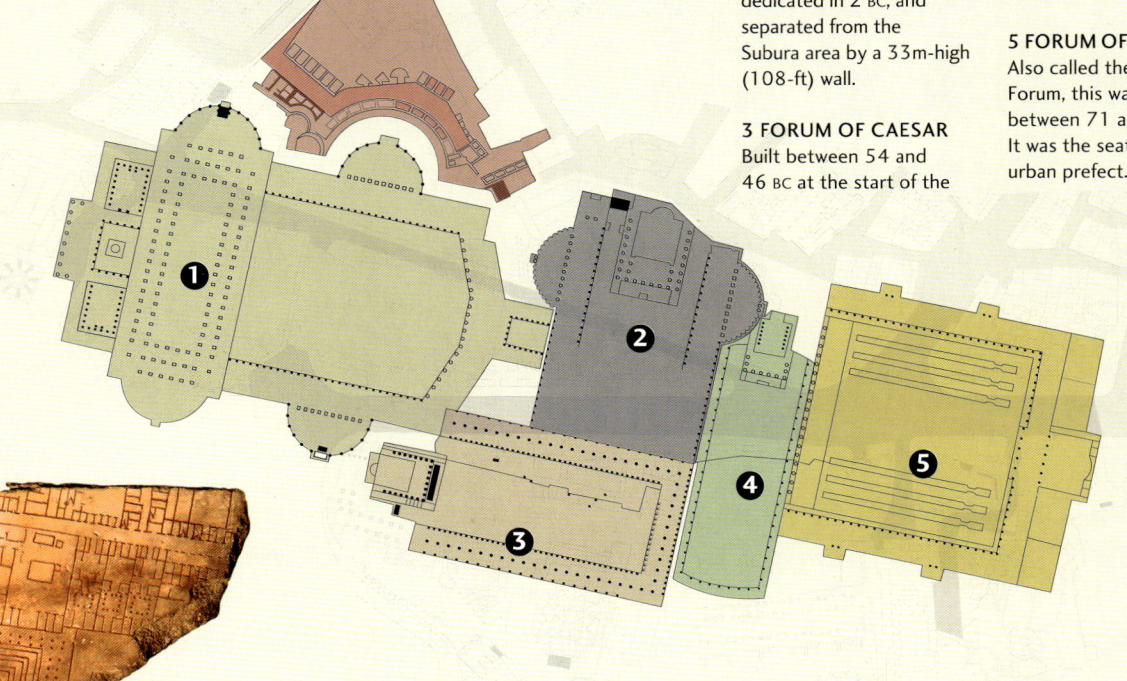

mythical characters, described in Ovid's *Fasti*, became the symbols of *pietas* and victory, the two foundational pillars of Augustine policy.

The Forum also portrayed Augustus's conquests with statues of victorious generals exemplifying Rome's military might. Arms of conquered enemies served as an expression of *maiestas imperii*, together with the crowns and sceptres won at war. The Forums of Caesar and Augustus initiated the progressive displacement of the capital's political, administrative and judicial activity from the old republican Forum to the new spaces created as symbols of imperial power. Vespasian was the next emperor to build an enclosure dedicated to his own exaltation: the Templum Pacis. Nerva, meanwhile, monumentalized the space between the Forum of Augustus and that of Vespasian, erecting a temple dedicated to Minerva. Trajan used loot from the Dacian Wars for an ambitious project. To obtain space for a square, its architect, Apollodorus of Damascus, destroyed a hill connecting the Capitol with the Quirinale, as attested to at the base of Trajan's Column, and in a passage by Dio Cassius. The earth removed was taken to the southeast section of the Forums and piled on the remains of Nero's Domus Aurea palace.

The Field of Mars
Like the Forums, during the imperial era the Field of Mars was transformed into a huge arena publicizing the rich families that held offices of State. The appearance of this vast plain along the Tiber and the first section of the Via Flaminia (or Via Lata) and bordering on the Quirinal and the Pincian hills was described by the Greek geographer Strabo: 'The works of art arranged around this plain, its terrain green throughout the year, and the crown of hills that can be seen up to the river bank, and that offer a scenographic view of it, make it difficult to divert one's gaze […]. Next to this plain are porticoes arranged in a circle, groves,

EMPEROR AUGUSTUS

THE PANTHEON
One of the most impressive buildings of classical Rome was built by Marcus Vipsanius Agrippa.

three theatres, an amphitheatre, and lavish temples, close to each other, in such a way that the rest of the city seems almost an appendix of it.'

In the northern area of the Field of Mars, next to the tombs of the most illustrious men and women of Roman history, Augustus erected his mausoleum, inspired by Etruscan burial mounds of the Eastern tradition. The *Ara Pacis* (Altar of Peace), dedicated on 30 January 9 BC, lay 300m (980ft) southeast of the tomb. Nearby was the Horologium, or Solarium Augusti, a large solar marker whose gnomon was a 30m-tall (98ft) obelisk of Psamtik II from Heliopolis. On 23 September, the day of the autumn equinox and Augustus's birthday, the shadow projected by the obelisk stretched inside the *Ara Pacis*, suggesting that the action of the princeps had ushered in an era of peace.

A large part of the central area of the Field of Mars was acquired by Agrippa (Marcus Vipsanius Agrippa) after victory at the Battle of Actium. It was adorned with buildings for public entertainment and dynastic celebration, with a set of iconographic elements hailing military victories.

The most spectacular building was the Pantheon, built between 27 and 25 BC. It was modelled on the Hellenistic *pantheia*, in which images of the gods were placed around a statue of the sovereign. Its original appearance is unclear, as it was reconstructed twice: once after a fire during Domitian's rule, and again under Hadrian (between 118 and 125). It then acquired the aspect that is admired today. The hemispherical dome measuring 43.3m (140ft) in diameter was incorporated, under which were placed, in exedras and aedicules, images of the gods, including Romulus-Quirine and Julius Caesar, deified. Statues of Agrippa and Augustus flanked the entrance to the enclosure at

THE ROMAN EMPIRE

Water supply in Rome

Strabo says in his *Geography*: 'So plentiful is the supply of water conducted by the aqueducts that word has it, rivers run through the underground channels in Rome. Houses are furnished with cisterns and fountains, due to Marcus Agrippa.' Rome's water supply was guaranteed by 11 aqueducts and 500km (310 miles) of pipelines (430km/267 miles underground) made by using a technique tested by Etruscans, Greeks and Persians. A collection basin at source directed the water along channels, which were supported on arches or excavated underground. A constant gradient of 2 per cent ensured the circulation of the flow.

To avoid leaks, the canal (*specus*) was waterproofed with *cocciopesto*, lime, sand, fragments of bricks or tiles and a vegetable binder, usually fig sap. Once it reached the city, the water filled drainage basins during the night, which were emptied the next day in hot springs and public fountains. Three of these are conserved in Rome: one at Sette Sale, in the Colle Oppio, one in the Baths of Caracalla and one at Caelian Hill, which fed the Colosseum. From the reservoirs, the water reached its final destination by means of tubes (*fistulae*) of different thicknesses, made of ceramic or lead, which flowed into bronze taps or valves. Above, the Cloaca Maxima; to the left, a network of basins and aqueducts.

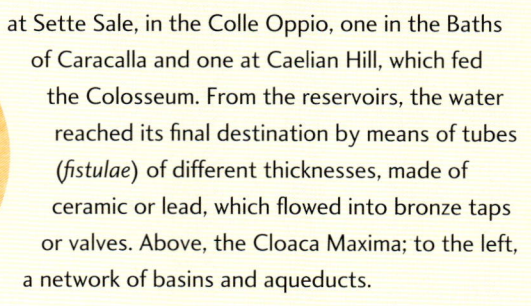

the rear of a portico featuring 20 monolithic granite columns imported from Egypt, standing 14.15m (46ft) tall and 1.48m (5ft) across.

In the vicinity of the Pantheon, Agrippa in ca. 25 BC installed the Agrippae Stagnum, a set of large baths and an artificial lake that served as a pool. He built an aqueduct (Aqua Virgo), which is still in use, from the Agro Lucullano (Casale di Salone). A part of the last section of the aqueduct was destroyed by Caligula, who planned to build an amphitheatre near the Pantheon, but was rebuilt by Claudius in 46 AD. Agrippa brought two paintings depicting Ajax and Venus from the town of Cyzicus and placed them on the walls of the caldarium; the artworks remained there until the time of Trajan. In front of the baths Agrippa dedicated the statue of Apoxyomenos of Lysippos. When Tiberius subsequently placed it in his private bedroom the people demanded that it be returned.

Also famous for its works of art was the Saepta Julia, a large square flanked by two porticoes known for their paintings as that 'of the Argonauts' and 'of Meleager'. It was converted into a market after the Roman assemblies ceased to be held there.

Other great works

The construction of permanent theatres in the southern part of the Field of Mars altered the appearance of the empire's capital. Pompey erected the first theatre in stone, but did so as if it were a ritual offering for the temple of Venus Victrix. This presided over the upper part of the cavea (seating) to remain consistent with the temple/theatre design scheme in place since ancient times in the late republican sanctuaries of Lazio.

Caesar commenced work on a

From the stadium of Domitian to Piazza Navona

Emperor Domitian restored the Field of Mars's buildings after the fire in AD 80, and built a stadium for athletics. In 217, a fire damaged the Colosseum, so the Stadium of Domitian held gladiatorial shows and *venationes* (animal hunts) instead. The outer perimeter of the stadium could seat 30,000 spectators. Houses and churches were built during the Middle Ages, like the one consecrated to the martyr Sant'Agnese. From the Renaissance, Roman families built palaces on the foundations of the stadium. Innocent X, owner of Pamphili Palace, gave the square (left) elegance via the architecture of Bernini and Borromini.

second theatre with capacity for 15,000 spectators, which Augustus concluded and dedicated to the recently deceased Marcellus, his nephew and the first candidate for his succession, in 11 BC. The third of the existing theatres, inaugurated in 13 BC, was commissioned by Lucius Cornelius Balbus the Younger, from Gades (Cádiz) in Hispania.

After the Augustan-era reforms, Nero ordered the construction of new baths in the Field of Mars and a new covered market (the Macellum Magnum) on Caelian Hill. The greatest project of the Julio-Claudian dynasty after 14 AD centred on the Palatine, where Augustus established his imperial residence. All the emperors who succeeded him followed his example. New construction included the camp for the Praetorian Guard, completed under Tiberius; the circus of the Ager Vaticanus, initiated by Caligula and concluded by Nero; and the two aqueducts built by order of Claudius (the Aqua Claudia and the Aqua Anio Novus). There was also a major effort to preserve previous works. In 27 AD, the Caelian Hill was devoured by flames; in 64 AD the most devastating fire Rome had ever suffered broke out, which Nero blamed on the Christians; in 69 AD the Capitol building burned down; and in 80 AD fire devastated the Field of Mars and, once again, the Capitol.

These catastrophes allowed for the redevelopment of Rome's districts in keeping with more rational criteria, in addition to the incorporation of new buildings linked to the new dynasties governing the empire and, therefore, conveying new political messages, symbolically encrypted.

The Rome of the Flavians

Rome's most iconic buildings were built during the Flavian dynasty, including the Flavian amphitheatre, or Colosseum. The lands that Nero had privatized were returned to the people by Vespasian and his sons, Titus and Domitian: the 100-hectare (247-acre) artificial lake in the Domus Aurea made way for the amphitheatre. Baths of the imperial house were supplanted with a new installation by Titus. The rest of the structures disappeared under a district set up to service gladiatorial games, including a hospital, homes for gladiators and shops.

TIBERIUS
The emperor wears the civic crown in this first-century marble bust that is preserved in the National Archaeological Museum of Naples. On the next page, a commemorative coin from the reign of Caligula shows the emperor haranguing his troops (Münzkabinett, Berlin).

TIBERIUS & CALIGULA

When Tiberius ascended the throne, young Romans had known no other political system than the monarchy, and the old ones feared the start of another civil war. Tiberius tried to implement a civil Principate in which participation would be subject to the Senate, but the intrigues of Livia and Sejanus propelled it to carry out great atrocities. However, his nephew Caligula exceeded Tiberius in cruelty.

After Augustus died in 14 AD, as the first princeps of the empire, his will was read out in the Senate, naming Livia Drusilla's son as rightful heir to the Principate. Suetonius accounts that this was more out of necessity than by the will of the testator. 'Adverse fortune took away my sons, Gaius and Lucius; I name Tiberius Caesar as my heir to two thirds.'

Tiberius's arrival to the throne was announced before the Senate as if it had been a game of destiny, since all the direct descendants of the Julian family who had been presented during Augustus's life before the people as hereditary princes had died. At the age of 56, Tiberius had, by removing his opponents, thus assumed the burden of government.

The remaining third of Augustus's inheritance was granted to Livia. The empress was adopted into the Julian family, as if she were a daughter of Augustus, and appointed to the government as a 'colleague' of her son so

THE ROMAN EMPIRE

The reign of Tiberius, the 'Sombre Prince'

42 BC
Tiberius was born on 16 November, son of Livia and Claudius Nero. Four years later, he moved to live with Octavian, Livia's second husband.

12 AD
Tiberius is linked to the Julio-Claudian family through his marriage to Julia, daughter of Augustus, who associated him with the Principality.

14 AD
Upon the death of Augustus, Tiberius is named his successor. He refuses the title of Imperator to maintain the civil nature of the Principate.

26 AD
After the murder of his two sons, Drusus the Younger and Germanicus (adopted), Tiberius retires permanently to the Villa Jovis, in Capri.

32 AD
Sejanus's plot is discovered. An altar to Providentia is erected, in which the salvation of the empire is celebrated annually.

37 AD
Tiberius dies in Miseno, aged 78. Senator Lucius Arruntius commits suicide upon the advent of Caligula.

that Livia, officially named Julia Augusta from then on, could receive the related inheritance. It was necessary to vote an exemption to the *Lex Voconia* that had been approved in 169 BC: this law prevented the hereditary transfer of property from citizens of a certain class to uphold *agnatio* (male civil kinship).

Portrait of a prince

Historians review Tiberius's reign in varied ways: for some he was a perverse, despotic prince from the start, guilty of all the disasters, comparable to Nero and Caligula in his wickedness. Others portray him as a model of bureaucracy, 'Rome's most capable emperor', as Theodor Mommsen wrote. The four main Roman sources on the public and private life of Tiberius (Suetonius, Tacitus, Dio Cassius and Veleius Paterculus) agreed on the shrewd running of the empire that Tiberius developed in his first years of government, all benefiting *res publica*. His late rise to power meant that he had more political and military experience than any other successor, following his successful military campaigns in the Alpine and Dalmatian plus battles against the Germanic peoples.

Among the first immoral acts credited to Tiberius by ancient historians is the murder of Agrippa Postumus, son of Julia the Elder and Marcus Vipsanius Agrippa and last descendant of the Julian family; he had been exiled to the island of Planasia at the age of seven so that Livia's son could take the throne. Tacitus narrates the elimination of the younger brother of Gaius and Lucius, according to which Tiberius and Livia, 'one out of fear, the other out of hatred', planned the death of the young man with the help of Passienus, nephew and adoptive son of the historian Sallust. According to this account, a slave of the deceased, Clemens, took the ashes of his master and, taking advantage of his physical resemblance to him, spread rumours that Agrippa Postumus was still alive and would incite an uprising against the new princeps. Clemens was captured and executed in the imperial palace.

Today it is thought that Agrippa Postumus could have died naturally at the same time as Tiberius became emperor, causing malicious stories to be spread by rivals. It is also very probable that the legend appeared years later, when the trials against anyone suspected of conspiracy against the State stained the emperor's brilliant career with blood.

An effective ruler

More than any other Julio-Claudian ruler, Tiberius sought support for the ideal of a civil Principate, in which the princeps and the Senate collaborated effectively. From the outset, he acted as one of the 300 members that made up the senatorial assembly and attended political debates. Just as Augustus had done, and following the advice expressed in his stepfather's will, Tiberius's counsellors guided him in legal matters and he took opposing opinions into account without resentment. He enjoyed discussion, cultivating a style similar to that of Theodorus of Gadara during his years of seclusion from public life in Rhodes. Somewhat

TRIUMPH OF TIBERIUS
This bas-relief scene adorns a beautiful silver cup that was part of the tableware found in a villa in Boscoreale, near Pompeii. Tiberius appears in his triumphal chariot; behind him, a slave holds the laurel wreath over his head as soldiers and lictors swarm around him. Tiberius was one of the Roman generals who achieved major military successes in his time: he spent much of his public life securing the borders of Germany and Armenia before ascending the imperial throne (Louvre Museum, Paris).

fussy and uncertain, he was also an admirer of the teachings of Corvinus.

The attempt to equalize his powers to that of the rest of the senatorial leaders, except for the authority awarded to him by his control over the legions, was displayed in Tiberius's refusal to accept the honours offered to him throughout his career. Tiberius refused to be named *pater patriae* (father of the fatherland), and used the name Augustus only in official documents, as it humanized a living god. He called himself Princeps Senatus (first head of the Senate), and only his soldiers addressed him by the title of emperor. He rejected all adulation, leaving the city on the first day of the year to avoid receiving gifts, a tradition started by Augustus, and vetoed public celebrations of his birthday.

Tiberius's disregard for the power invested in him and his resolve to behave in parity with the Senate created ambitions in those aspiring to take control of the State. His mother, Livia, and his Prefect of the Praetorian Guard, Lucius Aelius Sejanus, manipulated his indecision and forced him into leaving Rome, delegating the most important imperial decisions to them.

Livia turned her son into an instrument to fulfil her eagerness to rule the world. She controlled the official correspondence, received the Senate and behaved as if she had imperial power in her hands. She was not satisfied with acting as regent with Tiberius, whom she claimed to have made an emperor; nor was it enough for her name to be attached to the princeps in official documents: she also took charge of eliminating those she considered to be a danger to the stability of Claudian rule.

If there was a death, among the many that defiled the government of Tiberius, for which Livia was blamed and that shocked the entire Roman Empire, it was that of her own grandson Germanicus, who, despite having the support of the legions, had always been loyal to his uncle and adoptive father.

THE ROMAN EMPIRE

The northern borders: from Drusus to Germanicus

Augustus's *Res Gestae* warned about keeping the Rhine and the Danube as the northern limits of the empire; Drusus the Elder had been killed in military expeditions against the Germanic and Pannonian tribes, and Tiberius forced Germanicus to retire in 17 AD. As proconsul in Gaul, Germanicus, without Tiberius's approval, crossed the Rhine and invaded Germania; he was obsessed with emulating his father Drusus, who had died in 9 AD after submitting to the Marsi and Cheruscians. Germanicus fought the Chatti, Tencteri and Mattiaci tribes and built fortresses between the Rhine and the Weser, bribing eight legions stationed there, under Gaius Silius and Aulus Caecina Severus, for their loyalty. In an invasion of Germania in 14 AD, the Romans penetrated the Cesia Forest and massacred the Marsi. After pacifying the region west of the Rhine, Germanicus headed east of the river in 15 AD; there, Caecina was killed on the Pontes longi (long bridge), attacked by Arminius, a Cheruscian prince. A new campaign against the tribes of the Rhine and the Elbe in 16 AD saw Roman victory at Idistaviso, near the Weser. According to Tacitus, Tiberius envied Germanicus and sent him to the East. Below left is the Golden Age of Tiberius (National Archaeological Museum, Naples); on the right is the altar to the Victorious Sixth Legion, Lower Germania, dedicated to the god Oceanus in thanks for its protection.

For his part, Sejanus, who, in the opinion of Tacitus, 'hid under his meek exterior a thirst for power', aimed to be a favourite of the princeps, just as Agrippa had been for Augustus. Using a friendship established during the retreat of Tiberius in Rhodes to bolster a jealous hatred of the victorious General Germanicus, and his wife Vipsania Agrippina, who had greater authority in the army than his envoys, both Livia and Sejanus participated in murdering Germanicus and in the political neutralization of Agrippina and her children, who were supported by a powerful political party faction of the last descendants of Julians.

Tiberius's foreign policy

When Tiberius succeeded Augustus as head of the Principate, conflicts raged. The Gauls rebelled again. Alliances with the kingdoms of Cappadocia, Cilicia and Commagene failed upon the death of their kings, whose territories were annexed to the empire. To avoid depleting State coffers and in order to maintain the peace inherited from his predecessor, Tiberius pursued a foreign policy without expansionist zeal, mainly sustaining frontiers already won and pacifying the peoples already defeated.

The instability of the Lower Germanic region meant the emperor suspended military activity beyond the Rhine and ended the campaigns led by Germanicus to avoid war with the Marcomanni king Maroboduus. Tiberius let rows between the Germanic tribes ruin their leaders. Arminius, the chieftain of the Cherusci who had defeated the Romans at Teutoburg Forest, was assassinated by his own men for fear of his ambitions, and Maroboduus asked Tiberius for political asylum. He was exiled in Ravenna, 'accepting the loss of his fame for his great desire to live,' according to Tacitus.

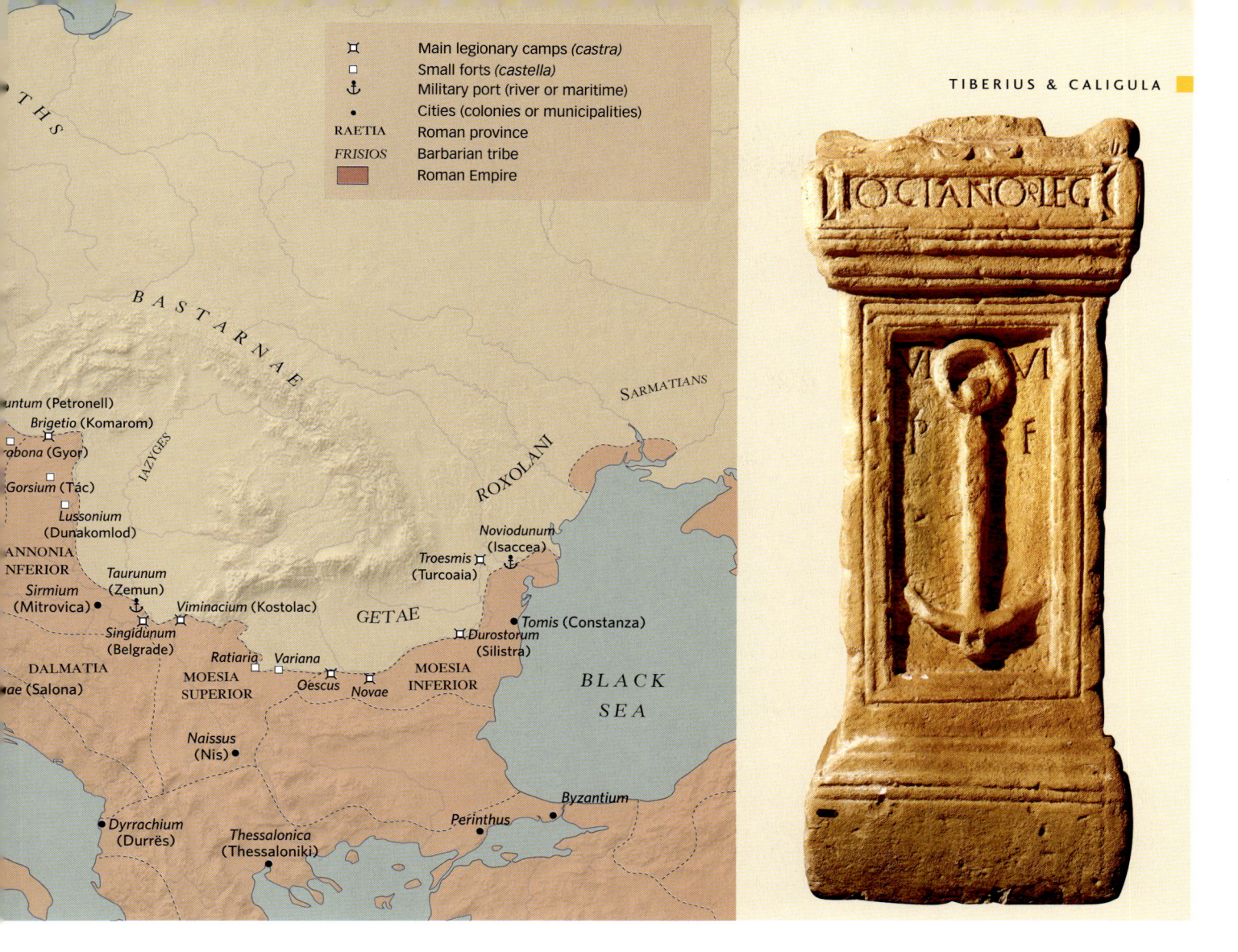

In 17 AD, a war began in North Africa, led by a Numidian named Tacfarinas. Aware of the discontent that many tribes felt for the Roman administration, Tacfarinas united the Musulamii, Mauri and Garamantes to rebel against their ruler, Ptolemy, a client king under the command of Rome, who was the son of Juba II and Cleopatra Selene, the grandson of Mark Antony and Cleopatra and the cousin of the future emperor Claudius. The warlike confrontation with the Berber tribes lasted for seven years, with intermittent flashpoints in a vast territory that extended between Sirte in the east and Mauretania to the west. After unsuccessful attempts by Quintus Junius Blaesus, the proconsul Publius Cornelius Dolabella defeated Tacfarinas in the fortress of Auzea. Meanwhile, in 21 AD, Tiberius was forced to end the Gallic tribes' revolt, led by Julius Sacrovir and Julius Florus, from the tribes of the Aedui and the Treveri, which had spread even to the Roman legions, who had witnessed the desertion of the Gauls enrolled in the auxiliary militias. The insurgents were defeated in the battles of the Ardennes Woods and Augustodunum, after which the leaders committed suicide.

Germanicus

In 17 AD, German military expeditions were still in motion as Germanicus suffered great losses among the legions. Tiberius opted not to pursue imperial expansion north of Germany and ordered his nephew to return to Rome. In 18 AD, he sent Germanicus east with the supreme power to rectify the civil discords that had arisen among the inhabitants of the eastern Roman provinces. At the same time, Drusus, Tiberius's son, was sent to Illyria to win the favour of the legion colonies.

THE ROMAN EMPIRE

The works of the great Roman historian Livy

In 17 AD, Titus Livy, the last of the Roman analysts, and one who had educated Emperor Claudius, died aged 77. Despite experiencing the rise of Augustus and the continuation of his family in power, Livy did not exalt the Julians, unlike Virgil and Horace, although he did praise the return to the ancient spirit of Rome and considered *pietas* and *virtus* as guarantors of the State's prosperity. Livy arrived in Rome from Patavium (Padua) aged 30, and began his life's work: *Ab urbe condita*, a history of Rome from its origins to Drusus the Elder's death. Pliny says the public reading of the first books earned Livy such a high reputation that citizens from remote provinces of the empire came to Rome to meet him. Livy's *History of Rome* comprised 142 books, published in groups of five. Only 34 are complete, but summaries of them have been preserved (*periochae* and *epitome*), and inspired the works of fourth-century Eutropius's breviary of Roman history and fifth-century Orosio's *Seven Books of History Against the Pagans*. Although the historical facts had been narrated by previous analysts, such as Celio Antipater, Polybius and Posidonium, Livy knew how to breathe a new spirit into his stories.
Image: Livy in a 19th-century engraving by the artist J.W. Fox.

From Brundisium, Germanicus sailed to Greece, where he crowned Artaxias III, son of Polemon I of Pontus, as king of Armenia, and started his second consulate. From Athens, he and his family went to Euboea and to Lesbos, where Agrippina the Younger gave birth to her youngest daughter. In the province of Asia via Byzantium, he went south, witnessing a prophesy of his premature death at the oracle of Apollo at Claros. Syria marked the end of his journey. Meanwhile, Tiberius appointed Gnaeus Calpurnius Piso as governor of the province, and Livia assigned him to spy on Germanicus. Plancina, wife of Calpurnius Piso and Livia's intimate friend, accompanied her husband in order to spy on Agrippina. As soon as they reached their destination, Piso and Plancina spread rumours against Germanicus and Agrippina, trying to corrupt the legions with bribes. Germanicus heard and declared his hatred of the governor sent by the emperor. On his return from Egypt and the provinces of the eastern Mediterranean in 18 AD, Germanicus fell ill, suspecting he was the victim of poisoning and of the curses of Piso and his wife, before dying aged 33. Tacitus states that he probably died from malaria.

A death that caused Rome to mourn

As news of Germanicus's death spread throughout Rome, the whole city mourned. Tacitus states that, upon Agrippina the Elder's arrival at the port of Brundisium with the ashes of her late husband and her six children (Nero, Drusus, Gaius Caligula, Agrippina the Younger, Julia Drusilla and Julia Livilla), 'crowds gathered visibly upset'. When they arrived in Rome, neither Tiberius nor Livia attended the funerals that were held in honour of the deceased. Their absence caused a public outcry, mixing grief for the death of a military hero with hatred towards the emperor and his mother.

Tiberius eventually conceded to the people's demands for justice, condemning Calpurnius Piso. The trial and verdict against Calpurnius Piso, as well as the posthumous honours that were decreed for Germanicus, were published in the portico of the Temple of Apollo Palatinus. Copies were distributed throughout the empire and were placed in the busiest place of each city.

One copy, preserved in the senate decree against Gnaeus Calpurnius Piso, which was found in the 1990s in the municipality of El Saucejo, near Seville, states that both Plancina and her son, Marcus Piso, were acquitted thanks to the direct intervention of Livia. Tiberius managed to mitigate the harsh sentence that was issued by the Senate, who condemned Piso not only for the death of Germanicus but also for having caused civil war in Syria after his death.

Tiberius's retreat to Capri

Public loathing towards the emperor after Germanicus's death and Livia's intrusion into State affairs drove Tiberius to retreat to the island of Capri in 26 AD at the age of 68. The emperor never returned to Rome, not even to bury his mother.

Officials gave his reason for leaving Rome as the fulfilment of a trip through Campania to dedicate a temple to Jupiter in Capua and another to Augustus in Nola. Once the ceremonies were over, Tiberius set course to the island. He stayed in the Villa Jovis, a palace three times larger than the Domus Tiberiana on the Palatine Hill, which became the main seat of the administration of the empire. The choice of Capri was a response to two different factors: first, since late republican times, Campania had become the ideal place of leisure for Roman aristocrats in retirement; second, added to the beauty of its landscape was the possibility of intellectual pursuits such as philosophical gatherings and recitals of verses among poets such as Virgil, Decimus Laberius and Blaesus. Capri was almost impregnable, located four hours by boat from the port of Misenum, the base of the largest Roman military fleet, and five hours from Puteoli (Pozzuoli), grain supply centre for Rome, one of the busiest ports in the Mediterranean. In addition, Tiberius also sought a cure for a condition that covered his body with ulcers.

The imperial administrative headquarters of Capri was constituted in the style of a Hellenic court, and Tiberius decided to surround himself with his most efficient advisers, such as the future emperors Vitellius, Galba and Vespasian; the senator Marcus Cocceius Nerva; the equites Sejanus and Curtius Atticus. Also present were his relatives who were most involved in his policy agenda, including the two sons of Germanicus: Drusus, along with his wife Aemilia Lepida, and Caligula, with his wife Junia Claudilla.

AGRIPPINA IN BRUNDISIUM

When Germanicus died in Syria in mysterious circumstances, his widow, Agrippina, accompanied by her children, arrived at the port of Brundisium (Brindisi) with his ashes in order to take them to Rome; this scene was recreated in 1767 by the American painter Benjamin West in an oil painting preserved in the Yale University Art Gallery, in New Haven. Germanicus was a true hero, as dear to the Roman people as his father, Drusus the Elder, who had also died young.

THE ROMAN EMPIRE

THE GREAT CAMEO OF FRANCE

The largest Roman cameo discovered to this day has been kept in the numismatic cabinet of the National Library of Paris since 1791. It probably arrived in France after being acquired by Baldwin II, Emperor of Constantinople, and became part of the French treasury, where it was conserved in 1279 according to the inventories of the Sainte-Chapelle. The relief, carved in five layers of onyx, 31cm high by 26.5cm wide (12 by 10in), represents the imperial family as it was around 23 AD. The scene highlights the dynastic continuity of the Julio-Claudians after the death of Augustus, while extolling his military victories over the barbarian peoples. The 24 figures depicted are distributed in three registers: the top represents the deceased in Olympus; in the middle strip the living are arranged around the two central enthroned figures of Tiberius and Livia; the lower register is dedicated to the vanquished peoples.

1 AUGUSTUS
Dressed as Pontifex Maximus and with the radiated crown, symbol of his divinization, he is led by Iulus, son of Aeneas, founder of the dynasty.

2 GERMANICUS
Shown ascending on Pegasus. He was adopted by Tiberius in 4 AD and died in 19 AD. In front of him is Drusus the Younger, son of Tiberius, who died in 23 AD.

3 GAIUS CAESAR
Younger son of Germanicus and Agrippina, here aged 11. He was nicknamed 'Caligula' and was a future emperor.

4 NERO JULIUS CAESAR
The eldest son of Germanicus, candidate for succeeding Tiberius through his marriage to his granddaughter Julia, daughter of Drusus and Claudia Livia Julia.

5 ANTONIA MINOR
The daughter of Mark Antony and Octavia and mother of Germanicus, Claudius and Claudia Livilla. She may have commissioned the cameo.

6 TIBERIUS
He presides over the scene, sitting on a throne with a footstool. He is dressed in the protective coat of Jupiter and carries the curved augural staff in his right hand.

TIBERIUS & CALIGULA

GEM CARVINGS
The use of seals in gold and cameo rings increased the demand for precious stones, which were imported from Asia Minor, Egypt, Arabia or India. Pliny says the seals were made using sardonyx, an orange-coloured translucent quartz from Sardis; onyx and, above all, agate, which allowed carvings to be made in superimposed layers or in different bands. Pliny cites Dioscurides among the most famous gem cutters; he created a portrait of Augustus that his successors used to seal official documents. Above, Augustus in a cameo preserved in the National Library of France.

7 LIVIA
She accompanies her son Tiberius, with whom she shared the Principate. She holds a bouquet of spikes and poppies – attributes linking her to the goddess Ceres.

8 DRUSUS JULIUS CAESAR
He raises a trophy towards his father. He was also adopted by Tiberius after the death of Tiberius's son Drusus.

9 CLAUDIA LIVIA JULIA
To her detriment, the sister of Germanicus and Claudius was compared with Agrippina, her sister-in-law, whom she managed to exile with the help of her lover Sejanus.

10 LOWER REGISTER
Here the barbarian captives are represented, probably freedmen (symbolized by the Phrygian cap) and Germans (with long hair).

THE ROMAN EMPIRE

Villa Jovis: Tiberius's refuge in Capri

In 1932, Benito Mussolini commissioned Italian archaeologist Amedeo Maiuri to excavate the Villa Jovis, which had been built on the highest promontory on the island of Capri. Maiuri's excavations revealed old cisterns that supplied the villa, plus a large portion of the residential complex, which combined spaces for housing, government and public administration. The palace layout did not conform to the typical structure of Roman leisure villas, but rather was inspired by Hellenistic architectural models adapted to the requirements of a government residence. Built on a single artificial terrace, more than 40m (130ft) high and with a surface area of 7000sq m (75,350sq ft), the Villa Jovis is a superb example of Roman engineering. Left, a marble statue of Tiberius (National Archaeological Museum, Aquilea).

The intrigues of Sejanus

Although he did not personally go to Rome, Tiberius kept contact with the capital from his island headquarters, keeping audiences small. He used as his intermediary and co-regent the Praetorian prefect Sejanus, whom Paterculus described as, 'a man full of eagerness; without asking anything, he amassed everything'. Sejanus did not belong to the senatorial class but was equal in honours to the emperor: his image was minted on coins; his name inscribed next to the princeps; and statues of him displayed with those of the Augustan family.

He was 'enraptured by his great power', remarks Dio Cassius, and 'exalted by the emperor himself.' Sejanus formed a party supported by 9000 soldiers of the Praetorian Guard that he commanded and plotted seizure of the throne. To legitimize his plan, he had to become related to the imperial family, making allies of the Roman aristocracy, supporters of the emperor, and to eliminate the rivals grouped in support of Germanicus's widow, Agrippina, and their children.

Sejanus began affairs with the wives of the most illustrious citizens of Rome, hoping to learn secrets about their cuckolded husbands. Claudia Livia Julia, wife of Drusus, the son of Tiberius, and sister of Germanicus and Claudius, became his focus, as his union with the Claudian family depended on her. Apicata, Sejanus's betrayed wife, later claimed that the eunuch Lygdus and Livia's doctor and friend, Eudemus, had provided the poison for Drusus's assassination, thus clearing the path to the dynastic marriage planned by Sejanus.

Meanwhile, in 23 AD, Agrippina the Elder left Rome, and was banished to Pandateria. She died of starvation a decade later, after her sons Drusus and Nero had been eliminated.

TIBERIUS & CALIGULA

1 ACCESS RAMP
This led to the imperial area, with a large semicircular chamber overlooking the Bay of Sorrento.

2 GREAT CENTRAL COURTYARD
Below were the cisterns that supplied the villa with water.

3 BATHS
These featured five different atmospheres. The caldarium was equipped with marble and bronze tubs for washing.

4 SERVANTS' QUARTERS
These were distributed on three floors, along lengthy corridors.

5 VILLA VESTIBULE
Accessed via a series of ramps, this was an atrium with four columns of Cipollino marble.

6 LIGHTHOUSE TOWER
This allowed boats to communicate with the mainland by means of light signals.

7 SPECULARIUM
The astronomical observatory was built for Thrasyllus, Tiberius's personal astronomer.

Tacitus says that Drusus, the son of Germanicus and Agrippina, also died of starvation in the Palatine prison. One rumour was that Tiberius had ordered, in the event that Sejanus rebelled against him, that Naevius Sutorius Macro should help Drusus escape from prison and make him leader of a movement against Sejanus.

Political terror in Rome
Sejanus's victims of the Julian law of majesty increased, and many who were accused of acting against his imperial majesty avoided the death sentence with suicide to prevent their children losing the family property. The Roman knight Lucius Ennius was prosecuted for melting down a silver statue of Augustus to make cutlery. He was spared, but Gaius Silius and Titius Sabinus, supporters of Agrippina and the descendants of Germanicus, were not. Aelius Saturninus was accused of writing verses against Tiberius, and Cremutius Cordus was tried for his writings on the deeds of Augustus in which he extolled Cassius and Brutus.

After Tiberius went to Capri, the persecutions increased. No citizen in Rome felt safe, as rewards from the treasury incentivized betrayals. Poverty drove children to accuse their parents of revolt just to claim rewards. This happened to Vibius Serenus (Proconsul of Spain), who was exiled to Amorgos. Tiberius remained unaware of events in the capital. His correspondence was edited and labelled responsible for the situation. Suetonius declared: 'Rome, this is the fate that awaits you: he who from exile comes to reign, reigns drenched in blood'.

The death of Livia and the fall of Sejanus
Livia died in 29 AD, at the age of 87. Tiberius

TEMPLE OF AUGUSTUS AND LIVIA IN VIENNE
Despite the dedication of temples such as that of the Colonia Julia Vienna (in modern-day Vienne, France), which dates back to ca. 20–10 BC, Livia yearned to be incorporated into the series of Roman gods, but her son Tiberius did not wish to espouse this position before the Senate. It was Livia's grandson, Claudius, who elevated her to the rank of goddess after he was proclaimed emperor.

did not travel back to Rome for the funeral. Angry at his mother's meddling in affairs of State, the emperor allowed only a funeral befitting a Roman aristocrat, before declaring Livia's will null and void.

Sejanus was sentenced to death after Tiberius's sister-in-law Antonia the Younger, the mother of Germanicus, Claudius and Claudia Livia Julia, informed Tiberius that the Praetorian prefect was a traitor. Shrewdly, Tiberius pretended he knew nothing of Sejanus's plot and began to govern in an unusual manner. In 31 AD, he made Sejanus his consular colleague and sent contradictory letters to the Senate, praising and then condemning Sejanus. Announcing Caligula as augur meant the public exaltation of his nephew and declared that Tiberius had chosen his successor to the throne, dashing the prefect's hopes. The public accepted this motion, projecting onto Caligula the qualities of his father. Thus assured of the Senate's support, Tiberius went on the attack against the prefect.

Naevius Sutorius Macro, Graecinius Laco and Publius Memmius Regulus, who were in charge of controlling the bodyguard, the *vigiles* (firefighters and police) and the Senate, respectively, conspired in Sejanus's collapse. Sejanus went to the Senate expecting to be honoured with tribunician power, a position associated with absolute power. His cohorts were led to the Castra Praetoria (the Praetorian Guards' barracks), expecting gifts. The Senate met in the Temple of Apollo. Regulus passed judgement on Sejanus and sentenced him to death. His sons and daughter were also condemned by senatorial decree. Apicata, Sejanus's former wife, committed suicide.

Among the Romans, the punishment of oblivion, *damnatio memoriae* or *atimia* – the

The dreadful death of Claudia Livia Julia, Sejanus's lover

Claudia Livia Julia, better known as Livilla, was the daughter of Antonia Minor and Drusus the Elder, and the sister of Claudius and Germanicus. Augustus had planned her marriage to Drusus the Younger, son of Tiberius and his cousin, in order to unite the rival Julian and Claudian families.

Shortly after the trial and execution of Sejanus in 31 AD, Sejanus's former wife, Apicata, whom Sejanus had divorced in 23 AD, wrote to Tiberius, accusing Sejanus and his mistress Livilla of having poisoned Drusus in 23 AD with the help of the physician Eudemus and a slave named Ligdus. Although all involved in the poisoning were executed by order of Tiberius (who believed Apicata's accusation), Dio Cassius records the rumour that, rather than being executed, Livilla was sent to her mother, Antonia, who then starved her to death. It is possible that the story of Livilla's death (depicted here in a statue at the Maremma Museum of Archaeology and Art) was fabricated by the people as a result of the values embodied by Antonia, who was a woman of irreproachable dignity, impeccable morality and chastity, and highly esteemed by Augustus and Tiberius. Tacitus writes that 'fame takes pleasure in surrounding the death of princes with tragic circumstances'. After Livilla's death, the Senate decreed her *damnatio memoriae* – destroying monuments portraying her or bearing her name.

---

elimination of their name from the public monuments of the empire – was one of the worst that could be suffered. In reference to the fall of Sejanus, Dio Cassius describes perfectly the behaviour of the people against tyrants, whom they had been forced to revere out of fear and whom they damned, directly or indirectly, when the situation of danger had been overcome. This happened with Sejanus, Tiberius, Caligula and Nero among the Julio-Claudians; it continued with the Flavians, and also with some Antonines who overstepped the limits of sovereignty and became tyrannical.

When Sejanus was prosecuted and executed on 18 October 31 AD, people continued to inflict wounds on his corpse, throwing it into the Tiber from the Gemonian stairs. With the disappearance of a leader like Sejanus, who had tried to emulate his power to that of Tiberius, all his supporters also disappeared, well aware that, if Sejanus had been the victor in the struggle for power, they would have been the beneficiaries and their adversaries those punished with death. Aware that the people were freed from the impositions of a tyrant, they raised a statue of Libertas in the Forum, an indirect commemoration of the end of an era and the recovery of lost freedom, not only from the direct actions of the tyrant, but also from the state of paranoia and fear instigated by the followers of the dictatorial regime.

The earth overwhelmed with fire

In the months after the execution of Sejanus, terror returned to ravage the streets of Rome, as proceedings against all those who had supported the insurrection against Tiberius began. The people began to persecute and kill those who had become powerful because of their support for the traitor. From 33 AD and as

LIVIA'S HOUSE (OVERLEAF)
Although the residence where Livia lived with her husband Augustus was on the Palatine Hill, the empress owned a lavish villa in Prima Porta. This villa, on the outskirts of Rome, next to the Via Flaminia and near the Tiber, was her favourite residence. It was decorated with beautiful, naturalistic frescoes such as the depiction of a garden shown here. The frescoes at Livia's house are among the best-preserved in Rome (National Museum of Rome, Palazzo Massimo, Rome).

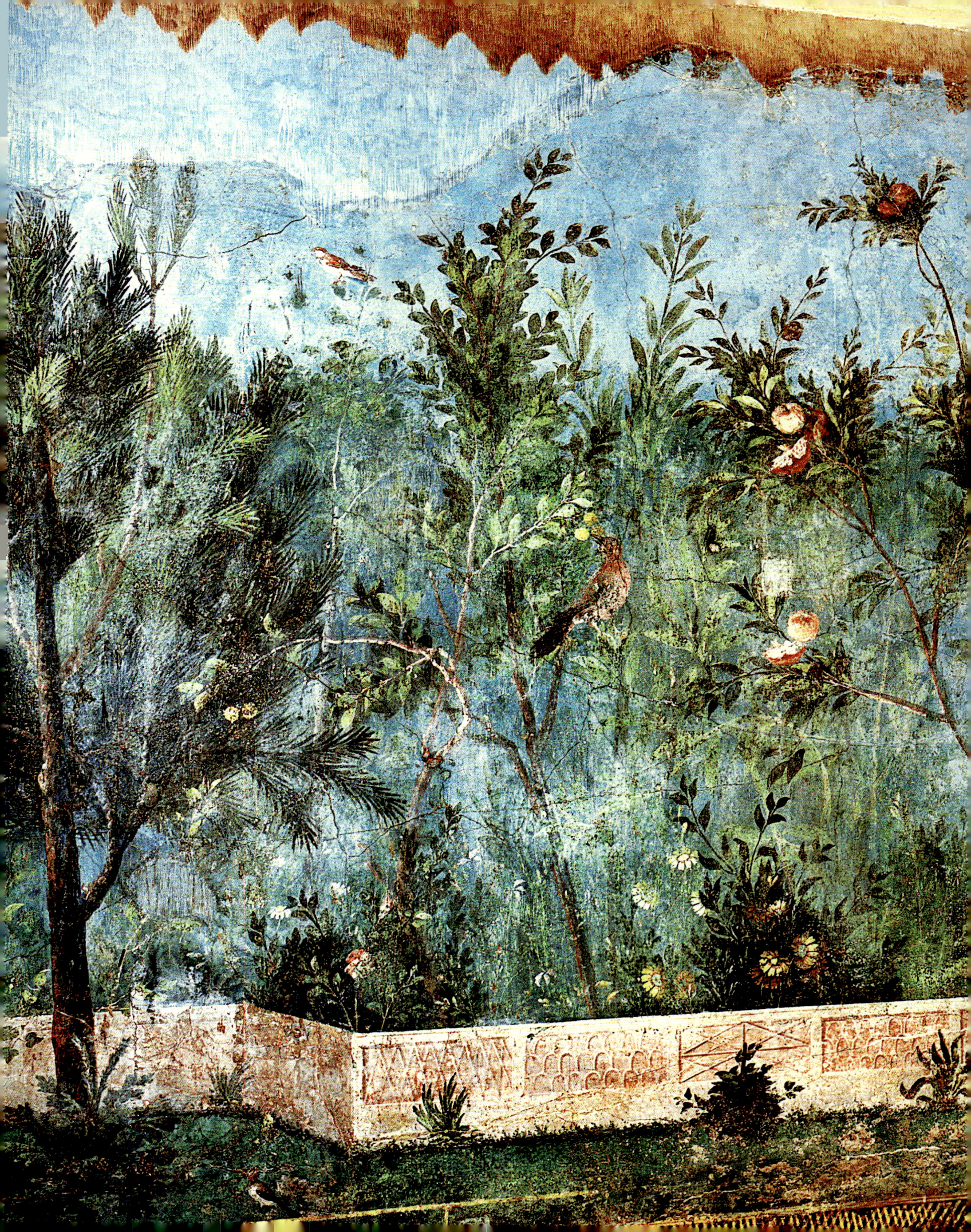

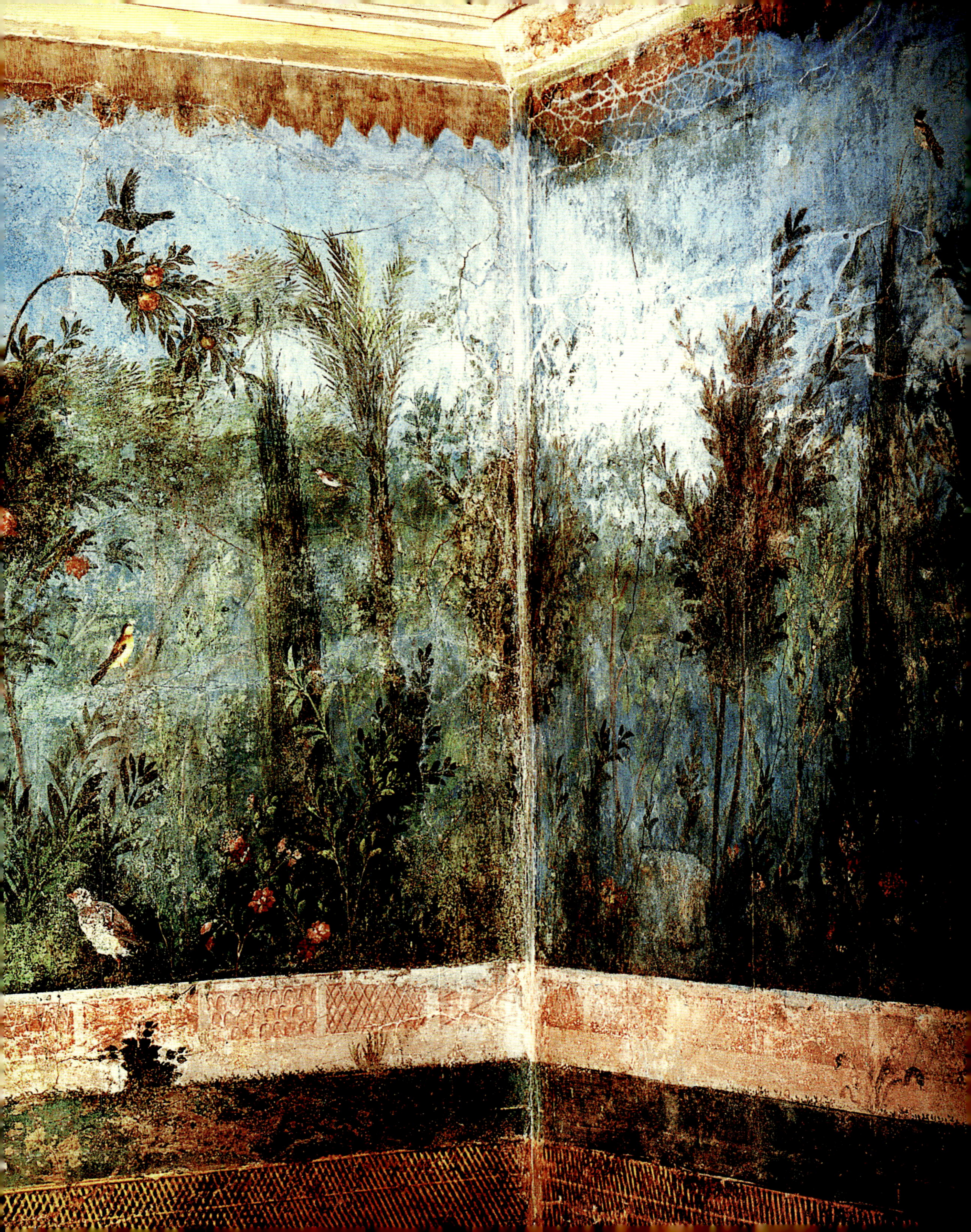

The Praetorian Guard: decisive in the imperial succession

On Sejanus's advice, between 21 and 23 AD, Tiberius gathered the Praetorian Guard, 'hitherto scattered in various accommodations', according to Suetonius, into a single barracks, the Castra Praetoria, between the Via Nomentana and the Via Tiburtina in Rome. Two equestrian prefects were placed in charge. Their excessive power spurred Constantine to dissolve the body in 312.

The Prateorian prefects exerted great influence on the government, as they commanded the only troops allowed to remain in Italy. Emperors bribed the Praetorian Guard for their loyalty with three times a legionary's salary and four years' fewer service. They also distributed major sums of money among the guards. The loss of the imperial guard's allegiance meant the end of a government and the rise of a new monarch. For example, they were decisive in bringing about Caligula's fall and the rise of Claudius. They were also involved in the conspiracy against Commodus, plotted mainly by Praetorian prefect Aemilius Laetus and Commodus's mistress, Marcia. Image: statuary found in the Forum (Louvre Museum, Paris).

a result of the death of Agrippina the Elder and her son Drusus, who were not even granted a grave worthy of their lineage, Tiberius gained the animosity of all Rome and gruesome stories began to circulate describing his revolting vices and malevolent cruelties.

The only child of Agrippina the Elder who was saved was Caligula; he was protected at first by his great-grandmother Livia and, after her death, by his grandmother Antonia the Younger. In 31 AD, he was summoned to Capri to live in the imperial residence, so that the last descendant of the Julians would be protected from the assassination plots of Messalinus Cotta and Sextus Vestilius, both allies of Sejanus. Two years before his death, Tiberius appointed as his heirs both Caligula and his grandson Tiberius Gemellus, knowing that the former, as soon as he inherited power, would end the life of the last offspring of his bloodline.

Ancient historians, aware of the atrocities that took place after the death of Tiberius, justify his choice of heir, as Caligula's future barbarities would in retrospect elevate the achievements of his predecessor. Dio Cassius states that Tiberius uttered the verse of an anonymous tragic poet, 'when I am dead, let fire overwhelm the earth', as if the princeps could have prevented the madness that characterized the behaviour of Caligula, the only surviving son of Germanicus.

Upon the death of Tiberius, at the age of 78, various accounts circulated, among them one that Caligula had hastened the emperor's death by depriving him of food. Tacitus claims that it was Macro who gave the order to asphyxiate the emperor, while Suetonius offers a third version of the events, according to which Caligula killed his uncle with poison or strangled him.

A few days before his death, Josephus states that, undecided about the appointment of his successor, Tiberius left the decision up to divine providence. Advised by an augur to give it to the first person to enter his room the next morning, Tiberius asked the tutor of his grandson Tiberius Gemellus to bring him to his room as dawn broke. However, Caligula visited him first, destined by the gods to inherit the throne.

History of Caligula's Principate

12 AD
On 31 August, Gaius Julius Caesar was born, son of Germanicus and Agrippina the Elder, and thus grandson of Tiberius.

37 AD
Ascent to the throne and service as First Consul for two months.

40 AD
Defeat of Arminius in Germania. Revolt in Mauretania and Jewish Uprising.

41 AD
Assassinated by the Praetorian Guard, incited by Cassius Chaerea and Cornelius Sabinus. His wife and daughter were also killed.

Caligula ascends the throne

Tiberius passed away on 16 March 37 AD. Gaius Julius Caesar Germanicus, known as Caligula, was proclaimed emperor and had to decide how he should commemorate his adoptive father. The people celebrated his death and clamoured that his remains be thrown into the Tiber, or that his body be dragged by a hook and thrown into the river from the Gemonian stairs. The moral and religious duties regarding the commemoration of an ancestor forced the descendant and successor to the throne to render funeral honours to his predecessor. Thus, the *funus publicum* (public funeral) was granted to Tiberius and his corpse was burnt in the Forum, according to custom, and not in the theatre, as agitated for by the people.

Caligula had to recover his popularity and extol the memory of his father, Germanicus, on whose fame and popularity he could form a power base. But at the same time, despite the public ill will against Tiberius, which had increased in the last years of his reign, he had to grant his predecessor a State funeral and commemorate him, depositing his remains in the Mausoleum of Augustus and to exercise his right to give the funeral speech; in this case not in order to praise the deceased, but to bring to mind Augustus and Germanicus and to associate his political aspirations with those of his two illustrious Julian ancestors.

Caligula tried to establish a succession of symbolic actions with propaganda as his motive. Among them was the recovery of the remains of relatives condemned by his predecessor. He reburied in the Mausoleum of Augustus the bones of his two brothers, Drusus and Nero Germanicus, and those of his mother, Agrippina the Elder. With this act, the popularity enjoyed by his family in the

CALIGULA

Son of Germanicus and Agrippina, Caligula came to power aged 25. He was enormously popular with the legions. His name was a nickname derived from his small size as a child, akin to soldiers' sandals (caligae). After the dark reign of Tiberius, the people also welcomed him with hope, especially remembering his father. The above image shows a marble bust of Caligula (Archaeological Museum, Venice).

Lavish apparel at the imperial court

The quality of fabrics, different dyes used and the types of folds and draping gave prestige to the finest Roman clothing. Augustus, to set an example of austerity, only wore wool robes woven by his wife Livia. In imperial times, the richest people wore cotton, linen and silk garments (*vestis serica*). Chinese silk, an incomparable luxury, could be replaced by a cheaper alternative from Cos, spun by silkmoth larvae. The tunic, stola and toga were cloths of varying lengths wrapped around the body and fastened with a pin or *fibula* (shown below). The style and colour of a Roman's shoes determined their social class. Patricians wore *lunules* (a crescent shape) on their sandals to distinguish themselves from plebeians, while consuls wore scarlet shoes. Thus, the term *mutare calceos* ('changing shoes') meant climbing the social ladder.

opinion of the masses would be directed at him. However, his extravagances and madness soon showed that Caligula was not heir to the virtues that had made his father so esteemed. His behaviour, based on a policy of terror, came to resemble that of a tyrant.

To the tributes to the dead were added those to the surviving members of his family. He renamed his grandmother, Antonia the Younger, Augusta and gave her the same honours that Livia had enjoyed; he made his uncle Claudius his fellow consul; his sisters, Drusilla, Agrippina and Livilla, were given the rights of the Vestal Virgins, and he adopted Tiberius Gemellus, son of Tiberius, giving him the title 'the prince of youth'.

The illness that twisted Caligula's mind

The first mandates of Caligula's government were an attempt to improve relations with the senatorial aristocratic class, which had completely deteriorated due to the abuses of power during Tiberius's reign. Caligula ended the prosecutions that still remained open and tried to ease the fears of the knights and senators who had been condemned under the previous regime.

In the eighth month of his reign, at the end of October 37 AD, Caligula contracted an illness that put him on the verge of death. To this was later attributed, in the standard account of his tyrannical reign, the cause of his madness. Suetonius was the only author who claimed that Caligula suffered a mental illness, and this was used to justify all the extravagant anecdotes attributed in his biography. But, as Tacitus warns, the accounts of Tiberius, Caligula, Claudius and Nero were falsified during their reigns and then rewritten after the fact, 'under the influence of the still fresh motive of

1 THE TOGA
The citizen was commonly portrayed with the classic toga, the most noble clothing, in which he was also buried.

2 THE TOGA PRAETEXTA
When emerging from youth to manhood, one changed the toga praetexta, worn here by a young Nero, for the toga virilis.

3 THE PEPLOS
Livia wears a peplos of Greek origin, which extended to her feet and wrapped around her waist, where it was folded. It was fastened to the shoulders with a fibula (brooch or pin).

4 THE TUNIC
One shoulder was left bare. Men wore it shorter than women, like this young first-century woman.

5 THE STOLA
A long-sleeved garment for women, at times adorned, and worn by Roman matrons, like this one from the second century.

resentment'. Although the madness of the princeps is disputed, all historians agree on his capricious financial management, cultural insensitivity, obsession with ceremonies, and political ineptitude. His reign eliminated the last vestiges of democracy that remained in Roman governance.

In any case, during the illness at the end of 37 AD, the serious issue of the succession of the newly appointed princeps was raised. The most obvious candidate was Tiberius Gemellus, proposed by Macro and Silanus, Praetorian prefects who had collaborated in Caligula's accession to the throne. However, Caligula took his first decision as supreme ruler and appointed his elder sister Julia Drusilla heiress 'of his property and the empire', in such a way that he made her the kingmaker, either to her husband, Marcus Aemilius Lepidus, with whom Caligula maintained a close friendship, or to any possible descendants that she, still only 22 years old, might have in the future. Caligula's high regard for his three sisters, which was reflected in their likenesses being reproduced on coins and statues and in the awarding of honours that were traditionally reserved for the wife of the emperor, was justified by the need to prepare the people to accept one of their descendants should they assume the throne.

After this promotion of the surviving female members of his family, accusations of incest were spread against Caligula, in addition to rumours of sexual depravity that were part of the standard historical accounts of every hated ruler. As a result of the succession issue having to be faced so early, Tiberius Gemellus was incited to commit suicide. He also eliminated the Praetorian prefect and his confidant, Macro, and Senator Silanus, both of whom had supported him. Drusilla died unexpectedly on

THE ROMAN EMPIRE

Caligula and the annexation of the Kingdom of Mauretania to the Empire

In 33 BC, Bocchus II, King of Mauretania, left Octavian his entire kingdom. After eight years, Augustus ceded it to Juba II, a Numidian married to Cleopatra Selene, the daughter of Mark Antony and Cleopatra, who had been educated at the Roman court by Octavia. Mauretania then joined Numidia and made Caesarea (now Cherchell) and Volubilis (near Meknes, pictured) capitals. After Juba II's death (in 23 AD), his son, Ptolemy (below, in a statue at Rabat Archaeological Museum) took charge of Mauretania. He remained loyal to Rome and the imperial family, to which he was distantly related through Mark Antony. In 17 AD, local Berber tribes, led by the Numidian Tacfarinas and the king of the Garamantes, revolted against Mauretania and Rome. Ptolemy supported the governor of the province, Publius Cornelius Dolabella, and was rewarded, says Tacitus, with 'an ivory sceptre and star-embroidered toga, and for him to be called king, ally and friend'. This alliance ended when Caligula annexed the territories to the empire, toppling Ptolemy and having him killed because, according to Suetonius, 'during a show he had attracted everyone's attention with his bright purple robe'. Under Claudius, Caligula's successor, Mauretania was divided into Tingitana and Caesarensis.

10 June 38 AD. She was the first deified woman in the history of Rome.

The emperor in the provinces

A few months after Drusilla's death, Caligula began his travels through the provinces of the empire. It had been 55 years since a princeps had left the peninsula, for Tiberius had never left Italy. The first trip began in Sicily; there Caligula built a large port next to Rhegium (Reggio Calabria), with warehouses for the grain that was imported from Egypt. According to Josephus, this was the most useful achievement of Caligula's reign. At the end of 38 AD, preparations were made for a military campaign against Germania, in which between 200,000 and 250,000 soldiers participated, resuming Caligula's father's deeds.

In fact, Caligula used the threat of the Germanic peoples as a pretext to confront the governor of Germania Superior, Senator Gnaeus Cornelius Lentulus Gaetulicus, a former supporter of Sejanus who had survived the fall of the Praetorian prefect. Caligula rushed from Rome in order to catch Gaetulicus off guard, whom he knew to be leading a conspiracy against him. Gaetulicus was executed and replaced by Servius Sulpicius Galba, the general who would ascend the throne a few decades later, although only for a few months. Already in Germania, the princeps learned of the plans of the conspiracy, in which his brother-in-law and friend Lepidus and his own two sisters, Agrippina the Younger and Julia Livilla, who had been displaced from the dynastic succession by marriage, were implicated. Lepidus was killed and Caligula's sisters sent into exile to the Pontine Islands.

The tyranny goes too far
The repercussions that the conspiracy had in Rome were dramatic: a state of absolute uncertainty was generated, especially after Caligula had ended the pretence of the equal division of power between the Senate and the princeps. Although the Roman Principate had proven the effectiveness of a consolidated system, Caligula counted on the teachings of masters of tyranny such as Herod Agrippa of Judaea and Antiochus IV of Commagene and other rulers with whom he liked to surround himself: they served as an example of how to replace the Roman Principate of which he was an heir with an absolute monarchy according to the patterns of deified Hellenic rulers. The accounts of the displays of Caligula's pride in the work of Dio Cassius, Suetonius, Tacitus, Philo of Alexandria and Josephus are so extensive that they cannot be cited in their entirety. However, they can be grouped into a string of actions that Caligula repeated with some variations throughout the three years and eight months of his government. He used all the mass media available to him to present himself before the people as a monarch who had assumed power by divine right. He placed statues of himself in the sacred sites; he had temples dedicated in his name; he spent large sums of money to commemorate dates related to his accession to the throne, and took bloodthirsty measures inspired by his lust for greatness; for example, ordering the death of all

The resurgence of Eastern cults during Caligula's reign

Unlike the official Roman religion, the Eastern cults imported to Rome from Egypt and the Near East guaranteed prosperity in this life and salvation in the hereafter. Eastern gods, such as Isis and Osiris, Cybele and Attis, and Mithras, who did not demand exclusive fidelity, were capable of dying, resurrection and suffering pain; initiates in the cult had to experience this through esoteric rituals.

During the Principate (27 BC–284 AD), Eastern cults were banned in Rome. Augustus forbade the Isiac cult, while Tiberius destroyed the city's largest temple to Isis and Serapis (*iseum campense*), built in the Field of Mars in 43 BC, and threw their statues into the Tiber. After many attempts to eradicate the cult, Caligula added Isiac festivities to the calendar and rebuilt the *iseum campense*. According to Prudentius, initiates to the cult had to bathe in bull's blood in a pit partially covered by wooden boards on which the animal had been sacrificed. During this ritual (*taurobolion*), the devotee uttered the enigmatic phrase: 'I have eaten from the eardrum, I have drunk from the harpsichord, I have learned the secrets of the cult'.

Mithraism was another popular Eastern religion of the imperial era, introduced to Rome after Pompey's campaigns in the East. The cult included foreign divinities amid figures and episodes from Hesiod's poem *Theogony*. Mithras, a god born of a stone, appeared sacrificing the primordial bull, which he ate during a sacred banquet in which the sun participated. On his sun chariot, Mithras crosses the heavens, welcomed by the Leontocephaline, a lion-headed figure entwined with a snake, representing cosmic time. Image: a relief of Mithras (National Roman Museum, Rome).

bald men. Any attempt to protest these actions was silenced by extreme violence, as happened in 40 AD, when the people gathered en masse in the circus to protest because the princeps had published in small type the harsh fiscal measures that would affect them and had this pronouncement placed at a high altitude, so that they could not read it, and those who did not comply were punished with extortionate fines. The protest was put down with the killing of all those present. 'After this episode everyone was silent,' writes Dio Cassius.

The policy of extortion

Sentencing citizens to death was in part motivated by Caligula's need to raise money; in his first year of government, Caligula had squandered the vast wealth inherited from Tiberius. Suetonius states: 'prodigal spending overcame the fantasies of all spendthrifts'. He bathed in hot or cold expensive perfumed oils dissolved in vinegar; he hosted banquets in which loaves and meats of gold were served; he threw gold coins from the top of the Basilica Julia to recreate a divine rain; and built Liburnian galleys with sterns adorned with precious stones, which included baths, porches and orchards with vineyards and fruit trees.

Caligula's pressing need for money meant the annulment or modification of numerous final testaments in which the emperor was not named heir. He justified the changes, alleging ingratitude on the part of the testators. He pocketed the savings of senior centurions. He sent poisoned sweets to kill citizens who had made a will. He raised new taxes or increased existing ones on all properties and commercial activities – measures that affected judges, artisans, prostitutes and slaves equally. He fixed auctions so that, with his bid, prices rose exorbitantly. One time, both Suetonius and Dio Cassius recount, the gladiators who had survived a circus battle were auctioned by him between consuls, praetors and people chosen by lot to participate in the purchase. Some went voluntarily to the auctions to spend large sums and thus please Caligula, in the hope of saving their lives and those of their descendants.

The conspiracy against the tyrant

The climate of denunciations for personal gain and the extermination of the senatorial class led to a plot to kill the tyrant. The Jewish historian Josephus's account of events state that two tribunes of the Praetorian Guard, Cassius Chaerea and Cornelius Sabinus, who counted on the support of centurions and Praetorian prefects, in addition to Lucius Annius Vinicianus and one Emilius Regulus from Corduba (Cordoba), plotted the conspiracy. The praetorian officers used by the emperor to torture and execute death sentences began to fear for their future. Chaerea remarked, 'we dirty ourselves by spilling the blood of those who we kill or torture until in the end others will do the same thing to us', Josephus writes.

It was key to choose the right moment to assassinate the emperor; not because of the difficulty of doing so, as Chaerea was close to him and had numerous opportunities to carry it out, but because the Praetorian Guard needed a replacement ready for the throne. Caligula's assassination was set for 24 January 41 AD. During a performance in a theatre on the slope of the Palatine, Caligula tired of the spectacle and retired to his quarters, accompanied by his uncle Claudius, Marcus Vinicius and Valerius Asiaticus. The conspirators separated the emperor from his entourage, and Chaerea and Sabinus escorted him.

The accounts of the end of the emperor differ, and no sources agree as to who struck the first blow. In any case, the wife and daughter of Caligula, Milonia Caesonia and Drusilla the Younger, were murdered immediately afterwards. The emperor's Germanic bodyguards, barely aware of his death, killed some of the conspirators.

In a few hours, the news spread from the palace to the neighbouring theatre to the rest of the city. The fear of reprisals meant that, 'even those who hated Caligula', states Josephus, 'on his death celebrated their joy in private, as they saw themselves just as close to death, without any hope of survival'.

ASSASSINATION OF CALIGULA
This oil painting by the British artist Lawrence Alma-Tadema (1836–1912) portays the critical moment when Caligula was assassinated. While the assassins celebrate their feat, the corpse lying nearby, a Praetorian Guard reverently salutes the new princeps, Claudius, Caligula's uncle. He had been hiding behind a curtain, trying to go unnoticed in order to avoid his proclamation (Walters Art Gallery, Baltimore).

THE AQUA CLAUDIA
This aqueduct was built by Claudius to alleviate the water scarcity suffered by the city of Rome. On the next page, a cameo shows Claudius (on the right) and his brother Germanicus with his wives (Kunsthistorisches Museum, Vienna).

A SCHOLAR ON THE THRONE

Surviving the tyrannical excesses of Tiberius and Caligula, Claudius came to the throne with the support of the praetorian and urban cohorts. A learned and educated man, although afflicted by physical problems, he restored judicial order and advocated a populist policy run by a central administration overseen by freedmen. The ambition of his last two wives, Messalina and Agrippina the Younger, led to his ruin and death.

The day after the successful plot against Caligula, concocted by Cassius Chaerea and other conspirators, 50-year-old Tiberius Claudius Drusus Nero Germanicus, known as Claudius, was hailed emperor by the praetorian cohorts. Literary sources, written by the senatorial class opposing the power held by princes, spoke of the moments after the assassination and describe Claudius's reaction with the intent of mocking him.

They stated that Claudius, also part of the conspiracy, fled in fear to hide behind curtains in a palace apartment (the hermaeum), where he remained until a sentry escorted him to the Castra Praetoria. On the night of Caligula's murder, the Senate met at the Capitol to discuss Rome's future. The senators were divided into those who wanted to restore the old Republic, those who proposed the continuation of the Principate, led by Marcus Vinicius, Valerius Asiaticus or Lucius Annius

THE ROMAN EMPIRE

Claudius: the most erudite emperor in Roman history

Dio Cassius said Claudius 'had a keen intelligence because he was constantly learning'. He was always interested in history, driven by his friendship with the historian Livy and the imperial tutor Sulpicius Flaccus. He was also fascinated by languages. He is credited with writing 20 books on the Etruscan language and culture, and eight on Carthage. Other than Etruscan and Carthaginian history books, written in Greek, Claudius wrote a comedy dedicated to his brother Germanicus, and a 43-book historical treatise of Rome, in Latin, spanning the assassination of Julius Caesar to the end of Augustus. In his books he reveals some very sombre family issues and shows sympathy for his grandfather, Mark Antony. Claudius's passion for Rome's past led him to promote to the highest positions in government the descendants of great investigators of republican times, including Aulus Caecina, friend of Cicero, and Venaio, friend of the poet Catullus. Regarding the study of languages, he claimed the need for orthographic reform and dedicated a speech in the Senate to the history of the alphabet, as Tacitus records in his *Annals*.
Image: A portrait of Claudius found in Thassos, Greece (Louvre Museum, Paris).

Vinicianus, and those who supported the only survivor of the Claudian family. The Jewish king, Herod Agrippa, served as arbitrator of a senatorial delegation that had been informed of the decision of the nine praetorian cohorts to support Claudius's succession. Urban cohorts also supported the praetors. Their support was won via an imperial donation of between 15,000–20,000 sesterces, more than their total salaries for one year. Facing military pressure, the Senate accepted the appointment of the new princeps, the last male in the family of Drusus the Elder.

The 'fool' educated to reign

Claudius was born under the reign of Augustus on 1 August in 10 BC in the city of Lugdunum (Lyon), in Gallia Comata, where his father, Nero Claudius Drusus the Elder (brother of Tiberius and son of Livia), commanded the legions. His father hoped that the old State would be restored. His mother, Antonia the Younger, daughter of Mark Antony and Octavia the Younger and niece of the first princeps of Rome, was the only blood tie that bound him to the Julian family.

During adulthood, Claudius had observed the degradation of the principality of his uncle Tiberius and survived the four years of his nephew Caligula's indiscriminate killings. He probably managed to stay alive due to a form of epilepsy prevalent in his childhood, characteristics useful to the writers Suetonius, Tacitus, Dio Cassius and Seneca, who were openly opposed to the populist policy of Claudius. They described him as a fool, unsuited for political life.

However, Claudius was not a 'parody of a man', nor 'an abortion of nature', as his own mother said; nor did he reach power by chance. Beyond his physical and psychological peculiarities, rejected by a society that despised the unseemly, he was an intelligent and cultured man, who knew how to stay alive in difficult times and who tried to restore peace and justice to the people. His early participation in religious ceremonies, his inclusion in the matrimonial strategies of the Julio-Claudian family, and his representation in public monuments to the dynasty show that even in youth he was prepared to occupy the position that fortune had reserved for him.

During the years in which Rome was subjected to the ambitions of Sejanus, Claudius disappeared from political life and remained absent until Caligula ascended the throne and appointed him as consul. The following year, Claudius married Valeria Messalina, granddaughter of Antonia the Elder and therefore of Julian blood, thus forging a new dynastic link to the founders of the empire.

Impunity for all

When Claudius was named successor of the Julio-Claudian dynasty, he was unsure about monarchical regimes. In his life he had suffered from the abuse of power. His government would restore order through moderation. According to Seneca, he abolished taxes

The Principate under Claudius

10 BC
On 1 August, Tiberius Claudius Drusus Nero Germanicus is born in Lugdunum (Lyon).

19 AD
On 10 October, his brother Germanicus dies, and supporters of Agrippina back his rise to power.

41 AD
After Caligula is assassinated, Claudius's son Britannicus is born.

48 AD
He discovers Messalina's plot and executes the conspirators. He marries Agrippina.

54 AD
On 13 October he dies, poisoned.

---

imposed by Caligula and freed those accused of crimes against him, invalidating sentences based on offences against imperial dignity. Claudius guaranteed impunity 'both to those who had openly defended the re-establishment of a republican regime and those who had had the opportunity to obtain power instead of him'. He condemned the leaders who had plotted against Caligula, because they had tried to eliminate him in the process. He granted magistracies to rivals and burnt the records kept by Caligula. As a demonstration of ancestral respect, his mother, Antonia the Younger, was given the title of Augusta; his father, Drusus the Elder, and his grandfather, Mark Antony, were commemorated with circus games on their anniversaries, and his grandmother, Livia, was deified. Suetonius states that, 'when it came to himself, he was frugal in refraining from using the praenomen of imperator (except when linked to military victories). He refused honours and celebrated the weddings of his daughter and the birth of his grandson with a simple ceremony'.

Claudius's relationship with the Senate was tense. He re-established his right to vote by renewing the Valeria Cornelia and Junia Pretoria laws, limiting their influence by centralizing power in his hands via systems run by trusted freedmen. In 47 AD, in his capacity as censor, he carried out a new selection for the Senate, replacing old members of the senatorial class he thought useless with ones selected from the class of provincial leaders. In Lugdunum (Lyon), Claudius's birthplace, a bronze tablet was found recounting the speech given by the emperor to announce the opening of membership of the Senate to Gallic provincials. The *oratio Claudii Caesaris de iure honorum Gallis dando* (the speech of Claudius Caesar on the

APOTHEOSIS OF CLAUDIUS
Preceded by the majestic Roman eagle, symbol of the empire and the ascent to the heavens of the souls of the dead, Claudius appears in his apotheosis, a prelude to divinization, in this cameo, made ca. 54. The emperor was deified by Nero and by the Senate almost immediately after his death (National Library, Paris).

THE ROMAN EMPIRE

IMPERIAL CULT: ADULATION OF THE SOVEREIGN

In order to reinforce the empire's new-found stability, after years of civil strife, it was necessary to sanctify politics. The establishment of certain ceremonies, such as the consecratio, the celebration of public holidays in commemoration of military victories, political offices and significant dates in the life of the emperor and his family, became indispensable to implement the new imperial policy and legitimize the government of the successors of the first princeps. The deifying of emperors, granted or denied by the Senate, meant the addition of the title divus to the emperor's official name, and the conferral of quasi-divine honours.

A GOD OUTSIDE THE FAMILY
Antinous, Hadrian's favourite, died in mysterious circumstances. The emperor expressed his fondness for him by decreeing his divinization, an honour hitherto reserved for members of the imperial family. Here he appears emulating Lycean Apollo (Archaeological Museum, Tripoli).

Heroic nudity was not associated with deification, but rather served to visually express the exalted virtues of the one portrayed.

A SCHOLAR ON THE THRONE

The wreath of oak or holm oak leaves that Claudius wears in this sculpture, kept at the Vatican Museums in Rome, alludes to his military successes, while the spear signifies his capacity to command.

1 HEROES OR GODS
In accordance with the iconographic traditions of the Hellenistic monarchs, established during the time of Alexander the Great and embraced by Rome in the second century BC, emperors were represented naked, or covered only by a cloak.

2 PATERA
In his capacity as the supreme pontiff and highest head of all the priestly colleges, the emperor carried a sacrificial *patera*, or plate, which was used for libations on the altars of the gods, in order to guarantee the *pax deorum* (the peace of the gods).

3 EAGLE
The incorporation of the eagle into the portrait had a dual significance. On the one hand, it identified the emperor with Jupiter, both being guarantors of justice. On the other, it alluded to the imperial apotheosis, as the flight of the eagle symbolized the ascent of the deceased's soul.

4 CLOAK
Wrapped over the left arm, the cloak (*himation*) was part of the Greek model to represent heroes such as Patroclus or Achilles, and that according to which some victorious generals and local leaders were portrayed. Sometimes the *chlamys* (cloak) was incorporated as a military symbol.

THE TEMPLES OF THE EMPERORS

The eastern provinces of the empire, ruled for centuries by tyrannical regimes and theocratic monarchies, were the first to build temples in honour of Rome and the princeps as testimony of their loyalty. The rest of the provinces followed suit and built temples like this one in Pula, Croatia (pictured). The emperor had to pre-approve the investment of public money to erect these temples. However, by accepting such signs of adulation he could be accused of tyranny, and some embassies sent to Rome to request the imperial permit were refused, such as the inhabitants of Baetica in the year 25. Tiberius, conscious of appearing ambitious and prone to tyranny before the Senate, rejected not only the construction of the temple, but the dedication of statues, which he equated with idolatry. Trajan's government also tended to refuse such honours, conscious, according to Pliny the Younger, that 'to choose flattery is hypocrisy stronger than truth, freedom and faith'.

concession to the Gauls of the right of access to public positions), collected in the *tabula Lugdunensis*, was pronounced in the Senate in 48 AD, as Tacitus affirms. Claudius achieved great success in this senatorial session.

The option of access to the Senate granted to the Gauls was one of the most important and innovative decisions of Claudius's reign: it recognized the right of the provincial ruling classes to obtain magistracies or to participate in the Senate and extended Roman citizenship to other social groups.

An agenda at the service of Rome
After re-establishing, as Seneca notes, 'everything the madness of the previous prince had shot to pieces', Claudius turned to justice. This he applied with intellect, overseeing procedures to help disadvantaged classes, for example, convicting the *domini* (masters) who left infirm slaves in the Temple of Asclepius on Tiber Island to a punishment equal to that of a murderer if the slave died. He introduced reforms to imperial administration and monitored senatorial attendance levels.

Claudius also attempted to curb real estate speculation by prohibiting the destruction of buildings in Rome and the regions of Italy. There was a man of high ranking who had become notorious for acquiring buildings, demolishing them and then selling the land for a higher price, as revealed in the Senate consultation *De aedificiis non deruendis* ('for the non-demolition of buildings'), which was discovered in Herculaneum. 'In the future, however,' added Claudius in his decree, 'others have been warned to abstain from such negotiation, especially when it is better to decorate rather than wreck the buildings of Italy, and thus end the negligence of times past.'

Linking policy to Augustan and Caesarian governance, Claudius resumed plans such as the pacification of Britain, the construction of the port of Ostia to keep the plebeians well supplied with wheat, and draining Lake Fucino. He improved health by taking care of the water supply. He built the Aqua Claudia, and finished the Aqua Anus Novus, begun by Caligula.

BRITANNICUS
This portrait of Claudius's young son, whom the emperor called 'Britannicus' in honour of the most prized of his conquests, presents him clad in a toga and with the demeanour of a young prince. Much loved by his father, Claudius could not, however, free him from his fate, determined by the ambitions of the emperor's fourth wife, Agrippina, and her son, Nero, who was ultimately Claudius's successor (Vatican Museums, Rome).

Roman dwellings under Claudius

As a result of the increasingly high price of buildable land, multi-storey apartment buildings known as *insulae* appeared in Rome. These made it possible to better exploit the land at a reduced cost. These blocks of flats generally stood four to five floors high and were divided into several apartments, each accessed through exterior corridors or galleries. The first floor was the only one equipped with toilets and water; the upper floors, with few windows, lacked plumbing. Building height was limited to 18m (60ft) in Augustus's time, but much higher ones were erected anyway, leading to frequent collapses. After the fire in 64 AD, Nero ordered there be a 3m (10ft) space between the buildings, as well as the construction of a portico along the façade (the picture shows a model of an insula in Ostia, Museum of Roman Civilization, Rome) in order to facilitate the work of firefighters. Hellenistic houses with an atrium and peristyle (domus) were reserved for the rich.

The marriages of Claudius
Historical sources agree that the emperor was a puppet of his wives, who enjoyed a position as privileged as his. The first two marriages of his life were used for the matrimonial strategies of the Claudians, in an attempt to unite members of the Augustan house with the important republican families. His first fiancée, Aemilia Lepidus, a great-granddaughter of Augustus, never married Claudius because her mother, Julia the Younger, was banished, accused of conspiring against Augustus. His second attempt at marriage was also fruitless, since Livia Medullina, a descendant of the Camilli, died on their wedding day. The regime assigned him a new wife, Plautia Urgulanilla, daughter of a confidant of Livia. The marriage, celebrated between 8 and 12 AD, was annulled ten years later to make possible a new matrimonial alliance with Aelia Paetina, from

1 PORTICO
Nero promulgated an anti-fire regulation that required the construction of a portico running along the front of the building, with a range of businesses along there.

2 WINDOWS
Houses received light from windows giving onto the street or interior patios. The most expensive insulae enjoyed shared landscaped spaces.

3 ROOFTOPS
The roofs of the buildings were made of wood covered with flat terracotta tiles (*tegulae*). The joints between two tiles were covered with a curved tile (*imbrex*).

4 BALCONIES
The first floor had access to a balcony that ran along the entire façade. Concrete and brick were the main construction materials.

5 FLOORS
Each building had two to six floors. The tallest known insula is preserved on the northern slope of the Capitol Hill.

the same family as Sejanus. From this marriage was born a daughter, Claudia, who was returned to her mother after divorce, as it was said that she was the daughter of the freedman Boter. Three years later, at the end of 38 AD, Claudius was divorced to marry Valeria Messalina, who was related to Augustus.

After ten years, Messalina plotted a coup d'état with her lover, Gaius Silius, in an attempt to ensure the accession to the throne of her son Claudius Tiberius Germanicus Britannicus. The conspirators were condemned to death and the princeps was forced to marry Britannicus to his niece Agrippina the Younger, the mother of Nero, born of her previous marriage to Gnaeus Domitius Ahenobarbus, whom Suetonius defines as a 'despicable and dishonest man'.

The intrigues of court that starred Messalina and Agrippina would have remained as mere anecdotes in literary sources had they not influenced the fate of Roman history. They manipulated the freedmen who directed the State administration, triggered illegal prosecutions against members of the aristocracy and the Senate and conspired to bring death sentences against whichever women they considered to have interfered in their succession plans.

Mauretania and the kingdom of Palestine

Claudius inherited the social and political disorder generated by the previous government. Problems affected the relationship of Rome with the provinces of the empire and with allied satellite states. One of the kingdoms under Roman influence from republican times was that of Mauretania, which Augustus had had restored to Juba II, a fellow student of the emperor. The murder of the son of Juba II, Ptolemy, by order of Caligula, gave rise to a

Herod Agrippa: A Jewish king at Claudius's Roman court

After Aristobulus IV, Prince of Judaea, was accused of treason against his father, Herod the Great, and condemned to death in 7 BC, his son, Herod Agrippa (aged three), was sent to Rome to join Tiberius's son, Drusus (aged seven), to be educated at the imperial court. Herod, Drusus and Claudius became great friends.

After Drusus's death, Herod Agrippa was forced to leave Rome and spent a few years in Idumea. He returned to Rome after a time and was welcomed by Tiberius, who entrusted him with educating his grandson, Tiberius Gemellus. Agrippa I forged close ties with Caligula, who assured him the title of king and parts of the Herodian Tetrarchy, including the Golan, Batanaea, Lajan, Auranitis and, later, Galilee and Perea. When the princeps died, Herod Agrippa (pictured, Museum of Israel, Jerusalem) supported Claudius's ascent to power and was rewarded with rule over Judaea and Samaria, becoming one of the most powerful rulers in the East. He died suddenly in 44 AD in Caesarea during games held in Claudius's honour.

popular revolt that Claudius subdued with two military campaigns in 41 and 42 AD, headed at first by Gaius Suetonius Paulinus and later by Gnaeus Hosidius Geta. Once pacified, the Mauretanian territory was divided into two imperial provinces, governed by two officials of equestrian rank: Mauretania Tingitana and Mauretania Caesariensis, with capitals in Tingis (Tangier) and Caesarea (Cherchell), respectively.

In the East, Caligula expelled Antiochus IV from the Commagene throne, three years after having enthroned him. Claudius returned him to the throne and enlarged his kingdom with a part of Cilicia, while another part of this same territory, Cilicia Trachea, was annexed to the kingdom of Polemon, king of Pontus. The government of Palestine was granted to Herod Agrippa, grandson of Herod the Great and childhood friend of Claudius, with whom he had been raised in Rome, under the protection of his mother, Antonia the Younger. In reward for the support shown during his accession, Claudius extended his dominions with Judaea, Samaria and some territories of Lebanon. But when Herod Agrippa died in 44 AD, the kingdom did not pass to his son Herod Agrippa II, who was only given the principality of Chalcis; instead his kingdom was incorporated as a province of the empire, so that Judaea fell under the caprices and pressures of the officials appointed by Claudius.

The revolts of Alexandria

The loss of political independence of the kingdom of Judaea and the fiscal pressure imposed by the new officials aroused hatred in the Hebrew population against Roman rule. The discontent of the Jews was not only apparent in the ancient kingdom of Herod Agrippa, but also in established Jewish cities of the empire, as in Alexandria in the first year of Claudius's rule. Under the government of Caligula, revolts in 38 AD had provoked a violent outbreak of anti-Semitism, encouraged by Governor Flaco, among the Greek population of the Egyptian city. In order to appease the two cultural and religious groups of Alexandria, an embassy was sent to Caligula, of which Apion went as a delegate of the Hellenic population. Philo represented the Jews and authored two works that narrate the events (*In Flaccum* and *Legatio ad Gaium*). Upon Apion's accusation that the Jews refused to honour the emperor with statues (which contravened the ancestral laws of the Jewish people), Caligula expelled Philo and his Jewish delegation from the court. This provoked a war, directed by Petronius, governor of Syria.

To end the situation in Alexandria, inherited from the previous government, and on the initiative of the kings of Judaea, Herod Agrippa II and Herod of Chalcis, Claudius sent a letter to the Alexandrian Greeks (now in the British Museum) trying to resolve the conflict by requesting tolerance. 'I am not going to dig into who was responsible for […] a war against the Jews. I am going to tell you if you do not stop fighting each other, this tolerant ruler will be forced to show his righteous anger.' In the same letter, published by the prefect of Egypt, Lucius Aemilius Rectus, on 10 November in 41 AD,

CAESAREA MARITIMA (OPPOSITE)
Herod the Great, Herod Agrippa's grandfather, was the founder of this city located on the Mediterranean coast, south of present-day Haifa, in Israel. In 13 BC, it was designated the capital of Judaea and the seat of the province's Roman governors. It was enhanced with large buildings, such as its circus, whose remains can be seen in the image.

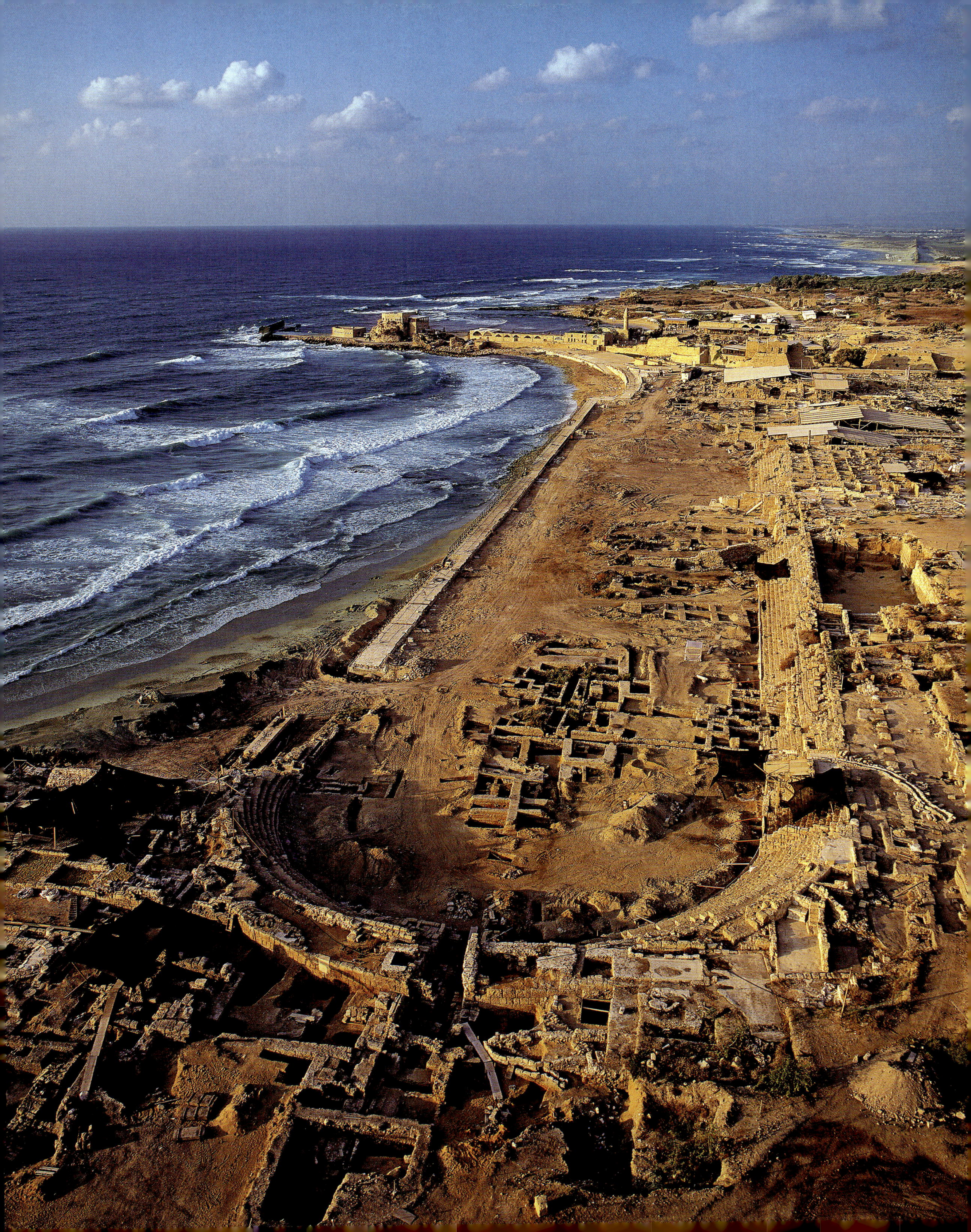

THE ROMAN EMPIRE

Claudius and the remodelling of Portus Augusti near Ostia

According to the geographer Strabo, Ostia lacked a safe harbour for the merchant ships that supplied Rome from the empire's western routes. The accumulation of silt in the Tiber and its narrow mouth (100m/330ft) made manoeuvring large vessels difficult. Most of the goods destined for Rome went to the port of Puteoli, but those that reached Ostia (1) were unloaded at sea onto smaller vessels that could navigate up the river to the capital. The famine in 42 AD spurred Claudius to start work on a safe harbour, north of the mouth of the Tiber (2), inaugurated under Nero, and dubbed the portus Augusti Ostiensis. (3) In 106, Trajan built the inland, more secure, hexagonal-shaped portus Traianus (4) (see image).

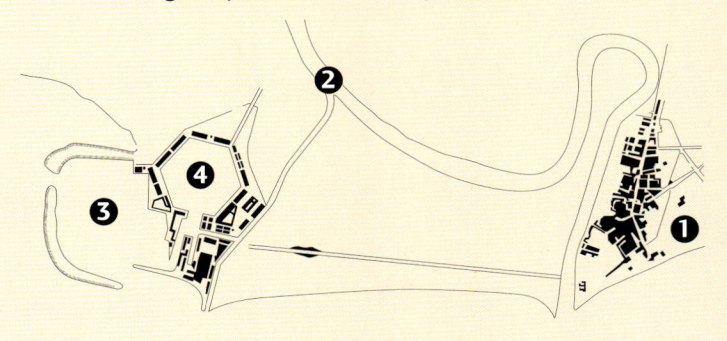

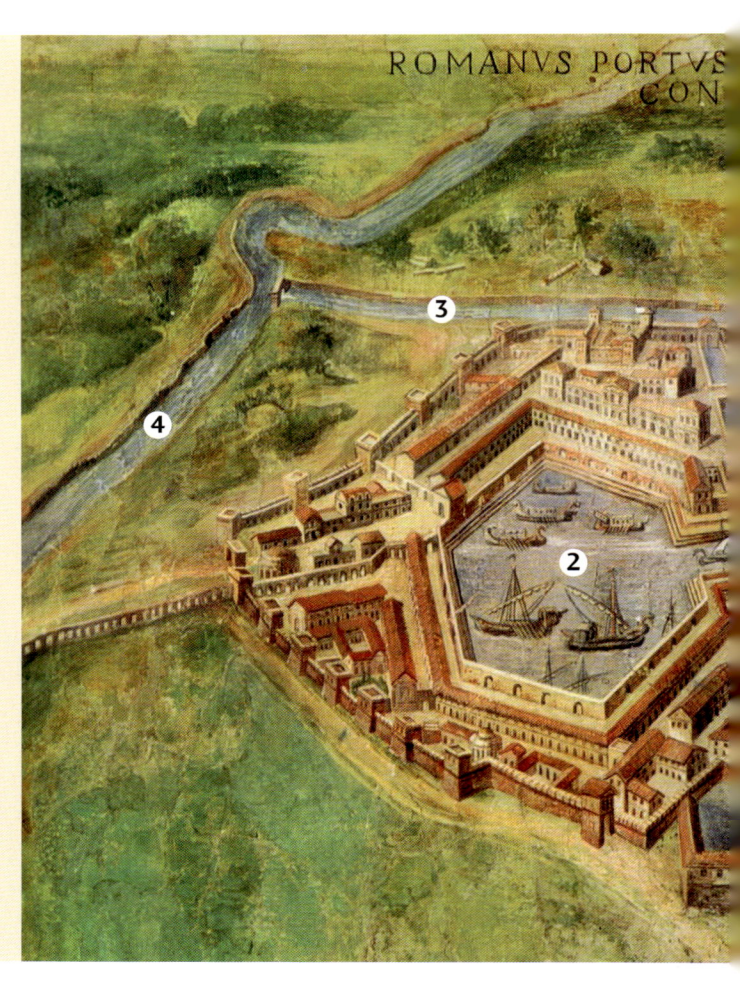

Claudius included a list of the rights restored to the Alexandrians and of the reforms that had been granted to the city.

The confrontation between Jews and Alexandrians was reignited between 53 and 54 AD, so a new embassy was sent to Rome, concluding in the execution of the Alexandrian Isidorus the gymnasiarch for publicly insulting the emperor. During those years, according to Suetonius, 'Claudius expelled Jews from Rome, who continually revolted, incited by Christ'.

The shortages of 42 AD

After the end of the conflict of Alexandria, a terrible famine arose in Palestine that affected Rome and Italy. Josephus recounts that the queen of Adiabene (a country to the east of the River Tigris), named Helena, alleviated the shortage in the city of Jerusalem by sending men to buy wheat from Alexandria and figs from Cyprus. Meanwhile, in Rome, this shortage moved Claudius to complete a project by Julius Caesar that would end the problem of the wheat supply, since between October and March impassable seas made it difficult to import grain from Egypt, the main supplier of grain to Rome.

Claudius commenced the building of a port in Ostia that guaranteed the safe approach of the ships to the mouth of the Tiber and storage for imported goods. The project consisted of a vast pier encircling part of the sea complete with an artificial island and lighthouse, cemented in a sunken ship – one that had brought the last of the Roman obelisks from Egypt. While the work was being carried out, Claudius oversaw wheat shipments from Africa and paid merchants for damage resulting from storms. With the help of his freedman Tiberius Claudius Narcissus and a workforce of 30,000 men, Claudius organized the creation of land that could be used for grain cultivation. For 11

1 PORTUS AUGUSTI
The port that was built on Claudius's initiative enclosed a large portion of the sea with a dock. Its shallow depths and width were hazardous for ships; 200 vessels loaded with grain were destroyed in 62.

2 PORTUS TRAIANUS
Between 106 and 113 AD, a second port was built, this one perfectly hexagonal, covering 32 hectares (80 acres) of surface area. It connected the port of Claudius with the Tiber by means of a canal, which was started by Claudius.

3 THE CANAL
The canal that linked the port of Trajan with the Tiber River (*fossa traianea*, the Fiumicino Canal) bounded an artificial island, later to be called the *isola sacra*, containing one of the most interesting necropolises in the Roman world.

4 THE TIBER RIVER
At its mouth in the Tyrrhenian Sea, the river was only 100m (330ft) across, and was not very deep. In 1557, a landslide transformed the configuration of the riverbed, and the meander that the ancient city of Ostia overlooked disappeared forever.

5 THE LIGHTHOUSE
Today lost, the lighthouse originally stood to the left of the dock at Claudius's port. It was constructed of three superimposed cubic structures, each one smaller than the one beneath. A fire, visible from 45km (28 miles) away, was lit at the top.

years, the workforce dug a 5-km (3-mile) drainage tunnel, at a depth of 30m (98ft), to drain the waters of the Fucine Lake to the River Liri. The project would be completed along with the Aqua Claudia, an aqueduct with a capacity to transport almost 192 cubic metres (6780 cubic ft) of water per day from more than 70km (43 miles) away.

The expedition to Britannia
The copying of Julian projects extended to plans to expand the borders of the empire. The conquest of Britannia, coveted by Caesar and undertaken by Caligula, became central to foreign policy, starting from 43 AD. Aulus Plautius, former governor of Pannonia, took command of four legions in 30 AD to begin an offensive against Caratacus, king of the Catuvellauni, who had shared with his brother Togodumnus the kingdom of their father, Cunobelinus. Their attempted expansion towards the southeastern part of the British Isles was slowed down by the intervention of Plautius, who caused the different tribes to retreat and managed to cross the River Medway with a group of German soldiers, accustomed to swimming in turbulent waters in full battledress. Accompanying him as his lieutenants were Flavius Vespasian, the future emperor, and his brother, Titus Flavius Sabinus.

After these early defeats, the Britons retreated to the mouth of the Thames and several tribes united their forces to avenge the death of Togodumnus. Plautius sent a messenger to Claudius informing him of these events. The emperor, who had prepared auxiliary troops, including elephants, undertook the trip to Britain. These troops were accompanied by a detachment of praetorians commanded by Rufrius Pollio, by the Eighth Legion and a commission, among whom were Valerius Asiaticus, Marcus Licinius Crassus

THE ROMAN EMPIRE

The conquest of Britannia: the realization of Caesar's dream

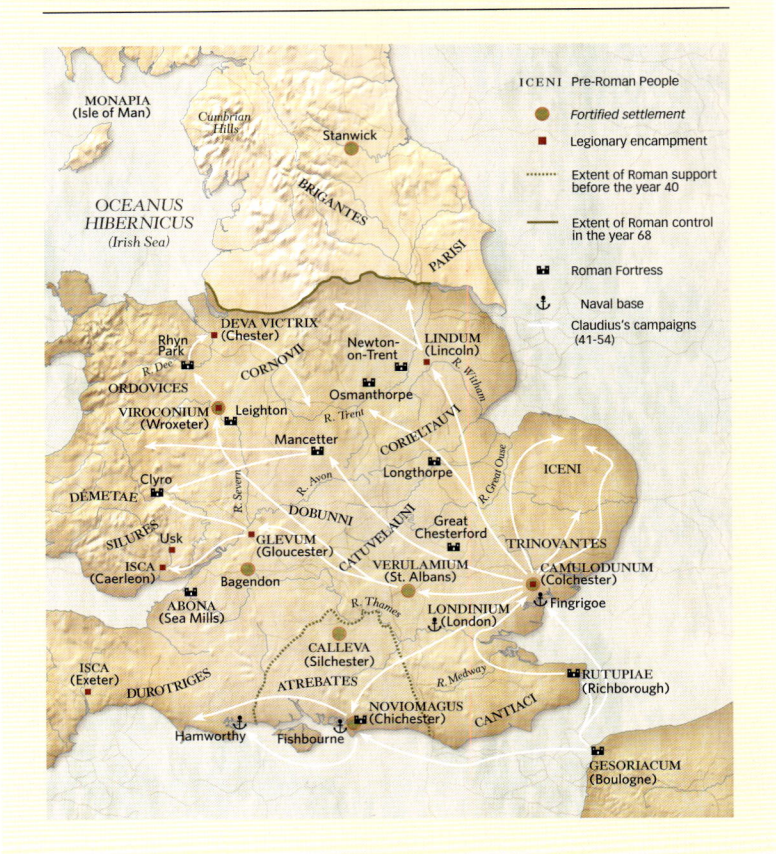

Britain had been the unattained goal of Caesar, Augustus and Caligula. Until 43 AD, when Claudius turned it into an imperial province under the control of a proconsul, Rome had only managed to maintain a cordial relationship with some vassal kings. Caesar tried to conquer the island during his campaign in Gaul; he led two expeditions aimed at this: a reconnaissance mission in 55 BC and an offensive in 54 BC. Unable to conquer the British tribes, the Roman general established a client system with some of them, such as the Catuvellauni, ruled by Tasciovanus, and the Atrebates, ruled by Commius, and exempted them from paying taxes as a reward for their loyalty. During the revolts in Gaul in 54 and 53 BC, Augustus planned three invasions, but his attempts were hindered by civil conflicts. Under Tiberius, a spontaneous arrival of the Roman fleet on the British coasts saw an unsuccessful expedition attempt in 39 AD. In 43 AD, Claudius invaded Britain and defeated the Catuvellauni at the battles of the Medway and the Thames. Camulodunum, modern-day Colchester, became the capital of the new province.

Frugi and his sons-in-law, Gnaeus Pompeius Magnus and Lucius Junius Silanus.

Once in Britain, he assumed command of the rest of the legions by the Thames, defeating the British tribes along with Camulodunum (Colchester). Pompeius Magnus and Junius Silanus were given the task of bringing news of the victory to Rome. The Senate granted the emperor the title of Britannicus and the right to a triumph. The subjugated territory was turned into a province, governed by a legate of senatorial rank and made into a number of municipalities such as Glevum (Gloucester) and Londinium (London).

Messalina and the freedmen of Claudius

The expedition to Britannia meant the emperor left Rome for over a year. His wife Messalina planned the ascension to the throne of her son Britannicus when Claudius, 30 years her elder, died. To eliminate all standing in the way of Britannicus assuming the throne, Messalina relied on the support of Tiberius Claudius Narcissus, in charge of the chancellor's office, the Secretary General of the State.

Claudius's wife enticed powerful families, the descendants of the great republican aristocracy, and surviving members of the Julians, by means of palatial and sexual intrigues, with the support of the freedmen of Claudius and with the confidence of the emperor, who had delegated to her State matters of the highest importance. This led to the death of a number of provincial commanders who had been in charge of the legions. First to die was Gaius Appius Junius Silanus, who Caligula had appointed governor of Hispania Tarraconensis. Messalina convinced Claudius to make Silanus a close confidant and even married him to her mother, Domitia Lepida, a widower since 20 AD. Once included in the court inner circle, the freedman Narcissus, after a premonition, accused Silanus of rebellion. It is possible that Silanus, whom Caligula sent to Tarraconensis with three legions, was suspected of rebellion and that the marriage to Messalina's mother was the first step to eliminate him.

MESSALINA: THE TWO FACES OF AN EMPRESS

Almost all the scandalous episodes in the life of Valeria Messalina that Tacitus, Dio Cassius, Suetonius and Pliny reported were meant to tarnish Claudius's government. Little is known, in fact, about this empress, who was related to the Julians through Octavia, other than her desire to place her only son, Britannicus, on the throne. She appears next to him in the few depictions that remain of her, such as the statue at the Museum of the Louvre (shown right), due to the *damnatio memoriae* to which she was condemned in 48 AD.

THE COURTESAN

The poet Juvenal's account in his *Satire VI*, according to which Messalina prostituted herself in the palace under the alias Lycisca, inspired painters such as Agostino Carracci, Mélanie Quentin and, here, Gustave Moreau (below, Musée Gustave Moreau, Paris).

Agrippina Minor: the last descendant of the Julians

Julia Agrippina Augusta, aka Agrippina Minor, was the fourth daughter of Germanicus and Agrippina. She was married to her uncle, allowing her to place her son Nero on the throne, who had been removed from Caligula's dynastic plans. When Claudius was appointed emperor in 41 AD, none of Agrippina's siblings were alive: Nero Julius Caesar Germanicus; Drusus Julius Caesar; Caligula; Julia Livilla; and Julia Drusilla. Agrippina was the last surviving link to the Julians and, conscious of the power conferred by her blood, fought for her right to wield it as a genuine empress. Her ambitions were realized when her uncle, Emperor Claudius, whom she had married in 48 AD, adopted her son Nero, the result of a forced marriage at the age of 14 to the despicable Gnaeus Domitius Ahenobarbus. Her maternal authority would soon become insufferable to Nero, who plotted her murder in 59 AD. Shown left, a seated statue of Agrippina (National Archaeological Museum, Naples).

The plot between Messalina and Silius

Silanus's murder in 42 AD led to a plot against Claudius, who was oblivious to the machinations of his wife and freedmen. The leader of the plot was Lucius Annius Vinicianus, who had plotted against Caligula, supported by Lucius Arruntius Camillus Scribonianus, governor of Dalmatia and at the head of two legions. The plot failed because of fear of a new civil war. The legions involved decided to end the conspiracy and remain loyal to the emperor. Scribonianus fled to the island of Issa, where he committed suicide. Vinicianus and his accomplices shared the same fate.

Messalina sought to rid every enemy to Claudius and his son. Julia Livilla, niece of the emperor, daughter of Germanicus and Agrippina the Elder, great-granddaughter of Augustus and sister of Caligula, was accused of adultery with the senator and philosopher Lucius Annaeus Seneca and banished for the second time in 47 AD because Messalina wanted to see the decline in influence of her husband, Marcus Vinicius, the favourite of the Senate. Livilla died of starvation shortly after, and Messalina was to blame for the death. To make sure that Marcus Vinicius would avenge her death, Messalina ordered his assassination. Next to fall out of favour was Publius Valerius Asiaticus, head of the Germanic legions, as well as lord of a large area of Gallia Narbonensis. Accused by the empress of committing adultery with Poppaea, wife of Scipio, he was arrested in Baiae, subjected to an interrogation and condemned to death without trial in the Senate.

Many others were driven to ruin, such as Pompeius Magnus, the son-in-law of Claudius, or Lucius Silanus, the great-great-grandson of Augustus. However, Messalina also met her undoing after making a false accusation against Polybius, the freedman in charge of a *studiis* (the department for government papers). Devoid of the support of the freedmen, Messalina tried to usurp power in 48 AD by marrying Gaius Silius, the last of her lovers, while Claudius was away in Ostia.

When Messalina knew that Claudius had learnt of this, she tried to appease him by paying the Vestal Virgin Vibidia to request imperial clemency. However, the freedmen of Claudius prevented the imperial couple from meeting, preventing the presence of the empress and their children from swaying the princeps, and forced him to decree the death of the two lovers. Narcissus ordered the execution of Messalina and the Senate decreed *damnatio memoriae* upon her – the elimination of any memory of her name.

The ambition of Agrippina

After the death of Messalina, Claudius married his niece Agrippina the Younger, sister of Caligula and Livilla, whom he had brought back from exile. Agrippina and her son Nero turned Britannicus into the focus of their hatred. Deprived of the honours his mother had bestowed on him, they condemned him to live in seclusion, so that people would forget he existed, lending credence to Agrippina's rumours. Another period of 'judicial terrorism' began with the aim of eliminating any rivals who could prevent her son the succession.

The poisoning of Claudius
Trials formed by the accusations of the two last wives of Claudius against the members of the aristocracy created a whole class opposed to a monarchical government; this motivated the condemnation of his legacy, with accounts for the highlighting of his physical and mental incapacity and the immorality of his wives.

Agrippina became permanent co-regent and accepted honours such as the title of Augusta and the dedication of her name to cities such as her birthplace Colonia Claudia Ara Agrippinensium (Cologne) in Germania. Her greatest ambition was fulfilled in 50 AD: Claudius adopted Nero, appointed him guardian of the British and promised him in marriage to his daughter Octavia. Seneca, who had been exiled to Corsica for his adulterous liaison with Livilla and had not been pardoned by Claudius despite numerous pleas, returned from exile, and was appointed tutor to Nero.

The crimes of Agrippina that had led to the deaths of people such as Titus Statilius Taurus, a proprietor of great wealth, reached Claudius. Before he could react, aware that, as Suetonius states, 'his destiny was to suffer the wickedness of his wives and then punish them', Agrippina hastened his death with the help of Locusta, an infamous poisoner, and the complicity of Halotus, his taster, and Xenophon, his doctor. The emperor died from poisoning on his return from a trip to the south coast of Latium, although his death was not made public until days later. On 13 October 54 AD, Nero appeared before the people escorted by the Praetorian Guard, and was acclaimed emperor by the soldiers with the approval of the Senate.

MESSALINA'S DEATH
Forced to commit suicide by order of her husband Claudius, Messalina, despite encouragement from her mother, who was present, was unable to kill herself, so she was decapitated with a centurion's sword. This is the moment portrayed in the oil painting by Victor-François-Eloi Biennoury (1823–1893), from the collection of the Museum of Fine Arts of Grenoble.

THE ROMAN EMPIRE

The legions of Rome

Over and above the politics and diplomacy, the legions were the essential instrument for Rome to achieve its supreme ambition – to build an empire that would dominate the world.

Rome's continual territorial expansion, its capacity to subject countless peoples to different customs, languages and religions, and to incorporate disparate territories, was made possible by a highly rigid institution, the legion, whose creation, according to Livy and Plutarch, went back to the mythical figure of Romulus, founder of Rome. Livy puts words into Romulus's mouth, imbued with Roman military pride, descendants of an ancient mindset in which self-denial and courage prevailed. He declared that '[…] by heaven's will my Rome shall be the capital of the world. Let them learn to be soldiers. Let them know, and teach their children, that no power on earth can stand against Roman arms.'

An army of citizens

Before Servius Tullius, any patrician citizen could serve in the army. It was not considered a duty, but rather a privilege that gave him access to a political career. The city had no army other than its own citizens, who were selected and mobilized according to current needs and only during wartime. In peacetime, the legions dissolved. This levy system was based on the original distribution of the patrician families into tribes and curias. Each one of the 30 curias had to contribute 100 men for the infantry and ten for the cavalry, so that the city's defence was guaranteed by 3000 infantry and 300 horsemen.

TRAINING IN THE TESTUDO
(TORTOISE) FORMATION
This was one of the formations most used by the Roman legions in combat and in the siege of cities. Relief on Trajan's Column (second century).

THE EMPIRE'S SPEARHEAD

578–535 BC
The first organization of the Roman army has been attributed to Servius Tullius. The military is distributed, according to the census, into five categories, and the basic tactical organization is the phalanx.

446–275 BC
The maniple-based legion is established, replacing the phalanx-based one, due to the difficulty of manoeuvring it. Age becomes the main criterion for the distribution of the legionaries.

157–86 BC
Gaius Marius allows the poor to enlist in the army, and grants them a salary for their service in the legion. The cohort, a group of 600 soldiers, replaces the maniple as a tactical unit. The Eagle is introduced.

100–44 BC
Julius Caesar arranges the ten cohorts into three lines: 2400 men are placed on the first line, in four cohorts of 600 men, while the remaining two rows have three cohorts.

76–138 AD
Emperor Hadrian places at the head of the Legion a single cohort made up of the 1000 best soldiers (*cohors miliaria*). Behind it, in three rows, are 10 cohorts of 500.

AQUILA (EAGLE)
Standard of the legion from the Circus Maximus, Rome.

Servius Tullius (578–535 BC) introduced the first major reform in the Legion by modifying the recruitment criteria: no longer was priority given to patrician families and an age for levies was established. The census was divided into five groups (*classis*): the first were the richest, who formed the cavalry (*equites*) and the body of princes; the other four classes were divided into infantry (*hastati*, *triarii* and *velites*) and the auxiliary services. Each group was divided in two according to age. The youngest formed the active army, while the oldest remained in the reserve, in charge of defending the city (*legio urbanae*).

To mobilize the soldiers on the battlefield, the first tactical units were organized, the *centuriae* (centuries), comprising 100 men each. Thirty centuries were grouped in phalanx (rectangular) formation, six ranks deep with 500 men each. The first two ranks comprised the richest citizens, called princes. They wore full armour, including a helmet (*galea*), breastplate (*lorica*), red bronze shield (*hasta*) and leg armour (*ocreae*), and carried a sword (*gladius*), a spear (*hasta*) and a javelin (*telum*). The third and fourth ranks of the phalanx comprised second-class men, the *hastati*, with a square shield (*scutum*) and no helmet. Third-class citizens formed the last two ranks, the *triarii*, without leg armour. Twelve centuries of citizens registered in the fourth and fifth *classis* formed the body of lightly armed *rorarii*, who marched in front of the phalanx. To this 4200-men strong infantry were added 300 knights, arranged in two lateral wings divided into five *turmas* (groups of 30

ARMY EQUIPMENT

Weapons and armour used in the Roman army varied depending on the period and the speciality or category to which each soldier belonged. The basic components of their equipment, however, were always the same.

1 HELMET This imitated the Attic or Celtic helmet, adorned with a plume or three red or black feathers. There was also a small protective element for the back of the neck.

2 MAILCOAT A mesh of intertwined metal rings that was donned over the tunic (*lorica hamata*). In the time of Trajan, the *iorica segmentata* (segmented cuirass) was used, made of superimposed metal sheets.

3 GLADIUS The gladius represented an improvement on the Iberian sword. The blade was straight, 50cm (20in) long, and with a short tip.

4 PILUM The pilum was a type of spear or javelin, 2m (6ft 6in) long, featuring a squared iron section, and a pyramidal tip, attached to a wooden stick with nails or a wooden rivet.

5 SHIELD Those of princes and spearmen were rectangular. Those of the velites (light infantry), tribunes and consul were round.

6 GREAVES These bronze shinguards were worn by spearman only on the right leg, as the left was protected by their shields. Officers had both their legs protected.

7 TUNIC The basic attire of the *velites*, or light infantry; they could not afford more expensive garments and went without breastplates or mail.

8 SANDALS *Caligae* were leather and covered the ankle. Metal studs were sometimes added to the sole, to enhance the footwear's grip.

---

horsemen), and five centuries of builders (*fabri*), musicians (*cornicines* and *tubicines*) and additional soldiers, *accensi volati*, who were only given weapons in case they had to provide cover for casualties.

The wars against the Samnites revealed the difficulty of manoeuvring and displacing the compact masses of the soldiers of the phalanx and prompted reform, which established age as the main criterion for the distribution of the legionaries and incorporated the *manipulus* as a tactical unit. The maniple legions, established between the time of Marcus Furius Camillus (446–365 BC) and the Pyrrhic War (280–275 BC), were divided into three battle lines of ten maniples each, spread 40m (130ft) apart. The youngest (*hastati*) marched in the first line, enduring the first enemy wave, then the middle-aged (princes), who replaced fallen soldiers. The maniples of the first two ranks comprised 120 men. In the third rank were the veterans (*triarii* or *pili*), consisting of 60 combatants.

In the maniple legion, the princes' and *hastati*'s equipment were almost identical. Both had a rectangular shield 1.2m (4ft) high, made with two circular wooden planks glued with oxtail, covered by a linen canvas and, under it, a calf skin, and reinforced with an iron border. They wore a breastplate, which could be a simple brass one or a sophisticated chainmail (*lorica hamata*) type, depending on the available assets of each soldier. They carried the Spanish sword (*falcata*), with a blade affixed by both edges, introduced by Scipio during the Second Punic War, and a javelin (*pilum*), which became the Roman legion's characteristic weapon. The *hastati* wore a crown of three red or black feathers, one elbow height.

The 1200 legionaries of the light infantry (*velites*), deriving from the ancient *rorarii* and *accensi volati*, were younger and poorer than the rest and, therefore, wore no armour, but a simple short tunic and a helmet, over which they placed a wolf skin. They could fight alongside the heavy infantry or independently, just as the cavalry contingent could.

The system of the manipled legion endured until the wealthy classes stopped supplying the army with its

The Roman fleet, a support force in military campaigns

In war, the Roman navy played a secondary role in relation to that of the land-based contingents. The naval infantry were considered inferior to legionaries of their same rank, and were applied in naval combat tactics used on land. The boats used were copies of Carthaginian and Etruscan ships.

Polybius tell us the Romans used a stranded Carthaginian quinquereme in the Strait of Messina to study the enemy's warship construction techniques, as they were more skilled in navigation. The quinquereme, devised by Corinthian ship builders ca. 700 BC, replaced the trireme in the fourth century BC. A trireme had three orders of rowers on each flank. During the wars against Macedonia, Rome deployed the *lembus*, a lighter and more agile vessel. This ship had no sails and just one bank of oars. From these derived the Roman *liburnias* (see fresco of the House of the Vettii in Pompeii, and, above, on a *denarius*), which were used in the Wars of the Rhine and the Danube.

1 CORVUS
A naval boarding system consisting of a 10.9m-long (36ft) bridge-like gangway for boarding Carthaginian ships.

2 CREW
According to Polybius, a trireme comprised 300 rowers manning 184 oars, 120 soldiers and 50 sailors.

3 OARSMEN
Distributed in three banks below deck, with 29 oars on each flank in the two upper banks and 34 oars in the lower bank.

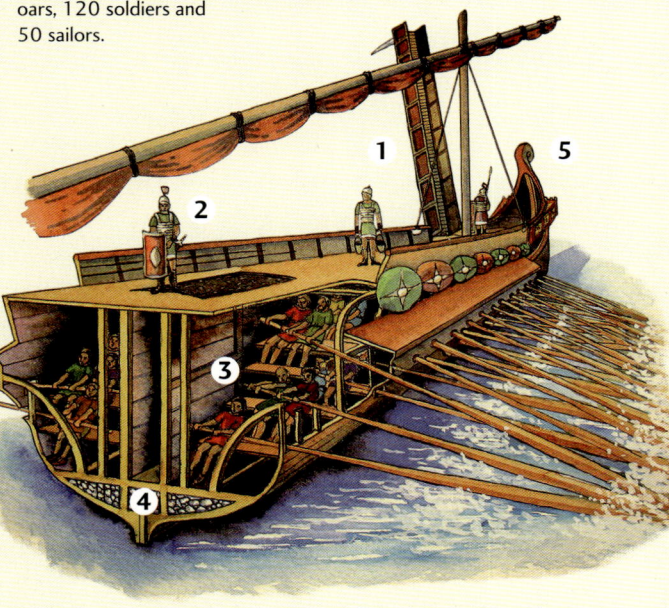

4 CELLAR
The triremes had little space for transporting goods, which was limited to armament and provisions for the crew.

5 ROSTRUM
Although the Roman warships had a rostrum (large brass ramming head), they did not use it as a battering ram, but rather to fight the collision.

THE ROMAN EMPIRE

War machines

The effectiveness and invulnerability of the Roman legions was based not only on strict discipline, guaranteed by the control wielded by their officers, but also by highly effective military technology, gradually improved through innovation and battlefield experience. Many mechanical instruments used for launching projectiles and assault on enemy defences were copies of Hellenistic experiments. The catapult, scorpion and the ballista, built, according to Vitruvius, to launch a range of projectiles, exploited the torsion provided by stretching the nerves, tendons or manes of animals to generate propulsive force. If these were cut, the machine was disabled, as happened with an enormous ballista used at the Battle of Bedriacum in 69 AD, according to Tacitus. To prevent their destruction, replaceable metal cylinders were added to protect the tension cords. For sieges there were different types of battering rams and towers, already in use during Caesar's time. The instructions for their construction and usage are described in Apollodorus of Damascus's *Poliorcetica*. He stated that these machines ought to be 'easily repairable, difficult to neutralize, mobile, stable, non-flammable, invulnerable, solid and capable of being disassembled'. Siege towers similar to those seen in the image were commonly used (Trajan's Column, second century).

citizens, many of whom were ruined or exhausted by the continuous battles. General Gaius Marius (157 BC–86 BC) was then obliged to enlist the poor into the legion; they would become willing soldiers and serve indefinitely in exchange for a secure salary and part of the spoils of war. The 'democratization of the army', in the words of French historian Fustel de Coulanges, meant the elimination of any distinction of standing or armaments among the legionaries. The infantry corps now comprised ten homogeneous groups, the cohorts, formed of 600 men each, distributed in two rows and subdivided into three tactical units, maniples, or six administrative units, centuries.

The soldier's salary

Although the division into cohorts did not change for centuries, there was an important transformation in the internal composition of the legion and in the soldiers' quality of life. After the Battle of Actium (31 BC), Augustus dissolved 32 of the 60 legions that had fought against Mark Antony, and discharged nearly 200,000 veterans, who he established in newly built colonies in different provinces of the empire. The other 28 legions, reduced to 25 after the Battle of Teutoburg Forest (9 AD), were mainly supplied by provincial natives, who were granted citizenship upon entering the legion, as well as monetary gain. Only in cases of extreme necessity were levies used, since legionary service continued to be obligatory for all Roman citizens.

Any man at least 1.7m (5ft 10in) tall and over the age of 13 could start in military service as an apprentice (*tiro*), until being registered in the army list and branded with a glowing iron. Once admitted to the legion, a soldier could serve for 36 years. The sub-officers and the centurions could remain for more

LEGIONARY ON HORSEBACK
This legion soldier appears armed with a javelin and in the heat of battle in this funerary relief dating from the second century BC (Capitoline Museums, Rome).

than 40 years and obtained many more benefits than a simple soldier. The first to establish a fixed salary for the legionaries had been Furius Camillus, during the Siege of Veii in 406 BC (two pence per day, 120 denarii per year); Caesar increased this to 225 denarii per year; and Domitian to 300 denarii per year. Although the State deducted expenses for food, arms and supplies, the soldiers were given incentives and rewards on the occasion of triumphs, visits of emperors, or revolts, whose repression was paid in gold. However, not all the donated money was given to the legionaries – half was kept in a deposit under the protection of the standards and was returned to each of its owners upon retirement, along with any interest generated. In this way, the State tried to prevent soldiers from spending all their savings and remaining in poverty if they were forced to leave the army before retirement. If they died in service, the deposit went to their father or heirs appointed by will. Those who completed their full term of service were honoured with the honourable discharge which granted them land in a colony of Italy or the provinces, and a lump sum of money, which rose in the time of Augustus to 3000 denarii.

As well as these benefits, soldiers could ensure the construction of an honourable tomb and a dignified funeral by paying into a State-controlled fund, which the State gave to a funeral society. In case of death, change of legion or discharge, the insured or his heirs received 500 denarii, which paid for the grave, or to enrol in a new professional organization.

The standing army
The creation of a standing army meant important changes to the civil status of enlisted men and the activities they had to carry out, since the legion was not always engaged in war. Military regulations forbade soldiers to marry during service and considered the women with whom they had relations concubines and any children born of them illegitimate. However, since the legionaries' sons ended up being incorporated into their family and received the same name and family name of the father, as if they were legitimate children, the emperors softened these conditions until, according to Herodian, Septimius Severus authorized the legionaries to

THE ROMAN EMPIRE

The legion camp

The camps the legions set up while stationed were built according to very precise standards and rules that guaranteed safety, although some aspects varied depending on how long the legion would stay. During the Republic, Polybius tells us that the *castra stativa* – permanent fortresses/camps – could accommodate 24,000 legionaries and were organized in a square measuring 666m (2185ft) each side, fortified by a stone wall. Unlike stable encampments, temporary *castra* – even those that were to last a day (*castra tumultuaria*) – were reinforced with a palisade, erected under a centurion's supervision using the shafts (*pila muralia*) that each soldier carried as part of his equipment. Some camps originally built as temporary wooden forts were later replaced by stone ones, such as Vindolanda in England, next to Hadrian's Wall, depicted here in a watercolour by Peter Connolly.

live with their women and attend the military camp only to exercise and to fulfil their duties for a few hours a day.

A useful force
In peacetime, beyond the troops' routine exercises, Flavius Vegetius describes in his work *Epitoma rei militaris* that the legionaries could work in provinces or cities next to their base camp. Epigraphic inscriptions give evidence of numerous constructions undertaken by the legions, including roads, bridges, recreational buildings, tunnels, cisterns, temples, aqueducts and fountains.

During the reigns of Augustus (27 BC–14 AD) and Gallienus (260–268 AD), a single permanent chief (*legatus legionis*) was entrusted to command the legion, elected from the former praetors of the senatorial class by the emperor, the supreme commander of the army. When Gallienus banned the senatorial class from the army, the legions came under the control of prefects from the equestrian class. They were assigned to the General Staff of the legate in charge of special missions (*beneficiarii*), administrators entrusted to the registers and archives of the legion (*commentariensis*), the head of the accountants (*cornicularius*) and a person in charge of the administrative acts (*actarius*).

The tribunes of the army, who in the time of the Republic had been the direct spokesmen for the consuls or the dictator and had held power over the army, became officers and administrators in the imperial era. This office was usually occupied by young people of the equestrian class keen to build a senatorial career. Of the six tribunes in a legion, the most important was the laticlavius, who wore a purple band on his tunic and, after a short time in office, was given a job in the Senate. The other five were called angusticlavii.

When the legate was absent, the praefectus castrorum took charge of the day-to-day running of the camp and also over all the legionaries based in it. He was also responsible for the conservation of buildings, barracks and camp facilities, the maintenance of weapons, medical care, soldiers' meals, the water supply and the manufacturing and storage of construction materials.

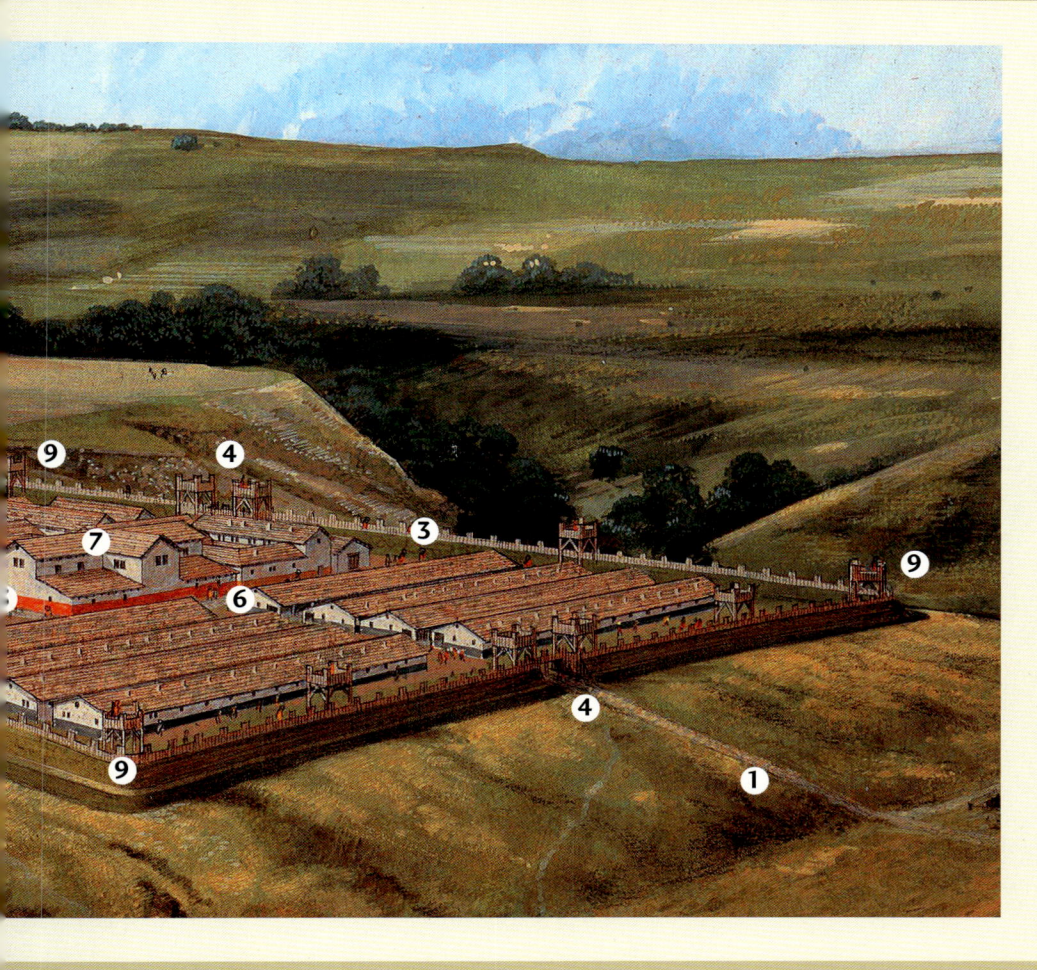

1 EMBANKMENT (AGGER) Made from the earth left from the excavation of a pit, this stood 1m high and 3m wide (3 by 10ft).

2 WALL (VALLUM) This served to reinforce the agger and was constructed using poles (*pila muralia*). Each metre of wall required 13 poles.

3 INTERVALLUM A 60m (200ft) portion of land cleared between the vallum and the camp's inhabitable area.

4 GATES Camps had four doors, each named after the way to which they provided access.

5 VIA QUINTANA AND VIA PRINCIPALIS These were the two parallel axes that crossed the camp. The centre of the space demarcated by both was reserved for the forum.

6 VIA PRAETORIA OR DECUMANA This ran perpendicular to the Via Principalis and Via Quintana to divide the camp into two halves.

7 HEADQUARTERS AND PRAETORIUM This was located in the centre, and occupied a higher position. In the middle was the commander's tent.

8 BARRACKS Long and narrow, they could lodge a century of 60 men, with its officers. A fort could contain up to 60 blocks of these.

9 WATCHTOWERS The camps of the Late empire included circular towers on their walls, with the number of gates being reduced to one.

10 CIVILIAN SETTLEMENT The prolonged occupation of a camp occasionally spawned veritable cities, due to the settlement of civilians around it.

In the military hierarchy, below the legates, tribunes and prefects, were ranked the centurions, a promotion in imperial times after serving in lower command posts in different legions. They were in charge of managing those assigned to them and enforcing discipline. Among the 60 centurions of a legion was the primipilus, the custodian of the Eagle. During a battle he was on the frontline, in charge of the *tubicines* (tuba players) who sounded the signals for attack or retreat.

Under the centurions' orders were sub-secretaries or specialists with very precise functions. The tesserarius was responsible for the communication of orders and received a password written on a tessera, which he circulated. The standard bearers were in charge of the legion's banners: the aquilifer with the Eagle standard; the signiferi with the teachings of the maniples; the imaginifer with the images of the emperor, who were in the first cohort. There were also heads of the musicians (*tubicines*, *cornicines* and *buccinatores*), doctors, vets, architects and engineers, the ministers of the religious cults and those in charge of administering provisions.

The number of legions
During Augustus's life there were 25 legions, known by an ordinal number and an honorific nickname. Five were added by Claudius, Nero, Galba and Trajan; the Flavians replaced some, as mentioned in a *laterculus legionum* dated 120–170 AD.

Hadrian introduced reforms in armament, recruitment and disposition in the battlefield. He brought back the phalanx formation for the first cohort, formed by the 1000 best soldiers (*cohors miliaria*). Septimius Severus increased salaries and allowed soldiers to take a wife, and three more legions were instituted: the I, II and III *Parthica*.

In the fourth century, under Diocletian and Constantine, the legion's function was divided between border defence (*legiones limitanae*) and protection of the sovereign (*legions palatinae* or *comitatenses*). Since the legions were divided into detachments of around 1000 infantrymen to fulfil different functions, the legion's prefect and legate duties were unnecessary and replaced by a tribune.

BUST OF NERO
Nero was the last emperor of the Julio-Claudian family and, for successive generations, an archetype of cruelty and madness (Capitoline Museums, Rome). On the next page: a gold coin depicts Nero and his mother, Agrippina (British Museum, London).

THE MONARCHY OF NERO

Nero ascended the throne supported by the praetorian cohorts. His government, a Hellenic court, bureaucratized the administration and separated the senatorial class from State affairs. His populist reforms and his attempt to transform Roman traditions with a cultural revolution of which he himself set an example led to a confrontation with the landed aristocracy – a conflict that formed the monstrous image of the last Julio-Claudian emperor.

After Claudius's murder in 54 AD, Agrippina the Younger ascended the throne, ahead of the first-born of her uncle and husband, her son Lucius Domitius Ahenobarbus, called Nero after his adoption on 25 February 50 AD. His paternal lineage was of plebeian nobility, since the Ahenobarbi – named after their copper-coloured beards – had entered Roman patronage around the first century BC; Nero legitimized his right to succession by his blood ties to the Julians, inherited from his mother, and so began his controversial 13-year reign.

Nero received a painstaking education via Hellenic tutors, such as Berillus, Chaeremon of Alexandria and Alexander of Aegae, who encouraged the arts and oriental culture. Nero's inexperience in politics left the empire at the mercy of those who, during the first years of his reign, wielded de facto power in government: Agrippina and Seneca. With the guidance of the senator and philosopher, Nero made his

The Principate of Nero

Year 54
Nero Claudius Caesar Augustus Germanicus ascended the throne at the age of 17, with the support of Praetorian prefect Sextus Afranius Burrus.

Year 57
Nero's definitive divergence from the interests of the Senate. A State bureaucratic apparatus is created run by freedmen.

Year 59
Agrippina Minor is murdered by order of Nero, on the advice of Seneca. Nero meets Poppaea Sabina, whom he married in 62.

Year 63
Claimants to the throne Rubellius Plautus and Sulla are eliminated, at the instigation of the Prefect Ofonius Tigellinus.

Year 64
Rome is devastated by a terrible fire and reconstruction begins. Gaius Calpurnius Piso leads a plot against the emperor.

Year 68
After the rebellions of Vindex and Galba, Nero, who is dethroned and fears for his life, commits suicide. With him the Julio-Claudian dynasty, of which he was the fifth emperor, is extinguished.

first speech before the Senate, as well as the funeral eulogy in honour of the late princeps, which, at the same time, Seneca slandered in a virulent satirical pamphlet, *Apocolocyntosis (divi) Claudii*. In this pamphlet, Seneca cruelly described the ascent to the sky of Claudius dragged by an *uncus*, a hook used to throw corpses of assassins into the Tiber.

The fate of Britannicus

Ancient accounts of Nero forged the image of a deviant emperor to discredit a government in which the powers of the senatorial class and the landowners, who wanted to ensure their class privileges, were curtailed. Modern historiography, based on direct sources of the time (mainly through numismatics and epigraphy), offer a more balanced portrait of the 'cursed emperor', giving recognition to Nero's reign as a period of economic and cultural dynamism.

It is possible that one falsehood added to the biography of Nero is the murder of his stepbrother, Britannicus. Tacitus's version of the fratricide argues that Agrippina, cut off from power by Nero, threatened to ally herself with her stepson, who could claim the throne as soon as he assumed the *toga virilis* aged 14. The murder of Britannicus was done, according to the Latin historian, with the help of the poisoner Locusta, who added a fast-acting poison to fresh water served at a banquet. While the diners attended the sudden death of Britannicus, Octavia and her husband, Nero, continued as if nothing had happened.

The aloof behaviour of the imperial couple and the exclusion of the episode from the list of crimes of the emperor written by non-Roman historians, such as Plutarch or Josephus, have given rise to the hypothesis that the death occurred due to natural causes, such as an aneurysm caused by an epileptic attack, a disease that Claudius's son suffered. The reasons Tacitus gives are rendered less valid when we note that the death occurred at the end of January of 55 AD, when Agrippina was at the height of her power, as indicated by the monetary stamps of that period.

Seneca and the politics of the young princeps

The philosopher Lucius Annaeus Seneca, who Agrippina, Nero's mother, brought out of exile to tutor her son, tried unsuccessfully to instil in his pupil a conservative political disposition. During the first eight years of Nero's reign, Seneca became one of the most influential men at the court, a direct participant in the life of the palace, along with Nero's mother and Praetorian prefect Sextus Afranius Burrus. However, in 62 AD, Nero rebelled against the interference by his collaborators and conceived a government calling for revolutionary political and economic reform. Seneca's gradual discrediting then began. His role as Nero's adviser (portrayed here in Eduardo Barrón González's sculpture of 1904, Prado Museum, Madrid) was interpreted to be that of a *tyranno didáskalos* (educator of a tyrant). His Stoic teachings were branded as hypocritical, as he was a man who, according to Dio Cassius, 'recriminated the rich for being so, while he himself possessed a fortune of 300 million sesterces'.

The consolidation of the bureaucracy

A fratricide committed by the newly appointed emperor would have contravened one of the primary policies of the Neronian principate: clemency, the imperial virtue exalted by Seneca in a treatise (*De Clementia*) published the same year as the alleged crime. Eight years would pass until the elimination of the dynastic suitors who threatened Nero on the throne – Rubellius Plautus and Cornelius Sulla – would begin.

The first five years of the Neronian government, which Trajan cited as prosperous, were characterized by administrative, fiscal and legal reforms benefiting the disadvantaged classes. Beginning with the bureaucratic system that Claudius had set in motion, Nero surrounded himself with efficient collaborators, mostly freedmen, as administrative personnel with great autonomy, though disallowed from reaching the ranks of the praetorship and quaestorship, whose admittance was restricted to the senatorial class. The aristocracy's reluctance to see the power of the freedmen increased led to situations of violent opposition between the emperor and the Senate in 57 AD, when the 400 slaves of Lucius Pedanius Segundus, prefect of Rome, were condemned to death for a crime that only one had committed. That conflict, in which Nero had to submit to the law imposed in the Curia, marked the beginning of his estrangement from the senatorial class.

After renouncing the participation of the senators in the imperial administration, Nero created a genuine State bureaucratic system, led by Phaon as financial secretary (*a rationibus*); Doryphorus and Xenophon of Cos as legal ministers (*a libellis*); Polyclitus and Berillus, in charge of the imperial correspondence in Latin and Greek (*ab epistulis*); Patrobius, whose ministry organized circus games; Epaphroditus, personal secretary of the emperor, and Aelius, who deputized for Nero when he was absent from Rome. The *concilium principis* was added as an advisory body, made up of 30 councillors of the senatorial and equestrian classes.

Currency devaluation

One Neronian reform was the suppression of the *intracubiculum principis* processes, which had been carried out frequently during the time of Claudius. These involved the arbitrary conviction or salvation of the courts in cases that had not received a regulatory judgement in the Senate. To avoid mutual influence, a custom was established that pre-trial collaboration between experts was forbidden until after the proceedings had been concluded, and a day of reflection was granted prior to the passing of a verdict.

THE ROMAN EMPIRE

Commerce and taxes under Nero

Italy produced little, so depended on imported goods. Marble, textiles, cereals, meats and fish, oil and slaves all arrived mainly by sea, as land transport was much more expensive.

The voyage of a merchant ship was slow and dangerous. A ship took nine days to get from Alexandria to Puteoli, the main port on the Italian peninsula; and, from there, three more to reach Ostia in smaller vessels. Ships normally sailed at night, between 5 March and 11 November. Imported products were subject to taxes such as the *quinta et vicesima venalium mancipiorum* (25 per cent on the sale of slaves) and customs fees, paid at all provincial borders (*portorium*), which Nero wanted to stop. Merchants, like the one shown in this relief, from Cabrières-d'Aigues (France), were protected by the Laws of Rhodes: this said that if a ship was saved from sinking by throwing part of its cargo overboard, the losses were borne by the owner of the goods and the owner of the ship.

1 AMPHORAS OF OIL
Most oil was exported from the province of Baetica, and North Africa.

2 AMPHORAS OF WINE
They were covered inside with fish and sealed with a clay plug.

3 THE CAPTAIN
He holds the rudder and keeps the ship on course during its voyage.

The tax reform of 58 AD had serious repercussions: it began with the attempt to remove all indirect taxes (*vectigalia*), those on levied goods by two and a half per cent (if imported from the western provinces) or by five per cent (if imported from elsewhere); its aim was to activate commerce and stimulate people's participation in it. The Senate aborted the proposal, as it involved the elimination of a vast part of the public treasury (25 million sesterces, or 15 per cent of its income), but they really aborted it because it harmed the privileges of the senatorial class, owners of large estates in Italy. In order to reduce the price of imported grain, Nero decreed the exemption of the patrimonial taxes to mercantile ships and limited the benefits of the exaction practised by the publicans (tax collectors).

The fiscal reforms defeated in 58 AD by the Senate were passed between 63–64 AD through more practical reform: the devaluation of the currency. Nero ordered a decrease in the purity in gold and silver in the denarii and circulated more money in the market, which caused inflation linked to a period of frenzied construction. This reform turned around an economic depression.

One motivation for reducing the amount of silver in the denarii by up to a quarter was an insufficient supply of silver sourced from Hispania, the province that contributed the most metals to the empire. Supplies were depleted by the military campaign in Armenia, whose defeat provided reserves.

The attempted matricide

In the first four years of his tenure, Nero forged his own style of rule, conscious of the personal interests that confronted him: not only the Senate, but also Agrippina, his mother, whose

4 BARRELS
They mainly contained cereals, from the province of Egypt.

5 THE CABOTAGE BOAT
Small river ships were towed from the shore.

6 THE RUDDER
The *gubernaculum* was formed by an axis holding a *palmula* (blade).

7 THE SAILORS
They helped the ship to get up the river in the shallowest areas.

desire for dominance, described by Tacitus as 'of almost virile energy, with great severity and arrogant pride', threatened to displace the princeps from the throne. Agrippina had disposed of all her rivals and compromised the policy of clemency that Nero tried to instil, so with the advice and help of Seneca, the princeps plotted the elimination of his own mother.

The first step was to deprive her of the freedman Pallas and the Praetorian Guard before forcing her to leave the palace. By 55 AD, Agrippina, according to the accusation of Junia Silana and Domitia Lepida, Nero's aunts, was planning her marriage to Rubellius Plautus, a descendant of Augustus via his mother, and attempting a coup d'état, similar to the one Messalina had plotted with Gaius Silius. The empress involved Praetorian prefect Afranius Burrus and others. Nero denied the accusations and interrogated her through an inquiry involving the Praetorian prefect, which left Rubellius unscathed and Silana condemned. The two who had filed the complaint, Iturius and Calvisius, were exiled.

In 58 AD, Agrippina tried to win over the senators, using the conflict between them and the emperor, but Seneca prompted Nero to halt her plans.

Anicetus, commander of the Misenum fleet, attempted to dispose of the mother of the princeps on the coast of Bauli, when the ship taking her to Baiae was scuttled. However, the ship did not sink and Agrippina swam ashore. That night, on 23 March 59 AD, Anicetus, together with Herculeius and Obaritus, went to the village and murdered her.

Adultery with Poppaea

Nero feared reprisals after his mother's murder and did not return to Rome for four months.

BANQUETS IN IMPERIAL ROME

For a Roman, the main meal of the day was dinner, conceived as a social event in which the host displayed his wealth and generosity. Both breakfast (*iantaculum*) and lunch (*prandium*) were small. At dusk, wealthy Romans invited guests at the baths or the porticoes of the Field of Mars. Guests were greeted at the home by slaves, who helped them remove their uncomfortable clothes, took off their shoes, and offered them more comfortable attire. Dinner took place in the *triclinium*. It began with an invocation of the gods, with the words '*dii propitii*', followed by three to seven dishes, served on sumptuous tableware. It was not considered appropriate to drink wine with food, as this prevented one from appreciating the taste of the different dishes served. With the dessert the last phase of the banquet, the *comissatio*, began. Plenty of drink was offered, along with a variety of entertainment, such as musicians, dancers, mimes and even gladiators. In the centre, a mosaic from Pompeii (National Archaeological Museum, Naples).

SUMMUS IN IMO
(the place of the host)

LECTUS IMUS
Right side of the *triclinium*

TRICLINIUM IN HERCULANEUM
Some aristocratic houses, such as that of Neptune and Amphitrite in Herculaneum, featured a summer *triclinium* in the garden, with stone divans on which mattresses and cushions were placed.

1 TRICLINIUM
The Romans ate reclined, which is why their dining areas were equipped with divans (*kliné*, in Greek), generally on three of their sides.

2 CLEANING
A slave washed and dried the feet of the guests, and stretched fabrics over the mattresses on the divans, as recorded in a Pompeiian inscription.

3 WOMEN
They also attended dinners. Graffiti from Pompeii read: 'Do not throw lascivious glances or fix your eyes on another man's wife'.

LOCUS CONSULARIS
(the place of the main guest)

① LECTUS MEDIUS
Central side of the *triclinium*

LECTUS SUMMUS
Left side of the *triclinium*

4 CLOTHING
When a guest arrived at the home, a slave removed his toga, replacing it with a lighter and more comfortable garment (*vestis cenatoria*), and took off his sandals.

5 SERVANTS
The dinner dishes (between three and seven) were served one after another by the slaves, under the direction of a master of ceremonies (*tricliniarcha*).

6 EXCESSES
At the end of the banquet (*comissatio*) people drank wine in abundance. Some had to be taken home by their slaves.

THE ROMAN DIET

WINE
Wine was drunk diluted in hot or cold water. Amianthus celebrates the pleasure of its consumption in a mosaic on his grave, found in Thaenae (Tunisia).

FRUIT
Fruit was consumed raw, dried or cooked, with honey as a garnish for meats. In Pompeiian frescoes, like this one at the National Archaeological Museum, Naples, still lifes of fruit are common.

FISH
The Romans consumed different types of fish, such as those depicted in this mosaic (Baths of Diocletian, National Museum of Rome).

THE ROMAN EMPIRE

The naumachia: a major Roman spectacle

Julius Caesar was the first to stage a recreation of a naval battle in Rome to commemorate his triumphs. Known as a *naumachia*, this featured slaves, prisoners and criminals dressed as different combatant groups, and used biremes and triremes to re-enact battles. Augustus ordered the construction of a building to host these events. Nero celebrated a public banquet there during the Juvenalia festivities in 59 AD.

NAVMACHIA NERONIS

For the *naumachia* of 46 BC, Caesar ordered the excavation of the Field of Mars up to the aquifer of the Tiber, creating a deep artificial lake. Shortly thereafter, the lake was blamed for originating a terrible, city-wide epidemic. Augustus furnished Rome with a building adapted for these spectacles, creating a lake measuring 533 by 355m (1750 by 1165ft) in Trastevere with a capacity for 200,000 cubic metres (7,063,000 cubic ft) of water, which was brought from the Alsietinus (Martignano) lake. The ships used in the naval combat came via a channel connected with the Tiber; the same one Nero used to return to the palace after the *naumachia* in 59 AD, shown in this 17th-century engraving. Claudius decided to use Fucine Lake, before attempting to drain it, to offer the people an unprecedented *naumachia*. Tacitus reports that the emperor had 19,000 men in triremes and cuatriremes creating a circle of boats manned with infantry and cavalry from the praetorian cohorts. Claudius attended, wearing a splendid cloak, and Agrippina a golden one. The actors fought heroically until the emperor suspended the massacre. Claudius's naval combat was equalled in magnificence only by the one offered by Titus at the inauguration of the Colosseum in 80 AD. Trajan built a new *naumachia* site at the Vatican in 109 AD.

Shortly afterwards, another woman appeared in his life, to whom he would again be subjugated: Poppaea Sabina, 'beautiful and majestic', as described in the anonymous drama *Octavia*. Poppaea was married to Marcus Salvius Otho, after a first marriage with the senator and prefect Rufrius Crispinus. As soon as the emperor fell prey to the charms of Poppaea, Otho was removed from Rome and sent to be the governor to Hispania Lusitania.

Poppaea caused political consequences in 62 AD when she became pregnant, and Nero was forced to renounce his wife Claudia Octavia, at the risk that divorce and a union with a woman who had no connection with the imperial families would nullify his legitimacy to the throne. To justify the divorce before the Senate and public opinion, which believed the daughter of Claudius to be a virtuous woman, Nero accused her of adultery with Eucareus, an Egyptian slave, and exiled her to Campania; 12 days later, Nero married Poppaea. However, public opinion demanded the emperor return to his former wife. This provoked a public riot against Poppaea, resulting in the destruction of all the images of the new empress. This display of popular animosity led to the death sentence for Octavia; she was accused of adultery with Anicetus, who had murdered Agrippina. Octavia was exiled to the island of Pandateria, where an assassin of Nero chained her up, cut her veins and submerged her in boiling water.

The first daughter of Nero, born on 21 January 63 AD, lived for only four months. Two years later, Poppaea became pregnant again, but no child was born. According to Suetonius, a kick from a drunken Nero caused the death of the mother and foetus at the same time. Nero showed great repentance and embalmed the body of his wife with spices before burying her in the Mausoleum of Augustus after a public funeral granting divine honours. Soon after, he married the eunuch Sporus, because, according to Dio Cassius, he reminded him of Poppaea.

The first executions of the reign

The death of his half-brother, his mother and Octavia inspired the image of Nero's bloodthirstiness with which the last Julio-Claudian monarch went down in history. The policy of clemency that his government advocated was muffled by crime, justified by the need to perpetuate power by eliminating rivals.

Any plots against Nero were exposed by spies commanded by Praetorian prefect Ofonius Tigellinus and Faenius Rufus (*praefectus annonae*) from 62 AD, when Afranius Burrus died. His zeal to safeguard the throne saw new accusations of *lèse-majesté*, which had claimed victims in the days of Tiberius and Claudius. At the instigation of Tigellinus, misgivings against Nero's most dangerous rivals, Rubellius Plautus and Cornelius Sulla, were renewed. Both were linked to the imperial family, the former as a descendant of Augustus through his mother, and the second as the husband of Claudia Antonia, the first daughter of Claudius. Both had been accused of conspiracy in 55 AD and pardoned by the emperor. The increase in Plautus's popularity led him to be considered the successor announced by celestial omens; this encouraged Nero to remove him from Rome and send him to Asia. The accusation of an imperial freedman, Graptus, against Sulla in 58 AD condemned him to exile in Massilia (Marseille).

These exiles allowed Plautus and Sulla enough time to ensure the faithfulness of the legions stationed in the respective provinces and the support of powerful supporters. Tigellinus alerted Nero of the imminent danger; according to Tacitus, both were condemned to death with no legal process. Nero survived another conspiracy led by Piso in 65 AD.

The Armenian dispute
Nero had to preserve his inherited empire to keep his privileged position. It extended from the southeastern part of Britannia and the confines of the Rhine and the Danube to

AGRIPPINA'S DEATH
In this oil painting by Antonio Rizzi, Nero leans over the body of his mother, whom he had murdered by his assassins. In the eyes of Romans, parricide was one of the worst crimes a citizen could commit, and was devastating to the emperor's reputation (Museo Cívico Ala Ponzone, Cremona).

THE ROMAN EMPIRE

The Arsacids: between Parthia and Armenia

In 54 AD, Vologases I of Parthia, son of Vonones II, whose effigy is found on coins (below), conquered Armenia and handed the kingdom over to his brother Tiridates, under the pretext that the Parthians deserved the throne more than the foreign, treacherous usurper Rhadamistus. This violated the treaty that Augustus had established with the king of the Parthians, Phraates IV.

Through this treaty, the Parthians granted Rome the right to crown the kings of Armenia. After the Armenians crowned Tiridates king in 55 AD and expelled Rhadamistus, who fled to Iberia (Georgia) with Queen Zenobia, Nero took action to end Parthia's excessive influence on Armenia. He sent Gnaeus Domitius Corbulo to take command of Eastern operations, which ended with a diplomatic agreement recognizing the Roman protectorate. In 66 AD, Tiridates, founder of the Arsacid dynasty, went with his wife to Italy to swear obedience to Nero. From Naples, Nero and Tiridates proceeded to Rome with a large entourage, decorated with lights and garlands. At the Forum, full of citizens dressed in white and crowned with laurels, and soldiers carrying weapons, Nero, clad in triumphal dress, crowned Tridates King of Armenia. Image: the Parthian king Vonones II (British Museum, London).

Tingitana and Egyptian Africa, and from Lusitania to Cappadocia and Syria. Beyond the eastern borders extended Armenia, serving as a defence against the powerful kingdom of the Parthians, adversaries of Rome. Neither Romans nor Parthians could allow Armenia to fall into the hands of a rival power; in such a case, the two great empires would go to war.

In 54 AD, King Vologases I of the Parthian dynasty of the Arsacids placed on the throne of Armenia his brother Tiridates, replacing the Roman allies who had ruled there before. The loss of control in Armenia gave the Parthians access to Syria, a rich province. Nero therefore appointed Gnaeus Domitius Corbulo as commander with the aim of recovering Armenia. Two legions were combined and given to Corbulo, one previously commanded by the governor of Syria, Numidius Quadratus, to which the IV *Scythica* legion, based in Germania, was added.

In nine years of war with Parthia there were both victories and defeats. A solution came through a diplomatic agreement and was the first peaceful victory of Roman history, although it was celebrated with the character of a military triumph. Rome agreed to recognize Tiridates as King of Armenia if he in turn recognized Armenia as a client kingdom to Rome. To sanction the agreement, Tiridates laid down his crown at the foot of a statue of Nero in Artaxata, capital of Armenia, in 63 AD. Three years later he was crowned king by the emperor in Rome. Payment for his journey and ceremony depleted the revenues of an entire year from the public treasury, but peace with the Parthians was an achievement for Nero.

A new rebellion in Britannia

The instability of the Britannic borders secured after Claudius's victory led Nero to consider abandoning the island between 54 and 56 AD or to convert Britannia into an independent state allied to Rome, ruled by Tiberius Claudius Cogidubnus. His military disinterest was at odds with the expansionist and warmongering zeal of the Senate. Nero was forced to organize an expedition to Wales under the command of the governor Quintus Veranius in 58 AD and, after his death, under Suetonius Paulinus.

While Paulinus engaged in the conquest of the island of Mona (Anglesey), which served as a base for the organization of guerrillas, the Iceni tribe from the east of Britannia rebelled against Rome after the death of their vassal king Prasutagus, who named Nero as heir to the kingdom with his two daughters. One of them, Boudica, who Tacitus described as a strong leader, declared war on Rome and allied herself with the neighbouring Trinovantes tribe, who had been stripped of land in the time of Claudius due to the establishment of a fortress in their ancient capital, Camulodunum (Colchester). The first Brittanic raids destroyed the cities of Londinium (London) and Verulamium (St Albans), causing a death toll of 70,000 Romans. Suetonius Paulinus occupied the area with two legions and ended the rebellion led by Boudica, who committed

LEGIONARIES IN BRITANNIA

This relief, from the funerary stele of the soldier Longinus, shows him on horseback, in a triumphant pose, with one of the conquered barbarians at his feet. The stele was found in the British city of Camulodunum (modern-day Colchester), considered the oldest city in Britain. Camulodunum was the capital of the tribe of the Trinovantes, and was established around 25 BC. After a first attempt by Tasciovanus, the king of the Catavellauni tribe, his son Cunobelinus, conquered it. After the Roman victory, the XX legion, Legio vigesima Valeria Victrix, *or XX Victorious Valeria Legion, was established in Camulodunum, with the camp growing into a new colony and the seat of the Roman provincial government. (Colchester Castle Museum).*

suicide rather than surrender. After the victory, and against the opinion of the procurator Julius Classicianus, Suetonius tried to impose reprisals, which Nero prevented, replacing the general in 61 AD by the consul Petronius Turpilianus. Pacification and reconstruction began in Londinium, which became the new capital of the province.

All for art

The peaceful inclination of Nero's foreign policy and his aversion to the bloodthirsty policies that had led him to confront the Senate, such as the condemnation to death of the slaves of Lucius Pedanius Secundus, was also manifest in his program of social re-education, in which he substituted ancient Roman traditions for others inspired by Hellenic culture, which he considered more civilized and learned. Nero's cultural revolution relied on venues for the teaching of the new syllabus, such as gymnasiums, arenas and imperial schools, in which young aristocrats were schooled to compete in competitions that were gradually incorporated into Roman festivals. Five hundred of these youngsters formed the society of Augustani, professionals involved in the propagation of a Hellenic outlook to culture and sports.

The Hellenic cultural program of 'Neronism' that was forced on the upper class allowed them to portray Nero as a megalomaniac. Roman men liked violent combat to celebrate male virtues. Artistic expressions of poetry and music were private matters. Greek culture emphasized the *agon*, non-brutal contests demonstrating beauty and spirit. Nero banned fighting to the death, and organized theatres, such as the Neronia, which required the participation of Roman senators and knights. Nero's own performances as a citharist (the cithara being an instrument like a lyre), singer, actor and charioteer began in Naples in 64 AD. He not only pursued educational and cultural ends, but also the creation of a politics of spectacle, of which he was a pioneer.

The fire that devastated Rome
In the same year of Nero's artistic debut, a fire broke out in Rome that devastated ten of the 14 regions into which Augustus had divided the city. The accusation that the emperor started the fire so he could build a new capital for the empire was developed by Suetonius and Dio Cassius almost a century after the event, but does not appear in contemporary accounts, such as those by Josephus, Martial, Cluvius Rufus or Clement, bishop of Rome. Nowadays there is no doubt about the accidental nature of this catastrophe.

The fire of 64 AD started in the vicinity of the Circus Maximus, very close to the Palatine and the Caelian Hill, an area populated with warehouses, markets, houses and taverns. Flames spread through streets near the Roman Forum, the Velabrum and the Forum Boarium. Nero was in his villa in Anzio and hurried to the city.

Rome burned for three days. As the water hoses feebly tackled the blaze, Nero ordered the creation of a firebreak on the Esquiline Hill, cutting down houses and trees. On the seventh night, the fire seemed under control. Three neighbourhoods had burnt down; seven others were severely damaged, leaving four intact (Esquiliae, Porta Capena, Alta Semita and Transtiberim). The emperor set up shelters for the homeless in the Field of Mars, the gardens of Agrippa, the Saepta Julia, the Porticus Vipsania, and in the Pantheon, and brought in necessary aid and supplies from the surrounding municipalities.

The reconstruction of Rome
The fact that the fire started on the slopes of the Palatine and the Aemilian gardens, owned by Tigellinus, caused suspicion of an attack against the emperor. In 64 AD, the suspects were thought to be Christians, who believed Rome to be a new Sodom and Gomorrah and predicted their own salvation through burning. After the fire, Tigellinus's spies infiltrated Christian circles, in which hymns were composed indicating their satisfaction with what had happened. Soon the Cornelian laws respecting assassins and poisoners and the Julian laws on public violence were passed. Many Christians were tortured to extract confessions and 300 were burned alive, crucified or thrown to wild animals.

By applying these vile punishments, Nero went down in history as a monster. However, he rebuilt Rome in the same summer of 64 AD, using functional urban plans. Tacitus writes that 'the layout of the areas was well measured, where broad streets were built; the height of the buildings was limited to 25m [82ft]; courtyards were opened, to which porticos were added to protect the front part of houses'. Workforces comprised of citizens were rewarded for punctuality and quality of construction. Debris was cleared from the city on ships that returned to Ostia after unloading the wheat with which they arrived in Rome.

Nero's building policy included the completion of the Ostia port, begun by Claudius, along with large-scale projects carried out in Leptis Magna (Libya), Thrace, Syria, Bithynia and Galia Narbonensis. The most acclaimed work was the Domus Aurea, the new royal residence. This integrated series of buildings was erected between the Palatine and the Viminal hills, surrounded by forests and meadows, lakes, temples and majestic buildings adorned with masterpieces of Greek sculpture.

The buildings of the Neronian residence built on the Oppian Hill were the residence of the Flavians. They were converted into the Domus Titi and into thermal baths, which were opened in 80 AD. In 104 AD, a fire destroyed the last remains of the palace, which were buried under the Trajan baths.

The conspiracy of Calpurnius Piso
Tacitus recounts that, during the fire, Nero was seen running madly among the flames, alone and without a bodyguard, and that the tribune Subrius Flavius wanted to take advantage of this

APOLLO PLAYED THE CITHARA
Nero's passion as a player of the cithara (a lyre-like instrument) has placed him in popular imagery as playing the instrument while Rome burned. In this first-century statue, the cithara accompanies Apollo as a symbol of culture and music. Ludovisi Collection (National Roman Museum, Palazzo Altemps, Rome).

THE FIRE OF ROME (OPPOSITE)
The immense architectural structures of Rome at the mercy of fire are depicted in an oil painting by the Frenchman Hubert Robert in 1787 (Hermitage Museum, St Petersburg).

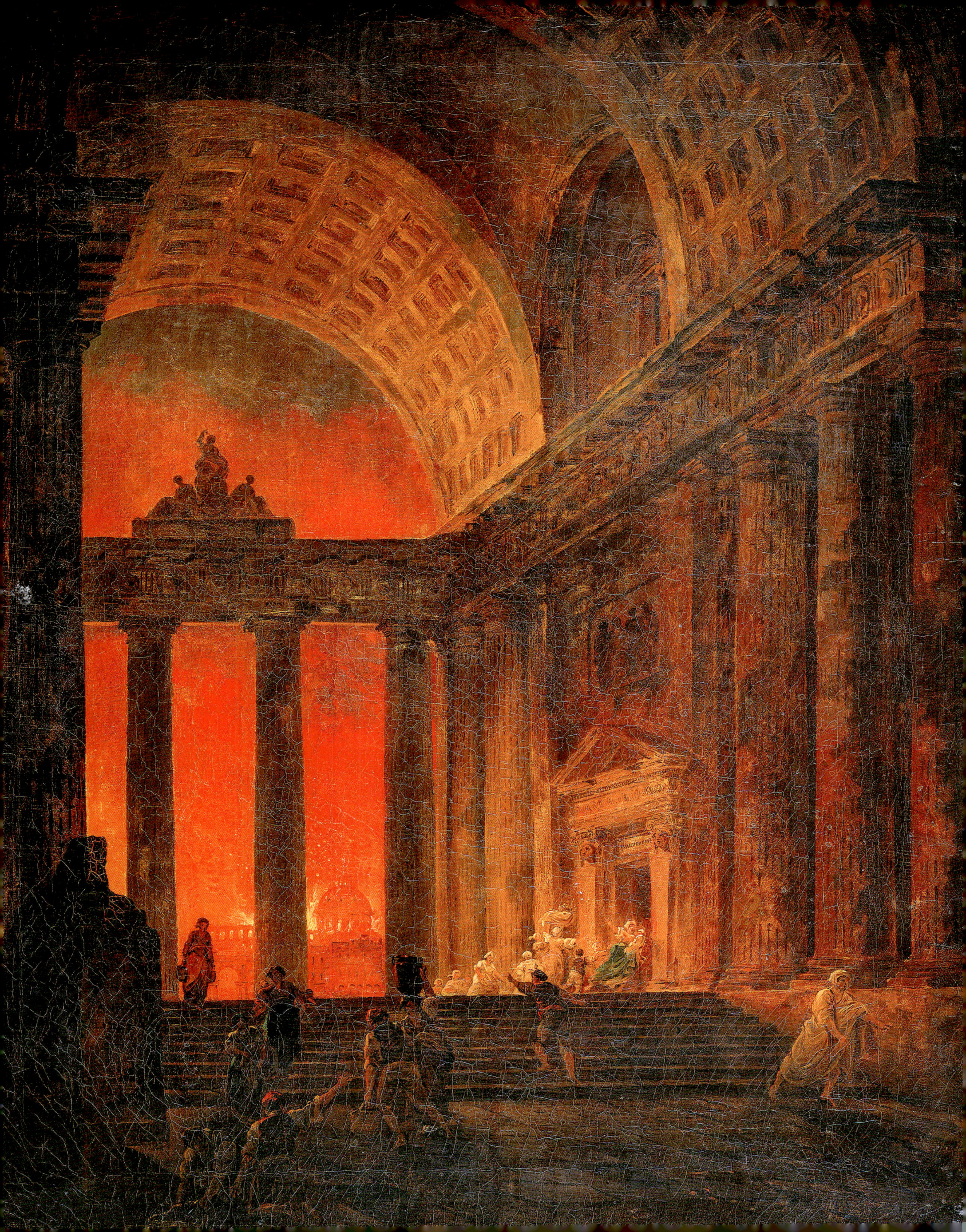

THE ROMAN EMPIRE

The Domus Aurea: the emperor's golden palace

Peter Connolly reconstructed in magnificent watercolours the Domus Aurea, the imperial residence Nero had built after the fire of Rome in 64 AD. Suetonius describes it: 'Its vestibule was large enough to contain a colossal statue of the emperor, 36m [120ft] high [...]. There was also a large lake, surrounded by buildings as big as cities next to ploughed fields, vineyards and woods ...'. Below, the Octagonal Room.

event to carry out the assassination that Gaius Calpurnius Piso and a group of Roman senators and knights had been plotting. Piso's conspiracy was motivated by the rupture of the *concord ordinum*; that is, because the interests of the landed senatorial class had been ignored and the government gave preference to the *novi homines*, knights, career soldiers and provincials. Monetary reform benefited the plebs, but harmed the interests of large landowners, while Nero's cultural reform, with its attempt to Hellenize Roman traditions and transform monarchical principles along the lines of Hellenic monarchies, were scandalous in the eyes of traditional republican families.

In addition to Piso, who was elected to replace Nero when he had been killed, the group of plotters included senators such as the poet Luca; knights such as Claudius Senecio, an old friend of the princeps; soldiers and centurions, and one of the Praetorian prefects, Faenius Rufus, who was jealous of the power wielded by his colleague Tigellinus. It was decided to carry out the assassination in the Circus Maximus during the celebration of the Cerealia. Plautius Lateranus was to take advantage of a planned commotion to get close to Nero and throw him to the ground, while Flavius Scaevinus was to strike the first blow. Meanwhile, Piso would wait in the Temple of Ceres for Faenius Rufus to take him to the Castra Praetoria, where, with the support of Claudia Antonia, daughter of Claudius, Piso would be proclaimed emperor. The plot fell down when Epicharis, the lover of Seneca's brother, tried to involve the commanders of the fleet in Misenum in the plot. One of them, Volusius Proculus, one of the murderers of Agrippina, denounced the conspiracy to the emperor, after which Epicharis was arrested.

THE MONARCHY OF NERO

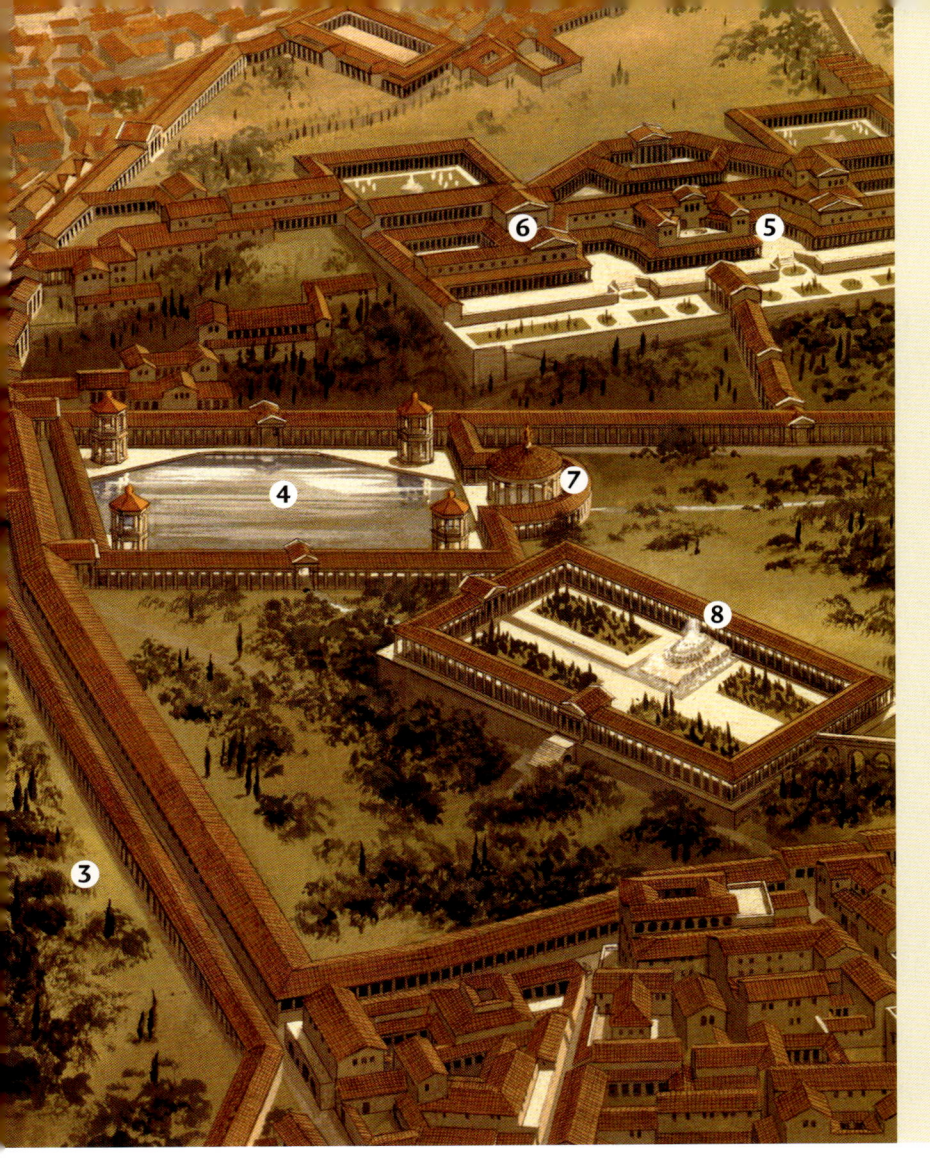

1 DOMUS TIBERIANA
The first true imperial palace on the Palatine Hill was attached to the Neronian buildings of the Oppian Hill.

2 COURTYARD
This housed a colossal statue of Nero, portrayed as the Roman god of the sun, Sol; this gave the Flavian Amphitheatre its other name: the Colosseum.

3 ENCLOSURE
The buildings were surrounded by fields, vineyards, pastures and woods, where there were large numbers of domestic and wild animals.

4 THE LAKE THAT 'SEEMED LIKE THE SEA'
According to Suetonius, this lake occupied a vast area of the Oppian Hill, over which Vespasian had the Flavian Amphitheatre erected.

5 GARDENS OF MAECENAS
Located on the Esquiline Hill, they were connected with the Palatine residence through the Domus Transitoria, the first nucleus of the Domus Aurea.

6 THE PALACE
In the words of Suetonius, 'it was covered with gold and adorned with precious stones and mother-of-pearl'.

7 OCTAGONAL ROOM
The most important room of the remains of the Domus Aurea that were buried under the Baths of Trajan complex between 104 and 109 AD.

8 NYMPHAEUM
This was a monumental fountain surrounded by gardens; it was built next to the remains of the burned-down Temple of Divus Claudius.

Seneca's suicide

On 18 April 65 AD, Scaevinus freed his slaves, organized a banquet, met secretly with Antonius Natalis, another conspirator, and ordered his servant Milichus to fasten the dagger and prepare bandages. The latter, suspecting the crime, went to the palace and met with Epaphroditus and Nero and confessed to 'the grave and terrible things' that were to happen the following day. Nero had Scaevinus interrogated first, from whom he obtained no information, and then Natalis, who implicated Piso and Seneca of leading the plot.

Once the plot had been revealed, the accused began to betray the names of other conspirators; only Epicharis maintained silence under torture. Nero ordered the German soldiers to guard the walls and access roads to the city and declared a state of siege in Rome. Piso committed suicide as the emperor's soldiers appeared. Seneca, who had been removed from Nero's inner circle in 62 AD and whom, according to Pliny the Elder and Dio Cassius, was plotting to prevent Piso from ascending the throne, was in his villa several miles outside Rome, with his wife Pompeia Paulina and two friends. The tribune Gaius Silvanus, who had also participated in the plot, appeared before him demanding to know what had happened, and Seneca claimed his innocence. After recounting his pleas to Nero, the emperor ordered Silvanus, 'Go back and tell him he must die'. The tribune sent a centurion to communicate the sentence to Seneca.

The death of the philosopher as told by Tacitus is a replica of the suicide of Socrates. Seneca and his wife, Paulina, had their veins cut at the wrists and ankles, but before he died, Nero responded to Seneca's plea to spare the innocent Paulina. Her wounds were bandaged

On the *Satyricon* and the 'arbiter of delicacies'

While researchers were integrating different parts of the Roman novel *Satyricon* from fragments included in manuscripts of the 15th and 16th centuries, attempts to identify its author, Petronius, began with a character of the same name. He was described by Tacitus as *arbiter elegantiarum* (arbiter of delicacies), who was included in Nero's court for his love of luxury. Tacitus's Petronius was Titus Petronius Niger, consul in 62 AD, an indolent man and a 'refined opportunist'. Nero considered him a close friend and trusted his good taste, which caused the envy of Tigellinus and the ruin of Petronius, who eventually committed suicide. Before he died, he wrote a libel in which, 'under the name of impudent youth and depraved women, he described the unprecedented refinement of the prince's orgies'. Although the identification of this libel with the *Satyricon* has been ruled out, in a satire of the Roman aristocratic world, here illustrated by G.A. Rochegrosse (1902; private collection), Titus Petronius is identified as the author.

and she did not attempt to follow her husband to the grave. Since Seneca was still not dying, he asked his friend Statius Annaeus to give him poison, but this did not work either. Finally, his friends submerged him in a hot bath, where he suffocated and bled to death.

The Judaean revolt

After the Great Fire of Rome and the Pisonian Conspiracy (for which Petronius, author of the *Satyricon*, was executed, along with Claudia Antonia, Marcus Annaues Mela and the senator Thrasea Paetus, among others), a new conflict arose in the eastern provinces, which increased discontentment with Nero's government and precipitated its end.

In May 66 AD, while Gessius Florus was procurator of Judaea, a revolt erupted against the confiscation of the treasures of the temple in Jerusalem and the ruthlessness and greed with which both the procurator and his wife Cleopatra behaved. The population fought the Roman legions, and Florus had to request the help of Gaius Cestius Gallus, a legate from Syria, who brought him 30,000 men to quash the rebellion. Palestinian guerrillas defended Jerusalem and forced Gallus to return to his province. In February of 67 AD, Nero sent Flavius Vespasian, a decorated military general with victories in Thrace, Germania and Britannia, to Judaea. With the collaboration of his son, the future emperor Titus, Vespasian quashed the revolt and reconquered Jerusalem in 70 AD.

Simultaneously with the conflict in Judaea, a new conspiracy was hatched in Rome, led by Lucius Annius Vinicianus (son of Annius Vinicianus, the main culprit behind the assassination of Caligula), in which many provincial governors and senior military officers participated, including Corbulo and Proculus Escribonius, commanders of the legions of Superior and Lower Germania. The assassination was set to take place in Benevento, at the beginning of Nero's excursion to Greece in 66 AD. Tigellinus's spy network uncovered the plot. The traitors were ordered to die, along with many high-profile figures.

From that date, the rupture between the emperor and the Senate was definitive. In that same year, 66 AD, Nero embarked on his first and only trip out of Italy. He left for Greece, where he spent more than a year, accompanied by his third wife, Statilia Messalina, his eunuch Sporus, 1000 praetorians and a retinue of more than 5000.

The unpopularity of the emperor
If Vinicianus's conspiracy revealed a lack of respect for the emperor among the highest officers of the army and among the aristocracy, Nero also lost the support of the common people during his absence from Rome. The trip to Greece seemed to prove his desire to replace the centre of power of the empire with a new one, Corinth. This was the quintessential Greek city, rife with oriental tendencies. This illuminated the principles of the new monarchy that Nero was attempting to impose.

Nero embodied this revolution himself, performing as a citharist in the four main panhellenic games that took place in that year: the Olympics, the Pythian Games, the Isthmian Games and the Nemean Games. He won medals and was declared *periodonica*, a title granted to those who had triumphed in all four of the festivals.

On his return to Corinth, Nero started a grand project to dig a canal through the 6km (4 miles) of land on the Isthmus of Corinth to avoid the circumnavigation of the Peloponnese. For this enormous work, Vespasian, commander of the legions that had suppressed the Judaean revolt, sent 6000 prisoners to add to the 10,000 who were condemned to forced labour. The work exalted the monarchy and the empire and Nero's inclination for the eastern province, to which he gave economic and political freedom on 28 November 67 AD. While Nero spent the little money left in the State coffers, discontent increased in Rome. People faced delays with the distribution of wheat; the army and the senatorial class suffered confiscations; and public finances wavered as the emperor strutted like a star of the arts, indifferent to the problems of his people.

ROMAN BATHS IN CORINTH
The Ancient Greek city, which was destroyed after the Achea War in 146 BC and rebuilt by Julius Caesar's design in the first century BC, had become a culturally important Roman city. The weight of the Corinthian past and its dominant position in the Hellenistic age were decisive in the choice of the city by Nero, who showed a great passion for Greek culture.

EMERITA AUGUSTA
Partial view of the Roman theatre of Mérida, one of the Hispanic cities that supported Vespasian, victor in the contest that faced the four emperors. On the next page is shown a lamp found in a Roman tomb in Veneto, near Este; the relief portrays the goddess Fortuna (National Atestino Museum, Este, Italy).

FOUR CAESARS IN A SINGLE YEAR

In his *Histories,* Tacitus summarizes events following Nero's death as a: 'period rich in disasters, terrible with battles, torn by civil struggles, horrible even in peace [...]. Italy was distressed by disasters [...]. Cities on the shores of Campania were overwhelmed; Rome [...] had ancient shrines consumed and the very Capitol burned by citizens' hands.'

To persuade Nero to return to Rome, his freedman Helius had been forced to go to Greece in January 68 to convince the emperor of the situation. In a first in the empire's history, a provincial governor, Gaius Julius Vindex, defied the princeps, claiming, by the coins he issued, that Nero jeopardized the 'restoration of Rome'. Although his military forces were limited and the capital of the province over which he ruled, Gallia Lugdunensis, did not support him, Vindex sought assistance from Galba (Servius Sulpicius Galba Caesar Augustus), the governor of Hispania Citerior, pledging aid if he accepted him as emperor. At the same time that Vindex was urging Galba to revolt against Nero, the governor of Aquitaine was asking him to put down Vindex's revolt.

Galba was one of the empire's richest men, of high-born bloodline traced paternally to Jupiter, containing several consuls and praetors

The year of the four emperors

June 68
After the death of Nero, Servius Sulpicius Galba, governor of Hispania Tarraconensis, declared himself emperor.

1 January 69
Aulus Vitellius, legate of Rome in Upper Germania, is acclaimed emperor in the city of Colonia Agrippina (Cologne) by the Germanic legions.

15 January 69
The praetorians acclaim Marcus Salvius Otho as emperor and assassinate Servius Sulpicius Galba.

14 April 69
First Battle of Bedriacum. Otho's troops are defeated by Vitellius's German legions, commanded by Aulus Caecina and Fabius Valens.

24 October 69
Second Battle of Bedriacum. The Danubian legions, which support Vespasian, defeat Vitellius's forces.

29 December 69
After the assassination of Vitellius in Rome, the senate appoints Vespasian, who was then in Alexandria, emperor. The Flavian dynasty is restored.

---

of the Roman Republic. At the age of 30, he rose to the rank of consul thanks to Livia's intercession, and obtained the command of the legions of Germania, replacing Gaetulicus (Gnaeus Cornelius Lentulus), on Caligula's orders. Galba belonged to Claudius's close circle, was proconsul in Africa and, in 60 AD, Nero appointed him governor of Tarraconensis, where he had acquired a reputation for cruelty and greed.

Galba was over 70 years old when he decided to assassinate the emperor – according to Plutarch, because he had intercepted a letter from Nero in which the emperor had ordered his death. On 2 April 68, Galba proclaimed himself Legate of the Senate and of the Roman people, in a tribunal chamber full of portraits of figures condemned and murdered by Nero. An enthusiastic throng cheered him, enthused by the promise of freedom. Galba united the *Legio sexta victrix* (Victorious Sixth Legion) and other auxiliary troops. He also secured the support of the legate of the province of Lusitania, Otho (Marcus Salvius Otho Caesar Augustus), whose wife, Poppaea Sabina, Nero had taken from him years prior.

The legions of Lucius Verginius Rufus

In Hispania, only the governor of La Baetica kept his oath of loyalty to the State and the princeps. When Nero heard of Galba's revolt, he did not vehemently defend the throne, but considered sharing the empire with him and retiring to Alexandria, to dedicate himself to art, poetry and the cithara. Nero did not want to fight, as he had received only modest military training from Afranius Burrus. Reluctantly, Nero had the Senate label Galba an enemy, sending legions under Publius Petronius Turpilianus and Rubrio Gallo after him.

Nero's fate and that of the more than 100,000 rebels led by Vindex in Gaul depended on the position assumed by the neighbouring governor of Germania Superior, Lucius Verginius Rufus, who commanded troops in the western part of the empire, camped by the Rhine. In 68 AD, according to Dio Cassius, Verginius Rufus attacked the insurgents, besieging the city of Vesontio (Besançon) defended by Vindex. After negotiations between the two generals, Vindex moved his soldiers towards the city. This was interpreted by Verginius's troops as an unforeseen attack, spurring them to fall upon their adversaries. The defeated Vindex took his own life. The legions of the Rhine acclaimed Verginius Rufus as Caesar and Augustus, titles he refused.

Verginius Rufus's victory, along with that of the governors of Dalmatia and Pannonia, and the commander of Germania Inferior, Fonteius Capito, placed Nero in an advantageous position, forcing Galba to Hispania. Nero's hesitation to counterattack spurred those who had not yet taken up a position to back Galba's cause. The monarch's fall came about by two Praetorian prefects: first, Ofonius Tigellinus, who abandoned his post and left Rome; and second, Gaius Nymphidius Sabinus, who tricked the Praetorian Guard with false promises.

'What an artist dies in me!'

Nymphidius Sabinus urged Nero to leave his Domus Aurea and shelter in the Gardens of Servilianus, informing soldiers in the praetorian camp that the emperor had abandoned the throne to go to Egypt, as he had said he would on other occasions. He also promised that Galba would pay 30,000 sesterces to each praetorian, and 6000 to each legionary, if they proclaimed him the new princeps of the empire. It was clear that Rome's military forces lacked discipline, which could alter the course of the empire's history. On that occasion, Nero's death not only put an end to the Julio-Claudian dynasty, but echoed Tacitus's concern about unrest.

On 9 June, Nero woke alone, stripped of everything by those who had hailed him emperor 14 years prior. He had even been deprived of a quick death. His loyal supporters Epaphroditus, Neophytus, Sporo and Phaon offered the emperor a villa several miles from Rome as a refuge. They left disguised as slaves, urging Nero to take his own life, as Galba's soldiers would torture him if they caught him. The emperor repeated the lament '*Qualis artifex pereo!*' ('What an artist dies in me!'). He ordered that a tomb be dug, and for him to be given the minimum rituals due the deceased. Upon hearing the approaching horses, Nero cut his own throat. His freedmen buried him between the Via Salaria and the Via Nomentana. The Senate, which had been stripped of all power during his reign, condemned Nero to *damnatio memoriae*, such that all his statues and inscriptions be erased.

Galba's unpopularity

After Nero's death, Galba headed for Rome, saluted by Verginius Rufus and, at Narbo Martius (Narbonne), a diplomatic contingent of the Senate where he was declared emperor.

NERO'S SUICIDE
The end of the last emperor of the Julio-Claudian dynasty was conveyed by the Russian painter Vasily Sergejevitsch Smirnov in a famous oil painting on canvas of 1888 (Russian Museum, St Petersburg). According to Tacitus, the death of Nero was received with joy by the Senate and the Roman upper classes, but with pain by the people. This account, however, does not tally with other historians' views.

THE ROMAN EMPIRE

Four emperors in the shadow of the Julio-Claudians

By making Servius Sulpicius Galba emperor in 68 AD, the Senate sanctioned a decision taken by the army and placed in charge of the empire an exponent of the aristocracy. His proximity to the Julio-Claudian family meant he received the bulk of Livia's will. In reward for his excellent military career, he was granted rule over Tarraconensis. He then went to Rome, where he was acclaimed emperor. Otho was also among Livia's clients and owed her his inclusion in the Senate; Nero confined him in Lusitania as governor to separate him from his wife, Poppaea Sabina. Vitellius had grown up in the shadow of the Julio-Claudians: his grandfather had been the procurator of Augustus's fortune, while his father had established the custom of worshipping Caligula as a god; he had flattered Claudius so much that the emperor put him in charge of the empire during his absence in Britain. Vespasian was the only one of the four who reached the position of emperor through military merit.

GALA UNIFORM
At military parades the Roman officers wore feathered helmets and beautiful armour. Marble (Museum of Roman Civilization, Rome).

The city had been cared for by Nymphidius Sabinus, proclaiming himself Rome's benefactor for causing Nero's demise. Claiming kinship with the Julian family, he named himself a son of Gaius Caesar (Caligula), making allies of the people by persecuting the tyrant's supporters.

Events that took place when Galba reached Rome triggered a civil war opposing the imperial legions. Galba, the new emperor, shed his reputation as moderate, proving to be a greedy old man manipulated by close advisers such as Titus Vinius, 'a man overcome by avarice', according to Plutarch, and Cornelius Laco, appointed Prefect of the Praetorium, replacing Nymphidius Sabinus. The latter, removed from a position he assumed for life, undertook a revolt, but was killed by his own men.

Galba's entry to Rome was stained by violence in which the members of the navy loyal to Nero were killed, along with supporters of the last Julio-Claudian, except Tigellinus, whom they considered to have inspired the tyranny. The repression brought tough measures to refill public coffers. Galba failed to deliver the promised donations to praetorians and legionaries and tried to recover what Nero had given him, earning the disgust of the people and the Praetorian Guard.

Vitellius and Otho

Discontent among the soldiers spread to the legions of Germania. Witnessing how Galba favoured the Gallic tribes that had revolted with Vindex, who had been given citizenship and reduced taxes, while their loyalty and support were not rewarded, they acclaimed Vitellius as emperor. The general, known for his bravery, was in Cologne, commanding the troops of Lower Germania. 'Choosing him',

1 SERVIUS SULPICIUS GALBA
Born in Terracina on 23 December in 3 BC, he died aged 72 after seven months of rule. Suetonius describes him as 'totally bald [with] dark blue eyes, aquiline nose and hands and feet completely deformed', and attributes him a cruel and greedy character despite his great wealth (Borghese Gallery, Rome).

2 MARCUS SALVIO OTHO
Descended from a patriotic Ferentinum family, he lived 37 years and was emperor for the last three months of his life. He was reputedly reckless, vile and extravagant. According to Suetonius, he was small, with deformed feet and a near-feminine elegance. He always wore a wig and shaved daily.

3 AULUS VITELLIUS
From Nuceria Alfaterna, Aulus succeeded Otho on 16 April 69. He had a reputation for greed and gluttony, and was ambitious and licentious. He was acclaimed emperor thanks to support from Aulus Caecina Alienus and Fabius Valens, commanders of two legions of the Rhine (Uffizi Gallery, Florence).

4 TITUS FLAVIUS VESPASIANUS
Born in 9 AD into an equestrian family in the Vicus Phalacrinae. He married Flavia Domitila and had two sons, Titus and Domitian, who succeeded him in 79 and 81, respectively. He was affable, sarcastic and mocking, and enjoyed good health (Capitoline Museums, Rome).

Plutarch wrote, 'shows all we are worth more than the Hispanos and Lusitanians when it comes to naming an emperor'. Vitellius accepted the name of Germanicus, but refused the title of Caesar, on 2 January 69 AD.

Like the legions of Germania, the *Legio tertia Augusta* (Third Augustan Legion), based in Africa under the command of Lucius Clodius Macer, refused to acknowledge Galba's imperial acclamation, and threatened to cut off the shipment of grain from Egypt to Rome. Threatened with a supply shortage, the legate of Mauretania Tingitana was sent to eliminate Macer, who was replaced by Valerius Festus.

Galba heard of Vitellius's acclamation, prompting him to secure a successor. To Otho's surprise, as he was consul along with Titus Vinius that year, and the main candidate for succession, Galba chose instead Lucius Calpurnius Piso Licinianus, son of Crassus and Scribonia, a modest man. Upon being deprived of the throne, Otho sought out discontented cohorts willing to name him emperor and proceeded to eliminate all opposition. First he killed Galba, his newly adopted son, then his two advisers, Titus Vinius and Cornelius Laco, followed by his most fervent supporters. Otho was sworn in before the Senate on 15 January 69 AD, and acclaimed as Caesar and Augustus.

The Battle of Bedriacum
That year, two men had been appointed emperors simultaneously: one in Germania, the empire's most fortified region, and the other in the capital. When Otho heard of Vitellius's acclamation, he set off to place Italy under his dominion, along with the provinces that had supported his opponent. He had four legions: the *Legio septima Gemina*, which had been mustered by Galba in Hispania and sent

THE ROMAN EMPIRE

The two battles of Bedriacum in 69

Bedriacum, a Roman settlement on the banks of the Oglio near Cremona, was the scene of two bloody battles, on 14 April and 24 October 69 AD. The results led to the start of the Flavian dynasty ruling the empire. In the First Battle of Bedriacum, Otho's troops, plus legions from Media and Illyria, fought against each other and the German legions that supported Vitellius: legions XXI and V *Alaudae*, led by Aulus Caecina and Fabius Valens, to which several contingents of the legions of the Rhine and auxiliary troops of Batavia were added. Otho defeated Vitellius at Locus Castorum; Vitellius won at Bedriacum. The Danubian legions that had arrived too late to aid Otho switched their loyalty to Vespasian, persuading the VII *Galbiana* and XIII *Gemina* to join them. When Vitellius learnt that Vespasian was marching his legions to Rome, he went to meet him. The Second Battle of Bedriacum, at which Vitellius was defeated, took place on 24 October. The Senate proclaimed Vespasian emperor in December 69.

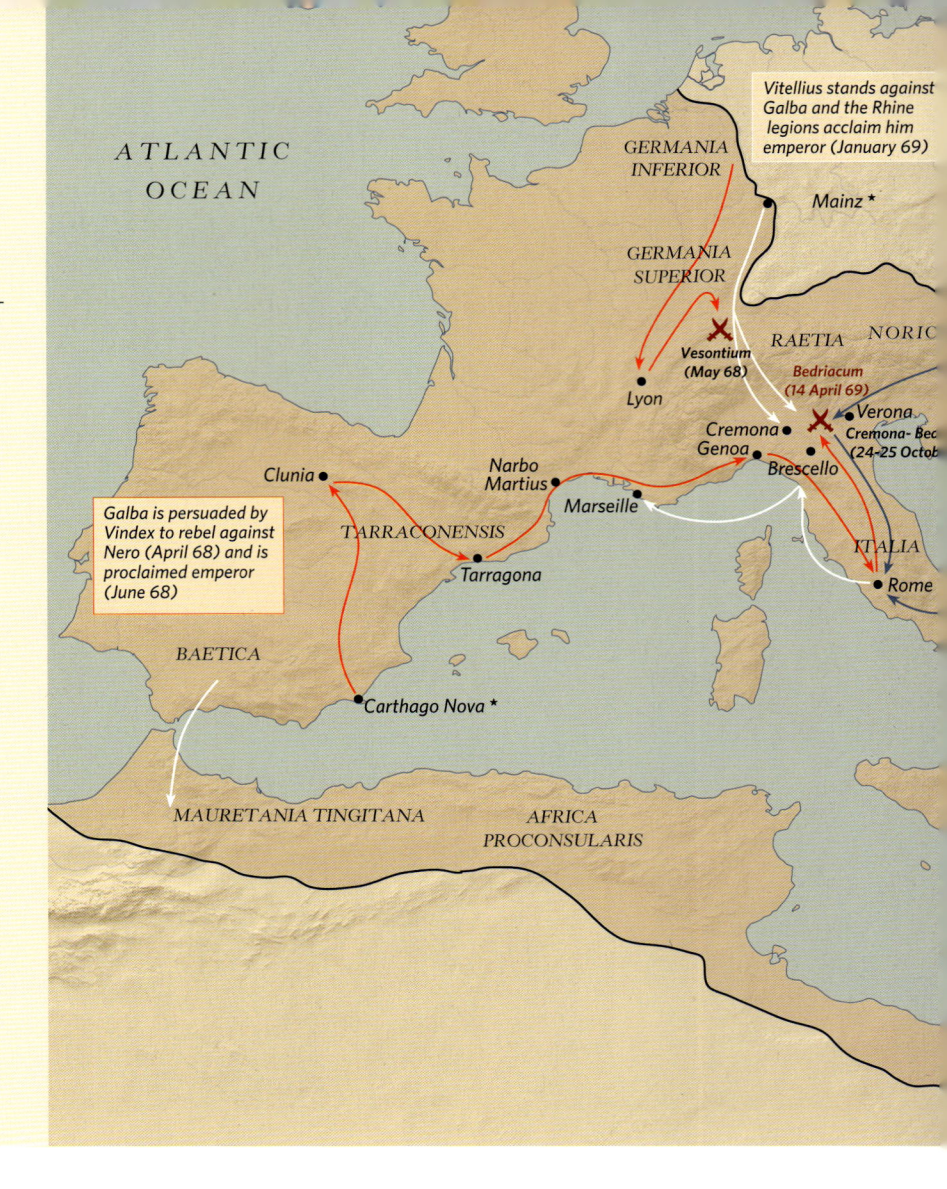

Vitellius stands against Galba and the Rhine legions acclaim him emperor (January 69)

Galba is persuaded by Vindex to rebel against Nero (April 68) and is proclaimed emperor (June 68)

later to Carnuntum, in the province of Pannonia, with Marcus Antonius Primus; the *Legio undecima Claudia* (Claudius's 11th Legion); the *Legio tertia decima Geminia* (Twinned 13th Legion), settled in Poetovium (Ptuj), featuring the Anglo-Slavic tribune Suetonius Laetus, the father of the historian Suetonius; and the *Legio quarta decima Gemina* (Twinned 14th Legion). The legions' 8000 men were joined by auxiliary infantry and cavalry troops, five praetorian cohorts, and 2000 gladiators. Appius Annius Gallus, who had gone ahead with Titus Vestricius Spurinna to occupy the banks of the Po, commanded all of them. Otho's troops outnumbered those of Vitellius but lacked discipline. The first encounter between Otho's and Vitellius's forces was in Liguria, on the shores of Gallia Narbonensis. Vitellius's troops were almost defeated. Otho attacked, disregarding advice from Gaius Suetonius Paulinus and Aulus Marius Celsus, and abandoned his troops in the final battle, which took place in Bedriacum on 14 April 69. Otho's absence influenced the fight; some of the praetorian cohorts retreated before the battle, leaving the soldiers demoralized. Aulus Caecina Alienus and Fabius Valens, the two commanders of the Vitellian troops, took advantage of their enemy's imprudence to score victory. Upon hearing the news, Otho, age 37, took his own life, leaving imperial power in the hands of Vitellius.

A dissolute and licentious emperor

Forty days after the battle, Vitellius visited Bedriacum and saw hundreds of still unburied bodies strewn across the land. After celebrating sacrifices to thank the gods, and oblivious to his impending destiny, Vitellius headed for Rome, spending empire funds on parties and donations

FOUR CAESARS IN A SINGLE YEAR

Map Legend:
- The Roman Empire when Nero died
- ★ Acclamation of an Emperor
- ✕ Battle
- Displacements and Military campaigns:
  - → Vindex – Galba (May 68 – January 69)
  - → Otho – Vitellius (January – April 69)
  - → Vitellius – Vespasian (July – December 69)
- RAETIA Roman Province

Vespasian's army enters Rome and Vitellius dies (December 69). Vespasian becomes emperor in Rome (summer 70)

Vespasian is proclaimed emperor by his troops in Judaea (July 69)

1 GALBA
In 67, while proconsul in Tarraconesis, he went to Rome leading the VII *Hispana* legion, which he had organized in Hispania. To avoid looking like a military usurper, he sent his Spanish legion to Pannonia to replace the X *Gemina* legion by the Danube.

2 OTHO
He left Rome with insufficient forces (around 25,000 men) to prevent the legions commanded by Fabius from meeting with those of Aulus Caecina. During the First Battle of Bedriacum he was in Brixellum, and learnt of his defeat there. Without waiting for the Illyrian and Median legions, he committed suicide.

3 VITELLIUS
After winning the First Battle of Bedriacum at the head of his Germanic legions, he faced the Vespasian-supporting Danubian legions. They fought in front of the XXI *Rapax*, the V *Alaudae*, the I *Italica* and the XXII *Primigenia*, in addition to auxiliary troops and *vexillationes* (temporary detachments) of seven more legions.

4 VESPASIAN
He tried to end the Jewish Revolt with his son Titus. Syrian and Judaean legions supported him, as did VII *Hispana*, led by Marcus Antonius Primus. When he was emperor, the VII legion was rebuilt with soldiers of the I *Germanica*. Renamed VII *Gemina*, it was sent to guard the gold mines of Gallaecia.

---

to the soldiers. Legions from Germania that had acclaimed him emperor suffered the fury of the Senate and fear of the praetorian cohorts. The soldiers formerly faithful to Otho, like those of the XIV Legion, were sent to fight the Batavi and then relegated to Britain.

Vitellius and the 70,000 armed men accompanying him to Rome fell into debauchery, besieging the cities through which they passed. Vitellius entered Rome donning the *toga praetexta*, preceded by a military procession, at the head of which the eagles of four legions and the banners of 12 cavalry squadrons were paraded. Soldiers ceased to train and abandoned discipline. Tacitus states in his *Histories* that when the army of Germania recommenced its march to face Vespasian's legions: 'no vigour was there in their bodies, no ardour in their tempers; their march was disorderly, their weapons, neglected; their horses, gaunt; their men, soft to the elements, the sun and the dust; they were ripe for discord and incapable of enduring fatigue'.

Vespasian's acclamation
Vitellius's corruption of his legions led to the first defections of the troops camped in the East. They were instigated to rebel by Gaius Licinius Mucianus, the governor of Syria, who extolled the virtues of Vespasian, the perfect candidate for the administration of the empire due to his lineage and military prowess.

In Syria, Judaea and Egypt they had nine complete legions, with soldiers not spoiled by discord, in addition to squadrons of cavalry, naval forces, auxiliary cohorts and faithful kings in the East. After the decision to wage war against Vitellius, Vespasian travelled to Caesarea Maritima, and his legate, Mucianus, to Antioch, the capitals of Judaea and Syria.

WAR CHARIOT (OVERLEAF)
Drawn by four horses, the quadriga *was the war chariot of the victorious generals of the Roman army. Later, it was used for chariot races. Relief of the first century.*

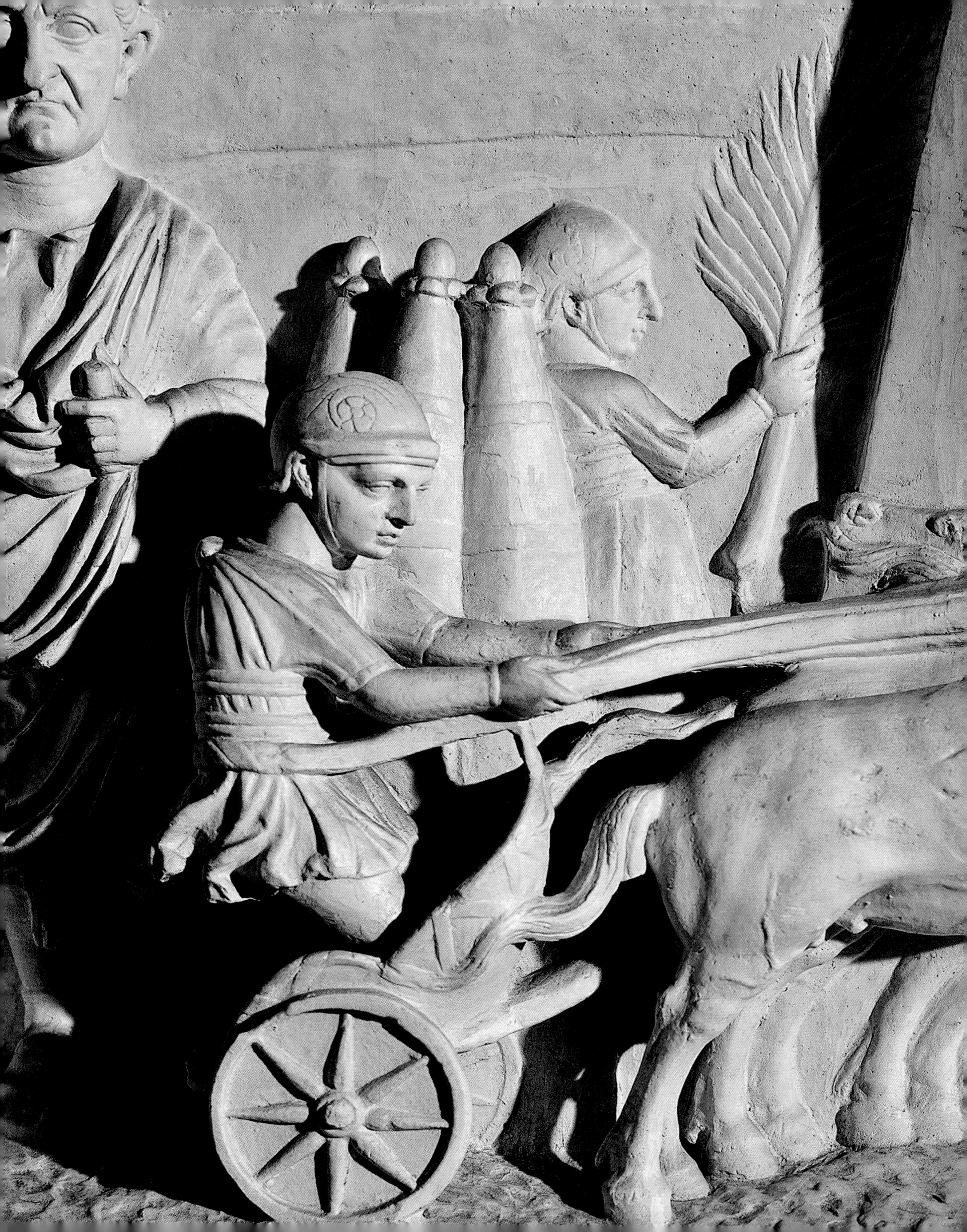

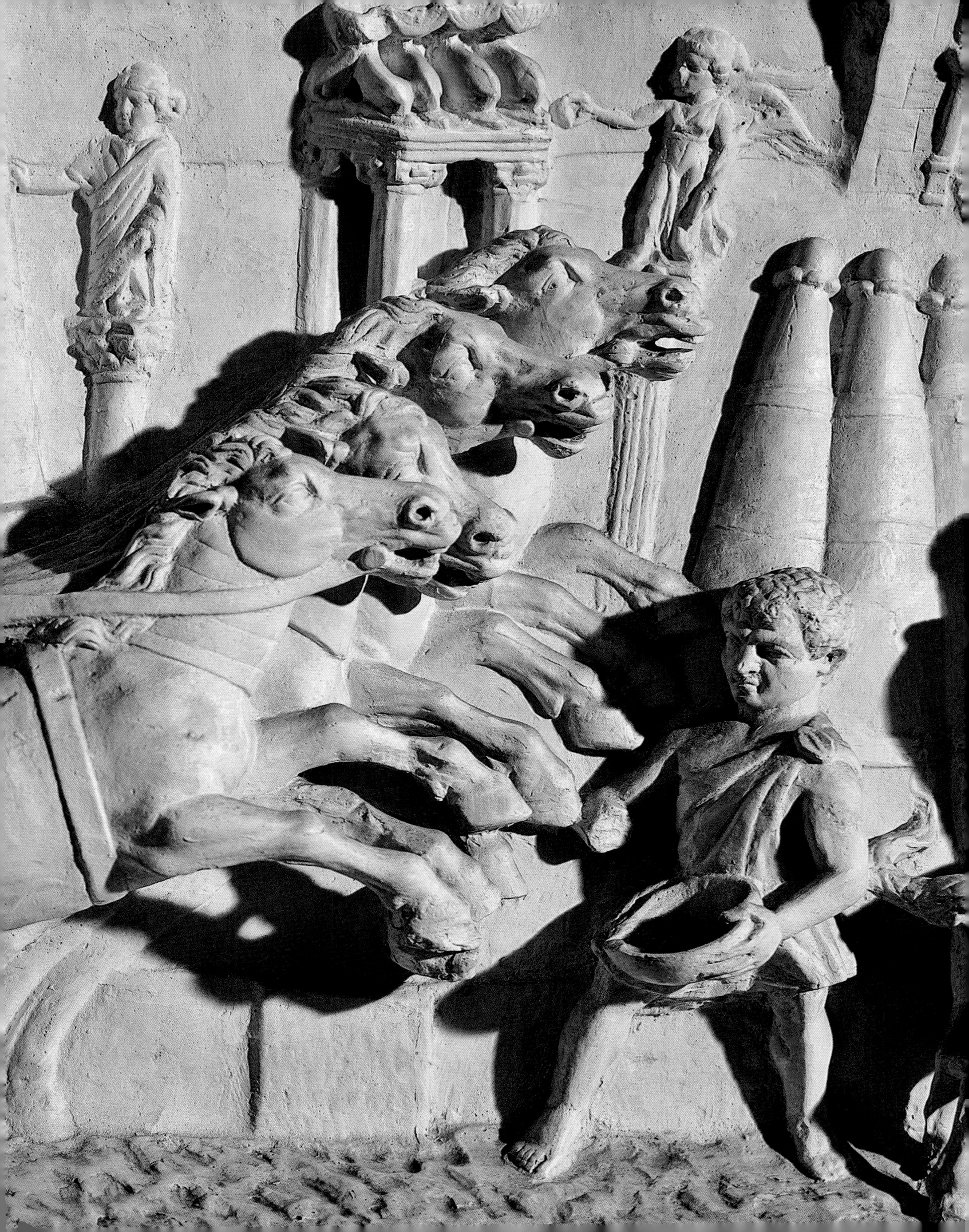

THE ROMAN EMPIRE

Tacitus before the events of 69

In the 14th century, Italian writer Giovanni Boccaccio took from Montecassino Abbey a codex containing the end of Tacitus's *Annals* and the first books of his *Histories*. These narrate the year of the four emperors and the start of Vespasian's reign, the first of the Flavians.

When civil war broke out in 69 AD, Tacitus (pictured) was a teenager. Therefore, in order to write his *Histories*, intending to span the time from 1 January 69 AD until Domitian's death in 96 AD, he needed historical sources or direct witnesses. It is likely that he and Plutarch, who dedicated two of his biographies to Galba and Otho, were inspired by Pliny the Elder, author of *A fine Aufidi Bassi*, now lost. He also used his father-in-law, Agricola, as a source, since Agricola had served as military tribune under Suetonius Paulinus at the start of his military career. As Tacitus was finishing writing his *Histories* – dedicated to the happy kingdom of Nerva – he began his *Annals*, spanning the death of Augustus to the end of the Julio-Claudian dynasty. He omitted the last months of 68 AD, perhaps to avoid the delicate issue of the revolt in Gaul led by Vindex.

From Alexandria, in turn, a contingent representing the Prefect of Egypt, Tiberius Julius Alexander, departed to confer imperial power upon Vespasian on 1 July. Two days later, the Army of Judaea spontaneously swore allegiance to him. Mucianus urged his soldiers to swear obedience to Vespasian at the theatre in Antioch, where he instilled animosity towards Vitellius by stating that he was planning to transfer the legions in Germania to Syria and take Syria's troops there. All the provinces between Pontus and Armenia, and those along the coast between Asia and Greece, backed Vespasian's acclamation. Also mustered to fight were the praetorians, hostile to Vitellius, and other disgruntled legions, such as the XIV, relegated to Britain, the legions of Moesia (III, VII and VIII *Claudian*), Pannonia (XII and VI *Galbian*), Dalmatia and the soldiers that formed the *Legio prima adiutrix*, which had ended up in Hispania after the Battle of Bedriacum.

The Danubian army, former supporters of Otho, also backed Vespasian's revolt. They marched to Rome under the command of Primus (Marcus Antonius Primus) without waiting for the arrival of troops from the East. After reaching Aquileia, Patavium (Padua) and Este, in September, Vitellius placed his defence in the hands of the generals Fabius Valens and Caecina (Aulus Caecina Alienus), but the former was ill, and the latter planned to betray him. On 24 October, Flavian troops were victorious at the Second Battle of Bedriacum, and the Vitellians' camp at Cremona was razed.

Vespasian's ascent to the throne

After the first Flavian victory, Marcus Antonius Primus marched on Rome in November, while the remaining Vitellian forces headed north. The two armies met at Carseoli (Carsoli) on 13 December, but the Vitellians, demoralized by the death of Fabius Valens, withdrew. In Rome, Vespasian's brother, Titus, prefect of the city, pleaded with Vitellius to resign peacefully. However, the legions of 16,000 men led by Titus Julius Priscus confronted him, and forced him to seek refuge in the Capitol building, which they burned on 19 December, one day after Vitellius's abdication. The next day, Marcus Antonius Primus entered Rome with his legions and took on the last of the Vitellian resistance. Vitellius was seized and killed and his body thrown into the Tiber.

The Senate appointed Vespasian emperor in his absence on 21 December 69. Titus, the new emperor's son, was appointed consul along with his father. He was put in charge of Judaea while Vespasian headed towards Rome, where he was awaited by Mucianus and his second son, Domitian. He arrived in the capital in the summer of 70 AD, a few months before Titus put down the Jewish Revolt and levelled Jerusalem.

With Vespasian and the *gens Flavia*, a new era dawned. Provincial elites who had risen under the Julio-Claudians took over the administration of the empire; with the vital support of the legions and the praetorian cohorts, they proved that any region of the empire could place a new emperor on the throne. The revival of the Republic would remain an unfulfilled dream of the aristocracy, as the monarchical system established by Augustus would, in essence, endure until the final days of the empire. The Flavians established a system of dynastic succession, thus addressing one of the Principate's weaknesses.

The events of the year 69 AD were repeated 27 years later, at the end of the Flavian dynasty, with Trajan's rise to power. His predecessor, Nerva, faced a revolt by the praetorian cohorts similar to that faced by Galba. Like him, Nerva shored up his power through close ties with an army commander – in this case, Trajan, who was in Germania Superior at the time. Nerva appointed Trajan as his successor from Hispania Baetica (modern-day Spain). He appeased the legionaries' revolts, and a period of greater freedom under the Principate began.

ROMAN FORUM OF AQUILEIA
Founded in 181 BC, and connected to the Padan Plain by the Via Annia, Aquileia was a settlement on the mainland, not far from the Adriatic coast. It was located there for military reasons and as part of Roman expansionism towards central Europe and the Balkans. Soon it acquired great strategic, economic and cultural importance as a hub of communications; in the imperial era, it grew to 200,000 inhabitants. The image shows the ruins of the city's forum.

THE ROMAN EMPIRE

Roman villas and imperial palaces

The grandeur of Roman society, its power and wealth during this time, is reflected in the villas and palatial residences dating from it, scattered all across Italy.

Rome's wealthiest families owned residences in the city's most exclusive neighbourhoods and the most idyllic mountain areas, or on the Italian coast at places such as Tusculum, Antium and Baiae. In Rome, the hills of the Palatine, Velia and the Capitol were the preferred enclaves of both the traditional elite and the new ruling class. The hilltop locations provided fresh air, views over the Forum, and a chance to display their wealth through refined domestic architecture.

The Palatine hill boasted sites evoking Rome's legendary origins. According to Dionysius of Halicarnassus, a group of Arkadians from Pallantion, led by Evander, son of Hermes and Themis, reached the Tiber and founded a village, which they dubbed the *madre patria*, or 'mother country'. At the foot of the new city, Pallantium, they founded a cave sanctuary, Lupercal, which included a forest and a grotto, in which water flowed, and a *Ficus Ruminalis* fig tree. Legend had it that Romulus and Remus had been discovered by a shepherd, Faustulus, while the two were being suckled by a she-wolf, and that they had been reared very close to there, in the *tugurium Faustuli* or *aedes Romuli*.

SHELTERED BY THE GODS

Villa owners used to show their illustrious lineages, sometimes linked to the gods, through paintings and reliefs, like this one from the village of Tiberio in Sperlonga, which shows the image of Venus Genetrix, ancestor of the Julio-Claudians (Archaeological Museum, Sperlonga).

FOUR CAESARS IN A SINGLE YEAR

WALL PAINTINGS ON VILLAS

The eruption of Vesuvius in 79 AD buried Pompeii and Herculaneum, among other settlements, under ash and volcanic rock. Many of the frescoes adorning their walls were left intact; some examples, made by *redemptores* (coordinators), *parietarii* (decorators) and *imaginarii* (portrait painters), remain in the village of Agrippa Postumus in Boscotrecase (see image). However, in local villas like Hadrian's (left), only fragments of the room decorations remain.

In republican times, noble families keen to live near those legendary sites built houses on the Palatine. From the top of the mount, in the Cermalus area, among others, you could see the house of Quintus Caecilius Metellus Celer, consul in 60 BC and husband of Clodia (Quadrantaria), the poet Catullus's lover, nicknamed 'Medea Palatina' for allegedly poisoning her husband in 56 BC; and that of Cicero, demolished by order of his hated neighbour, Clodius (Publius Clodius Pulcher), tribune of the plebs, and converted into a temple consecrated to freedom during the orator's exile. The domus of these noble families, which did not usually exceed 1200sq m (12,020sq ft), stood on several terraces on the hill's slope. The internal spaces were distributed in traditional Roman domus style, with the entrance hall leading to an atrium with an *impluvium* and a *tablinum*. By the rear façade of the domus there was usually a porticoed courtyard, a peristyle, and a small *hortus*, or garden.

Eminent generals such as Caesar and Pompey, and new rulers such as Atticus, Cicero's friend and banker, whose power was rooted not in oratory and legal knowledge, but rather in the force of arms and wealth, preferred to live in large villas far from the Forum, on the outskirts of Rome. The hills of the Quirinal, the Viminal, the Caelian and the Pincian became the sites of large mansions surrounded by lush gardens, decorated with fountains, *nymphaea* and statues with typical Hellenistic splendour. Some of these *horti* were owned by emperors of the different dynasties, such as the Gardens of Sallust, next to the Colline Gate in the Quirinal, originally belonging to Caesar but later acquired by the historian Sallust with the fortune he had amassed while proconsul in Numidia. The villa was returned to the Julio-Claudians under Tiberius and, according to Latin sources, was lived in temporarily by Nero, Vespasian, Nerva and Aurelian. However, after a long hiatus in Rhodes, Tiberius chose the Gardens of Maecenas instead, located on the Esquiline, which Augustus had inherited from his late friend and adviser Gaius Cilian Maecenas.

The Palatine Hill
Many of the noblest and wealthiest people who lived on the Palatine were bitter enemies of Julius Caesar, and some backed armed revolt against

141

THE ROMAN EMPIRE

Mark Antony and Octavian, supporting tyrannicide. Among them was Quintus Hortensius, son of the famous orator. He murdered Mary Antony's brother and was imprisoned in Philippi, eventually having his throat slit on his victim's grave. Hostility against Caesar was the main reason his name appeared on the lists of proscriptions in 43 BC; his properties were expropriated and sold at public auctions. In 42 BC, Octavian acquired five houses on the Palatine, on whose land he commenced the construction of the house that would years later become the first imperial palace.

The house built by Octavian, accessed via the Vicus Apollinis (a street on the Palatine), featured two peristyles arranged on both sides of a large central atrium, typical of a Greco-Hellenistic palace layout. Around the western peristyle were private rooms, located very close to the *aedes Romuli*, near the chamber where, according to Suetonius, Augustus slept for at least 40 years. Around the eastern peristyle were the house's public and reception areas. The spaces were distributed on two floors: a lavish upper floor, its rooms decorated with frescoes exuding Egyptian-style exoticism; and a bottom floor, with rooms with lower ceilings and less sophisticated paintings. Its proximity to the slope of the mountain gave the palace exceptional panoramic views of the Circus Maximus and the Aventine quarter.

The architectural complex, on which construction began in 42 BC, was short-lived. In 36 BC, lightning struck the heart of the house, which Octavian took as a sign that Apollo, his protector god, demanded part of his residence. The emperor then decided to demolish the first palace and build another on top of it. The new project involved the expansion of the estate and the incorporation of the adjoining houses, including those of Livia and Publius Cornelius Sulla, in addition to the transformation of part of the residence into a shrine to Apollo, which included, besides a temple, a curia (meeting house) for Senate members to assemble, and a library, lined with gardens. The new palace tripled the surface area of the first residence, covering 24,546sq m (264,210sq ft). The Temple of Apollo, built to honour a vow after the victory at Naulochus, was built over the vestibule and atrium of the preceding house. Across from it was the Portico of the Danaids, where Augustus held official hearings. To the left was the domus privata, which Propertius called 'Remo's house', and to the right was the domus publica, to which Augustus moved in 12 BC after being named Pontifex Maximus.

After Augustus's death in 14 AD, Livia stayed in the palace of Cermalus until 29 AD; Claudius and Nero used it for Senate meetings. Tiberius resided in the casa paterna, between the Temple of Apollo and the Roman Forum. The Domus Tiberiana was expanded by Caligula, who converted the Temple of the Dioscuri (Temple of Castor and Pollux) in the Forum into the palace's vestibule. Under Claudius, the different nuclei of the Domus Palatinae Caesarum were transformed into an architecturally unified palace occupying the whole western section of the Palatine. It was on the steps of Claudius's palace that Nero was named emperor in 54 AD at just 17 years old.

The mansion of a Roman ruler

The houses of rich Roman families were designed according to social status. The domus, the single-family house, was usually a two-storey building entered via a small lobby leading to an atrium, with an *impluvium* to gather rainwater, *maiorum imagines* (wax images of ancestors) and a *Lararium* (a shrine for the *Lares*, the household gods). The *tablinum* (the owner's study) was accessed from the atrium, as was the *triclinium*, the main dining room where lavish dinners were enjoyed, the *culina* (kitchen) and *cubicula* (small bedrooms). There were also spaces for bathrooms. The second century saw the adoption of the Greek-influenced peristyle, which gained prominence to the detriment of the atrium. The ashes of Vesuvius preserved many Pompeiian houses in perfect condition, allowing us to study Roman domestic architecture. This painting by Peter Connolly (1935) shows the house of Lucius Caecilius Iucundus.

1 VESTIBULE
This was decorated with mosaics and wall paintings. Clients lined up here each morning to be greeted by the master.

2 ATRIUM
The nerve centre of the house, where the master exhibited his wealth and received his visitors. It was also a women's work space.

3 TABLINUM
The office or study of the owner of the house. Here he kept his account books and his money. The room was often beautifully decorated.

4 PERISTYLE
This room, landscaped and open-air, had a more domestic character than the atrium and was sometimes adorned with *trompe l'oeil*.

Nero's palace

Wishing to recreate idyllic landscapes in the heart of Rome, by then considered too urbanized, Nero decided to connect the Palatine residence with the nearby Gardens of Maecenas. For this he devised the Domus Transitoria, his first palace, which was rebuilt and extended to the Oppian Hill after the fire in 64 AD, and renamed the Domus Aurea (Golden House). Nero's palace encompassed the different areas of the previous domus by means of internal hallways or external paths, as if it were a large urban complex, auguring the way that Hadrian's Villa in Tibur (Tivoli) would be designed.

After 64 AD, expropriations continued on the Palatine and Oppian hills, which allowed Nero to build a new royal residence organized as a huge suburban villa, in accordance with plans produced by the architects Severus and Celer. The scenography of the different buildings that comprised it were arranged on artificial terraces at different heights, joined by arcaded paths. The valley between the two hills was occupied by the Stagnum Neronis, a large artificial pond where years later the Colosseum would be erected. The complex architecture was lavishly decorated, and the most up-to-date technical innovations were applied. This can be seen in the preserved archaeological remains and descriptions, such as that by Suetonius in relation to the *cenatio rotunda*: 'The ceilings of the banquet halls were built using moveable and perforated wooden dowels, in such a way that guests could be showered with flowers and perfumes. The main room was round and rotated all day, continuously, like the Earth'. The generous use of gold and precious stones, also mentioned by Suetonius ('everything was covered in gold, precious stones and mother-of-pearl'), seemed to allude to the *aurea aetas* (golden age) that Nero aspired to give the Roman people.

The easternmost part of the Palatine, on which some private residences had been preserved until 64 AD, was definitively integrated into the Flavians' palatial residence, consisting of an extension of Augustus's domus eastwards, for which it was termed the Domus Augustana. The Flavians'

THE ROMAN EMPIRE

CALDARIUM OF THE HOUSE OF MENANDER
Beautiful mosaics and wall paintings decorated this room, which was part of the bathroom of this Pompeiian domus.

palace featured a large peristyle, around which the different rooms were arranged. The throne room, or *aula regia*, located to the north, was a 30m-long (98ft) apsidal nave, designed to exalt the emperor's majesty and to awe visiting diplomats.

Villas for leisure time
The need to escape from the busy life of the capital and the longing for a quiet retreat spurred Roman nobles to seek a refuge for *otium*, or leisure time, in some of Italy's most beautiful places. The Gulf of Naples, known in antiquity as Crater, was a favourite location. The imperial family built villas in Oplontis (Torre Annunziata), Baiae, Stabiae and Posillipo to use as summer residences; only the most influential aristocrats could dream of owning a villa nearby. The fertile lands of Campania produced the finest wines on the peninsula, such as Falernian and Caleno; the bay's fishermen always had fresh fish to offer; and the sulphur-rich lands around Mount Vesuvius promised to heal respiratory and skin diseases at the spas that filled the region. Meanwhile, the bustling and prosperous Port of Puteoli (Pozzuoli), one of the largest in the Mediterranean, offered access to the most select products: wool, silks and rugs from Asia; spices and pearls from Arabia and India; and marble, precious stones and slaves from every region of the ancient world. The aristocracy built luxurious villas in the mountains near the sea. Over time they approached the coast, closer and closer. Some were even built right on the water, thanks to the discovery of hydraulic malt, made with local pozzolanic ash (*pulvis puteolanus*), which hardened on contact with the water and made it possible to build sturdy pillars in the sea.

When the capital's nobility withdrew to Campania in search of tranquillity, according to Strabo, it adopted the way of life and clothing of the Greeks and devoted its days to *otium*: reading, philosophical reflection at gatherings, dinners among friends, and *ars topiary*, recreating landscapes from epics and mythology in private gardens. The spirit that inspired the construction of these villas was well reflected in the names they received: Apragopolis ('the city of no work') was Augustus's villa in Capri; Pausilypon ('where worries end') was the name of Publius Vedius Pollio's villa. He was also the owner of a palace on the Aventine so scandalously opulent that Augustus, upon inheriting it, had it demolished to build a public building in its place: the Portico of Livia.

The Imperial Villa at Posillipo, also inherited by Augustus when Vedius Pollio died, is one of the most extraordinary examples of a Roman villa dedicated to *otium*. Like the royal structures on the Palatine, the architecture of the villa's different buildings was integrated into the natural surroundings, thereby creating a kind of scenographic landscape. Each wing of the villa was assigned a different function, in such a way that there was a residential area, a spa area, another reserved for spectacles, and another one to welcome and receive visitors. The extraordinary theatre at Vedius Pollio's Imperial Villa could seat 2000 and was equipped with a lake for aquatic shows. For poetry recitals and concerts there was a *teatrum tectum*, seating 100. From the spa facilities, passing porticoes and *nymphaea* adorned with the most refined statues, a path led to the residential area, with several buildings

FOUR CAESARS IN A SINGLE YEAR

The statuary of aristocrats' villas

Roman aristocrats could spend fortunes converting their villas into true art galleries. Many of the sculptures exhibited were plundered by generals such as Marcus Fulvius Nobilior or Lucius Aemilius Paullus Macedonicus, who brought 250 carts full of statues to Rome.

In the trial against Verres, Cicero describes the village of a certain Heius in Messina, in which you could see, in a small private chapel, a Cupid by Praxiteles, a Hercules in bronze by Mirón and two cancleras by Policleto. Cicero himself had commissioned Atticus 'whatever you deem appropriate for the palaestra and gymnasium of the village', and he went into debt to decorate his mansions of Tusculum, Pompeii and Arpinum. Although many of the statues that adorned these houses of leisure ended up transformed into lime in medieval ovens, others were saved. These include the female figures that supported the porch of the Canopus of Hadrian's Villa (above), which were hidden under the mud of the pond into which they had accidentally fallen, and the sculptural group of Polyphemus from the village of Tiberius in Sperlonga, which was submerged under the sea.

THE VILLA OF TIBERIUS
Located in Sperlonga, it was built next to a marine grotto, in which the emperor installed a sculptural group that recreated the scene of the *Odyssey* in which Ulysses and his companions blinded the Cyclops Polyphemus (on the left).

■ THE ROMAN EMPIRE

Hadrian's villa

The most famous of all the imperial villas was Hadrian's, built in Tibur (Tivoli). It was built in several phases (118–134 AD) from a unitary project in which the emperor participated. It covered 120 hectares (300 acres) on a plain between two moats: the Ferrata water and the Rocca Bruna, in which a suburban villa was built after the end of the second century BC.

The buildings of Hadrian's villa were connected by underground passages where slaves, merchandise and oxen-pulled carts could move around unnoticed. Galleries and porticoes linked the external areas of this vast complex. The emperor's buildings included winter and summer residences with open-air *triclinia* equipped with individual latrines, libraries, baths and gardens surrounded by porticoes around large swimming pools topped with nymphs and fountains, two theatres and several belvederes. Aelius Spartianus, author of a biography of Hadrian, says that in the town you could admire the most famous places in the empire, such as the Lyceum, the Academy of Athens, the Pecile, the Vale of Tempe and the Canopus of Alexandria. A series of buildings with secondary accesses was dedicated to high-ranking personnel, and the servants' quarters were often located under vaulted lodges that maintained the artificial terraces of the town.

Hadrian's villa, like many other Roman villas, was plundered in medieval times. The precious marble that covered floors and walls was used to build new residences, and the rich decorations and artworks were progressively dispersed into public and private collections throughout Europe.

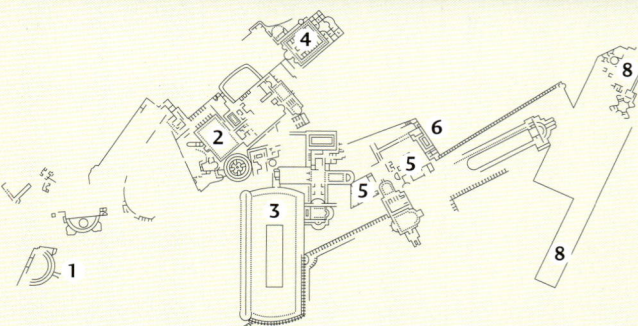

1 GREEK THEATRE
On the periphery of the village was a Greek-style theatre, with the cave resting on the slope of the hill and the straight scenic front.

5 THERMAL DISTRICT
Endowed with large hot springs, which included a *sudatio* or Turkish bath, and small hot springs for lower-ranking people.

FOUR CAESARS IN A SINGLE YEAR

arranged on terraces decorated with spectacular paintings and fine molten glass mosaics. These villas also included pools, nurseries, and oyster and fish hatcheries – symbols of the aristocracy's status and their owners' extravagance. Some even adorned their eels with earrings. According to one source, Vedius once threatened to throw a slave into the pond for a careless act, but he was pardoned. The Roman villas at the Phlegraean Fields, meanwhile, functioned as an architectural laboratory where new techniques were developed and later introduced at other imperial villas. One of the most popular inventions, attributed to Caius Sergius Orata, was the hanging bath, or *balinea pensilia*, by which bathing waters were heated by hot air rising from volcanic fumaroles.

THE YOUNG CENTAUR
Found in Hadrian's Villa, this beautiful oriental marble statue is preserved in the Capitoline Museums of Rome.

2 PATIO OF THE LIBRARIES
Despite its name, these were summer dining rooms that gave access to a miniature domus, known as the 'maritime theatre'.

3 PECILE
At the heart of the village there was a large square with a pond in the middle, resting on the *Cento Camerelle*, where the slaves lived.

4 IMPERIAL PALACE
Built on a late republican villa. Inside, a large complex ('the golden square') was dedicated to parties and banquets.

6 PRAETORIUM
Accommodation for service personnel was arranged beneath the artificial terrace that supported the main palace buildings.

7 CANOPUS AND SERAPEUM
A canal stretched for 119m, (390ft) at the end of which rose the Serapeum, for the celebration of banquets.

8 ACADEMY AND TOWER OF ROCCA BRUNA
Reproductions of the Academy of Plato and Tower of Rocca Bruna were used in the villa as a belvedere.

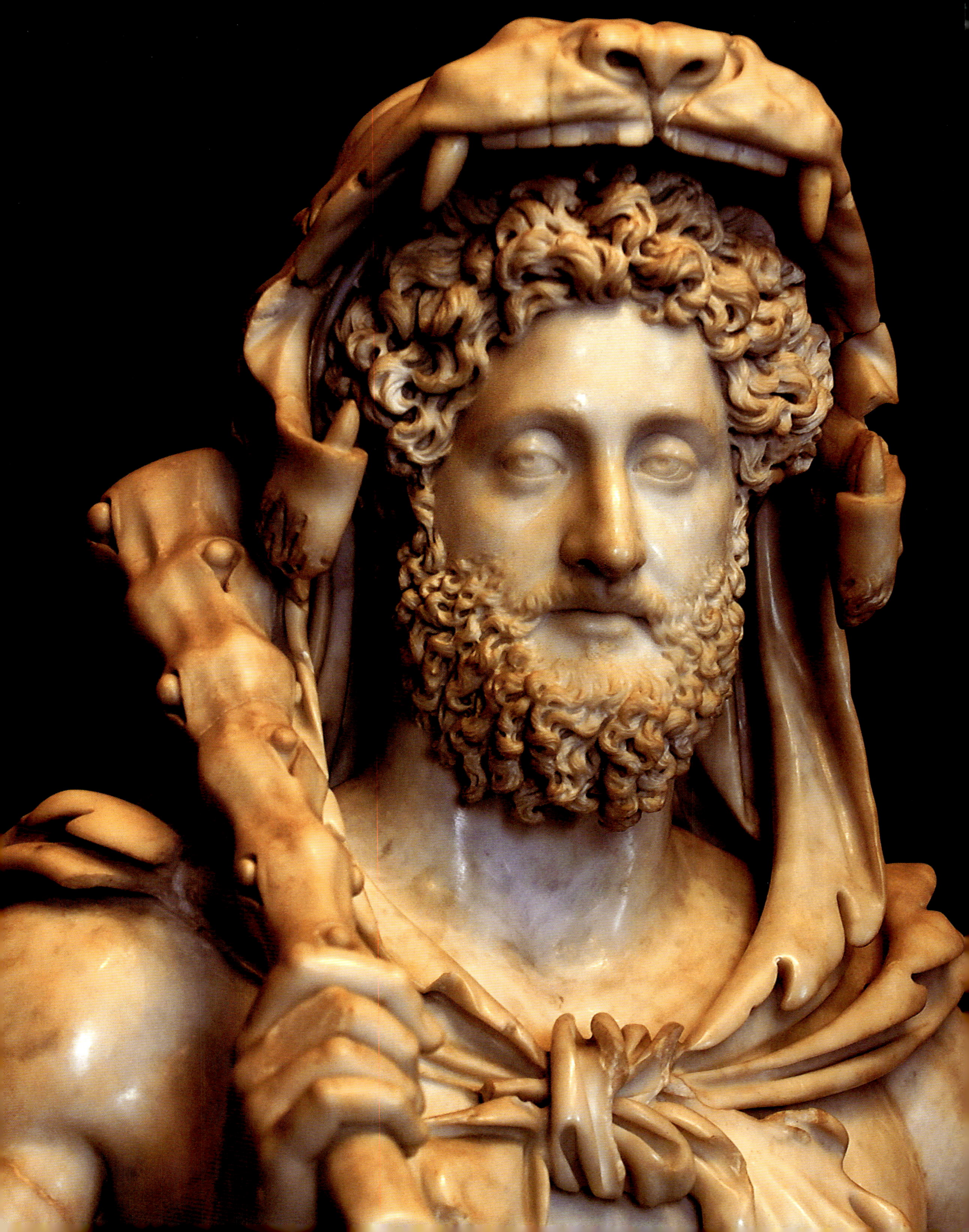

PART II

ROME DOMINATES THE WORLD

ROME DOMINATES THE WORLD

The Roman Empire under the Flavian and Antonine dynasties

THE FLAVIAN DYNASTY

Legend:
- Roman Empire
- Allies or under Roman protection
- Territory annexed
  - By Trajan
  - By the Flavian and Antonine Dynasties
- GOTHS Barbarian tribes

THE RISE OF VESPASIAN
This relief found in the Apostolic Chancery of Rome shows the founder of the Flavian dynasty with his two sons and successors, Titus and Domitian (Vatican Museums, Rome). Opposite page: The reverse of a Vespasian aureus with the image of a bull.

THE FLAVIAN DYNASTY

The civil war that followed the death of Nero left the empire battered and divided. The general who finally rose to power, Titus Flavius Vespasianus, came from an Italian family without a noble pedigree. He turned out to be a skilful politician and capable ruler who cleaned up the economy, defeated the enemies of the empire and restored prestige to the position of emperor.

Titus Flavius Vespasianus came from a well-to-do Italian family. He was born on 17 November 9 AD in Falacrinae, near Reate (modern Rieti), in the Sabine hills. His father was Titus Flavius Sabinus, who served as a customs official in Asia and then became a moneylender among the Helvetii. His economic success was rewarded with promotion to the rank of equestrian. The mother of the future emperor, Vespasia, came from a wealthier Nursian family, evidenced by the fact that her brother was a member of the Senate.

The efforts of Vespasian's father and maternal uncle allowed the two sons of the marriage to develop political careers in Rome. Vespasian's older brother, Titus Flavius Sabinus, was a skilled politician who became consul in 47. Later he governed the province of Moesia and, from 56 onwards, was prefect of Rome. Vespasian's early political career was not as dazzling as that of his older brother. He began as a military tribune in Thrace in around 27. Back in Rome, he took a role as a minor magistrate in the *vigintivirate* (group of 20 administrators), probably taking charge of

ROME DOMINATES THE WORLD

Vespasian's rise to power

Year 27
Tribune in Thrace. Aged 18, takes his first position in the imperial administration in Thrace, as a military tribune.

Years 35–38
Quaestor and aedile in Rome. Is appointed quaestor for the province of Crete-Cyrenaica. Under Caligula, he takes the position of aedile in Rome.

Years 43–47
Conquest of Britannia. Emperor Claudius gives him command of Legion II *Augusta* in Germania, then he accompanies it to the conquest of Britannia.

Year 51
Consul of Rome. After his success in the Britannia campaign, Vespasian is elected consul for the last two months of the year.

Years 62–63
Proconsul of Africa. During the 50s, he disappears from the public sphere, finally returning to it as proconsul of Africa.

Year 66
General of the Eastern armies. To quell the Jewish rebellion against Rome, Vespasian is appointed commander in chief of the Eastern legions. After the death of Nero, his road to power opens during the Year of the Four Emperors.

street cleaning. The story goes that, during his tenure, Emperor Caligula publicly humiliated him by throwing muck at his toga to draw attention to the dirty streets. This event did not affect his political career, for he was appointed praetor in the year 40. He then received the command of the Legion II *Augusta*, stationed in Germania, with which he also took part in the military operations that Claudius carried out in Britannia in 43. His generalship during the conquest of southwestern Britain and the Isle of Wight drew him commendations. As a reward for his services, he was awarded triumphal regalia (*ornamenta triumphalia*) and honoured with two priesthoods. At the end of 47, Vespasian returned to Rome, but only managed to be elected consul four years later and during the last two months of the year, which were the least prestigious.

His next promotion came in 62 under the auspices of Nero, when he was appointed proconsul of Africa. Vespasian accompanied Nero himself on his lavish journey through Greece in 66. However, during the journey, Vespasian nearly lost his life for committing the discourtesy of falling asleep while the emperor was speaking. In spite of this, at the end of that year he was commissioned to reconquer Judaea for the empire. He was given command of three legions, to which were later added five additional legions. This broad military command placed him in an advantageous position when different Roman notables began their bids for power after the death of Nero. In fact, the reason why he was granted such a powerful role was that he had a combination of proven war experience and an obscure lineage, which made him an unlikely candidate to turn against the emperor who had appointed him.

The rise to power

The struggles between Galba, Otho and Vitellius during the years 68 and 69 forced Vespasian, at that time occupied in the defeat of the Jews, to choose between the different candidates who were attempting to gain control of the empire. At the end of 68, Vespasian sent his son Titus to Rome to congratulate the new

The death of Vitellius

'Yet I was your emperor.' These were, according to Tacitus, the last words of Vitellius and those that unleashed the murderous wrath of the legionaries. Before Vespasian's troops arrived in Rome, the defeated Vitellius tried to hand over power to Titus Flavius Sabinus, prefect of the city, but the crowd and his own legionaries prevented him from doing so. When Rome surrendered to Vespasian's army, Vitellius tried to escape, but he was an easy man to recognize, so he returned to the palace to hide. There, dressed as a slave, the triumphant troops discovered him. They led him to the Forum, while the crowd and legionaries mocked and beat him. Finally, he was murdered and hurled down the stairs that ascended the Capitol from the prison, the Scalae Gemoniae. His remains were thrown in the Tiber. According to some authors, his severed head was exhibited throughout the city. This 19th-century engraving shows the death of Vitellius.

emperor, Galba. Yet while Titus was on the way to Rome, the young man learned of the assassination of Emperor Galba, which took place on 15 January 69, orchestrated by Marcus Salvius Otho, one of Galba's closest allies. Otho was now proclaimed emperor, and Titus returned to his father. Even before Galba's death, the legions of Germania had refused to take the oath of loyalty to the emperor, and had proclaimed the commanding general of Lower Germania, Aulus Vitellius, as emperor. The empire was plunged once more into civil war. Although he carried out no military action in his support, Vespasian sided with Otho. Only after the defeat of Otho's army in northern Italy, at the Battle of Bedriacum, near Cremona, and his subsequent suicide on 16 April 69, did Vespasian swear loyalty to Vitellius. However, the generals of the East now chose Vespasian himself as a candidate for the imperial throne.

At that time there were eight legions in the Roman East: two of them stationed in Egypt, three in Syria and three more in Judaea, all under Vespasian's command.

The uprising of the Eastern armies began in Egypt, whose prefect, Tiberius Julius Alexander, together with his troops, proclaimed Emperor Vespasian on 1 July 69. From that moment, events gathered pace. On 3 July, the legions under Vespasian's charge in Judaea proclaimed him emperor, followed by those stationed in Syria, whose governor, Gaius Licinius Mucianus, had enthusiastically joined the rebellion by the middle of that same month.

Vespasian and his son Titus remained in Egypt, while Mucianus left for Italy in mid-August by a land route through Asia Minor and the Balkans. Meanwhile, the legions of the Danube also decided to swear allegiance to Vespasian, and the general of Legion VII, Marcus Antonius Primus, marched in front of all the troops towards Italy. Antonius Primus, originally from the Gallic town of Tolosa, was a sympathizer of Galba, who had given him command of his legion; he was, therefore, the sworn enemy of Vitellius. Vitellius responded to the threat of the Danubian legions by sending his lieutenant Aulus Caecina Alienus to northern Italy. Vitellius could only count on the legions that were already in the peninsula, because those located on the Rhine were struggling under attacks by the Batavians.

The confrontation between the two armies took place, as had been the case shortly before, near Cremona, and is known as the Second Battle of Bedriacum. Vitellius was severely defeated, and the city was plundered by the victors. From that moment, the road to Rome was open. Vitellius was being abandoned by many of his supporters. Even his own

AULUS VITELLIUS

According to Suetonius, 'he was abnormally tall, his face red from too much wine, with a big belly and a crippled leg from when he was rammed by a quadriga while he was in attendance on Caligula at the races'. Marble bust (Archaeological Museum, Vienna).

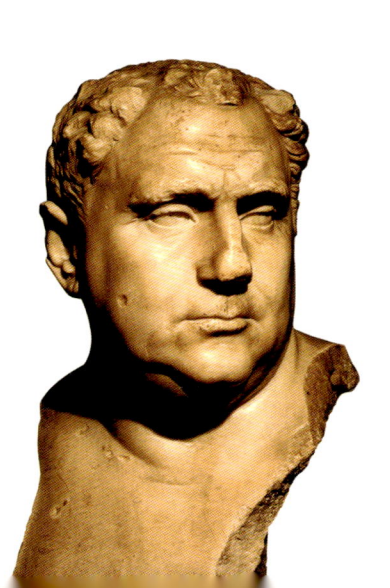

ROME DOMINATES THE WORLD

Praetorian Guard, who were dispatched to stop Antonius Primus's advance, joined Vespasian, as did the legions of the provinces of Hispania, Britannia and Gaul. Seeing the terrible situation he was in, Vitellius opened a dialogue with Vespasian's brother, Flavius Sabinus. The emperor apparently expressed a willingness to give up his power. However, another faction of the Praetorian Guard decided to defend his cause, and the privileges it gave them, to the bitter end. These troops attacked Flavius Sabinus and other supporters of Vespasian, including his youngest son, Domitian. They all took refuge in the Capitol, where they were besieged on 18 December. The confrontation ended the next day with the burning of the Temple of Jupiter Capitolinus and the lynching of Flavius Sabinus by a furious mob. Domitian managed to escape only by disguising himself as a worshipper of Isis.

The troops of Antonius Primus finally arrived in Rome on 20 December and began the fight for the city itself. The praetorians were crushed and Vitellius was put to a cruel and ignominious death. His body was dragged to the Tiber and thrown into the river, depriving him of a burial, as was the custom with common criminals. Rome was now in the hands of the soldiers who had plundered Cremona, and its citizens feared they faced looting. Domitian was swiftly appointed praetor and the Senate recognized Vespasian as emperor. A few days later, Mucianus arrived in the city: the general had been delayed on the way by fighting against the Sarmatians and Dacians, who had taken advantage of the empire's weakness to make incursions into the province of Moesia. As soon as he was in the capital, Mucianus assumed command in the name of the emperor, relegating Antonius Primus and Domitian. In the nine months it took Vespasian to return to Rome to enjoy the power he had gained, the political situation remained unstable.

Pacifying the empire

When Vespasian seized power and began his rule, first from Alexandria and then from Rome itself, most of the empire was pacified. However, the emperor had to respond to old problems, such as the war in Judaea, and to new conflicts resulting from the chaos and power vacuum that had shaken the empire during 69, the 'Year of the Four Emperors'. The Batavian insurrection was one of these conflicts. The Batavians, who inhabited the region of the Rhine delta, took advantage of the absence of Vitellius's troops during 69 to rise against the empire. Leading the rebellion was Julius Civilis, a local prince who had served in the auxiliary troops of the Roman legions.

Under the pretext of supporting Vespasian, the Batavian leader began a war of liberation in the summer of 69. He was soon joined by Germans from the other side of the Rhine, together with eight cohorts of Batavians who had been dispatched from the Italian peninsula by Vitellius.

VESPASIAN
The first ruler of the Flavian dynasty came to power after a long and fruitful military career. Suetonius described him thus: 'He was square-built, his limbs strong and robust, and he always frowned as if he were concentrating.' Marble bust of the emperor found in Ostia (Museo Nazionale Romano, Rome).

Vespasian's victory in the Second Battle of Bedriacum did not end the Batavian uprising: Julius Civilis continued with his campaign. In the winter of 69, the Germanic uprising spread to Gaul. The Treviri joined the conflict, led by the commanders Julius Classicus – who was considered a descendant of Julius Caesar – and Julius Tutor, and the Lingones, under Julius Sabinus. In addition, a large part of the indigenous auxiliary troops of the Roman army deserted to join the rebels. The insurgency had such impetus that even the regular legions, after reluctantly accepting Vespasian, ended up swearing allegiance, according to Tacitus in his *Histories*, to the *Imperium Galliarum* (Empire of Gaul) established by Julius Classicus. To this new union, however, neither Civilis nor the Batavians submitted.

At the start of 70, once military operations in Italy were concluded, Vespasian could finally devote the necessary efforts to resolving this conflict. The large armed contingent he mobilized shows how seriously he took the situation. Eight legions – five from Italy, two from Hispania and one from Britannia – went to the war zone under Quintus Petillius Cerialis. After the first Roman triumphs, the weakening of the insurgents was not long in coming, largely because of the internal disagreements between this heterogeneous group of allies. The main obstacle was the traditional tensions between the Gauls and Germans, but in fact the tribal enmities among the Gauls themselves were the first to explode. The Sequani attacked and defeated the Lingones under Julius Sabinus. The Remi, who were sworn enemies of the Treviri, summoned a council of the Gallic towns in Durocortorum (Reims). Here it was decided to condemn the insurrectionists.

THE JULIUS CIVILIS CONSPIRACY
The Batavians were a Germanic people who lived in the region of the modern Netherlands. With the birth of modern Dutch national consciousness in the 16th century, the Dutch, who considered the Batavians as their forebears, placed great importance on Batavian struggles for independence from Roman rule. In 1661, Rembrandt (1606–1669) painted this oil for the city of Amsterdam, depicting the oath of the Batavians before Julius Civilis, leader of the uprising (National Museum, Stockholm).

ROME DOMINATES THE WORLD

The fall of Jerusalem

The capital of Judaea was a populous, rich and well-protected city. Yet, after Titus's conquest, only a few fortified towers and part of the walls remained standing. In April 70, Titus laid siege to Jerusalem using a typical Roman technique: the construction of four fortified military camps linked together by a wall (*agger*) that surrounded the entire city. The struggle for the city was fierce. In July, the Romans took the Fortress of Antonia, and in August they managed to penetrate the Temple, which was soon alight. The rest of the city fell the next month. Below is a Vespasian sestertius with the legend *Iudea Capta* ('Judaea conquered') and the image of a Jewish woman seated in an attitude of mourning and a captive with his arms bound behind his back. To the right is an oil painting by Francesco Hayez (1791–1881) depicting the destruction of Jerusalem. On the far right is a plan of the Temple, by Peter Connolly.

Cerialis's troops overcame Julius Tutor's Treviri, then defeated the combined forces of Civilis, Classicus and Tutor in Vetera. Vespasian offered conciliatory peace terms to the tribes that participated in the uprising, but he asked for the death of the ringleaders. We do not know for certain what happened to Civilis and Classicus, but Sabinus remained hidden for nine years, until he was arrested and executed. The conflict convinced Vespasian of the need to maintain a greater military presence on the German border, where he quartered eight legions and built a set of military camps.

The end of the Jewish war

The first of the three clashes between Rome and the Jews that took place during the first and second centuries began in the spring of 66. The area inhabited by the Jews had long seen strife due to internal political instability, conflict between religious factions and the continuous greed and plundering of local and Roman rulers. The events that triggered the rebellion were, first of all, the taking of silver from the treasury of the Temple of Jerusalem by the procurator of Judaea, Gessius Florus; and, second, the refusal of the Jews to carry out the traditional sacrifice in honour of the emperor, which to them was idolatrous. These triggers took place during the reign of Nero, who had sent Vespasian to get the area under control.

The future emperor made remarkable strides during 67 and 68; so much so that, when the Roman political crisis began at the end of Julio-Claudian rule, Judaea was back under control, with the exception of Jerusalem, where the surviving protesters had fled, and a handful of fortresses. The events of the Year of the Four Emperors stopped Vespasian's work in Judaea, although Jerusalem remained under

THE FLAVIAN DYNASTY

1 THE SECOND TEMPLE
The Zealots, led by Eleazar ben Simon, built forts in the Temple.

2 COURT OF THE GENTILES
A confused struggle took place in the outer Court of the Gentiles.

3 THE PORTICO
The temple precinct was bounded by a portico with a perimeter of 1 km (3280ft).

4 THE BASTION
The Fortress of Antonia, formed by four towers, was captured and demolished by the Romans at the start of the siege.

5 THE FIRE
In the final assault, Roman soldiers burned the wooden structure of the temple to the ground.

siege. Once control of Rome was secured thanks to Antonius Primus and Mucianus, Vespasian gave the mission of concluding the Jewish conflict to his son Titus, assisted by Tiberius Julius Alexander, while Vespasian himself awaited developments in Alexandria.

Titus had four legions at his disposal, to which were added detachments of the Egyptian legions and Syrian and Arab auxiliary troops. The battle for the capture of Jerusalem was fierce, despite the fact that within Jerusalem's walls were opposing factions fighting among themselves. At the head of each of these groups was a rebel leader, of whom three are known: Simon bar Giora, John of Giscala and Eleazar ben Simon. After a long struggle, the Romans managed to breach the city's three defensive walls and finally took the upper town at the end of the summer of 70. A terrible massacre followed, with most of the killing carried out by the Romans, although the most radical Jews also murdered some of those who tried to flee or surrender to the invaders.

The Jewish historian Flavius Josephus at first took an active part in the rebellion, but then defected to the Romans and became Titus's lieutenant. In his book *The Jewish War*, Josephus described the horror of the siege and the fall of Jerusalem. According to Josephus, the Roman general tried to save the city from its fate, even attempting to extinguish the burning Temple. However, this testimony is probably down to Josephus's need to curry favour with the son of Vespasian. The reality is that Jerusalem was burned and razed, its property stolen and the Second Temple, Judaism's most important holy place and monument of the people's collective identity, was burned and demolished. The holy treasures that were kept there were plundered.

Rome Dominates the World

THE VICTORY OF TITUS
In this oil on panel by the British artist Sir Lawrence Alma-Tadema (1836–1912), Vespasian is dressed as Pontifex Maximus, followed by his son Domitian, who accompanies his wife Domitia Longina, and finally Titus, on his return from his victorious campaign in Jerusalem. The look exchanged between Longina and Titus is the painter's nod to their supposed love affair, as described by Cassius Dio and Suetonius (Walters Art Museum, Baltimore).

The following year, Titus returned to Rome to celebrate the victory with his father. A triumphal procession took place, carrying the remains of some of the vanquished. Coins with the legend *Iudea Capta* ('Judaea conquered') were minted. Altogether, this military success was used as political propaganda for the power of the dynasty and the strong government that the Flavians were inaugurating in Rome. Two of the leaders of the rebellion were arrested and taken to Rome: Simon bar Giora was sentenced to death, while John of Giscala was sentenced to life imprisonment. Flavius Josephus states that there were more than one million Jewish deaths during the fall of Jerusalem, while Suetonius reduces this number by a half. The exact figure is unknown, but the enormity of the numbers, especially that indicated by Josephus, have led many researchers to think that these figures must have been the total of all casualties throughout the armed conflict. Whatever the case, it is clear that Jerusalem suffered terrible violence as a result of the Roman victory.

The war against the Jewish rebels continued for several years, first under the generalship of Lucilius Bassus and then Lucius Flavius Silva, who faced the thankless task of wiping out the armed Jewish sects that remained active, even though they had lost all hope of victory. The epilogue took place in 73 with the taking of the mountain fortress of Masada by Silva's troops. There, a particularly recalcitrant Jewish sect called the Sicarii had taken refuge. It was necessary for the Romans to build a spectacular set of siege works, including a 3km-long (2-mile) siege wall around the hill on which Masada was built and a ramp that allowed the troops to roll a battering ram to the top. According to the account of Josephus (*The Jewish War*, VII, 402–408), when the conquest was inevitable, the Jews took their own lives to escape capture by the invading army. The taking of the fortress put an end to the war.

Reconstructing the borders
The fall of the Julio-Claudian dynasty and the Year of the Four Emperors had confirmed the importance of the Praetorian Guard in the political struggles of Rome. On the other hand, the crisis also showed clearly that no one could forget the regular legions, key protagonists in the conflict's main events. The political opposition that the Senate might raise was important, but control of the Roman armies was clearly the fundamental tool for access to power. The Flavians, fully aware of this, devoted much of their efforts to reorganizing the army and stabilizing the borders. This mission was put before any new conquests.

The first task was to ensure the loyalty of the available troops, which was carried out by dismissing the majority of the units loyal to Vitellius, especially the Praetorian Guard, whose number was reduced (Vitellius's 16 cohorts became first 9 and then, under Domitian, 10). From then on, army recruitment took place only in the most Romanized provinces and in Italy itself. The total number of legions was increased to 29. The length of military service remained at 20 years.

The new army, reformed and adapted by the Flavian regime, was applied almost entirely to the maintenance of the borders. Here began the policy of militarized borders that would be consolidated in the second century. Within the empire, most of the provinces were left without legions, which were stationed along the Rhine, the Danube and the eastern border.

Some places needed special attention. In Britannia the unstable situation typical of the island had deteriorated due to the power vacuum and the transfer of troops to the continent to serve in the armies of the aspirants to the empire. The Brigantes tribe rebelled in the north of England, as well as the Silures in Wales and the Caledonians in Scotland. The region needed fast military intervention, a job entrusted to Quintus Petillius Cerialis, the victor against the Batavians and Gauls. The continuous campaigns of Cerialis and his successors, Sixtus Julius Frontinus, author of important works on Roman engineering, surveying and military tactics, and Julius Agricola, father-in-law of the historian Tacitus, restored peace to the island. Wales and England were subdued, while the northern tribes were forced back into Scotland. This military undertaking, which lasted until the reign of Domitian, was accompanied by the creation of a stable defensive system of fortified camps and bastions, alongside the courting of local rulers with the aim that their Romanization would make a widespread rebellion more unlikely.

Along the Danubian border, the transfer of legions enabled rebellious tribes, especially the Sarmatians and Dacians, to be brought under

THE LOOTING OF JERUSALEM
After the capture of the city, Roman troops plundered the riches of the Second Temple and exhibited them in the triumphal procession that took place in Rome. In this detail in the relief of the Arch of Titus, the most important symbol of the subjugated people is clearly seen: the Menorah, or seven-branched candelabrum. Located next to the Via Sacra, in the Roman Forum, the Arch of Titus was built after the death of the emperor, in around 81.

THE DIFFICULT CONQUEST OF MASADA

The rock plateau of Masada rises about 360m (1180ft) from the narrow plain that separates the western coast of the Dead Sea from the Judaean mountains. It is an unbeatable defensive location, since the outcrop is bounded by steep cliffs and the only access is along a winding path that climbs its eastern face, known as the Snake Path. The first defensive constructions on the site date from the Hasmonean period, but it was Herod the Great who endowed Masada with a strong fortress wall, warehouses for provisions and cisterns for the collection of water, as well as a palace for recreation.

SUICIDE OF THE SICARII

Along with the Zealots, the Sicarii, who took their name from the *sica*, the curved dagger they carried, gained control of Masada during the early days of the First Jewish–Roman War. There they held out until 73, when the legions subdued this last Jewish stronghold. According to Flavius Josephus, on the night before the final assault, the leader of the Sicarii in Masada, Eleazar ben Ya'ir, convinced his followers to kill themselves. According to Josephus, he proposed that a lottery be drawn to choose ten men who would be in charge of killing the rest. A second draw would decide who was responsible for eliminating the remaining nine. Finally, the last one would commit suicide. On the right is an ostracon (potsherd) with the name of Ben Ya'ir, excavated in Masada.

1 ASSAULT RAMP
Taking advantage of a rock formation, the ramp was 200m long and 60m high (656 by 196ft). It allowed the Roman troops to push a siege tower with a battering ram up to the wall.

2 SNAKE PATH
The gateway to the Snake Path, the only existing route up Masada's steep cliffs, was walled up. The Zealots turned the gateway into a living space.

3 ROMAN CAMPS
Eight camps were built by the Romans, of which two have been excavated, one 700m (2300ft) from the fortress to the southeast, the other 300m (984ft) to the northwest.

4 SIEGE TOWER
The tower was covered with iron and erected on a platform of stone slabs. Here the Romans brought the battering ram that broke down the wall.

5 FIRE
The Romans threw a rain of flaming torches onto a second, wooden, wall raised by Masada's defenders, entirely destroying it.

6 SIEGE WALL
This fortified wall was similar to the one that Titus had built around Jerusalem. It encircled Masada to isolate the Sicarii and prevent their escape.

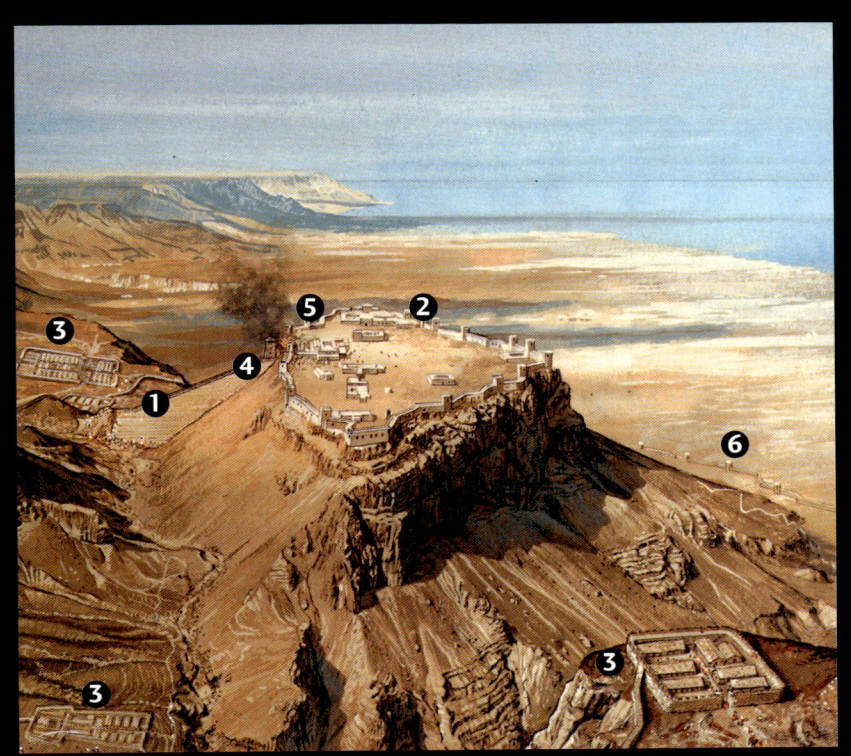

ROME DOMINATES THE WORLD

Deva Victrix: A Roman fortification in Britannia

The Deva fortress was built during the Flavian dynasty to house Legion II (about 5500 men) in the northwest of England, near the sea and the Welsh border. Later it was the main site of Legion XX, which was in charge of military control of that area of Britain.

The legionary fortresses had a high degree of uniformity in both their layout and facilities. They were large, between 20 and 25 hectares (Deva is 594 x 415m/1948 x 1360ft). They were shaped like a playing card, with a rectangular plan and rounded corners. Many of these camps became cities that have survived to this day, as is the case with Deva, which lies beneath Chester. Numerous camps first constructed in wood were later rebuilt in stone.

LEGION XX *VALERIA VICTRIX*
The 20th legion 'Valeria Victorious' was one of the combat units with which Claudius invaded Britain in 43 AD. This triangular antefix bearing the arms of the legion is kept in the Museo della Civiltà Romana, Rome.

control. Strong military camps were also built in the Rhine region, such as the one at Vindobona (Vienna), while the number of legions was increased to seven. The ground troops received the support of the navies of Pannonia and Moesia.

Problems were also felt in the East. Around the Black Sea, Anicetus, a freedman of King Polemon II of Pontus, rebelled against Vespasian, but was defeated by the Roman army. However, a provincial reorganization was needed in Asia Minor and the annexation of independent client kingdoms, such as Armenia Minor and Commagene. The Alans made an incursion into the Caucasus, invading the eastern territories of the Parthian Empire, the great power neighbouring the Romans in Asia. For the Romans, this merely accelerated the process of creating a stronger militarized border, with camps and auxiliary fortresses, and with a greater legionary presence that bounded the empire from the Black Sea to Arabia. Yet the Parthians, with whom Vespasian initially kept peace, attacked the Roman Empire in Syria in 75. The cause of the conflict was the fact that the Romans had refused requests for help from their Parthian allies in the face of the Alan invasion. The assault was stopped by Marcus Ulpius Traianus, father of the future emperor Trajan. Shortly afterwards, the Parthian king who had ordered the attack died, which allowed the signing of a peace treaty that remained in force for the rest of the period.

The new emperor's powers

Vespasian's legal position as Head of State was legitimized by a decree of the Senate called the *Lex de Imperio Vespasiani*, of which a partial copy has been preserved in a bronze plaque. With this document, the Senate sanctioned the

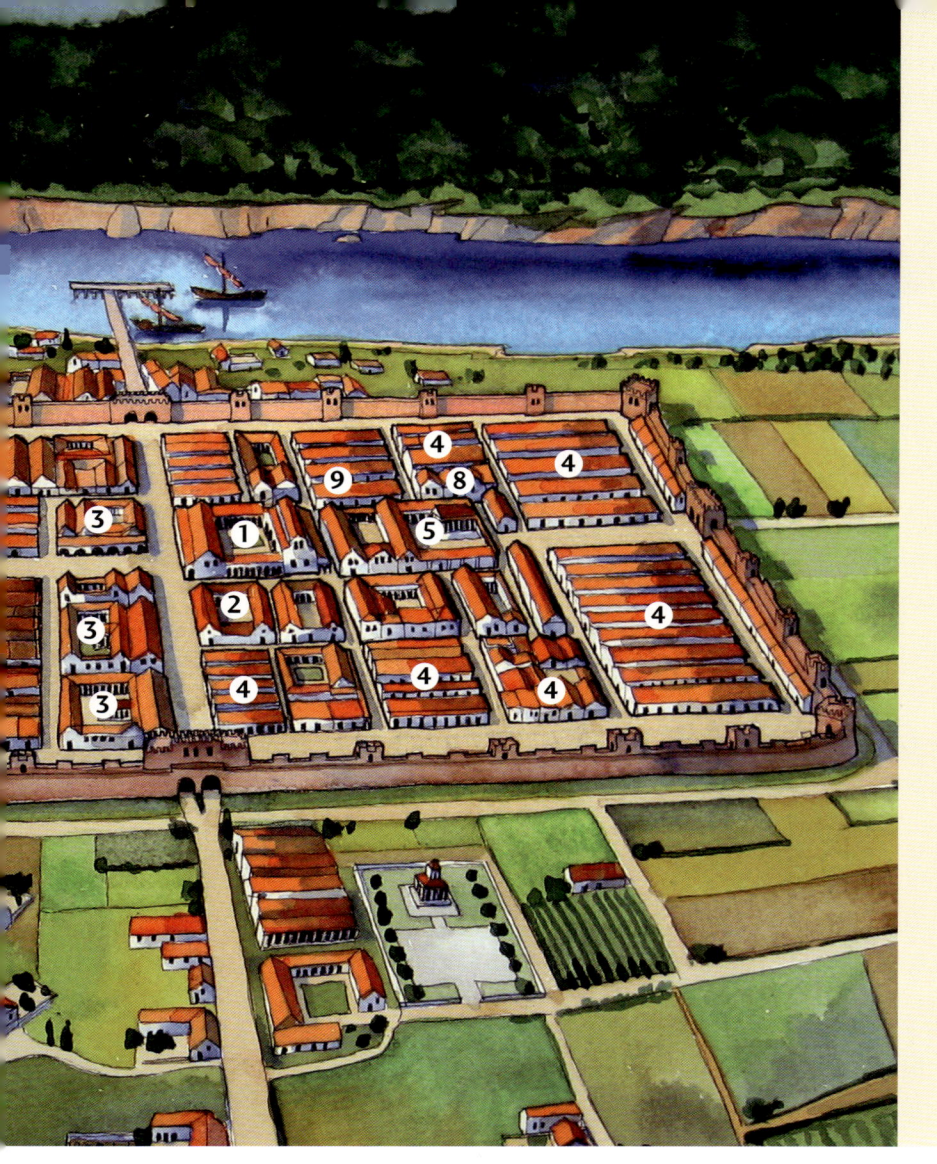

1 PRINCIPIA (HEADQUARTERS)
The legion was administrated from this building. It also served as an archive and a regimental sanctuary, to keep the banners and images of the emperors.

2 PRAETORIUM
This was the home of the commander of the legion. Its features are reminiscent of those of any aristocratic country house of the period.

3 HOUSES OF OFFICIALS
Other officers, such as the tribunes, prefects and senior centurions, had their own private houses.

4 BARRACKS
Each century had its own barracks, in which sleeping space was reserved for the men and a larger room for the centurion.

5 HOSPITAL
Made up of rooms with space for eight beds, the hospital was equipped with operating rooms.

6 AMPHITHEATRE
There was sometimes an amphitheatre to keep the troops entertained.

7 BATHS
The legionaries were not denied the comforts offered by this building.

8 WAREHOUSES AND WORKSHOPS
Buildings here were designated for the storage of food and the manufacture of tools.

9 ELLIPTICAL BUILDING
The function of this building is uncertain, although it may have been a temple.

---

position that the new emperor had already forged with the strength of his army. The objective of the law was clear: to grant to Vespasian all those rights enjoyed by the previous Julio-Claudian emperors. Although historians are divided among those who believe that this was the first time such a law was enacted and those who think that similar decrees had been approved before, the crucial fact is that the use of the Senate legitimized the power of an Italian who did not have the authority and ancestry of the Julio-Claudians. The power that this law ratified was absolute in terms of both internal and foreign policy. Thus, the *Lex de Imperio* established that Vespasian could 'make treaties with whomever he wished, as could the divine Augustus, Tiberius Julius Caesar Augustus and Tiberius Claudius Caesar Augustus Germanicus'. At the same time, he was granted the power to call the Senate, to present and reject proposals, to approve decrees and to elect the Roman magistrates. In short, his authority was legitimized to carry out all those actions 'that he deemed useful to the State or served the greatness of divine, human, public and private things'. His power, finally, was not subject to laws or plebiscites or to the Senate and people of Rome.

The consolidation of the State

Vespasian's arrival on the throne was a sea change, as all the previous emperors had belonged to the family of Augustus, the founder of the empire. But Vespasian not only lacked Roman noble blood, but was of Italian origin, an upstart who lacked the traditional authority (*auctoritas*) of the great Roman potentates. However, Vespasian's rise was a sign of the new times, for the empire was no longer the exclusive concern of the city of Rome and the

Lex de Imperio Vespasiani: the first Flavian's key legislation

The law setting out Vespasian's powers is one of the most studied and controversial documents of the imperial period. The law was recorded in a bronze plaque (pictured) that was found by the Roman politician Cola di Rienzo (1313–1354) in the basilica of St John Lateran. Currently the plaque can be seen in Rome's Capitoline Museums. This law granted absolute power to the emperor, although republican forms were maintained since the Senate was the organ that sanctioned this privilege. Vespasian's legislation did not limit itself to setting out this status quo, but, in its eagerness to restore the peace and prosperity that the empire had lost, carried out numerous reforms, among which it is worth mentioning those of an economic nature: Vespasian was in dire need of money to rebuild the State after the reign of Nero and civil war.

old leading families of the Republic. The development of Italian cities and the incorporation of their oligarchies into State politics precipitated the arrival of their members at the imperial throne. As the historian Tacitus affirmed in his *Histories*, the civil wars revealed that 'an emperor could be named in another place besides Rome'. For this reason, much of Vespasian's initial efforts were directed at the assertion of his imperial power by laws and decrees. This affirmation also had a clear dynastic inclination. From the beginning, Vespasian's children were closely involved in the work of government.

To Vespasian's political and legal actions was added enormous propaganda activity carried out with all the means at the Flavians' disposal. Coins were minted on which the new government was praised and legitimized. Important public constructions were undertaken to spread the magnificence of the new imperial family, including the Colosseum, Arch of Titus, Temple of Peace and Temple of Jupiter Capitolinus. The propaganda even resorted to stories of miracles and portents, like Vespasian's fabulous cures in Egypt, which helped to create an aura of majesty that the dynasty lacked in its origins.

Economic reform

Another pillar of the reconstruction of the State had to be economic recovery. All testimonies are unanimous in the description of the chaos, not only political, but especially economic, after the reign of Nero and the terrible civil war. A tight economic policy had to be implemented for the proper maintenance of the empire. There was a lot to do, but with very little money. Vespasian was a skilled politician in this respect. He immediately applied austerity measures to the expenses of the imperial house, earning himself the reputation of a miser and even some mockery.

Historians describe Vespasian as an avid money grabber, by any means possible, even seizure and robbery. Among his money-collecting activities were the incorporation into the State coffers of the booty from the Jewish war, the creation of a new tax on the Jews, and similar measures for Egypt and Asia. Among the novel taxes attributed to Vespasian – although the original idea seems to have been Nero's – is the urine tax (*vectigal urinae*) that was paid for the right to use the urine collected in latrines and amphoras placed for this purpose on public roads: this was used for tanning leather and cleaning clothes.

Vespasian also collected back taxes and the debts that had been allowed to accrue during the period of civil strife. He also eliminated the fiscal privileges that Galba had granted to Hispania and Gaul to win them to his cause, and again subjected the cities of ancient Greece, the province of Achaea, to imperial authority.

Another important measure in the colonies was laying claim to the *subseciva*, or unclaimed imperial land that was being squatted, and that detracted large revenues from the treasury.

This action was so unpopular that, in the end, Domitian had to abolish it, as it proved impracticable. However, despite criticism and ridicule, the general assessment of the emperor's economic policy was positive, since, according to Suetonius, 'he certainly made good use of money he had acquired so badly'. This favourable judgement, echoed by modern historiography, is largely due to the fact that income was not dedicated to Vespasian's own enjoyment, but to the embellishment of Rome and the reconstruction of the empire.

Social reform

Economic reform was accompanied by social reform, affecting in particular the privileged classes: the senatorial and the equestrian. In 73, Vespasian purged the Senate, dismissing those who were not worthy of the position or sufficiently in favour of his cause. Vespasian also allowed entry to the Senate to the most distinguished Roman citizens from Italy and the provinces, reflecting the social change that had allowed him to take the imperial throne. He also elevated equestrians to positions of power formerly reserved for the Senate.

Pliny the Elder affirms that the will to include the provinces in the march of the empire was behind the granting of Latin rights to all Hispania. Researchers do not agree about when the measure was taken: some maintain it was during the civil war in 69; others think it was in 73. Regardless of the date, the change rewarded these provinces and brought them closer to Rome. The *peregrini* (free provincial subjects who were not Roman citizens) of the Iberian peninsula came to have the same rights as the citizens of Latium. In addition, all Hispanic provincials who were involved in city government through working as magistrates or

PUBLIC LATRINES, IN DOUGGA, TUNISIA
The tax on urine was the origin of one of the most humorous anecdotes, although of doubtful veracity, that were told about Vespasian and collected by both Cassius Dio and Suetonius. According to these authors, Vespasian's son Titus reprimanded him for introducing a tax on urine. The emperor put a coin from the first tax collection under his son's nose and asked if he was bothered by the smell. When Titus said no, his father said: 'Yet it comes from urine.'

ROME DOMINATES THE WORLD

The Colosseum: masterpiece of the Flavian dynasty

The Flavian emperors, who came to power without the family pedigree of the Julio-Claudians, wanted to win the favour of Rome's people, in which cause they undertook the construction of the Colosseum, an immense building that would house gladiatorial games, the spectacle the Romans enjoyed even more than animal fights and prisoner executions. The gardens of Nero's Domus Aurea were replaced by the amphitheatre, whose elliptical floorplan measures 188m (617ft) on its main axis and rises to almost 50m (164ft) in height. The building's name derives from the gigantic bronze statue known as the Colossus of Nero that presided over the entrance to the late emperor's residence. Some 50,000 spectators could attend the bloody events that took place in the arena. Thus, Vespasian and Titus sent the Romans a clear message: the new dynasty gave back to the town, for its recreation and delight, the space a tyrant had appropriated for his own enjoyment. Below is the Colosseum represented on Titus's sestertius from 80 AD. Spectators are in the stands, while beside the amphitheatre are, on the left, the Meta Sudans fountain and, on the right, a two-storey portico.

ARCH OF TITUS (ABOVE RIGHT)
The arch of Titus celebrates the emperor's triumph in the Jewish wars. The ruler is depicted during the triumphal procession, crowned by the goddess Victoria and accompanied by two allegorical figures of the people and Senate of Rome.

AQUEDUCT OF SEGOVIA (OVERLEAF)
Although the date of construction is uncertain, it is believed to have started during the reign of Vespasian or Titus. With a length of 728m (2390ft) and height of 29m (95ft), the aqueduct is one of the most impressive feats of Roman engineering.

as a decurion – a member of the municipal Senate – were given Roman citizenship. The promotion extended to the wives, parents and legitimate children and grandchildren of the beneficiaries, a crucial change that accelerated the incorporation of Iberian oligarchies into positions that had importance beyond provincial government.

With all this accomplished, Vespasian seemed to the Romans like a second Augustus, the refounder of the empire. He had proved that he knew how to rebuild the State and establish new foundations for the emperor's powers, while still linking his actions to all that was best about the Julio-Claudian past.

The brief reign of Titus

Vespasian's rule had a profoundly monarchical and dynastic character. According to Suetonius, the emperor affirmed in the Senate that on his death either his children would succeed him or nobody. To prepare the way, both Titus and Domitian received all kinds of honours and shared much of their father's dignities and powers. Titus received the title of 'Emperor Titus Caesar, the perfect and popular youth' in 69, and shared the consulship with his father on seven of the eight occasions on which Vespasian held the position. He also shared the censorship with Vespasian in 73 and was granted tribunician power in 71; powers that in practice made him co-regent. Similar manoeuvres were put into practice with the younger brother, Domitian, although his roles were more ceremonial. He was also named 'Caesar' and 'Prince of Youth' and obtained six consulships during his father's reign. The idea of dynastic power was also stressed in propaganda, especially in coinage, in which Vespasian frequently appeared with his two sons.

It is not surprising that on Vespasian's death in 79, Titus took his place without difficulty and, in addition, maintained the privileged position of Domitian, whom he named as associate in power and successor. Both circumstances were endorsed in coins, such as those on which Vespasian is pictured giving the orb and sceptre to his son, or on which the brothers are pictured shaking hands. Titus ruled from 24 June 79 to 13 September 81, a brief reign that is difficult to differentiate from that of his father and during which he won general affection, to such an extent that, according to Suetonius, 'for his qualities, skill and good fortune, he was the darling and delight of the human race'. The information that we have about the character of Titus's reign, and the way in which he exercised his power, is all positive. The sources highlight in particular the removal of lèse-majesté powers, or laws originally intended to punish treason, which had been abused in previous reigns, especially those of the last Julio-Claudians.

Public affection for Titus had been in much shorter supply before his father's death, since many had seen in him a libertine heir whose youthful vices made them fearful of a new Nero. Titus's poor reputation had been partly created by his role during Vespasian's rule as commander of the Praetorian Guard, which made him effectively the armed enforcer of the regime. Another episode that had antagonized the Roman people was his relationship with the daughter of King Herod Agrippa, Berenice, with whom he fell in love during his stay in Judaea. This tragic love affair with the beguiling foreigner, in whom some historians have wanted to see a second Cleopatra, was a key obstacle to Titus's career. However, according to Suetonius, when Titus gained the

THE REIGN OF EMPEROR TITUS

24 June 79
Titus takes power on the death of his father, Vespasian.

Aug–Sept 79
The eruption of Vesuvius and the fire of Rome take place.

80
The Colosseum is inaugurated with lavish festivities.

13 Sept 81
Titus dies from a fever, apparently in the same villa where his father died.

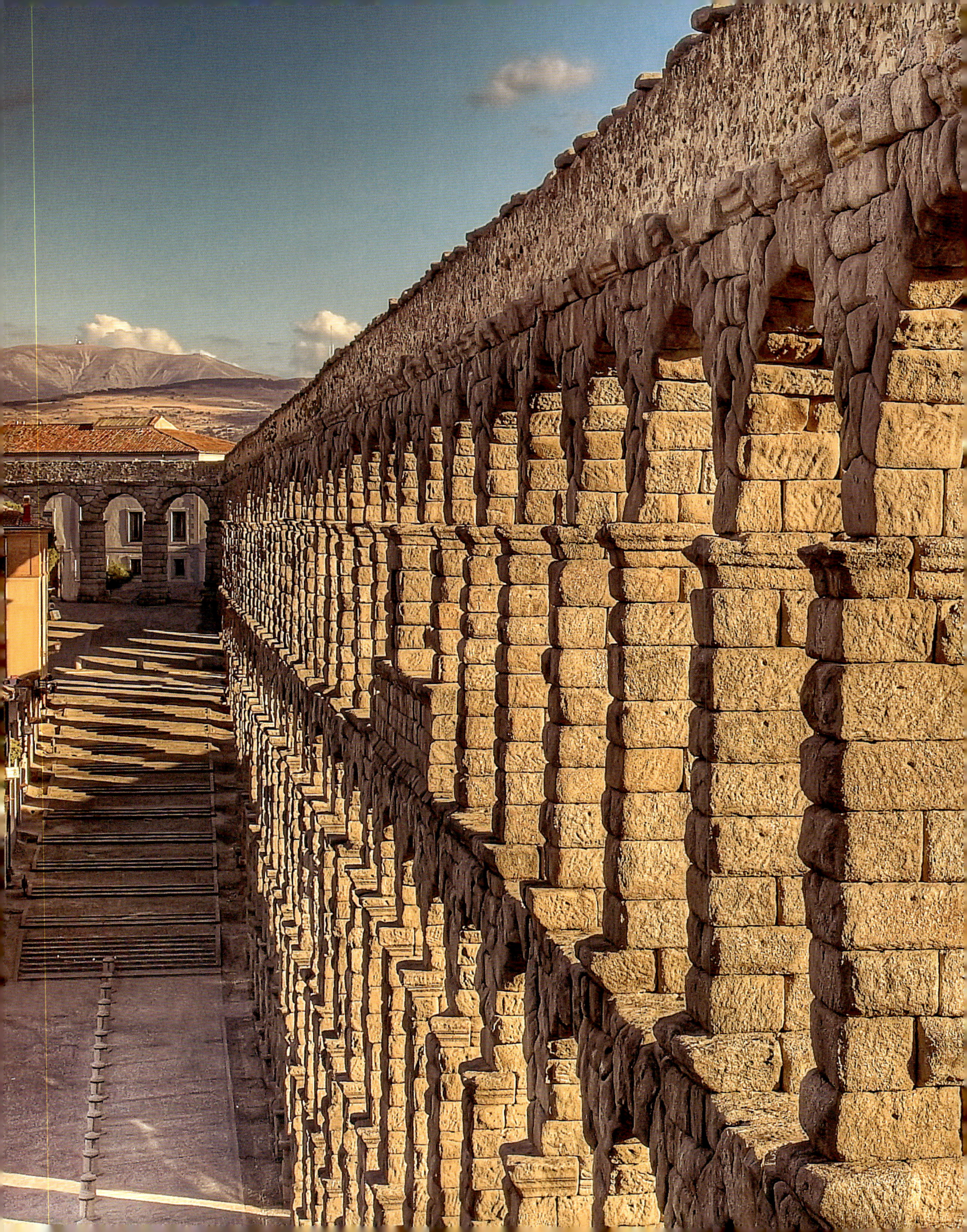

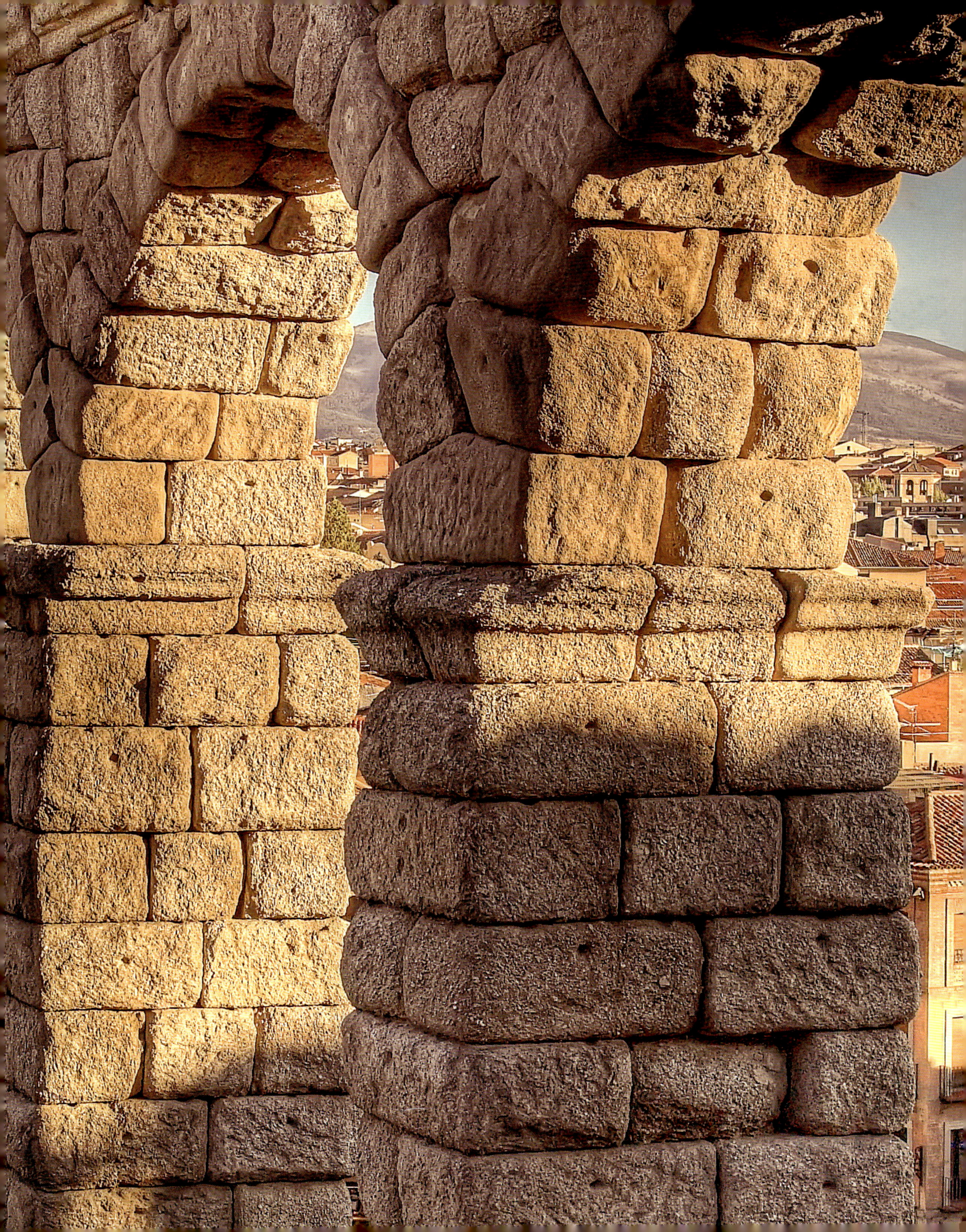

Titus and Berenice of Cilicia: public duty versus love

The impossible love between Titus, heir of the Roman Empire, and Berenice, daughter of Herod Agrippa I, inspired works of art through history, including the opera by Metastasio and Mazzolà, *La Clemenza di Tito*, which Mozart set to music. The lovers met in Judaea, when Titus commanded the Roman armies in the region. The princess financially supported Vespasian in his campaign to become emperor and stayed with Titus while the military operation lasted. However, Berenice could not accompany him in the celebrations to mark his triumph, although they met again in Rome in 75. According to the historian Cassius Dio, they lived together in the palace as if they were married. Public criticism forced Titus to send Berenice to Judaea, from where she returned in 79, after Titus took power. However, the new emperor had to separate himself from his lover to ingratiate himself with the Romans. In the image, Berenice is depicted in an 1805 illustration by Philippe Chéry for the play *Bérénice* by the French playwright Jean Racine (1639–1699).

---

throne he rejected his lover 'to the great regret of both' and forced her to leave Rome. The renunciation of his forbidden love brought Emperor Titus closer to his subjects and cemented his new image as a decent man and rightful ruler. He also moderated his excessive behaviour and removed from his retinue the idle people who had surrounded him.

During his reign, Titus had to face two major disasters. The first was the eruption of Vesuvius on 24 August 79, which buried the cities of Stabiae, Herculaneum and Pompeii. His response was quick and effective: he appointed a commission of ex-consuls to organize the reconstruction of the cities and provide funds for the relief effort. Part of the relief fund was donated from Titus's personal fortune, which helped to further strengthen his reputation as a generous ruler. He also used the assets, held in the treasury, of those who had died without heirs. The emperor himself went to the area to supervise the relief effort.

The second catastrophe faced by Titus was the fire in Rome, which occurred shortly after the Pompeii disaster. Again the emperor put his own funds towards the reconstruction of the city. The fire burned for three days and three nights, destroying many buildings in the Campus Martius and Capitol. The Temple of Jupiter itself, which had been rebuilt just a short while earlier by Vespasian, was again consumed by flames. The fire was swiftly followed by a terrible plague that was, according to Cassius Dio, a consequence of the ash from Vesuvius. To coordinate efforts to restore normalcy in the city, Titus appointed a commission of equestrian rank. In addition to paying for the start of the works, which were completed mainly by his brother, Titus donated works of art from his private villas to beautify the damaged monuments. The message that the ruler wanted to convey was very clear: unlike Nero, who had spent large sums of money on his personal pleasures, the new Flavian emperor put a good part of his wealth and treasures at the disposal of the people.

The culmination of Titus's public works in Rome was the inauguration of the Flavian

JULIA FLAVIA
The daughter of Titus's second marriage to Marcia Furnilla, and his only descendant, Julia Flavia married the consul Titus Flavius Sabinus in 82, although she became famous for an alleged incestuous relationship with her uncle Domitian, who was then married to Domitia Longina. Domitian, however, did not abandon Domitia for his niece, as the people would have disapproved. When her father and husband died, Julia lived with Domitian, and died, according to the historian Suetonius, when she was forced to abort his son. After Domitian's death, again according to Suetonius, a wet nurse secretly mixed the ashes of both lovers in the Temple of the Flavians. Bust in marble (Museo Nazionale Romano, Rome).

amphitheatre, the Colosseum, named for the colossal statue of Nero, and the lavish baths that stood next to it. According to Cassius Dio, the inauguration was celebrated with a hundred days of games, during which there were continuous gifts to the populace, who could watch gladiatorial battles, *naumachiae* (naval battles) and animal shows in which 9000 wild beasts were sacrificed.

When Titus died on 13 September 81, from a fever, the affection of the people and the respect of the Senate favoured his inclusion among the Roman gods, as had already happened with his father Vespasian. A temple was consecrated to both divinities in the Roman Forum. A memorial to Titus's deeds was the triumphal arch that bears his name, completed by Domitian. The decoration of the arch pays special attention to the triumphal procession that was granted to Titus for his success in the conquest of Jerusalem. The rest of the decoration, which still stands today in the Roman Forum, recalls the divinization of the late ruler, who rises to the sky on an eagle.

The good reputation which the late emperor enjoyed among the Romans was unanimous, according to the preserved sources, who observed with relief the way in which he moved away from excesses that had presaged a second Nero. However, the last of the Julio-Claudians was not so easily forgotten, especially in the Greek East, where even during Titus's reign there arose a pretender 'Nero' who gained many adherents. This phenomenon, known as the 'false Neros', was repeated several times afterwards. Neither did the Jews share the positive opinion that the Romans held about the second Flavian: for them, Caesar's early death was the punishment God imposed on him for the destruction of the Temple of Jerusalem.

ROME DOMINATES THE WORLD

Pompeii: Precious Victim of Vesuvius

Pompeii is one of the best-known ancient sites. Its optimal state of conservation allows us to know what daily life was like in a city of the Roman Empire. The site's preservation was due to protection from air and moisture, during the hundreds of years it remained buried.

In February 1787, the German writer J.W. Goethe visited the ruins of Pompeii, because it was an essential stop on the cultural tour ('the Grand Tour' that upper-class Europeans of the time customarily undertook). Later, in his *Italian Journey*, he wrote, recalling that visit, that 'many misfortunes have happened in the world, but only a few have procured so much happiness for posterity'.

Today, the tourists that fill the streets of the excavated city continue to show the same enthusiasm as these early visitors, particularly because of the sense of closeness to the distant Roman past that the site's extraordinary state of conservation allows the contemporary observer. The same can be said of nearby Herculaneum and other localities scattered in the neighbouring countryside. These cities have become an essential field of study for historians of the ancient world, to the point that much of what is currently known about the daily life and society of the Roman Empire is a consequence of the

BEWARE OF THE DOG

Several homes in Pompeii, such as the House of the Tragic Poet and House of Paquius Proculus, decorated their vestibules with striking mosaics of chained dogs, either pets or guard dogs. In the House of the Tragic Poet, the dog was accompanied by the warning '*Cave canem*', or 'Beware of the dog'. This example is in the National Archaeological Museum of Naples.

VICTIMS OF VESUVIUS

The eruption of Vesuvius had two phases: first, a column of ash belched over the Bay of Naples; then, a fiery cloud of gases poured down on the cities. Six hours after the start of the eruption, the walls and roofs of Pompeii had collapsed, and the inhabitants had been killed by the scorching cloud. The image on the left is of Pompeii's Temple of Apollo. In the photograph above, plaster casts of the moulds left by the victims' buried corpses are seen in the so-called Garden of the Fugitives.

'fortunate' misfortune of Pompeii, Herculaneum and their inhabitants.

The first excavations at Pompeii took place in the mid-18th century, when the area was under the rule of the future King Carlos III of Spain, then sovereign of Naples, who acted as patron. Until that time, the region had remained sparsely populated and had only received attention, even in the Roman imperial period itself, from occasional looters. After 1763, however, visits to the site began. The French occupation, between 1806 and 1815, accelerated the pace of archaeological work, but it was mainly during the excavations that were carried out in the second half of the 19th century that the most well-known and surprising remains of the city were uncovered. The excavations led by the great archaeologist Amedeo Maiuri, from 1924, focused particularly on the daily personal lives of the inhabitants. Maiuri was the last to carry out excavations of large areas of the site.

The disaster

The eruption of Vesuvius, which is located a few kilometres from Pompeii and Herculaneum, dominating the Bay of Naples, began on 24 August 79. Stones and ash rained onto Pompeii, burying the city under a layer between 4 and 6m (13–20ft) thick and causing the death of some 2000 people. Herculaneum was buried under about 20m (65ft) of mud, although the testimonies suggest that the inhabitants of this city had more time to escape, so the death toll was lower than in Pompeii. Some of those who tried to escape were trapped on the beach, where their corpses have been found.

Pompeii and the other settlements affected by the volcano are unique not only for the state of conservation of the sites, but also for the vivid story of their last days, told by an exceptional eye witness: the Roman writer Pliny the Younger, who was in the area with his uncle Pliny the Elder, the famous author of *Natural History*. The latter commanded the Roman fleet of Misenum; on hearing of the eruption, he took his ships to the site of the catastrophe to help the victims. He would never return: he was caught up in the cataclysm and died from the effects of volcanic gases.

Everyday life in a city of the Roman Empire

The eruption of Vesuvius resulted in the abandonment and oblivion of ancient Pompeii. However, this tragedy also preserved the city under a thick layer of ash. The ruins of Pompeii became a unique opportunity to see first-hand what life was like in a medium-sized Roman city. The destruction wrought by the volcano also occurred so quickly and suddenly that it is not only possible to study in detail the public and private buildings of the city, but also to investigate other aspects of daily life, such as utensils, furniture, clothing and food.

THE HOMES OF THE WEALTHY
In Pompeii, there were many houses of wealthy and aristocratic families, who flocked there for respite from the oppressiveness of Rome and were attracted by the mild climate of Campania and the beauty of the landscape. With their atriums, gardens, colonnades, frescoes and mosaics, the beautiful Pompeiian homes, like the House of Menander (above), are silent witnesses to the long-ago lives of privileged Romans.

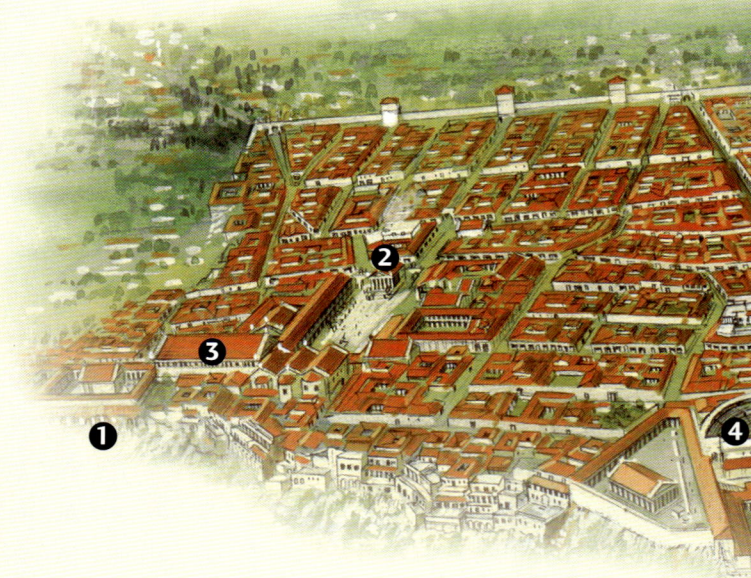

THE BATHS
In Pompeii, as in all Roman cities, the baths were one of the centres of social life. Those in the forum had male and female sections equipped with a dressing room (*apodyterium*), cold bath (*frigidarium*), warm bathroom (*tepidarium*) and hot bath (*caldarium*). Both the *tepidarium* and *caldarium* were heated by a hypocaust, an underfloor heating system. In the image above is the *caldarium* with a *labrum*, a shallow marble bath for washing.

THE BROTHEL
A lesser-known aspect of male leisure pursuits in Roman cities is that of prostitution. In Pompeii, a building dedicated exclusively to this business has been preserved, the famous *lupanar* located east of the forum, although there are records of many other buildings (apparently more than 35) in which prostitution was practised in the city. Inside, the brothel was divided into small rooms and decorated with erotic themes.

THE FLAVIAN DYNASTY

THE SHOPS
The shops, *tabernae* in Latin, available to the inhabitants of Pompeii stocked all the products and services that were needed for daily life. There were wineries, greengrocers, butchers, potteries, bakeries and barbershops. The image shows the counter of the 'Abundancia' store, which served, as indicated by a sign engraved in stone, 'chicken, fish, pork leg, turkey and game meat'.

THE SPORTS FACILITIES
Several places in Pompeii were dedicated to sport: citizens could exercise in the large palaestra (exercise ground), Samnite palaestra or in the thermal baths. The presence of these sports facilities testifies to the profound influence exerted by the Greek world in the city. The image above shows the building that was used by Nero for the training of gladiators. It consists of a large, rectangular open area surrounded by a continuous four-sided colonnade.

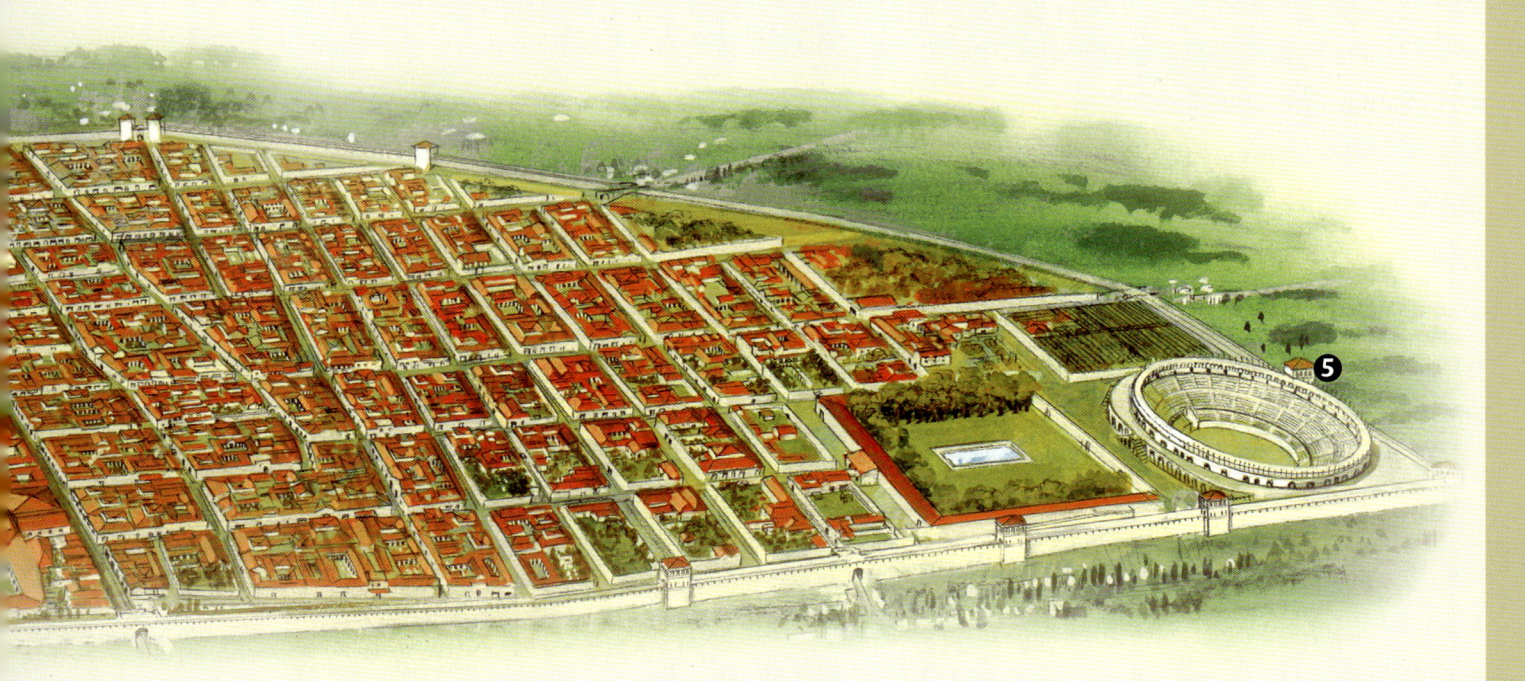

1 TEMPLE OF VENUS
Immediately after entering the Porta Marina, visitors found this great building, the largest temple in Pompeii, surrounded by porticos. It was consecrated to Pompeii's divine patron, testifying to the city's devotion.

2 TEMPLE OF JUPITER
Presiding over the forum was this large temple on its 3m-high (10ft) podium. Originally it was consecrated only to Jupiter, but later it also embraced Minerva and Juno, creating a sanctuary for the Capitoline Triad.

3 BASILICA
This was one of the city's most imposing buildings, more than 50m (164ft) in length, with a main entrance on the forum. It was originally a covered market, but by the first century was the city's law courts.

4 LARGE THEATRE
The Large Theatre could seat about 5000 people, who were sheltered from the sun with an ingenious system of awnings. Next to the theatre was the odeon, a covered theatre that was reserved for music and recitals.

5 AMPHITHEATRE
This amphitheatre, built in 80 BC, had capacity for 20,000 people. A feature that differentiated it from other similar buildings is that access to the stands was from external ramps.

ROME DOMINATES THE WORLD

FORUM OF POMPEII
This great porticoed square measured 38 by 157m (125 by 515ft). It was the heart of the city, home to buildings central to the administrative and religious life of Pompeii, such as the basilica and the Temple of Apollo.

The destruction of the cities was preceded in 62 by a strong earthquake, which caused major damage. Before the repair work had been completed, the next and final scourge of nature took place.

The city and its buildings

At the time of its destruction, some 20,000 people lived in Pompeii. The urban core was surrounded by a wall dotted with defensive towers, protecting an area of some 66 hectares (163 acres). On the scale of the empire, Pompeii was a medium-sized city, with a regular plan and cobblestone streets and pavements. The roads around the forum have a less ordered layout than the rest of the road system, which extends to the north and east.

The forum, near the Porta Marina, was the political and economic centre of Pompeii. Around the central square stood the most notable sanctuaries, such as the Capitol and the temples dedicated to the Lares, Vespasian and Apollo. Nearby was the immense temple to Venus Pompeiana. Alongside these sacred buildings were other buildings central to the functioning of the city, such as the basilica, treasury, archives, curia and comitium. No less significant were the two markets, one for grain and a larger one for food, which were also located around the forum. Part of the forum's eastern side was occupied by the rectangular building whose construction was financed by the wealthy matron Eumachia, and whose purpose is still the subject of debate.

In the southern part of Pompeii was a complex of buildings dedicated to leisure – the theatre, odeon and Samnite palaestra (exercise ground) – accompanied by two other temples, one dedicated to Isis and the other to Zeus Meilichios. The amphitheatre and the large palaestra are further away, although still within the walls.

Alongside these public buildings, the visitor to Pompeii can today wander through more intimate and evocative spaces, such as baths, taverns, latrines and even brothels.

House of Venus

Standing out among Pompeii's many treasures are a large number of townhouses, which allow us to examine the typical home of a wealthy Roman family: the domus. There is much variety among the plans of Pompeiian domus, due to the free combination of two main elements: the atrium, which is a small arcaded courtyard, and the peristyle, which consists of a large garden, also porticoed. Around these two open spaces, which are the main source of light and air for the property, all the rest of the rooms are arranged, such as the dining room, the bedrooms and the servants' rooms. One of the key spaces in the domus was the tablinum, positioned between the atrium and the peristyle, which housed the altar to the lares (*lararium*) and the family's most important documents and goods. In this room, as well as in the atrium and peristyle, the best works of art were usually concentrated. These photographs show the peristyle of the House of Venus, named after the magnificent painting of the goddess who presides over the garden.

■ ROME DOMINATES THE WORLD

Mosaics in Pompeii

Pompeii's mosaics, which decorated the floors of houses and public buildings in the city, are as splendid as its wall paintings. On the left, musicians prepare for a concert; below, a striking composition combines a skull, butterfly, level and plumbline, and a wheel, indicating that *'Omnia mors aequat'*, meaning 'Death renders all equal' (National Archaeological Museum, Naples).

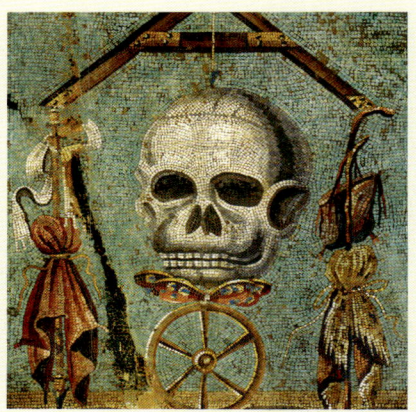

Pompeiian painting
The paintings found in Pompeii and Herculaneum are exceptional tools in the advancement of knowledge about the ancient world. The best examples of Roman painting are found on the walls of the mansions of these cities, and only the city of Rome itself begins to match their wealth. Thus, it is not surprising that academic works on Roman painting began in the 18th century, coinciding with the first excavations at Pompeii. The systematization of styles was the work of German archaeologist and scholar August Mau, whose classification, published in 1882, is still used today.

Other than murals, other types of Roman painting are known, such as painting on statues, ivory or wood.

However, very few examples have survived: some of the most notable are funeral portraits discovered in Egypt. For this reason, descriptions collected from ancient sources are important, such as the accounts given by Pausanias of Greece in the second century, which describe many different mediums that, being easily damaged, have largely not survived. The works of two writers from the Roman imperial era are also important to our understanding of Roman art. One of them is Vitruvius, who, in his *De Architectura*, focused on technical aspects; the other is Pliny the Elder, who, in his *Natural History*, was interested in the origins of artistic expression in Rome.

Mau's first style of mural painting, also called the incrustation style, was used in Pompeii during the second century BC. It was an adaptation of the forms, tastes and techniques of Hellenistic Greece. Frescoes in this style reproduced architectural elements, especially marble, with the aim of imitating ostentatious building materials. The walls were divided horizontally into three parts, topped with a stucco cornice. Panels of painted stucco were fixed to the wall to give the impression of blocks. Examples of this style can be found in the Houses of the Faun, Sallust and Silver Wedding, all of them in Pompeii.

The second style, or architectural style, appeared at the beginning of the first century BC and fell out of use at the end of this century. Its main feature was the profuse use of perspective and

HOUSE OF THE MYSTERIES
In this great work of ancient art, 17m (56ft) of wall painting and 29 figures narrate the initiation of a young woman (seen here waving her cloak) into the 'mystery' cult of Dionysus.

shading techniques to replace the previous incrustations in the evocation of architectural elements. As this style progressed, so did the complexity of paintings, with several perspective views represented on the same wall. Finally, to these complex compositions other elements were added, depicted as if seen through a window, such as bucolic landscapes, with views of temples and sanctuaries, as well as human figures. This style also made frequent use of *trompe l'oeil* devices, such as the representation of everyday utensils as if jutting from the wall.

In Rome, there are superb examples of the second style in the House of the Griffins and the Houses of Augustus and Livia, on the Palatine Hill. In Pompeii and its surroundings, the best were in the Villa of P. Fannius Synistor in Boscoreale; the Villa of the Mysteries, in the city itself; and in the neighbouring site of Oplontis.

The third style, or ornate style, was popular between around 20 BC and 20 AD, although there are authors who suggest a later end date of 40–50 AD. This style is characterized by the abandonment of visual effects and games. A typical fresco consisted of panels in white, red or black, on which were meticulously painted scenes of gardens, myths and Egyptian motifs. The idea was not to imitate a scene glimpsed through an open window, but to give the impression of a picture or tapestry hanging on the wall. The most admired examples are in the imperial villa in Boscotrecase, near Pompeii.

The fourth style, or intricate style, includes a greater variety of shapes, motifs and techniques than the previous styles. It may have been a reaction to the restrictive forms of the previous period. Compositions consisted of a neutral and homogeneous background on which were placed an intricate succession of small figures, paintings, views, garlands and fantastic architectural elements. The most outstanding examples of this style are found in the Domus Aurea of Nero in Rome, and in the House of the Vettii in Pompeii.

ARLES AMPHITHEATRE
Able to seat 25,000, the amphitheatre was built by Domitian in Arelate, a key city of Gallia Narbonensis. Opposite is a marble statue depicting Mithras emerging from a rock, from the Dacian site of Sarmizegetusa (Museum of Dacian and Roman Civilization, Deva).

THE REIGN OF DOMITIAN

On Titus's death in 81 AD, Domitian took the title of emperor without any difficulty. His rule was characterized by a continuation of the policies of previous governments, yet Domitian's careful administration of the empire was eclipsed by his excesses and cruelties. Domitian's autocratic policy, especially the scorn with which he treated the Senate, led to his assassination and the condemnation of his memory (*damnatio memoriae*).

When he was proclaimed emperor, Domitian was perfectly familiar with the exercise of power. Although his father never named him as his co-regent, the youngest of the Flavians held positions of responsibility and fulfilled important ceremonial roles during the tenures of his father and brother. During Vespasian's lifetime, he served as consul six times. In addition, during the period between the fall of Vitellius in December 69 and the arrival of his father in Rome in the autumn of 70, Domitian was the family's highest authority in the city.

Domitian had an autocratic conception of the power he had received from his family, so he wished to fully exercise the authority granted to him as Roman emperor. He had plenty of the political drive of his predecessors, but took their style of government to extremes not seen in the previous emperors. In particular, he differed from the rest of the Flavians in the way

ROME DOMINATES THE WORLD

Domitian: timeline of his reign

Year 81

Ascension to the throne. On Titus's death, Domitian takes the throne, already armed with an understanding of imperial administration.

Year 83

Victory over the Chatti. Domitian attempts to pacify the Rhine border and carries out two successful military campaigns against the Chatti, a Germanic tribe.

Year 84

Battle of Mons Graupius. General Agricola destroys the Caledonian army in Scotland, achieving the end of hostilities in Britain.

Years 85–88

Dacian War. After several setbacks, the Romans manage to defeat the Dacian king Decebalus at the Battle of Tapae.

Year 89

Rebellion of Antonius Saturninus. A military uprising in Germania is quickly put down, but prevents Domitian from taking advantage of the victory in Dacia.

Year 96

Assassination of Domitian. His relationship with the senatorial aristocracy deteriorates in the final three years, leading to the emperor's death.

---

he related to the Senate, since he never moderated the expression of his power, as the experienced Vespasian knew was necessary, nor was he diplomatic and propitiatory with the senators, as Titus had been. Domitian always appeared as he really was: an authoritarian monarch who considered himself a benevolent despot. He placed justice and fairness over all other considerations, and the senators learned the bitter lesson that the harsh penalties laid down by imperial laws also applied to them.

Tensions between Domitian and the Senate began from the very start of his government. In a break with traditional behaviour, the new emperor claimed many honours. He obtained the right to hold the post of consul continuously. In 85, he became censor for life, which was a blow to the senators, as it gave him control over the appointment of new senators and set him up as a moral authority for the whole of Roman society. The strengthening of the emperor's court, to which flocked Domitian's friends from all social classes, also meant a setback for the senators, who saw their practical reach greatly diminished.

Domitian's accumulation of honours led him to rename the months of September and October as 'Germanicus' – an epithet adopted by the emperor in 83 as a result of his military campaign in Germania – and 'Domitianus'. His break with the republican-tinged modes of behaviour that Augustus had initiated was evident in the profusion of statues and monuments that were erected in his name in Rome. A colossal equestrian statue, erected in the Roman Forum in commemoration of his victories in Germania and Dacia, aroused the senators' strongest criticisms. The statue must have had spectacular dimensions, judging by its base, which measures 11.8 by 5.9m (38 by 19ft).

However, it was undoubtedly the harshness with which he treated any hint of rebellion in the senatorial ranks that earned him the most hatred. Many Roman aristocrats were condemned to exile or death. The names of 14 of his victims are known, among them relatives Titus Flavius Sabinus and Flavius Clemens, grandsons of his uncle Flavius Sabinus, alongside whom he suffered during the assault on the Capitol. Although, at first, Domitian continued his brother's policy of punishing informers, he later used them extensively to expose traitors and to increase his income at the expense of the fortunes of those he condemned.

The last of the wrongs that have been attributed to Domitian is the supposed demand to be called '*Dominus et Deus*' (lord and god). However, modern historiography doubts this information from ancient literary sources, as no inscription, coin or other archaeological evidence has been preserved to support it.

The 'Bald Nero'

Domitian's desire to exercise his power without the support of the Senate fundamentally affected the way the literary sources tell his life story. They mostly have a contrary take on the emperor. The *damnatio memoriae* after his death also meant the removal of his name from many inscriptions and monuments, which has further complicated a just assessment of his reign.

Except for the writings of Flavius Josephus, who was clearly favourable to the Flavians; the poems by Martial written in the emperor's lifetime; and the work of Statius, all the preserved literary testimonies portray Domitian as an aberrant pervert who deserved to be forgotten. They liken him to the bad rulers who preceded him, such as Tiberius, Caligula and Nero. For example, in his *Satires*, Juvenal called him the 'Bald Nero' in reference to Domitian's hair loss. However, these opinions came from a small fraction of the population: the aristocracy. Ultimately, these invectives were caused by the way Domitian behaved to this small group of privileged people, who were sometimes severely punished and deprived of their traditional prerogatives.

The senatorial hatred towards Domitian was also helpful to the emperors who succeeded him, as it was a necessity for them to legitimize a position they had obtained thanks to his murder. Nerva, Trajan and, to a lesser extent, Hadrian consented to, and benefited from, the publication of numerous works contrary to the emperor and that magnified their own achievements in comparison with his evils. Tacitus, Pliny the Younger and Suetonius wrote during the reigns of Trajan and Hadrian and are clearly opposed to the emperor. The section of Tacitus's *Histories* dedicated to the Flavians has been lost. However, from what has been preserved of his work, especially concerning Domitian's behaviour when he was in command of Rome before his father arrived, it seems that Tacitus's opinion was extremely negative. This was despite the fact that Tacitus prospered under the Flavian dynasty. Perhaps

DOMITIAN'S DEPARTURE
This relief, discovered in the Apostolic Chancellery of Rome, shows the emperor preparing to leave for a military campaign. Domitian became enormously popular among his soldiers, whose salaries he raised and with whom he spent three years on campaign (Vatican Museums, Rome).

DOMITIAN IMPERATOR
In Rome, the title of imperator (commander) was theoretically reserved for the rulers who had won it on the battlefield. This marble statue of the emperor shows him in military attire (Vatican Museums, Rome).

PIAZZA NAVONA (OPPOSITE)
This famous Roman square still retains the shape of the stadium that Domitian had built in the Campus Martius for staging athletic competitions.

this was precisely why Tacitus openly criticized Domitian, in an attempt to distance himself from one of the rulers who had elevated him but who was no longer well regarded. In *Agricola*, Tacitus accuses Domitian of being a bad strategist and of precipitating the fall of Tacitus's father-in-law, hero of the story, because he envied him his victories against the Caledonians. Recent studies question Tacitus's version of events and give proof that Domitian and Agricola were friends.

For his part, Pliny the Younger, in his *Panegyric in Praise of Trajan* and in *Epistulae*, took Domitian as a negative counterpoint to the new emperor. For everything that Trajan was, did and promised, he offered a contrary action by Domitian, who is portrayed as arrogant, cowardly, cruel and greedy. Again, despite the invectives in both works, Pliny politically matured under the Flavians, taking on increasingly important public roles.

Finally, the *Life of Domitian*, written by Suetonius during the reign of Hadrian, is the longest preserved account of Domitian and the one that has most influenced posterity's opinion of the emperor. However, Suetonius's text is contradictory, sometimes describing Domitian as a conscientious, concerned and moderate ruler, while also portraying him as vicious, depraved and cruel. Suetonius gives a series of malicious anecdotes about the emperor, such as fights with his brother, his taste for torturing flies, his lasciviousness and his cruelty.

The biased and negative interpretation of Domitian in the reigns immediately following his death only continued during the second and third centuries. Cassius Dio, the historian who was a senator under the Severans, echoed Suetonius's opinion, beginning his description of the emperor with the words: 'Domitian was not only reckless and quick to anger, but he was also treacherous and secretive.'

To this set of Roman sources must be added other literary testimonies unfavourable to the emperor. For example, there were the opinions of the Christians who suffered persecution under Domitian's government, mainly because of the importance Domitian placed on the practices of the imperial cult. The construction in Ephesus of a colossal temple in his honour and the obligation to render him divine honours, which went against the practice of the Christian faith, seems to make up the historical context of the *Book of Revelation*. The beast that the Christians were forced to worship might be Domitian himself, although for some authors it is Nero. According to Lactantius, Christians considered Domitian one of the worst emperors, as well as a sworn enemy.

The portrait of the emperor built up from the study of historical sources is so clearly biased that most contemporary historians admit that Domitian's true character is a mystery. Current historiography, following authors like Theodor Mommsen and Ronald Syme, prefers to make a more impartial and complete reconstruction of the history of the empire under Domitian, avoiding slanderous anecdotes and invective. This necessary revision has led to the presentation of Domitian as an autocratic but effective ruler, according to the words of Brian W. Jones, one of his last biographers.

Administration of the empire

Despite the criticisms of the pro-senatorial sources, Domitian was deeply concerned about the proper functioning of the empire. On one of the few occasions when he wrote favourably about the emperor, Suetonius said, 'He also knew how to manage the magistrates of Rome and the governors of the provinces, who were never more virtuous or more righteous.' The epigraphic and archaeological information confirms these words and gives proof of the empire's prosperity under Domitian. This evidence also suggests Domitian was a conscientious, meticulous administrator, personally directing as much as he could and interfering in the decisions of his provincial governors when they were not to his liking.

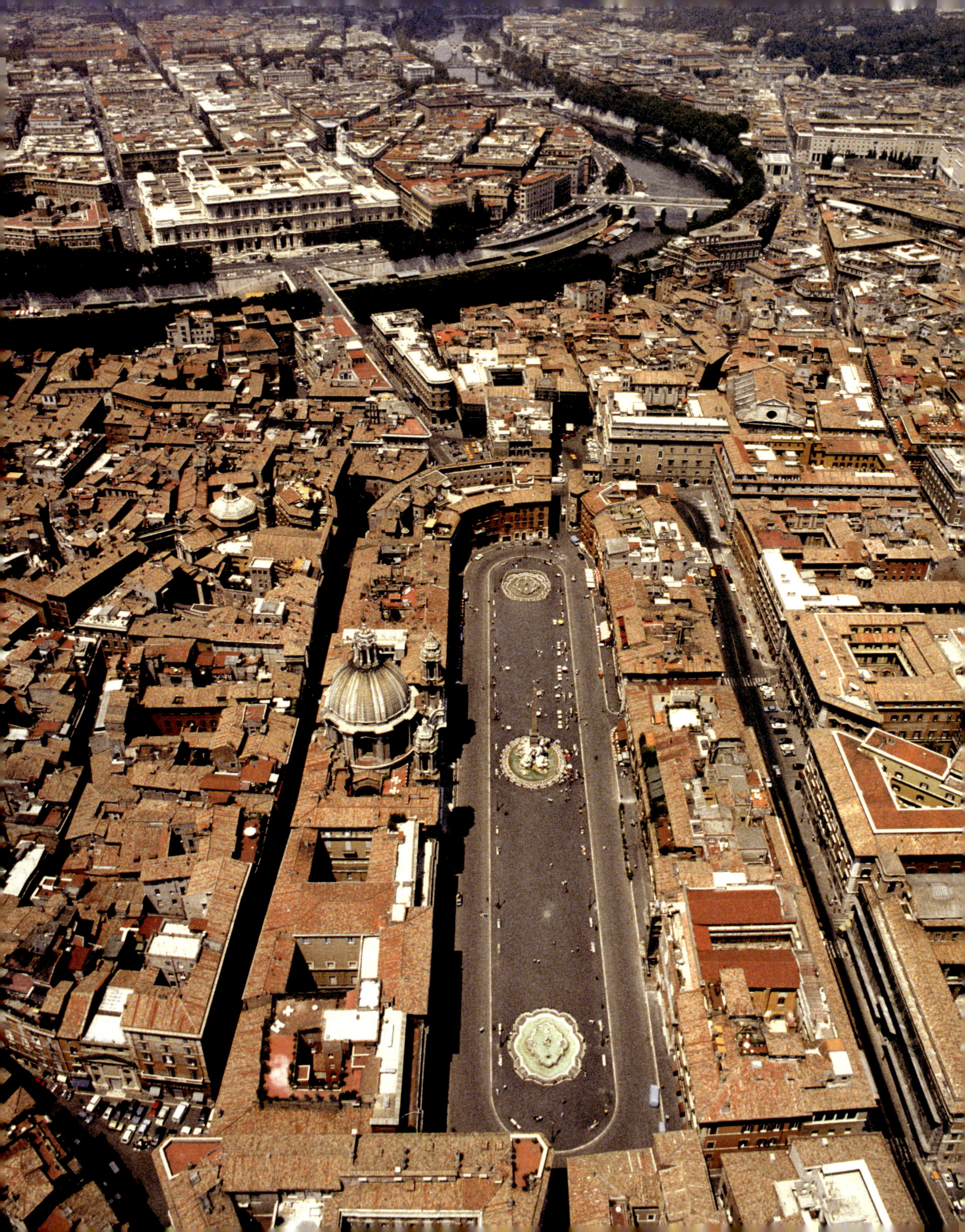

Equestrians in the imperial administration

Under Augustus, men of equestrian rank were allowed to be procurators and prefects, but the first emperors relied on their own freedmen to take most roles in the civil service. The Flavians began to hand over more posts to equestrians. In doing so, they made equestrians the second largest group of officials (the largest was the senators) dedicated to the government of an increasingly centralized empire. The senators took the positions of greater importance, although the equestrian order took roles such as the governorship of Egypt, the praefectus annonae (prefect of provisions) and the Praetorian prefect, in charge of the Praetorian Guard. The career of equestrian procurators was ranked according to their salary: the sexagenarians, who had a salary of 60,000 sestertii; the centenarians, who received 100,000; the ducenarians, who received 200,000 sestertii; and, finally, the trecenarians, with 300,000 sestertii. In this image, an equestrian is seen on a tombstone (Museo Nazionale Romano, Rome).

AUREUS OF DOMITIAN
On the reverse of the coin, the emperor appears triumphantly on his chariot with the legend 'Germanicus', alluding to his victories in Germania.

Domitian drove the empire with a firm hand, promptly collected taxes and did not tolerate the traditional arbitrariness of the provincial authorities. To this end, he gave more power to the equestrian order and the procurators. In short, Domitian began the long process of the bureaucratization of the imperial administration that would continue with the 'good emperors' of the second century.

In the Western empire, Hispania again monopolized the emperor's attention. Vespasian had granted Latin rights to all the *provinciales* of the Iberian peninsula and made possible the acquisition of Roman citizenship for local leaders. By doing so, he promoted Romanization and the incorporation of the most powerful Hispanics into the administration and politics of the empire. Domitian continued with his father's efforts. The cities that had been promoted to municipalities thanks to Vespasian's measure needed legal statutes to organize their political and economic life. Domitian organized the new city charters, such as those of Salpensa (Utrera), Malaca (Malaga) and Irni (Algámitas).

Domitian's dedication to government can also be observed in the Eastern empire. His policy towards the Greek world was that of a Hellenophile, always showing respect for institutions and customs, while trying to funnel the dynamism of the Greek region towards the interests of the State. Here he also raised the legal status of many populations, especially in Asia Minor, and funded from his own estate works in cities such as Aphrodisias, Lindos, Megalopolis, Stratonicea, Ephesus and Delphi. In the last community, he also mediated in internal conflicts in the Amphictyonic League, a religious league of Greek cities that had met for centuries in Delphi's sanctuary. In Athens, he was appointed chief magistrate, the eponymous archon. In this role, he even punished the most influential noble of his time, Hipparchus, with the confiscation of all his property, in response to the many accusations of tyranny against him.

In his desire to improve the economy of the empire, Domitian also paid great attention to agriculture and the land. Vespasian had tried to regain for the State the plots of land that the coloniae had usurped as public land, thereby removing a source of revenue. Domitian decided to allow the cities to maintain the management of these properties, in a way that significantly improved their economic capacity. Domitian's desire to effectively manage the land is also behind one of his best-known measures, the vine edict, dated to 90 or 91. This law prohibited the planting of new vines in Italy and ordered the destruction of half the vineyards in the provinces. This was the only occasion on which legislation on economic matters was created in one block for the whole empire. Contrary to traditional interpretation, the emperor was not trying to protect the interests of Italian farmers against provincial wine, but to prevent famine. An excess of mediocre vineyards was reducing space that would be better dedicated to grain cultivation.

Domitian's careful management of the empire allowed him to implement a broad policy of public charity, as the emperor wanted to be seen as a benefactor by his subjects. On three occasions, he made public donations (*congiaria*), in which he gave 300 sestertii per citizen, and also paid for several public banquets. In addition, new festivities were organized, such as those dedicated to Minerva and the Capitoline games (*ludi capitolini*). Nor did he forget the gladiatorial contests, which

STADIUM OF APHRODISIAS
The Hellenic city of Aphrodisias was located in the region of Caria, in present-day Turkey. The Roman stadium is one of the Mediterranean's best preserved. It measured 262 by 59m (860 by 193ft) and could hold more than 30,000 spectators.

MINERVA
The goddess was the Roman version of the Greek Athena, patron saint of wisdom, strategic warfare and artisans. The Romans celebrated her festival from 18 to 23 March. This statue, made of marble and golden onyx, dates from the second century (Louvre Museum, Paris).

were held frequently, nor the circus races, for which he showed great enthusiasm, adding two new teams to the traditional four.

The imperial program in Rome
In less than 20 years, Rome had suffered two fires – in 64 under Nero and in 80 under Titus – and a civil war, and the city's architecture had suffered terribly. Domitian continued the construction policy of Vespasian and Titus and even surpassed his predecessors, probably driven both by his autocratic character and his desire to appear a benevolent ruler.

Domitian's building activity was vast, making him one of the emperors who left the deepest mark on Rome. He carried out a huge campaign of reconstructing the buildings damaged by the vicissitudes of recent years: the Circus Maximus, Curia Julia, Temple of Augustus, House of the Vestals, Temple of Castor and Pollux and Forum of Caesar; the Porta Capena on the Caelian Hill; the Temple of Apollo and the library in the Palatine; and, in the Campus Martius, the Pantheon, Baths of Agrippa, Porticus Octavia, Saepta Julia, Temple of Isis and Serapis and Theatre of Balbus. He also oversaw the renovation of the Temple of Jupiter Capitolinus, which was damaged in 69 and, after Vespasian's reconstruction, was again damaged by the fire of 80. Just the cost of this single project was a fortune: it is believed the gold for the temple cost 288 million sestertii.

Domitian also completed projects started by Vespasian and Titus. He completed the Colosseum, which, despite having been inaugurated twice, was not yet finished. He fitted out the network of underground chambers and corridors that were essential for the proper functioning of the building. He also commissioned the building of several gladiatorial schools, among them the Ludus Magnus next to the Colosseum. According to recent archaeological studies, Domitian erected the Arch of Titus at the beginning of his reign, while also completing the Baths of Titus. In addition, the Temple of Vespasian and Titus, in the Roman Forum, dates back to his reign.

The emperor and the vestal virgins

Despite his own amoral behaviour, Domitian promoted measures to support virtue, such as the punishment of vestal virgins who broke their vows. According to Roman law, it was the obligation of the Pontifex Maximus – the high priest, a role the emperors reserved for themselves – to watch over the behaviour of the virgins and punish any infraction. Shortly after the start of Domitian's rule, three vestal virgins were accused of breaking their vow of chastity. In a gesture of magnanimity, the emperor allowed them to choose their method of execution. The second trial was of Cornelia, the chief vestal, who was apparently accused unfairly. Domitian was inflexible and imposed the traditional penalty: the vestal was buried alive. Her supposed lovers were beaten to death, except one, who admitted his guilt and was exiled. The drama is depicted in this engraving by Giuseppe Mochetti, based on work by Bartolomeo Pinelli (1781–1835).

Domitian also undertook the construction of new monuments in which the will to extol the imperial house and to create recreational spaces for the people were cleverly combined. The list of buildings he commissioned is astounding. In the Campus Martius, there was a stadium, whose shape can still be seen in the Piazza Navona; the Divorum Temple, consecrated to Titus and Vespasian; and a Temple of Fortuna Redux, in commemoration of his triumphal return after the campaign of 93 against the Sarmatians. He also built a temple in honour of the Flavian dynasty on the Quirinal Hill, the Meta Sudans fountain adjacent to the Colosseum, and a basin excavated on the banks of the Tiber for *naumachia* (naval battles). Concerned about Rome's supplies, the emperor commissioned the construction of several warehouses for provisions such as spices and grain.

Among Domitian's achievements in construction, the restructuring of the area around the imperial forums deserves a special mention. The forum that is traditionally called the Forum of Nerva, or the Transitional Forum, was, in reality, constructed by Domitian and dedicated to the goddess Minerva, the emperor's favourite deity. This square served as a link between the Temple of Peace, built by Vespasian, and the Forum of Augustus, restored by Domitian. Recent research suggests that the Forum of Trajan, one of the main achievements of that emperor, was actually begun under Domitian. Yet the highlight of Domitian's building work was the construction of a colossal palace complex on the Palatine Hill. The palace incorporated the old Domus Tiberiana but extended the apartments to occupy most of the hilltop. The majestic structure became the official residence of the emperors in Rome.

Along with these larger constructions, Domitian adorned Rome with numerous statues, mostly of himself, including his equestrian statue in the Roman Forum; as well as arches and altars, like the one he dedicated to Vulcan in commemoration of the fire of 64. Domitian's construction projects in Rome had their echo in the rest of Italy and the provinces, where numerous works were also undertaken, either under the direct patronage of the emperor or as a consequence of the prosperity that his reign brought to the Mediterranean.

Consolidating the borders

Domitian's military campaigns, like those of his father, had the main objectives of creating a stable border and the punishment of rebellious barbarian populations. However, this emperor departed from the usual Roman practice by abandoning wars of conquest in favour of

DOMUS FLAVIA: PALACE OF THE ROMAN EMPERORS

The Romans believed that the Palatine was the hill on which the wolf that raised Romulus and Remus lived, and the oldest buildings in the city have been found in this area. During the Republic, it became the home of a large part of the Roman aristocracy, who built their villas on the slopes of the hill, which was conveniently close to the forum. In the imperial period, the emperors appropriated most of the hill until Domitian chose it for the site of his immense palace, which became the official residence of the emperors in Rome until the fall of the empire.

The Palatine Hill gave its name, by extension, to this type of construction, the palace. The palace of Domitian, which was known in antiquity as the Domus Augustana, or palace of the emperors, consisted of three different parts: the Domus Flavia, which is the modern name given by historians to the public area of the complex; the Domus Augustana, which is the private part of the building; and the stadium. The private area, which has not been well conserved, had an underground structure that connected with the stadium. The palace complex, designed by the imperial architect Rabirius, was immense, with an area of about 40,000sq m (430,560sq ft).

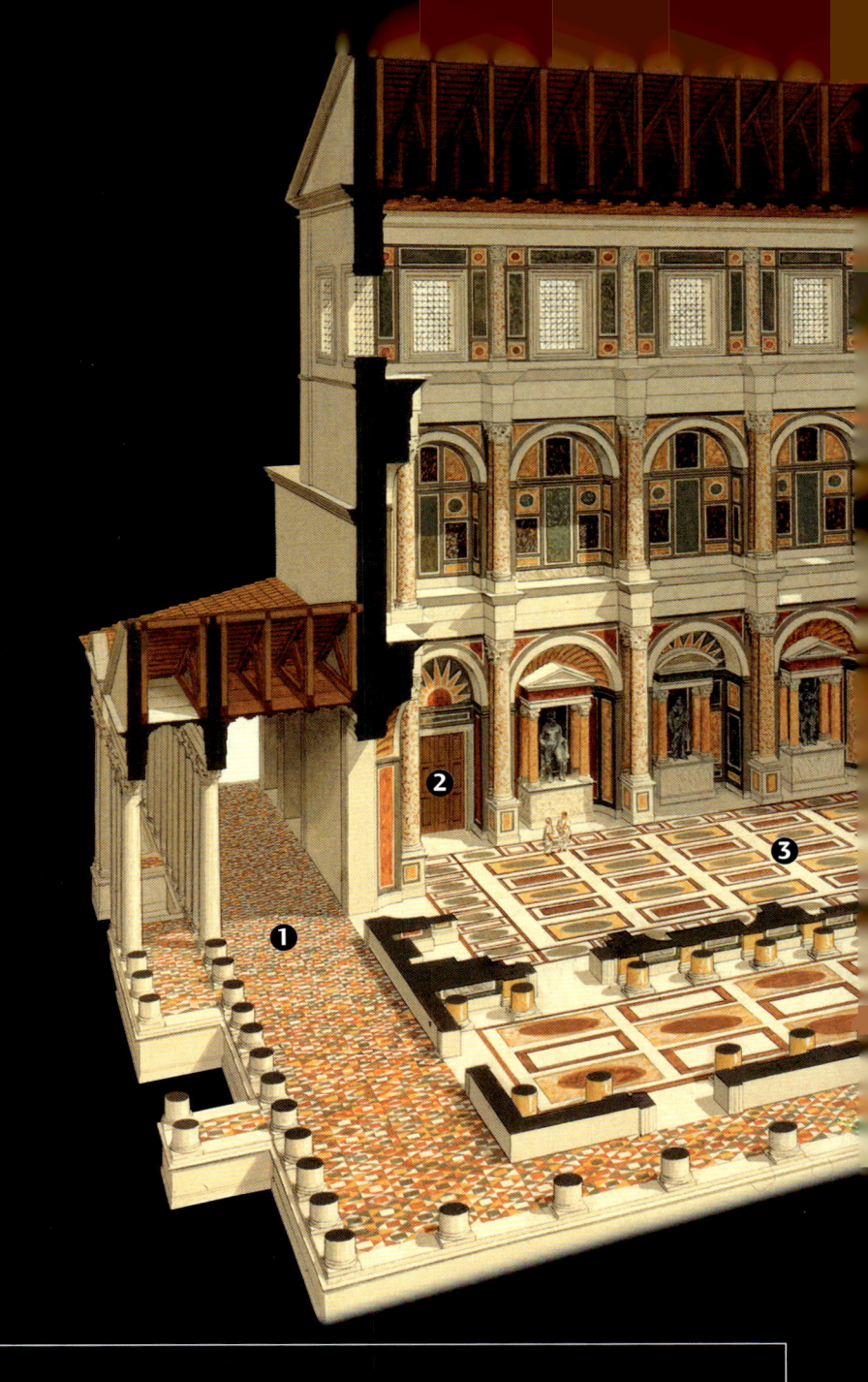

OPUS SECTILE

The Domus Flavia still conserves some portions of the sumptuous mosaic that covered the floor of the enormous dining room. It was executed according to the *opus sectile* technique, in which mosaics were created by cutting differently coloured marbles into large, shaped pieces to form geometric patterns (as in the image) or figures of animals, flowers or people. In other Roman mosaic techniques, such as *opus vermiculatum,* which was of Egyptian origin, the *tesserae* (tiles) were tiny; this allowed the creation of very detailed figures, soft contours and compositions of great complexity. For the Romans, mosaics were a luxury that they lavished on their public and private buildings.

The public part of the palace was arranged on a north–south axis and centred on a huge peristyle courtyard with a fountain. On both sides of this courtyard were the most important rooms: the *Aula Regia* and the *Cenatio Iovis*.

1 ENTRANCE DOORWAY
The northern entrance to the palace opened onto a wide mosaic-decorated square with a portico. This area gave access to both the public and private parts of the palace.

2 LARARIUM
The *lararium* was traditionally the location of the household shrine, but today it is believed that this small room housed a detachment of the Praetorian Guard.

3 AULA REGIA
This hall was the official audience chamber, where ceremonies presided over by the emperor took place. It was an immense room, about 30m (98ft) high.

4 BASILICA
This room was divided by columns into three naves and topped with an apse. It was where the emperor heard legal cases and was the seat of the imperial council.

5 CRIPTOPORTICUS
From the basilica, a stairway gave access to the *criptoporticus*, an underground passageway built by Nero to connect the Domus Aurea with the Palatine.

6 PERISTYLE
The portico of this garden, according to the first-century poet Statius, was formed 'not by a hundred columns but by as many as could shoulder the gods and the sky if Atlas were let off'.

7 CENATIO IOVIS
The southernmost room has usually been identified as the lavish banquet hall of the palace. It was elaborately decorated with an inlaid floor of coloured marble using the *opus sectile* technique.

8 NYMPHAEUM
The dining room was flanked by two *nymphaeums*, with monumental fountains dedicated to nymphs. Oval-shaped, they were once decorated with polychrome marbles.

THE IMPERIAL PALACE
The structures that remain from the Domus Flavia, and above all the intricate underground spaces, allow us to grasp the extraordinary grandeur of the complex. The ruins of the ancient palace of the Caesars are still impressive and, as Pliny the Younger wrote, appropriate 'for a nation that had conquered the world'.

The Agri Decumates and Limes Germanicus

The Agri Decumates was the only region that the Romans conquered and kept in their power on the right bank of the Rhine. It is the triangular area between the River Main and the sources of the Rhine and Danube. The incorporation of this zone, which inserted a dangerous wedge of hostile territory between the provinces of Germania Superior and Raetia, allowed the Romans to considerably reduce the length of the border and the number of troops necessary for its defence. This annexation took place during the reign of the Flavians, especially Domitian. The defence of the Agri Decumates, like the rest of the Limes Germanicus, alternated the positions of great legionary fortresses with small bastions and forts. Continuous walls were also occasionally built. To the right is a reconstruction of a guard tower of the Limes Germanicus in Hessen. On the left is a marble bust of Domitian (Capitoline Museums, Rome).

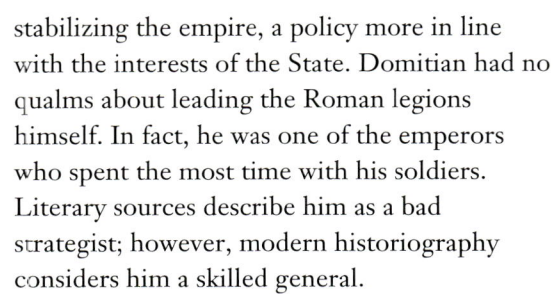

stabilizing the empire, a policy more in line with the interests of the State. Domitian had no qualms about leading the Roman legions himself. In fact, he was one of the emperors who spent the most time with his soldiers. Literary sources describe him as a bad strategist; however, modern historiography considers him a skilled general.

The emperor was aware that one of the pillars of his power was the army, so he strove to keep it happy. One of his greatest successes was raising soldiers' salaries, which had not changed since the reign of Augustus. He moved the Praetorian Guards from 750 to 1000 denarii a year, and the salary of the legionaries from 255 to 300 denarii. The increase also affected the auxiliary troops, with 200 denarii for the cavalrymen and 100 for the infantrymen.

At the beginning of his reign, the territory that required the most attention was the Rhine border, where Domitian undertook campaigns, in 83 and 85, against the Chatti. The objective was not so much the conquest of new lands as to endow the empire with a frontier, the Limes Germanicus, that was solid and with good communications, and would allow the defence of the rich provinces of the interior. Both campaigns concluded successfully and the right bank of the Rhine was pacified. In 83, Domitian granted himself a triumphal procession and the epithet 'Germanicus'.

The need to find a solution for this problematic territory was the result of Augustus's failed project to create the province of Germania Magna with territories on both sides of the Rhine. Thanks to Domitian, the defensive system was definitively established on the river and two regions, Germania Inferior and Germania Superior, were created with a heavily militarized border. Domitian gave them

THE REIGN OF DOMITIAN

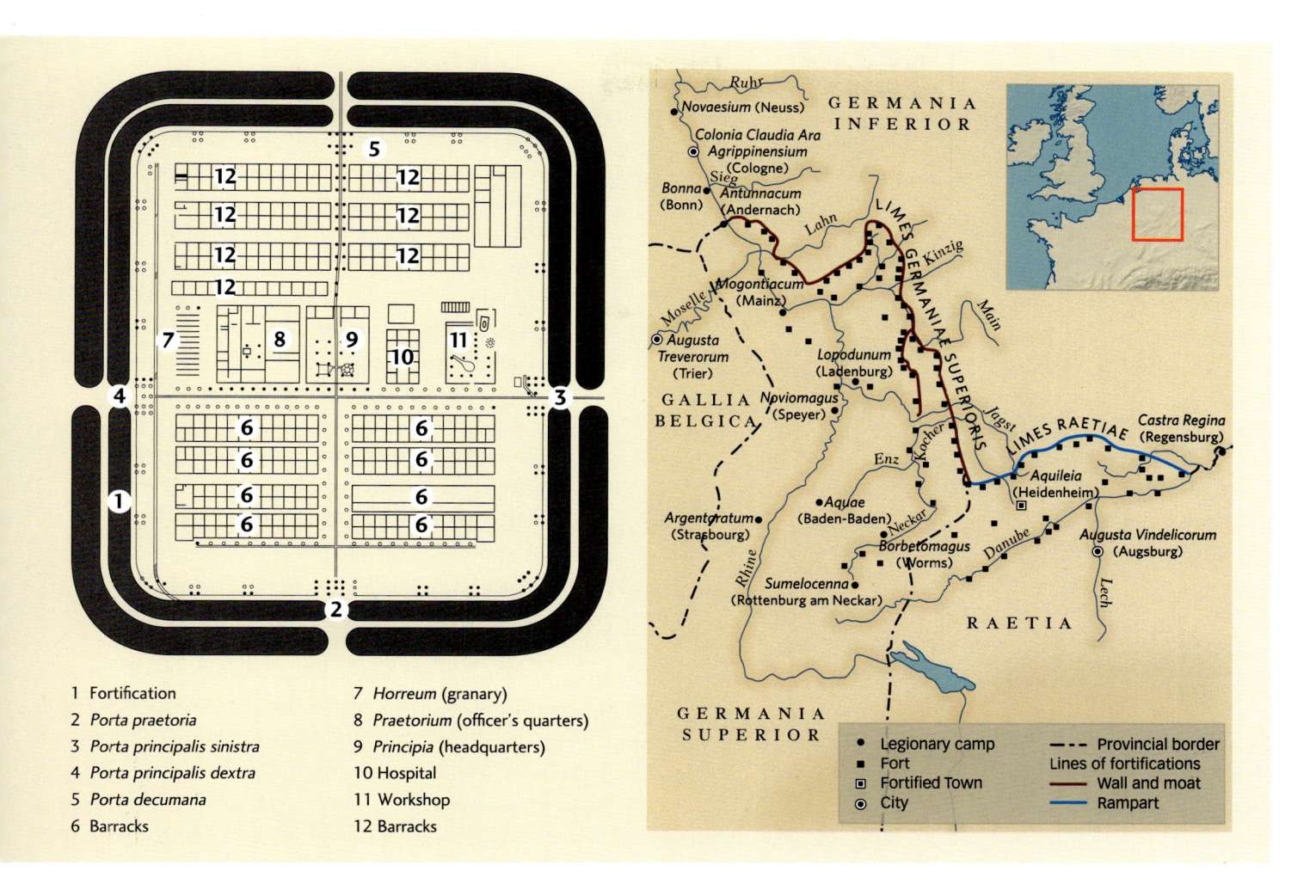

1 Fortification
2 *Porta praetoria*
3 *Porta principalis sinistra*
4 *Porta principalis dextra*
5 *Porta decumana*
6 Barracks
7 *Horreum* (granary)
8 *Praetorium* (officer's quarters)
9 *Principia* (headquarters)
10 Hospital
11 Workshop
12 Barracks

the rank of provinces with capitals in Colonia Claudia Ara Agrippinensium (Cologne) and Mogontiacum (Mainz). The general plan of this frontier was completed with the incorporation of the Agri Decumates region, lying between the Rhine and Danube. A lengthy defensive line was thus formed, running along the Rhine in Germania and linking through the Agri Decumates with the Danube in Raetia. A wide network of roads allowed the easier transfer of legionary columns.

During this period, Julius Agricola continued battling in Britain, an island that cost the empire more than it offered. The peoples of the north, especially the Caledonians, kept up a continuous struggle against the invader, but were defeated in the Battle of Mons Graupius in 84. However, the advances made by Agricola from 78 to 84 could not be consolidated, because he was recalled to Rome. Tacitus states that the decision to halt Agricola's campaign was due to Domitian's jealousy over Agricola's victories. However, the truth is that Britain was a military objective of secondary importance and the army's attention had to be directed to the problematic Danubian border, which was under pressure from the Dacians. In 85, the Roman governor of Moesia, Oppius Sabinus, perished in a Dacian attack. The situation on the Danube was serious enough for Domitian himself to head to the area. The first confrontations were resolved in favour of the Romans. However, shortly after the emperor's departure for Rome to celebrate his triumph, the Dacians once again defeated the commander of the legions, Cornelius Fuscus, which prompted Domitian's rapid return to the theatre of operations, with reinforcements. He reorganized this border region into two provinces, Upper and Lower Moesia.

ROME DOMINATES THE WORLD

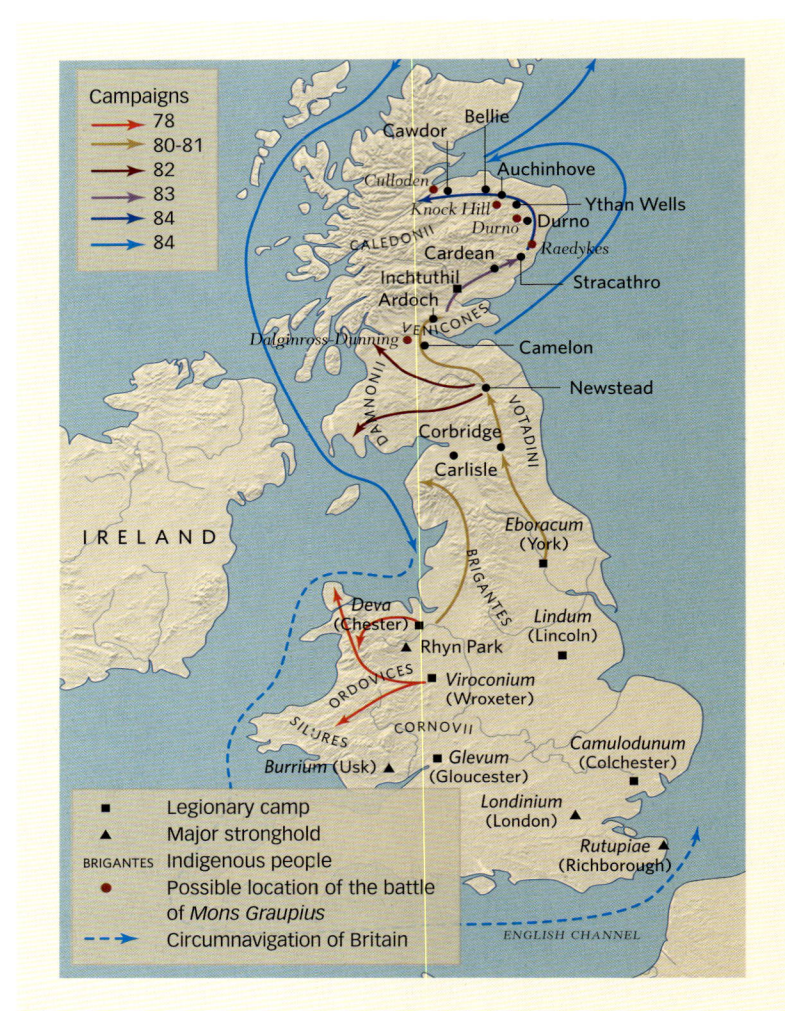

The campaigns of Julius Agricola in Britannia

The campaigns of Julius Agricola are known thanks to the work of his son-in-law, the Roman historian Tacitus. When recalled, Agricola was on the verge of definitively conquering the whole island. However, he helped to pacify Britain more by his capacity for persuasion and diplomacy than his military power. When Julius Agricola arrived in Britannia as governor, in 77, the Ordovices, who occupied the northern part of modern Wales, had revolted. Agricola moved quickly against the tribe, which he defeated and subdued; then, during the following years, he attacked the north of England and the south of modern Scotland. In 84, he faced the fierce Caledonian warriors on Mons Graupius, inflicting a terrible defeat, in which, according to the sources, some 10,000 barbarians were killed. He also ordered the Roman fleet to explore the north coast of the British Isles. Although there is no agreement about the particulars of this naval mission, the general's objective was met, since the insularity of the territory was confirmed.

Domitian's efforts were rewarded by a great victory over the Dacians, who were led by King Decebalus, in the Battle of Tapae in 88. However, he could not take advantage of this success, because there was now a military uprising in Germania led by governor Antonius Saturninus, who added to his legionary forces the support of some local tribes. Although Domitian contained the rebellion, in 89 there were conflicts with the Swabians in Pannonia. Needing his troops elsewhere, in that same year Domitian agreed to peace terms with Decebalus: the Dacian became a client king of the Romans in exchange for 8 million sestertii per year. This measure earned Domitian severe criticism, as well as a blow to the imperial economy, but allowed him to focus on the conflict in Pannonia. The rest of his reign was spent battling on this front, which absorbed most of the legions, although expeditions were sent to Africa, both to Mauretania and to Numidia. The empire's eastern border also received attention, as Domitian continued the fortifications his father had begun.

Economic policies

During his reign, Domitian had to face significant expenses, among them the increase in military salaries, the construction of a fortified border, military campaigns, the payment to the Dacian king Decebalus, beautification of the city of Rome, donations to the people and the organization of celebrations.

To some historians, Domitian did not have any of the answers to the problems of the Roman economy, especially to the expenses for the maintenance of the war machine and to the debts that his brother Titus had incurred. However, others have argued that he left a significant surplus in the imperial coffers. The fact that Nerva had sufficient funds to pay for the ongoing expenses of the empire, and could even lower some taxes, suggests that Domitian was not such a bad financial administrator.

The strength of the Roman economy during Domitian's reign was manifested in the increase in the silver content of the denarius, which was implemented in 82. With this increase, the weight of the coin was equal to that of Augustus's denarius. However, in 85, thanks to the increase in legionaries' salaries, the weight had to be taken down to around that set by Nero in 64, but it was still greater than the standard during the reign of Vespasian.

Everything seems to indicate that 85 was a turning point in imperial economic policy. The increase in expenses caused by military expenditures forced Domitian to modify the currency and look for alternative incomes. New revenues were obtained through a change in the policy regarding confiscations and informers. Confiscations of property became more frequent, and the informers, as had been the case in previous reigns, became the – not always just – instruments for the enrichment of the imperial coffers. Other measures taken by Domitian when he was self-appointed perpetual censor may also have been related to the need for money. Such measures included the application of the laws on luxury, adultery and immorality, which earned significant amounts of money in fines. However, it seems that Domitian's real financial success derived from the personal control he exercised over the Roman economy, his meticulous study of detail and the efficiency with which he collected taxes and governed the provinces.

A good example of the emperor's concern for the correct administration of the empire was his stress on the fact that only the central power could demand taxes. A letter has survived from Domitian to his procurator in Syria, Claudius Athenodorus, telling him to avoid putting pressure on the *provinciales* with burdensome demands. The letter stresses that the provincial cities were exhausted and scarcely meeting the needs of the local population – and, above all, the autocratic prince reserved the power to

DECEBALUS

Carved on Trajan's column, the Dacian ruler is leading his men into a fortress during the Dacian Wars. Below, the victor, Domitian, is pictured on the obverse of a contemporary silver sesterce.

Domitia Longina: accomplice in the assassination?

Domitia Longina was born into an aristocratic family in the middle of the first century. Her father, Domitius Corbulo, was a general under Nero but fell into disgrace and was ordered to commit suicide. Her mother, Cassia Longina, was the last living descendant of Augustus, her ancestor being the emperor's only daughter, Julia the Elder. Domitian fell in love with Domitia and was determined to marry her, even though Vespasian had other ideas and Domitia was already married. The relationship between Domitian and his new wife was not without difficulties, caused fundamentally, according to the surviving testimonies, by the emperor's high libido, which led him to seduce even his own niece. However, the real rift came in 83, when Domitia was accused of adultery and exiled. Her lover was a young actor named Paris, whom Domitian, according to Cassius Dio, murdered with his own hands. Shortly afterwards, the empress was forgiven. Another of her supposed lovers was her brother-in-law Titus, although the ancient authors are not unanimous. The sources point to the empress being an accomplice in Domitian's assassination, although there is no agreement among historians about her guilt. Domitia long outlived her husband, dying between 126 and 130, and was well respected by later emperors. Marble bust of Domitia (Louvre Museum, Paris).

create new taxes. No one should oppress his subjects except himself, because, 'if the farmers are disturbed, the land will remain untilled.'

The *damnatio memoriae*

Domitian's reign was marked by frequent conspiracies that made the emperor increasingly distrustful, as well as severe in his punishments. In 82, he ordered the execution of his first cousin once removed, Titus Flavius Sabinus. According to Suetonius, the execution was prompted because, on the day Flavius Sabinus was appointed consul, 'the herald, by a slip of the tongue, had announced him to the people not as consul, but as emperor', although perhaps the real reason was his marriage to Julia, Domitian's niece and lover. The most important of the conspiracies was the one led by Antonius Saturninus, governor of Germania Superior, in 89. Senatorial opposition was manifested among the philosophers, especially the Stoics, who were expelled from Rome on several occasions. The situation clearly worsened from 93. Historians describe three years of terror during which the slightest suspicion of treason could cost someone their life. The number of informers multiplied, as well as the sentences of death and exile, especially among the Stoics. In 95, Domitian ordered the execution of his first cousin once removed, Flavius Clemens, shortly after he became consul, despite having adopted his children as heirs to the throne.

The feeling that no one was safe led to more intrigue. And supposed conspiracies led to new convictions in a vicious circle of terror. Finally, Domitian's own wife, Domitia Longina, also fearing for her life, joined in with the plot by the prefect of the Praetorian Guard and several freedmen to assassinate him on 18 September 96. We do not know if other senators were involved in the plot, although the speed with which decisions were made after the success of the assassination, as well as the quick rise of Nerva to the throne, suggests that at least the future emperor was aware of the plans.

The last of the conspiracies against Domitian proved the truth of the words that Suetonius attributed to the emperor: 'The lot of princes was very miserable, for no one believed them when they discovered a conspiracy, until they were murdered.' Suetonius, together with Cassius Dio, offers an account of how the assassination played out. The conspirators could not agree on the place or time when they should attack the ruler, who had become extremely wary. The solution was furnished by a steward of Empress Domitia, Stephanus, who had come under suspicion and was in fear for his life. Stephanus pretended for a while to have a wound in his left arm, which forced him to wear a bandage, in which, on the appointed day, he hid a dagger. He asked the emperor for an audience, on the pretext that he had information about a conspiracy. Once admitted to the emperor's room, as Domitian was reading Stephanus's denunciation, the steward stabbed him in the stomach. The emperor hurled himself on Stephanus, while appealing to a young slave to bring the dagger that he always kept under his pillow. The assassins, however, had left no loose ends, because the weapon had disappeared and all the doors were locked. Several guards and gladiators appeared to help finish off Domitian, who was stabbed seven times. He only received a burial thanks to his former nurse, who cremated his corpse and, secretly, deposited the ashes in the Flavian temple in the same urn as the remains of his lover, Julia Flavia.

Now all the factions opposed to the regime were able to step into the open, with a literature intensely critical of Domitian soon developing. The poet Martial was the first to contrast the evils of the prince with the benign governments of his predecessors, even claiming that Domitian's deeds besmirched the memories of his father and brother. For Cassius Dio, Titus's supposed dying words – 'I have only made one mistake' – referred to the election of his successor, Domitian. However, the reactions to Domitian's death were both positive and negative, which attests to the fact that we should not rely only on the accounts of a portion of the Roman aristocracy when it comes to weighing up Domitian's reign.

In general, the members of the Curia rejoiced over the end of the ruler who had been their scourge. Upon hearing of his death, they marched, cheering, to the Senate. In their jubilation, the senators passed *damnatio memoriae* on Domitian, condemning his name to oblivion. They had Domitian's coins and statues melted, his arches torn down and his name erased from all public records. However, the army was much aggrieved by his death and, according to Suetonius, did not rebel only because they lacked a determined leader.

'STADIUM' OF DOMITIAN
Following in the footsteps of his imperial predecessors, Domitian chose to live on the Palatine Hill. The stadium in his Domus Flavia was either a Greek-style construction intended for pedestrian races, or perhaps a private garden built in the shape of a stadium.

■ ROME DOMINATES THE WORLD

Early Christianity

Christianity was born and developed under the Roman Empire. At first it was a small, persecuted religion, but the faith became the empire's sole authorized religion under the emperors of the fourth century.

The history of early Christianity is one of the themes on which a great deal has been written and that has awakened many conflicting opinions. The main reason for this interest is the importance that this religion still has today. However, the religion is also interesting in its historical evolution, going from a minority sect to becoming the ideological sustenance of the empire. Christianity emerged in Palestine under the aegis of the first emperors. Its original teachings derived from the Jewish religion and interpretations of it by a preacher named Jesus of Nazareth. This movement, which was initially limited to the Jewish faithful, managed to survive the martyrdom of its leader. It seems that internal divisions among the original group of followers were there from the start, so there were soon communities of the faithful with doctrinal discrepancies, whose number and diversity did not stop growing. The most successful of the variants, from a historical point of view, was the one that was converted, thanks above

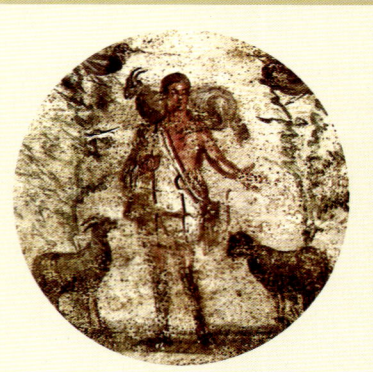

JESUS OF NAZARETH

Images of 'The Good Shepherd' were among the first iconographies of the founder of the Christian religion, Jesus of Nazareth. Some examples are found in Rome's catacombs. Little can be said about the true historical figure, although he has undoubtedly been one of the figures that has received the most attention from historians throughout the eras.

SCENES FROM THE PASSION OF JESUS
This palaeochristian sarcophagus dates from the fourth century and is preserved in the Vatican Museums of Rome.

all to Paul of Tarsus, into a universal religion, deeply Hellenized, that began to gain followers among the polytheist populations of the empire. But many sects remained within Jewish practices: they are the so-called Judeo-Christians, from whose practices the non-Jewish Christians diverged.

These first communities, otherwise diverse, had a minimal internal organization that gravitated, initially, around an apostle, who was soon joined by a group of elders or priests. The churches that were founded subsequently, growing from the preaching outside Palestine, were also endowed with priests or episcopates – literally, inspectors – who were in charge of doctrinal questions, and deacons, who were entrusted with the administration of material matters. It was in the second century, and not synchronously throughout the empire, that bishops emerged, a new position that was at the head of the community and exercised absolute power, with the help of a group of priests and deacons.

The first Christian communities accepted a series of beliefs that separated them from the rest of the Roman subjects, such as the resurrection of the dead, the need to lead a life of chastity and the existence of a single god. This last difference was very important, because it led Christians to abandon the pagan rites practised by their fellow citizens, which they considered sacrilegious, especially animal sacrifices. Their actions led to their being suspected of atheism and of conspiring against the social order, and made them victims of the animosity of the population.

The persecutions
The harassment of Christians was not continuous; nor was it carried out systematically throughout the empire. It was more a matter of specific actions, limited to specific regions, which only rarely became organized attacks in all territories subject to Rome. Such general attacks, which captured the imagination of later Christian Europe, were limited to the third century, under the reigns of emperors such as

THE CHRISTIANS BEFORE THE LIONS
The persecution of Christians during the reign of Nero was recreated in this painting by the English Pre-Raphaelite artist Herbert Schmalz (1856–1935).

Decius, Valerian and Diocletian. This was a time when Christians had increased in number and importance.

The oldest mention is found in Suetonius, who states that in the reign of Claudius, the Jews were expelled from Rome, perhaps for following the teachings of Christ. However, the first definitive mention of a persecution of Christians was after the fire of Rome during the reign of Nero. Tacitus relates that the emperor feared the rumours that blamed him for the fire. To direct suspicions elsewhere, he pointed the finger at Christians, and punished them as the cause of the catastrophe. After this terrible episode, there were frequent persecutions both in Rome and in the East, especially under the reign of Domitian. With Trajan, the question of Christians and their treatment was discussed again; it seems that a norm of action was established that was maintained throughout the rest of the pagan empire, even in the great persecutions of the third century. The information comes from the letters exchanged between Pliny the Younger, then governor in Bithynia-Pontus, and the emperor. In one of them, the author asks the emperor for guidance about what to do with the Christians who had been brought before him. Pliny states that his procedure was to ask the accused if they were Christians. If they said yes, the question was repeated on several occasions; if those questioned did not deny belonging to the religion, they were finally executed. The condemned who enjoyed Roman citizenship were sent to the capital of the empire to be judged there. Those who denied being Christians were subjected to a rapid religious exam, consisting of making offerings to the gods, and the obligation to publicly deny the name of Christ. If they passed the exam, they were released.

Expansion and consolidation

At first, Christianity lacked importance in terms of its number of followers. Estimates of the empire's population in the first century place it at around 60 million, the vast majority being pagans, while some four or five million were Jews. At the end of the first century, the number of Christians was not more than 10,000 and, according to most researchers, did not exceed 200,000 at the beginning of the third century. Christians were, therefore, an insignificant fraction of the emperor's subjects, which explains the scant interest given to this religion.

The social composition of Christian groups also contributed to their going unnoticed. The first Christians were among the most disadvantaged groups. Only occasionally did Christians belong to the empire's urban oligarchies and, even less frequently, to the senatorial aristocracy. This situation changed during the third century, although, even when Christianity received the attention of Constantine and was accepted by Rome, the religion did not have a large following. The religion's growth took place under the Christian emperors of the fourth century, especially under Theodosius the Great.

The Catacombs

In the outskirts of Rome, there is a series of underground complexes in which thousands of people were buried. For a long time it was thought that these catacombs were exclusively Christian cemeteries, but today we know that the reality was more complex: both pagans and Jews used this burial system; in many cases, before the birth of the new religion.

This mode of burial was not practised right across the empire and was mostly concentrated in Rome, although there are also catacombs in Sicily, Malta, Tunisia, Syria and Naples. Many catacombs were mixed, because the beliefs of the first Christians did not force them to bury themselves apart from the rest of the pagan population. Therefore, crucial figures in the religion, like Paul and Peter, shared a place of eternal rest with those of other faiths. This situation changed from the second century, when Christians began to look for their own spaces in which to better attend to their particular funeral rites and ensure that all the faithful, even the poorest, had an appropriate grave. The main differences between Christian and non-Christian catacombs were only in technical details, such as the greater pictorial richness in Christian catacombs. Above, the miracle of the loaves and fishes is depicted in the Roman Catacombs of Priscilla; to the left is the Crypt of the Popes, in the second-century Catacombs of Callixtus.

TRAJAN
Marcus Ulpius Traianus was the first emperor of the Antonine dynasty and also the first of the provincial emperors. This marble bust shows him wearing the civic crown of oak leaves (Bevilacqua Palace, Verona). Shown opposite is a bronze head of Medusa dating from the first century (Museo Nazionale Atestino, Este).

THE 'GOOD EMPERORS'

The reign of Nerva was characterized by good relations between the Senate and the emperor. Trajan, the first emperor from the provinces, continued this positive relationship, which earned him the title *Optimus princeps* ('the best ruler'). During his reign, Roman forces conquered Dacia, the kingdom of the Nabataeans and Mesopotamia. The income from these new lands allowed Trajan to carry out an extensive programme of public works and donations to the people.

In 1776, the English historian Edward Gibbon, in his *History of the Decline and Fall of the Roman Empire*, described the second century: 'If a man were called to fix the period in the history of the world, during which the condition of the human race was most happy and prosperous, he would, without hesitation, name that which elapsed from the death of Domitian to the accession of Commodus. The vast extent of the Roman Empire was governed by absolute power, under the guidance of virtue and wisdom.' It is a period that the writer called the 'Good Emperors' but has also been given other names, such as the 'Adoptive Emperors', because of their manner of ascension to the throne. However, the most frequent term used by historians today is the 'Antonine dynasty', which is used to designate the emperors from Nerva to Commodus. This nomenclature is mainly the work of European writers, who, from Gibbon himself, chose the Emperor

ROME DOMINATES THE WORLD

NERVA
Upon his accession to the throne, Nerva was 65 years old and had dedicated his life to the service of the empire during the reigns of his four predecessors. Marble bust of the emperor (Museo della Civiltà Romana, Rome).

Nerva: Timeline of his reign

Year 96
Ascension to the throne. Nerva is named emperor on 18 September, the same day as Domitian is assassinated.

Year 97
Adoption of Trajan. To ensure a peaceful succession, Nerva adopts the Baetican general of the legions of Germania Superior, Marcus Ulpius Traianus.

Year 98
Death and divinization. On 27 January, Nerva dies and power passes to Trajan.

Antoninus Pius, the third after Nerva, to designate the entire dynasty. Unlike his two predecessors, Antoninus did not come from Hispania Baetica – his family was from Nemausus (Nîmes), in Gallia Narbonensis – and he was the first to use the name Antoninus. Recently, the term 'Ulpian-Aelian dynasty' has been proposed as more in keeping with the facts, since all the emperors who reigned in the second century, from Trajan to Commodus, belonged to one of these families, including Antoninus after being adopted by Hadrian.

Regardless of the term used, this was the period when the Roman Empire was at its most splendid, when the economy prospered, cities grew and multiplied, and the arts developed thanks to stable governments and internal peace, which facilitated trade and improved the quality of life in the Mediterranean. However, grouping all these emperors under one name should not disguise the fact that this was a complex and diverse time, inaugurated by the consensus government of Nerva and ending with the murder of Commodus, the last Aelian.

Nerva's brief reign

When Domitian was assassinated, Marcus Cocceius Nerva immediately ascended to the throne, as had been agreed in advance to avoid the terrible situation, burned into the memory of many Romans, that arose after the death of Nero. The man chosen as emperor by the conspirators was also considered the best candidate by the Senate. Nerva belonged to the Roman nobility. Through a maternal uncle, his family was connected to the Julio-Claudians. This association was immediately reinforced by the commemoration in coins of 'Divus Augustus', the deified first emperor, and was underlined at the end of Nerva's reign with his burial in the Mausoleum of Augustus. Although Nerva held the consulship with Domitian in 90, he was not noted for his services to him. He was even related to senators reprimanded by the regime, which was another argument in his favour. The new Caesar was about to turn 66 and had no children, a circumstance that must also have been very satisfactory for the Curia.

Emperor Nerva and the Transitional Forum

Inaugurated in 97 by Nerva, this forum was actually the work of Domitian, who used this space to improve communications in the centre of Rome, while honouring the goddess Minerva. The Transitional Forum was named for its position between the Forums of Augustus and Caesar and the Temple of Peace, erected by Vespasian, and also because it allowed access from the populous suburb of the Suburra to the Roman Forum. The space between these zones was planned in such a way that the resulting plaza, with an elongated plan (120 x 45m/393 x 148ft), allowed for easy passage. The centrepiece was a temple dedicated to Minerva. Today, little of the square remains, but among the ruins are the columns of the perimeter, joined to the wall by architraves. In the image is a detail of the attic supported by these paired columns, with a high relief of Minerva and scenes of craft activities in the frieze below.

The ruling class was happy, but the city was less so. However, the populace was pleased by the delivery of a monetary gift, as was the custom on any ascension to the throne. Nevertheless, the army, which also received a *donativum* (gift of money), was on the verge of revolt, especially the praetorians. However, the praetorians found themselves short of ringleaders since their two prefects had been involved in the conspiracy against Domitian. The army's unhappiness presented a problem, since Nerva's government needed the support of the legions. To prove the point, there was soon a rebellion among troops on the Rhine. Stability was not achieved until Nerva adopted as his successor to the throne the governor of Germania Superior, Marcus Ulpius Traianus, in October 97, putting him above, according to Cassius Dio, his own relatives. The adoption of Trajan was the culmination of a plan by influential senators of Spanish origin, such as Lucius Julius Ursus Servianus, Lucius Licinius Sura and Quintus Sosius Senecio.

Nerva's short reign was characterized by the propagation of the idea, also taken up by Trajan and his successors, of public liberty. According to Tacitus, who was known for his republican inclinations, the new regime was able to harmonize two concepts that until that moment had remained separate: freedom and the government of the Caesars. In spite of the briefness of his tenure, the emperor undertook some important projects. He is credited with setting up the system of *alimenta*, or funds for the care of poor and orphaned children, which Trajan built on. He also gave back to the Senate many of its privileges, halting treason trials and vowing not to condemn senators to death. Nerva also reduced the tax burden on the poorest Romans.

The emperor died in Rome on 27 January 98. The transfer of power to Trajan was uneventful. A young Spaniard, the future emperor Publius Aelius Hadrianus, who was also in Germania, broke the news of Nerva's death to his first cousin once removed, Trajan. The new emperor did not hurry to the capital. Conscious of the dangerous situation in the Rhineland-Danubian border, he remained on the *limes*. He did not return to Rome until the following year, when he immediately deified Nerva as well as his biological parents.

Optimus princeps

Domitian had been an autocrat who treated senators like any other social group – he was their lord and master. When the members of the Curia did not comply with his orders, he eliminated them without hesitation. However, Domitian was assassinated and the Senate

Emperor Trajan in Dante's *Divine Comedy*

According to a medieval legend, St Gregory the Great, pope of Rome between 590 and 604, saved Trajan from hell with his prayers. The reason for the Christian saint's intercession on behalf of the pagan was an episode when the emperor, during one of his campaigns, stopped to comfort a widow who begged for justice. This anecdote, which the ancient sources actually attributed to Hadrian, served to grant salvation to Trajan. Dante echoed this story in his *Divine Comedy*. In the Italian poet's famous work, Trajan is already redeemed, thanks to the magnanimity he showed to the widow, in the Sixth Heaven or Sphere of Jupiter, devoted to justice. The poet included Trajan, along with four other righteous spirits, in the eyebrow of the mystical eagle, where was written: 'Love justice, you who rule the world.' The 15th-century illuminated manuscript above is a representation of a passage from Dante's *Purgatorio*, in which we see Trajan and the supplicant, as well as those being punished for their pride by being crushed by boulders.

condemned his memory to oblivion and deprived him of the divine status that Titus and Vespasian had received. When Nerva, and then Trajan, ascended the throne, the way in which the emperor related to the Senate changed completely, even though the emperor's powers remained unchanged. Deference and respect took the place of the dislike and contempt of Domitian's rule. Pliny the Younger, in his *Panegyric in Praise of Trajan*, provides numerous examples of this transformation, which, on the one hand, did not undermine imperial power, since 'everything is under the control of only one [the emperor]', but, on the other, restored the senatorial position and privileges, to the point that the emperor swore in public that he would never condemn a member of the Curia to death. In effect, Trajan was a moderate ruler who considered the will of the Senate, treated its members as equals, and offered the highest magistracies and governorships to both former supporters and opponents of Domitian.

In effect, the characteristic that made Trajan the 'best ruler' was his respect for the Senate. For the rest, many of his policies were a continuation of Domitian's. The good opinion of the senators and related social groups was reflected in laudatory writings – such as the works of Pliny the Younger and Cassius Dio – that immortalized his memory to this day. In these sources, Trajan is described as a superb general and skilled administrator, disciplined, firm but fair, and concerned about his people; a tolerant and patient ruler who assumed power as a service to the political community. It was a set of virtues that matched the Stoic model of a good ruler that was to become the benchmark for most of his successors.

The idea that Trajan was a good emperor was forged early on. As early as 103, he was named Optimus princeps, and in 114 he formally adopted the title Optimus ('the best'). For more than a century, successive emperors based their right to the throne on their kinship to Trajan. According to Eutropius, the Senate acclaimed new Caesars with the expression '*Felicior Augusto, Melior Traiano*' ('More fortunate than Augustus, better than Trajan').

ALCÁNTARA BRIDGE
This great structure was built on the orders of Emperor Trajan between 104 and 106. Located on the Tagus River at Alcántara, Spain, the bridge was designed by Caius Julius Lacer. Trajan's public works went beyond Rome and Italy to stimulate the provinces.

Trajan's closeness to the Senate, and public propaganda about his virtues, allowed him to escape the criticism that any other ruler would have received from the ancient historians, given his fondness for wine and boys (Cassius Dio, *Roman History*). He also avoided criticism over the disaster that his megalomaniac campaign against the Parthians was for the Roman army and economy. The prestige enjoyed by Trajan in pagan Rome was so great that it survived into the Christian era. A medieval legend tells us that Pope Gregory the Great (590–604) asked God to forgive Trajan for being a pagan because of his just government. God accepted the papal plea and allowed Trajan to leave purgatory. The success of the medieval legend and Trajan's fame as the best of rulers is attested in Dante's *Divine Comedy*, in which the emperor is described as having been freed from limbo. And this despite the fact that Trajan, in addition to the behaviour attributed to him by Cassius Dio, which was not in accordance with Christian morality, had persecuted Christians, according to Pliny the Younger. This Christianized Trajan was a role model for later kings, especially for the Spanish Habsburgs, who considered him their ancestor.

A provincial leading the empire

Trajan was born in Italica (Santiponce, Seville), in the province of Hispania Baetica, in 53. He was the son of a senator of the same name who had made a career under Nero. Some historians think that Trajan's family origins were entirely among the indigenous Turdetani, following the writings of Eutropius and Cassius Dio; others maintain that his lineage was Italian and the family settled in Italica during the Republic, either around the time of the founding of the settlement by Scipio in 206 BC, or later.

ROME DOMINATES THE WORLD

TRAJAN WEARING IMPERIAL ARMOUR
This marble statue was part of the Borghese collection and is today housed in the Louvre Museum in Paris. Trajan's reputation as a general survived him, yet he was also a great statesman and a philanthropist who cared about the welfare of his citizens.

Whatever the case, the family's origins were not decisive in Trajan's rise to power, as his father held a consulship under Vespasian and served as commander of a legion during the First Jewish–Roman War. He was governor of Syria between 73 and 77, during which time he prevented a Parthian invasion. Later, Traianus the Elder governed Baetica and the province of Asia, one of the empire's richest territories.

The son also held important positions before his adoption by Nerva. He first served beside his father in Syria. While legate of Legion VII *Gemina* in Hispania, he was called on by Domitian to supress the rebellion of Antonius Saturninus on the Rhine. He was consul in 91, and in 97 was governor of Germania Superior, having under his command all the legions stationed in the province.

The career of both great men is testimony to the integration of provincial aristocracies in imperial politics. This integration was the result of the inclusive attitude of the Julio-Claudians, especially Claudius and Nero, who knew how to put to their service the energies that were born in the provinces, creating an aristocracy that stretched beyond Rome and even Italy to encompass the whole Mediterranean. The Flavians continued and accelerated the process. The fact that these new occupants of the Curia could even dominate it is proof of the strength that the provinces had acquired, of their economic development and of the deep Romanization in some Mediterranean regions.

With the Flavians it had become clear that the rank of emperor was not the exclusive prerogative of the noble families of the old Republic. Trajan's arrival on the throne was a further step, as it showed that not only Italy held the empire in its hands, but the most Romanized provinces must also be taken into account. In short, a political community had been formed that shared common cultural features and in which the wealthiest Mediterranean families could participate, regardless of their birthplace. This association of interests was perceived as such in Antiquity.

The Greek Sophist Aelius Aristides said, at the end of the second century, that 'no one worthy of rule or trust remains foreigner, but a civil community of the world has been established as a free Republic under one, the best, ruler and teacher of order'. It can be argued that the creation of a political community of this type was the foundation on which the success of the Roman Empire was based, and what distinguishes it from the imperial powers of modern Europe, who jealously reserved the positions of power for their own elites and prevented the promotion of provincials to the centre of power.

The reforms introduced by Caesar and Augustus transformed the Spanish economy, particularly that of the south, which went from only importing to exporting essential goods to Rome and the rest of the provinces. The exploitation of the mines, the growth of the fishing industry and the production of oil and wine turned local businesspeople into rich provincial aristocrats. In 73 and 74, four of the 14 families from the whole empire that entered the patriciate, the noble class, were from Baetica or had close relations with it. The economic power of the new aristocrats, as well as their extensive political and social connections, explains how the first Baetican tycoon became emperor.

The Dacian Wars

The bas-reliefs on Trajan's column shed much light on Roman military life and warfare. However, they do not provide much useful information for reconstructing the events of the conflict that the monument commemorated. Additional information is very scarce. It is known that the peace agreement between Domitian and King Decebalus of Dacia had left the most conservative and warmongering nucleus of the Roman Senate and army unsatisfied. The payments to the Dacian king were seen as a sign of weakness. Decebalus, according to the preserved sources, was also not happy about the treaty and had begun to conspire with neighbouring tribes to resume the war against the empire.

A TALE OF THE CONQUEST OF DACIA

Among the most famous constructions in Rome is Trajan's Column, a monument about 30m (98ft) high, made up of 20 carved Carrara marble blocks. The work presents around 155 scenes, including 2662 figures, which spiral upwards, relating the campaigns of the last great Roman conqueror, Emperor Trajan, in Dacia. On the death of this 'best of rulers', a chamber at the base of the column was used as a repository for his ashes and those of his wife, Plotina. The column is topped with a statue of St Peter, which occupies the emperor's former position.

AN ETERNAL EXAMPLE
The construction has been a model for other victory columns, such as the Vendôme column, commissioned by Napoleon I in Paris to commemorate French victory at the Battle of Austerlitz, and even Nelson's column in London's Trafalgar Square.

RIVER TRANSPORT
The Danube was the biggest obstacle to seizing Dacian land, but also the best transport route for men and food. Trajan's fleet was made up of *triremes*, with three banks of oars.

A CONQUERED PEOPLE
The majority of the Dacian population was enslaved and distributed throughout the empire. According to Trajan's procurator Criton, 500,000 Dacians were enslaved.

SACRIFICE
Trajan, in travel dress and bare-headed, makes a sacrifice at a garlanded altar to win the favour of the gods. He uses a *patera* (bowl) to pour a libation on the altar's flame.

ROME DOMINATES THE WORLD

The maximum extent of Trajan's empire

Emperor Trajan was the last great Roman conqueror. Under his rule, the empire extended beyond the Danube, incorporated the Nabataean kingdom, and briefly glimpsed the Persian Gulf. This diverse empire covered an area of about 6 million sq km (2.3 million sq miles) and contained between 60 and 100 million inhabitants – almost half the world's population. It was one of the largest and most powerful empires that has ever existed. This huge state was divided into provinces (more than 30 during the reign of Trajan) and was defended by an army of about 400,000 men. However, a surprisingly small number of people participated in the administration of this vast empire, probably about 10,000. On the sesterce below, minted in Rome around 104, is the acronym of the Roman Senate. In the photo on the far right is a reconstruction of the victory monument erected by Trajan in 109 in Tropaensium (Adamclisi, Romania).

Trajan was the first to attack. In 101, he left Rome for the Danube, where he prepared for an assault. He assembled at least 12 legions and numerous auxiliary contingents, as well as the Danubian fleet. Some 100,000 men were ready for combat. He also undertook crucial infrastructural works, such as several roads and a canal to improve river transport.

That same year, Trajan led his army to Dacia, where he won a first victory in Tapae. Decebalus responded by attacking Roman army bases, crossing the Danube and penetrating Moesia, forcing the Romans to come to the rescue of the troops stationed in that province. The legions' rapid intervention frustrated Dacian plans. In 102, Trajan unleashed further hostilities and, after a successful campaign, managed to sign a new treaty with Decebalus on much more advantageous terms. Payments to the Dacian king were stopped and he was forced to demolish several forts and to relinquish part of his territory to Moesia. A permanent garrison of Roman soldiers occupied Sarmizegetusa, the capital of the kingdom. The emperor then commissioned his architect, Apollodorus of Damascus, to build a bridge over the Danube, a colossal work more than 1km (3280ft) long. Trajan returned to Rome and, in December 102, processed through the city in the triumph granted him by the Senate. The epithet 'Dacicus' was added to his name.

However, hostilities resumed in 105 in the conflict known as the Second Dacian War, as a result of Decebalus's dissatisfaction with the harsh conditions imposed on him. The Dacians invaded the border provinces in the spring of 105, but were repulsed. Trajan returned to lead the army, although it was not until 106 that he could execute a plan designed to definitively end the barbarian threat in the Danube region.

THE 'GOOD EMPERORS'

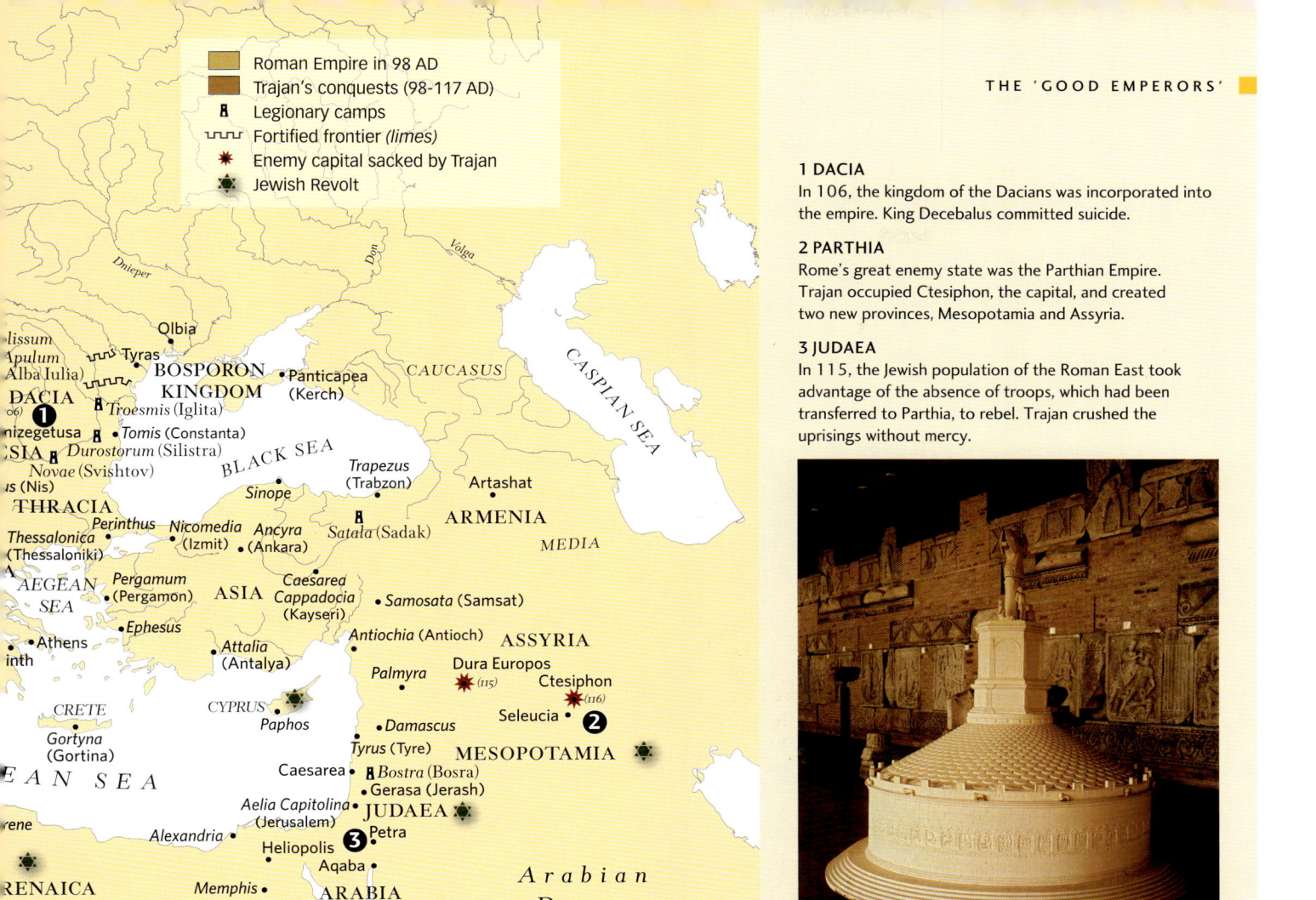

Legend:
- Roman Empire in 98 AD
- Trajan's conquests (98-117 AD)
- Legionary camps
- Fortified frontier (*limes*)
- Enemy capital sacked by Trajan
- Jewish Revolt

1 DACIA
In 106, the kingdom of the Dacians was incorporated into the empire. King Decebalus committed suicide.

2 PARTHIA
Rome's great enemy state was the Parthian Empire. Trajan occupied Ctesiphon, the capital, and created two new provinces, Mesopotamia and Assyria.

3 JUDAEA
In 115, the Jewish population of the Roman East took advantage of the absence of troops, which had been transferred to Parthia, to rebel. Trajan crushed the uprisings without mercy.

This plan consisted of attacking the Dacian capital with two main columns. The first crossed Apollodorus's bridge over the river, while the second advanced through the Aluta Valley. Sarmizegetusa could not endure the two-pronged attack and capitulated.

Decebalus escaped and was pursued. Not wanting to be captured by the Romans, he committed suicide; a courageous gesture that was immortalized by the victors in both Trajan's Column and the coins that were issued in 106 to commemorate the victory. In 107, Trajan was able to return to Rome to celebrate his second triumph over the Dacians. The glory of being a great conqueror and skilful warrior was forever linked to Trajan's name.

The victory brought the incorporation of a vast territory that would also help to maintain peace in the Balkan provinces. To ensure the annexation of the territory, the province of Dacia and a Roman *colonia* were founded. Looting of the territory and the seizure of the royal treasury brought, according to the ancient sources, a total of 165,000kg (363,760lb) of gold and twice as much silver. According to some sources, the Romans took 500,000 slaves. Dacia was rich in gold mines, whose appropriation was undoubtedly one of Rome's first objectives. Although the figures may be exaggerated, it was thanks to the income from this victory that Trajan could afford numerous public works and an immense programme of public munificence. Some historians believe the conflict resulted in the genocide of the indigenous population, with most Dacians killed, enslaved or emigrating. Romanization of the province was so intense that the inhabitants of the region later gave their country the name of the conqueror, Romania; Trajan's name is even invoked with pride in the national anthem.

Trajan's city in Dacia: Colonia Ulpia Traiana Sarmizegetusa

The defeat of King Decebalus brought the annexation of Dacia and its conversion into a Roman province. To secure the territory, a *colonia* was built, its full name Colonia Ulpia Traiana Augusta Dacica Sarmizegetusa, in honour of the emperor who played a leading role in the conquest and in memory of the ancient capital of the subjugated kingdom. Sarmizegetusa is in present-day Romania. The new *colonia* had all the comforts and features of a typical Roman city. It was built close to, but not on the site of, the old Dacian capital, and populated with veterans of the legions. It had an estimated 20,000 inhabitants. Throughout the second century and much of the third, it was the main city of the region, until it was finally abandoned during the reign of Aurelian (270–275). In this century and a half of occupation it was a bulwark of Romanization in a recently conquered land. The forum, basilica, several temples, homes and industrial buildings are partly preserved. In this photograph are the remains of the site's most famous construction, the amphitheatre.

Trajan's government

It is rare for documents about the daily administration of the empire to survive. However, there is a valuable source concerning the reign of Trajan: the correspondence between the emperor and Pliny the Younger while the author was governor of the province of Bithyna-Pontus, in present-day Turkey. This resource allows us to better understand Trajan's conscientious and paternalistic involvement in the empire's administration. All matters could be raised for the emperor's consideration and his answer was decisive, although, in general, it left a wide margin of manoeuvre for provincial governors. The correspondence also points to the continual process of broadening the responsibilities of the imperial bureaucracy. It was now not a matter of enlisting freedmen, as during the Julio-Claudian dynasty, but of an increase in officials of equestrian rank. These equestrian procurators depended solely on the emperor and testify to his increasing power, the gradual diminution of the executive importance of the senators and the desire to create a more effective central and provincial administration.

The empire also benefited from the extensive and continuous construction projects that the emperor commissioned or helped finance, a task for which the enormous Dacian booty was fundamental. For example, several *coloniae* for veterans were founded, such as that of Sarmizegetusa in Dacia; the Colonia Ulpia Traiana (Xanten), in Germania Inferior; and the Colonia Marciana Ulpia Traiana Thamugadi (Timgad), in Numidia.

However, Emperor Trajan was initially occupied with the reconstruction of Italy itself, which had been in a long period of decline. Nerva's *Institutio Alimentaria* was improved (some historians even suggest that it was one of Trajan's innovations). The system consisted of granting mortgages on Italian farms, using money from the public treasury. The beneficiaries of the loans paid five per cent interest into the funds that each municipality created for that purpose. The money was dedicated to the maintenance, including food and education, of the impoverished or orphaned children who were registered in each locality, to whom a fixed amount was given per month. Despite much historical interest in the measure, there is no agreement on its real purpose. Some believe the intention was to increase the birth rate in Italy, to provide manpower both for the army and political institutions, which more and more foreigners were entering. It has also been argued that the intention was purely to improve the living conditions of the most disadvantaged citizens. However, some historians suggest it was just a token of imperial beneficence, spreading the word of the emperor's goodwill.

Italy also benefited from important public works, clearly aimed at stimulating the economy. New roads were built, such as the Via Traiana, which linked Beneventum (Benevento) with Brundisium (Brindisi) and improved communications with Greece and the East. A port was built in Ancona to facilitate access to Rome from the Adriatic Sea, and another in Centumcellae (Civitavecchia). The Arch of Trajan in Benevento is homage to all these efforts by the ruler to improve the peninsula's prosperity and a major piece of political propaganda. The coins minted in the period, in which Trajan raises a kneeling Italia, also publicize the emperor's efforts to improve the peninsula. However, it is interesting to note that, despite minting far more denarii than his predecessors, in 107 Trajan actually decreased the silver purity of the coin.

Important work was also carried out in Rome. Trajan built a new harbour in Ostia, supplementing the one built by Claudius and improving the capital's communications and trade. The hexagonal harbour could berth up to 100 ships. Warehouses were also built along the Tiber. In line with his paternalistic policies

TIMGAD
Located 35km (22 miles) from the city of Batna, in present-day Algeria, Timgad was founded ex nihilo *(from scratch) in 100 AD as a veterans' colony. The city is one of the best examples of the grid plan used in Roman town planning. Veterans of the Parthian War were installed here, rewarded with lands in recognition of their years of service.*

THE PLUTEI OF TRAJAN: TESTAMENTS TO THE RULER'S GENEROSITY

There is no agreement among historians regarding the protagonist of the Plutei Traiani (also known as the Anaglypha), the carved stone balustrades that today are on display in the Curia Julia. Some believe that the works commemorate the emperor Trajan's *alimenta*; for others, however, the events depicted took place in the reign of Hadrian. The faces of the figures have been systematically destroyed, which makes it difficult to decide between the different interpretations. However, the works show how much the emperors of this period wanted to be seen as magnanimous by their people. The upper scene depicts the burning of the citizens' debt records. In the lower scene, the emperor institutes the *alimenta*, a charitable system for feeding orphans and other needy children.

1 STATUE OF MARSYAS
Placed in the Forum Romanum in the third century BC when fines were imposed on usurers, the statue symbolized freedom from the slavery of debt.

2 SERVANTS
A group of imperial servants carries the registers of the debts contracted by the citizens so that they can be destroyed.

3 RECORDS
The debt records are piled on a pyre to be burned in front of the plebeians and senators, who watch the event closely.

4 TEMPLES
The buildings depicted are the Temples of Saturn and of Vespasian and Titus, in the Forum Romanum, next to the Capitol.

5 TRAJAN
The emperor addresses the people from the speakers' platform to announce the development of the *alimenta*.

6 FORUM ROMANUM
The buildings are those of the Forum Romanum: the Arch of Augustus, the Temple of Castor and Pollux and the arches of the Basilica Julia.

7 ALIMENTA
Trajan sits on a podium accompanied by the personification of Italy holding a child in her arms, demonstrating his care for the poor children of Italy.

8 *FICUS RUMINALIS*
According to legend, it was under this fig tree, possibly recreated in the Forum as a statue, that Romulus and Remus arrived and were suckled by the she-wolf.

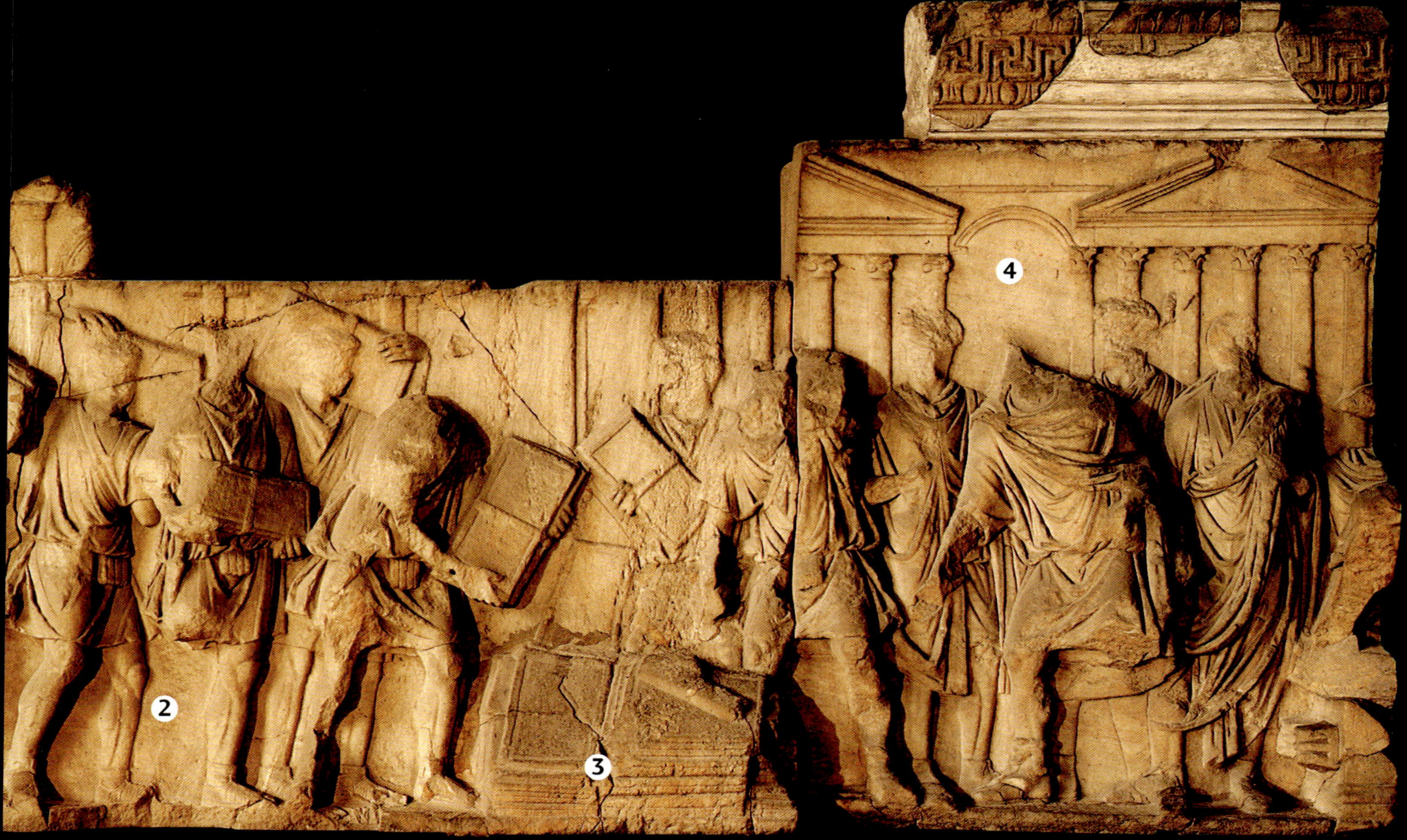
2
3
4

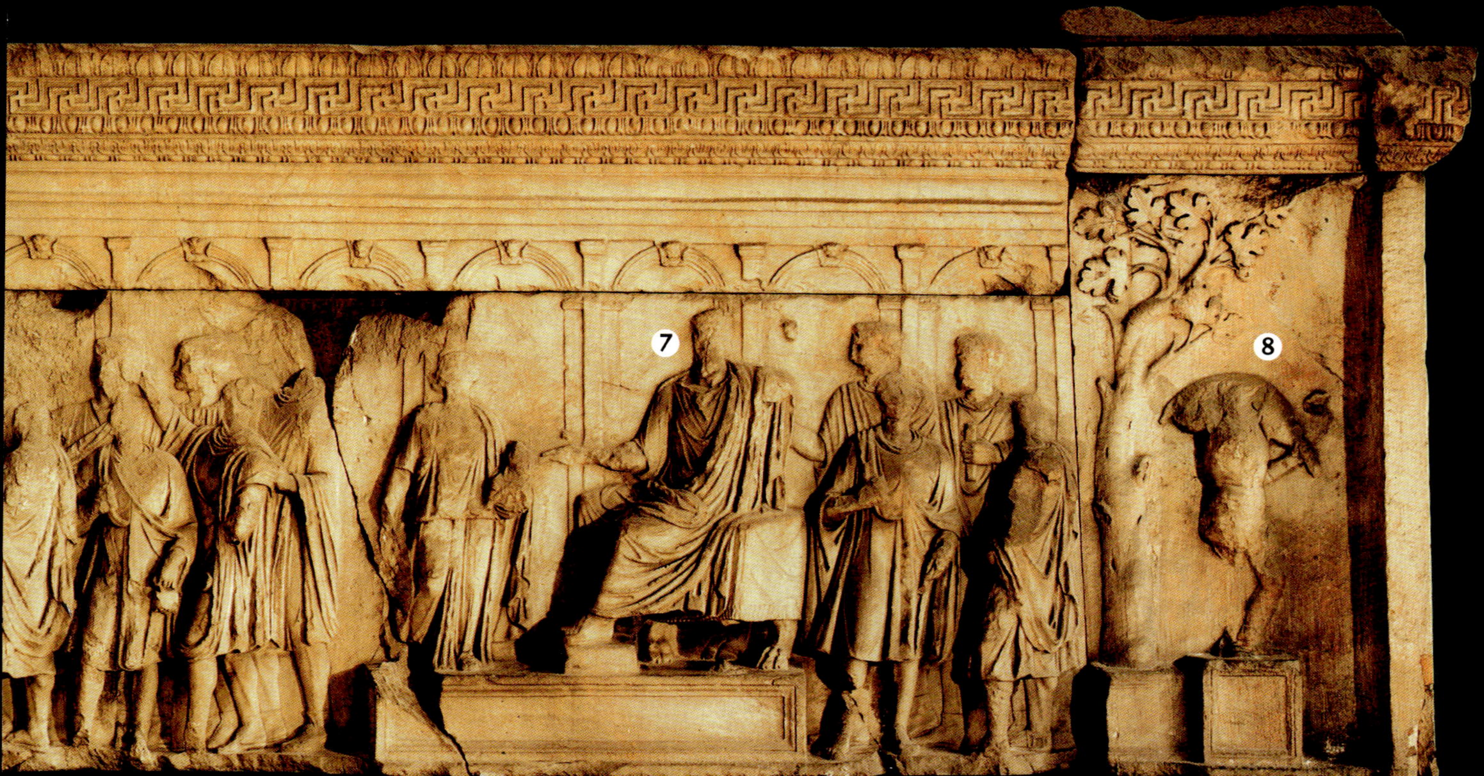
7
8

A basilica instead of a temple: the novelty of Trajan's Forum

The Forum of Trajan marked a profound departure in Rome's urban planning. Its size (300 x 185m/984 x 607ft) exceeded that of the rest of the imperial forums put together. Trajan's own column testifies to the magnitude of the work, especially the earth removal that was entailed: as explained by the inscription on the column's base, its height, about 30m (98ft), was the same as that of the hill that previously rose in this spot. This forum became the political, economic and administrative epicentre of the city.

The architect Apollodorus of Damascus, who built the bridge over the Danube for the military invasion of Dacia, was commissioned to design the square. Its design, very different from that of previous forums, was intended to echo that of a military camp. As in a legionary barracks, the open plaza was closed across its front by a basilica. The basilica of the Forum of Trajan, or Basilica Ulpia, takes its name from the dynasty of Emperor Marcus Ulpius Traianus. It was the largest ever built in Rome, about 60m (197ft) wide with a maximum length of 170m (558ft). Inside, four rows of colossal columns created five naves. Reminiscent of the layout of a military camp was the position of the two libraries that flanked Trajan's column (one contained documents in Latin; the other documents in Greek), located to the north of the basilica, in the same place occupied by the archives in military camps. Finally, the column was located where the sanctuary was usually placed with the legionary insignia. Under Hadrian, the link with the military plaza was loosened by the erection, in 121, of a temple to the deified Trajan. This brought the forum closer to the traditional model of other imperial forums. This illustration of the Basilica Ulpia is by Peter Connolly.

across the peninsula, he also gave a determined boost to the institutions dedicated to feeding the people, especially those that dealt with the free distribution of grain. To facilitate this, Trajan granted privileges to the miller-bakers and corn traders – *negotiatores* and *navicularii* – who worked for the State, resuming a policy that had been inaugurated by Claudius.

In addition, several donations (*congiaria*) were made to the Roman populace to celebrate the successes of the regime. In 99 and 102, 75 denarii were given per person. In 107, after victory in the Second Dacian War, 500 denarii were given to each citizen. Trajan also arranged lavish celebrations during which gifts, monetary or in kind, were combined with gladiatorial games, races and all kinds of shows. According to Cassius Dio, on his return to Rome after the conquest of Dacia, Trajan organized 123 days of festivities during which 10,000 gladiators fought and 11,000 wild animals were killed.

Trajan's care over the grain supply for Rome and the whole peninsula, together with the many festivities, large constructions and donations to the populace, seems to have made him popular among the Roman populace, not only among the senatorial oligarchy, in as much as we can determine this from the preserved sources. His military campaigns, especially the conquest of Dacia, provided the necessary additional resources. A list of just some of the projects begun after the Dacian campaign is extraordinary. In 109, there were the Baths of Trajan, his *naumachia* basin and the Aqua Traiana aqueduct, which supplied water to Rome. In 112 and 113, the centre of Rome saw the inauguration of Trajan's Forum, the Basilica Ulpia, Trajan's Column, with its famous scenes of Dacian victories, and the Temple of Venus in the Forum of Caesar. Also during this period were large infrastructural works in Italy, especially road-building, and the ports of Ancona and Ostia. If the extraordinary festivities mentioned above and the grain donations are added to all this construction activity, we can begin to see the magnitude of the financial effort made by Trajan in a very short period.

Finally, it must be stressed that the enormity of the tasks completed by the emperor are clearly the manifestation of an autocratic power, in which respect Nerva's successor was, in essence, continuing the policy of the Flavians, in particular of the hated Domitian. This ambivalence in Trajan's government, the discrepancy between the all-powerful Caesar and the political aspirations of the senatorial class, anchored in the republican ideal, was not exclusive to his reign, but rather derives from the nature of the political system created by Augustus. The tension between monarchy and republic created the power struggles that took place during the reigns of Nero and Domitian. Trajan, however, thanks to his skilful political management in Rome and, above all, thanks to his strict observance of traditional forms in his relationship with the Senate, which allowed its members to maintain their dignity, as well as a successful military career, was able to maintain this difficult balance and thus put all the forces of the Roman State behind achieving the political objectives that he had set himself. However, this complex harmony, which largely accounts for the achievements of an entire era, would be destoyed once more with the next ruler, Hadrian.

The Parthian War

The cause of the Parthian War was a disagreement over who should occupy the throne of Armenia, a state over which the Romans and Parthians shared hegemony. Each power had its own candidate and both refused to yield to the other. As a result, the treaty signed by Nero in 63 was broken. Trajan arrived in Antioch (in Turkey) in early 114 and began to prepare for what promised to be his most important campaign.

TRAJAN'S MARKET
This market, the world's first covered shopping mall, was constructed next to Trajan's Forum between 101 and 110 by the architect Apollodorus of Damascus. The market had six levels: the three lower ones were occupied by tabernae selling oil, bread, fruit and other food products; the upper levels were for offices.

ROME DOMINATES THE WORLD

Trajan's spoils of war and Decebalus's plan

Trajan was the Roman Empire's last great conqueror. The huge booty that he seized with his victories was used to fund vast public works and donations. The exact amount of plunder that Trajan took from Dacia is unknown. Historians think he was able to seize 165,000kg (363,760lb) of gold and 330,000kg (727,525lb) of silver, an unimaginable fortune at the time. It seems that Decebalus wanted to prevent his fortune from falling into the hands of the Roman victors. In attempting to do so, he diverted the course of the Sargetia River, which passes near Sarmizegetusa, and buried the riches of the Dacian monarchy in its bed. Once the treasure was buried, the river was returned to its original route. The king's stratagem was discovered by a comrade of the defeated leader, who told the secret to the invaders. However, excavations carried out in the capital of the Dacian kingdom have uncovered several hidden treasures, about 700kg (1543lb) of gold in total, which suggests that part of the city's wealth could have been hidden from the grasping Romans. The photograph to the right shows a detail from Trajan's column, depicting a confrontation between Roman legionaries and Dacian soldiers. On the left is an aureus of Trajan.

This was not the first time the emperor had taken an interest in the East. Between 105 and 106, in order to consolidate the southern frontiers of the empire, the Nabataean kingdom, known for the rock-cut architecture of its capital, Petra, had been annexed. This territory, along with regions further north, became part of a new province called Arabia Petraea, with its capital in Bostra. A fortified border was built from Damascus to the Gulf of Aqaba. The canal that linked the Nile with the Red Sea was also renovated to facilitate the empire's trade with Arabia and India.

To attack the Parthian Empire, Trajan gathered a large army from all over the East and the Danube. Historians disagree about what benefits the emperor hoped to gain from the conflict. For some, the victory would allow control over the trade routes with the Far East and stabilize the empire's eastern border, thus concluding the campaigns begun in Arabia Petraea. However, there are sources, such as Cassius Dio, who suggest an additional factor: the *aemulatio Alexandri*, the desire to imitate the conquests of Alexander the Great, acquiring fame through world domination. According to these sources, the conflict could have been resolved diplomatically, but the disagreement provided Trajan with an excuse to initiate hostilities. It is said that, when Trajan arrived in the Persian Gulf and saw a ship leaving for India, he expressed regret at not being young enough to follow in Alexander's footsteps. According to another anecdote, his respect for Alexander led him to make sacrifices in his honour in the room of the Babylonian palace where he died. But it is not necessary to distinguish between the two motives: Trajan's desire for glory could be accompanied by geopolitical and economic objectives.

The attack by Roman forces began in the spring of 114 with an offensive in Armenia. During the following two years, Trajan conquered that entire region and penetrated into Mesopotamia, where he took control, through battles and pacts, of the territory west of the city of Dura-Europos (in Syria). In 116, the Senate granted him the title 'Parthicus', and coins were minted to celebrate the new provinces of Armenia and Mesopotamia. That same spring, Trajan's army resumed operations to the south and occupied the great Parthian cities of Seleucia, Ctesiphon and Babylon.

Shortly after, concluding his rapid conquest, the emperor reached the Persian Gulf. Rome celebrated the victories, and the Curia granted Trajan new honours, including the erection of a triumphal arch. However, the problems began almost immediately. The regions that had submitted to the Parthians revolted against the Roman garrisons. The Parthian army arrived from Media to join the conflict and, although the fighting was not decisive, Rome's control over the area began to crack. An additional difficulty reared its head: taking advantage of the absence of troops, the Jewish populations of Cyrenaica, Egypt, Cyprus, Syria, Judaea and Mesopotamia rebelled, forcing a large part of the army to head for the Levant.

Trajan recognized the impossibility of keeping hold of all his conquests, so he tried to secure those territories that could be defended with relative ease. To maintain the appearance of victory, he crowned Parthamaspates, a Parthian prince, as a client king in Ctesiphon. He gave him all the territories south of Dura-Europos. Tired of the conflict and growing ill, Trajan set off for Rome. On the way, in Selinus (Gazipasa) in Cilicia, Trajan died at the beginning of August 117.

HADRIAN'S WALL
This photograph of the Roman Empire's northernmost border was taken from Vercovicium, today known as the Roman fort of Housesteads, in present-day Northumberland. On the opposite page is a detail of the mosaics that adorn the Academy of Hadrian's Villa in Tivoli, dating from the second century (Capitoline Museums, Rome).

THE TRAVELLING EMPEROR

In contrast with Trajan's military expansion, Hadrian's focus was on the development of the empire's interior. To achieve this goal, he travelled through most of the provinces, becoming directly involved in the government and progress of the peoples subject to Rome. He also devoted himself to improving imperial administration and law. He built great frontier walls that separated civilization from the barbarous enemy on the other side.

When Trajan died in 117, he had no legitimate children and had not indicated with clarity who was to succeed him. Numerous rumours circulated, such as the possibility that Trajan had chosen Neratius Priscus or Lusius Quietus, two influential senators, or even that he had drawn up a list of candidates for the Senate to elect the next ruler. The official version of the succession was, however, very different. According to this version, the emperor had adopted Hadrian shortly before dying in Cilicia, on his way back to Rome. A written adoption document, as well as the word of Plotina, Trajan's wife, and the prefect of the Praetorian Guard, Acilius Attianus, who were both present in Cilicia, were proof of the last wish of the dying Caesar. The news of the adoption and the subsequent death of Trajan arrived with Hadrian, who was in Syria, almost simultaneously, perhaps on 9 August. Shortly afterwards, on 11 August,

ROME DOMINATES THE WORLD

HADRIAN'S REIGN: A TIMELINE

Year 117
Takes power. After Trajan's death in Cilicia, on his way back to Rome from Mesopotamia, Hadrian is acclaimed emperor in Syria.

Years 121–125
Hadrian's first journey. In the spring of 121, Hadrian leaves Rome to travel through part of his domains, from Britannia to the Black Sea.

Years 128–132
Hadrian's second journey. This trip focuses on the eastern part of the empire and leads to the founding of the Aelia Capitolina colony in Jerusalem.

Years 131–132
Founding of the Panhellenion. During his second journey, Hadrian attends the inauguration of this new Greek institution, a league of Hellenic cities, which is based in Athens.

Years 132–135
Bar Kokhba revolt. The last of the Jewish rebellions breaks out when the emperor is in the East. When the revolt is finally suppressed, the Jewish population of Judaea is devastated.

Year 138
Adoption of Antoninus Pius. In February, Hadrian adopts his successor. In July, the emperor dies in his villa at Tivoli.

Hadrian was acclaimed by his army, the most powerful of the time. Plotina wrote to the Senate reporting what had happened, and accompanied her husband's remains to Rome. Hadrian also sent letters, in his case apologizing for not having waited for the approval of the Curia before letting his troops acclaim him.

However, the official version of events was already doubted by contemporaries. In his *Roman History*, the historian Cassius Dio wrote that the empress was in love with Hadrian, which led her to falsify the adoption. In addition, Trajan's death was hidden for a few days, with the connivance of Acilius Attianus, so that the adoption could be announced before the death. The relative proximity of Hadrian and his army did the rest.

The sources that are available for reconstructing the course of events do not allow us to be conclusive. There are many indications that Trajan's wish was to be succeeded by Hadrian, which is irrespective of the fact that, because of the speed of the emperor's illness on his journey back to Rome, a hasty adoption or falsification after his death was necessary. Hadrian was Trajan's closest male relative, his first cousin once removed, and he had married Vibia Sabina, Trajan's great-niece. Like the emperor, he came from a family from Italica, in southern Spain. Hadrian's ancestors had probably reached the Iberian peninsula from the Piceno region of Italy some time in the republican era. After the death of Hadrian's father, in 86, when he was 10, he became the ward of Trajan and Acilius Attianus. The future emperor had accompanied Trajan throughout his life and was his quaestor (administrator). He participated in key military campaigns, such as the two Dacian Wars, during which he was decorated for bravery, and the Parthian War. Finally, a compelling reason to justify his accession is that, when Trajan was taken ill in Mesopotamia and left for Rome, he asked Hadrian to assume power over the region as general commander of the eastern army.

The supposed irregularities of the adoption, together with Hadrian's changes in imperial policy, made the beginning of his reign difficult. In 117, shortly after the arrival in Rome of Acilius Attianus, four senators, including Lusius Quietus, were convicted *in absentia* of conspiracy against the emperor, hunted down and killed. According to the ancient sources, their only fault was being too rich and influential. In this way, the new emperor silenced the voices opposed to his government. However, Hadrian, who was still in Syria during these trials and executions, blamed them on Attianus's excessive zeal. Relations with the Senate were clouded, and they never recovered. The period of peace between the Curia and the emperor was broken, even though Hadrian's general behaviour was not too different from Trajan's.

Building walls

The construction of Hadrian's Wall in Britain is the best testimony to his change in the

---

Hadrian's Wall: fortifying the *limes*

In northern England, Hadrian's Wall travels more than 119km (74 miles), from the North Sea to the Irish Sea. It was built to protect the British peoples from the attacks of the Picts to the north. A causeway along the wall facilitated the transport of troops and supplies; the construction of a bridge over the Tyne, where Newcastle now stands, markedly improved communications. Along the wall, palisades of wood and earth alternated with stone walls that were in places 5m high and 3m wide (16 by 10ft). Every 1.5km (1 mile), a fortified gate allowed the transit of civilians and soldiers. Troops were stationed in 15 forts attached to the wall, many of which became towns, as well as in nearby camps. Surveillance towers were built every 500m (1640ft). The defences were completed with a ditch 8m (26ft) wide. It took more than ten years to finish the works, which began during Hadrian's trip to Britannia in 122.

THE TRAVELLING EMPEROR

1 HADRIAN'S WALL
The wall ran along the perimeter of the fort itself, thereby improving the defence of both.

2 THE CAMP
It had a principia, praetorium, hospital and stores, which made it an almost independent entity.

3 THE LATRINES
These had running water, supplied by rainwater collection, and are one of the best-preserved areas in the fort of Vercovicium.

4 CIVILIAN SETTLEMENT
This was next to the fort's wall, on its southern side. Only a few vestiges remain. The settlement was at its largest in the third century.

THE FORT OF VERCOVICIUM. *This was one of the 15 forts along Hadrian's wall in which legionaries were stationed. Once home to about 800 soldiers, it is one of the best-preserved Roman forts.*

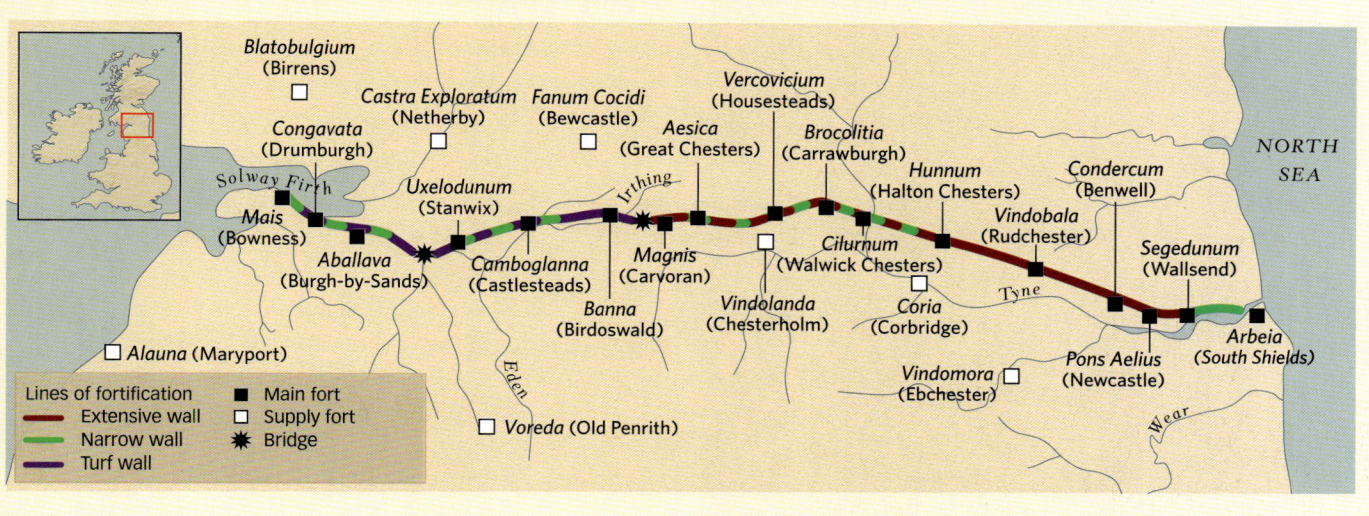

direction of foreign policy. However, this wall was just one example of a strategy aimed at turning away from conquest and towards strengthening existing borders as a preliminary step to improving Roman life. Similar measures were introduced along the Rhine and Danube borders in 121, as well as, later, in Africa and the East. The empire closed its borders and, in this way, as the *Augustan History* affirms, it drew the line between civilization and barbarism. It was a novelty that surprised the world. In the words of the Greek Aelius Aristides: 'To place the walls around Rome itself as if you were hiding her or fleeing from your subjects you considered ignoble and inconsistent with the rest of your concept, as if a master were to show fear of his own slaves. Nevertheless, you did not forget walls, but these you placed around the empire, not the city ... Beyond the outermost ring of the civilized world, you drew a second line, quite as one does in walling a town, more widely curved and easily guarded ... An encamped army encloses the civilized world like a rampart.' A faction of the Roman aristocracy was against this policy, which seemed to many an act of cowardice that announced the end of the idea of Rome as an empire without limits. Perhaps it was this disaffection that provoked the rapid execution of the four senators. However, this new policy should not be seen as the decision of a pacifist philanthropist: Hadrian was a seasoned military man. There were numerous occasions when the emperor presented himself wearing the complete military panoply both in statues and coins, never forgetting this facet of his position at the head of the State. The *Augustan History* compares him to the great generals of the Republic, such as Scipio Africanus, and his own adoptive father, Trajan, especially in the way he

AUREUS OF HADRIAN
On the obverse of this gold coin, Hadrian is shown with a firm profile and a full beard, which he apparently grew to hide his facial imperfections or blemishes. Around his head are the laurels of the Roman emperor.

No pacifist: Hadrian's military career

His love for Greek letters and his decision to abandon wars of conquest have marked Hadrian down in history as a benevolent and even pacifist prince. However, this is a distortion of his true character, as the emperor led an active military life. Calling an end to the expansion of the empire was a strategic decision and not the result of an anti-war policy. When he took power, Hadrian was a military veteran. His career began in 95, when he was 19 years old, as a military tribune in Pannonia, in the city of Aquincum, on the site of modern Budapest. He later served as a tribune in Moesia, in 96, and in Germania Inferior, in 97. There are no precedents for a man of senatorial rank occupying the post of tribune in three different legions. Alongside Trajan, Hadrian fought in the Dacian Wars (101–102 and 105–106) and the Parthian War, battling in Armenia and Mesopotamia. To this war experience we must add the years of government of border provinces, such as Pannonia Inferior and Syria.

THE CIVIC CROWN
During the republican era, this crown of braided oak leaves was a military decoration, given for saving a Roman citizen on the battlefield. From Augustus's time, it became a typical attribute of the emperors.

THE BREASTPLATE
A typical motif of the reign of Hadrian decorates his breastplate: the goddess Athena is standing on the Capitoline she-wolf, which is depicted with Romulus and Remus, while two victories crown the goddess. It is a symbol of Hadrian's desire to unite Greece and Rome.

THE DEFEATED ENEMY
The general's pose, trampling on the vanquished, is typical of ancient art and was frequently used by the Romans.

---

shared the soldiers' hardships: he ate the usual rations, participated in training and slept in a regular tent like any other legionary.

Hadrian also paid great attention to the reorganization of the army that needed to accompany his reforms at the borders. As the army moved from being an offensive to a defensive weapon, he needed to maintain strict discipline. To create an iron order, Hadrian deified Disciplina, who was to be worshipped in military barracks. He also forced soldiers to live in the camps. Yet he also in some ways softened the life of legionaries, since he allowed their children to inherit, even though Roman soldiers were forbidden to marry and, therefore, have legitimate children. Perhaps with this measure he aimed to make the army more attractive and to improve recruitment.

Hadrian began to apply these rules as soon as he came to power and continued to set out his dictates during his numerous trips through the empire. Thus, in 118, after putting the army on a firm footing in Syria, and before even returning to Rome, he toured the Danube and Rhine borders, looking into training and strengthening positions. The most significant artefact that reveals Hadrian's military concerns is the inscription found in Lambaesis, in what is now Algeria, which includes the words he addressed to the soldiers during his stay in that military camp. He exhorted them to train daily in the handling of weapons, the construction of fortifications and physical exercise, including running, jumping and marching. According to the *Augustan History*, Hadrian 'trained his soldiers as if there were an impending war'. It is also worth pointing out that Hadrian's change in military policy also energized the border regions thanks to the economic and cultural contact that resulted from the continued presence of large contingents of troops.

Hadrian's travels

The move from conquest to strengthening the borders was fundamental to Hadrian's desire to drive the empire's progress. This was an aim that he carried out through diverse actions, from his continuous preoccupation with the application of the law and the enormous correspondence he maintained with his subjects to his inexhaustible construction activity and travels. Hadrian was a travelling emperor, who passed through most provinces and knew first hand the problems of his subjects, to whom he offered help when necessary. According to Cassius Dio, 'he visited many cities, more than any other emperor, building in some aqueducts and ports, giving others wheat, public works, money and honours.'

A reconstruction of Hadrian's great journeys has been carried out through the meticulous study of literary, numismatic and epigraphic sources. However, there is no agreement on the exact itinerary of the emperor and his delegation. Leaving aside the details, the emperor's pilgrimage through his domains continued to surprise his subjects, although it did not always make them envious, as verses by the poet Florus prove: 'I do not want to be an emperor, to tramp round the Britons, and suffer the cold of Scythia'. To which his friend Hadrian replied: 'I do not want to be Florus, to tramp round taverns, and suffer the food of the wine shops, and be bitten to pieces by fleas.'

In the spring of 121, Hadrian left Rome and probably did not return until the summer of 125. During this period, he toured the provinces of the Rhine and Danube, reached the north of Britannia, where he busied himself with the wall that bears his name, then went to Hispania through Gaul and perhaps later toured North Africa on the way to Asia Minor and the Black Sea. It is possible that it was during this time that he met Antinous, the young man who would accompany him on all his trips until he died in mysterious circumstances on the Nile, after which he was divinized by the emperor.

HADRIAN'S VILLA
Built as a retreat (it was said that Hadrian detested the Palatine Hill palace), this villa in Tivoli was where the emperor lived the last years of his life, ruling the empire from its precincts. The villa was able to house the whole court and was kept in communication with Rome through an efficient postal service.

ROME DOMINATES THE WORLD

HADRIAN'S TRAVELS AROUND THE ROMAN WORLD

Many Roman emperors had travelled through the empire before Hadrian: Augustus, Claudius, Nero, Domitian and Trajan. However, all of them, except Nero, with his cultural pilgrimage to Greece, did so to annexe new territories. Hadrian also paid attention to military matters, especially in his first great journey, made between 121 and 125. However, his focus was on the maintenance of legionary discipline and the strengthening of borders, as he was concerned with defence rather than expansion. This emperor was driven to travel for reasons very different from those of his predecessors: he was keen to learn more about his domains, especially the Greek Mediterranean; improve the management of his vast empire; and implement a policy of – and a passion for – construction that led him to fill the empire's cities with beautiful buildings and to provide them with infrastructures that would improve the daily life of their inhabitants.

THE PHILOSOPHER'S BEARD
Hadrian was the first emperor who allowed himself to grow a beard, a style that brought him closer to the Hellenic world, since a beard was typically worn by the Greek philosophers. His decision became a fashion that was soon adopted by all Roman social classes (Museo Nazionale Romano, Rome).

1 BRITANNIA
In 122, Hadrian arrived at the northern border of his empire and built the wall that bears his name to separate the Romans from the barbarians.

The Travels of Hadrian

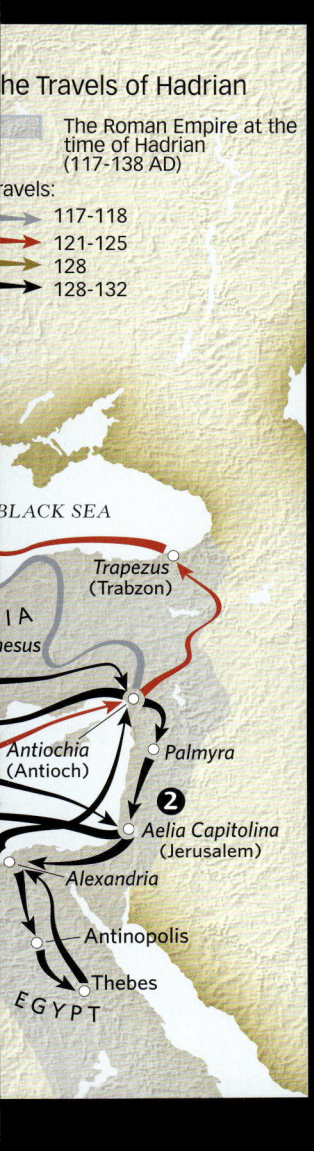

The Roman Empire at the time of Hadrian (117-138 AD)

Travels:
- 117-118
- 121-125
- 128
- 128-132

(Map shows locations including Black Sea, Trapezus (Trabzon), Antiochia (Antioch), Palmyra, Aelia Capitolina (Jerusalem), Alexandria, Antinopolis, Thebes, Egypt)

2 JUDAEA
The emperor visited Jerusalem in 130, when he founded a colony, Aelia Capitolina, on the site of the old city, which was in ruins.

3 ATHENS
This city was the one that received the most gifts from Hadrian and to which he returned most frequently both before and after his accession to the throne. Here he built many public buildings, plus an aqueduct.

HADRIAN'S PASSION FOR CONSTRUCTION

Hadrian's abandonment of conquests brought a long period of peace and prosperity to the empire. This, along with the emperor's passion for art and architecture, made this era one of the most prolific in the history of Roman building. In addition to the magnificent buildings Hadrian financed in Rome, he took advantage of his trips to undertake numerous projects, from the forum and basilica of Londinium (London) and Ratae Corieltauvorum (Leicester) in Britannia, to the elegant buildings of Gerasa, in present-day Jordan. Roads and aqueducts were also built, and numerous buildings left unfinished by previous rulers were completed. Some cities received special attention, such as Italica, in Spain, where an immense temple was built in honour of Trajan, and Athens, which saw the Temple of Olympian Zeus completed, as well as the new Hadrian's Library.

HADRIAN'S ARCHITECTURAL LEGACY
At the top is the remains of the Temple of Hadrian in Ephesus, with its famous semicircular entablature. Directly above is the Arch of Hadrian in Gerasa, one of the city's most remarkable monuments, built to commemorate the emperor's visit in the year 130. The colossal construction measures 25m (82ft) in width and more than 20m (66ft) in height.

Antinous: Hadrian's favourite

Antinous was originally from Bithynia, in present-day Turkey. He was born around 110 and joined the court of Emperor Hadrian when he was still very young, perhaps during the first great journey that the ruler made to Asia in 123. The emperor was captivated by the boy's beauty and soon began a relationship. From the moment of their meeting, Antinous accompanied the emperor on all his trips. In 130, the young man died in strange circumstances in Egypt. Although the official version was that his death had been accidental and that he drowned in the Nile, some ancient authors stated that the boy sacrificed himself or, according to others, was offered in sacrifice to guarantee a long and fruitful life for the ruler. Whatever the truth, the death plunged Hadrian into despair. To honour the young man's memory, Hadrian built a city in the place where he died, which he called Antinopolis, and deified him, encouraging both Greeks and Romans to worship him with festivals, priests and temples. The emperor oversaw the creation of the divine image of the deceased, which he then distributed, especially in the form of statues, throughout the Mediterranean. More than 90 of these works remain; one of them is the marble bust on the left, which is in the Museo Nazionale Romano, in Rome. Antinous's enigmatic figure has caught the attention of artists from the Renaissance to the present day.

THE RETURN OF HADRIAN (OPPOSITE)
The emperor returns to Rome after one of his frequent trips in this relief from an arch erected by Emperor Antoninus Pius in honour of his predecessor (Museo del Palazzo dei Conservatori, Rome). Hadrian is welcomed by the goddess Roma and personifications of the Senate and people.

On the way back to Rome, Hadrian stopped in the Balkans, Greece and Sicily. Between 128 and 132, the emperor undertook another great trip, although he also devoted 127 to touring Italy. He departed during the summer of 128, heading for North Africa, and in the autumn was already in Athens, where he was initiated into the Eleusinian Mysteries. He dedicated the following year to the cities of Asia, Syria and Judaea. In Jerusalem, he decided to found a *colonia*, Aelia Capitolina, a decision that motivated a Jewish revolt. In 130, he was in Egypt. On the way back to Rome in 131, he stopped in the province of Asia and in Athens.

Some authors think that Hadrian then returned to the East to direct the campaigns against the Jews, while others suggest he went directly to Rome. In 134, he was definitely in the empire's capital, which he never left again, as he was already afflicted with the disease that would kill him in 138. Many epigraphic and numismatic artefacts commemorate Hadrian's journeys through his dominions and his concern for the progress of the State and the prosperity of the cities that composed it. Particularly significant are the many coins on which the emperor raises the prostrate provinces. These are the clearest representations of the governmental objective that the ruler was pursuing with his travels.

The government of Hadrianus Augustus

Hadrian cast off most of his honorary titles to be called only Hadrianus Augustus, showing that he saw his rule – and that he wanted it to be seen – as the continuation of the mission initiated by the founder of the empire. For this reason, he ordered the construction of a large mausoleum for his dynasty, copying the plan of the one erected by Augustus. Today, this structure is known as the Castel Sant' Angelo, which is linked to Rome by a bridge over the Tiber also built at Hadrian's request.

Like Augustus, Hadrian devoted himself to extensive building work in the capital, the most visible example of which is the Pantheon, in the Campus Martius. He also built a sanctuary in honour of Trajan to top off the forum of that emperor; and, between the Forum Romanum and the Colosseum, an immense building consecrated to Venus and Roma, which was the city's largest temple. Hadrian's administrative work focused on improving the condition of the empire. By expanding the imperial bureaucracy, he gave a huge impetus to the centralization of the State, a process that had begun under the Flavians and was continued by the other second-century rulers. Among his reforms was, in 127, the division of Italy into four regions governed by legates, who administered justice in their regions, thereby taking Italian cases out of the Roman courts. By this measure, Hadrian reduced Italy's status to that of a province, a fact that did not please the Senate and aggravated relations with them. He also expanded the number of procuratorships for the equestrians, and created the position of advocatus fisci (counsel of the treasury). It was a

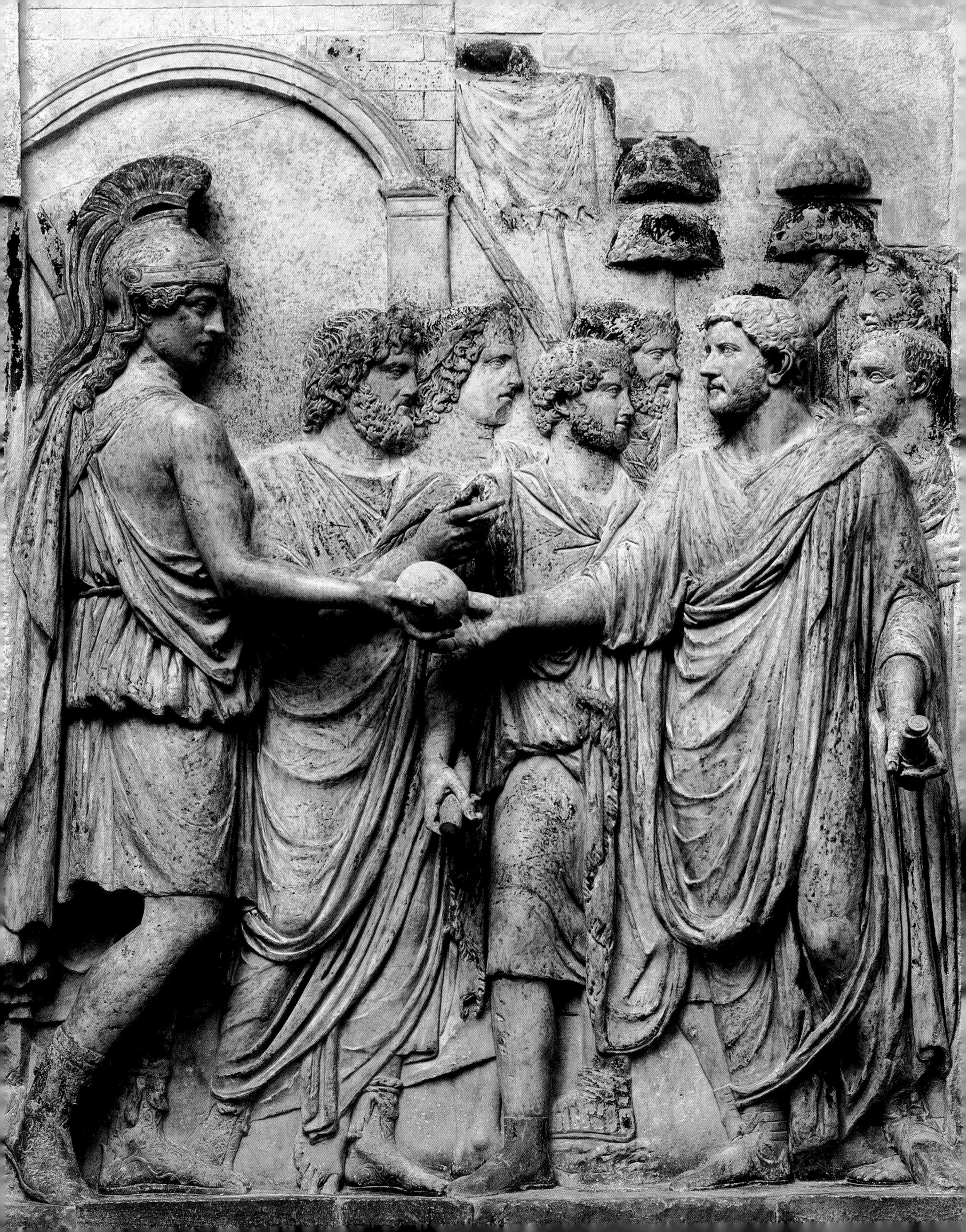

The reconstruction of Agrippa's pantheon

Hadrian was an innovator in the field of architecture, although in the visual arts he demonstrated a more classical taste. He took part in the design of his buildings and his preference for originality was reflected in many of them. The Pantheon of Agrippa was his most innovative project. His taste for experimentation and the search for new architectural solutions led him to conceive a building that combined a classic portico of large monolithic columns with an immense dome faced with austere brick, which hid a lavish and colourful interior. The old forms joined with new ideas to create a building that continues to surprise today. It was completed in 125.

post for equestrians that allowed them to enter directly into the coveted procuratorships, without going through the army. The job of the treasurer was to protect the interests of the treasury when demands were filed by taxpayers. Also in the area of public finance, another measure was the cancellation of debts with the treasury, whose records were burned publicly in the Forum, as is recalled in a bas-relief preserved inside the Julia Curia.

Hadrian also paid great attention to the development and rationalization of the law. He made the first attempt to codify Roman law, ordering the famous jurist Salvius Julianus to write the *Edictum perpetuum* (Perpetual Edict). The text, which was approved by a senate consultation, aimed to give coherence to civil law, because in the second century it was still customary for each incoming praetor urbanus to issue an edict at the beginning of his year of office, setting down the positions on which he would impart justice. In principle, all praetors could change these precepts at will, which could cause confusion and instability. The emperor wanted to avoid these dangers with the creation of a single edict that, as the name suggests, could no longer be changed by successive praetors. With the same aim in mind, Julianus was also given the task of determining the edicts that the provincial governors, the praetor urbanus and the curule aediles had to publish each year.

To improve the application of the law, the emperor established that when the opinion of the legal experts, called *iuris prudentes*, was unanimous on some matter, it was imposed on the will of the magistrates; if they were not unanimous, the final decision would fall on the emperor himself, who from now on had a *consilium principis*, consisting of salaried legal

THE TRAVELLING EMPEROR

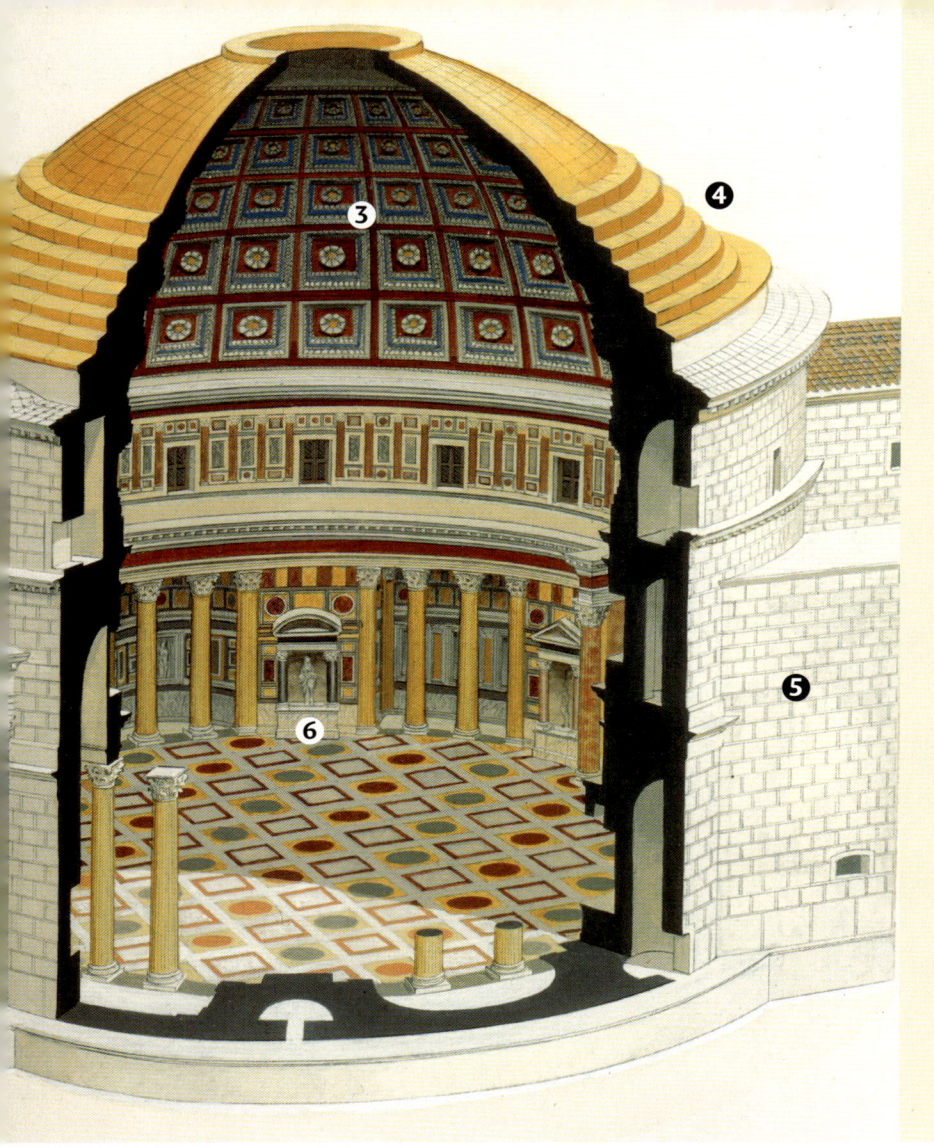

1 THE FOUNDER
The inscription that appears in the frieze on the portico refers to Marcus Vipsanius Agrippa, right hand of Emperor Augustus, as the founder of the original temple in 27 bc. It reads: 'Marcus Agrippa, son of Lucius, built this when consul for the third time.'

2 THE PORTICO
The pediment, facing north, is supported by eight columns with Corinthian capitals. Just behind, two groups of four columns divide the space into three naves.

3 INTERIOR OF THE DOME
This is the largest unreinforced concrete dome ever built, even surpassing that of St Peter's in the Vatican. The dome's interior is faced with five rows of sunken panels (coffers), which were once ornamented with rosettes or stars, culminating in an oculus of 8.9m (29ft) in diameter.

4 EXTERIOR OF THE DOME
The construction is topped by a structure formed by seven overlapping rings, which distribute the weight of the dome onto a concrete wall.

5 DIMENSIONS
The height of the dome is 43.3m (142ft), which is the same as its diameter. The architect of this extraordinary construction was Apollodorus of Damascus.

6 THE GODS
The temple had seven exedrae, which were reserved for the Roman celestial deities: the Sun, the Moon, Mercury, Venus, Mars, Jupiter and Saturn.

---

specialists, to resolve such issues. In this way, Hadrian aimed to unify jurisprudence.

Hadrian's legislative work also affected the economic sphere. For example, he passed legislation that encouraged farmers to take over and cultivate any unused lands in Africa. A series of detailed laws on the exploitation of imperial mines, which were usually leased to private individuals, have also been preserved in bronze tablets found in the mining district of Vipasca (near Aljustrel, in Portugal). A similar meticulousness can be observed in provisions for the exploitation of imperial forests, in this case referring to the mountains of Lebanon.

Also dating from Hadrian's reign is a measure that appears in the *Digest* (the collection of Roman law made between 529 and 534 by order of the emperor Justinian I) and expressly certifies the control by the *annona*, the office for the distribution of foodstuffs, over the supply of olive oil, a provision that endorses the increase of State interventionism against private trade. Finally, Hadrian also modified the Latin rights so that decurions of colonies with 'Latin' status, as opposed to 'Roman' status, could receive Roman citizenship, rather than just the magistrates, as had been the case until now.

A toga with a beard

Hadrian's vast empire, which had never before been subjected to a single power, had the Mediterranean Sea and 90,000km (56,000 miles) of roads to facilitate communication and the passage of people, goods, ideas and gods. The empire shared some cultural and moral values, but also had great regional diversity. The author Marguerite Yourcenar in her novel *Memoirs of Hadrian* described the complexity and uniformity of the empire, with words put into the mouth of Hadrian himself:

HADRIAN'S MAUSOLEUM (OVERLEAF)
This wonderful travertine mausoleum, which rises on the right bank of the Tiber, was begun in 135 by Hadrian as a place of eternal rest for him and his family. It was finished by his successor, Antoninus Pius, four years later.

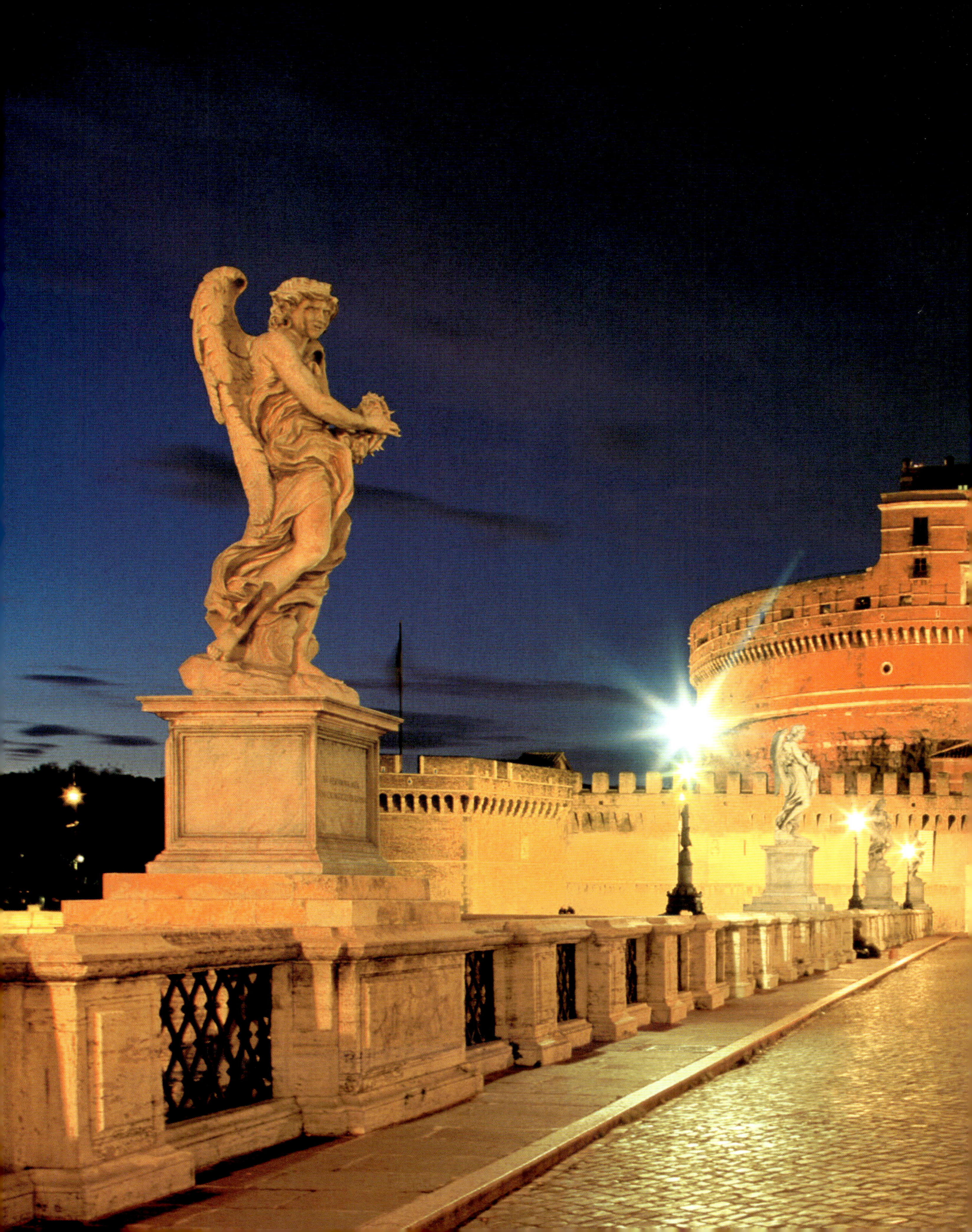

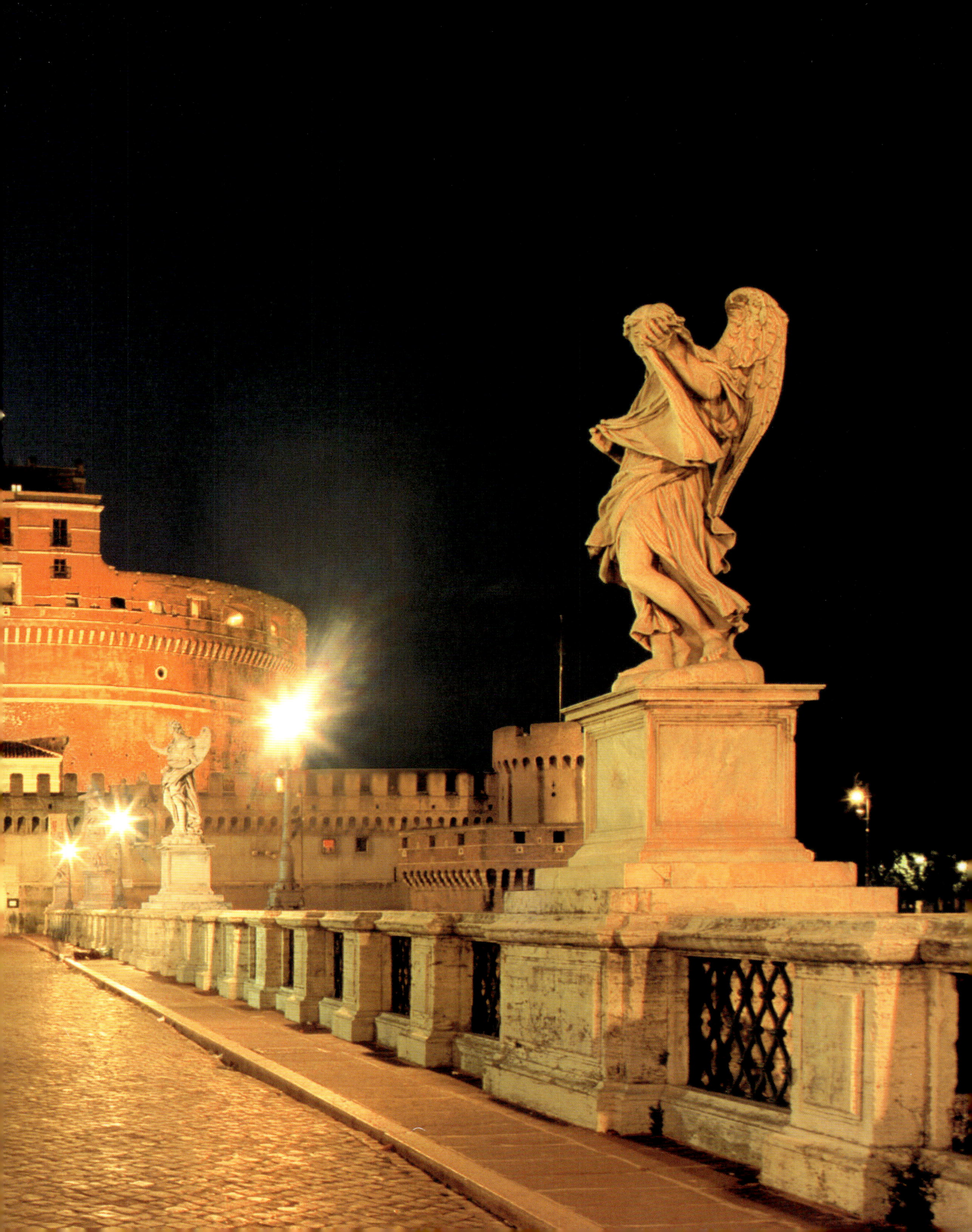

ROME DOMINATES THE WORLD

'In a world more than half dominated by forest, desert, fallow plains, there is no more beautiful sight than a paved street, a temple to no matter which god, public baths and toilets, the shop where the barber chats with his clients about the news from Rome, the pastry and sandal stalls, maybe a library, a doctor's sign, a theatre where one enjoys from time to time a play by Terence. Fussy people complain about the uniformity of our cities: they dislike seeing everywhere the same statue of the emperor, the same aqueduct. They are wrong: the beauty of Nimes differs from that of Arles. But this same uniformity, found across three continents, comforts the traveller like a milestone; our most insignificant cities keep their reassuring promise of inn, post and shelter.'

The cultural and political foundations of this empire were a combination of Greek history with the addition of Roman baggage. In this mixture of two traditions it is difficult, and unnecessary, to hunt for the origins of the constituent parts, because a community had been forged that can be defined as Greco-Roman and that had been taken up by the aristocracies of the entire empire.

An obvious symptom of this unity is found in the integration in State government of men from the Eastern Empire, who performed roles within both the Western and Italian oligarchies. A good example is found in the Spanish province of Baetica, which had both a governor and a legate from Greece. The first was the historian and military commander Flavius Arrianus, who wrote the *Anabasis* about Alexander the Great; the latter was Gaius Julius Eurycles, a member of an influential Spartan family. Roman architecture of the period also testifies to the integration of East and West: there are great stylistic similarities between the new district built in Italica, in Baetica, and the extension of Athens. The magnificent palace that the emperor built near Rome for relaxation and recreation, the villa of Tivoli, is also a clear example of this integrated style.

However, the most striking physical manifestation of these cultural affinities was the emperor himself, who grew the beard of the Greek philosophers, although the *Augustan History* maintains that his true objective was to hide his facial imperfections. All his successors until the third century would continue with the fashion. Hadrian is also credited with the adoption of a rule that obliged senators and equestrians to always wear a toga when in public, and it seems that he led by example, at least when in Italy. In this way, Hadrian became a toga-wearer with a beard. And this combination, which to the uninformed observer may seem to be the quintessence of Romanity, was in fact an innovation, an unprecedented revision of what it was to be Roman and how this identity was externalized.

THE GODDESS APHRODITE
Copies of Greek statues profusely adorned Hadrian's Villa, the imperial residence in Tivoli. In his choices, the admiration that the Spanish emperor felt for the Greek aesthetic can clearly be seen. This marble statue was copied for Hadrian from a Greek original made in the third century BC (Museo Nazionale Romano, Rome).

The Greek league: the Panhellenion

Hadrian was a Hellenophile but also a skilled politician who realized the economic and social possibilities of the Greek world. His new league of Greek cities was based in Athens. For a city to be part of this union and send representatives to the council, it had to demonstrate the Greek roots of its population. Cities from all over mainland Greece, Asia Minor and more remote areas, such as Libya, participated. The councillors were priests of Hadrian and wore ceremonial crowns bearing a bust of the emperor. In Attica, the league had several meeting places, among them the Temple of Olympian Zeus, which Hadrian paid for in Athens (pictured on the right). There is no agreement on who was the instigator of this federation, whether the emperor or the Greeks themselves. However, perhaps the best answer is that the Panhellenion was born from the combination of the political aspirations of the Greeks and Hadrian's desire to energize the Eastern Empire.

Hadrian and the Greek world
If you visit the agora of Athens, you will find a headless statue of Emperor Hadrian in a place of honour. In his breastplate, a very significant

scene is carved: Athena stands on the Capitoline she-wolf as she suckles Romulus and Remus. Flanking this group are two winged victories. This was a frequent motif in sculptures of Hadrian, who was widely seen as bringing about the resurgence of Athens, and all Greece.

Hadrian's taste for the Greek world began in childhood, proof of which is his childhood nickname of Graeculus, 'Greekling'. Through his life, he spent a lot of time in Greece, especially in Athens, a city with which he had a close relationship. Before becoming emperor he was the city's eponymous archon, and he also participated in the celebrations of the Eleusinian Mysteries. His predilection for Athens led him to complete the colossal Temple of Olympian Zeus, which had been started and left unfinished several times. In the area surrounding this sanctuary, he also developed a new neighbourhood of the city.

Here an inscription on the Arch of Hadrian bears witness to his work as a founder of the city. Hadrian also endowed Athens with a library, perhaps with the purpose of serving not so much as a place for reading but as a government building in which laws and administrative documents were compiled.

Although the capital of Attica was the focus of the emperor's attention, the rest of the Greek East also benefited from the ruler's Hellenophile interest, as evidenced by the numerous constructions and donations he made throughout his travels, as well as the attention he devoted to solving problems of civic life, as evidenced by the imperial letters. The culmination of this close relationship was the creation of a new institution, the Panhellenion, an assembly of cities of Hellenic origin that met in Athens, probably in the Temple of Olympian Zeus.

SANCTUARY OF DEMETER IN ELEUSIS
This temple, dedicated to Demeter and her daughter Persephone, also known as Kore, was where the Eleusinian Mysteries were celebrated. Hadrian visited Eleusis, which was in Attica, about 18km (11 miles) from Athens, and took part in the rites during his trip through the Roman East.

Hadrian wanted to give a voice to Greece and put its energies behind the empire, as he had done in the West with the expansion of Latin rights. This was an objective that was undoubtedly achieved and that initiated the long process of displacement of the nucleus of the Roman State towards the East. The cities chose their representatives in the Panhellenion among their most distinguished men. These notables could then gain social promotion and occupy positions of importance in the imperial administration. The results did not take long to appear, with an increase in the number of senators and bureaucrats of Eastern origin.

The Greeks acknowledged the emperor's attention by erecting many shrines consecrated to Hadrian as founder and saviour. Just within Athens were more than a hundred of these altars, which testify to the enthusiasm, at least officially, that the cult of the emperor aroused.

The ruler was associated with the god Zeus and a colossal statue of him was erected inside the precinct of the Temple of Olympian Zeus.

The Jewish rebellion

A feature that differentiates the Roman Empire from most of the great political constructions of the modern age, such as the British or Spanish Empires, was the lack of a single religion upheld from the centre. As long as its subjects maintained order, paid their taxes and carried out the mandatory tokens of adherence to the regime, the Roman State did not interfere in their beliefs. Apart from exceptions such as human sacrifice in the Celtic religion or the Christian refusal to worship the gods, pagan Rome had no issues with other beliefs; nor was it a protagonist of religious wars.

Judaism was also among the exceptions. The tumultuous relationship between Rome and this religion had its final and definitive act during the reign of Hadrian. The revolt during Nero's reign, suffocated by Vespasian and Titus, was surpassed by a new rebellion, the so-called Bar Kokhba revolt, after the rebel leader. The conflict was confined to Judaea and lasted from 132 to 135. It was characterized by the use of guerrilla tactics that greatly impeded the Roman reconquest and caused many legionary casualties. The emperor was so worried about the progress of the conflict that he sent numerous reinforcements to the region and even went to the field himself.

There is no agreement among historians as to exactly what triggered the conflict. Some argue that the cause was the founding of a new Roman *colonia* on the site of Jerusalem with the name of Aelia Capitolina, perhaps on the occasion of the imperial visit to the region. Others think it was due to an alleged ban on circumcision by the emperor.

The insurgents waited for Hadrian's departure in 132 to rise up in arms. During the first two years of fighting, they managed to occupy a good part of Judaea and take Jerusalem. The rebels organized themselves as an independent state, appointing local authorities, minting coins and leasing public

Aelia Capitolina: Hadrian's new Jerusalem

It is not known for certain when the Roman *colonia* of Aelia Capitolina was founded on the site of old Jerusalem. The city was almost deserted after being destroyed by Titus, and was only occupied by a legionary contingent. The Bar Kokhba revolt was in response to the establishment of the colony consisting mainly of veteran legionaries, in addition to other measures contrary to Jewish practices. Therefore, the foundation, following the testimony of Cassius Dio, had to occur prior to the outbreak of hostilities, perhaps coinciding with Hadrian's visit to the area in 130. However, the inauguration was not the start of a fertile period of construction, and there is very little archaeological evidence for this stage of the city. Ancient Jerusalem became a pagan monument in honour of the ruling family (Aelia was Hadrian's family name), but did not regain its pre-eminence in the region until the time of Constantine and the Christianization of the city. On the right is a coin minted by the Jewish rebels.

1. Temple of Jupiter
2. Temple of Venus
3. Temple of Asclepius
4. Temple pools
5. Encampment of Legion X
6. Forum
7. Baths
8. Gate
9. Tetrapylon
10. Theatre

lands. Simon bar Kokhba, some of whose letters were found preserved in the Judaean desert, was a general and ruler who took pains over the maintenance of the morale and discipline of his troops, as well as adhering to strict religious principles. At the time of the uprising, the Romans had only one legion in the area, X *Fretensis*. Four others had to be sent from the East – from Syria, Egypt and Arabia – as well as several detachments of troops stationed in the Danube *limes*. Even so, victory was not easy, and the Roman army suffered major defeats, such as the destruction of the legion that had come from Egypt. The general in charge of bringing the area under control was Sextus Julius Severus, who had to travel from Britannia, where he was governor. In 134 he managed to recover Jerusalem; the following year, he annihilated the rebels. Bar Kokhba died during the assault on the insurgents' last stronghold.

The Jewish population of Judaea was devastated, with the majority killed, exiled or enslaved. Jewish religious and political authority was suppressed. Those Jews who remained were forbidden to go to Jerusalem more than once a year. The territory was reorganized administratively with the creation of the province of Syria Palaestina with its capital in Aelia Capitolina and a permanent garrison of two legions.

Hadrian's efforts to control and reorganize this new province, in addition to the founding of the veterans' colony, resulted in the creation of an extensive network of roads that was the first of its kind in the area. Some 12 roads are known, thanks to the milestones found in the region. The new city – although it did not recover from the destruction caused during the Titus era and the Bar Kokhba revolt – served as the focus of Romanization in the region.

ROME DOMINATES THE WORLD

Eastern cults in Rome

During the first two centuries of the common era, and especially during the Flavian and Antonine dynasties, when the Mediterranean enjoyed a lasting peace and stable governments, a series of gods and cults of Eastern origin were incorporated into the religious practices of the inhabitants of the Roman Empire.

Chief among these cults were those of Isis, Mithras and Cybele, divinities of ancient origin among the cultures of the Mediterranean basin, which transformed their exotic characteristics to become very popular cults among the Romans.

The mystery cults

The most important feature of these cults was their mystery component, which derived from their fundamental religious practice, initiation, a feature that they probably acquired through the rituals that were celebrated in the sanctuary of Eleusis in honour of Demeter and Kore. The worshippers of these Greek gods were initiated into secrets that only those who had gone through the ceremony could know. During the rite of initiation, the faithful followed a sacred itinerary that led them to direct communication with the divine entity of their choice, and through this arcane ceremony the neophytes entered a sacred community and were joined by a vow of silence.

The Eastern mystery cults became completely integrated into the rituals of the Roman Empire, and some of their ceremonies, such as those dedicated to Cybele and Isis, became cornerstones of the official Roman religion. However, the initiation always maintained its confidentiality and sectarianism, a hallmark that radically separated these new cults from most of the religious practices that were carried out in honour of the traditional gods of the Roman pantheon, since the secrecy of the mystery rites was totally opposed to the public displays in the Forum that characterized the Roman divinities.

In addition to this sectarian aspect, the Eastern gods shared a feature that differentiated them from the usual Roman divinities, since in their myths they incorporated their own death and resurrection, associated with the natural cycle of the seasons and the farming year. This event in the mythical life of the gods, death and resurrection, was crucial to adherents, since the most precious asset offered by the Eastern deities, as a consequence of this special relationship between the divinity and death, was the salvation of the faithful. Salvation was, in addition, double, as initiates enjoyed a fuller and happier earthly existence, while, after death, they could enjoy the eternal company of their protective deity.

Some historians have argued that the Eastern cults were the precursors of Christianity, as they paved the way for the new religion. In fact, the caesura between Christianity and the other Eastern religious practices conceals the fact that Christianity was also an Eastern cult that grew up alongside the other religions of the region. Therefore, it seems more accurate to conclude that it is not that all these cults 'paved the way' for Christianity, but that Christianity and the other cults were largely similar because they provided similar solutions and shared both their origins and the social groups for whom they were intended.

ALTAR TO MITHRAS
Underneath the Basilica of San Clemente al Laterano, in Rome, is one of the 45 Mithraea that existed in the city during the imperial era. In this altar carving from the sanctuary, Mithras is seen slaying the sacred bull.

THE CRUEL INITIATION INTO THE CULT OF CYBELE

The priests of Cybele, the *galli*, followed the example of Attis by castrating themselves during an ecstasy that was brought on by extreme music – with cymbals, tambourines and drums, all under a pine, the symbol of Attis – the consumption of hallucinogenic substances and self-flagellation. After this rite, the new servant of the deity dressed in women's clothes to indicate that the *gallus* was no longer a man. In the reign of Antoninus Pius, the figure of the *archigallus*, the high priest of the *galli*, was introduced, who did not have to sacrifice his genitals to take the job. It was, in short, a position that allowed Roman citizens, especially those of higher status, to participate in ritual practices. Around the same time, a ritual was introduced of sacrificing a bull and giving its testicles as an offering to the goddess. Above is Cybele wearing a Phrygian cap (Christie's, London).

ROME DOMINATES THE WORLD

TRAJAN AND THE TEMPLES OF ISIS

The isle of Philae, in the Nile, was submerged by the Aswan dam. The temples built there by the pharaohs were moved to Agilkia Island, along with Trajan's Kiosk for the barque of Isis (above). On the right are the goddesses Isis and Nephthys with the sacred crocodile, in a fresco in the Pompeian Villa of the Mysteries.

Cybele, mother of the gods

Cybele was a mother goddess of Anatolia, with healing ability and associated with mountains and nature, a characteristic that was symbolized by the lions that usually accompanied the deity. In her myth cycle, the young priest Attis, who had sworn eternal love to the divinity, broke his vow in order to marry a beautiful Phrygian heiress. During the nuptial ceremony, the jealous Cybele appeared in all her glory, sending the men into a crazed passion. Attis used a flint to cut off his own genitals under a pine, a tree that became the symbol of the god.

The Roman State adopted the cult of Cybele, called Magna Mater, during the Second Punic War (218–201 BC), after dire prodigies, including a meteor shower, failed harvest and famine, warned of Rome's defeat. Under the Julio-Claudians, the spring festivities were celebrated in honour of the deity, to promote a good harvest. During these celebrations, in which branches of Attis pine were carried, those who aspired to be *galli* (priests of Cybele) castrated themselves.

The Egyptian cults

Isis was one of the most important goddesses of the traditional Egyptian pantheon. During the Hellenistic period, when Egypt was ruled by Greeks, and later under the Roman Empire, the deity was linked with Serapis, a reinterpretation of Osiris, the husband of Isis, who was created by the Ptolemies to sustain their power in Egypt by establishing a bridge between their Greek and Egyptian subjects. Serapis was a union of the god Apis, who was related to death, and Osiris (Osiris + Apis = Serapis); but to this conjunction of Egyptian deities was joined the characteristics of Pluto, from whom he took his appearance. Thus, the resulting divinity became sovereign and protector of the dead. Later, in Hellenistic and Roman worship, he also became a healing god.

The cult of Isis was not exclusive to those initiated in its mysteries. Temples to Isis outside Egypt were built in a largely Greco-Roman style but, like Egyptian temples, were surrounded by large courtyards. They were decorated with Egyptian-themed artwork. Daily worship was in the hands of shaven-headed priests. An annual festival, the Isia, from 26 October to 3 November, celebrated the death of Osiris and his resurrection by Isis. Another festival for the Egyptian goddess was the Navigium Isidis, on 5 March, which marked the start of the sea-going season.

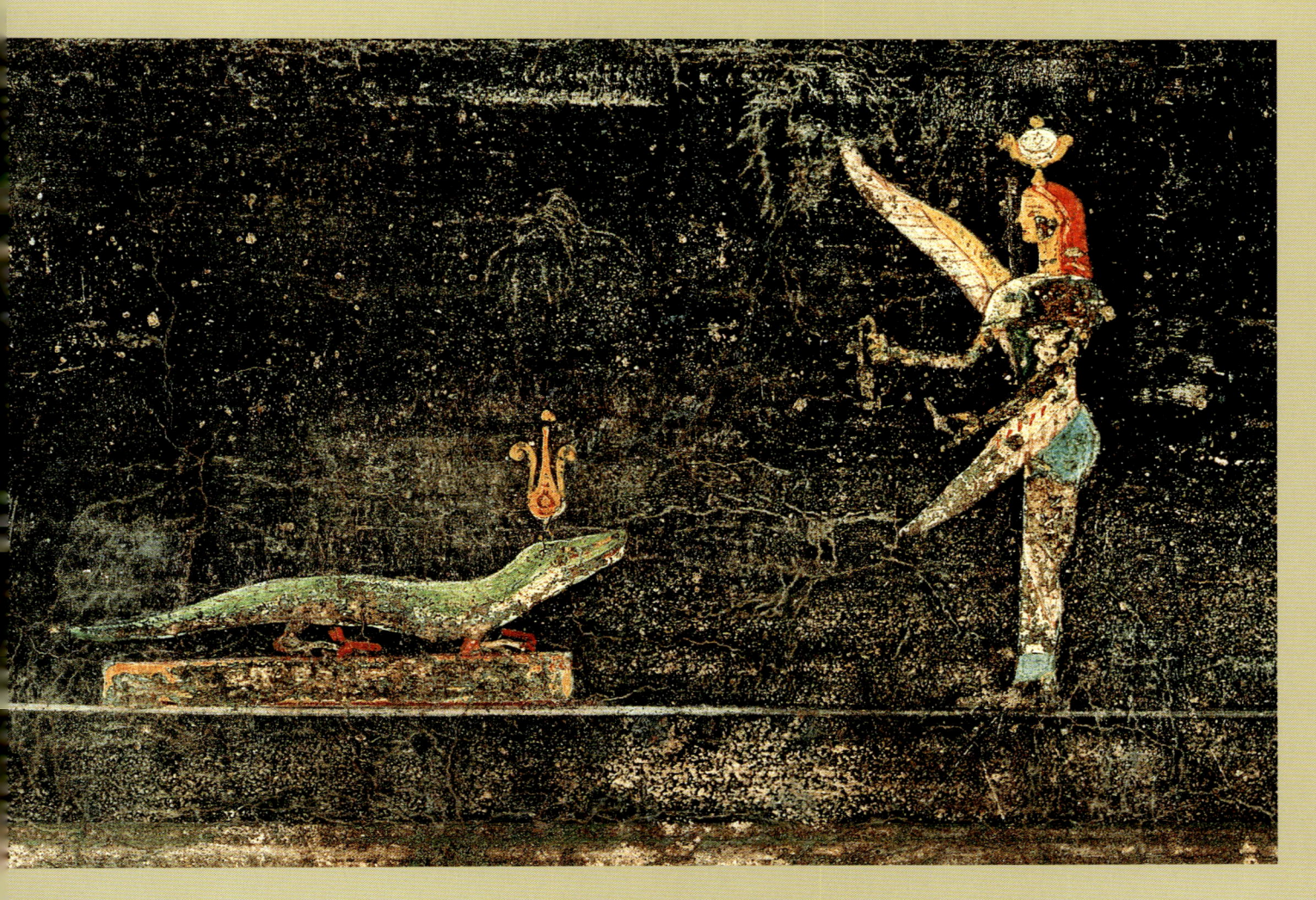

At the start of the imperial period, the cults of the Egyptian divinity had already spread through the Hellenic East and reached Rome, where they were banned by Augustus and even persecuted by Tiberius. However, Caligula put the Isia in the official Roman calendar. In the Flavian era, cults of Isis received the support of the emperors, after which they spread rapidly throughout the West, especially in ports, and through the means of river communication reached Hispania, Gaul and central Europe.

Mithras, the Unconquered Sun
Mithras was a god of Indo-Iranian origin who was related to contracts and pacts, cattle breeding and twilight. It is unknown how he became part of the Roman pantheon during the empire, and how he went on to become the patron divinity of a mystery cult. Undoubtedly, the Roman deity retained the main attributes of the Asian god, which were manifested in his sunlike qualities – he is *Sol Invictus* (the Unconquered Sun) – and in his role as killer of the sacred bull; however, it seems that the transformation process of Mithras, as with Isis and Cybele, was also very profound.

The preserved information about this cult is mostly archaeological and epigraphic. Mithraea, the temples consecrated to the divinity, were long, narrow and often underground, like caves. The most revealing artefacts are tauroctonies, depictions of Mithras killing a bull, which presided over shrines dedicated to the god.

Mithraism was secret and did not count on occasional participants: those who took part in the rituals were initiated and a strong hierarchy was established between them. All were men, mostly soldiers and low-ranking officials, as well as freedmen and slaves. It was not until the fourth century that Mithraism became a religion of the Roman ruling class, who used it to oppose the rise of Christianity.

MARCUS AURELIUS
In this bronze statue of the emperor on horseback, made in 176, the ruler has his arm outstretched in a gesture of mercy. He is also without armour, conveying the image of a lover of peace (Capitoline Museums, Rome). On the opposite page is an aureus minted by Marcus Aurelius.

THE MATURE EMPIRE

Through his succession plan, Hadrian chose the rulers of the empire for more than half a century, which was a period of maturity and consolidation for the State that saw an increase in imperial power, development of the law and expansion of the administration. The rule of Antoninus Pius was calm and prosperous. Marcus Aurelius, the philosopher emperor, who shared power with his adopted brother Lucius Verus and his son Commodus, engaged in continuous wars and conflicts.

Hadrian had no legitimate children, so when he fell ill after his return from the East, in 136, he began to plan his succession. He adopted Lucius Ceionius Commodus, a young senator who was then consul. The reason for choosing him is not clear. Contemporary sources describe him as incapable of carrying out the role; some modern researchers think he was Hadrian's illegitimate son, although there is no firm proof. The emperor's decision provoked outrage among Roman nobles, particularly those who fancied the throne for themselves, including Hadrian's brother-in-law Lucius Julius Ursus Servianus and his grandson, Pedanius Fuscus Salinator, whom Hadrian had groomed as his heir. The pair created problems and were forced to commit suicide. Hadrian's reign was thus closed in the way that it had begun: with the death of senators.

After his adoption, Lucius Ceionius Commodus changed his name to Lucius Aelius

ROME DOMINATES THE WORLD

Antoninus Pius: Timeline of his reign

Year 138
Adoption and accession. In February, Antoninus is adopted by Hadrian. In the month of July, the new ruler ascends the throne.

Years 139–142
Construction of the Antonine Wall. The legate Lollius Urbicus builds a new defensive wall in Britannia, to the north of Hadrian's Wall.

Year 141
Apotheosis of Faustina. The wife of Antoninus Pius, Faustina, dies and is deified. A temple is built in honour of them both in the Forum Romanum.

Year 147
Anniversary of the foundation of Rome. The 900th anniversary of the founding of the city is commemorated with great festivities, including arena shows.

Years 154–155
Problems in Britain. The submission of Britannia is celebrated in Roman coinage, but shortly afterwards the Antonine Wall is abandoned.

Year 161
Death and succession. The death of Antoninus Pius and the ascension to the throne of Marcus Aurelius follow Hadrian's succession plans, more than 20 years after his death.

Caesar. To celebrate, games were organized in Rome and a donation was given to the people and legionaries. However, the heir apparently died of natural causes on 1 January 138, reopening the question of succession.

Hadrian then made a convoluted decision that would mark out the future of the empire for 50 years: he would adopt a prestigious senator from a family from Nemausus (Nîmes), Titus Aurelius Fulvus Boionius Arrius Antoninus, who would later be known as Antoninus Pius. It was a measure that satisfied the Curia and, above all, the emperor himself, as the new successor was older and had no living descendants – which facilitated the rest of Hadrian's plan. He forced Antoninus to adopt two young Romans: the son of Marcus Annius Verus, the future Marcus Aurelius, who was then 17 years old; and the seven-year-old son of Lucius Aelius Caesar, who would be known as Lucius Verus. Marcus Aurelius was the nephew of Antoninus Pius's wife Faustina. Hadrian also got Lucius Verus engaged to Faustina the Younger, daughter of Antoninus Pius.

This complex set-up surprised Hadrian's contemporaries and continues to surprise today. Many possible explanations have been given. Perhaps Hadrian sought to form his own dynasty and, to that end, decided to construct kinship with members of the most influential senatorial clans. It has also been suggested that, just as Lucius Ceionius Commodus could have been Hadrian's son, there could also have been some kinship between Marcus Aurelius and Hadrian. The most solid suggestion, although it cannot be definitively proved, is that Rupilia Faustina, the wife of Annius Verus, Marcus Aurelius's grandfather, was the daughter of Matidia, who was also the mother of Vibia Sabina, Hadrian's wife. If this hypothesis were correct, Annius Verus and Hadrian would have had the same mother-in-law, Matidia, who was Trajan's niece and an influential character in the court early in the second century.

Hadrian's dynastic wrangling worked. Antoninus Pius fulfilled his part of the pact, although he slightly modified Hadrian's orders by undoing the engagement between Lucius Verus and his daughter Faustina, to unite her with the future Marcus Aurelius, thus pointing to him as clear successor.

A long period of prosperity

From the beginning of his reign, Hadrian was not close to the Senate, which disliked his independence, the curtailment of some of its traditional privileges and the elimination of some of its members. On his death, the latent animosity was evident, because the Curia tried to condemn his memory and prevent him being deified. According to the sources, Antoninus Pius stood firm and approved Hadrian's apotheosis. This was one of his first actions when he came to power at the age of 52. Much was at stake, since the new emperor owed his position to being adopted by the previous one. It is probable that he received the name 'Pius' for the devotion he showed in defending the interests of his predecessor, which were, in fact, also his own. He finished Hadrian's mausoleum and built a temple to extol his divinity in the Campus Martius, the remains of which can be seen today. The recourse of deifying members of the imperial family as a means to strengthen the position of the emperors at the head of the Roman State and society was a well-established procedure. In this reign, the practice was taken a little further with the deification of Faustina, the wife of the emperor, when she died in 141. For her a sanctuary was erected that Antoninus would later share; it is among the most outstanding buildings in the Forum Romanum.

In spite of this first confrontation, Antoninus Pius enjoyed harmonious relations with the Senate, an institution in which he and several of his relatives had participated. The emperor was born into a senatorial family that had acceded to the consulate on several occasions. Antoninus Pius himself was consul in 120 and, around 135, he occupied the prestigious proconsulate of Asia. In the period between these two roles, he was administrator of one of the four regions into which Hadrian had divided Italy, the creation of which had so annoyed the Senate. One of the first signs of rapprochement that he gave to the Curia was, in fact, the elimination of these regions.

With Antoninus Pius, the Senate exerted its maximum level of executive power, although the Caesar maintained his autocratic position at the head of a State that continued centralizing and whose main organ of government was the *Consilium principis* ('council to the emperor'). In fact, among the measures included in the *Digest*, the compilation of Roman jurisprudence commissioned by Emperor Justinian in 529, Antoninus Pius is credited with the maxim: 'I am indeed lord of the world'.

TEMPLE OF ANTONINUS AND FAUSTINA
Situated in the Via Sacra is the best-preserved building in the Forum Romanum (seen on the far left). It was commissioned by the emperor in 141 on the death of his beloved wife. When Antoninus died in 161, the Senate, after deifying him, consecrated the temple to the imperial couple. Directly above is the reverse of an aureus minted by Antoninus.

GATE OF ANTONINUS PIUS IN SBEITLA

In this city, in the high plateaus of Tunisia, the emperor ordered the construction, between 138 and 161, of this magnificent archway into the forum. Its inscriptions refer to the emperor and his two adopted sons, Marcus Aurelius, who would be his successor, and Lucius Verus.

Despite his lack of interest in travel (he never left Italy), Antoninus Pius's policy continued the activities of his predecessor, both in administration and the development of law. He legislated in favour of the less socially advantaged, such as slaves, and introduced measures such as the presumption of innocence and limits on the use of torture for obtaining confessions. However, these humanitarian reforms occurred in parallel with the official approval of two groups of citizens, the *honestiores* and *humiliores*, who were treated differently under the law, especially in the application of sentences, which were less harsh for the former. The *honestiores*, although it was never clearly defined, were senators, equestrians, decurions, merchants and veterans.

The emperor also continued with the good works that had characterized the previous reigns. He gave nine cash donations to the people of Rome and the army, and also helped the provincial cities, as in the case of Ephesus, which received aid after an earthquake. Like Hadrian, he showed a marked interest in the provinces, as evidenced by his numerous letters to cities throughout the empire. He maintained the *alimentaria* and created a new programme for the help of girls, which he named *Puellae Faustinianae* in honour of his wife.

The cordiality that marked relations with the Senate and the general prosperity of the period in which he held power – between 138 and 161 – may have had something to do with the affable, hard-working and calm character attributed to Antoninus by the sources, especially Marcus Aurelius, who praised him in his *Meditations*. However, beyond the character of the emperor, the achievements of these decades lie in the governmental machinery created by the emperors of this dynasty.

The apotheosis of Emperor Antoninus Pius

The political and religious power of the emperor separated him from his subjects, to an extent that favoured his inclusion among the gods, both in the official religion and in the collective imagination. However, in this deeply hierarchical society, the ruler did not occupy the same position for all levels of subject. After Augustus, in Rome as well as the colonies and army, the tradition was that the emperor would only become a god after his death. Although some transgressed the model, such as Caligula or Nero, the second-century rulers followed the custom. After the death of the emperor, the Senate met to discuss his fitness for deification. A ceremony accompanied the change of official status and, finally, a place of worship, priests and festivals were assigned to the new god. However, among subjects who did not enjoy Roman citizenship, the emperors were treated as gods in life. In this relief on the base of the Antonine Column, the apotheosis of Antoninus Pius and Faustina is represented.

1 THE IMPERIAL COUPLE
Antoninus Pius and Faustina are depicted as they ascend to the heavens.

2 TWO EAGLES
On both sides of the couple, eagles symbolize their consecratio (sacred status).

3 WINGED GENIUS
A winged genius carries the new gods to their heavenly abode.

4 CAMPUS MARTIUS
The place where the deification ceremony was held is personified as a reclining young man.

5 ROME
The goddess Roma salutes the deifed couple. Her shield depicts the city's founders, Romulus and Remus.

6 DECURSIO
Flanking the main scene are depictions of two processions by the Praetorian Guard.

The *Pax Romana* of Antoninus Pius

The reign of Antoninus Pius was the period's most peaceful. In 147, the emperor was able to celebrate the 900th anniversary of the founding of Rome, satisfied with the role that the eternal city was playing in the world. Armed conflicts were confined to the borders, where the emperor knew how to continue the prodigious work done by Hadrian, keeping confrontations outside the empire and solving disputes with firm, but intelligent, diplomatic work. This was demonstrated in the treatment of the Quadi on the other side of Danube, over whom he appointed a suitable king (140–141), and in the Armenian question, which was also resolved by the appointment of a pro-Roman client king (144). The same strategy was followed with the Bosporan Kingdom, Colchis and the Kingdom of Iberia. He also avoided confrontation on the eastern border with the Parthians, whose kings, Vologases II and III, made preparations for war. The military presence of Rome in the area, reinforced during the reign of Hadrian, was also a deterrent to the neighbouring empire.

However, fighting took place at the borders of the Mauretanian provinces – Caesariensis and Tingitana – between 145 and 152, a situation serious enough for Antoninus Pius to send detachments from Syria, Hispania and the Danube. In order to prevent future attacks, an attempt was made to integrate some of the enemy tribes into the imperial peace, particularly the Bacuatae, by granting Roman citizenship to their chief. It is also possible that defensive fortifications were built in this part of the empire. In addition, the legions were busy in Dacia and in the *limes* of Germania Superior between 140 and 145. In the latter province, the frontier was moved to the east and fortified with a wall, defensive towers and stone forts.

ANTONINUS PIUS
This emperor boasted the longest reign since Augustus, surpassing by two months that of Tiberius. After holding power for 23 years, Antoninus died of a fever and was buried in the Mausoleum of Hadrian. This marble statue belonged to the Ludovisi collection (Museo Nazionale Romano, Palazzo Altemps, Rome).

COLUMN OF MARCUS AURELIUS (OPPOSITE)
This column was erected in the Campus Martius either after Marcus Aurelius's triumph in the Marcomannic War, or after his death in 180, as a pedestal for a statue of the emperor. Its reliefs, arranged in a spiral, commemorate Marcus Aurelius's victories against the Germanic and Sarmatian tribes. It measures almost 30m (98ft) in height.

A similar decision was made in Britain. The legate Lollius Urbicus defeated the Brigantes at the beginning of Antoninus Pius's reign, then, between 139 and 142, ordered a 100-km (62-mile)-long wall to the north of Hadrian's Wall. It stretched between the Forth and Clyde estuaries. The wall's design copied that of the previous one, but was not so imposing: it consisted of an earth bank about 4m (13ft) high, with stone foundations, protected by a wide moat and forts, located every 3km (2 miles). However, conflict continued in the area. Roman coins from 154 and 155 celebrated the island's submission, but at the same time the legions were defeated in Trimontium (Newstead), a fort located between both walls. Soon after, the Antonine Wall was abandoned and the forts burned, although it is unknown if the destruction was carried out by the Romans before retreating or by their enemies.

Marcus Aurelius, the wise emperor

Antoninus Pius died on 7 March 161 and was deified soon after. His place was taken without mishap by Marcus Aurelius, who had shared in his predecessor's administration from early on. The Senate planned to confirm Marcus Aurelius alone, but he insisted they name his adopted brother, Lucius Verus, alongside him. Finally, the two were granted most of the same titles, most importantly 'Augustus'. Although Marcus Aurelius reserved the position of Pontifex Maximus for himself and always held more authority, he saw to it that, for the first time, the empire was governed jointly.

The reign of the new Caesar was marked by the fact that he was a practitioner of Stoicism. Thanks to his untitled writing, known today as *Meditations*, we can understand the thinking of this great philosopher. His submission to Stoic principles led him to avoid the honours and praises of the court, and to conceive 'the idea of a State based on equality and freedom of speech, and a sovereign who honours, above all, the freedom of his subjects'. Stoicism also instilled in him the need to put duty before his own personal needs. To him, it seems, government of the empire was a burden imposed by his birth. The ideals and ethical code that came from his Stoic beliefs are clearly seen in one of the most well-known quotations from his work: 'Keep yourself, therefore, simple, good, pure, upstanding, without arrogance, the friend of justice, godly, kind, gracious, firm in the performance of duty.'

Marcus Aurelius's behaviour was undoubtedly marked by these philosophical principles, as can be seen in the way he governed, particularly in his care for the cities and in his treatment of the Senate. Perhaps also as a consequence of the application of these ideals in the administration of the State, his rule has more continuist than innovative characteristics, as evidenced by the fact that the process of centralization of power that defined the previous reigns was now accelerated. The imperial bureaucracy increased considerably, and the State continued adding to its powers and intervening in matters in which it had not traditionally been involved. One example is the restoration of the administrative divisions of Italy that Hadrian had carried out.

Marcus Aurelius also set great store by the ruler's duty to carry out good works, to which all his predecessors had given so much importance. He showed significant largesse to Rome by seven donations and the institution of two new food programmes, one in commemoration of the marriage of Lucius Verus with his daughter, and another in honour of his late wife. He also tried to respond to a plague that devastated the empire during his tenure with the creation of a programme for the care of orphaned children. He placed much importance on legislative activity that protected the most disadvantaged, such as orphans, slaves and widows. In addition, following the examples of Trajan and Hadrian, he cancelled all debts to the treasury for the previous 46 years, the records of which were burned in the Forum. Marcus Aurelius also continued with the policy of previous emperors in favouring legislative measures that brought the activity of sellers and transporters of wheat and oil within the framework of the *annona* (the office of food distribution).

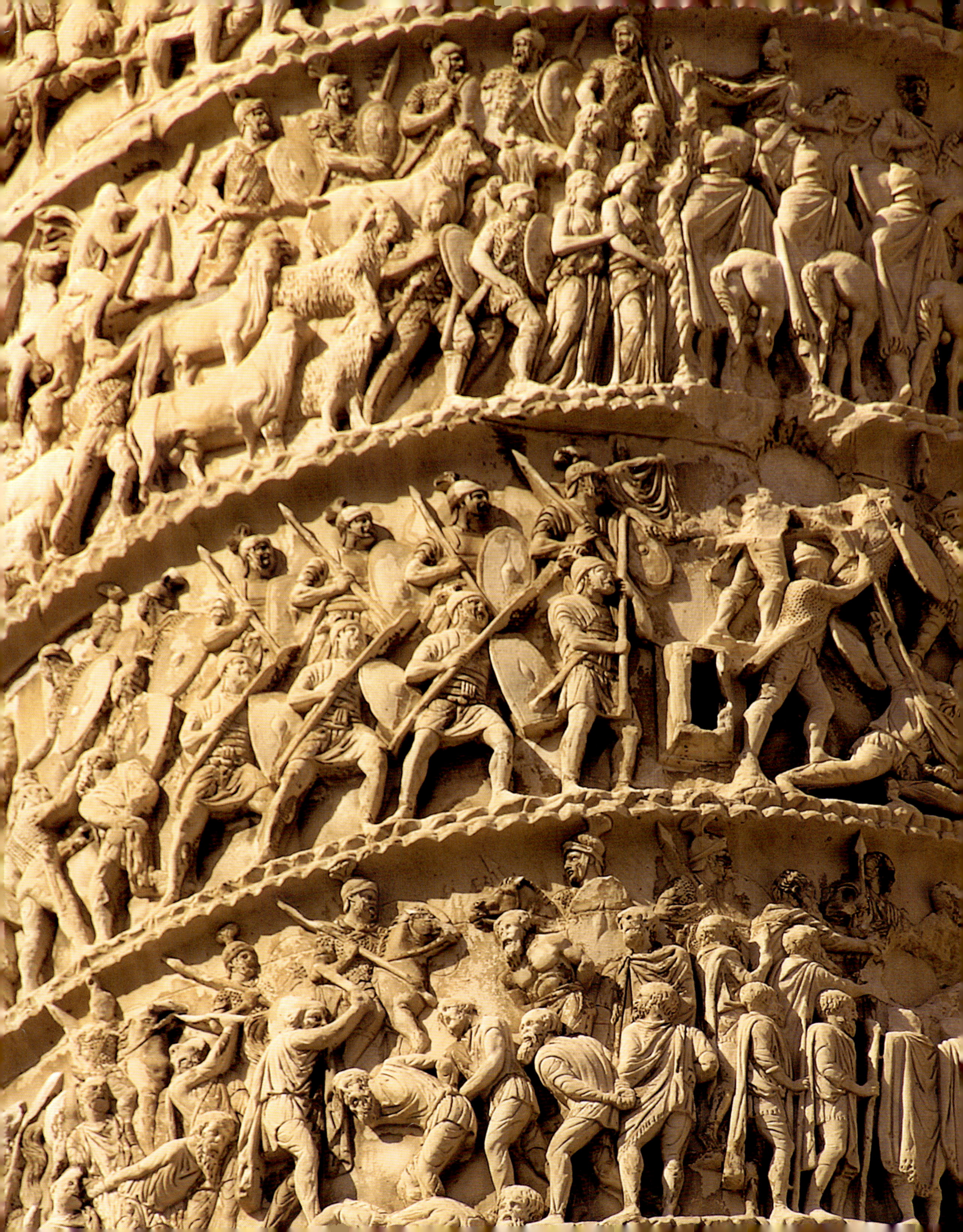

The writings of Marcus Aurelius, the philosopher emperor

Emperor Marcus Aurelius adopted the teachings of Stoic philosophy and tried to live up to them. He collected his thoughts in a work known as the *Meditations*, written in Greek. In it is revealed a straightforward ruler, weighed down by the gravity of his position, but firm in the fulfilment of the mission that had been entrusted to him. The emperor wrote this work almost at the end of his life, while he was taking part in military campaigns away from Rome, and the only copy existing today is in the Vatican Library. The themes covered by the *Meditations* are very broad, describing the teachings that the ruler followed and who had taught them to him, as well as his own reflections on life, death, religion, power and many other issues. Although the character of Marcus Aurelius has been subject to conflicting assessments by researchers, especially in terms of the weight that each one of them gave to the statements contained in the *Augustan History*, in the case of the *Meditations* the vast majority of scholars agree in their praise for the text and its author. The work was already influential in antiquity, although it is unknown how it was published. According to some researchers, Marcus Aurelius simply jotted down his thoughts to remind himself of the precepts he had learned in happier times while he was away from Rome and in dangerous circumstances. This marble bust of the emperor is in the British Museum, London.

CTESIPHON (OPPOSITE)
This city, one of the largest in Mesopotamia, was one of the recurring objectives of the Roman Empire thanks to its strategic position on the banks of the Tigris. It was conquered by Trajan and Hadrian before being taken in the Parthian War during the reign of Marcus Aurelius. Avidius Cassius had to return the city to the Parthians when a peace was agreed. All that remains of that city today is the ruins of the sixth-century Sasanian palace.

Marcus Aurelius helped cities such as Izmir, which suffered a devastating earthquake, and assigned administrators (*curatores*), as other emperors had done before, to those cities that had problems, especially economic ones. This allocation of administrators eventually meant the loss of the self-government enjoyed by the cities of the Mediterranean, accelerating the process of centralizing the empire.

The Parthian War

From the beginning of the joint reign of Marcus Aurelius and Lucius Verus, the large-scale wars that characterized the period began. The first major confrontation occurred in the East against Rome's greatest enemy in the region: the Parthian Empire. This rival of the Roman Empire had experienced a renaissance and expansion thanks to the stable government of King Vologases IV (147–191). This monarch took advantage of the change of emperor to send his armies into Armenia and Syria.

The Parthian assault began in 161 with the rapid advance of two forces, which both defeated the Roman legions. Vologases put a Parthian prince on the Armenian throne. However, the Roman response was fast. In 162, a powerful army was sent to the region under the leadership of Lucius Verus. Yet Marcus Aurelius retained supreme command and even appointed Lucius Verus's lieutenants. It is interesting to note that Lucius Verus was described in the *Augustan History* as a bad emperor, of amoral, dissolute, jealous and undisciplined habits. This work blames him for how he entertained himself on the journey from Rome to the front, which he reached in 163. It also reproached him for staying in Antioch during the campaigns, indulging himself in a life of gambling and excess. However, the testimony of this source does not coincide with the writings of Marcus Cornelius Fronto, tutor to both rulers. The letters that this author exchanged with Antoninus Pius, Marcus Aurelius and Lucius Verus seem to exculpate the young prince of the iniquities attributed to him by the *Augustan History*; they even describe him as a good general and emperor.

The Roman offensive began in 163. Statius Priscus recovered Armenia in 164. The following year, Avidius Cassius pushed into Mesopotamia, even penetrating Media. During the advance, the Romans captured Ctesiphon, home to 400,000 people and the largest Greek community outside the Roman Empire. The Greeks allowed the Roman legions to enter, but the city was destroyed anyway and with it this stronghold of Hellenism in the East.

Not long afterwards, in 166, Avidius Cassius managed to make Mesopotamia into a Roman protectorate. The war thus ended with a great victory, and the emperors were able to organize the first triumphal procession in Rome since the one posthumously given to Trajan in 118. Lucius Verus received the title of 'Pater Patria' (father of the fatherland), which lifted his status closer to that of Marcus Aurelius. Both added to their names the epithets 'Armeniacus', 'Medicus' and 'Parthicus Maximus'. However, this victory could not be exploited to its fullest, because major conflicts were breaking out on the Danube frontier.

The Marcomannic War

While Lucius Verus was fighting against the Parthians, new revolts had to be put down in Britain and the Rhine. Neither situation was too worrying, but there were two consequences of the Parthian War that were disastrous for the empire.

REIGN OF MARCUS AURELIUS

Year 161

Ascension to the throne. On the death of Antoninus Pius, Marcus Aurelius assumes power, with Lucius Verus, the other 'Augustus', as co-ruler.

Years 162–166

Parthian War The invasion of the empire by the Parthians unleashes a war, which is directed by Lucius Verus and ends in Roman victory.

Year 166

The empire suffers a plague. The victorious troops of Lucius Verus bring a plague from the East that ravages the empire and results in many deaths.

Years 167–175

The Marcomannic War. Barbarian tribes from the north, including the Marcomanni, penetrate the empire. The result is a war that continues through much of the reign.

Year 175

The Avidius Cassius revolt. The most important general of the East proclaims himself emperor, but is soon assassinated.

Years 177–180

Commodus is co-ruler. Marcus Aurelius gives his son Commodus the title 'Augustus' and adds to his governmental roles, paving his way to the throne.

ROME DOMINATES THE WORLD

The Portonaccio Sarcophagus: testimony of war

In the second century, interment generally took the place of cremation. Noble families ordered lavish sarcophagi in order that the social differences so obvious in life would continue after death. Although historians have looked for autobiographical elements in the reliefs that adorn them, the scenes were carved with standardized motifs that tell us more about society than the particular individual entombed. This sarcophagus, perhaps that of one of Marcus Aurelius's generals, was found in Portonaccio, near Rome (Museo Nazionale Romano, Baths of Diocletian, Rome).

The first was the plague brought back from the East by the legions. The magnitude of the disaster is not known, but it must have severely affected Italy and Rome itself, which in 167 suffered many deaths. 'The dead were carried away in carts ... the plague extinguished thousands of people, many even among the aristocrats.' This is how the *Augustan History* describes the situation in the capital, in a vision that recalls descriptions of the Black Death during the European Middle Ages. The plague was still claiming victims more than ten years later, although by then it had lost intensity.

The second consequence of the Parthian War was the weakening of the Danubian border, as at least three legions were removed from their barracks to swell the Roman army in the East. This was done in full knowledge of the barbarian danger: while the troops were moved, two new legions were recruited and trained to strengthen the *limes*. In addition, diplomatic contacts were made with the barbarians. Yet, before the Romans could complete these projects, the attacks began.

The situation on the Danube border was complex and historians do not know much about most of the tribes who harassed the empire. Nor did the Romans themselves have a precise knowledge of the enemy of a thousand faces that confronted them. For this reason, this conflict, which took up most of the reign of Marcus Aurelius, was called at the time both the Germanic War and the Marcomannic War, from the Proto-German for 'frontier tribes'.

The principal tribes who participated in the war were the Marcomanni tribal confederation and the Quadi, both of Germanic stock, whose lands bordered the provinces of Raetia and Noricum; and facing Pannonia and surrounding Roman Dacia, the Sarmatians, with their many

1 CENTRAL SCENE
This portion of the relief depicts the general leading a charge of the Roman cavalry during a battle of the Marcomannic War. His face is unfinished, perhaps because the work was created speculatively.

2 LOWER SCENE
Below the cavalry charge, other Roman units of infantry and cavalry attack and defeat the enemy. In defiance of perspective, these figures are slightly smaller than those further back.

3 THE DEFEATED
The foreground of the composition is covered with the bodies of defeated enemies, who are trampled by Roman soldiers.

4 THE END OF THE CONFLICT
The battle scene is flanked by trophies and barbarians with tied hands, who reveal that the outcome of hostilities was victory for the Romans.

5 UPPER FRIEZE
This narrates crucial moments in the life of a man, beginning on the left with the purification ceremony on the ninth day after birth. In the centre is a wedding.

6 CLEMENCY
The upper right corner of the sarcophagus presents a typical scene showing clemency on the part of the victorious general, who accepts the submission of the barbarians.

tribes, such as the Iazyges, Bastarnae and Roxolani. These tribes were accompanied by others of whom we know little and of which in some cases only the name has been preserved.

Clashes began in 167 after Balomar, leader of the Marcomanni, came to an agreement with the main enemies of Rome, who attacked in concert. The Quadi assaulted Pannonia, while the Sarmatians made for the Dacian gold mines; the Marcomanni crossed into Noricum, trying to reach the port of Aquileia, in Italy itself. Although the barbarians were met by local forces, Lucius Verus and Marcus Aurelius could not respond in person because they had to stay in Rome, where the plague was raging.

In the spring of 168, the emperors marched on Aquileia and then north. Although there were no decisive victories, the barbarian tribes decided to agree a peace. In January 169, the Caesars set out for Rome. On the way, Lucius Verus died, perhaps of apoplexy, although some sources maintain that Marcus Aurelius had him poisoned to get rid of an unruly and inefficient co-ruler. Whatever the truth, Marcus Aurelius officiated at his adopted brother's funeral and deified him. The emperor then returned to the Danubian front in the autumn of 169.

Meanwhile, the legions quartered in northern Italy, in a second defensive line that guarded the Alps, were decimated by the plague. The Marcomanni and Quadi took advantage of the moment to attack again. In the spring of 170, the clashes resulted in a Roman defeat in hostile territory beyond the Danube. Then the barbarians invaded and plundered the north of Italy, besieging Aquileia. Other tribes took advantage of the space created by these powerful tribes to plunder the Balkans. The Costoboci even reached Eleusis. The empire was facing a threat of extreme gravity.

ROME DOMINATES THE WORLD

GALEN AND MEDICINE IN THE ROMAN EMPIRE

In second-century Rome, the practice of medicine enjoyed great prestige. Those who practised it were usually of Greek origin and were part of the period's select group of enlightened scholars. Medical knowledge was the subject of numerous diatribes and discussions and was undergoing important changes and advances. From the literary works of the time, it can be concluded that medicine was in fashion. The foremost Greek doctor of the period was Claudius Galenus, usually anglicized as Galen, who was born in Pergamon (present-day Bergama, Turkey) in 129. He travelled extensively, exposing himself to a wide variety of theories and discoveries before settling in Rome. His fame was already so great in antiquity that Marcus Aurelius himself asked him to be his personal doctor. Galen was able to describe the symptoms of the great plague that broke out after the Parthian War. In the central image, Telephus, King of Mysia, wounded by Achilles, is healed by the hero who scrapes the rust from his spear into the wound, in a relief in the House of Telephus, in Herculaneum.

CLAUDIUS GALENUS
Galen's work decisively influenced Western medicine. He was a prolific writer, and numerous of his works on medicine, surgery and philosophy have been preserved. This anonymous portrait was painted in the 16th century (Library of the Faculty of Medicine, Paris).

THE MATURE EMPIRE

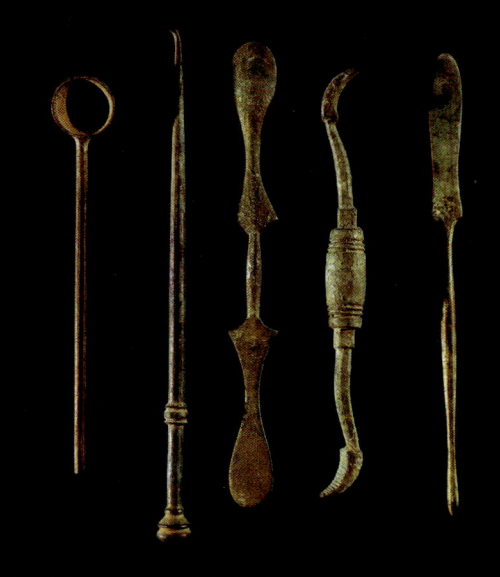

SURGICAL INSTRUMENTS
Although their knowledge of surgery was held back by major deficiencies in the field of anaesthesia, the Romans could carry out surgical interventions that, judging from the archaeological remains and artefacts, were made in rooms built for this purpose, with sterile material and decent instruments. The central instrument shown here is a spatula for stirring and spreading medicaments. To its right is a lever for putting fractured bones into position.

MEDICATION
The medicine of the time lacked the complexity of the modern pharmacopoeia, but the Romans could treat a very broad set of diseases, and many ancient remedies have their current correlate. For example, Galen medicated Marcus Aurelius, who was suffering from some type of ulcer, with potent analgesics whose base was opioids. Not only the rich, but also the lower classes and, above all, the Roman soldiers, enjoyed medical assistance.

Rome Dominates the World

Faustina the Younger, wife of Marcus Aurelius

Faustina the Younger was born in around 125, the youngest daughter of Antoninus Pius and Faustina the Elder. In 145, she was married to the future emperor Marcus Aurelius. The ancient sources collect numerous rumours about her licentious and scheming behaviour. However, when she died in 175, her husband had her deified. The question of Faustina must be understood in the context of the importance and influence enjoyed by the women of the imperial family in the second century. Matrons such as Matidia, Vibia Sabina, Plotina and Faustina the Elder were decisive during successions to the throne, and not always as compliant pawns. Faustina the Younger was used by Hadrian to build his succession plans through her engagement to Lucius Verus, but Antoninus Pius married her to Marcus Aurelius, with whom she had 13 children. Cassius Dio and the *Augustan History* present her as an evil empress who condemned her opponents to death. They accuse her of adultery with gladiators, with one of whom she was said to have conceived Commodus. The list of her infamies also included disloyalty, since she was presented as the instigator of the Avidius Cassius rebellion. At present, however, most historians question the veracity of the sources. This marble bust of the empress is in the Louvre Museum, Paris.

Efforts at containment by provincial governors and the emperor himself, with the support of local militias recruited on the march, allowed Rome to halt the enemy advance. The slow campaign to expel the barbarians was not completed until 171. In Carnuntum (in Austria), the emperor signed a peace treaty with the Quadi and other tribes, which enabled him to start a new campaign, this time offensive. Between 172 and 174, the legions crossed the Danube several times and succeeded in defeating the Marcomanni and the Quadi (who had broken their treaty), even though they had improved their combat techniques, having learned from their enemies. The plague and the barbarian invasions had sown panic in Rome, which feared disasters equal to those of the Cimbri and Teutones during the Republic. All this surrounded the conflict with a halo of legend, with some Roman victories attributed to divine intervention. In 174, the Marcomanni and Quadi accepted terms very favourable to Rome, with conditions such as the return of loot, the location of garrisons in their territories and the prohibition to approach the *limes*.

Marcus Aurelius could now focus on the Sarmatians, whom he also defeated and forced to agree harsh treaties. The sources report that the barbarians returned 10,000 captives as a result of the agreements, a figure that testifies to the magnitude of their incursions.

The Avidius Cassius revolt

While these events were taking place on the Danubian border, the East was not completely calm either. There were still problems in Armenia, where the king had to be defended from a pro-Parthian faction by the Romans. More worrying were the ravages of the Bucoli of the Nile Delta, which even endangered

Alexandria, the capital. Avidius Cassius, the general who had defeated the Parthians in Mesopotamia, suppressed this revolt.

At the end of April 175, this same man was proclaimed emperor. It was a conspiracy about which many interpretations were offered both then and now. Cassius Dio and the *Augustan History* tell the same story, although it is questionable. According to these sources, Faustina, Marcus Aurelius's wife, feared that her husband could die at any moment, as he had fallen ill. Faced with the possibility that her son Commodus would be left helpless, the empress tried to persuade Cassius to take over the empire and marry her. While weighing the proposal, the general got a message announcing the death of the emperor, which encouraged him to act. When, shortly after, another letter corrected the previous information, he decided to continue with his plans.

Marcus Aurelius heard the news while still on the Danubian front. The Senate, meanwhile, declared the usurper a public enemy. According to Cassius Dio, the emperor was surprised at the betrayal of someone he considered a good friend and hoped that no harm would befall Avidius Cassius so that he would be able to pardon him. Marcus Aurelius decided to head for the East to suppress the revolt, just when he was about to subjugate the Sarmatians definitively, and before he could conclude a restructuring of the region, which would probably have involved creating several new provinces in the Danube borderlands. The Empress Faustina, who was in the *limes* with her husband, accompanied him to the East. Commodus was summoned from Rome to join his parents and he was awarded the title 'prince of youth'. It was clearly an attempt to save the dynasty. However, the revolt was short-lived.

MOSAIC OF A FISHING SCENE
This mosaic from Tripoli, in Libya, the Roman Tripolitania, is indicative of the splendour that the North African provinces achieved at the time of the Antonines. It was an African scholar, Fronto, a native of Cirta in Numidia, who served as tutor to Marcus Aurelius and Lucius Verus.

The reliefs of Marcus Aurelius: his symbology

Few rulers of antiquity enjoyed greater authority and had a field of action as broad as the Roman emperors. The long process of concentration of power begun by Augustus was well established in the second century. The emperor had absorbed the powers of the previous republican State and assumed new ones. The emperor's powers were frequently manifested in art. A good example is this magnificent set of reliefs of Marcus Aurelius, perhaps created to decorate a triumphal arch lost today. Some of them are in the Museum of the Palazzo dei Conservatori (Rome); others were reused by Emperor Constantine, who placed them in their own triumphal arch in Rome. Caesar appears as general in chief, Pontifex Maximus and first citizen of the Senate. His attitude is that of a moderate and just ruler, victorious over his enemies but lenient with them. In 1, Marcus Aurelius, armoured and on horseback, shows himself benevolent with the barbarians, who fall to their knees in supplication. In 2, his head covered, the ruler acts as Pontifex Maximus and makes libations on a portable altar in front of the Temple of Jupiter Capitolinus. Also in the scene is the animal destined for sacrifice. The emperor's attendants carry a box of incense and a flute. In 3, he is the victorious emperor, travelling through Rome in a *quadriga* during a triumph. A winged Victoria crowns him. To the right, an arch marks the entrance to the city.

In July 175, the soldiers of Avidius Cassius assassinated their general, perhaps when they realized that the true emperor was still alive or when they saw the recklessness of his enterprise. Marcus Aurelius received the news of the death before he left for the East – the usurper's head was sent to him – but he did not change his plans. He dedicated the rest of the year and a good part of the next to touring the East, completing the pacification of the territory and ensuring the troops' loyalty. The emperor was benevolent about punishments for the rebellion. The family of Avidius Cassius was left unharmed and the penalties imposed on his followers were in most cases financial.

During the imperial journey, Faustina died in Cappadocia. Cassius Dio suggested that the empress had committed suicide to avoid retaliation from her husband. While in Greece, Marcus Aurelius was initiated into the famous Mysteries of Eleusis, something that Lucius Verus had done a few years before, confirming the central position occupied by Greece for the emperors from the time of Hadrian. Back in Rome, Marcus Aurelius deified his wife and, in December 176, celebrated the triumph over the Germans along with his son, whom he began to rule jointly with in 177, granting him, as he had done with Lucius Verus, the title of 'Augustus'.

The besieged fortress

The emperor's philosophical ideals did not prevent his reign from being marked by war. Sometimes the events of the Marcus Aurelius era – especially the border struggles against the Germanic tribes – have been interpreted as the prelude to the empire's crisis of the fifth century. Although this idea goes too far, it is true that Rome's power was entering a new era. On the one hand, the problems were no longer confined to one place, as they were springing up across all borders, and even in the interior in the form of piracy and banditry; on the other, the enemies of Rome had been transformed from long years of cultural contact. The Germanic tribes of the frontier had learned from the Romans, and would continue to do so. They were Romanizing, so they were no longer brave but easy to conquer tribes, but well-trained forces who understood their enemies.

One of the additional difficulties faced by Marcus Aurelius was the endemic problem in Britannia, where an extra military contingent had to be sent in 175. Likewise, it was essential to face the resurgence of piracy in the Mediterranean, which had been almost completely eradicated, and also banditry, especially in Gaul. However, the worst crisis was in Hispania, due to the invasions of the Moors, from North Africa. The first incursion was in 172 or 173, when the Moors crossed the strait and attacked Baetica, which was devoid of legions. The province sought help from neighbouring Tarraconensis, which received reinforcements from the Balkans and expelled the invaders. But the Moors again attacked the Iberian peninsula around 175, endangering even such important cities as Italica. The governor of Lusitania was in charge of ending the invasion, chasing the Moors to the province of Mauretania Tingitana.

As had been the case under Antoninus Pius, Marcus Aurelius sometimes combined strength with diplomacy, as happened during the period when Commodus was co-ruler. A bronze plaque, called *Tabula Banasitana* because it was found in the town of Banasa (Morocco), reports the granting of citizenship to Julianus, chief of the Zegrensi, and his family, in an attempt to win the friendship of a rebellious tribe.

COMMODUS
This marble bust of Emperor Commodus can be found in the Capitoline Museums, in Rome. On his breastplate is the head of the gorgon Medusa. On the opposite page is the helmet of a Roman gladiator of the second century, found in Pompeii (National Archaeological Museum, Naples).

THE END OF AN ERA

The second century, which historians have called the golden age of the Roman Empire, closed with the government of Commodus. The young prince was associate ruler with his father, Marcus Aurelius, and as sole emperor ended the empire's military campaigns of expansion. Commodus imposed a regime of terror to maintain his autocratic control over Rome, and his death marked the beginning of a long and terrible civil war.

Commodus was the first emperor to succeed his father since Titus. Marcus Aurelius appointed him co-ruler in 177. At only 15 years old, Commodus was also given the post of consul. Soon after, both leaders left for the Danube, from where Marcus Aurelius would not return.

The conflict on the Danubian front was a result of the peace terms imposed on the Quadi and Marcomanni. It seems that the barbarian tribes complained about the garrisons stationed in their territories to control their movements. The war began in 177. The Germanic tribes tried to create a great coalition of peoples like the one forged in the previous conflict, but the Sarmatians did not join them, as a result of the milder conditions of their treaty with Rome. In 178 there was progress for the Romans, but it was the following year that an important victory was achieved, allowing the stationing of 20,000 soldiers in enemy territory. During that year, coins were minted with the legend *Propagatores*

Commodus: timeline of his reign

Year 180
Sole government. After several years of sharing government of the State with Marcus Aurelius, Commodus puts himself at the head of the empire.

Year 182
Lucilla's conspiracy. The emperor's sister, widow of Lucius Verus, allies herself with influential characters in the court to conspire against him.

Year 185
The end of Perennis. The Praetorian prefect had replaced Saoterus as the emperor's chief of staff. He now falls after a revolt of legionaries.

Year 188
War on Deserters. Pescennius Niger stops the uprising of the legionaries discharged after the abandonment of hostilities on the Danube.

Year 190
Revolt against Cleander. A popular uprising over a grain shortage in Rome causes the fall of Cleander, Commodus's favourite.

Year 192
Murder of Commodus. The hatred that the emperor awakens provokes plots against him that, finally, succeed when the athlete Narcissus strangles him.

Imperii ('Enlargers of the Empire'), which, together with other testimonies, such as the *Augustan History*, suggests that Marcus Aurelius had decided to restart the project, paused by the Avidius Cassius revolt, of creating new provinces north of the Danube. Still according to the *Augustan History*, these new territories would be called Marcomannia and Sarmatia. However, before the military campaign of the year began, the emperor died in Sirmium (in present-day Serbia), on 17 March 180, leaving Commodus with the Danubian problem. Marcus Aurelius's body was sent to Rome, where he received the honour of an apotheosis.

Military campaigns were not the only activities carried out by father and son during their joint government. They also passed many laws. A decree was issued urging governors and magistrates to assist the owners of escaped slaves; provisions were made to fight banditry; and a new law defended the rights of freed slaves. Another notable measure was a decree for a limit on the costs of staging gladiatorial games. Through this measure, which was another example of State interventionism in civic affairs, they were attempting to protect the fortunes of local notables, who were sometimes ruined by competing to stage the most lavish events. Likewise, they wanted to avoid the abuses of gladiator trainers, who took advantage of high demand to ask for excessive fees. This situation had worsened since 169 and 170, when a forced levy of gladiators was made for the legions, raising costs for the nobles who had to finance the festivities.

The first solution that the emperors put into practice to solve this serious problem – at least in Gaul – was to allow the purchase of death-row inmates to use as fighters in the arena, but soon innocent people were being sentenced to death to increase the number of gladiators. It seems that the increase in the persecution of Christians during the reign of Marcus Aurelius was linked with this shortage of gladiators more than with an anti-Christian policy. The second solution was the decree about costs. However, this measure was also intended to prevent wealthy provincials from using the games as a means to gain fame that would allow them to prosper politically: the emperor reserved the position of top benefactor for himself.

A controversial reign

Commodus has traditionally been considered a bad emperor, a category he falls into with Caligula, Nero and Domitian. His reputation as a villain has been popularized today thanks to literature and cinema. The origins of this bad reputation are the historians of antiquity: all the sources denounce him. The *Augustan History* presents him as a lascivious, vicious, immoral and ruthless emperor. Cassius Dio excuses him in part from these defects, but dismisses him as weak-minded and cowardly. According to this source, it was his easily influenced character that left Commodus at the mercy of degenerate careerists, who led him into lust and cruelty. In *History of the Roman Empire*, the third-century

---

The *Tabula Gladiatoria* of Italica

One of the most important documents for our understanding of the gladiatorial games in the Roman Empire is the so-called *Tabula Gladiatoria*, which was found in the Roman amphitheatre of the city of Italica, in Hispania. The inscription sets down legislation by the emperors Marcus Aurelius and his son Commodus during the period of their joint reign, perhaps during 177 and 178. The text was engraved on several bronze plaques, of which one has survived, measuring 156 by 92cm (61 by 36in), in the National Archaeological Museum of Madrid. The law on the *Tabula* focuses on the control of the prices that the owners and trainers of gladiators, the *lanistae*, could request from the organizers of these celebrations, who were usually the cities' priests of the imperial cult and who had to pay out of their own pockets. The measure aimed at maintaining the celebrations without bleeding dry the local notables. On the right is the amphitheatre of Italica.

writer Herodian also portrayed him as easily led on account of his youth.

The testimony of these last two historians is especially significant, because Cassius Dio actually lived in Rome during the reign of Commodus, as, probably, did Herodian. However, their stories are mediated by the political circumstances in which they were composed and by the social position of their authors. Cassius Dio was a senator and had to suffer the continuous confrontation between the Curia and the emperor that characterized the government of Commodus. The *Augustan History*, a source in which historians have less confidence, also suffers from a clear pro-senatorial slant. Finally, Herodian used his work to explain the terrible state in which the empire found itself at the time he wrote, and considered that the origin of the third-century crisis was in Commodus's excesses. However, it should not be our aim to exonerate Commodus, but rather to attempt a dispassionate reconstruction, for which it is essential to appeal to other literary testimonies, as well as to epigraphy, numismatics and archaeology.

A rule of iron and rust

When concluding his description of Marcus Aurelius's reign, Cassius Dio stated that a golden age was ending and one of 'iron and rust' beginning. The key issue with Commodus's government was the enmity between the Senate and the emperor. Like Domitian, Commodus did not grant privileges to the Curia and did not hesitate to do away with its members. He imposed additional taxes on senators, with which he paid for the court's lavish lifestyle and the continuous gladiatorial games he held in Rome, which the members of the Curia were obliged to attend.

ROME DOMINATES THE WORLD

The Germanic peoples at the end of the second century

Beyond the border of the Roman Empire, which followed the course of the Rhine and Danube, vast stretches of land were inhabited by tribes, such as the Frisii, Burgundians, Costoboci, Marcomanni and Quadi. Some had been in contact with Rome for centuries, either peacefully or violently. Many of these tribes assaulted the borders looking for new lands and the riches of their southern neighbours. Others, like the Goths, advanced from the East, pressing the groups closest to the empire. The second-century emperors carried out numerous campaigns beyond the *limes*. From the mid-second century, and especially in the following centuries, the tables turned, and the barbarians seized the Roman Empire's traditional territory to form new states. The configuration of Europe was to change profoundly, beginning the long period during which a good part of the current nations were born. In contrast to the popular image of the barbarians, many of these peoples had evolved thanks to their contact with Rome. Most of the barbarous nations that took advantage of the disappearance of the empire – and contributed to its fall – were no longer backward and uneducated, but were deeply Romanized, which turned these groups into formidable enemies. To the left is a bust of Commodus (Capitoline Museums, Rome).

The problems began soon after the death of Commodus's father and had their origin in the political decisions taken by the young emperor, mainly in abandoning the campaign on the Danube. The ancient writers attributed the end of the war effort to the emperor's cowardice and softness, saying he wanted to enjoy the pleasures of the capital as soon as possible. They also attributed the decision to Commodus's fear for his health, since the plague had spread among the troops. According to the sources, he unexpectedly concluded the campaign and returned immediately to Rome.

However, Marcus Aurelius died in March and Commodus did not arrive in Rome until the end of October, which proves that he did not accelerate his departure. The conditions imposed on the Quadi and Marcomanni were harsher than those conceded by Marcus Aurelius. They were forced to return prisoners, to offer up warriors to fight as auxiliary troops in the Roman army and to pay tribute in kind. They were forbidden to approach the river. When Commodus deviated from his father's plans, he did not make a frivolous decision: he decided to conclude an overly onerous war that would, in any case, not allow for the construction of more solid border defences, because the best protection was provided by the Danube itself. His decision was in line with the policy already practised by Hadrian, aiming at the internal development of the empire and the containment of the enemy beyond the *limes*. But as was the case with his predecessor, the change brought him fierce criticism and the loss of the support of the military aristocracy.

Back in Rome in 180, the ruler, who was only 19, sought the support of new counsellors, tending to govern through these intermediaries.

THE END OF AN ERA

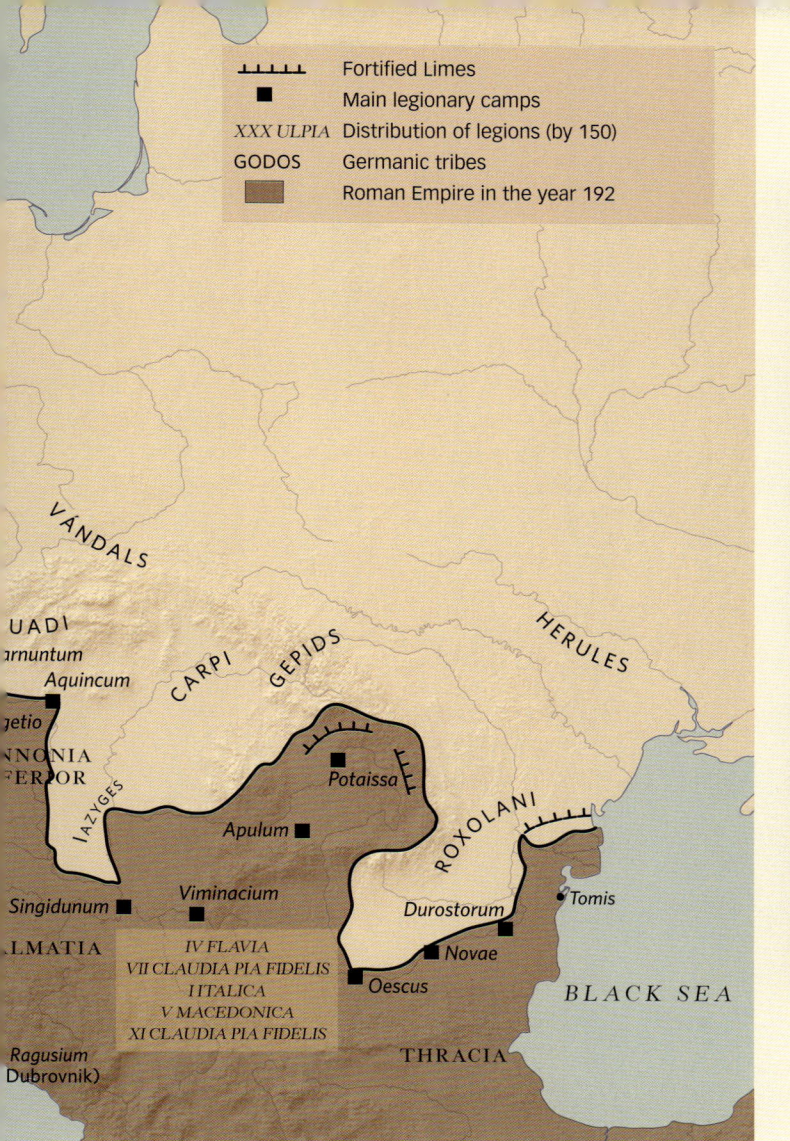

PARTHIAN MONUMENT FROM EPHESUS
Erected to honour Lucius Verus, this monument combines battle scenes with the victory of the Roman general. This fragment depicts a soldier striking a kneeling enemy (Ephesus Museum, Vienna).

This further deteriorated relations with the Senate. However, Commodus did not ignore the Senate, since he held the consulate in 181, as well as on four other occasions, and attended meetings of the Curia. Yet the defection of most of the high-ranking men of the previous regime soon led to problems. In 182, a conspiracy against Commodus involved his own sister, Lucilla, who had been married to Lucius Verus. The conspiracy included other members of the imperial family and influential senators. They planned to assassinate Commodus when he arrived to preside over some games. The magnicide would be carried out by Claudius Pompeianus Quintianus, who was promised to Lucilla's daughter. The setting and the manner in which the murder was to be perpetrated recalled the tyrannicide of Caligula, a similarity undoubtedly sought by the conspirators. The result, however, was not as expected.

Quintianus approached Commodus, showed him the dagger and said, 'This is what the Senate sends to you.' This gave the emperor's guards time to react, and Quintianus was overwhelmed. This event must have shown the young ruler the truth of his situation in Rome. From that moment, Commodus was always on the watch for conspiracies, leading to demagogy and terror as a means to protect himself and strengthen his absolute power. Those most affected were, of course, the senators, who suffered continuous persecution and humiliation, although equestrians also came under fire. This first conspiracy resulted in the deaths of many members of the Curia, both those who had taken part and those who aroused suspicion or were simply accused by anonymous informers. The emperor's sister was banished to Capri, where she was soon murdered.

Lucilla, the plotting sister of Emperor Commodus

Lucilla, the second daughter of Marcus Aurelius and Faustina the Younger, was an influential woman who carried the title of 'Augusta'. Accustomed to power, she held a prime position in her father's succession plans. At the age of 11, she was engaged to Lucius Verus, whom she married in 163 or 164, in Ephesus, when he was commander of the Roman armies during the Parthian War. When she was widowed, and before the end of her period of mourning, in 169, Marcus Aurelius forced her to marry a much older general, Tiberius Claudius Pompeianus, who was one of his main supporters. Her father's death probably made Lucilla aspire to greater power, but her brother Commodus had other plans. Two years after the young emperor's return to Rome, Lucilla was the main instigator in a conspiracy against him. Her motives are unclear: she might have been concerned about the discontent caused by Saoterus, the imperial chamberlain, or she may have been resentful at losing a good part of her privileges in favour of Commodus's wife. The objective of the plot was to kill the ruler and replace him with one of the nobles involved. The plan, however, was not successful. Lucilla was sent into exile on Capri in 182; Commodus ordered her execution that same year. On the left is an aureus bearing a bust of Lucilla Augusta.

The gladiator emperor

All the sources agree that Commodus had a great fondness for public shows, especially chariot racing, *venationes* (animal hunts) and gladiatorial games. The emperor trained as a warrior and charioteer, and on several occasions participated in the festivities himself. According to some ancient authors, he charged the public treasury one million sestertii for each of his appearances, an extraordinary sum, enough to feed a thousand families for a whole year. He also took part in the animal hunts. For example, it is reported that in two days he killed a rhinoceros, five hippos, two elephants and a giraffe, while in another celebration he slaughtered 100 lions, throwing spears from a podium built for that purpose in the arena.

Commodus was a skilled archer. On one occasion, he shot several ostriches in the neck with arrows that had crescent-shaped points, so that their heads were cut off and they carried on running without them. According to Cassius Dio, after carrying out one ostrich hunt, he cut off the head of one and, grinning, held it in the faces of the senators present to show them he would be happy to treat them the same way.

The emperor's fondness for shows also generated many fanciful or false stories, such as his killing of 'giants' in the arena. These were apparently people who were lame and he had dressed up as mythological giants, with 'serpents' wrapped round their legs. He killed them with his club while they threw sponge 'stones' at him. It was also said that Faustina, the wife of Marcus Aurelius, had fallen in love with a gladiator who was Commodus's real father. The story did not end there, as it was also said that the empress bathed in the blood of this same warrior to heal herself.

Supposedly, Commodus's taste for shows, along with his dissolute and orgiastic life, led him to delegate power to flatterers whose sole objective was to keep him happy while increasing their wealth and pre-eminence. However, Commodus's search for support outside the usual circle of Roman aristocracy was a symptom of his need to surround himself with people whose fidelity was beyond doubt. After Lucilla's conspiracy in 182, several obscure individuals shared the ruler's favour. First was Saoterus, a former slave who was his chamberlain. The general dislike that this character provoked led to his murder at the hands of the two Praetorian prefects, Tigidius Perennis and Tarrutenius Paternus. Then, Perennis got rid of his companion and took over the reins of government from 182 to 185, when he was denounced by legionaries from Britannia, for reasons that are not fully known. Commodus then got rid of him. The chaotic situation had to be controlled by the future emperor Pertinax. The emperor's trust then fell on Marcus Aurelius Cleander, another freedman of dubious reputation, who was Praetorian prefect and enjoyed favour until 190.

Through Cleander's years of office there were murders of senators and equestrians who opposed the ruler's autocratic plans, their fortunes swelling the emperor's treasury. Nobody was safe. Even his wife, Bruttia Crispina, whom he married in 178, was murdered after being accused of adultery. Military and political posts, such as the consulate, were sold to the highest bidder regardless of social extraction, which was a new outrage to the senators. The climax of this policy was in 190, when there were 25 consuls simultaneously, among them the future emperor Septimius Severus. Commodus named new members of the Curia among those who bought their favour or whom he found useful. Cleander met his end in 190 because of a popular revolt, perhaps orchestrated by the senators, who blamed him for a food shortage. The shortage was in fact caused deliberately by Papirius Dionysius, prefect of the *annona* (food office), who had been deprived of the post of prefect of Egypt by Cleander. Commodus, who placed great importance on the feeling of the people, gave his right-hand man to the mob.

Commodus's government of the empire

Many historians argue that, during the second century, the State administration had reached such a degree of maturity that it operated independently of the emperor. According to this theory, the specific character and behaviour of the ruler affected the capital and the nobles, but life in the provinces continued obliviously thanks to the well-run bureaucracy. This argument echoes the opinion that Tacitus put in the mouth of the Roman general Quintus Petillius Cerialis in a speech to the Gauls: 'You enjoy the advantages of the good emperors as much as we do ourselves, although you die far from the capital; nevertheless, you do not suffer the cruel emperors who overpower those closest to them.'

POLLICE VERSO
The Latin phrase pollice verso *means 'with a turned thumb'. In this 1872 oil painting by Jean-Léon Gérôme, a triumphant gladiator awaits the emperor's verdict, which he will give by turning his thumb up or down. Gladiatorial shows were loved by Emperor Commodus, who took part in some of them, doing little to improve his image among the senators.*

ROME DOMINATES THE WORLD

TRADE IN IMPERIAL ROME

At the end of the second century, Rome was the most important city in the Mediterranean and the nerve centre of a flourishing trade network where products from all over the empire and beyond its borders converged. The general peace enjoyed during this century explains the great boom in trade, because it allowed the free movement of people, ideas and merchandise. The Greek orator and author Aelius Aristides, in his speech known as 'Regarding Rome', offers the best description of the centrality of the city in imperial trade: 'Here is brought from every land and sea, the fruits of all seasons and the produce of all the regions, rivers and lakes, as well as the arts of the Greeks and the barbarians, so that, if someone wanted to take a look at all these things, they would need to travel the whole earth, or just visit this city ... So numerous are the cargo ships that arrive carrying all the goods from everywhere during every hour and day that the city looks like a workshop shared by the whole earth.' In the central image is a relief depicting a knife seller showing his customer several cutting instruments. It decorates the altar-ossuary of an ironmonger, Lucius Cornelius Atimetus, which is today in the Museo della Civiltà Romana, in Rome.

A BAKERY
A customer buys from a Pompeiian bakery the same type of loaf that has actually been preserved intact under the ash that erupted from Vesuvius during the first century.

THE END OF AN ERA

FABRICS AND CUSHIONS
This relief depicts seated customers, with their slaves standing beside them, who are being shown a range of wares by salespeople (Museo della Civiltà Romana, Rome).

A BUTCHER
Fresh, good-quality meat, including boar, pork, beef and lamb, was a luxury product. Poorer Romans, who often lacked cooking facilities, could buy ready-cooked sausages, tripe and blood puddings.

A TAVERN
An innkeeper fills a jug with wine from a barrel in the funerary stele of Sentia Amarantis, wife of the owner of such a premises (National Museum of Roman Art, Mérida).

BRONZE COIN
The obverse of this coin bears the image of Emperor Commodus, while on the reverse is a depiction of the Temple of Jupiter Capitolinus. To finance the extraordinary expenses of his reign, Commodus increased taxes on the senatorial class, which generated huge tensions.

Undoubtedly, the Roman State had achieved great effectiveness in the hands of good managers who were outside palace intrigues. The interesting thing is, therefore, to know to what extent government was different under Commodus than under the emperors who preceded him. And despite the negative portrayals, there are also sources, both literary and otherwise, that suggest that the last emperor of the dynasty was also dedicated to the work of State, although not in the way that Marcus Aurelius might have liked. For example, differing greatly from the apocalyptic portrait that has been given of this reign, Tertullian, a Christian writer under Commodus and the Severans, praised the happiness of the empire during this time: 'Every day we know more about the world; it is better cultivated and more civilized than in the past. Everywhere there are roads, all regions are known, all countries open to trade. Fields have invaded forests. Sheep and cattle have driven away wild beasts … Where there are vestiges of life there are houses, human dwellings and right governments.'

The key issue in Commodus's reign was the hostility between emperor and Senate, which caused the annihilation of many notable families and precipitated the State into a terrible and costly civil war. However, in other areas, the government of Commodus was continuist, especially in the tendency to bureaucratization and the professionalization of the administration, which was based on the promotion to power of equestrians and the creation of new jobs for them.

In line with his predecessors, during Commodus's term the law was not neglected, as is attested by legislation approved by him and included in the *Digest*. A new push was given to the concentration of power in the figure of the emperor, a process that explains the emperor's religious policy, especially the measures he carried out in his last year in office, but also the turbulent relations with the Senate and the continuation of the good works and paternalistic policies of the dynasty. In fact, although he did not carry out major works in the capital (only a few baths and a temple are known to have been erected), Commodus gave the citizens several donations and financed continuous games, with which he managed to make the people his great ally.

With the people in mind, the emperor was concerned about the supply of grain. He took care to regulate the situation in North Africa, where there had been abuses of the regulations set by Hadrian. He built a new fleet to transport grain to Rome. Commodus also had to face the ongoing plague that was unleashed after the Parthian War. The number of victims is not known, but it is estimated that during the most virulent outbreak, between 187 and 188, there were 2000 daily deaths in the capital.

The reign of Commodus brought tranquillity to the Mediterranean. His father worked hard to bequeath Commodus a pacified territory, but with his return to the foreign policy stance of Hadrian and Antoninus Pius,

The production and distribution of wheat

The city of Rome had grown into an overpopulated megalopolis whose inhabitants were unable to produce the food they needed to live. This problem was especially serious in the empire's capital, but it also affected other big cities of the Mediterranean and much of Italy, whose fields were largely in the hands of wealthy landowners who did not devote them to cultivating cereals. Sicily, North Africa and Egypt were the city of Rome's bread basket. The emperors put great efforts into ensuring the proper functioning of the vital wheat supply chains, subsidized by the State but also involving private traders. Any failure in the production and distribution of wheat could be disastrous for Rome's governors, because grain shortages or increases in its price could unleash popular revolts. On the right is a third-century Roman mosaic from Uthina (near modern Tunis) depicting an allegory of Ceres harvesting wheat (Bardo National Museum, Tunisia).

the young ruler encouraged peace and the internal strengthening of the empire. There were, however, some confrontations, mostly on the borders, such as in Africa and in Germania Superior and Pannonia in 185. In Dacia, in 184, the fighting was briefly resumed without causing great problems, but the situation necessitated the extension of the Danube fortifications. Three years later, in 187, conflicts re-emerged, but they were put down quickly. In Britannia there were easily repelled incursions by northern tribes.

To these problems at the borders we must add an internal rebellion, known as the War on Deserters, which affected Gaul and Hispania. It seems that the uprising began at the beginning of the reign among the troops that had been demobilized after the Danubian peace, who were joined by the dispossessed and outlawed. The revolt lasted several years, perhaps up to 188, and the rebels even managed to plunder cities. Reinforcements had to be sent to the governor of Aquitaine, Pescennius Niger, who, supported by the future emperor Septimius Severus, then legate of the Lugdunensis province, wiped up the insurgents.

The leader of the revolt was a soldier named Maternus, the subject of an interesting story whose veracity has been questioned by some researchers. According to several sources, after the defeat of the revolt, Maternus managed to flee, but instead of hiding, he decided to go to Rome to kill the emperor. Several of the insurrectionists followed him, although by different ways. His plan was to take advantage of the spring festivities consecrated to Cybele to approach the ruler and assassinate him. However, Maternus was denounced by one of his colleagues, caught before he had the chance to act, and executed.

ROME DOMINATES THE WORLD

BATTLE BETWEEN ROME AND THE BARBARIANS
This second-century relief depicts the struggle between the empire's legionaries and the frontier peoples in all its harshness. In the background, a hut and an oak tree suggest the peasant lifestyle of the barbarians (Louvre Museum, Paris).

LIFE IN THE FORUM (OPPOSITE)
This fresco portrays the usual civic animation in the forum, the centre of every Roman city's social life (National Archaeological Museum, Naples).

The reign of Lucius Aurelius Commodus, relatively short compared to that of his predecessors, was marked primarily by the continuity of his economic and social policies with those of his dynasty. The emperor's main deviation was the treatment he gave the Senate and his open desire to be considered a divine ruler. These were not, however, the worst of the empire's problems: the real threats were in the scourge of the plague, the persistent assaults of barbarian tribes and the increasingly arduous effort of maintaining the unity of the empire under the aegis of a single caesar in Rome. Since the days of the Flavians and, particularly, during the second century, the emperors had been assuming new governmental roles and expanding the areas over which they had power. It was precisely this increase in government tasks and the primacy of the emperors that meant overcoming the limits that had characterized the imperial government since the time of Augustus. This explains the search for new ideological and religious formulas with which to sustain the increasingly autocratic figure of the emperor. This difficult task did not end until the fourth century, with the adoption of Christianity as the empire's only religion.

The end of Commodus

The emperor's final years were, according to the pro-senatorial sources, the peak of madness and depravity. After Cleander died in 190, Commodus leaned on Eclectus, husband of his mistress, Marcia, and Quintus Aemilius Laetus, who was the new prefect of the Praetorian Guard. He now moved towards a more marked absolutism, in which the figure of Caesar was equated with the State. The emperor introduced eccentric changes that have been interpreted as the ravings of a megalomaniac madman, but which are better explained by considering his actions as aimed at ideologically sustaining the totalitarian figure of the ruler.

To show the absolute primacy of Commodus, the people, the Senate and the legions – and all other institutions of power – received the epithet 'Commodianus'. The very epoch was renamed *Saeculum aureum Commodianum* ('the golden age of Commodus'). Even the months were given new names, all related to the emperor: Lucius, Aelius, Aurelius, Commodus, Augustus, Herculeus, Romanus, Exsuperatorius, Amazonius, Invictus, Felix and Pius. The capital was renamed Colonia Lucia Aurelia Nova Commodiana, turning the ancient city into a mere colony.

Commodus linked himself to Hercules, calling himself Herculeus Romanus and choosing a priest for his cult, a proposal that was approved, as with all official cults, in a session of the Senate. The aim was to elevate the emperor to the divine sphere during his own lifetime, a customary procedure in the cultures of the ancient Mediterranean and in Rome itself, but which the attitude of the Antonine dynasty had softened by delaying the deification of the emperor until after his death.

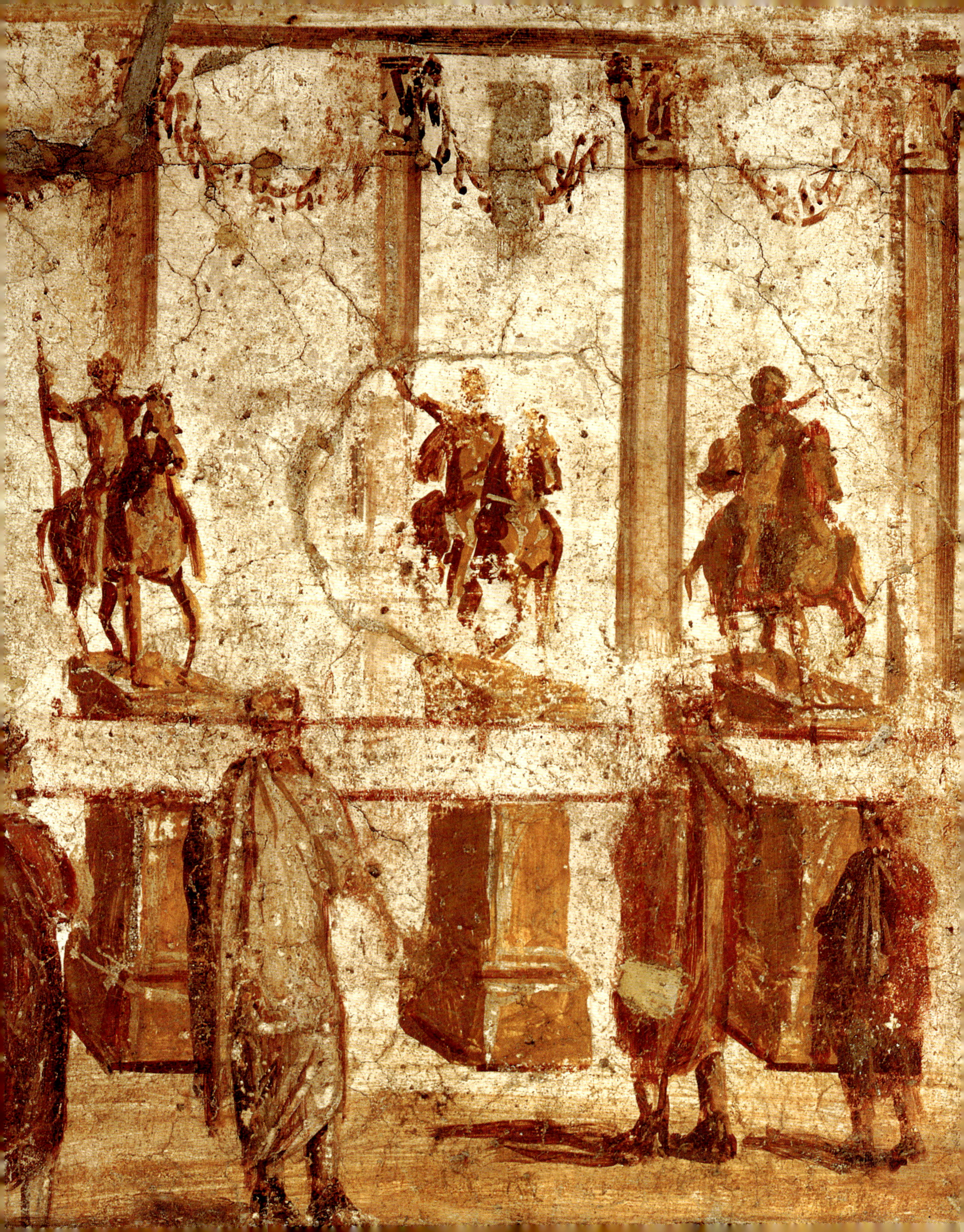

The 20 names of Emperor Commodus

In Rome it was customary to add other names to the one given at a child's birth. Some names were honorific and were passed down in a family, but others were received as a personal reward for a successful political career; for example, after taking part in a military campaign against the barbarian peoples.

Year 161
At his birth, the future emperor is named by his father, Emperor Marcus Aurelius: Lucius Aurelius Commodus.

Year 166
When he is named heir to the throne, Caesar is added to his name.

Year 172
After his father's victory over the Germanic peoples, he receives the title Germanicus. His name is now Caesar Lucius Aurelius Commodus Germanicus.

Year 175
He receives the name Sarmaticus in honour of the victory over the Sarmatians.

Year 176
He becomes his father's co-ruler, who grants him the titles of Imperator and Augustus. Thus, his official nomenclature is Imperator Caesar Lucius Aurelius Commodus Augustus Germanicus Sarmaticus.

Year 180
He is named sole emperor after the death of his father. He adds Antoninus's name to his official nomenclature and, later, changes his praenomen from Lucius to Marcus in memory of his father.

Year 182
He adds Pius to his name, then adds to Germanicus the qualification Maximus. At this point he has the title Imperator Caesar Marcus Aurelius Antoninus Commodus Augustus Germanicus Maximus Sarmaticus Pius.

Year 184
He now also takes the title Britannicus.

Year 185
With the addition of the title Felix, the emperor is now called Imperator Caesar Marcus Aurelius Antoninus Commodus Augustus Pius Felix Germanicus Maximus Sarmaticus Britannicus.

Year 191
He restores his praenomen and adds the name of the gens Aelia, to which the Emperor Hadrian belonged.

Years 191–192
He drops Antoninus's name but adds other titles: Imperator Caesar Augustus Pius Felix Invictus Exsuperatorius (Supreme, a title reserved for Jupiter) Lucius Aelius Aurelius Commodus Sarmaticus Germanicus Maximus Britannicus Amazonius (a name attributed to Hercules). Shortly after, Commodus also assumes other titles: Pontifex Maximus, Pater Patriae (Father of the Fatherland), Pacator Orbis (Pacifier of the World) and Dominus Noster (Our Lord), which completes his 20 appellations as they appear in the sources.

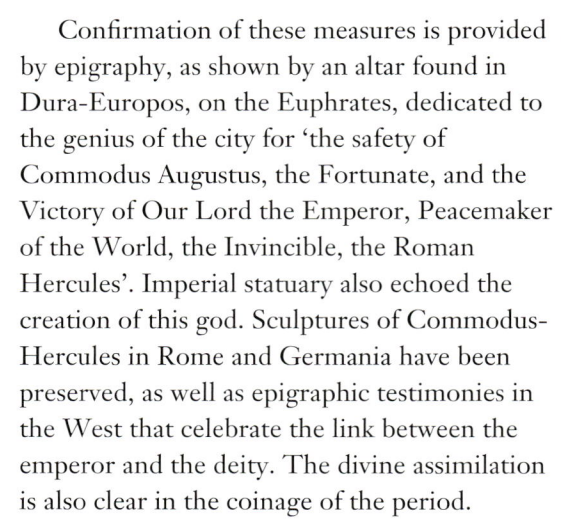

Confirmation of these measures is provided by epigraphy, as shown by an altar found in Dura-Europos, on the Euphrates, dedicated to the genius of the city for 'the safety of Commodus Augustus, the Fortunate, and the Victory of Our Lord the Emperor, Peacemaker of the World, the Invincible, the Roman Hercules'. Imperial statuary also echoed the creation of this god. Sculptures of Commodus-Hercules in Rome and Germania have been preserved, as well as epigraphic testimonies in the West that celebrate the link between the emperor and the deity. The divine assimilation is also clear in the coinage of the period.

The death of the emperor was the result of a new conspiracy. According to the ancient sources, Commodus intended to preside over the opening of the Senate on 1 January 193, at the front of a gladiatorial troop and dressed as one of them. The procession was to be preceded by the symbols of Hercules: a lionskin and club. This histrionic plan did not enjoy the approval of even Commodus's intimate collaborators. To prevent him from carrying it out, Marcia, Eclectus and Laetus planned to kill him. His mistress served him poisoned wine, but he vomited it up. They then sent in an athlete, Narcissus, to strangle him. The Senate rejoiced at the death of its nemesis and declared the condemnation of his memory.

This anecdotal version of the assassination has been reinterpreted by modern historiography, which backs the idea that there was a calculated plan to kill Commodus, orchestrated by influential figures of the time, including Pertinax. The death of Commodus was the beginning of a long period of political instability and civil war that would not conclude until the arrival of a new dynasty, initiated by Septimius Severus. Curiously, the vilified emperor became the ideological and legitimating reference point for the founder of the new lineage. Thanks to the first of the Severans, Commodus would leave the limbo of the forgotten and climb the Roman Olympus after the celebration of his apotheosis.

It is interesting to note that the vindication of Commodus's character under the Severans, as a link between the powerful dynasty of the second century and the new imperial family of the next century, although placing him among the gods, failed to alter his image as a corrupt and licentious emperor. The historians of antiquity, like Cassius Dio, have therefore exercised a greater influence on posterity than ideological constructions made by other emperors. Commodus, like Domitian, served, and continues to serve, as a model of the bad ruler who puts his personal whims before good government. The pro-senatorial writers could not tolerate that the government that had known how to keep the autocratic reality of its power camouflaged for almost a century, in that period Gibbon had called the happiest and most prosperous in all history, was once again openly independent, autonomous and despotic.

The moderation and benevolence that had characterized the previous emperors came to an end with Commodus. The broken ideal had its staunchest ideologues among writers close to the senatorial oligarchy. One of the clearest statements of how a good emperor should behave, according to the Curia, was given by Cassius Dio: 'How will they not all see you as a father, a saviour, and how will they not love you, when they see you always worthy, virtuous, good at warfare and yet peaceful; if you do not act with excess, nor do you defraud; if you address them as equals and do not enrich yourself while demanding money from others ... but instead you make your life in every way equal to theirs?' That equality between senators and emperor had been definitively broken. The last of the Antonines was the precursor of a new empire in which profound transformations would crystallize in all areas of life and, especially, in the conception of power. A new order was emerging.

THE MURDER OF COMMODUS
According to the sources, the emperor was strangled by Narcissus in the presence of Eclectus, Marcia and the Praetorian prefect Quintus Aemilius Laetus. This engraving was made around 1810 by Giuseppe Mochetti, based on a drawing by Bartolomeo Pinelli (Archiv für Kunst & Geschichte, Berlin).

ROME DOMINATES THE WORLD

'Panem et circenses'

'Bread and games', a phrase believed to have been coined by the satirist Juvenal, was the Roman emperors' formula for keeping the populace happy. Even today, centuries after the celebration of the last gladiatorial fight in Rome, these entertainments continue to fascinate for their brutality, their magnificence and their desperate human drama.

The Roman shows were much more than just entertainment: they established a powerful dialogue between rulers and the governed. For the emperor, in Rome, they offered an optimal space in which to present his political slogans, celebrate his glory and show his generosity. On a smaller scale, local aristocracies in the different cities of the empire put shows to the same use. But in an unequal and ruthless society like Rome's, the shows that the citizens liked so much had much broader semantics. They expressed the dominion of Rome over the rest of the world, demonstrated by the killing in the arena of slaves and prisoners of war from all corners of the empire and beyond.

Gladiatorial bouts and the re-enactment of battles demonstrated the pre-eminence of Rome, while remembering that this dominion had been obtained by force of arms. The combats restored the city's martial tradition, but in a domesticated manner that was useful for the emperors' political purposes. The presence in the amphitheatre and circus of exotic and dangerous beasts captured in remote regions – elephants, bears, ostriches, panthers, tigers, lions, hippos, crocodiles, rhinos – also confirmed this sense of universal domination.

On the other hand, the shows were the clearest reflection of the internal inequality of Roman society and actually contributed to maintaining these differences, since the social order was made concrete in the circus, amphitheatre and theatre. The imperial family presided from the position of honour. The senators took the first rows, which offered a better view of what was happening on the stage or in the arena, and that also allowed them to show themselves off before their fellow citizens. Next, the equestrians occupied the following rows. The rest of the population was also organized strictly. Married citizens sat in better areas than single citizens, and all of them were separated from the military. Freedmen, if they wanted to take the seats available to them, had to dress as citizens, by wearing a toga. Women and poor citizens, without a toga, occupied the worst, highest spots, with the exception of the vestal virgins, who could sit in the first rows.

The Flavian amphitheatre

In 80 AD, Emperor Titus inaugurated, with 100 days of celebrations, the largest building in the world dedicated to gladiatorial games, the Flavian amphitheatre – commonly known as the Colosseum because of the colossal statue of Nero that stood beside it. The building soon became Rome's central landmark.

The Colosseum lives up to its name: it is an immense building whose design not only impresses with its large dimensions, but also with the clever organization of the stairs, ramps and *vomitoria* (exits) that allowed ingress and egress in just a few minutes. The stands were in five sectors, the lower four of marble and the last of wood.

THE COLOSSEUM
On the left bank of the Tiber, this amphitheatre, which could hold 50,000 spectators, is one of the most famous monuments of classical antiquity.

THE FLAVIAN AMPHITHEATRE: 2000 YEARS OF HISTORY

Year 71
Work on the amphitheatre begins on the initiative of Emperor Vespasian, founder of the Flavian dynasty.

Year 80
Titus inaugurates the Colosseum with a *naumachia*, gladiatorial battles and huge animal hunts.

Year 82
The works are completed during the reign of Domitian, who adds a fourth floor to the building.

Year 217
Lightning starts a fire that significantly damages the building, which will be restored in 238.

Year 404
The emperor Honorius prohibits the celebration of gladiatorial games in Rome.

Fifth and sixth centuries
Two earthquakes, in 442 and 508, damage the structure of the building, which undergoes repairs.

Year 523
The last show in the Colosseum takes place in the time of the Ostrogothic king Theodoric.

GLADIATOR AUREUS
The fighter is depicted with the palm of victory (first century).

The bowels of the giant

Rome's Colosseum has an elliptical plan that measures 527m (1729ft) in diameter. It rose to almost 50m (164ft) in height and offered seating for 45,000 people, plus room for another 5000 standing. Its internal structure is radial: it rests on 80 pillars with travertine walls oriented towards the arena. Concrete vaults support the stands. The pilasters and arches are travertine, set without mortar. Tuff was used for the lower sections and the basement, set in the same way. All the seats were wooden until the great fire of 217. The illustration is a reconstruction of the Colosseum by Peter Connolly (1935). On the left is an oil lamp with the image of a gladiator during a workout.

The exterior façade was in four levels. The first three had 80 arches, each flanked by semi-columns of the three classical styles, Doric, Ionic and Corinthian, in ascending order. The second and third levels were lavishly decorated with statues. The fourth level had windows rather than arches, in addition to the posts and anchorages that held the awnings to protect the audience from the sun.

In the centre of the structure was the large area dedicated to fighting. Its surface was sand, on top of wooden planking. Under the arena, an underground complex, built in Domitian's time, served as storerooms and allowed the transfer of men, animals and merchandise. A system of ramps, trapdoors and lifts could create spectacular effects, such as the sudden appearance of beasts or new enemies.

The idea of building this majestic monument was Vespasian's, but he did not live to see it finished. The funds for its erection were obtained mainly from the booty from the Jewish Wars, although the demolition of Nero's old palace also contributed. In fact, the Colosseum was erected on the site of Nero's artificial lake.

A day at the amphitheatre

Before enjoying a day of shows, the Romans had to hand over their tablets (*tabellae*), equivalent to modern tickets, at the entrances. These cards indicated the door through which they had to enter, as well as the seat reserved for them. Once inside, attendees could enjoy the programme of festivities, which was almost always the same.

The animal shows (*venationes*) were held in the mornings (*ludus matutinus*), starting with the presentation of the beasts. The events could then be of various types. Sometimes there were hunts, either on horseback or with spears and arrows, and often gladiators were pitted against beasts. Other events were fights between animals, such as tigers against lions, or bulls against bears. Although the ancient sources may have exaggerated the figures, the number of beasts used in the *venationes* was very high. Augustus offered 26 shows of this type, in which 3500 animals participated. Pompey used 500 lions in five days, and Caesar,

THE END OF AN ERA

1 VELARIUM
A row of 240 protruding supports on the cornice fitted masts to which the rigging was attached for an immense awning, the *velarium*, which provided shade for the spectators.

3 WOODEN SEATS
The seats of the fifth level were wooden, to reduce their weight and the consequent pressure on the outer wall.

5 VOMITORIA
The *vomitoria*, the gateways through which spectators entered and exited the stands, had barriers to prevent falls in the stairwells.

7 MARBLE SEATS
The marble of the seats in the four first levels has not been preserved. The seats were reserved for, in this order: the senators, equestrians, citizens and plebeians.

9 ARENA
The major and minor axes of the elliptical arena were 75m and 44m (246 and 144ft). The floor is believed to have been wooden, with stone next to the stands.

11 THE FAÇADE
The façade (50m/164ft high) had four levels. There were 76 general entrances and four reserved ones, such as that for the emperor.

13 PENS FOR ANIMALS
Under the arena, a series of vaulted holding rooms was where some of the animals that performed in the shows were housed. Ramps and lifts took them to the surface.

2 UPPER PORTICO
A portico protected the upper tiers. Its columns were carved from grey granite or cipollino (green-veined marble from Euboea, Greece). The bases and capitals were white marble.

4 SAILORS
Sailors from the fleets of Misenum and Ravenna were employed to operate the rigging of the gigantic awning.

6 IMPERIAL BOX
On the south façade was the door reserved for the emperor (perhaps with a triumphal arch), who from there accessed the imperial box, which was located very close to the arena.

8 PODIUM
The senators, vestals, foreign ambassadors and other dignitaries sat on the first level of the stands, the *podium*, which was about 4m (13ft) above the arena.

10 ACCESS TUNNELS
Four concentric tunnels, whose walls were plastered and painted, allowed spectators to access the different levels via stairs.

12 MAGISTRATES' BOX
Opposite the imperial box was the box for consuls and other magistrates, who accessed the Colosseum through a special door.

14 DEEP FOUNDATIONS
The foundations of the Colosseum are concrete and about 12m (39ft) deep. The concrete was cast directly on the floor of the old lake, then encased in walls of brick.

surpassing his political enemy, offered 400 in a single day. During the days of empire these figures did not stop increasing. Titus, for example, put more than 5000 beasts in the arena during the festivities with which the Colosseum was inaugurated.

The midday hours were dedicated to the execution of criminals and prisoners of war, for which wild beasts were also used. In these events, the condemned person's deliverance was not an option and the animals were not intended to suffer harm, so the victims were thrown into the arena unarmed and generally tied. Although repugnant to us today, these events aroused such enthusiasm among the Romans that sometimes death-row prisoners were purchased, and even innocent people were condemned, so that these bloody intermissions could go ahead. Sometimes, the executions were not inserted between two performances, but were the core of the day's celebrations, as, for example, in the great naval battle organized by Claudius in 52 AD, in which 19,000 condemned men participated. The taste for naval clashes even led some emperors, such as Augustus and Trajan, to build special basins for them to take place, although they were also held in the amphitheatres. These shows were called *naumachia*.

Finally, the day closed with the climax: the gladiatorial bouts. Normally they were fought in pairs, but there were also many times when larger battles were staged, as when Julius Caesar commemorated the death of his daughter in 46 BC, when he faced infantry squads with units of cavalry and even elephants.

The gladiators

Historians do not agree on the origins of the gladiatorial games. Some argue that it was an Etruscan tradition that came to Rome along with many other customs from that civilization. They base their hypothesis on frescoes found in the Etruscan tombs of the city of Tarquinia, as well as on the opinion of classical authors such as Nicolaus of Damascus. However, other researchers maintain that this type of event originated in southern Italy. They base their theory on pictorial evidence, also found mainly on tombs. The first

Blood and sand

'Gladiator' literally meant 'warrior who fights with a sword', but the term was used to refer to any fighter in the arena. The gladiators were divided into types, of which 20 are known. The shows were designed to match pairs of gladiators whose weapons and protection were opposed, as, for example, the *retiarius* with the *secutor*: the former was able to move fast because he wore little armour, and could reach his enemy from afar with his trident; the latter had a large shield that allowed him to defend himself, but his weapon was short, so he had to come close to his opponent to kill him. The *hoplomachus*, *murmillo* and *Thraex* also used to fight each other. The origins of the gladiators were very diverse. Some were prisoners of war or convicted criminals. The best, however, were slaves who were taught by a professional trainer (*lanista*). This profession was not exclusive to men, as it is known that women also fought in the arena. On the right are two third-century mosaics from the National Archaeological Museum, Madrid.

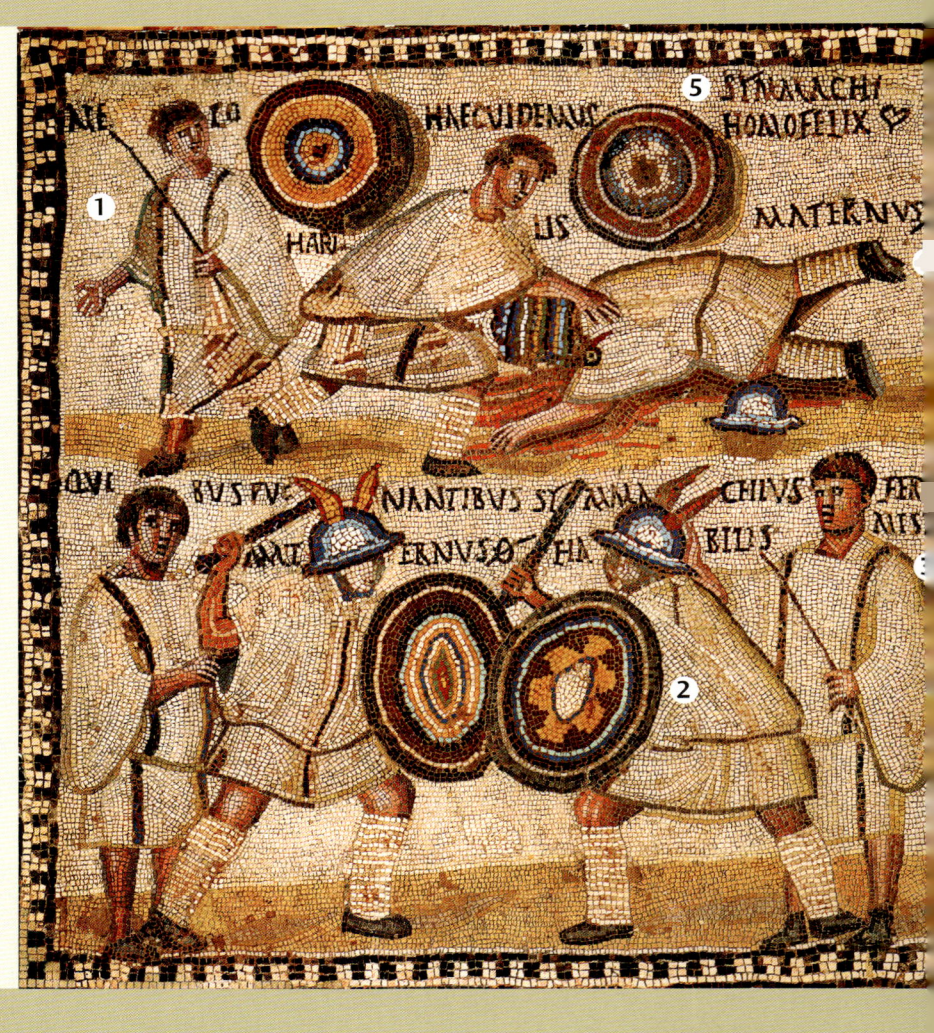

Roman mention of gladiatorial combats was in 264 BC, when Marcus and Decimus Junius Pera had three pairs of gladiators, who were prisoners of war, fight to commemorate the death of their father. In 216 BC, Marcus Aemilius Lepidus's sons put on three days of fighting, with 22 gladiator pairs, also to commemorate their father's death. On this occasion, the bouts took place in the Roman Forum.

Thanks to Rome's increasing wealth during the second century BC, the result of Mediterranean conquests, the fighting became more frequent and involved a greater number of warriors, but always kept the context of honouring the illustrious dead.

The end of the Republic, with its struggles between nobles to take power, meant an increase in the magnitude of games. Julius Caesar, for example, employed 320 pairs of gladiators to honour his father. This period also marked the start of the games' diffusion across the provinces. During the High Empire, gladiators became one of the most important entertainments, as evidenced by the construction of at least 200 amphitheatres in the Mediterranean.

The gladiatorial games were carefully structured, with organizers trying to make the most of the bloody skills of the fighters, pitting different types of gladiators against each other. The *Samnite* or *hoplomachus* wore a crested helmet with a visor, and a high greave on his left leg. He carried a long spear, dagger and small, round shield.

The *Gallus* ('Gaul') or *murmillo* carried a long shield and a short sword. His heavy helmet was topped with a fish-shaped crest, from which the name *murmillo* is derived, as *mormylos* meant 'sea fish' in Greek. A short greave on his left leg, as well as a guard of metal plates, called a *manica*, on his sword arm, completed his armour. The weapon of the *Thraex* ('Thracian') was a curved sword. He wore a helmet with a long visor and high greaves on both legs, and carried a small rectangular shield. The *secutor* ('pursuer') carried the long rectangular shield and short sword of the Roman legionary, as well as a segmented guard on his sword arm. His most distinctive feature was his smooth and heavy helmet, designed to hinder the work of his usual enemy,

THE END OF AN ERA

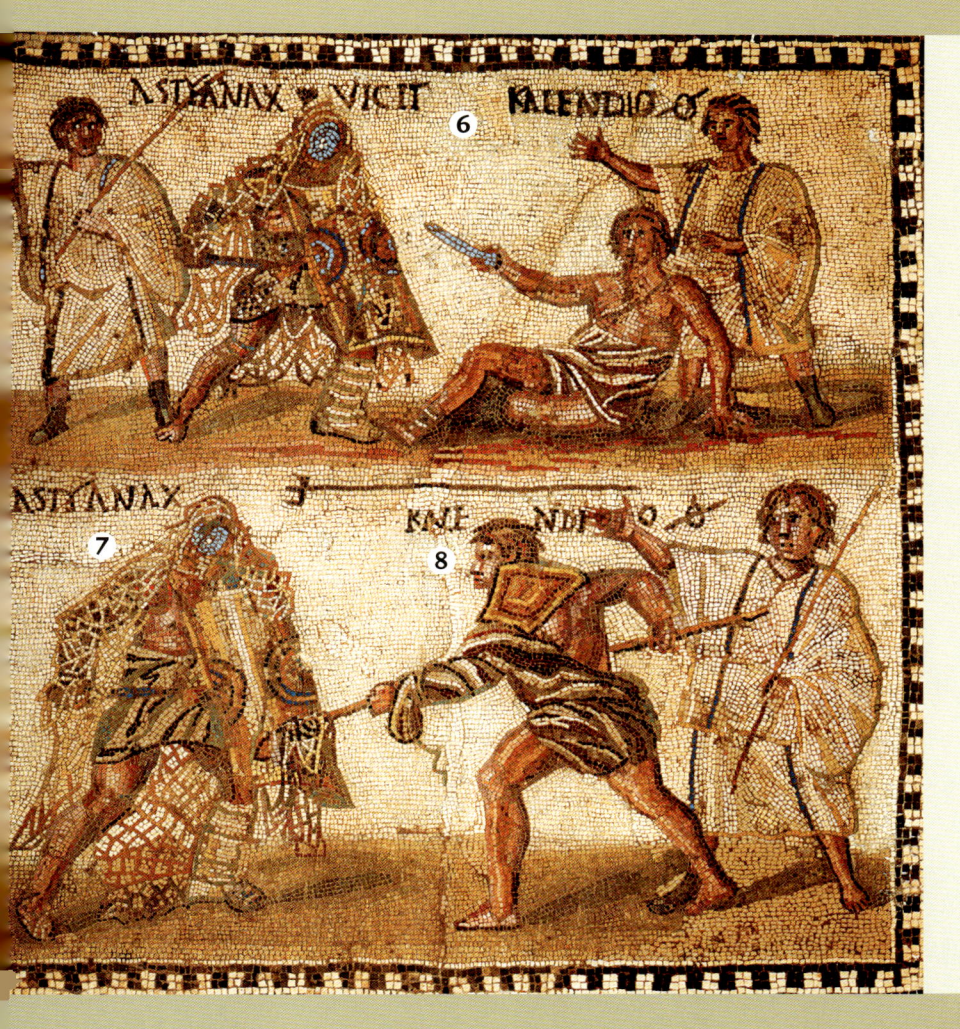

1 A COMBAT
This scene depicts the battle between two gladiators called Habilis and Maternus. The struggle is presented in two sequences, which begin in the lower portion of the mosaic.

2 GLADIATORS
The attire of the two contenders is very similar, with a tunic, protective bands for the legs, short swords, small round shields and feathered helmets.

3 REFEREES
The two men in tunics on either side of the gladiators are probably referees in charge of fair play.

4 THE RESULT
Habilis, the victor, bends over the defeated Maternus, whose name appears with the Greek letter *theta*, which indicates the death of the combatant.

5 SPONSOR
The text '*Symmachi homo felix*' (Symmachus, lucky man) could refer to a character who does not appear in the scene, perhaps the organizer of the games.

6 A FIGHT
This mosaic shows the struggle of a *secutor* named Astyanax against a *retiarius* named Kalendio. The story begins in the lower portion of the mosaic.

7 SECUTOR
The *secutor* Astyanax, covered by his opponent's net, has a helmet, protection on his right arm, a short skirt, bands on his left leg, a large shield and a sword.

8 RETIARIUS
Kalendio points his trident at his opponent. He wears a robe and a *galerus*, a metal shield to protect the shoulder and the nape of the neck.

---

the *retiarius*. The name of this type of gladiator comes from the *rete* (net), with which he caught his enemies. To facilitate speed of movement, this gladiator wore no helmet or greaves, but he did have a larger arm guard and sometimes a shoulder shield to protect the neck. He also fought with a trident.

Other entertainments

Although some Roman entertainments, like those in the amphitheatre, offered bloody battles and deaths, others resembled the entertainment that can be enjoyed today, such as chariot or horse racing, theatrical performances and Greek-type sports (*agones*).

To host these events, lavish venues were constructed, which are among the most well-known and admired vestiges of the classical past. Of note, of course, are the amphitheatres, which have a clear model in Rome's Colosseum and boast many well-preserved examples, such as those of Pompeii and Verona (Italy), Nîmes and Arles (France), El Djem (Tunisia), Pergamum (Turkey) and Italica (Spain).

The theatre, with its semicircular shape and richly decorated *scaenae frons* (architectural backdrop), continued to be used in Rome, although its mission changed, as performances of classical comedies and tragedies gave way to mime dramas and pantomimes. Theatres were also used for political activities, such as the reading of letters from the emperor in the provincial cities or the giving of speeches. Likewise, the theatres of the Greek East were adapted to stage gladiatorial games and animal shows, by closing the fronts of the stands with stone slabs to separate the fighters from the public.

A type of venue that arrived late to Rome was the stadium, of Greek origin and used mainly for athletics competitions. It had an elongated plan, with a length of about 200m (656ft). Stadiums are scarce in the Roman West but common in the eastern part of the empire, where they alternated between their traditional employment for sporting events and the staging of gladiatorial and animal shows. The current Piazza Navona in Rome is a magnificent example of the conservation of ancient spaces in modern cities; it retains the shape of the stadium that Domitian had built.

■ ROME DOMINATES THE WORLD

Charioteers

The teams that organized races provided horses, charioteers, chariots, doctors, veterinarians and trainers. They were identified by colours. In the republican era, there were only red and white, but at the beginning of the first century, green and blue appeared. The young charioteers aroused passion in their followers, as did their horses. The fans' devotion to their colour often degenerated into altercations. In the upper relief is a race in Rome's Circus Maximus. The main elements of the building and event can be seen: on the terrace, presiding over the event, is the *editor spectaculorum*; to the left are the gates of the *carceres*, where the chariots were kept. On the track, divided by a central spine, are the chariots, as well as horse riders who encourage them and assistants who soak the sand. On the right, a mosaic depicts charioteers of the four colours (Museo Nazionale Romano, Rome).

WHITE CHARIOTEER
These were the charioteers of the *Anemoi*, gods of wind and winter.

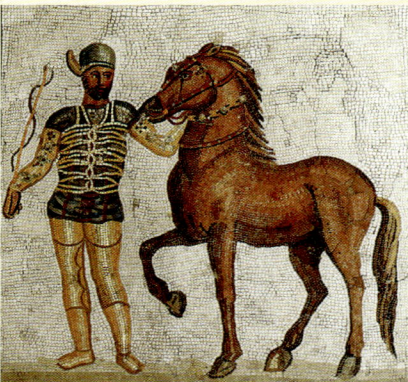

BLUE CHARIOTEER
Dedicated to the sky and sea or autumn, they reigned supreme in the third century.

RED CHARIOTEER
These charioteers were dedicated to the god Mars, and also to summer.

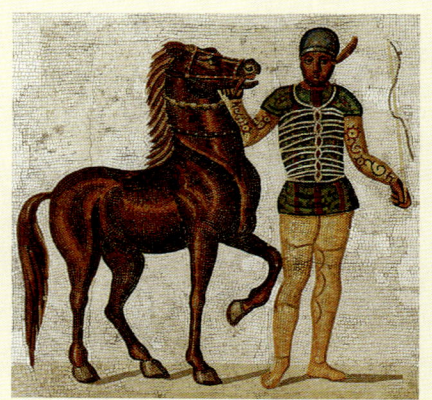

GREEN CHARIOTEER
Dedicated to Mother Earth, in the third century this team was the favourite.

THE END OF AN ERA

CIRCUS MAXIMUS
Twelve chariots could race abreast on this track, the only remnant of the Circus Maximus, alongside a small section of the stands.

The circus

The entertainment that, along with the gladiatorial games, enjoyed most prestige among the Romans was horse and chariot racing, which was held in the circus. To house these events, colossal buildings were constructed; due to their size and versatility these could also be used for animal hunts or athletic competitions. The circus was at least 400m (1312ft) long, with the racing area divided in two by a high and elaborately decorated barrier called the *spina* ('spine'). The Circus Maximus of Rome, built on the plain between the Aventine and Palatine Hills, was the empire's largest venue, with a length of 540m (1770ft) and capacity for more than 250,000 spectators. Other well-preserved examples are found in Leptis Magna (Libya), Tyre (Lebanon) and Tarragona (Spain).

Chariot racing was enthusiastically followed by the Romans, who, like fans of modern football teams, took a decisive stand for one of the four factions (white, blue, green and red). Huge amounts of money were placed as bets. The number of people who attended the circus was so high that the emperors soon realized the importance of their presence in this building and the possibilities of communication with the people it offered. For that reason, the imperial palace on the Palatine Hill had direct access to the imperial box of the Circus Maximus, so the emperors could participate in an entertainment so loved by their subjects.

As was the case with other entertainments in Rome, the circus was not just a show but had an important religious meaning that is crucial to understanding its success and dissemination. The horse races and the sacred rituals were closely related, both in the circus and in religious festivities, such as the Consualia (harvest festival) and Equirria (racing festivals in honour of Mars). This link was demonstrated in the circus shows by the procession with deities that preceded the races during the *pompa* (opening parade) and the presence of statues of gods in the building, particularly in the *pulvinar*, or emperor's gallery.

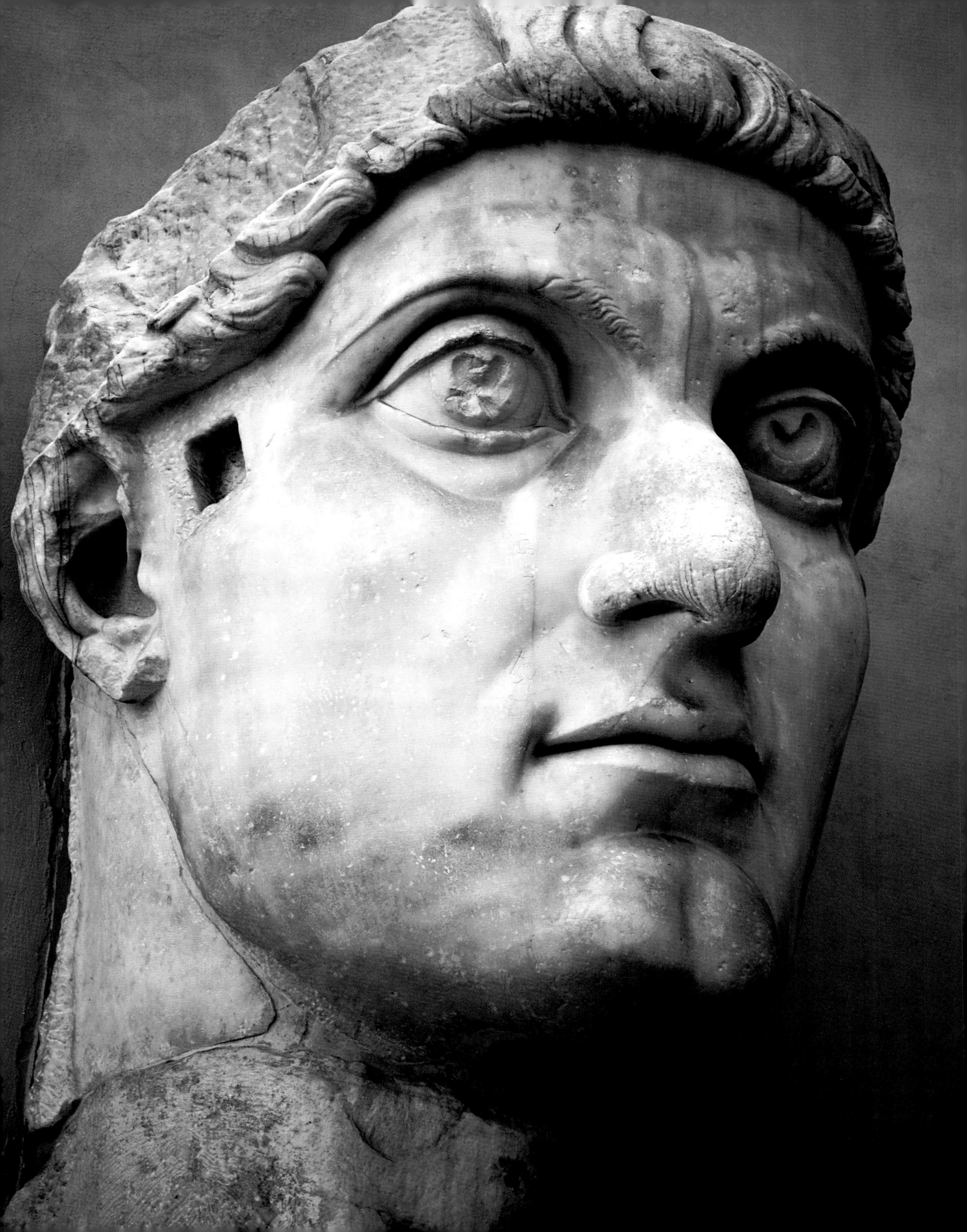

PART III

THE FALL OF ROME

THE FALL OF ROME

Europe in 476

FROM THE SEVERANS TO THE TETRARCHY

■	The empire at the time Romulus Augustulus was deposed (476)
■	Territories abandoned by Rome
■	Regions out of imperial control
■	Barbarian Kingdoms
■	Byzantine Empire
SUEBI	Barbarian tribes
MOESIA	Dioceses and kingdoms
——	Lines of *partitio imperio* separating the Western Empire from the Eastern (395)
◆◆◆◆	Odoacer's kingdom 476

SLAVS

AVARS

HUNS

BULGARS

GEPIDS

us (Nis)
Serdica (Sofia)
HRACIA
Hadrianopolis (Edirne)
alonica (aloniki)
Athenae (Athens)
tus (th)

BLACK SEA

Sinop
Trabzon
Constantinople
Nicomedia (Izmit)
Nicaea (Nicea)
Ancyra (Ankara)
PONTUS
ASIA
Smyrna (Esmirna)
Ephesus
Caesarea Cappadocia
Edessa
Tarsus (Tarso)
Attalia (Antalya)
Antiochia (Antioch)
Arsinoe (Famagusta)
ORIENS
Damascus
Tyrus (Tyre)
Aelia Capitolina (Jerusalem)
Petra

CASPIAN SEA

SASANIAN EMPIRE

MEDITERRANEAN SEA

Alexandria

ARABS

AEGYPTUS

RED SEA

289

THE TETRARCHS
This sculpture from St Mark's Basilica in Venice depicts members of the first tetrarchy: Diocletian, Maximian, Galerius and Constantius Chlorus. Facing page: A fourth-century cameo of the Persian king Shapur I and the Roman emperor Valerian engaged in combat. (National Library, Paris).

FROM THE SEVERANS TO THE TETRARCHY

During the third century, severe political and economic crises erupted that brought the Roman Empire to the brink of collapse. There were frequent civil wars as rival generals fought each other for the imperial throne. As a result, borders were often left undefended and subjected to raids by foreign tribes. Eventually, stability was restored thanks to Diocletian and his establishment of the tetrarchy.

The Romans had always struggled to maintain peaceful relations with the Germanic tribes on the empire's northern frontier. From the third century, the pressure from these tribes increased as they sought to move into the empire for farmland or to escape their enemies. Since the time of Marcus Aurelius, emperors had been settling migrating tribes within the empire and even recruiting tribesmen into the Roman army. By the third century, Germanic tribes had settled the territories along the empire's borders, east of the Rhine and north of the Danube and Black Sea. This policy of pacifying tribes by inviting them into the empire seemed to work for a time. However, from 238, one tribe, the Goths, broke the uneasy peace and began launching raids on Roman provinces in Asia Minor and the Balkan peninsula. By the late 250s, the Goths controlled Crimea and the Bosphorus and had captured several wealthy Greco-Roman cities

THE FALL OF ROME

The Severan Dynasty

Years 193–211
Septimius Severus, founder of the Severan dynasty, made major changes to the structure of the imperial government, giving the army a dominant role in the State and reducing the power of the Senate.

Years 209–211
Geta, son of Severus and younger brother of Caracalla, was named co-emperor in 209. Severus intended his sons to rule together after his death, but Caracalla murdered Geta in 211.

Years 198–217
Caracalla was co-ruler with his father Severus from 198 and with his brother Geta from 209. Caracalla's reign was marked by political instability. He was killed by his Praetorian prefect Macrino, who took power.

Years 218–222
Elagabalus, cousin of Caracalla, defeated Macrino at Antioch and took power. He developed a reputation for eccentricity and decadence.

Years 222–235
Alexander Severus came to the throne after his cousin Elagabalus's assassination. His attempts to bring peace by bargaining with the Germanic tribes alienated many in the Roman army and led to his assassination.

on the Black Sea coast.

Meanwhile, to the east of the empire, the Sasanian Persians became a growing menace to Rome. Under Shapur I (ca. 240–270), the Sasanians invaded Roman Mesopotamia in 242, and in 260 they defeated a Roman army at Edessa. To complete the humiliation, the emperor Valerian was captured – the first time a Roman emperor had ever fallen into the hands of an enemy. Valerian would remain Shapur's prisoner for the rest of his life.

The era of the Severans

After the emperor Commodus was assassinated in 192, he was succeeded by Pertinax, who ruled for just 86 days before being killed in March 193 by his Praetorian Guard. Three powerful generals refused to recognize his successor Julianus as emperor, and each decided to claim the throne for himself. One of these generals was Septimius Severus.

Born in Leptis Magna in the Roman province of Africa, Severus rose through the *cursus honorum* (sequence of public offices) during the reigns of Marcus Aurelius and Commodus; by 193, he was governor of Pannonia Superior. Severus was proclaimed emperor by his legion at Carnuntum. He advanced rapidly to Italy, gathering support along the way, and reached Rome before either of his rivals. The Senate declared Severus emperor, and Julianus was killed, having reigned for just four months.

One of Emperor Severus's first acts was to disband the notoriously treacherous Praetorian Guard and replace them with a new 15,000-man guard, made up of loyal veterans from his own Danubian legions. Next, he turned his attention to his rivals, Pescennius Niger in Syria and Clodius Albinus in Britannia. Severus bought Clodius Albinus's loyalty by offering him the rank of Caesar, hinting that Albinus would be chosen as his successor. He then moved east and defeated Niger's forces at Issus. After Severus declared his son Caracalla as his successor, Albinus rose against him. Severus defeated and killed Albinus at Lugdunum in February 197, establishing himself as the sole ruler of the empire.

In 198, Severus led a campaign against the Parthian Empire. His forces sacked the royal city of Ctesiphon and, by 199, northern Mesopotamia had been annexed to the empire. Despite his victories, Severus remained unpopular with the Senate, who distrusted his reliance on military force. It didn't help when, in 197, he executed 30 senators suspected of supporting Clodius Albinus. Severus mostly ignored the Senate, recruiting his administrators from the equestrian rather than the senatorial class. As a result, the Senate declined dramatically in power.

Severus cemented his popularity with the army by offering soldiers a sizeable bonus in 197, by permitting them to marry, and by raising their annual wages from 300 to 400 denarii. To prevent the emergence of rivals to his throne, he reduced the number of legions

FROM THE SEVERANS TO THE TETRARCHY

under each general's control.

In 208, Severus, accompanied by Caracalla and his younger son Geta, led an army to Britain with the aim of conquering Caledonia. He strengthened Hadrian's Wall and reoccupied the Southern Uplands as far as the Antonine Wall. By 210, despite suffering heavy casualties against the fierce Caledonians, Severus had won control of the Central Lowlands. However, in 211, as he was preparing for another campaign, Severus fell ill and died at Eboracum. Caracalla and Geta inherited the throne as joint rulers. They continued the campaign, but soon sued for peace and returned to Rome. The Romans would never advance so deep into Caledonia again.

Relations between the two brothers grew increasingly hostile, and in December 211 Caracalla had Geta assassinated. He then ordered the massacre of Geta's friends and supporters and the removal of his name and image from all artworks, coins and records. In 212, Caracalla issued an edict declaring that all free men in the Roman Empire were to become Roman citizens – hitherto, citizenship had been restricted to free men within Italy. He may have done this to increase tax revenues, and also because he recognized that the continued survival of the empire now depended on the support of those living at its edges.

In 213, Caracalla departed Rome, never to return, leaving his mother Julia Domna to administer the empire. The emperor headed north to deal with the Alamanni, a confederation of Germanic tribes that had broken through the frontier at Raetia. After a successful, if brutal, campaign against the Alamanni, Caracalla launched an expedition against the Parthian Empire in 216. By this time, he had become obsessed with the

SEVERUS AND SONS
A relief from the Arch of Septimius Severus showing the emperor Severus and his sons Caracalla and Geta. The white marble arch is at the northwestern end of the Roman Forum at the foot of the Capitoline Hill. It was built in 203 to commemorate Severus's victories against the Parthians in 194 and 198–9. Following Geta's assassination in 211, his image and inscriptions were removed from the arch.

THE FALL OF ROME

Leptis Magna, home city of Emperor Septimius Severus

Leptis Magna was a city in Roman Libya in the region known as Tripolitana. As the birthplace of Septimius Severus, it reached its greatest prominence during his reign. Severus gave orders for building works in the city, including a spectacular arch, a new basilica and forum and a colonnaded street leading to an enlarged harbour. This transformed Leptis Magna into a major city to rival Carthage and Alexandria. However, during the third century, as trade declined, Leptis diminished in importance; by the fourth century, parts of the city were abandoned. In later centuries it fell under the control of the Vandals and Byzantines while suffering Berber raids. By the time it was conquered by the Arabs in around 647, the city had just 1000 inhabitants. By the tenth century, Leptis was in ruin.

Macedonian conqueror Alexander the Great, adopting his clothing, weapons, travel routes and even battle plans.

Other signs were emerging of his unstable mental state: while in Alexandria preparing for the Parthian campaign, he was upset by a satirical theatrical performance, which he believed was mocking him, and ordered the massacre of the city's leading citizens. In April 217, while he was preparing to wage a new campaign against Parthia, Caracalla was assassinated on the orders of Macrinus, his Praetorian prefect, who took the throne. Macrinus made peace with several kingdoms, but his attempts to introduce fiscal reforms were unpopular with the army. Caracalla's aunt, Julia Maesa, saw the opportunity to start a rebellion and restore Severan rule under her 14-year-old grandson Bassianus. Macrinus was defeated at Antioch in June 218, and Bassianus was proclaimed emperor. After his death, Bassianus became known as Elagabalus (the name of the Syrian sun god he worshipped) and it is by this name that history remembers him.

On taking power, Elagabalus decided to replace Jupiter with the god Elagabalus at the head of the Roman pantheon. The emperor continued to stoke controversy by marrying the Vestal Virgin Aquilia Severa – a major violation of Roman tradition – claiming their union would produce godlike children. He further shocked Roman society with his personal behaviour, showering titles on male courtiers thought to have been his lovers, 'marrying' his charioteer, and allegedly prostituting himself in the imperial palace. His grandmother Julia Maesa and mother Julia Soaemias wielded power behind the scenes, but could do little about Elagabalus's increasing eccentricity and decadence, which alienated the Praetorian

FROM THE SEVERANS TO THE TETRARCHY

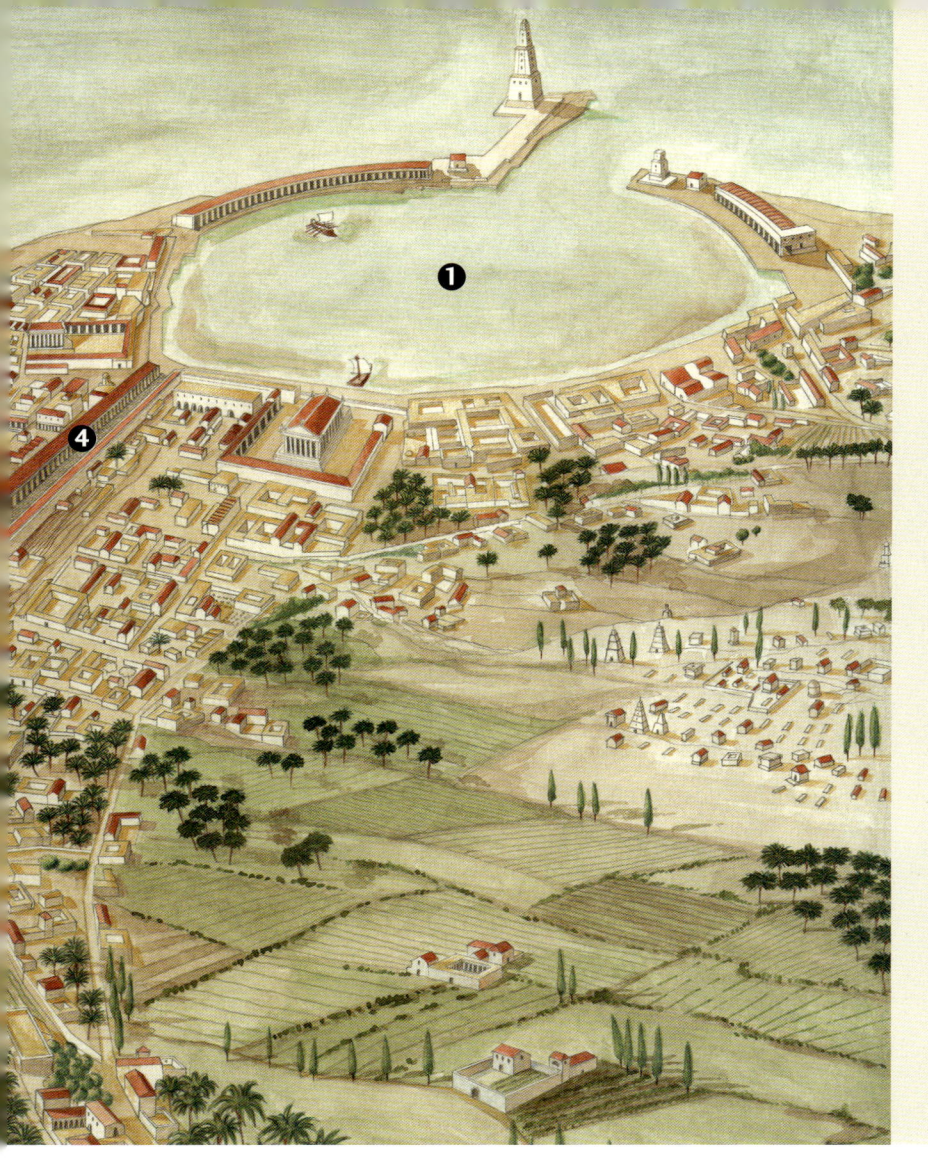

1 HARBOUR
Septimius Severus ordered the building of the eastern pier of the harbour to prevent flooding caused by the frequent rise of the Wadi Lebda. Unfortunately, sand brought in by the tide could now no longer escape back to the sea, and the harbour quickly silted up.

2 OLD FORUM
Built in the time of the emperor Augustus, the old forum was located close to the sea front on the site of the original centre of the Carthaginian town. It featured several small temples and statues of the emperors. It remained the heart of the city until replaced by the new forum.

3 NEW FORUM
The new forum and basilica commissioned by Emperor Septimius Severus was completed five years after his death, in 216. Inscriptions on the marble walls celebrate all the emperors since Nerva, helping to legitimize Severan rule. The sculptural decorations include several giant heads of Medusa.

4 COLONNADED STREET
A colonnaded street linked the new forum to the harbour. It was 20.5m (67ft) wide (42m/138ft including the side paths) and 400m (1312ft) long. The street was bounded on either side by 125 arches made of green cipollino marble. At the forum end was a large *nymphaeum*, or monumental fountain.

Guard, the Senate and the citizenry. In 222, he was summoned before the Praetorian Guard where he was assassinated, with his mother.

Elagabalus was succeeded by his 13-year-old cousin Alexander Severus. Being so young, Alexander was heavily influenced by his mother Julia Mamaea. Under her direction, Alexander lowered taxes, encouraged the arts and reduced the extravagance of the imperial court. He reversed Egalabalus's religious changes, but was tolerant towards Jews and Christians (although his proposal to build a temple to Jesus was rejected by Roman priests). He also did much to improve the rights of soldiers, protecting their property rights and allowing them to name heirs and free slaves in their wills.

Alexander's domestic reforms may have been popular, but he failed as a military leader, and this would prove his undoing. In 231, the Sasanian king Ardashir I invaded Roman Mesopotamia. In response, Alexander launched a three-pronged counter-offensive. He personally led the main body into northern Mesopotamia, while another army progressed north towards Media, and a third headed south towards Babylon. While the northern army had some success, the southern army was wiped out by Persian horse archers. Alexander's own advance stalled, partly because of his own indecisiveness and the indiscipline of his troops. Nonetheless, the Sasanians withdrew from Mesopotamia, enabling him to celebrate a triumph in Rome in 233.

In 234, the Alamanni crossed the Rhine at Moguntiacum (Mainz). Following his mother's advice, Alexander attempted to bribe the barbarians in order to buy himself some time. This decision incurred the disdain of the army, especially after the near debacle of his Parthian campaign, and the generals concluded that he

DENARIUS OF ALEXANDER SEVERUS
This silver denarius, minted in 235, shows the head of the last Severan emperor (National Roman Museum, Palazzo Massimo alle Terme, Rome).

THE FALL OF ROME

THE BATHS OF CARACALLA: A WONDER OF THE ROMAN WORLD

Septimius Severus ordered the construction of a great new bathhouse in the southwest of the city of Rome. It opened in 216 during the reign of his son Caracalla, for whom the baths are named, but the complex was only finally completed in 235. The site covered an area of around 25 hectares (52 acres). The main building was 214 by 114m (700 by 374ft), built on four levels – two above ground, two below. Water was carried there from a newly built aqueduct, the Aqua Nova Antoniniana. The complex was adorned with mosaics, statues and fountains, and contained, as well as baths, gymnasiums, temples, libraries, gardens and shops. The baths could accommodate more than 1600 visitors at a time, and received up to 8000 visitors each day, including women, although they were officially banned. The baths remained in use until 537 when invading Goths cut off the city's water supply, after which the complex slowly fell into ruin.

ARCHAEOLOGICAL REMAINS
The remains of the Baths of Caracalla. Much of the complex was destroyed by an earthquake in 847.

1 THE ENTRANCE
The baths were surrounded by a grand portico of which little remains. Visitors could enter through either of two entrances, in the northwest and the southeast.

2 THE HOT ROOM
The circular *caldarium* had seven pools, each measuring 9.5 by 5m. (31 by 16ft). It was topped by a dome 35m (115ft) in diameter. Glass windows helped to heat the room.

3 THE COLD ROOM
The *frigidarium*, the central room of the complex, measured 58 by 24m (190 by 79ft) and consisted of four pools. Its high roof was supported by eight huge granite columns.

6 STEAM ROOMS
Between the *palaestra* and the *caldarium* were a number of rooms whose function is unclear; they may have operated as saunas or steam rooms kept at varying temperatures.

7 THE WARM ROOM
Visitors would begin in the *tepidarium*, which consisted of two pools. Here they would warm up and scrape off dirt and sweat using oil and a strigil.

8 THE SWIMMING POOL
The pool, measuring 50 by 22m (164 by 72ft), had walls 20m (66ft) high and no roof. Bronze mirrors mounted on the walls directed sunlight into the pool.

4 SCULPTURES
The baths were lavishly decorated with more than 120 sculptures. Among the statues that have survived are one of Hercules and a colossal statue of Asclepius.

5 THE CHANGING ROOM
Visitors could leave their clothing and belongings in cubicles or on shelves in a changing room, or *apodyterium*. A slave called a *capsarius* would guard them for a fee.

9 SUNBATHING TERRACE
According to some scholars, the flat roof of the portico surrounding the *palaestra* may have been used for sunbathing. The roof may have been accessed via a set of wooden stairs.

10 THE PALAESTRA
The complex housed two *palaestra*, gymnasia where visitors could perform physical exercises before heading into the bathhouse. Wrestling and boxing matches were also held here.

THE EMPEROR CARACALLA
The baths were inaugurated during Caracalla's reign (bust of the emperor from the Capitoline Museums, Rome).

THE FALL OF ROME

Princes of the Military Anarchy

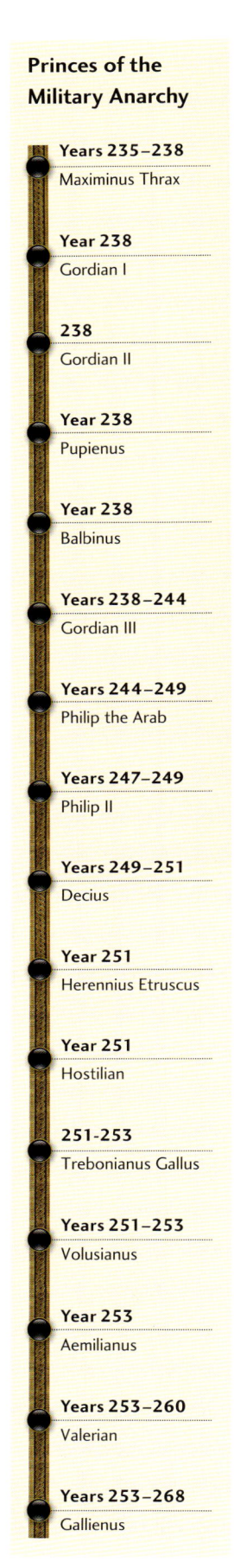

Years 235–238
Maximinus Thrax

Year 238
Gordian I

238
Gordian II

Year 238
Pupienus

Year 238
Balbinus

Years 238–244
Gordian III

Years 244–249
Philip the Arab

Years 247–249
Philip II

Years 249–251
Decius

Year 251
Herennius Etruscus

Year 251
Hostilian

251-253
Trebonianus Gallus

Years 251–253
Volusianus

Year 253
Aemilianus

Years 253–260
Valerian

Years 253–268
Gallienus

was unfit to be emperor. On 19 March 235, Alexander and his mother were killed during a meeting with his generals, bringing an end to the Severan dynasty.

The Military Anarchy

The period between the fall of Alexander Severus in 235 and the rise of Diocletian in 284, known as the Military Anarchy, was one of the most turbulent in the history of the Roman Empire. It was a time of civil war, economic collapse, violent seizures of power and external invasions. For several years, the empire fractured into three separate political entities. There were at least 26 claimants to the imperial throne during the 50-year period, and most reigns ended violently. The lack of a clear policy for imperial succession opened the way for the domination of politics by the military. 'Legitimacy' for an emperor in these times was based almost solely on proclamation by the army, with little respect given to a candidate's dynastic or ancestral heritage. The crisis was made worse by inflation caused by the devaluation of the currency by successive emperors. This, and the breakdown of trade, led to economic depression. The empire was further destabilized by outbreaks of plague and a series of earthquakes.

The Military Anarchy is considered to have begun with the death of Alexander Severus and the rise to the throne of Maximinus Thrax, commander of the Italian Fourth Legion. Maximinus was of peasant stock, the son of a Goth, and purportedly a giant of a man. The Senate regarded him as a barbarian and only reluctantly confirmed him as emperor. Maximinus moved quickly to consolidate power, eliminating Alexander's supporters and crushing two plots to overthrow him. He then launched a campaign against the Alamanni, crossing the Rhine and triumphing in a fierce battle near Baden and Wurttemberg.

Having secured peace on the Rhine frontier, albeit temporarily, Maximinus moved to Sirmium in Pannonia on the Danube, where he attacked the Dacians and Sarmatians. The cost of these campaigns, along with Maximinus' decision to double soldiers' pay, led to steep tax rises, which made him even more unpopular with the Senate. When the province of Africa revolted in 238, the senators saw their opportunity to move against him. The revolt began when Maximinus's procurator in Africa used the corrupt court system to impose high taxes and fines on local landowners. The furious aristocrats killed the procurator and proclaimed their governor Gordian I and his son Gordian II co-emperors of Rome. The Senate threw its support behind the Gordians, giving them the title Augustus.

When Maximinus heard what was happening, he immediately set out for Rome. But before he could get there, the governor of Numidia, neighbouring province to Africa, decided to take matters into his own hands. The governor, Capelianus, who hated the Gordians, attacked Carthage and killed Gordian II. The elder Gordian then hanged himself. The Gordians had reigned for just 21 days. On hearing of their deaths, the Senate appointed two of its own men, Pupienus and Balbinus, as joint emperors. Neither was popular with the public, so the Senate decided to raise 13-year-old Gordian III, grandson and nephew of the elder Gordians, to the rank of Caesar, making him heir to the throne. Meanwhile, Maximinus was having troubles of his own. During his march to Rome he laid siege to the city of Aquilela. The city put up unexpectedly fierce resistance, supplies to

THE ROMAN AMPHITHEATRE AT EL DJEM
The amphitheatre at El Djem (the Roman city of Thysdrus) is the biggest in Africa and fourth biggest in the Roman world. It was built in 238 by proconsul Gordian during the reign of Maximinus Thrax.

GORDIAN II (OPPOSITE PAGE)
Emperor for just three weeks, Gordian II died in battle at Carthage at the age of 46. According to the historian Edward Gibbon, he had 22 concubines and a library of 62,000 books (marble bust, Louvre Museum, Paris).

THE FALL OF ROME

War with Sasanian Persia: Shapur I versus Rome

Shapur I was the son of Ardashir I, founder of the Sasanian dynasty. Following his defeat by Gordian III at Resaena in 243, Shapur signed a peace treaty with Gordian's successor, Philip the Arab. Around 250, Shapur conquered Armenia, turning it into a Persian satrapy. He then turned on the Roman legions occupying Mesopotamia, defeating an army of 60,000 at the Battle of Barbalissos. In 253, Shapur invaded the Roman province of Syria and conquered Antioch. The Roman emperor Valerian marched against him and took back control of Syria. Valerian pursued the Persians to Edessa in 260, where Shapur defeated him and took him prisoner. Septimius Odenathus, ruler of the Palmyrene Kingdom, fought against Shapur, forcing him to withdraw across the Euphrates. He besieged Shapur at Ctesiphon but was unable to take the city. In this relief at Naqsh-e Rustam, Valerian appears before Shapur, pleading for his life. Left: A bust of Philip the Arab (Uffizi Gallery, Florence).

Maximinus's forces were cut off, and his soldiers began to starve.

The soldiers had become disenchanted with Maximinus, and in May 238 they killed the emperor. Pupienus and Balbinus were now sole emperors of Rome, but their rule did not last long. On 29 July 238, the praetorians, who resented serving Senate-appointed emperors, dragged them from their palace and hacked them to death. Thus, young Gordian III became emperor.

Because of the new emperor's immaturity, responsibility for administering the empire passed to the Senate. In 241, Gordian was married to Furia Sabinia Tranquilina, daughter of Praetorian prefect Timesitheus, who soon became de facto ruler of the empire. When the Sasanians under Shapur I invaded Mesopotamia in 242, Gordian and Timesitheus led a large army east. They drove the Sasanians back across the Euphrates and defeated them at the Battle of Resaena in 243. Gordian was planning a further campaign against the Persians when his father-in-law suddenly fell ill and died. His replacement as Praetorian prefect was Philip the Arab, who proceeded with the campaign. The Roman advance stalled at Ctesiphon and, on 11 February 244, Gordian suddenly died. The circumstances of his death are disputed – Sasanian sources claim he was killed in battle, but according to Roman accounts he was far from the battlefield at the time, and may have been murdered on the orders of Philip the Arab.

Whatever the case, Philip was proclaimed emperor. He immediately made peace with Shapur I, managing to retain the reconquests of Osroene and Mesopotamia at the cost of an

FROM THE SEVERANS TO THE TETRARCHY

1 SHAPUR I
The victorious king, mounted on a horse, is larger than life size and wears the distinctive Sasanian crown, emphasizing his authority. His left hand leans on the hilt of his sword, symbolizing his power over the eastern territories of the Roman Empire.

2 KARTIR
Standing behind the mounted Shapur is his high priest Kartir, who is saluting the king with the gesture of the fist and index finger (a gesture commonly found on Sasanian rock reliefs). Kartir was instrumental in promoting Zoroastrianism as the Sasanian state religion.

3 VALERIAN
The defeated emperor kneels before Shapur I. Accounts vary about how he was treated in captivity. Some allege Shapur used him as a human footstool, and that after he died he was skinned and his skin stuffed with straw. According to other accounts he was treated with respect.

4 ANAHITA
This female figure may be a representation of the Indo-Persian deity Anahita, goddess of the waters, fertility, medicine and wisdom.

5 SHAPUR'S HORSE
The horse occupies the centre of the scene in acknowledgement of the central role of heavy cavalry in Persian armies and strategy during this period. The Sasanian cavalry were known to breed war horses of impressive height and size.

---

enormous indemnity to the Sasanians. Philip returned to Rome in 244, where he was confirmed as emperor. Desperately short of money, Philip increased levels of taxation and ceased paying subsidies to the tribes north of the Danube.

As a result, the Carpi crossed into Roman territory, and Philip had to assemble an army and chase them back to Dacia. In 248, he returned to Rome to celebrate the one thousandth anniversary of the founding of Rome. The festivities were spectacular, but storm clouds were gathering. In late 248, the legions of Pannonia and Moesia rebelled and proclaimed Pacatianus emperor. At the same time, barbarian tribes began crossing the Danube frontier at Pannonia, Moesia, Dacia and Thrace. Simultaneously, in the East, there was an uprising against the oppressive rule of Philip's brother Priscus. Philip was overwhelmed by so many rebellions and invasions, but the Senate refused to accept his offer to resign. So Philip sent Gaius Decius (a senator who had expressed strong support for the emperor) to the Danube to suppress the Pacatianus uprising and drive back the barbarians. Instead of dealing with the rebellious legions, Decius allowed them to proclaim him emperor in early 249.

Decius immediately marched on Rome, and his forces met Philip's near Verona. Decius won the battle and Philip was killed. The Senate immediately recognized Decius as emperor and made his son Caesar. In January 250, Decius issued an imperial edict ordering all Roman citizens to publicly perform a religious sacrifice. When many Christians refused to comply, Decius's commissioners tortured and executed them. Victims included the bishops of Rome, Jerusalem and Antioch.

THE LUDOVISI BATTLE SARCOPHAGUS (OVERLEAF)
This beautiful third-century marble relief depicts a battle between Romans and barbarians. The central character is, allegedly, Hostilian, son of Emperor Decius. (National Roman Museum, Palazzo Massimo alle Terme, Rome.)

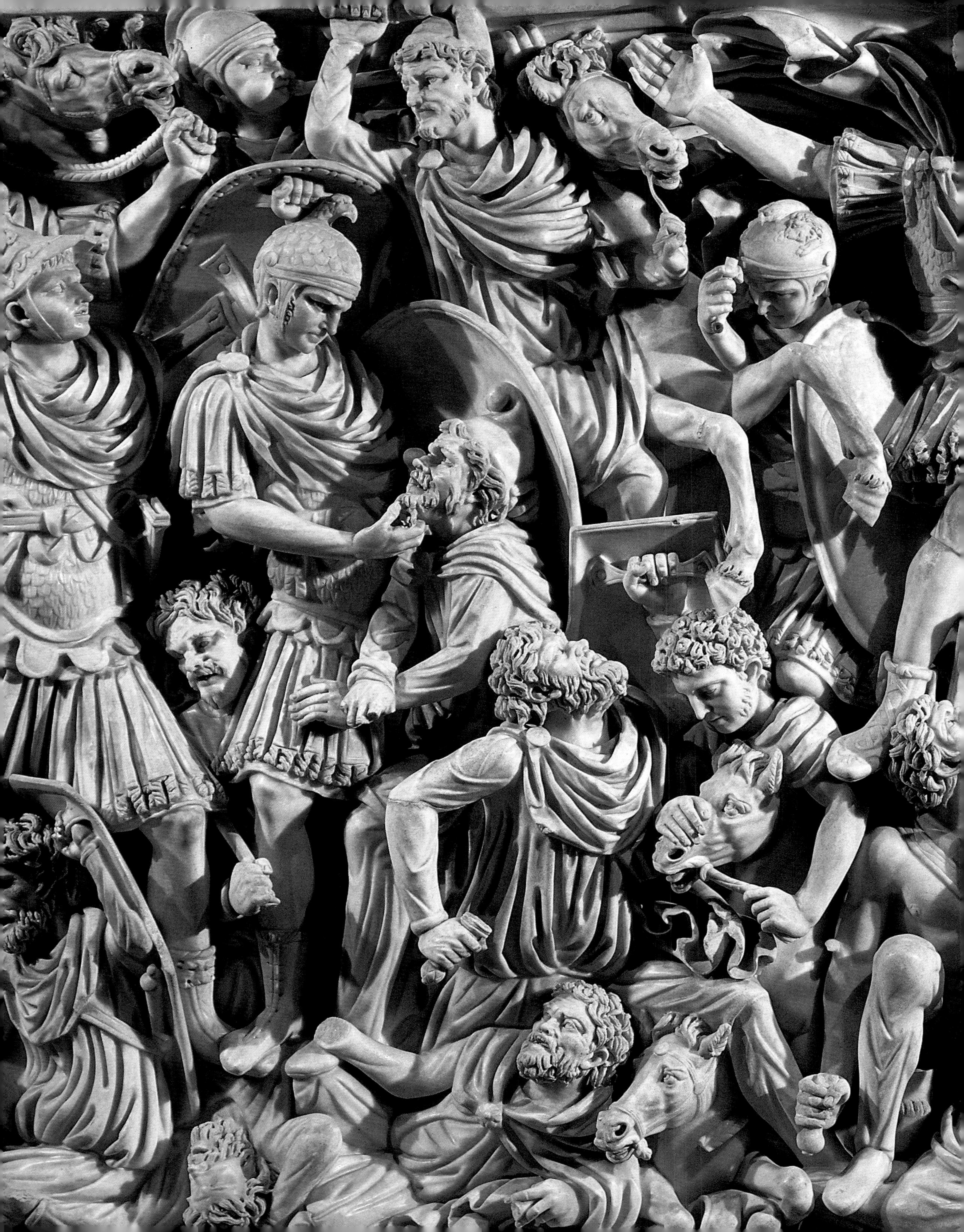

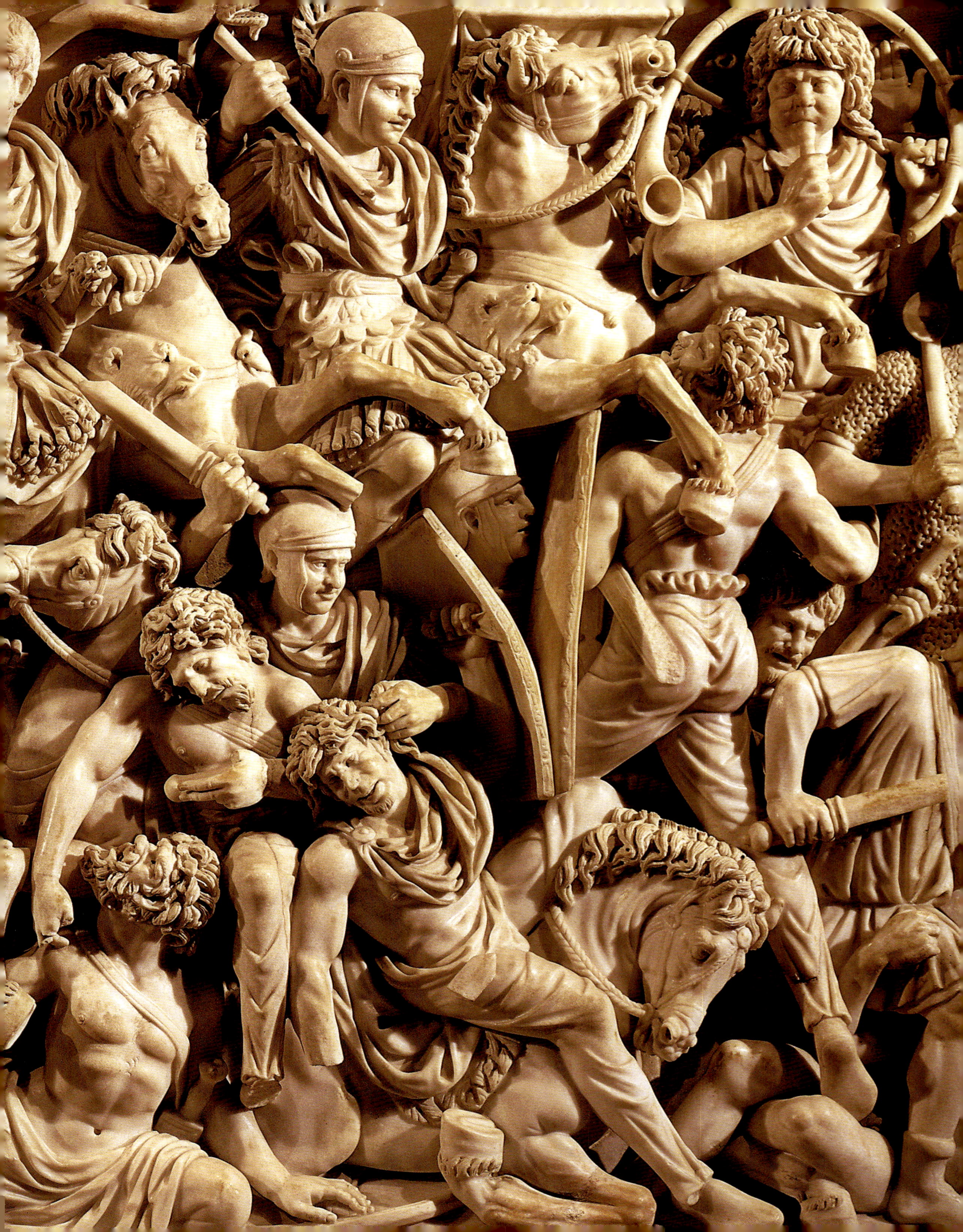

THE AURELIAN WALLS
As barbarian incursions continued through the third century, the city of Rome felt increasingly vulnerable. The Aurelian Walls were built during the reigns of the emperors Aurelian and Probus between 271 and 275, to defend the city from attack. The walls ran for 19km (12 miles), were 3.5m (11ft) thick, with a watch tower every 100 Roman feet (29.6m).

The persecution horrified many Romans and ended up strengthening Christianity in the empire. Decius's attention was soon drawn back to the Danube as Goths under King Cniva invaded Moesia and Thrace, besieging and plundering cities. Decius rushed to the frontier, accompanied by his son Herennius Etruscus (who was by now co-emperor), determined to punish the barbarians.

At the Battle of Abritus in around July 251, the Roman army was routed by Cniva's forces, and both Decius and Herennius were killed. Decius was the first Roman emperor ever to have been killed in battle against a foreign enemy, and the news of his death sent shockwaves through Rome. Two years of anarchy followed this incident, in which five imperial proclamations followed one after the other, as the army and the Senate each put forward their preferred candidates for succession. Finally, in October 253, the Senate and the army agreed to recognize Valerian as emperor and his son Gallienus as Caesar.

The Military Anarchy reached its climax during the reigns of Valerian and Gallienus. External threats were constant, from Germanic tribes attacking along the Rhine and Danube frontiers, from nomadic Berbers in northern Africa, and above all from the Sasanians in the east. The crisis reached a peak in 260 with Shapur I's victory over the Romans at Edessa and the capture of Emperor Valerian. Following this catastrophe, his co-emperor Gallienus lost control of much of the Western empire. A general named Postumus declared himself emperor of a new realm, known today as the Gallic Empire, consisting of Britain, Spain and parts of Gaul and Germania. Gallienus was also forced to grant greater autonomy to Septimius Odenathus, governor of the East, in order to contain the Sasanian threat. Odenathus remained nominally loyal to

FROM THE SEVERANS TO THE TETRARCHY

Rome, but governed the Eastern empire from Palmyra, Syria, as an independent kingdom.

When not dealing with any of the many crises engulfing his empire, Gallienus managed to make some important military reforms, opening up opportunities for promotion for the most talented soldiers and creating new cavalry units that could be dispatched swiftly anywhere they were needed.

The Illyrian emperors

Gallienus died in 268, assassinated by his own officials, and was succeeded by Claudius, his military deputy. Claudius was the first of the so-called Illyrian emperors, who hailed from Illyricum and came through the ranks of the army. All were able and experienced soldiers, and between them they managed to recover most of the territories lost by their predecessors. Claudius routed a huge Gothic army at Naissus, driving them back across the Danube and earning the title Gothicus (conqueror of the Goths). Next he crushed the invading Alamanni at Lake Benacus. With the frontiers temporarily secure, he turned his attention towards the breakaway Gallic Empire. Claudius managed to regain control of Spain and part of Gaul, but then fell ill from plague and died in January 270.

Claudius's successor Quintillus reigned for just a few months before dying in mysterious circumstances. He was followed by Aurelian, a talented general who had fought with Claudius at Naissus. In late 270, Aurelian led his forces against the Vandals, Juthungi and Sarmatians, expelling them from Roman territory. In 271, the Alamanni and Juthungi invaded Italy. Aurelian drove them out, and ordered the construction of new defensive walls around Rome. Next, Aurelian turned his attention east. In 272, Aurelian reconquered the Eastern empire, which had seceded from Rome under Queen Zenobia to become the Palmyrene Empire. Two years later, he reconquered the Gallic Empire, this time largely through diplomacy. Aurelian was hailed as a hero, and the Senate awarded him the title *Restitutor Orbis* ('Restorer of the World').

Aurelian increased the distribution of free food for poor plebeian families in Rome. To promote religious unity across the empire, he placed the sun god Sol Invictus at the head of the Roman pantheon, hoping that this would become a god that all peoples could believe in without betraying their own gods. He also tried to reform the coinage system, which had suffered from decades of debasement by previous emperors. In 275, Aurelian was about to launch another campaign against the Sasanians, when a group of officers, misled into thinking the emperor was about to execute them, murdered him.

Two short-lived emperors followed Aurelian – Tacitus and Florianus. After them came Probus, commander of the eastern armies. Probus spent most of his reign fighting barbarian tribes on the Rhine and Danube and putting down rebellions in Britain, Gaul and the East. He was killed by his troops who

The Illyrian emperors

Years 268–270
Claudius Gothicus
Inflicted a famous defeat on the Goths; died of plague in Illyria.

Year 270
Quintillus
May have been killed by his soldiers, by Aurelian or by his own hand. Sources vary.

Years 270–275
Aurelian
Reconquered the breakaway empires and gave Rome a new defensive wall.

Years 275–276
Tacitus
Elected by the Senate to replace Aurelian.

Year 276
Florianus
Elected by the army in the West to replace Tacitus.

Years 276–282
Probus
Commander in the East. Defeated the Goths, but was murdered.

Years 282–283
Carus
Died on campaign in Persia, near Ctesiphon.

Years 283–285
Carinus
Son of Caro, died in a battle against Diocletian.

Years 283–284
Numerian
Second son of Caro, killed by his Praetorian prefect Aper.

305

THE FALL OF ROME

REIGN OF DIOCLETIAN
This relief adorns the base of one of five honorary columns erected by Diocletian in the year 303 to celebrate the 20th anniversary of his accession to the throne, as well as the first decade of the tetrarchy. The columns were originally located behind the Rostra in the Roman Forum.

resented his strict discipline, and was succeeded by his prefect Carus. On campaign against the Sasanians in 283, Carus suddenly died and the throne passed to his sons Carinus and Numerian. In 284, Numerian was killed, and Diocletian, commander of the household guard, was proclaimed emperor. Carinus moved against Diocletian, and the forces met at the Margus River in mid-285. During the battle, Carinus was killed by his soldiers, leaving Diocletian sole ruler of the empire.

Diocletian

Diocletian's reign marks the end of the Military Anarchy. A soldier but also a talented administrator, he dedicated himself to the task of reorganizing the empire in a way that would bring long-term stability. In 286, he surprised many by appointing his loyal friend and fellow officer Maximian co-emperor. Diocletian knew the empire was too big for one man to administer, especially with crises erupting often simultaneously in far-flung places, so Maximian was given authority over the Western half of the empire, while Diocletian ruled the East. Rome remained the imperial capital, but Maximian would reside in Milan, and Diocletian in Nicomedia, placing both emperors close to the frontiers they needed to defend.

In 293, Diocletian split the administration further by bringing in two more trusted colleagues, Galerius and Constantinius Chlorus. Galerius was made Caesar to Diocletian and was installed at Trier, and Constantinius was made Caesar to Maximian and was based in Sirmium. Under this 'tetrarchy', each of the four ruled over one-quarter of the empire. To further strengthen the union between them, each Augustus adopted his Caesar, and the Caesars married their respective Augustus's daughter. The system worked well: Diocletian brought stability to the frontiers, defeating the Sarmatians, Carpi and Alamanni and putting down rebellions in Egypt. Galerius, with Diocletian's help, triumphed against Sasanian Persia, sacking their capital Ctesiphon, and achieving a durable and favourable peace. Meanwhile, Maximian was able to put down a revolt of the Bagaudae in Gaul, and in 297 Constantinius successfully reconquered Britain for Rome after Carausius had declared himself emperor there.

Diocletian also made important reforms to the civil administration of the empire and the army. He centralized power within the imperial administration, so the Senate no longer collaborated on law-making or appointed consuls. He professionalized the government, creating a class of imperial counsellors with clearly defined areas of responsibility, and greatly increasing the size of the bureaucracy from around 15,000 to 30,000. Diocletian was keen to re-establish the rule of law after so many decades of arbitrary rule by powerful men, and he ordered the rewriting of Rome's legal codes to preserve ancient traditions regarding marriage and the family, private property and creditors' rights. Diocletian also placed strict limits on the use of torture.

FROM THE SEVERANS TO THE TETRARCHY

THE TETRARCHY: A FORMULA FOR STABILITY

Following the crisis of the third century (235–284), Diocletian established a system of government known as the tetrarchy. He named Maximian his co-Augustus in the West (286); he made Galerius his Caesar (deputy) in the East (293); and he made Constantinius Chlorus Caesar to Maximian (293). Each ruler had his own specific area of responsibility but there would be no territorial division of the empire, because Diocletian reserved for himself the ultimate authority over the other rulers. In order to avoid power becoming concentrated in one person's hands, the Augustuses were supposed to retire after 20 years to be succeeded by the Caesars who would name new Caesars to replace them.

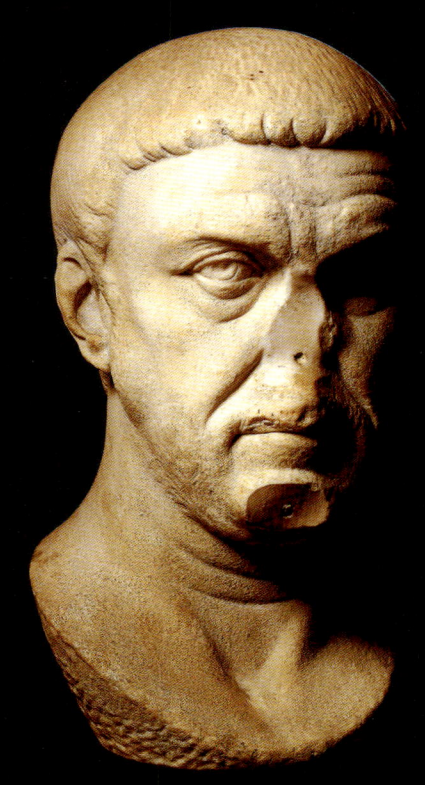

DIOCLETIAN
He held power between 284 and 305, establishing his base at Nicomedia (the modern Turkish city of Izmit, in whose museum this marble head is preserved).

MAXIMIAN
He reigned between 286 and 305. Primarily a military man, he left politics to Diocletian. (Marble bust, Archaeological Museum of Milan.)

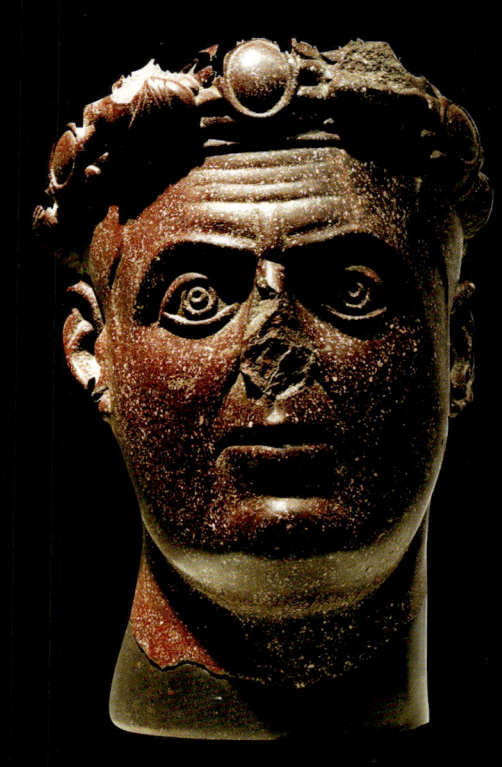

GALERIUS
He became Augustus of the East when Diocletian abdicated in 305, ruling until 311. (Porphyry head, National Mueum, Zajecar, Serbia.)

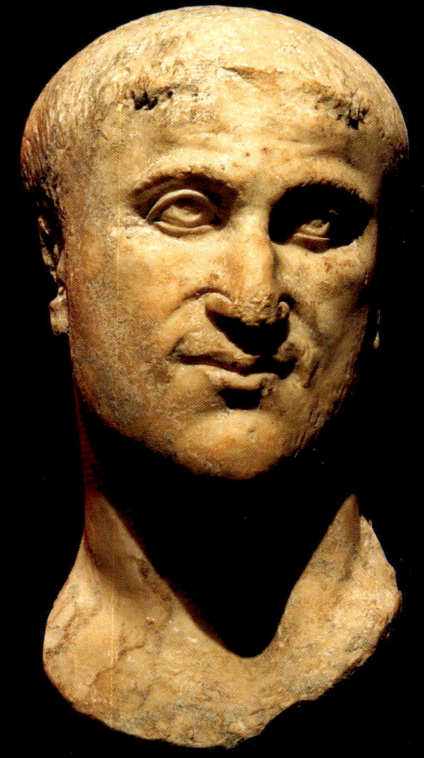

CONSTANTINIUS CHLORUS
Caesar from 293 to 305 and Augustus from 305 to 306, he was the father of Constantine the Great. (Bust, Ny Carlsberg Glyptotek, Copenhagen, Denmark.)

Diocletian: reorganizing the empire

Diocletian wanted to end political instability and make it easier to deal with Rome's enemies. To this end, he put in place a new structure that avoided concentrating power in the hands of provincial governors and army generals – in other words, the kinds of people who had led uprisings in the preceding era.

Each tetrarch ruled one-fourth of the empire. From his base in Nicomedia, Diocletian ruled Thrace, Asia and Egypt; Galerius, from Sirmium, took care of the southern Danubian provinces from the Alps to the Black Sea; Maximian (portrayed in the gold coin on the opposite page) was based in Milan and exercised command over Italy, Sicily and Africa; and Constantinius had his headquarters in Trier, from where he ruled Gaul, Spain and Britain. Diocletian doubled the number of provinces from 50 to almost 100. The provinces were grouped into 12 dioceses, whose territories prefigure those of some modern nations such as Great Britain (Britannia), France (Gaul) and Spain (Hispania). Each diocese was governed by an appointed official called a vicarius. The dioceses were in turn grouped into four Praetorian prefectures, each commanded by a tetrarch. This system not only allowed better control of the territories but also reduced the possibility of military rebellion by governors and enabled a swift response to external threats.

Diocletian's military reforms aimed at reinforcing the discipline and effectiveness of the army as well as improving the lot of ordinary soldiers. The army was reorganized to make it more flexible and to improve its mobility during periods of external threat. The legions were divided into *limitanei*, guardians of the borders, and *comitatenses*, troops quartered in the imperial capitals yet capable of rapid deployment to the frontiers to reinforce the *limitanei* when necessary.

In support of these reforms, Diocletian also ordered the construction of a more robust infrastructure along the empire's borders, consisting of military roads, walls, fortifications and castles. The army was increased in size from 39 to 60 legions. This may not be quite as impressive as it sounds, as legion sizes did become smaller. Nevertheless, scholars estimate that overall soldier numbers increased by at least 33 per cent. To raise troop numbers, Diocletian introduced systematic annual conscription of Roman citizens. He may also have been responsible for the decree ordering sons of serving soldiers and veterans to enlist. But Diocletian also showed concern for soldiers' welfare. Soldiers could retire after 20 years of service and limits were placed on the prices of basic goods to reduce their cost of living.

To reduce the likelihood of rebellion, Diocletian separated military from civilian command in the provinces. Command of the troops stationed in each province was taken away from the local governor, who remained in charge of administering justice and collecting taxes. Military command was handed over to officers called *duces limitis* (border commanders). At the upper levels of the hierarchy, military and civilian command remained united, however, so the vicarii and, ultimately, the tetrarchs,

FROM THE SEVERANS TO THE TETRARCHY

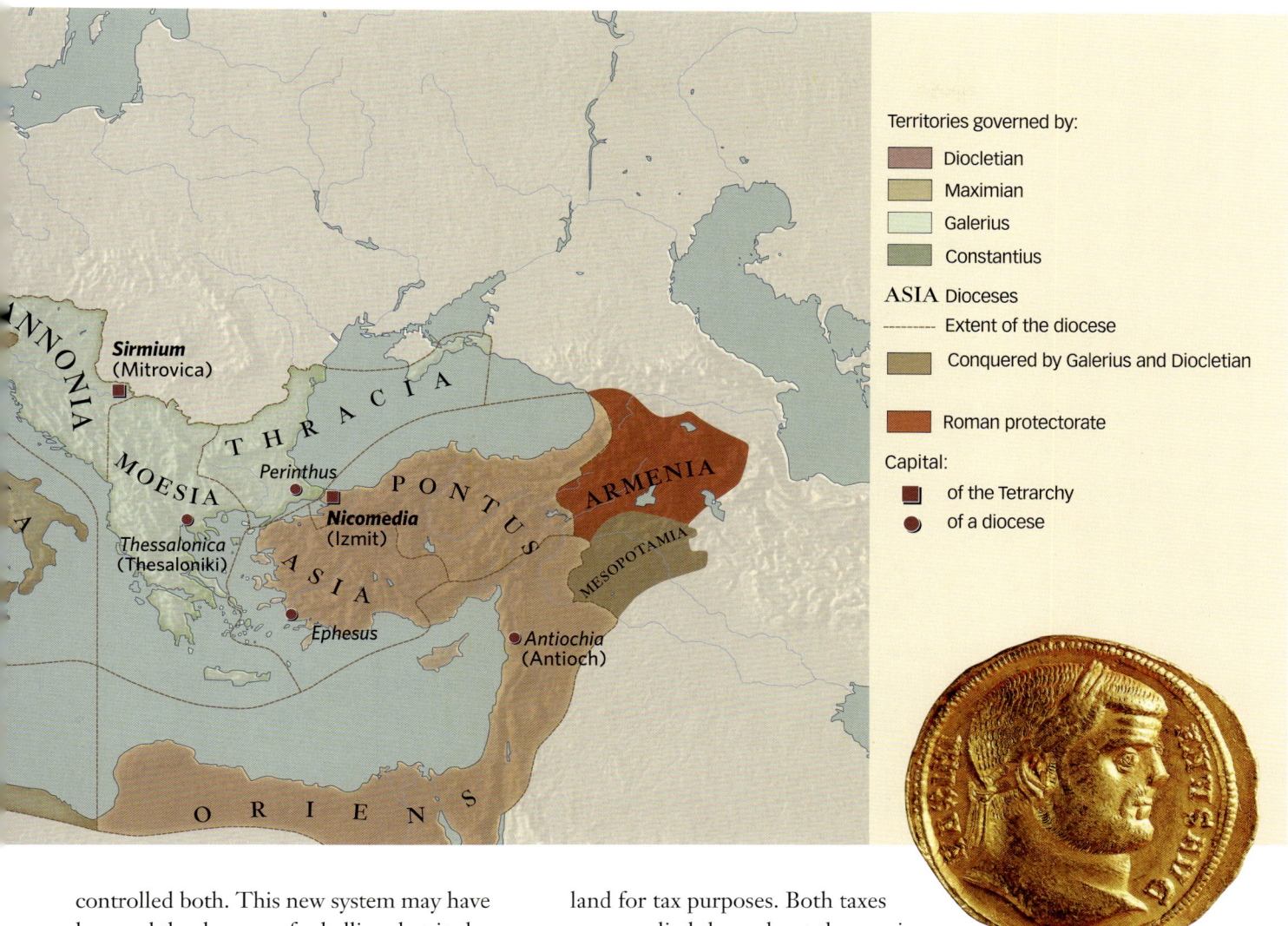

controlled both. This new system may have lessened the dangers of rebellion, but it also lessened a governor's prestige and so limited his ability to control local landed elites, especially those of senatorial status.

The expansion of the government bureaucracy and the army, the constant campaigning, and an ambitious new building programme all placed a major strain on the imperial finances.

Diocletian responded by introducing a new tax system based on cultivable land (*iugera*) and individuals (*capita*). One *iugerum* equated to around 0.26 hectares (0.65 acres), adjusted according to the type of land and crop and the amount of labour required. The *caput* was also variable, with women often valued at half a *caput*. Every five years, census officials would travel around the empire, counting the population and reassessing the productivity of land for tax purposes. Both taxes were applied throughout the empire, including Italy (though not the city of Rome), which had previously been exempt from land taxes. The new taxes gave rise to some anger, but had the advantage of being based on fair principles, contrasting with the arbitrary levies imposed by previous emperors. Tax records were also made public, so people could see how much everyone was paying.

Previous emperors had resorted to debasing the coinage, reducing the amount of silver in the denarius as a money-raising measure. This had led to rampant inflation, rendering the denarius virtually worthless. In his attempt to reform the currency, Diocletian introduced a new system of coinage based on five coins, each containing a fixed percentage of gold, silver or copper: the *aureus*, the *argenteus*, the *follis*, the *radiatus* and the *laureatus*. When this measure

309

THE FALL OF ROME

The persecution of Christians during the reign of Diocletian

In the year 303, Diocletian and his fellow tetrarchs issued a series of edicts abolishing the rights of Christians throughout the empire and demanding that they comply with traditional religious practices. Thus began the bloodiest persecution of Christians in the history of the Roman Empire. Diocletian was not the first emperor to be concerned about the rapid rise of Christianity during the third century. Decius and Valerian had both instituted persecutions. However, Diocletian, urged on by the fanatically anti-Christian Galerius, went much further. The tetrarchs expelled Christians from the army and ordered churches to be razed and scriptures to be burned. Executions soon followed, prosecuted with extreme violence throughout the empire. The persecution was unsuccessful, however. Most Christians escaped, and the sufferings of those who did not escape strengthened the resolve of the rest. In 311, Galerius ended the persecution, admitting that it had failed to bring Christians back to the official religion. The image shows the catacombs of San Sebastiano in Rome. According to tradition, they contain the preserved relics of saints who suffered martyrdom in the time of Diocletian.

failed to prevent another spike in inflation in 301, Diocletian issued his Edict of Maximum Prices, fixing wages and establishing maximum prices on more than a thousand goods. Violating the edict was punishable by death. Yet the edict ignored the law of supply and demand: the fact that prices vary from place to place depending on product availability and transportation cost. Inevitably, prices continued to rise and the edict was later revoked.

Diocletian saw himself as a restorer whose task was to return the empire to an era of peace, stability, justice and moral virtue. To bring about such an ambitious vision, he needed to vest himself with great power. Political authority was centralized in the hands of himself and his fellow tetrarchs and they ruled the empire as absolute monarchs. As such, they needed to present themselves as figures of great authority – not as gods, as earlier emperors had done, but as representatives of the gods, enacting their will on earth. This shift from military or dynastic legitimacy to divine sanctification had another great advantage: it reduced the power of the army or powerful families to challenge the tetrarchs' authority.

To emphasize his pre-eminence, Diocletian took great care with his public image. In contrast with the low-key, quasi-republican persona of the first emperor Augustus, Diocletian wore a gold crown and jewels, and banned the wearing of purple cloth for all but the emperors. His appearances at the games and other public events were carefully stage-managed. Subjects were required to prostrate themselves in his presence. A fortunate few were permitted to kiss the hem of his robe.

Diocletian was a conservative on matters of religion, and a staunch upholder of the traditional Roman pantheon. He saw rising faiths like Manichaeism and Christianity as threats to Rome's religious traditions. Manichaeism, he believed, corrupted the morals of the Roman people. Moreover it was supported by Rome's great enemy, Persia, another reason to distrust its followers. In a 302 edict, issued from Alexandria, Diocletian ordered that low-status Manicheans should be executed by the blade, and those of high status should be sent to work in the quarries of Proconnesus (Marmara Island, Turkey) or the mines of Phaeno in southern Palestine. This, however, was merely a prelude to his repression of the Christians (303–11), the largest, the bloodiest and the last official persecution of Christianity by the Roman Empire.

In May 305, after a near-fatal illness, Diocletian announced his retirement, making him the first Roman emperor to voluntarily abdicate. Maximian retired with him, and, in accordance with the rules of the tetrarchy, Galerius and Constantinius became the new Augustuses. Everyone expected the new Caesars to be Constantine (the son of Constantius) and Maxentius (the son of Maximian). Instead, Severus and Maximinus were elevated to this role. This may have been Galerius's influence: Maximinus was Galerius's nephew, and Severus was his former army comrade. Whatever the reason, the exclusion of two favourites from the succession bred resentment and did not bode well for the future of the tetrarchy.

Diocletian, meanwhile, retired to the small town of Spalatum on the Adriatic coast, where he lived peacefully until his death in 312. He had come to power at a time when the empire was in a state of near collapse, battered by rebellions, secessions and invasions, when emperors ruled sometimes for mere months before meeting violent ends. Diocletian restored peace to the frontiers, strengthened the army, gave the empire a durable administrative structure and established a professional government bureaucracy. In so doing, he prolonged the life of the empire for a further 150 years.

The success of Diocletian's reforms can be measured in the fact that he reigned for 21 years and was able to abdicate voluntarily. His failure can be demonstrated by the way his tetrarchic system collapsed soon afterwards and the empire fell once more into civil war. Despite all his achievements, Diocletian failed to solve the problem that bedevilled the late Roman Empire: the imperial succession.

PALACE OF DIOCLETIAN IN SPLIT

During his retirement, Diocletian lived in an enormous, heavily fortified palace in Spalatum in the Roman province of Dalmatia. The palace was made of white limestone and high-quality marble and was decorated with granite columns and sphinxes taken from ancient Egypt. Today, the palace forms around half of the historic town of Split in Croatia. This monumental court, called the Peristyle, formed the northern access to the imperial apartments.

THE FALL OF ROME

FROM THE SEVERANS TO THE TETRARCHY

The Nabataeans and the Palmyrenes

In this section we shall look at the stories of two peoples, the Nabataeans and the Palmyrenes, dwelling in the Levant on the eastern rim of the Roman Empire, and at the fate of their two great trading cities, Petra and Palmyra.

The Nabataeans originated as one of several nomadic tribes wandering the Arabian Desert with their herds in search of pasture. The first to write about them was Diodorus Siculus in 30 BC; he described them as a strong tribe of some 10,000 nomadic warriors engaging in a profitable trade in frankincense, myrrh and other spices. Their extensive trading activities brought the Nabataeans into contact with other cultures, and this impacted on their religion. The main gods worshipped at Petra were Dushara and al-'Uzzá, which they represented as featureless pillars or blocks.

The Nabataeans spoke an early form of Arabic, but the language of their inscriptions is a version of Aramaic, the lingua franca of Arabian peoples at that time, used for commercial and legal purposes. The Nabataean alphabet developed out of the Aramaic alphabet, but used a cursive script, which was the ancestor of the Arabic alphabet.

Founding a kingdom
In the fourth century BC, the Nabataeans settled in northern Hejaz, Edom and the Negev, creating a kingdom with Petra as their capital. The first known king was Aretas I, his name found in an inscription in the Negev. The Nabataeans grew wealthy on the spice trade that passed between the Arabian interior and the coast, and by harvesting bitumen from the Dead Sea, which they sold to Egypt. In 312

THE TREASURY
The impressive façade of Al-Khazneh (the Treasury) in the city of Petra. It is believed to be the tomb of King Aretas IV.

RISE AND FALL OF THE KINGDOM OF THE NABATAEANS

312 BC
Antigonus I Monophthalmus (One Eye), king of Anatolia, sends three expeditions against the Nabataeans; all are defeated.

168–167 BC
Aretas I, the first known Nabataean king, helps the Maccabees of Israel in their revolt against the Seleucids.

84 BC
The Nabataeans defeat Antiochus XII, who dies in battle.

63 BC
Pompey conquers Jerusalem and creates the Roman province of Syria. His troops attack the city of Petra, but cannot capture it.

9 BC–40 AD
Aretas IV wins the favour of Rome by sending troops against the Jews. Under him, the kingdom reaches its greatest splendour.

106 AD
Trajan, the Roman emperor, incorporates the Nabataean kingdom into the Roman Empire, to form part of the new province Arabia Petrea.

ZENOBIA
The queen of Palmyra with a servant. Funerary relief from the third century.

BC, King Antigonus I Monophthalmus, a former general of Alexander the Great and founder of the Antigonid dynasty, became aware of the wealth of the Nabataeans and sent three raids against them. The Nabataeans successfully fought them off, taking advantage of the mountainous terrain surrounding Petra, which effectively acted as a defensive wall.

Another of Alexander's generals, Seleucus, founded the Seleucid dynasty, which battled Egypt for control of Jordan, emerging victorious in 198 BC. The Nabataeans remained untouched and independent throughout this period, although their art and architecture was influenced by their Hellenistic neighbours. As the Seleucids grew weaker in the second century BC, the Nabataean kingdom grew in strength, expanding its borders northward into Syria in around 150 BC. They started to mint coins, and Petra was ranked with Alexandria as a major world city.

The Romans arrive
In the early first century BC, the Nabataeans reached the zenith of their power, defeating both the Judaeans and the Greeks in battle and greatly increasing their territory. But then they came up against the might of Rome. In 62 BC, the Romans laid siege to Petra, and the Nabataean king Aretas III agreed, for the sake of peace, to pay tribute to them and become a Roman vassal. When they fell behind in their tribute payments in 32 BC, the Roman vassal King Herod the Great invaded them twice.

THE FALL OF ROME

Empire of the caravans

The Nabataean kingdom was at the nexus of several major trade routes, linking Egypt, Persia, Syria and beyond the sea to Greece and Rome. Silk, spices aloe, frankincense, myrrh and incense would come by sea and camel caravan from Asia or the Horn of Africa. From Petra, these products would be sent to the sea ports of the Mediterranean, destined for Rome and Alexandria.

1 THE NORTHERN ROUTE
This route connected several cities, such as Jerash and Damascus, to Petra.

2 THE ROAD TO THE RED SEA
The routes towards the West connected Petra with diverse ports of the Mediterranean and with Egypt, after crossing the deserts of the Negev and Sinai.

3 THE DESERT TRAIL
An exhausting route across the Arabian Peninsula linked Petra with Hegra, from where the route divided into three: one to the Red Sea, another to Yemen and the third towards the East.

During the second invasion in 31 BC, Herod took control of a large area of Nabataean territory, including the northern trading routes into Syria. Nevertheless, as an ally of Rome, the Nabataean kingdom flourished, and Petra continued to be an important trading city. King Aretas IV (9 BC–40 AD) built a chain of settlements along the caravan routes to develop the prosperous incense trade. Gradually, the Nabataeans lost their warlike, nomadic character and became peaceful farmers and traders.

Although the Nabataean kingdom remained formally independent, the surrounding territories were slowly annexed by the expanding Roman Empire: first Egypt, then Judaea. Finally, in 105–6 AD, the Nabataean kingdom was itself annexed by the Roman emperor Trajan and became part of the new Roman province of Arabia Petraea, with Bostra rather than Petra as the provincial capital. Under Greco-Roman influence, the Nabataean gods became anthropomorphic and were represented with human features. By the third century, the Nabataeans had begun writing in Greek, and by the fifth century they had converted to Christianity.

The splendour of Petra

The city of Petra was located around 240km (149 miles) south of Jerusalem, roughly halfway between Damascus in Syria to the north and the Red Sea to the south, making it ideally located as a commercial hub in the ancient world. Surrounded by desert and rugged mountainous terrain, it stood out for its beautiful rock-cut architecture and sophisticated water system, reaching a peak of splendour during the reign of King Aretas IV. Yet the city itself remains mysterious. Even its original name is unknown. Petra ('rock') is what the Greeks called it, referring to its position as a natural fortress. The city has also been named, in various historical accounts, as Pel, Sela, Seir and Rekem, but we do not know what the Nabataeans called it.

The Petra that existed at the time of Antigonus's raids in 312 BC was probably a place of tents and simple structures, reflecting the semi-nomadic character of the Nabataeans at that time. By 100 BC, as the Nabataeans

FROM THE SEVERANS TO THE TETRARCHY

MADA'IN SALEH
The entrances to Nabataean tombs, carved out of sandstone, in the ancient Nabataean city of Hegra, in the northwest of the Arabian peninsula.

grew rich from the caravan trade, they began building houses out of stone.

Some dwellings were carved into the cliffs, while others were free-standing. By the first century AD, Greek architects were being used to build more substantial dwellings for the wealthy elite, containing internal columns and multiple rooms.

In his encyclopaedia *Geography*, written in the early first century AD, Strabo said of Petra: 'It is situated on a spot which is surrounded and fortified by a smooth and level rock, which externally is abrupt and precipitous, but within there are abundant springs of water both for domestic purposes and for watering gardens. Beyond the city-enclosure, the country is for the most part a desert.' The Nabataeans were able to build this city in the desert by controlling the water supply and creating an artificial oasis. They did this by using dams, cisterns, rock-cut channels and ceramic pipes to collect water from flash floods and store it for the prolonged periods of drought.

City of tombs

The city of Petra has many tombs, most of them built at the edge of the city. On the eastern edge of the city, at the bottom of a steep narrow gorge called the Siq (shaft), is Petra's most impressive tomb: Al Khazneh, or 'the Treasury', so-called because people once believed that it contained hidden treasure. However, archaeologists believe it to be a tomb, possibly of Nabataean king Aretas IV, who died in 15 AD. Its elaborate façade, hewn from the sandstone cliff face, has a Greek appearance with Corinthian columns and reliefs depicting figures from Greek mythology, including the twin brothers Castor and Pollux, and six axe-wielding Amazon warriors. There are also representations of griffins, eagles, winged 'victories' and a woman who may be a version of the Egyptian goddess Isis. The tomb's interior is relatively plain, consisting of a vestibule that branches off into three chambers. Beyond the Treasury, at the foot of the en-Nejr mountain, is another example of the strong Greek influence: an

■ THE FALL OF ROME

enormous amphitheatre, big enough to accommodate 6000 spectators, cut into the base of the mountain.

The pious nature of the Nabataeans is evident from Petra's numerous temples. One of these is located near the main street, known today as the colonnaded street, on the southern bank of the Wadi Musa. The temple is believed to date from the city's heyday in the first century AD, and is known as Qasr al-Bint (a shortened version of the Arabic for 'Castle of the Daughter of the Pharaoh'). A relief in the main hall suggests the temple may have been dedicated to the god Dushara. Another building, known as the 'Great Temple', contains a small theatre that may have been used for religious ceremonies. The temple's decorations include limestone sculptures of elephant heads. The city also contains many statues carved into the rock depicting the main god, Dushara, and the three goddesses, Al-'Uzza, Allat and Manāt.

Christianity had already taken root in Petra by the time Constantine legalized it in 313 – indeed, several of the Christians martyred under Diocletian had come from Petra. For many years afterwards, Christians co-existed peacefully with pagan worshippers in Petra. Then, in 423, a band of 40 monks broke into the city, bent on destroying the temples. However, their arrival happened to coincide with an intense rainstorm, and this so impressed the pagan priests (coming as it did after a period of prolonged drought) that they immediately converted to Christianity.

Petra continued to flourish for a hundred years or more under Roman rule. However, by the middle of the

ROYAL TOMBS OF PETRA
These underground chambers have been carved into the sandstone rock of a mountain. The closest one is the so-called Tomb of the Palace.

FROM THE SEVERANS TO THE TETRARCHY

THE FALL OF ROME

Palmyra: city at the crossroads

Situated halfway between the Roman and the Persian worlds, Palmyra was influenced by both East and West. The image shows the monumental arch and the Great Colonnade.

1 AGORA A caravanserai (resting place for caravans) containing a *triclinium* (dining hall).

2 GREAT COLONNADE Palmyra's main street is lined with more than 200 Corinthian columns.

3 TEMPLE OF BAALSHAMIN Small temple dedicated to a sky deity of Phoenician origin.

4 TETRAPYLON Cube-shaped monument with four gates marking the crossroads between the city's two main streets.

5 ROMAN THEATRE Unfinished theatre dating from the late second century Severan dynasty.

6 TEMPLE OF NABU A temple consecrated to Nabu, Babylonian god of writing.

7 MONUMENTAL ARCH Also known as the Arch of Septimius Severus and built in honour of the Roman emperor.

8 TEMPLE OF BEL Consecrated to the Mesopotamian god Bel, worshipped in triad with the lunar god Aglibol and the sun god Yarhibol.

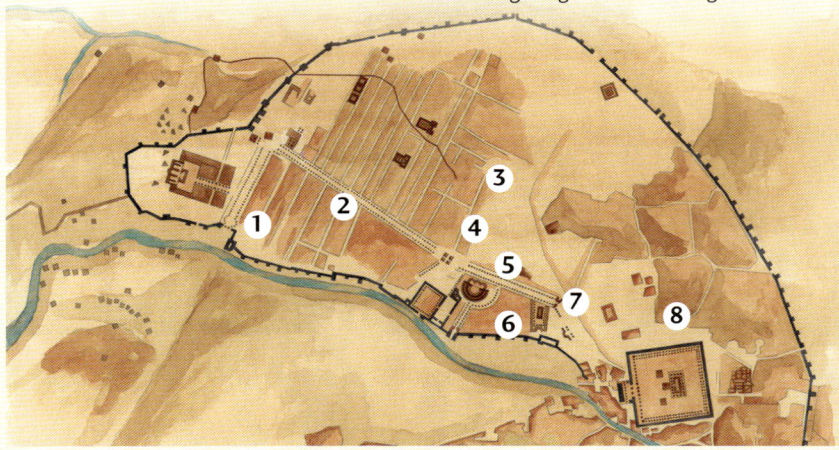

---

third century AD, as trade routes moved elsewhere, it began a slow and irreversible decline. An earthquake in 363 destroyed half the city and crippled the water management system. Petra was further weakened by another earthquake in 551, and was finally abandoned altogether when Arabs conquered the region in 663.

The magnificence of Palmyra

Like Petra, Palmyra was another city that grew wealthy on the caravan trade. Located in Syria between the Euphrates and the Mediterranean, it was an important staging post for traders travelling between east and west, and grew rich by charging heavy tolls on the caravans. The city was built on an oasis and surrounded by palms, from which it derived its name. Ethnically, its population was made up of Amorites, Arameans and Arabs.

Palmyra first emerged as an important trading centre under the Seleucids (312–64 BC). By the late second century BC, large-scale tombs and temples were being built there in the Hellenic style. In 64 BC, the Roman general Pompey conquered the Seleucid kingdom and established the Roman province of Syria, yet he left Palmyra independent, and the city continued to trade freely with both Rome and Parthia. That situation ended in 14 AD when the Romans under Tiberius conquered Palmyra, making it part of Syria. Palmyra remained relatively autonomous under Roman rule, with little asked of it except to pay its taxes and send its young men to fight in the legions. The city thrived, with Palmyrene merchants plying their trade under the protection of Roman garrisons and establishing colonies in surrounding trade centres. Its first walled fortifications were built at this time, and the great Temple of Bel was completed in 32 AD. Palmyra reached a peak of prosperity during the second century, helped by the Roman conquest of Petra, which shifted control of the southern trade routes from the Nabataeans to the Palmyrenes.

Towards the end of the second century, Palmyra's situation deteriorated as the Roman–Parthian war affected the city's trade. Worse was to follow in the third century with the rise of Sasanian Persia and the Roman

FROM THE SEVERANS TO THE TETRARCHY

Empire's decline into military anarchy, leaving Palmyra very vulnerable.

When the Sasanians took over the Palmyrene colonies on their lands, the Palmyrene council elected a lord for their city, Septimius Odenathus, to lead their army. In 260, Odenathus declared himself king and led the Palmyrenes to victory against the Sasanians. Odenathus then defeated and killed two usurpers, Quietus and Balista, and was rewarded by Emperor Gallienus with the title Corrector of the East with authority over the entire Eastern empire. Palmyra had become a de facto independent kingdom allied to Rome. Odenathus continued to triumph, driving the Persians back to their capital, Ctesiphon. But in 267 he was assassinated, succeeded by his ten-year-old son Vaballathus. The boy's mother, Zenobia, became de facto ruler. She had ambitions to expand Palmyrene power, but was careful to do so while appearing subordinate to Rome. In 270 she conquered Arabia and Egypt; the following year, she invaded Anatolia. The Palmyrene kingdom had become an empire, and Vaballathus and his mother assumed the titles of Augustus and Augusta. Their glory was short-lived. In 272, Emperor Aurelian reconquered all the territories Zenobia had taken and laid siege to Palmyra. Zenobia tried to escape but was captured by the Romans. The city fell soon afterwards. Aurelian spared Palmyra, but then it revolted a second time in 273, slaughtering the Roman garrison and declaring Antiochus, the alleged son of Zenobia, Augustus. This time Aurelian showed no mercy and razed the city to the ground, pillaging the Temple of Bel and seizing many of its treasures to decorate his Temple of Sol. Palmyra never recovered.

Emperor Diocletian later established a military camp in the ruined city as one in a line of fortresses marking the empire's eastern boundary. The Byzantine emperor Justinian I further rebuilt the city's defences in the sixth century. It survived, as such, as a military outpost, but the caravan trade had long since moved away. In 634, Palmyra fell to a Muslim army led by Khaled Ibn al-Walid, and the city all but vanished from the record. Its ruins, covered in sand, were rediscovered in 1678.

CONSTANTINE THE GREAT
This emperor changed the ancient world, adopting Christianity and moving the empire's centre of gravity to the East. This bronze statue is in the British city of York, where Constantine was on campaign when he became emperor. On the next page: aureus of Emperor Constantine II.

FROM CONSTANTINE TO THEODOSIUS

The Roman Empire recovered from the crisis of the third century thanks in large part to the leadership of emperors like Diocletian and Constantine. The tetrarchy helped to establish a more decentralized form of government, and also carried within it an implicit recognition that East and West were gradually diverging. The fourth century would witness the empire's political revitalization but also its permanent division.

With the retirement of Diocletian and Maximian in 305, the second tetrarchy took power. The Augustuses were Galerius (who ruled Asia Minor, Greece and the Balkans) and Constantius Chlorus (who ruled Gaul, Britain and Spain), while the Caesars were Severus (ruling Italy, Africa and part of Pannonia) and Maximinus Daia (ruling Egypt and Syria). This tetrarchy, however, would be short-lived: the following year, Constantius and his son Constantine were campaigning against the Picts in Britain when Constantius fell ill and died. His troops immediately proclaimed Constantine the new Augustus. When Galerius heard about this, he was furious. Under the rules of tetrarchic succession, Severus should have been the next Augustus. But Galerius knew that denying Constantine would mean civil war, so he compromised by granting him the title Caesar while making Severus the new Augustus.

THE FALL OF ROME

The battle that changed the face of the Roman world

When preparing for a siege, Maxentius destroyed the Milvian Bridge to cut off his enemy's access to the city. But then he changed tactics and rode out to meet Constantine, building a wooden pontoon bridge in place of the destroyed one so his army could cross the Tiber, and arraying his troops on the far side of the river.

Constantine's army drove Maxentius's troops back towards the pontoon, which collapsed under their weight: hundreds died in the muddy waters. The next day, Constantine made his entrance into Rome preceded by the head of Maxentius impaled on a pike. On the right of this painting of the battle by Peter Connolly (1935) is the symbol of Christ, which, according to legend, Constantine ordered to be painted on his soldiers' shields (Vatican Museums, Rome).

Constantine's promotion prompted Maxentius, the ambitious son of Maximian, to declare himself emperor. Avoiding the terms Augustus or Caesar, he styled himself *princeps invictus*, or 'undefeated prince' and asserted his authority over Italy and Africa. Galerius, fearing a return to the bad days of the Military Anarchy, sent Severus to Italy to deal with the usurper. Maxentius countered by encouraging his father Maximian out of retirement and appointing him co-emperor. When Severus laid siege to Rome, many of his troops deserted him, and Severus was forced to flee to Ravenna.

He eventually surrendered and was later killed. In mid-307, Galerius invaded Italy, but was forced to withdraw after Maxentius's bribes prompted many of his soldiers to defect. Maxentius, now master of Italy and Africa, sent his father to Gaul to try to forge an alliance with Constantine. Maximian appointed Constantine Augustus, and Constantine agreed to marry Maximian's daughter. Sadly, Maximian's second experience of power went to his head: he tried to depose first his son and then Constantine, was defeated by both, and committed suicide in 310.

Galerius tried to rescue the tetrarchy by hosting a conference at Carnuntum in 308, even persuading the elderly Diocletian to attend. If Maxentius had hoped that Galerius would accept reality and confirm him as tetrarch, he would be disappointed: instead, Galerius appointed Licinius, a close childhood friend, as Augustus in the West, entrusting him with the task of overthrowing the usurper Maxentius. However, by this time, Galerius's authority was fading. Maximinus Daia, Caesar in the East, rejected the promotion of Licinius, proclaiming himself Augustus. In 311, Galerius died of cancer, recanting his violent

FROM CONSTANTINE TO THEODOSIUS

1 CAVALRY
Constantine ordered his cavalry to charge at the enemy horsemen. The cavalry of Maxentius buckled before the impact and broke ranks.

2 INFANTRY
Maxentius ordered a retreat, hoping to regroup in Rome, but the only way to cross the river was the pontoon, creating a traffic jam.

3 RETREAT
Next, Constantine ordered his legionaries to advance. Most of Maxentius's troops fought back fiercely but began to be pushed back towards the Tiber.

4 THE TIBER
The bridge collapsed and the current dragged away the bodies of the fallen. Maxentius drowned while trying to cross the river on horseback.

persecutions of the Christians. His death was a further blow to the tetrarchy, as he was the last of its committed supporters, and very little trust existed between the remaining four emperors.

Defensive alliances were quickly forged between Maximinus Daia and Maxentius, and then between Constantine and Licinius, but these merely hastened the drift towards war. Maxentius felt surrounded by enemies (his ally Maximinus Daia was far away), and he began readying his troops for war.

Constantine struck first against Maxentius, crossing the Alps in spring 312 with 40,000 men. He won a series of victories in northern Italy, taking Turin and Milan. Maxentius advanced from Rome and offered Constantine battle near the Milvian Bridge, a crossing point on the Tiber, on 28 October 312. According to legend, Constantine had a dream the night before the battle in which a voice spoke to him predicting victory under the sign of the Christian *labarum* (military standard). *In hoc signo vinces*, it said ('with this sign, you shall win'). The legend tells that Constantine's soldiers arrived on the battlefield with the Christian sign on their shields. What cannot be doubted is that Constantine's forces won a crushing victory and Maxentius died during the battle, making Constantine the undisputed master of the West. The Battle of the Milvian Bridge was a major step towards establishing Christianity as the dominant religion in the Roman Empire, and consequently a crucial event in the history of Western civilization.

Constantine was received triumphantly in Rome. In February 313, he met with Licinius in Milan and cemented their alliance with the marriage of Licinius to Constantine's sister Constantia. During the meeting, the two emperors signed the Edict of Milan, granting

The baptism and death of Constantine the Great

In 337, Constantine was returning to Constantinople from a visit to Helenopolis, when he realized he was dying. He informed his bishops of his wish to be baptized. The decision to delay his baptism until just before death was not unusual in the early Church, when many Christians believed one could not be forgiven for sins committed after baptism. Constantine may have felt that a sin-free life was incompatible with his duties as emperor. For example, shortly before he died, he left orders for the elimination of certain contenders for the succession. He chose Bishop Eusebius, bishop of Nicomedia and future patriarch of Constantinople, to perform the baptism. In medieval and Renaissance depictions of this event, it is usually Pope Sylvester I who baptizes Constantine in Rome after his victory in the Battle of the Milvian Bridge, but there is no historical evidence for this. The image shows Pope Sylvester baptizing Constantine, a scene from the *Stavelot Triptych*, created around 1156 (The Morgan Library, New York City).

Milestones of the second tetrarchy

Years 312–313
Constantine defeats Maxentius and, later, issues the Edict of Milan.

Year 325
Council of Nicaea establishes the structure of the Church of Rome.

Year 330
Constantinople is the new capital of the empire. War against the Goths.

Year 337
Death of Constantine and ascent to the throne of Constantius II.

religious toleration throughout the empire and agreeing to the restoration of confiscated Church property. In April, Maximinus Daia led an army against Licinius, taking Byzantium and Heraclea. The two armies met at Tzirallum, where Licinius won a crushing victory. Maximinus died in August 313, leaving Licinius master of the East.

Despite their alliance, relations between the two remaining emperors quickly soured. Constantine accused Licinius of harbouring Senecio, a rebel accused of plotting against him. Then Licinius appointed Valerius Valens as his co-emperor without seeking Constantine's agreement. Their forces clashed at Cibalae in 314 and Mardia in 316–7; Constantine emerged victorious both times.

In a peace treaty signed in March 317, Licinius recognized Constantine's superiority and ceded all European territories to him except Thrace. He had his co-emperor Valens killed. Constantine's sons Crispus and Constantine II, and Licinius's son Licinius II, were named Caesars.

The uneasy truce did not last long. In 320, Licinius angered Constantine (according to Christian polemicist and Constantine supporter Eusebius) by reneging on the Edict of Milan and beginning a new persecution of the Christians, sacking Christian office holders and confiscating church property. The following year, when Constantine pursued invading barbarians across the Danube into Licinius's territory, Licinius complained that Constantine had broken the terms of their treaty. After several more skirmishes, Constantine declared war on Licinius in 324, defeating him at the Battle of Adrianople in July. Licinius fled, appointing Martius Martinianus as Caesar. Constantine triumphed over Martinianus at the

Hellespont and at Chrysopolis in September. Licinius and Martinianus surrendered to Constantine at Nicomedia. Constantine agreed to spare their lives, but in 325 he changed his mind and had them both killed along with Licinius's son. Thus Constantine became sole emperor of the Roman Empire.

Constantine, the Christian emperor

Following his triumph over Licinius, Constantine decided that the empire needed a new capital, further east, to better integrate the Eastern, Greek-speaking provinces. Various cities were considered, including Serdica, Sirmium and Thessalonica, but eventually he opted for Byzantium, due to its strategic importance controlling access to the Black Sea, and its good defences. Rebuilding work began in 324, and the city was officially dedicated in May 330, being renamed Constantinople.

With the emperor now residing in the 'New Rome' on the Bosphorus, the empire acquired a new centre of gravity. The old Rome continued as a wealthy, prestigious city, and would always remain the emotional heart of the empire, but it rapidly declined in political importance.

Throughout his reign, Constantine sought to promote Christianity, building churches, granting privileges to clergymen and encouraging the observance of saints' days. In 321, he declared that Sunday should be a day of rest for all citizens, and in 323 he decreed that Christians should no longer participate in State sacrifices. Pagan gods disappeared from his coins, replaced by Christian symbols: the *chi rho* and the *labarum*. In the 330s, the emperor seized control of the pagan temples and proceeded to melt down their gold, silver and bronze statues in order to mint new coins. Constantine disliked factionalism within the Church and was always

MAUSOLEUM OF CONSTANTINA
Known today as Santa Constanza, this church was built in Rome in the fourth century. Traditionally, it was believed to be the mausoleum of Constantina, daughter of Constantine the Great, who died in 354. However, recent excavations suggest it was built by Emperor Julian for his wife Helena, who died in 360. Circular in plan, it is one of the earliest Christian buildings in Rome.

THE FALL OF ROME

THE ARCH OF CONSTANTINE: A SYMBOL OF POWER

Located between the Colosseum and the Palatine Hill, the Arch of Constantine was erected by the Senate to commemorate Constantine's triumph over Maxentius on the Milvian Bridge. The arch spans the *Via triumphalis*, the route taken by all emperors when entering the city in triumph. Work began on the arch in 313, and it was officially opened in 315. The largest of all of Rome's triumphal arches, it is 21m (69ft) high, 25.9m (85ft) wide and 7.4m (24ft) deep. It contains three archways: a central one 11.5m by 6.5m (38 by 21ft), and two lateral archways 7.4m by 3.4m (24 by 11ft) each. Above the archways is the 'attic', made of bricks faced with marble. The attic contains a frieze depicting the Battle of the Milvian Bridge. Although dedicated to Constantine, much of the arch's decoration incorporated work from the 'golden age' of emperors in the second century. Several major reliefs from monuments built at the time of Trajan, Hadrian and Marcus Aurelius were reused in the Arch of Constantine, resulting in a collage of different styles.

ORIGIN OF THE ARCH RELIEFS

TRAJAN (98–117)
Two reliefs on the east and west sides of the attic and two more on the inside of the central archway depict scenes from Trajan's Dacian Wars. These came from a large frieze celebrating the Dacian victory. The original location of the frieze was probably Trajan's Forum.

HADRIAN (117–138)
The pairs of round reliefs above each lateral archway date to the time of Hadrian. On the north side they display scenes of a boar hunt, sacrifice to Apollo, a lion hunt and sacrifice to Hercules. On the south side they show hunters departing, sacrifice to Silvanus, a bear hunt and sacrifice to Diana.

MARCUS AURELIUS (161–180)
Flanking the attic's central inscription are four pairs of relief panels from the time of Marcus Aurelius, showing the emperor engaged in various activities. The faces of the figures were reworked between 313 and 315 so they resembled those of Constantine, Licinius and Constantius Chlorus.

FROM CONSTANTINE TO THEODOSIUS

1 VICTORY OVER THE BARBARIANS
A battle from the Dacian wars: after the massacre, cavalrymen finish off the survivors.

2 HUNTING SCENE AND SACRIFICE
The emperor is hunting a bear (left) and offering sacrifice to the goddess Diana (right).

3 PRISONERS BEFORE THE EMPEROR
Enemy prisoners are presented to the emperor, who appears on the left in both scenes.

CONSTANTINE (306–337)
The horizontal frieze that runs below the round reliefs and above each lateral archway is the main part of the arch dating from the time of Constantine. The frieze shows scenes from Constantine's Italian campaign against Maxentius, and immediately afterwards. It begins on the western face with Constantine's departure from Milan. The southern face shows (on the left) the Siege of Verona, a key victory for Constantine, and (on the right) the Battle of the Milvian Bridge, portraying Constantine victorious and Maxentius's army drowning in the Tiber. The eastern face shows Constantine and his army entering Rome, and the northern face portrays Constantine's activities after his arrival in Rome: on the left we see him speaking to the citizens in the Roman Forum, while on the right (the final panel of the frieze) he is shown distributing money to the people.

4 WINGED VICTORY OR CHRISTIAN ANGEL
The spandrels of the main archway depict victory figures that might also be angels.

THE FALL OF ROME

The house of Constantine the Great

Years 307–337
Constantine: Executes Crispus and names as Caesar Constantine II, Dalmatius, Constans and Constantius II.

Years 337–340
Constantine II: Named co-emperor alongside Constantius II and Constans.

Years 337–350
Constans: Defeated Constantine II to become sole emperor of the West.

Years 337–361
Constantius II: Names Julian as Caesar, then is forced to accept him as co-emperor and successor.

Years 360–363
Julian: Tries to restore paganism, persecutes Christians and dies in Persia.

HAND OF CONSTANTINE THE GREAT
A fragment of a seated statue (Palazzo dei Conservatori, Capitoline Museums, Rome).

keen to establish an orthodoxy where possible. Therefore, in 317, he declared the Donatists in North Africa heretics and sent them into exile. In 325, he summoned the bishops to Nicaea in order to arrive at a consensus on the Church's core beliefs. This resulted in the Nicene Creed, a fundamental statement of belief still used to this day in Christian liturgy.

In 326, Constantine decided to restrict senior administrative positions to people of senatorial rank. This reversed the trend since the mid-third century of giving greater power to the equestrian class at the expense of the old aristocracy. Now it was up to senators to elect praetors and quaestors. Although the Senate itself remained a weak body, the senatorial class were pleased to see some of their ancient authority restored. Constantine may have done this in an attempt to reintegrate the wealthy senatorial order, still largely pagan, within an increasingly Christian imperial court.

In 328, Constantine constructed a bridge across the Danube at Sucidava, and in 332 he led his armies into Dacia in an attempt to reconquer the province, abandoned under Aurelian. He inflicted a crushing defeat on the Goths living there, and in 334, he routed the Tervingi. With these victories, Constantine extended Roman control over Dacia, receiving the title Dacicus maximus in 336. However, this was not to last: within 40 years, the bridge at Sucidava was no longer in use. In his final years, Constantine began planning a campaign against Persia. Presenting this as a campaign to protect Persia's Christian subjects, he made plans for bishops and a church-shaped tent to accompany his army. However, the campaign had to be abandoned when Constantine fell ill in the spring of 337.

Constantine continued the work of Diocletian in restoring stability and order to the empire, re-establishing its military dominance and adding prestige to the office of emperor. His commitment to and promotion of Christianity laid the groundwork for its adoption at the end of the fourth century as Rome's official religion. Finally, his decision to shift the imperial capital from Rome to Constantinople was an implicit recognition that the future of the empire lay in the east.

The heirs of Constantine

When Constantine died in May 337, he left the empire under the control of his three surviving sons: Constantine II, Constantius II and Constans. Constantine's nephews, Delmatius and Hannibalianus, were killed before they could pose a threat to the succession. The three sons, elevated to Augustuses in September, divided the empire between them: Constantine took control of Britain, Gaul and Spain; Constans took the other European provinces; Constantius ruled the East. The brothers were soon at war with each other. In 340, Constantine II invaded Italy and was defeated and killed at Aquileia, leaving Constans in control of the whole Western empire.

Constantius would spend most of his reign defending the eastern border against Sasanian

The church and Constantine

In 325, Constantine summoned all the bishops of the Church to the Bithynian city of Nicaea (in present-day Turkey) to discuss Christian doctrine. The First Council of Nicaea was the first ever ecumenical council of the Church. Constantine organized it along the lines of the Roman Senate and presided over it but did not cast any official vote. The council produced the first uniformly agreed statement of Christian doctrine, the Nicene Creed. In part, this sought to resolve a dispute within the Church of Alexandria regarding the nature of the Son in relation to the Father. It decided against the Arian view on the matter, and Arianism was condemned as heresy. The council also agreed a date for Easter and adopted disciplinary rules. The image shows a meeting of the Council of Nicaea held in the Roman church of San Martino ai Monte, from a 16th-century fresco.

Persian invasions under their ruler Shapur II. This violent, bitter war ultimately proved inconclusive. In the West, Constans proved a cruel and unpopular ruler. A barbarian general in his army called Magnentius was elevated to Augustus in January 350. Finding himself without support, Constans fled and was killed by Magnentius's supporters. On hearing of this, Constantius II broke off his war with Persia and marched West. He defeated Magnentius at Mursa in September 351, but Magnentius survived and withdrew to Italy. The final confrontation between Constantius and Magnentius came at the Battle of Mons Seleucus in southern Gaul in 353. Constantius emerged victorious, and Magnentius committed suicide, leaving the empire once again under the control of a single ruler.

As a Christian, Constantius tried to promote Christianity and suppress paganism. He closed pagan temples and imposed the death penalty on those performing pagan sacrifices. He also exempted the clergy from paying taxes and from performing compulsory public service. Since Constantine's day, the Church had been split between two forms of belief: the Nicene Creed and Arianism. Constantius sought to unify Christians under a new, compromise creed later called Semi-Arianism. He convened councils to discuss this in 359 and 360, but no agreement was reached. Ultimately, Constantius would be remembered not as a unifier but as a heretic who tried to impose his will on the Church.

Constantius also imposed some harsh restrictions on the Jewish population of the empire. Early in his reign, together with his brothers, he issued edicts limiting the number of slaves that Jews could own, and banning marriage between Jewish men and Christian women. Later, when he was ruling as sole emperor, Constantius decreed that anyone

THE FALL OF ROME

The structure of the imperial government in the fourth century

Under Constantine and his sons, the empire resembled an absolutist monarchy, with hereditary rulers exercising divine right. After the founding of Constantinople, the Senate of Rome was reduced to the status of a municipal authority. The imperial court became the centre of political power, with the emperor advised by a ministerial council. Civil and military administrations were kept separate, each with their own structure. The emperor presided over both hierarchies and served as the only link between them. The provinces, governed by praeses provinciae (provincial governors), were organized into 14 dioceses, each under the authority of a vicar. The dioceses were grouped under four Praetorian prefectures: Gaul, Italy, Illyria and the East. Rome and Constantinople were administered separately, under a praefectus urbi (urban prefect). The image is a bronze statue titled *Genius of the Senate* (National Museum of Roman Art, Mérida, Spain).

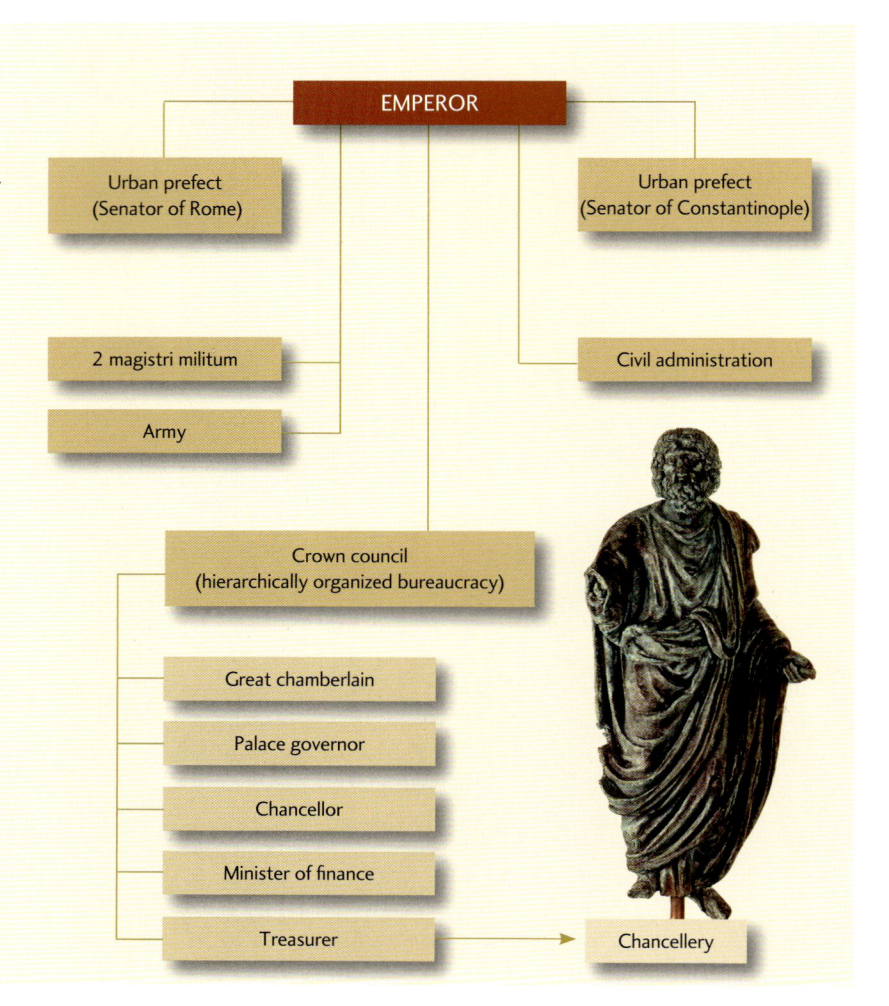

```
EMPEROR
├── Urban prefect (Senator of Rome)
├── Urban prefect (Senator of Constantinople)
├── 2 magistri militum
│   └── Army
├── Civil administration
└── Crown council (hierarchically organized bureaucracy)
    ├── Great chamberlain
    ├── Palace governor
    ├── Chancellor
    ├── Minister of finance
    └── Treasurer → Chancellery
```

converting from Christianity to Judaism would have all their property confiscated.

In 355, Constantius decided that too many threats faced the empire, and that he needed to share power. He appointed his half-cousin and brother-in-law Julian as Caesar with control of the Western empire. Over the next five years, Julian led his Gallic troops in a string of victories against invading Germanic tribes, enabling him to secure the Rhine frontier. In 360, Constantius sent orders for the Gallic troops to be transferred east to reinforce his army, which was currently struggling against the forces of Shapur II of Sasanian Persia. The Gallic troops refused to obey the order and instead proclaimed Julian Augustus in the West. Civil war seemed inevitable, although Constantius was too preoccupied with his confrontation with Shapur II to respond immediately. In 361, the eastern front became quieter and Constantius began preparations to face Julian. But then, in November 361, he fell ill and died, leaving Julian as sole emperor.

Julian the Apostate

The new emperor differed both in style and philosophy from his immediate predecessors. He viewed the Constantinian court as inefficient, corrupt and wastefully extravagant; shortly after his arrival in Constantinople, he dismissed thousands of palace staff. The imperial bureaucracy, he believed, had become bloated in its efforts to micro-manage the empire. The Constantinople government, in his view, had two functions: administering the law and defending the empire's frontiers. Day-to-day administration he preferred to leave to individual city authorities. This stripped-down view of the emperor's role was reflected in his ascetic style, which he based on his heroes,

Hadrian and Marcus Aurelius. Rejecting the ostentation of Diocletian and Constantine, he presented himself as *primus inter pares* (first among equals): a man of the people, operating under the same laws as his subjects.

Arguably the most important difference between Julian and the earlier Constantinians was that Julian was a pagan, not a Christian, and he wished to restore Rome's polytheistic religious tradition – hence his posthumous appellation, 'the Apostate'. He knew from studying history that persecuting Christians only made them stronger; his aim was not to destroy Christianity, merely to replace it with Hellenistic paganism as the State religion.

Soon after taking the throne, Julian began reopening pagan temples and restoring their confiscated properties. He repealed the special rights and privileges that Constantine had awarded to Christian bishops, and in February 362 he issued his Tolerance Edict guaranteeing freedom of religion and declaring all religions equal before the law. In the spirit of toleration, he allowed heretical Christian bishops to return from exile, most likely to sow discord between the Christian sects. In an edict on schools, Julian demanded that all teachers be approved by the emperor. This has been seen as his attempt to reduce the powers of Christian schools, which tended to present Christian scripture as superior to pagan texts.

No one knows why Julian made the fateful decision to invade Persia in March 363. There was no immediate threat to the eastern border. Perhaps he felt the need for military glory to strengthen his authority, especially with the Eastern army, recently under the command of his rival Constantius. His ambitious plan was to conquer the Sasanian capital Ctesiphon, overthrow Shapur II and replace him with his

EMPEROR JULIAN

Julian presiding over a meeting of the sectarians. In his youth, Julian studied under Eusebius, Arian bishop of Nicomedia. Aged 19, he continued his education first at Como and later in Greece where, in 351, he converted to the pagan philosophy of Neoplatonism. (Oil on canvas by Edward Armitage, 1817–1896, Walker Art Gallery, Liverpool.)

THE FALL OF ROME

SAINT AMBROSE
Born in 340 in Trier, Ambrose was appointed bishop of Milan in 374. He was a vehement defender of the primacy of the Church over the State and a strong adherent of the Nicene orthodoxy who has been accused of inciting persecutions of Arians, Jews and pagans. Ambrose was one of the four Doctors of the Church and the patron saint of Milan. Mosaic of Saint Ambrose from the Sacello de San Vittore (Chapel of St Victor) in the Basilica of St Ambrose in Milan.

Roman-friendly brother Hormizd. Julian marched his army east and laid siege to Ctesiphon, but was unable to take the city. His generals warned him that Shapur was approaching with a large force and they should withdraw. Instead, Julian destroyed the fleet that had brought them across the Tigris and advanced further east into the Persian interior. The Persian army harassed them with ambushes and scorched earth tactics. In June 363, Julian received a spear wound that proved fatal.

Julian's early death provides scholars with one of history's great 'what ifs'. Had he survived to continue with his religious reforms, would he have been able to reverse the Christianization of the Roman world, or would it have happened anyway?

The Church was organized, driven and homogenous, whereas paganism was barely a coherent religion, based as it was around diverse local traditions and deities, so perhaps Christianity's rise was inevitable. On the other hand, in the time of Julian, the people of the empire were still largely pagan, Christianity having largely been imposed from above. The future of the Christian faith was still uncertain at this time, and it may be that a Persian spear tipped the balance in its favour.

Valentinian dynasty

After Julian died, the army hastily proclaimed Jovian, commander of the imperial bodyguard, emperor. With the army still being harassed by the Persians, Jovian was forced to accept humiliating peace terms. On his return to Constantinople, he set about restoring Christianity to its former status. His reign would be short, however: in February 364, just eight months after his accession, Jovian died while travelling between Ancyra and Nicaea. Army leaders met with civilian officials at Nicaea to choose a new emperor. They eventually selected a former army commander and native of Pannonia named Valentinian.

An able soldier, Valentinian quickly established his authority over the army. To reassure civil administrators and prevent a succession crisis he appointed his younger brother Valens co-emperor, with responsibility for the Eastern empire. Valentinian took up residence in Milan while Valens based himself in Constantinople. Valentinian was very soon preoccupied in putting down border incursions and rebellions. In September 365, the Alamanni crossed the Rhine and invaded Gaul. Valentinian's forces were defeated twice by the Alamanni and two of his generals were killed before he managed to drive them out of Gaul.

In late 367, a combined force of Picts, Attacotti and Scots went on the rampage in northern and western Britannia, sacking and burning forts, settlements and cities. Valentinian sent a force under Theodosius in the spring of 368 to restore order. Theodosius discovered a province in disarray with deserted forts and local garrisons collaborating with the invaders. By the end of the year, the invaders had been driven back to their homelands and

Valentinian I and Valens, two ruthless emperors

In the early years of the double reign of Valentinian I and Valens, they were relentless in their efforts to eradicate the pagan restoration begun by Julian. They engaged in a ruthless persecution of the practice of magic, instigating the first witch hunt undertaken in the name of Christianity. Valentinian could behave with remarkable savagery towards his staff, and he often had servants and attendants executed for minor delays, omissions or perceived offences to his dignity. It is said that victims of his cruel 'justice' were placed in a cage with two bears to be torn apart. On the other hand, Valentinian promoted public health and education for the poor. As for Valens, he could equal his brother in cruelty, but also shared many of his virtues. During his reign he reduced the tax burden on his subjects by a quarter. Image: Medallion of Valentinian and Valens, made between 365 and 375 (Münzkabinett, Berlin).

SUBMISSION
The younger brother, Valens, expresses his more compliant character in a gesture of submission.

AGGRESSION
Valentinian, the elder brother, displays his boorish nature with a contemptuous, mocking smile.

---

order had been restored. Valentinian rewarded Theodosius by promoting him to magister equitum (Master of the Cavalry).

While Theodosius was busy in Britannia, Valentinian was once again fighting the Alamanni, who had recrossed the Rhine and plundered Moguntiacum. By 368, he had expelled the invaders at heavy cost. In 369, he ordered a strengthening of defences along the length of the Rhine. For four more years, Valentinian campaigned hard against the Alamanni, trying unsuccessfully to overthrow their powerful chieftain Macrian. In 374, the emperor's attention was diverted to the Danube frontier and an invasion of Pannonia Valeria by the Quadi and Sarmatians. After driving out the invaders, Valentinian crossed the Danube at Aquincum and set about pillaging Quadi lands in retaliation. In November 375, he received a deputation of envoys from the Quadi, who explained to him that they had launched the original attack because Roman forts had been built on their lands. Valentinian was so infuriated, he burst a blood vessel in his head while yelling at them, and died.

Valentinian was known to be a man with a violent temper who could be cruel and brutal in his punishments. However, he was also an accomplished soldier and a diligent administrator who cared for the poorer classes from which his father had risen. His good instincts were often thwarted by a poor choice of lieutenants and a stubborn faith in their merits despite all evidence to the contrary.

In the Eastern empire, Valens began his reign preparing a campaign against Persia to win back territories lost under the treaty signed by Jovian. But he was forced to postpone these plans when, in September 365, Procopius, cousin of Julian and last of the male

Valentinian dynasty

Years 364–375
Valentinian I (West). After campaigns in Pannonia, he died on the Rhine.

Years 364–378
Valens (East). Challenged by Goths, he met his doom at Adrianople.

Years 375–383
Gracian. The son of Valentinian I, he was overthrown by Magnus Maximus.

Years 375–392
Valentinian II. After a fight with his guardian Arbogast, he killed himself.

THE FALL OF ROME

The battle of Adrianople: The death of an emperor

The Gothic revolt, which began in 376, was followed by two years of inconclusive battles during which the Romans failed to gain control of the situation. In 378, Valens decided to take control of the situation himself, bringing troops from Syria and ordering Gratian to come with troops from Gaul.

On 6 August, Valens learned from his scouts that a Goth force was heading towards Adrianople from the north. He marched his army, which may have numbered up to 30,000, to Adrianople, where

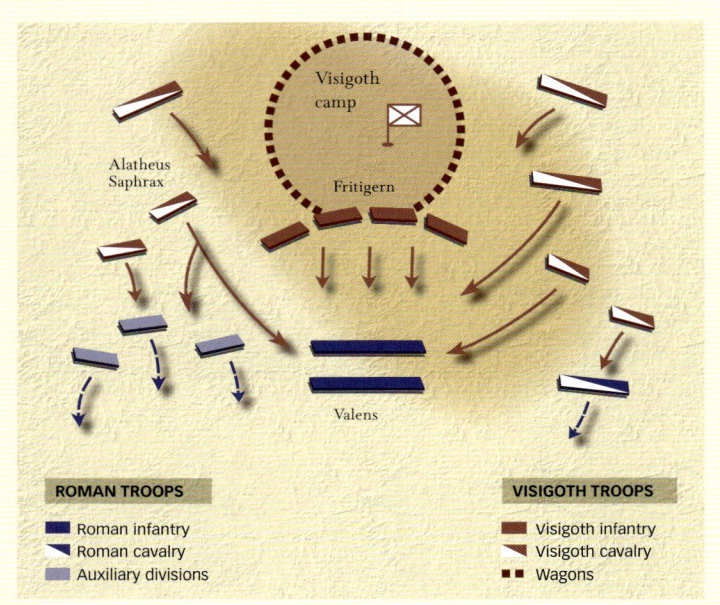

ROMAN TROOPS	VISIGOTH TROOPS
Roman infantry	Visigoth infantry
Roman cavalry	Visigoth cavalry
Auxiliary divisions	Wagons

he made camp. Fritigern sent an emissary to talk peace terms, but Valens, confident of victory, rejected the proposal. On the morning of 9 August, without waiting for Gratian's reinforcements, he led this army towards the Gothic camp. The Romans arrived exhausted to find Fritigern's Gothic army entrenched at the top of a hill defending a circular fortress of wagons. The Goths hoped to delay the battle until their cavalry had returned from a foraging mission, so they harassed the Romans with smoke and opened negotiations for an exchange of hostages. In the midst of these talks, an over-eager unit of Roman shield archers began to attack. Lacking support, they were easily pushed back. Then the Roman left wing advanced on the wagon circles. As they did so, the Gothic horsemen returned and surrounded them. The Romans were driven back to the base of the hill, but found it hard to fight back, weighed down by their armour and encumbered by their long shields. The Goth attack turned into a massacre that continued until nightfall. During the chaos, Valens was abandoned by his guards. His body was never found and his final fate is unknown.

Constantinians, declared himself emperor and seized control of the provinces of Asia Minor and Bithynia. Valens dispatched his available legions under generals Arinthaeus and Arbetio. In the spring of 366, they defeated Procopius in two battles, and the usurper was captured and executed in May. During the rebellion, a Gothic army under Ermanaric crossed the Danube in support of Procopius and began plundering Thrace. Valens drove them back and, in the spring of 367, he crossed the Danube and defeated a Visigoth army under Athanaric, a tributary of Ermanaric. Valens crossed the river again in 369, and once again defeated Athanaric.

With the Danube frontier secure for now, Valens could focus once more on trying to win back Armenia from Persia. His plan to reimpose the Roman-friendly King Papas on the Armenian throne was successfully achieved in 370. Shapur II counter-attacked in 371, but his forces were defeated by Valens's generals at Bagavan. A truce was agreed, which would hold for the next five years.

Following the death of Valentinian in 375, Gratian, Valentinian's son and Valens's nephew, was elevated to Augustus, as was Gratian's four-year-old half-brother, Valentinian II. In 376, trouble once more flared up on the Danube. Hordes of Huns were driving the Goths south, and a large group of Goths, led by Fritigern, requested permission to settle south of the river. Valens, a former ally of Fritigern, granted them admission with the intention of recruiting their members to swell his army's ranks. But Fritigern's group were soon joined by Ostrogoths, Huns and Alans. The resettlement began to turn into an invasion. Moreover, Valens's generals angered the Goths by charging them inflated prices for food. The Goths, and other groups, revolted and began to devastate the countryside. Roman legions attacked and temporarily checked them, but in the end were forced into retreat.

Valens, campaigning in the East, returned to Constantinople in May 378. His generals cautioned him to wait for Gratian to arrive with troops from Gaul. But Valens felt responsible for the disaster, for he had invited the Goths in.

He was also somewhat jealous of Gratian's successes on the Rhine, and wanted to win this one on his own. He led his forces against Fritigern's Gothic army at the Battle of Adrianople on 9 August 378. The result was a crushing victory for the Goths. Some 20,000 Romans were killed, including the emperor.

On the Rhine frontier, Gratian inflicted a devastating defeat on the Lentienses, a branch of the Alamanni, at Argentovaria in May 378. He then crossed the Rhine and successfully blockaded the Lentienses in their territory. The terms of their surrender included the forced recruitment of their young men into the Roman army. Following the catastrophe at Adrianople, hordes of barbarians began devastating the provinces south of the Danube. Gratian knew he could not leave the Rhine frontier, so he appointed a co-emperor, Theodosius (who had helped his father, Theodosius the Elder, restore order to Britannia in 368) to take charge of the East.

Gratian, meanwhile, continued to defend the Rhine frontier from attack. For some years he did so with energy and commitment, but he gradually lost interest, preferring to spend his time hunting with a group of Scythian archers who became his bodyguard. Gratian's behaviour alienated the army, and sparked a revolt in 383 by Magnus Maximus, commander of Britannia. Maximus invaded Gaul with a large army and Gratian, deserted by his troops, tried to flee beyond the Alps but was caught and killed in Lugdunum by one of Maximus's soldiers.

The reign of Gratian was a significant one for the development of Christianity. Valens had been an Arian, and with his death the cause of Arianism in the Eastern empire came to an end. Gratian, however, was a strong adherent of Nicene Christianity, and he promulgated an edict commanding everyone in the empire to follow the Nicene Creed. Also, under the guidance of Ambrose, Bishop of Milan, Gratian took steps to suppress paganism, closing pagan temples and shrines, and abolishing the privileges and appropriating the revenues of pagan priests and Vestal Virgins. He even removed the pagan Altar of Victory from the

OBELISK OF THEODOSIUS
The emperor Theodosius awards a laurel wreath to the victor of a chariot race. The scene forms part of a relief decorating the pedestal of a red granite obelisk. The ancient Egyptian obelisk, from the temple of Karnak, dates to the time of Thutmose III (1479–1425 BC). It was transported to Alexandria by Constantius II in 357, and from there to Constantinople in 390 by Theodosius, who installed it at the spina of the hippodrome.

THE FALL OF ROME

The death of Theodosius and the permanent partition of the empire

After his death in 395, Theodosius passed control of the empire to his sons Arcadius (18 years old) and Honorius (just 10). By this time the dynastic principle, reintroduced by Constantine, was so well established that it seemed natural for Theodosius's sons to succeed him, even though neither of them was temperamentally suited to the task of leadership. Arcadius became ruler in the East, with his capital in Constantinople, and Honorius became ruler in the West, with his capital in Milan and later Ravenna. This was not the first time the empire had been divided this way, and Theodosius certainly did not intend the division between West and East to become permanent. That it became so was due both to the severe challenges faced by the empire at the time of his death (with increasing pressure from barbarians and deteriorating finances), and the sheer incompetence of his successors. From this time forward, until the fall of the West in 476, the two halves of the empire would be governed separately, and West and East increasingly became independent territories with different, often conflicting, interests. Within a matter of decades, partition would come to seem like amputation, as the West began its final collapse. Image: Bronze coin with the image of Honorius.

Senate House in Rome, placed there more than 400 years earlier by the first emperor, Augustus. The tactic worked: one by one the chieftains agreed, in return for land and security, to be enrolled under the standard of the Roman Empire. Those who would not accept the terms were attacked and destroyed.

In 382, Gratian turned his attention to the Ostrogoths, luring their chieftains into crossing the Danube and then attacking them with Roman warships. With their leaders slain, the Ostrogoths sued for peace. A treaty signed in October 382 permitted large numbers of Goths to settle in self-governing communities in Thrace, south of the Danube frontier, and in Asia Minor, on condition that they supply a certain number of men to serve in the imperial army. There were problems with this solution: the barbarians were never fully integrated into the Roman legions, and there were many instances of troop desertions and defections, but it was perhaps the best Theodosius could have achieved in the circumstances.

With the death of Gratian in 383, Theodosius's attention turned to the Western empire. He was militarily too weak to challenge the usurper Magnus Maximus, now de facto ruler of the West, so he had to satisfy himself with the extraction of a promise from Maximus not to move against Valentinian II, the 12-year-old Augustus in Italy. Maximus kept his vow until 387, when a conflict between the Arian Valentinian and his Catholic subjects prompted the usurper to invade. Theodosius raised an army and marched against Maximus. They fought a two-month campaign in 388, ending in the Battle of the Save, which Theodosius won. Maximus was executed in August.

Theodosius appointed the Frankish general Arbogast as magister militum in the West, and guardian of Valentinian II. At 17, the emperor was still not ready to assume his imperial responsibilities, and Arbogast became the power behind the throne. He refused to allow Valentinian any military experience and, in 392, when Valentinian expressed his wish to lead the Gallic armies against a barbarian threat in Italy, Arbogast refused. Valentinian tried to dismiss his guardian, but Arbogast tore up the order. In May, Valentinian was found hanging in his palace in Vienne. It looked like suicide, but most contemporary sources believed that Arbogast murdered him or had him killed.

Arbogast, being Frankish, was ineligible to be emperor himself, so he appointed his trusted friend Eugenius to the role. In response, Theodosius raised his son Honorius to the position of Augustus of the West, then gathered an army to confront Eugenius. The two armies met at Frigidus in September 394. On the first day of the battle, Theodosius's forces were beaten back. On the second day, heavy winds blew at Eugenius's soldiers, disrupting the line. Eugenius's camp was overrun. Arbogast killed himself, Eugenius was executed, and Theodosius took control of the West. He would be the last to rule over the whole empire. Four months later, in January 395, he fell ill and died.

Under Theodosius, Nicene Christianity became the State religion of the Roman Empire. The First Council of Constantinople (381) defined orthodoxy and condemned all other forms of Christianity as heresy. In the same year, Theodosius began a comprehensive persecution of paganism, banning pagan feast days, blood sacrifices, taking auspices and witchcraft, disbanding the Vestal Virgins, and closing or destroying temples, shrines, monuments and objects of worship throughout the empire. He also ended the Olympic Games.

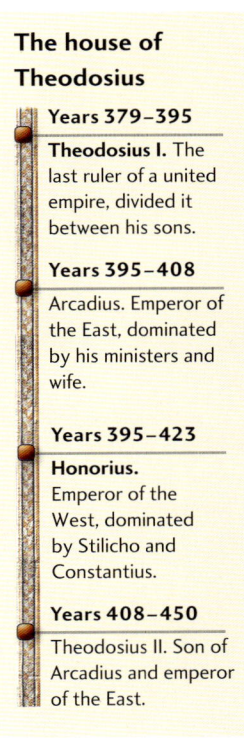

The house of Theodosius

Years 379–395
Theodosius I. The last ruler of a united empire, divided it between his sons.

Years 395–408
Arcadius. Emperor of the East, dominated by his ministers and wife.

Years 395–423
Honorius. Emperor of the West, dominated by Stilicho and Constantius.

Years 408–450
Theodosius II. Son of Arcadius and emperor of the East.

ROMANS AGAINST BARBARIANS
This battle scene decorates the front of the second-century Amendola sarcophagus (Capitoline Museums, Rome). Opposite: Roman helmet, iron and plated with silver-gilt, fourth century, discovered in Deurne, Holland (Rijksmuseum van Oudheden, Leiden).

THE FALL OF THE EMPIRE

The fifth century witnessed the final collapse and fall of Rome. Over the course of seven decades, the relentless pressure from barbarians coupled with the internal disintegration of imperial authority took its toll, culminating in the overthrow of the last emperor, Romulus Augustulus, by Odoacer. Rome fell and, with it, the Empire of the West, an event that has been and remains one of the most analyzed, mysterious and controversial in history.

Today we view the Mediterranean Sea as a border between the lands to the north and south. Yet in Roman times, the *Mare Nostrum* ('our sea') was the centre of the world, facilitating commerce and communications and acting as a conduit for the exchange of knowledge and ideas. It would remain so until the era of Islamic expansion brought it to an end. The division in the Roman Empire of late antiquity was never between north and south, but between east and west, and this rupture became permanent during the fifth century. The worlds of Rome and Constantinople began to diverge not only politically, but also in terms of language (Latin in the West, Greek in the East) and religion (Roman Catholicism in the West, Orthodox Church in the East). Despite this, the ideal of a unified empire refused to die. It remained a dream of rulers long after the fall of the Western empire, and there would even be attempts to revive it

THE FALL OF ROME

The last emperors of the West

Years 395–423
Honorius. Barbarians settle Gaul and Hispania. Alaric sacks Rome.

Years 425–455
Valentinian III. Huns ravage the empire. Assassinated by Scythians.

Year 455
Petronius Maximus. Very brief reign. Killed by Vandals.

Years 455–456
Avitus. A strong alliance with the Visigoths could not prevent his overthrow.

Years 457–461
Majorian. The last emperor to make a strong effort to restore the empire.

Years 461–465
Libius Severus. Puppet of the powerful magister militum Ricimer.

Years 467–472
Antemio. Tried to deal with Visigoths and Vandals. Killed by Ricimer.

Year 472
Olybrius. Puppet of Ricimer, his rule was not recognized by Eastern empire.

Years 473–474
Glycerium. Puppet of magister militum Gundobad, deposed by Julius Nepos.

Years 474–475
Romulus Augustulus. The last Roman emperor, deposed by Odoacer.

under Justinian in the sixth century and Charlemagne in the eighth and ninth.

Honorius

The younger son of Theodosius and Aelia Flacilla, Honorius was elevated to the rank of Augustus in January 323. His father died two years later, making Honorius ruler of the West aged only ten. His 18-year-old brother, Arcadius, became ruler of the East. A devout Christian, Arcadius had little interest in political or military matters; like Honorius, he was dominated by his ministers throughout his reign. Before he died, Theodosius appointed Flavius Stilicho to be Honorius's guardian. Stilicho, who was of mixed Vandal and Roman ancestry, was a seasoned military commander and hero of the Battle of Frigidus; he would be the power behind the throne for the first part of Honorius's reign. Stilicho had been brought into the imperial family by his marriage to Theodosius's adopted niece Serena. The couple had two daughters, Maria and Thermantia. In 398, Honorius married Maria, binding Stilicho yet more closely to the new emperor. Stilicho claimed that Theodosius had given him guardianship of Arcadius as well as Honorius. This claim was vehemently denied by Rufinus, the Praetorian prefect of the East, and the power behind the throne in the East. Rufinus and Stilicho would soon come into conflict over a crisis in the Balkans.

The Visigoths living in Lower Moesia had elected Alaric to be their first king. Alaric was a formidable warrior who had previously served in the Roman army as a leader of the *foederati* (irregular barbarian troops). Like Stilicho, he had fought with great distinction at the Battle of Frigidus. Alaric had hoped to be rewarded for his efforts with promotion to the rank of general. When this didn't happen, he turned against Rome and led the Visigoths on a raid into Thrace. Stilicho took an army into Thrace to confront them, and was poised to crush them when an order came through from Rufinus, recalling the army to Constantinople. As they were within the Eastern empire, they were, strictly speaking, under the command of

The Theodosian Wall of Constantinople

By the start of the fifth century, Constantinople had outgrown the original wall built by Constantine the Great between the Sea of Marmara and the Golden Horn. In 412–413, the Praetorian prefect of the East, Anthemius, constructed a new double wall west of the previous one, 6km (4 miles) long, with a moat 18m (59ft) wide and 96 towers. The Theodosian Walls protected the city for more than 1000 years. The image shows a reconstruction of the walls.

Arcadius, so the troops had no choice but to obey. Stilicho returned angrily to Italy and the army marched back to Constantinople. When Arcadius and Rufinus came out to greet them, the soldiers turned on Rufinus and killed him in front of the emperor. Many suspected Stilicho of being behind the assassination.

The next big clash between Eastern and Western empires occurred a few years later in the province of Africa. Gildo, governor of the province since 386, was proving to be a bloodthirsty tyrant. In 394, he had incited Theodosius's wrath by siding with Eugenius during the civil war. Although Theodosius died soon afterwards, Gildo still feared punishment from his successor Honorius (or more precisely, Stilicho), so he decided to place himself under the protection of Constantinople. By this time, Emperor Arcadius had fallen under the sway of his grand chamberlain Eutropius. Like Rufinus,

Eutropius loathed Stilicho, who was still pressing his claim to be guardian of Arcadius, so when Gildo requested his support, he was only too happy to oblige. For Stilicho, the situation was potentially very serious. Rome had already lost Egypt to the Eastern empire, and now depended on Africa for its grain, so he could ill afford to lose the province. In 398, he sent an expeditionary force of Gallic veterans under the command of Gildo's brother Mascezel. They quickly defeated Gildo, who later committed suicide. The failure of the rebellion was a blow to Eutropius's reputation, and led indirectly to his downfall and death.

In 401, Alaric led his army of Visigoths on an invasion of Italy, the heartland of the empire. At the time of the invasion, Honorius was in Milan, and he fled to Asti, pursued by Alaric. Stilicho, who was in Raetia, hurried back to Italy. He met Alaric at Pollentia on 6 April 402. Stilicho triumphed, albeit at considerable cost. Alaric retreated to Verona, where Stilicho defeated him again in June. The Visigoths then withdrew from Italy, but not before extracting a large subsidy from the Roman Senate. The invasion also prompted some other changes: the imperial court was moved from Milan to the more heavily defended Ravenna, and the Twentieth Legion was recalled from Britannia, where it had been stationed since the conquest in 43 AD, to defend the homeland.

The next major barbarian invasion came in late 405, when King Radagaisus led a force of around 20,000 Goths into Italy. A devout pagan, Radagaisus threatened to sacrifice the Christian senators of Rome to the gods and burn Rome to the ground. Stilicho struggled at first to assemble an army to confront them, and was forced to recall a contingent of troops from the Rhine frontier.

THE FALL OF ROME

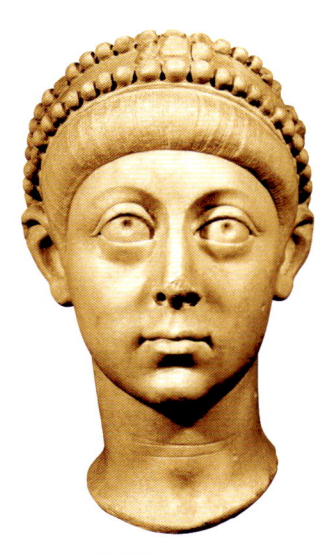

ARCADIUS, EASTERN EMPEROR
The eldest son of Theodosius the Great and Aelia Flaccilla was born in Hispania in 377, where his father was living in exile before his rise to the throne. Arcadius was married to Aelia Eudoxia, with whom he had four children. A weak ruler, his reign was dominated by a series of powerful ministers and by his wife. (Marble head, Archaeological Museum, Istanbul).

EMPEROR HONORIUS AND CONSUL PROBUS (OPPOSITE PAGE)
In this ivory diptych dating from 406, Honorius (on the left), second son of Theodosius the Great and emperor of the West, is accompanied by the consul Flavius Probus, who, in the inscription that appears at the foot, is declared famulus (slave) of the sovereign (Aosta Cathedral, Italy).

During the six months it took for the Romans to mobilize their forces, Radagaisus and his Goths overran northern Italy, sacking many cities, before laying siege to Florentia. Stilicho's army attacked the Goths at Florentia, driving them into the hills of Fiesole. Radagaisus abandoned his army and tried to flee, but was captured by Romans and later executed. Stilicho recruited 12,000 of his best Goth fighters into the Roman army; the rest were sold into slavery.

Crossing of the Rhine

On New Year's Eve in the year 406, the barbarian threat became a catastrophe when a vast horde of Ostrogoths, Burgundians, Alans, Vandals and Quadi crossed the frozen Rhine and invaded Gaul. They overwhelmed the Roman legions stationed there and began roaming the province at will, plundering the countryside and destroying cities. The invasion triggered military revolts and a general collapse in civic order in northern Gaul. Never again would Roman authority reassert itself in this region, and the invasion is therefore regarded as a decisive moment in the decline of the empire. Stilicho could do nothing about the disaster – it had been his decision to recall troops from the Rhine in order to defend Italy – and his reputation would never recover.

The invasion also deepened a developing crisis in Britannia. Cut off from the empire and too depleted in strength to defend themselves from Irish raiders, the British garrisons descended into open revolt. In 406, they proclaimed one of their soldiers, Marcus, emperor. Evidently, his rule did not please the army, and he was soon killed by them and replaced, in early 407, by a native British noble called Gratian. The army wished to cross to Gaul and confront the barbarian invasion, but 'Emperor Gratian' preferred to remain, so they killed him, too, after a reign of just four months. His replacement, Constantine III, was a common soldier and more to the army's liking, for he immediately ordered an invasion of Gaul. We do not know how many troops he took with him, but it is likely he left Britannia virtually undefended. While this was happening, trouble was brewing once again between Stilicho and the court at Constantinople. Stilicho believed that Honorius had a claim to Illyricum, currently part of the Eastern empire. He approached his former foe Alaric and made plans with him for a joint attack on the prefecture. War between East and West began to look extremely likely.

Meanwhile, Constantine III's invasion of Gaul was proving highly successful. He secured the Rhine frontier, and his authority was accepted by the legions in both Gaul and Hispania. Stilicho sent a force from Italy to oppose him, led by a Gothic general called Sarus, who won a victory against Constantine's vanguard. But then Constantine sent in another army, led by his magister militum Gerontius, which defeated Sarus, who was forced to withdraw to Italy. Constantine went on to occupy much of Gaul, and by May 408 he had established a base at Arles, former site of the empire's Praetorian prefecture. Constantine elevated Constans, his elder son, to Caesar, and sent him and Gerontius to Hispania to deal with a revolt started by some cousins of Honorius. The revolt was put down and Constans returned to Arles, leaving Gerontius in charge of Hispania.

Constantine's ongoing rebellion led Stilicho to shelve plans for an invasion of Illyricum. This greatly angered Alaric, who demanded a large sum of gold to cover the 'expenses of mobilization' and threatened to invade Italy again unless he was paid. The Senate wanted to refuse the ultimatum, but Stilicho persuaded them to promise payment. Stilicho, blamed for both the ongoing rebellion of Constantine III and the danger from Alaric, found himself increasingly isolated at court. His daughter Maria had died in 407, and in 408 he tried to shore up his position by offering his other daughter Thermantia to Honorius.

Stilicho's enemies at court were circling: in August, they spread rumours that Stilicho was manoeuvring to put his son Eucherius on the Eastern throne (Emperor Arcadius had died in May). On hearing this, the Roman army at

IN NOMINE
XPI·VINCAS
SEMPER·

DN HONORIO SEMP AVG

DN HONORIO SEMPER AVG

PROBVS·FAMVLVS·VC·CONS·ORD·

PROBVS·FAMVLVS·VC·CONS·ORD·

THE FALL OF ROME

Alaric and the sack of Rome: the beginning of the end of the imperial city

When Alaric and his Visigoths surrounded the walls of Rome in August 410, it was the third time they had besieged the city in as many years. The 408 siege was lifted after the Senate agreed to pay the Visigoths an enormous ransom. They lifted the second siege when the Senate agreed to support Priscus Attalus as emperor. This time, however, Alaric was in no mood to negotiate. On 24 August, the Visigoths entered Rome through the Salarian Gate and pillaged the city for three days. Many of the city's buildings were ransacked, tombs were destroyed and valuables stolen. By order of Alaric, the Visigoths did not engage in a mass slaughter of the inhabitants, and the two main basilicas of Peter and Paul were offered as places of sanctuary. Most of the city's buildings and monuments were left intact. When Alaric left the city, he took with him the emperor's half-sister Galla Placidia and thousands of barbarian slaves who he incorporated into his army. The sack of Rome sent shockwaves around the empire. Although no longer the imperial capital, Rome retained a unique status as the empire's spiritual centre, and this was the first time it had fallen to a foreign enemy since the attack by the Gauls under Brennus 800 years earlier. Thomas Cole's oil painting, *The Course of Empire: Destruction* (1836), interprets the event (New York Historical Society, New York).

Ticinum mutinied, killing at least seven of their senior officers who were known to be supporters of Stilicho. Honorius was then persuaded to give the order for Stilicho's arrest. On 22 August 408, Stilicho was executed, along with Eucherius.

The mutiny at Ticinum and the death of Stilicho prompted the Gothic general Sarus, along with his troops, to abandon the Roman army. This left Honorius and his court, still threatened by Alaric, with very little military protection. In 409, Constantine III sent envoys to Ravenna asking Honorius to forgive him for seizing power and promising him help against Alaric. Honorius had little choice but to accept this offer, so he sent Constantine an imperial robe and recognized him as co-emperor.

Then, in 409, Constantine faced a rebellion of his own by Gerontius, his magister militum in Hispania, who proclaimed his relative (possibly his son) Maximus emperor. Gerontius and Maximus defeated Constantine's armies several times over the next 18 months, and killed his son Constans at Vienne. In 411, they besieged Constantine at Arles. By this time Honorius had found a new, capable general named Constantius, and had no more need for Constantine III. Constantius led an army to Arles where he defeated Gerontius and Maximus, then persuaded Constantine to surrender with promises of a peaceful retirement. As soon as Constantine did so, Constantius had him executed and sent his head to Ravenna.

In the aftermath of Stilicho's execution, Honorius had foolishly incited the Roman populace to massacre the families of the Gothic soldiers who had been loyal to Stilicho. The soldiers defected en masse to Alaric, who marched on Rome to exact revenge. He laid siege to the city in 408 and again in 409. The Senate acceded to his demands for a subsidy and the freeing of Gothic slaves, but the court at Ravenna refused to give him what he most desired: command of the Western Roman army. In order to put pressure on Ravenna, Alaric forced the Senate to support the claims of the usurper Priscus Attalus, who was the Urban Prefect of Rome, as emperor. When Alaric besieged Rome for a third time in 410, his allies opened the gates, and the Visigoths sacked the city.

In 411, the beleaguered Honorius faced yet another rebellion: a Gallo-Roman senator called Jovinus was proclaimed emperor at Mainz, supported by the Alans and the Burgundians. Jovinus tried to make an alliance with the new Visigoth king Ataulf in 412. However, a problem arose when Sarus, now leading a band of mercenaries, offered his services to Jovinus. Sarus was a mortal enemy of Ataulf's, and Ataulf immediately ended negotiations with Jovinus and decided to ally himself with Honorius instead. He besieged Jovinus at Valentia in 413. When the city was taken, Jovinus was captured and executed and his head was sent to Ravenna.

Ataulf sealed the alliance with Honorius by marrying his half-sister Galla Placidia at Narbonne in January 414. But Honorius's general Constantius, who had become the new power at court, persuaded Honorius that Ataulf was actually his enemy. Constantius used the Roman navy to blockade the Visigoth port cities of Narbonne and Toulouse. In response, Ataulf proclaimed Priscus Attalus emperor, as Alaric had done before him. The blockade was successful, and Ataulf was forced to withdraw to Hispania. Attalus was captured and banished to a small island.

THE MAUSOLEUM OF GALLA PLACIDIA IN RAVENNA

Galla Placidia (388–450) was the daughter of Theodosius I, queen consort to the Visigothic king Ataulf (414–415) and wife of Constantius (417–421). She ruled the empire as regent to her son Emperor Valentinian III from 423 until he came of age in 437. It is believed that Placidia built this mausoleum for herself and her family. The building contains three sarcophagi. The central one reportedly once contained the remains of Placidia; the one on the left is attributed to her husband Constantius III, and the one on the right either to Valentinian III or Honorius. The building has a plain brick exterior. Inside, beautiful fifth-century mosaics cover the walls of the vault, the lunettes and the cupola. These feature geometric, animal and plant motifs, Christian symbols and depictions of the saints. The mosaics are highly representative of Christian art in late antiquity, during the transition from naturalistic classical art to the more stylized representations of the Byzantine period.

THE MAUSOLEUM
This was once linked to the narthex of Santa Croce, the church for the imperial palace, now in ruins.

THE FALL OF THE EMPIRE

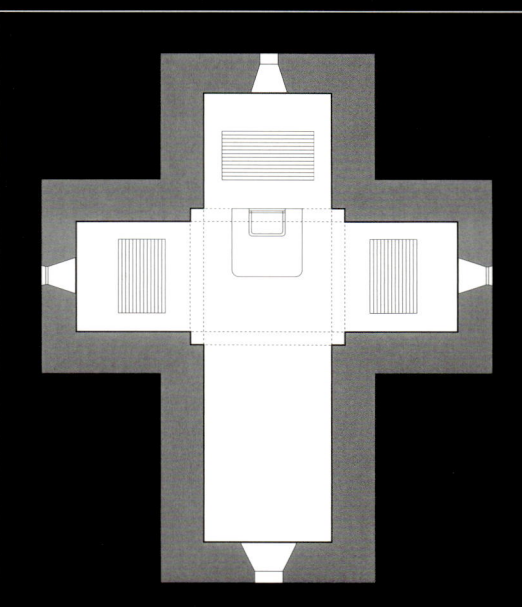

THE HEAVENLY CROSS
The mausoleum has a cruciform floor plan with a main nave of 12.75m (42ft) crossed by another of 10.25m (34ft). The four transepts are topped by barrel vaults converging on a central dome on pendentives. The dome's exterior is enclosed by a square tower. The interior is decorated with a mosaic with a giant gold cross in the centre against a blue sky filled with stars. The four evangelists appear in the pendentives; the four apostles are represented in the transept barrel vaults.

GALLA PLACIDIA
Although only briefly empress in 421, Galla Placidia exercised real political power for 14 years during her son's minority. Fifth-century golden coin.

THE FALL OF ROME

Barbarian migrations between the third and fifth centuries

The relationship between the Goths and the Roman Empire began with Trajan's conquest of Dacia in 106. It turned to conflict in the mid-third century when Goths began to cross the Danube to plunder Mesia and Thrace. Cniva, king of the Goths, defeated the Romans in 251, but after his death the unity of his kingdom was broken. The invasion of the Huns in 372 pushed the Goths towards the borders of the Roman Empire. The Roman reaction ended with defeat at Adrianople. The Visigoths of Dacia and the Ostrogoths from east of the Dnieper crossed the Danube en masse in 376, fleeing from the Huns, nomads of Asian origin. Swabians (Germanic farmers) were also pushed by the Hunnic invasion to the Upper Rhine, where they joined Iranian-speaking Alans and the Vandals (of Germanic descent) and tried in vain to cross the Rhine towards Gaul. At the end of 406, 250,000 Suebi, Alans and Vandals crossed the Rhine, defeated the border garrisons and went through Gaul towards Hispania. The Suebi settled northwestern Iberia, the Alans the southwest, and the Vandals moved on to Africa. Led by Rugila, the Huns crossed the Danube in 422; Theodosius II had to pay them 160kg (350lb) of gold to keep the peace. Rugila was succeeded by his nephews Attila and Bleda, who would return to the empire between 450 and 452. Opposite: a fourth-century diptych of Stilicho, a Roman general with Vandal ancestry (Treasure of the Cathedral, Monza).

Ataulf died in 415, and two years later his widow, Galla Placidia, married Constantius. They had a son, Valentinian, born in 419.

In 411, while he was fighting rebellions closer to home, Honorius wrote to the British advising them to look to their own defences; this was a tacit acceptance that Britannia was now lost. The empire's grip on Gaul and Hispania was also slipping. The Franks gradually embedded themselves in northeastern Gaul, while the Visigoths made their home in southwestern Gaul and Hispania.

In 418, Honorius acknowledged this new reality, at least with regard to the Visigoths, with an edict that relinquished Rome's administrative control over the seven Visigothic provinces. The Roman governors were withdrawn, and the settlers were given permission to operate as a dependent federation with their capital at Arelate.

In February 421, Honorius made Constantius co-emperor of the West. But his reign as Constantius III would be very short: he died just seven months later. Honorius himself died in August 423, leaving no heir. His closest male relative was Valentinian, Constantius's son by Galla Placidia, who was in Constantinople at the time. The power vacuum allowed an obscure court official named Joannes to seize the throne, with the support of the magister militum Castinus. Joannes was acclaimed as emperor in Rome, as well as in Gaul, Spain and Italy, although crucially he was unable to obtain the approval of Africa (source of the grain supply) or the Eastern emperor Theodosius II. Instead, Theodosius elevated Valentinian III to Augustus, and sent an expedition under Ardabur and his son Aspar to overthrow the usurper. Joannes captured Ardabur, but treated him well, as he still hoped

THE FALL OF THE EMPIRE

VISIGOTHS AND OSTROGOTHS
The Gothic tribes shared a common language and culture. Once settled within the empire they abandoned nomadism and became farmers looking for fertile land to settle, some of which would eventually become medieval kingdoms.

VANDALS, ALANS AND SUEBI
Before invading Africa, the Silingi Vandals were installed in Hispania Baetica and the Hasdingi Vandals in Asturia. The Alans were settled in Lusitania, and the Suebi in Gallaecia.

HUNS
Under Attila, the most famous of their rulers, the Huns invaded the Eastern and Western Roman Empires, but they were ejected from the West after failed campaigns in Gaul and Italy.

GERMANIC TRIBES ON THE RHINE BORDER
The Burgundians, Franks and Alamanni invaded Gaul for the first time in 253. In the fifth century the Burgundians and the Franks formed kingdoms in Gaul. The Alamanni came to occupy a territory comprising present-day Vorarlberg (Austria), northern Switzerland, Baden-Württemberg (Germany) and Alsace (France).

---

to persuade Theodosius to support him. But Ardabur convinced the garrison at Ravenna to betray Joannes, enabling Aspar to take the city. Joannes was captured and taken to Aquileia where he was executed. In October 425, the six-year-old Valentinian III became emperor of the West, with Galla Placidia serving as regent.

The reign of Valentinian III
The early part of Galla Placidia's regency was dominated by three men: Flavius Aetius, Bonifacius and Flavius Felix. Aetius, a military commander of Roman-Scythian origin, was initially Placidia's enemy. He arrived in Italy in the summer of 425 at the head of 60,000 Huns, ready to fight for the usurper Joannes. Hearing that Joannes was dead, Aetius made a deal with Placidia: in return for him sending the Huns home, Placidia gave him command of the Roman army in Gaul. Bonifacius was a senior administrator in Africa at the time of Joannes's usurpation, and his response was to cut off the grain supply to Italy. When Placidia came to power, she rewarded him for his loyalty with the position of comes domesticorum, or commander of the emperor's guard. Felix was a politician who had served under Valentinian III, and was appointed by Placidia to the powerful position of patricius in 425.

Aetius took up command of the army in Gaul in 426, and immediately proceeded to the city of Arelate, which was being besieged by the Visigoths, led by their king, Theodoric I. Aetius defeated Theodoric, lifted the siege of Arelate and drove the Visigoths back to their base in Aquitania. In 428, he defeated the Salian Franks, led by their king Chlodio, and drove them out of the lands they had occupied along the Rhine. The following year, Placidia promoted him to the rank of magister militum.

Attila the Hun: the lightning war against Rome

The presence of fierce nomadic warriors from the steppes, capable of shooting their arrows while galloping on their mounts, sowed panic in Europe and caused the flight of barbarian tribes towards the safety of Roman territory.

On their swift, armoured horses, the Huns descended from the hills and attacked the enemy with their swords and spears, and with their arrows, which they fired from the saddle, standing up on their stirrups. Attila, the last and most famous ruler of the Huns, created an empire that ran from central Europe to the heart of Asia, and from the Danube to the Baltic. The army of the Eastern Roman Empire was easy prey for the newcomers. In 440, the Huns crossed the Danube and laid waste to the cities of Illyricum. Over the next two years, they advanced through the Balkans, sacking city after city, and defeating two Roman armies sent out to stop them. Only Constantinople, protected by its double walls, was able to resist their onslaught. Stripped of his armed forces, Theodosius II had no choice but to negotiate a harsh peace, including an annual tribute in gold. In 447, Attila again rode into the Eastern empire, and again he defeated the Roman army. The Huns were left unopposed as they rampaged through the Balkans. Inevitably, Attila began to contemplate the rich opportunities for plunder that lay to the west, in the Empire of Rome.

While Aetius was busy campaigning in Gaul, tensions were growing between Felix and Bonifacius. In 427, Felix accused Bonifacius of attempting to form his own separate empire in Africa, and recalled him to Ravenna. When Bonifacius refused the summons, Felix sent an expeditionary force to Africa to confront him. The civil war dragged on for two years, and the Vandals under King Genseric took this opportunity to invade Africa. Placidia sent an envoy to Bonifacius and they made peace so that Bonifacius could deal with the Vandals. In 430, Genseric defeated Bonifacius at Calama, and then at Hippo, and Bonifacius fled to join forces with the Eastern Roman general Aspar. Bonifacius and Aspar confronted Genseric and, once again, the Vandal king won.

By the late 420s, Felix had become a powerful figure in Ravenna, having been elected consul for the West in 428 and appointed magister utriusque militae for Italy in 429. Yet in this era more than any other, Rome needed strong military leaders, not court politicians like Felix, who had risen mainly by plotting against his rivals. This may be why his fall, when it came, was so rapid. In May 430, Aetius was warned (possibly by Galla Placidia herself) that Felix was planning to assassinate him. Aetius ordered Felix's arrest, and he and his wife were executed.

With Felix dead, Aetius was now the highest-ranking of the magistri militiae, his prestige enhanced by successful campaigns in 430 and 431 against the Visigoths, Bagaudae, Juthungi and Franks. He was elected consul in 432 and seemed all-powerful, but then came a swift reversal of fortune: Bonifacius, by now back in Ravenna, had won the favour of Placidia, despite his failures in Africa. She made him patricius and magister utriusque militiae

THE FALL OF THE EMPIRE

Legend:
- Centre of Hun Kingdom in 400 AD
- Hun settlements by 435
- Hun control of Pannonia after 433
- ✗ Battle
- Campaigns of Attila and Bleda: 441–442
- Campaigns of Attila: 447–448, 451, 452

1 METZ DEVASTATED
In 451, the Huns invaded the Western empire and captured Divodurum (now Metz), then looted and burned it. Attila never occupied cities.

2 PARIS SAVED
Saint Genevieve led a prayer marathon that is said to have saved Lutetia (modern Paris) by diverting Attila's army away from the city.

3 ORLEANS BESIEGED
In June, the Huns laid siege to Aurelianum (modern Orleans). The staunch Alan defence of the city was Attila's first setback.

4 CHÂLONS
Two weeks later, at the Catalaunian Fields (near present-day Châlons), the army of Attila was finally defeated by Theodoric I and Aetius.

(titles formerly held by Felix), and Bonifacius immediately stripped Aetius of his command.

Rise of Aetius

Aetius, facing personal and political ruin, marched against Bonifacius. The two sides met at the Battle of Rimini in 432. Bonifacius won the battle, but was mortally wounded. He died a few days later, and his son Sebastianus was appointed in his place. Sebastianus ordered Aetius's assassination, but Aetius fled, for his own protection, to the court of his friend King Rugila of the Huns. Sebastianus attempted to raise an army against him, but Bonifacius's son was proving unpopular both with the army and at court, and was sent into exile. This left Aetius free to make a triumphant return to Italy, where his titles were restored and he was made official protector of Galla Placidia and Valentinian III. He was now the dominant figure in the empire, and would remain so for the next 20 years.

In July 437, Valentinian III turned 18 and began to rule as emperor in his own right. He confirmed the alliance with the Eastern emperor Theodosius II by marrying his daughter Licinia Eudoxia. Although Placidia's regency ended, she continued to exert influence behind the scenes until her death in 450.

The new emperor proved even less suited to the role than his predecessor Honorius. Spoiled and self-indulgent, Valentinian was a pious Christian and also, paradoxically, passionate about magic and astrology. His interventions in imperial affairs tended to be harmful, such as when he began expelling Jewish soldiers from the Roman army to prevent them from corrupting their Christian comrades.

Despite Aetius's military successes, the Western empire continued to face incessant

THE FALL OF ROME

The fall of the Roman Empire

Years 376–378

Adrianople. The Visigoths, fleeing from the Huns, cross the Danube, establish themselves in Thrace and defeat the Romans at Adrianople.

Years 401–402

Italy invaded. The Visigoths, led by Alaric, penetrate Italy, offering either to serve Rome or fight against it. Stilicho expels them.

Year 406

Crossing of the Rhine. Vast hordes of barbarians cross the frozen Rhine, hitherto one of the empire's most secure boundaries, and invade Gaul.

Year 410

Sack of Rome. The looting and pillaging of the eternal city by Alaric's Visigoths sends shockwaves through the empire.

Year 455

Rome sacked again. Genseric, ruler of the Vandals, keeps his promise to Pope Leo I not to burn Rome or commit murder, but they loot the city and carry away many of its inhabitants.

Year 476

Odoacer. The leader of a revolt by Herulian, Rugian and Scirian soldiers overthrows Romulus Augustulus, the last Roman emperor.

threats from the Visigoths in southern Gaul, the Suebi in Hispania and the Vandals in Africa.

In 438, Aetius won a major battle against the Suebi, but the following year the Visigoths defeated and killed his general Litorius. Aetius returned to Gaul and defeated the Visigoths and made a treaty with their king, Theodoric I. Aetius could not be everywhere, however, and while he was busy in Europe the Vandals were overrunning Africa, culminating with their capture of Carthage in October 439. This was a massive blow because the empire relied on Africa for taxes and grain. By 440, Vandal fleets were raiding Sicily. Aetius began negotiating with Constantinople to gather a joint force to attack Genseric. But these plans had to be abandoned because troops were needed to confront a large-scale invasion of Huns on the Danube frontier.

Aetius was left with no choice but to accept the Vandal conquest of Africa, as well as Sardinia and Corsica. During the early 440s, Hispania also began to slip away from Roman control, as the Suebi expanded across the peninsula. By 444, they had possession of all but Tarraconensis, which was itself under threat from the Bagaudae. As a result of all these territorial losses, the Western empire began to suffer severe financial problems and was struggling to fund its army. In 444, new taxes were levied on bureaucrats and the senatorial class. Even Valentinian was obliged to sacrifice part of his income to help pay the soldiers guarding what remained of his empire.

Uprisings continued through the rest of the decade: in 445, the Franks laid siege to Turonum and attacked Atrebatum; in 447, the Bagaudae of northwest Gaul revolted; and in 449, the Bagaudae of Hispania rose up and sacked three cities in Tarraconensis. Aetius did what he could to deal with these revolts, but the challenges he faced were about to be overshadowed by a far more devastating threat from the east.

Hun invasions

Under their king Attila, the Huns had established a vast empire in western Asia and eastern Europe. During the 440s, Attila left the Western empire alone, partly because of his good relations with Aetius, who had spent time in his youth as a hostage of the Huns. However, Attila's attitude changed in the spring of 450 when he received a letter from Honoria, sister of Valentinian III, enclosing her ring and requesting his help to escape her betrothal to a senator. Attila interpreted this as a marriage proposal, which he accepted, asking for half of the Western empire as his dowry. He gathered an enormous army of Huns, together with their vassals – Gepids, Ostrogoths, Rugians, Scirians, Herules, Thuringians, Alans, Burgundians and others – and began his advance west. Arriving in Gallia Belgica in 451, he attacked many cities in northern Gaul, including Divodurum, Rheims, Tongeren and Troyes.

Aetius assembled an army to oppose Attila, composed of Salian Franks, Armoricans, Saxons, Burgundians and Celts. He persuaded

Theodoric I, king of the Visigoths, to join the Romans in an anti-Hun alliance.

The combined army advanced on the Huns, who were engaged in a siege of Aurelianum. The Huns withdrew into open country, pursued by the Roman-Visigothic forces. The two armies met on 20 June 451 at the Battle of the Catalaunian Plains. It was an exceptionally bloody encounter, a tactical defeat for the Huns, ending their invasion of Gaul, but also a costly triumph for the victors, especially the Visigoths, whose king, Theodoric I, was killed. It boosted Roman morale, however, and destroyed Attila's aura of invincibility.

Attila returned in 452, still determined to assert his marriage claim with Honoria. This time, he led his army through Italy, laying waste to cities and prompting Valentinian III to flee to Rome. Aquileia was allegedly razed completely, leaving no trace behind. Refugees driven onto the small islands of a lagoon in northeastern Italy established communities there that would one day become the city of Venice. This time, Aetius could not muster an army strong enough to face the Huns in battle, so he used his forces to harass Attila's army, slowing its advance until it finally halted at the River Po. Valentinian III sent envoys to meet with Attila, including Pope Leo I. By this time, disease and lack of supplies were taking their toll on the Huns, and Attila was happy to agree a peace and return to his homeland. It would be his last invasion – he died in 453, and his empire collapsed soon afterwards.

In September 454, Aetius himself died at the hands of his own emperor. Valentinian III had never fully trusted Aetius, who had once supported Joannes against him. And when Aetius betrothed his son Gaudentius to Valentinian's daughter Placidia, the emperor perhaps believed that Aetius was planning to topple him and put his son on the throne.

THE MEETING OF LEON I AND ATTILA
In 452, Attila invaded northern Italy, ravaging cities and forcing Emperor Valentinian III to flee Ravenna and take refuge in Rome. Pope Leo I met with the Hun ruler to negotiate a peace. In exchange for payment of a tribute, he persuaded Attila to withdraw from Italy. Through his courage and leadership, Leo had placed the Church in the front rank of political power. Renaissance artist Raphael immortalized the episode in a 1514 fresco in the Stanza di Eliodoro at the Vatican (Vatican Museums, Rome).

THE FALL OF ROME

Why did Rome fall?

The fall of Rome has long been a source of fascination for historians, and the focus of much debate. What caused it, when did it begin, and was it inevitable? Today, historians question the traditional notion that Rome actually fell in 476, pointing out the many continuities of classical civilization beyond that date.

The fall of Rome had both internal and external causes. The empire was weakened from within by incompetent political leadership, an inability to establish a policy for the imperial succession, and the resulting civil wars. External and environmental factors included the irruption of barbarians into the empire, disease epidemics, climate change and a decline in the Italian birth rate. There were also economic causes: the debasement of the coinage; the contraction of agricultural and commercial activity and the social crises that arose from that; the breakdown of traditional loyalties, urban revolts and brigandry. Traditionally, historians argued that decadence and the loss of 'republican virtue' was the main cause of Rome's fall. Today, historians offer a more nuanced view, pointing out the other factors that weakened Rome. Continuists argue that the barbarians were not destroyers of the classical world, but merely gave a new direction to a process of transformation that was already underway. Image: a gold solidus portraying Romulus Augustulus.

It was relatively easy for an ambitious senator named Petronius Maximus and the chamberlain Heraclius to recruit Valentinian into their assassination plot. Aetius was delivering a speech when the emperor rushed at him and struck him on the head with his sword. Heraclius then finished him off.

Aetius was an exceptional military commander whose accomplishments almost certainly prolonged the life of the Western empire. As for Valentinian, his brutal and vindictive act would have consequences: six months later, he was assassinated by two Hun friends of Aetius. It is likely that Petronius Maximus was behind this assassination as well.

Death throes of the empire

Valentinian III left no sons or obvious successors, leaving the way clear for Maximus to take control. Well-placed bribes quickly gained him the support of the Senate and palace officials. To lend himself some legitimacy, he married Valentinian's widow, Licinia Eudoxia, and then married Licinia's daughter Eudocia to his son. This was a huge miscalculation, as it meant cancelling Eudocia's betrothal to Huneric, son of Genseric, which sent the Vandal king into a murderous rage. To protect himself against the Vandals, Maximus sent Avitus, his newly appointed magister militum, to the Visigoth king Theodoric II in Toulouse, to obtain his support. In May 455, panic swept Rome at the news that the Vandals were coming. Maximus soon gave up hope of the Visigoths' arrival, and fled. In the chaos he was abandoned by his bodyguard and stoned to death by an angry mob. The Vandals went on to sack the city.

News of Maximus's death reached Avitus while he was in Toulouse. Theodoric immediately proclaimed Avitus, who was Gallo-Roman, emperor. Gallic chiefs of seven provinces added their own support, as did the Roman Senate. On his return to Rome, Avitus found a city devastated by the sack, and suffering food shortages due to Vandal control of the seas. He sent his Germanic general Ricimer to Sicily to attack the Vandals. Ricimer inflicted some defeats, but the Vandals continued to raid the Italian coast. In Rome, Avitus soon caused resentment with his offers of key administrative posts to members of the Gallo-Roman elite. Popular discontent encouraged Ricimer to rebel against Avitus, who was forced to flee Rome. He returned to the city accompanied by an army of Visigoths, but was defeated and deposed by Ricimer.

Due to his barbarian origins, Ricimer could not be emperor himself, but his fellow magister militum Majorian could, and he was acclaimed emperor in April 457. Majorian was the last emperor to make a serious effort to revive the Western empire. After defeating a Vandal attack in Campania in 458, he saw that he had to make Italy stronger. He gave citizens the right to bear arms, expanded the army by recruiting barbarian mercenaries, and strengthened the navy to combat the Vandals at sea. Next, he attempted to restore the rest of the empire. Over the next two years, using a mixture of warfare and diplomacy, he succeeded in reconquering most of southern Gaul and Hispania and reducing the Visigoths, Burgundians and Suevi to federate status.

Majorian introduced several domestic reforms during his reign. In an effort to restore the imperial finances, he minted new coins and removed corrupt tax collectors. He tried to reverse the declining birth rate in Italy by raising the minimum age at which women could take religious vows to 40, and allowing young widows to remarry. Wary of the mistakes made by Avitus, Majorian took care to maintain the support of the wealthy senatorial classes both in Gaul and Rome by sharing out the key appointments between them. Consequently, he offered the consulship to a Gallic senator in 460, and then an Italian one in 461.

Majorian built a fleet in Hispania with the aim of reconquering the rich province of Africa, but disaster struck when the fleet was destroyed by traitors paid by the Vandals. Majorian had no choice but to cancel the operation and return to Italy. On his way back, he stopped at Arelate and disbanded his mercenary army, before continuing his journey with a few guards. This was a mistake. Near Tortona he was met by a military detachment led by Ricimer, a man Majorian may have thought of as an ally but who had secret ambitions of his own. Ricimer arrested and imprisoned Majorian. After five days of torture, he beheaded him. It was an ignoble end for the only fifth-century Roman emperor who had a claim to greatness.

Unable to wear the crown himself, Ricimer was determined to find an emperor whom he could control from behind the scenes. After a

SAINT CAESARIUS (CA. 470–542)
Arelate (modern Arles) was an important base for the Christianization of Gaul. Saint Caesarius, who became Bishop of Arles in 503, promoted asceticism as an important element of Western Christianity, and was famous for his dedication to people in need. Theodoric, king of the Ostrogoths, revered him, showering him with gifts, most of which Caesarius sold to raise money for the poor. This ivory belt buckle may have been a gift from Theodoric (Musée Departemental, Arles).

355

THE FALL OF ROME

Augustine of Hippo, *The City of God* and the fall of Rome

The pagans were quick to attribute the sack of Rome in 410 to the abandonment of Rome's traditional religion and its replacement with Christianity. They said the Christian god had failed to protect Rome, and that Christians were not proper Romans because they asked people to serve God and not the State.

The fifth-century Christian theologian and philosopher Augustine of Hippo responded to this attack with his great work *The City of God*. Augustine points out that Rome had suffered calamities before, even when the old gods were being worshipped. He says Romans became weak because of these gods, giving themselves up to moral and spiritual corruption. In the second part of the book, he describes two cities, one earthly and one heavenly, and explains how human history is a conflict between these two cities and is destined to end in victory for the latter. He writes that even if the earthly city of Rome were threatened, the City of God, where all true believers reside, would last forever. 12th-century manuscript of *The City of God* (Castle of Hradcany, Prague).

three-month search, he eventually selected an unremarkable senator called Libius Severus. Majorian's gains in Gaul and Hispania were quickly overturned, because the governors of the provinces that he had managed to win back would not recognize Severus as emperor. Neither did the Eastern emperor Leo the Thracian; he promptly took Illyricum back into his sphere of influence, leaving Severus only Italy to rule over.

The Vandals resumed their raids on the Italian coast. Genseric, now part of the imperial family through the marriage of his son Huneric to Eudocia, wanted Olybrius, married to Eudocia's sister Placidia, on the throne. Severus died in August 465, either from natural causes or being poisoned by Ricimer.

The throne remained vacant for nearly two years after that, as Ricimer and Leo searched for a suitable candidate for emperor. Genseric continued to push the case for Olybrius, widening his attacks to include the coastal cities of the Eastern empire to put pressure on Leo. Eventually, Leo and Ricimer agreed that Anthemius, a proven commander with experience on the Danube frontier, should be the next emperor. Anthemius, the last capable Western emperor, realized that the Vandals presented an ongoing threat, and in 468 he and Leo sent an enormous fleet to attack the Vandal capital of Carthage. But the fleet was defeated at the Battle of Cap Bon, and Anthemius was forced to accept that Africa was permanently lost. He turned next to the reconquest of Gaul, now controlled by the Visigoths under King Euric. Anthemius recruited Britons to help in the fight, but his army was defeated. His downfall came when he clashed with the kingmaker Ricimer. The struggle between the two men led to a civil war. After five months of fighting, Ricimer besieged Anthemius and his supporters in Rome, and on 11 July 472 the emperor was captured and beheaded.

Anthemius was succeeded by Olybrius, but he died of dropsy seven months later. By then, Ricimer, too, was dead, and the new power behind the throne was his nephew Gundobad.

The next emperor was Glycerius, who was proclaimed by Gundobad but not recognized by Leo, who wanted his own candidate, Julius Nepos, on the Western throne. Nepos invaded Italy in early 474 and Glycerius, hastily abandoned by Gundobad, was forced to surrender and abdicate. Nepos ruled until August 475, when he was deposed by his magister militum Orestes. Nepos then fled to Dalmatia, where he continued to rule as 'Emperor of the West' until his assassination in 480, although his power did not extend beyond Dalmatia. Orestes took power in Ravenna, installing his teenage son Romulus Augustulus as puppet emperor. A few months later, a coalition of barbarian mercenaries, led by a Scirian chieftain called Odoacer, demanded that Orestes give them a third of the land in Italy. Orestes refused and Odoacer revolted. He captured and killed Orestes in August 476, then captured Ravenna. On 4 September, Odoacer forced the young Emperor Romulus Augustulus to abdicate.

That event, which is traditionally regarded as marking the end of the Western Roman Empire, may not have seemed particularly significant at the time. The Western empire had already ceased to exist in all but name, and in those final troubled years, barbarian generals had already deposed or killed a number of emperors. The difference this time is that Odoacer did not feel it necessary to appoint another puppet to rule on his behalf. Instead, he informed the Eastern emperor Zeno that the West no longer required an emperor of its own, and that he would rule it as Zeno's client. This was said purely out of courtesy, however. The Eastern empire had no power in Italy, and Odoacer would now rule there as king.

THE DECADENCE OF ROME
Many Roman commentators, as well as 19th-century historians, argued that the decline of Rome was due to its decadence. In other words, it became weak and immoral, its citizens too preoccupied with banquets and orgies to be able to defend themselves when the barbarians invaded. This view was represented by Thomas Couture (1815–1879) in his oil on canvas, The Romans of the Decadence, *painted in 1847 (Fogg Art Museum-Harvard University Art Museums, Cambridge).*

GORDIAN III
The emperor in 238, aged 13, when he was proclaimed emperor. Roman sarcophagus of the third century (Roman National Museum, Baths of Diocletian). Opposite: a bronze belt of the second century, showing a battle scene between Romans and barbarians (Regional Archaeological Museum, Aosta).

SOCIETY IN THE LATE EMPIRE

To understand the instability detailed in the previous chapters, it is necessary to take account of the complex social conditions of the late empire. It was a time of demographic change, economic crises and natural disasters. Emperors tried to exercise greater control through bureaucratic expansion and by binding people to their land and their professions. Yet it was also a time of social mobility, with new opportunities for talented people from the lower classes.

During the third century, the structure and composition of the Roman aristocracy began to change. The *cursus honorum*, the traditional means by which ambitious men of senatorial rank could rise to positions of power, was displaced by a more bureaucratic system that was opened up to men of much lower social status. Top positions in the imperial administration and the army, which had formerly been the preserve of the Italian senatorial and equestrian classes, were increasingly being offered to people from the provinces. This trend began during the early empire when Augustus started promoting the primus pilus (chief centurion) of each legion to the *ordo equester* (equestrian rank) after a year in post, resulting in around 30 soldiers entering the order annually. Most of these were from the Danube provinces – Pannonia, Moesia, Thrace, Illyria and Dalmatia – where around half the Roman army was deployed.

THE FALL OF ROME

CURRENCY CHANGES
Reverse of a gold solidus of Constantine II. During the reign of Constantine I, the gold coin was replaced by the solidus, which became the most common currency during the late Roman Empire and the Byzantine Empire. In about 320, to avoid inflation, two silver coins were issued, the smaller of which was worth a quarter of the solidus. Silver and copper coins were used in everyday transactions, while gold ones were used for savings or important purchases.

Rise of the new men

These new men of the equestrian order and their descendants formed a group known as *equites primipilares* who were distinct from the wealthy Italian aristocrats who made up the rest of the order. The military skills of the *equites primipilares* became increasingly important to emperors over the following centuries as the barbarian threat increased.

However, there was a problem: as equestrians they were not eligible for the top military command, legatus legionis (legion commander), which was open only to those of senatorial class. In the later second century, emperors resorted to elevating *primipilares* to senatorial rank by means of *adlectio*, a process used to fill vacancies in the Senate. When senators objected to this, Septimius Severus (193–211) simply appointed *primipilares* to top commands by calling them 'temporary substitutes' (*praeses pro legato*). This expedient worked, and by the time of Gallienus (253–268), every legion was commanded by *primipilares*, with the Italian aristocratic class completely sidelined. Diocletian (284–305) completed the revolution by explicitly excluding Italian aristocrats, both senatorial and equestrian, from all military commands, as well as all administrative posts, except those in Italy, Sicily, Africa, Achaea and Asia. In their place, he created a new class of mainly provincial administrators to staff his massively expanded bureaucracy. Under Diocletian's reforms, the Roman Senate was also rendered politically irrelevant. In this way, the old Italian aristocracy, which had held such civic and military power in centuries gone by, gradually became neutered.

Despite this, the old aristocrats retained a great deal of prestige, due to their noble ancestry and their role as guardians of Roman tradition and culture. They were also extremely wealthy as owners of enormous landed estates (*latifundia*), yet they continued to be immune from most taxation. The richest received annual rents worth over 5000 pounds (2268kg) of gold, equivalent to 360,000 solidi, compared to a common soldier's salary of just 4 solidi per year.

Lugo, the Roman city of 80 towers

The city of Lugo was founded in the first century BC in northern Iberia during the Roman conquest of Hispania. Its defensive walls still stand. More than 2200m (7218ft) in length, the walls are up to 7m (23ft) thick and 12m (39ft) high, with 80 towers and 10 gates, and enclose an area of 34 hectares (84 acres). They were built between 260 and 325, following guidelines by engineer Vitruvio.

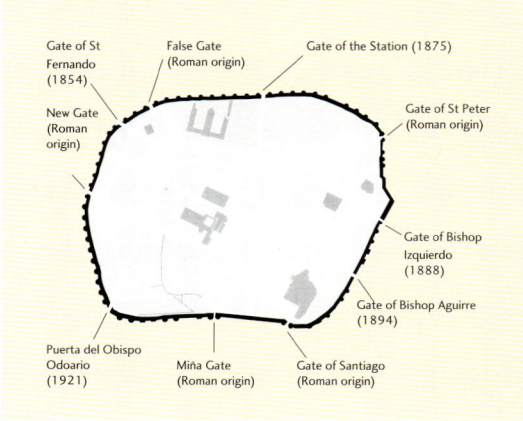

Gate of St Fernando (1854)
False Gate (Roman origin)
Gate of the Station (1875)
New Gate (Roman origin)
Gate of St Peter (Roman origin)
Gate of Bishop Izquierdo (1888)
Gate of Bishop Aguirre (1894)
Puerta del Obispo Odoario (1921)
Miña Gate (Roman origin)
Gate of Santiago (Roman origin)

They were denounced by commentators such the fourth-century Ammianus Marcellinus for their extravagant and decadent lives spent in pure idleness and frivolity. Yet in many ways this was the inevitable consequence of being excluded from their traditional role of governing provinces and commanding armies.

The increasing employment of equestrians by emperors in civil and military roles led to a proliferation of new ranks, as the new men attempted to distinguish themselves according to status. Three classes of equestrian emerged: the *viri egregii* (select men), the *viri perfectissimi* (best of men) and the *viri eminentissimi* (most eminent of men). The highest class, the *viri eminentissimi*, was confined to just two individuals, the two commanders of the Praetorian Guard. This rose to four under Diocletian, being the four praefecti praetorio who assisted the tetrarchs, each of whom governed a quarter of the empire. The viri perfectissimi were the top military commanders, the *vicarii* who ran the dioceses, and the men who managed key parts of the empire; they were responsible for civic order or the grain supply, for example. They were members of the emperor's inner circle and were usually appointed by him. The *viri egregii* comprised the rest of the equestrian order.

From the reign of Constantine the Great (312–337) onwards, there was a dramatic increase in the size of both senatorial and equestrian orders. By 376, even commanders of military regiments could be made senators, and membership of the Roman Senate had increased from 600 to 2000 – similar to the number of *equo publico* equestrians (those eligible to hold public office) in the early empire. The equestrian order experienced an even bigger expansion, with many officials in the imperial bureaucracy granted this status. Decuriones (local councillors) were automatically elevated to equestrian rank, as were some lower-ranked officials, such as actuarii (accountants), as a reward for good service. The inevitable result of this inflation was the debasement of the order's prestige, with the result that, by the year 400, equestrians were no longer seen as part of the aristocracy, but rather as mid-level administrators.

Constantine introduced a third tier of nobility, the *comites* (companions of the emperor), who were drawn from the ranks of both senators and equestrians. These started out as a very exclusive group, made up of the most senior officials in the army and bureaucracy. However, later emperors started to devalue the title by handing out appointments as a form of patronage, and by 450 it had become meaningless.

Military changes of the late empire

Diocletian and Constantine introduced important reforms to the imperial army in their efforts to make it more effective against the threats from barbarian tribes to the north and Persians to the east.

Diocletian increased the size of the army by at least 33 per cent to around half a million men. Constantine changed the way units were organized; he altered campaign and battle tactics, and even weapons. His main strategic innovation was a major expansion of the *comitatus*, the permanent mobile field unit used to support the garrisons (*limitanei*) at the frontiers during barbarian incursions. The *comitatus* had two field commanders: a magister peditum led the infantry, and a magister equitum, the cavalry. Mobility was key, so cavalry units were given priority over infantry, and were probably better armed and trained. Historians estimate that the *comitatus* numbered around 100,000, so about a fifth of the entire army. Constantine completed Diocletian's work of separating military and civil administrations: the vicarii and praefecti praetorio lost their military commands and became purely administrative roles. However, they did retain responsibility for military recruitment, pay and supply. As can be seen in this relief from the Arch of Constantine, which represents the Battle of Verona in 312, the Roman army was already using the oval shield that from the third century had progressively replaced the curved and rectangular scutum.

Bureaucracy and corruption

During the Principate, the empire was run by a mere 250 senior officials, who relied on local administrators and private contractors to collect taxes and deliver services. Corruption existed in those days, expressing itself according to an aristocratic, patron–client code that recognized ties of kinship and class. Its currency was not money but favours and services. By the late third and early fourth centuries, the imperial bureaucracy had swollen to more than 30,000 men, mostly from lower social classes. Corruption flourished within the newly expanded administration, but now the only currency that people recognized was money. An office holder expected to extract money for himself both from those ranked below him and from the citizens with whom he came into contact. All sorts of things were bought and sold: army commands, bishoprics, judges' verdicts, tax assessments, access to the emperor. As office holders essentially bought their appointments or promotions by bribing the right people, they expected to recoup their expenses and enrich themselves still further by extortion of citizens or by selling favours to those beneath them in the hierarchy. Small farmers were particularly vulnerable to tax collectors making unfair assessments of their property's worth. Many, threatened by huge tax bills, had no choice but to sell their farms to wealthy landowners and become their *coloni* (tenant farmers).

The authority of the emperor was never challenged, as it was the stable foundation upon which this complex web of corruption had grown up. Yet imperial power was constantly undermined by the thousands of private transactions that would flow from the emperor's commands. Thus, officials charged with investigating corruption would use this authority to set up a protection racket, selling their silence. Military commanders would try to avoid serious fighting, preferring to use the threat of violence to extort money from the local population. They would embezzle army supplies, sell exemptions from onerous duties to lower-ranked soldiers, and fail to report losses

BANQUET AND SPECTACLE

This mosaic was found in a villa in El Djem, in Tunisia. In the amphitheatre of El Djem, built in around 238, they hosted gladiatorial contests and venationes *(animal hunts). The upper part of the mosaic shows a banquet offered to the* bestiarii, *the beast hunters who will perform at the games the following day. Below the diners are two men playing dice. They are the animal keepers who care for the beasts intended for the show, which included lions, tigers, elephants, bears and wild boars.*

in battle in order to continue collecting dead men's pay and rations.

Due to this fraudulent inflation of troop numbers, some historians believe the actual size of the Roman army may have been a lot smaller than indicated by the 'paper' numbers recorded in such documents as the *Notitia Dignitatum*. This may be one explanation for the army's relative ineffectiveness during the fourth and fifth centuries.

There were, of course, honest commanders, bureaucrats and tax collectors, and records show cases of individuals being dismissed and sometimes executed for corruption, yet root-and-branch reform was never undertaken. For most people, this was seen as normal behaviour. In the late empire, patriotism and loyalty to the idea of Rome had become eroded by a pervasive culture of selfishness and greed, which only the unusually honest and brave could resist.

Agriculture

By the second century AD, wealthy landowners had bought up many small and medium-sized farms to create enormous *latifundia*. At first these were worked by slaves, but as the empire ceased expanding and the supply of slaves slowed, slave labour grew more expensive. So landowners parcelled up their estates into smaller farms that they leased to tenants, called *coloni*, many of whom were former soldiers. By the end of the third century, the crisis in the empire had left many *coloni* destitute and unable to pay their rent and taxes. They gave up their farms to find other jobs, often in the cities. Thus land fell into disuse, and tax revenues

INSCRIPTIONS IN ROMAN SOCIETY

Romans inscribed their most important texts on stone, bronze, silver, gold and ivory, in order to make sure they lasted. Much of what we know about ancient Rome has come down to us in the form of these epigraphic texts. Law codes have been preserved in this way, as well as engravings on tombstones and funerary monuments and even the names of the stonemasons and sculptors who created them. Engraved on milestones placed on the sides of many Roman roads are the name of the reigning emperor as well as the distance in Roman miles (1479m/4852ft) from the place of origin.

FUNERARY STELE OF THE HORSEMAN BASSO
According to the inscription, Basso was stationed in Noricum, squadron of Fabio Pudens. He was the son of Mucala and died aged 46, after 26 years of service. His heirs dedicated this monument to him.

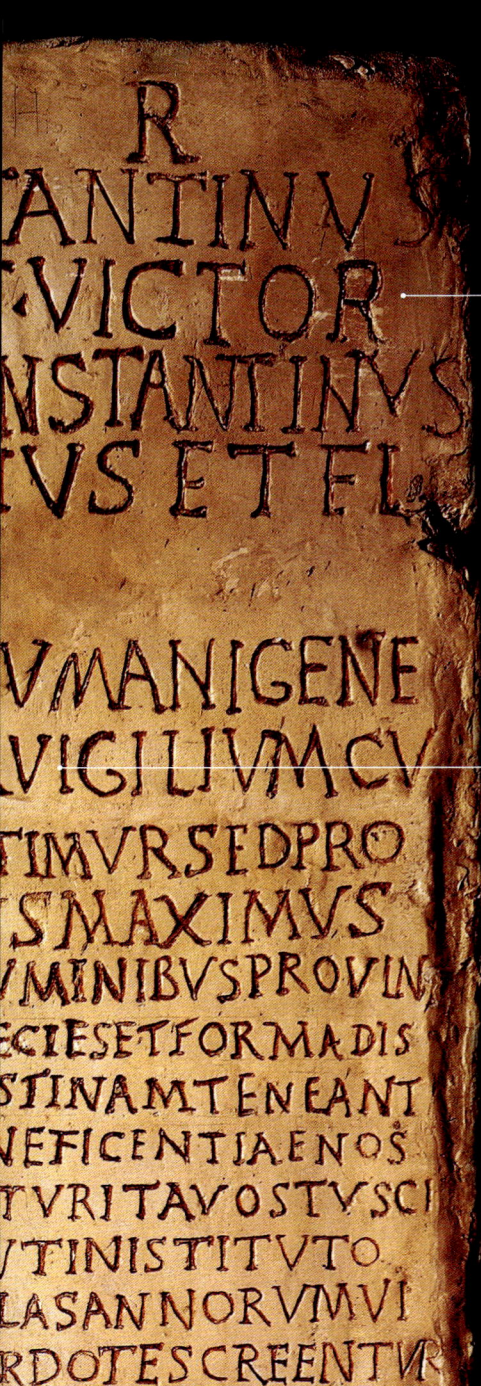

SOCIETY IN THE LATE EMPIRE

Mention of the emperor and Caesar Constantine, and his three offspring, Constantine, Constans and Constantius.

Inscription of an imperial edict ordering the foundation of a temple for the imperial family in Spello, renamed Flavia Constans.

This monumental tombstone, found in Spello, Perugia, is conserved in the Lapidary Gallery of the Archeological Museum of Perugia.

THE MONUMENTAL ROMAN LETTER

This is the earliest Roman typeface, whose origin dates back to the sixth century BC, to the western central region of Italy (Umbria), at that time Etruscan territory. The monumental capital letter has been present ever since then in Latin inscriptions. It was originally used to venerate the gods or praise magistrates, but in the Republic it came to be used in daily life. After the empire fell, it appeared on tombstones, titles and signs in the Carolingian period, and variants were later designed for the printing press. Currently called the capital letter or 'print', it is used in newspaper headlines and as the initial letter in books.

EPITAPH
Lapidary inscription and relief of *scriba librarius* (scribe or clerk) C. Stazio Celso. He appears in a toga, escorted by a lictor (magistrate) (Museo della Civiltà Romana, Rome).

THE FALL OF ROME

The extraordinary mosaics of the Villa Romana del Casale

The Villa Romana del Casale, excavated between 1929 and 1950, has the best-preserved collection of mosaics yet discovered. They were perfectly preserved because of a flood that covered them with a protective layer of mud in the Middle Ages.

The villa, located near the Sicilian town of Piazza Armerina, was built between 285 and 305. Its most likely owner was Lucius Aradius Valerius Proculus, governor of Sicily (327–331), who was consul in 340 during the reign of Constantine II. The mosaic decorating the indoor gym reproduces a chariot race at the Circus Maximus in Rome. The *frigidarium* is decorated with a large mosaic of fishermen, newts, nereids and seahorses, whose figures surround the octagonal enclosure. The ambulatory is a corridor where different hunting scenes are represented, among them a wild boar hunt. Other mosaics show representations of animals such as ostriches and felines attached to carts and chariots. Another features Orpheus playing his lyre, taming animals with his music. The so-called 'bikini mosaic' shows women performing sports, including weightlifting, discus throwing, running and ball games. Differences in style are evident among the mosaics. This may indicate that they were created at different times, or that they were made by different craftsmen.

declined. Diocletian, who needed a stable tax base to pay for his expanded army and bureaucracy, made the *coloni* compulsory tenants, legally obliged to farm their land, as their children were after them.

The *coloni* remained free men, not slaves, and so were legally entitled to the land they worked and unable to be moved or sold. If a landlord sold any part of his estate, he was not allowed to retain the *coloni* who worked this land. Yet if a *colonus* tried to abandon his farm, this was regarded as an act of 'theft', and he would be hunted down like any fugitive slave.

The reforms restricted the powers of landlords in some ways – for example, they were unable to charge their *coloni* exorbitant rents. But in other ways, their powers over their *coloni* grew, as the State entrusted them with the responsibility to collect their tenants' taxes, administer justice and conscript soldiers from those living on their estate. As barbarian attacks increased in the fifth century, landowners would build defensive walls around their *latifundia* and recruit private armies for protection. Many people would voluntarily offer themselves up as *coloni* in order to gain the protection offered by a landowner within his fortified estate. As commanders of their own private armies, landowners would often adopt the military title of *duc* (duke). Thus, a relationship based on loyalty and protection developed between *coloni* and their *duc*, later adopted by invading Goths and Franks, which would eventually evolve into feudalism.

The *latifundia* of Roman Italy cultivated olives for olive oil, grapes for wine, vegetables, herbs, and flax and hemp for linen. Some were devoted to rearing cattle or sheep. Many produced grain – wheat, emmer, spelt and barley – for bread.

SOCIETY IN THE LATE EMPIRE

1 ATRIUM
A three-arched gateway gives onto a horseshoe courtyard surrounded by marble columns with a square fountain in the centre.

2 PERISTYLE
This rectangular garden is decorated with a three-basin fountain decorated with representations of fish swimming among waves.

3 GYMNASIUM
This room, with apses at the ends, is decorated with scenes from the Circus Maximus in Rome.

4 FRIGIDARIUM
This octagonal room has six niches: two served as doorways to the pools; the others were used for changing clothes.

5 AMBULATORY
This corridor 66m long by 5m wide (216 by 16ft) has a double apse featuring mosaics of beast hunts.

6 TRICLINIUM
Overlooking an oval peristyle, the *triclinium* contains remarkable mosaics, including one of Hercules performing his 12 labours.

However, they did not produce it in anything like sufficient quantities to satisfy the vast population of Rome – for bread was the cheap, staple food on every Roman table. Most of Rome's grain came from Egypt and Africa, and after the loss of Egypt to the Eastern empire, from Africa alone. So, in effect, Rome outsourced production of its staple food to its provinces across the Mediterranean, and therefore depended not only on farmers but on the ships bringing the grain across the sea. This vulnerability became a crisis in the fifth century when Rome lost Africa, and control of the Mediterranean, to the Vandals, with ultimately fatal consequences for the empire.

Cities
Many of the peasants and small farmers who lost their land due to the expansion of the *latifundia* moved to the cities for work. This greater concentration of the population in cities had various impacts. It created a class of urban poor who could scarcely afford to feed themselves and became reliant on the *Cura Annonae* (grain dole). An emperor's popularity, and often the longevity of his reign, would come to depend to a large extent on his ability to provide bread and circuses for the masses, and specifically the *Cura Annonae* to the poor of Rome. Another impact of urbanization was a decline in population in many parts of the empire. Farming families tend to produce lots of children because of their relative health and greater need for helping hands. By contrast, the terrible sanitary conditions of Roman cities led to epidemics of disease and a consequent drop in population.

This situation would have serious consequences in later centuries when the empire, whose armies were already depleted by

THE FALL OF ROME

civil wars, could no longer manage to recruit soldiers in sufficient numbers to defeat the barbarian invaders.

As he did with the *coloni* on their farms, Diocletian also introduced an element of compulsion to the trades that the state relied on. Therefore, the captains of the vessels carrying grain across the Mediterranean were tied to this job, as were their sons. Furthermore, they were made legally responsible for the safe arrival of their cargo, and in sufficient quantities to meet the needs of the *Cura Annonae*.

The same principle applied to workers in other essential industries, including bakers, makers of weapons and armour, clothes manufacturers, and even producers of purple silk (the material worn by the emperor). Workers in these industries had to join *collegia*, or guilds. Members of a *collegium* were required to remain in their trade for life and to be succeeded by their sons. They also had to supply a portion of their output to the State, usually at a greatly discounted price. In reality, the State found this rigid system difficult to enforce. In former times, it may have been profitable for a son to follow in his father's footsteps, especially if his father's capital was invested in a bakery or a ship – but this became less attractive with all the burdens the State placed upon workers in these industries.

In the empire's heyday, well-to-do members of a Roman town or city would consider it an honour to carry out the unpaid duties of local administration. A seat on the curia, or municipal senate, was highly sought after, and membership of this class of curials meant being part of the local elite. However, during the crisis of the third century, the number of people willing to take on this role declined. To reverse this trend, Diocletian once more resorted to compulsion. The job of curial became obligatory and hereditary. They were tied to the town of their birth, unable to sell their land or move away. Furthermore, the role became loaded with additional duties. Not only did curials have to perform all the usual tasks of local government, they also had to collect the *iugera* or land taxes of their urban district; what is more, the curials were collectively liable for any shortfall in the amount they collected. They were also responsible for providing fresh horses and mules for the imperial post, even though the use of the post was limited to government officials. It is little wonder that many curials wished to escape their lot. Yet a curial was forbidden to leave his town without permission from the provincial governor, and he could only renounce his role by forfeiting all or part of his property. The fact that some people were forced to become curials as a punishment for misdemeanours demonstrates the unpopularity of the position.

The civil wars and barbarian invasions of the third and fifth centuries left many Roman towns and cities in a state of crisis. During the third century, when the army became increasingly influential in the elevation and overthrow of emperors, the power of the military was also felt in urban centres by ordinary citizens who suffered harassment and extortion from the troops stationed among them. The raising of taxes to fund the growing demands of the military and the tendency of soldiers to interfere in civilian government were common causes of complaint. Some of this reaction may have been motivated by xenophobia, for the army was increasingly recruited from barbarian tribes.

In the fifth century the situation grew even more perilous. Towns on the front line of attack, in the Rhine and Danube provinces, were often pillaged or destroyed, after which they might be abandoned or relapse into a more primitive, pre-Roman state.

Those that survived shrank in size and defensive walls were thrown up around them. Civic life began to disappear as the tax-collecting system deteriorated and governors and prefects no longer had the funds to maintain law and order or public services or endow the cities with entertainments. The wealthy elite withdrew to their fortified villas. The expansive spaces occupied by the forum and basilica in town centres would be repurposed as a place for artisanal shops,

STATUE OF A ROMAN ORATOR
This statue, possibly of a senator, dates from the fourth century and comes from Heracleopolis Magna, near modern Beni Suef, in Egypt. In Rome, oratory was an essential skill that had to be mastered by politicians and lawyers.

SLAVES (OPPOSITE PAGE)
Votive altar with a relief showing two slaves, one carrying a basket of fruits and the other an umbrella. It is preserved at the Roman National Museum, Baths of Diocletian.

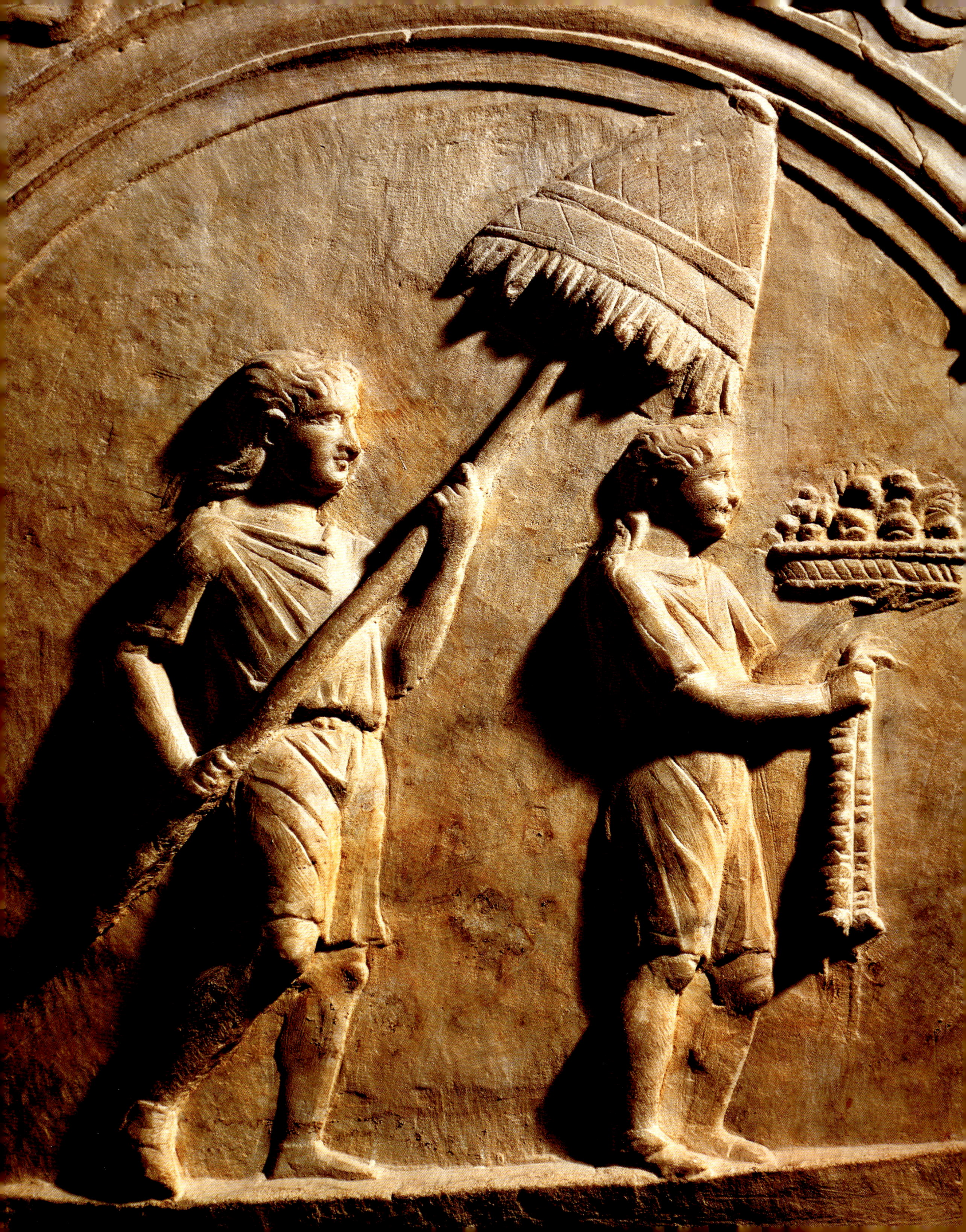

THE FALL OF ROME

Farmers in the late empire: bound to the soil

Diocletian decreed that *coloni* had to pay a tax, the *capita*, based on their place of origin. If a *colonus* deserted his farm, the landlord would be liable to pay the *capita*, so landlords had a strong incentive to hunt down the *colonus*.

The *colonus* could marry, have a family and live in relative freedom. His only duty was to produce harvests, pay the *capita* to the State and rent to his landlord. Children born to a *colonus* were listed on a census; when they reached maturity, they would start to pay the *capita*. From 419, the rules were altered to allow tenants who had been freed from their land by their landlord for 30 years to lose the *colonus* bond. Image: Farmers at work, funerary bas-relief preserved in the Roman National Museum, Baths of Diocletian.

informal markets, burial grounds and shrines to saints. Sometimes they were even dug up to grow crops. The urban population dramatically declined. In the third century, Rome was the most populous city in the world, with around 800,000 people. By the sixth century, its population had dropped to 30,000. The role of cities as commercial centres ended with the disappearance of long-distance trade, as people reverted to local production and consumption.

Climate and disease

No analysis of the late Roman Empire, or explanation of its decline, would be complete without an assessment of the role played by climate and disease. The Romans enjoyed remarkably benign climatic conditions when they began building their empire. During the period between 200 BC and 150 AD, the Mediterranean climate was warm, wet and stable, and conducive to high agricultural productivity. This began to change in the late second century, when the climate cooled and the Alpine glaciers began to advance. This was a period characterized by long droughts when the rains often came late in southern Egypt and central and southern Europe and many areas suffered from famine. For an agrarian society, this was destabilizing, and may have been a factor that contributed to the crisis of the third century, as well as to the widespread abandonment of farms described above. Roman farmers often made matters worse by, for example, stripping forested land for agriculture, causing soil erosion.

Certainly, the general health of the population dropped around this time, as evidenced by skeletal remains, which show that people were generally smaller than both their ancestors and their medieval descendants.

The expanding borders, increasing urbanization and greater connectivity of the empire opened the way, as never before, to epidemic diseases. Densely packed cities with poor sanitation were breeding grounds for gastro-enteric diseases such as typhoid and shigellosis, which spread through contamination of food and water. Roman roads and merchant ships connected cities and communities by land and sea, and germs travelled with them. Malaria, for example, travelled from Africa to Italy in the bloodstream of traders, leading to a major outbreak in the fifth century in Lugnano near Rome. Even slow killers, such as tuberculosis and leprosy, tended to flourish in such an interconnected world.

Worst of all were the pandemics – the Antonine Plague, which ravaged the Roman world from 165 to 180 AD, and the Plague of Cyprian, which arrived 70 years later. The Antonine Plague, which killed an estimated five million people, was probably the first appearance of smallpox. It devastated the army, but the empire was resilient enough at that time to recover. The Plague of Cyprian first appeared in 250, further weakening an empire that was already reeling from the Military Anarchy. It was probably a viral haemorrhagic fever similar to the ebola virus. At its height, 5000 people were allegedly dying per day in Rome. The epidemic lasted some 20 years and claimed the lives of two emperors, Hostilian in 251 and Claudius Gothicus in 270. Many Romans blamed the Christian community, and it may have partly prompted the persecution of Christians under Emperor Decius. Today, historians look back on it as a significant factor in Rome's decline and fall.

REMAINS IN TURIN
In the centre of this modern city, Roman structures still survive, like the Palatine Towers (above). Below: the Roman colony Julia Augusta Taurinorum (modern Turin), as it appears in the Codex Palatinus *(1564).*

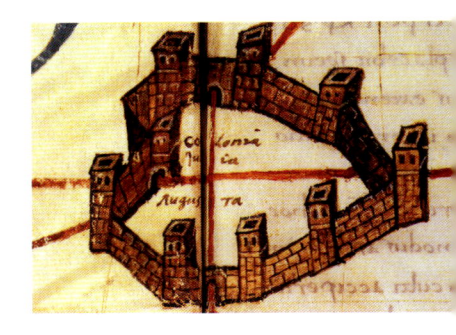

■ THE FALL OF ROME

SOCIETY IN THE LATE EMPIRE

The Fayum mummy portraits

From the first to the third centuries, a new kind of art form, the mummy portrait, flourished in Roman Egypt.

About a thousand of these images survive, painted on wooden boards and attached to the linen wrappings of Egyptian mummies in the place where the face would have been. Each painting shows the head and shoulders of a man, woman or child. The faces depicted are remarkably naturalistic and appear in many ways quite modern, in contrast with the stylized iconography of the medieval era that would follow.

The paintings have been found all over Egypt, but particularly from two locations in the Fayum Basin, hence their description as the Fayum mummy portraits. The locations are Hawara and el-Rubayat (respectively, Arsinoe and Philadelphia in Roman times). The subjects depicted in the paintings were native Egyptians, all of them members of the province's wealthy elite: military commanders, civil servants, politicians and priests. Although Egypt had become Romanized by this time, the mummy portraits suggest that the people still adhered to Egyptian beliefs about the afterlife.

Style and techniques

These works are products of the multicultural society of Roman Egypt – part of a school of Greco-Roman painting, yet created for a traditional Egyptian purpose: inclusion in the funerary ornamentation of mummies. Most of the images show a single figure, looking towards the viewer from a slight angle. The paintings feature

FEMALE FUNERAL MASK
This plaster mask is from Fayum and dates to the second century (Egyptian Museum, Turin).

TIMELINE OF THE FAYUM MUMMY PORTRAITS

30 BC
Roman conquest. Fayum mummy portraits start around this time, or soon after.

2nd century
Maximum splendour. Heyday of Fayum mummy portraiture, in the Antonine era.

3rd century
Final period. The portraits begin to decline, just before the Christianization of the empire.

1616
Pietro della Valle. An Italian nobleman brings the first mummy portraits to Europe.

1888–9
William Matthew Flinders Petrie. The British archaeologist excavates tombs containing portraits in Hawara.

20th century
The collection is scattered. The Fayum mummy portraits are dispersed to the world's major museums, where they remain on display.

PORTRAIT OF A YOUTH
This encaustic Fayum mummy portrait probably dates from the second century (Louvre Museum, Paris).

realistic shadows and highlights on the faces, examples of an art form that was regarded by contemporaries as among the highest achievements of Greek culture – yet these examples, preserved by Egypt's arid climate, are the only ones to have survived.

The portraits offer a tantalizing glimpse into the fashions in clothing, hairstyles and jewellery in Roman Egypt. There are undoubtedly strong influences from the imperial court at Rome, but with particular eastern Mediterranean characteristics, such as the curls in some of the female hairstyles. The paintings have proved very difficult to date, although the hairstyles depicted are an important clue, as these changed frequently according to fashion.

The majority of Fayum mummy portraits were painted on thin rectangular panels made from imported hardwoods such as oak, lime, sycamore, cedar, cypress, fig or citrus. The portraits were set within the layers of wrapping, framed by bands of cloth, giving the impression of a window-like opening through which the face of the deceased could be viewed. Some portraits were painted directly onto the mummy's wrappings.

The surface of the panels was smoothed and sometimes given a primary coat of plaster. A few of these primed layers reveal preparatory sketches. Most of the portraits were painted using the encaustic technique, in which the pigment is mixed with beeswax. Encaustic paintings have a glossy surface, with subtle treatment of light and shade, giving them a three-dimensional appearance.

■ THE FALL OF ROME

The art of cartonnage and the mummies of Fayum

Cartonnage is the name for a type of material used to make mummy cases or funerary masks in ancient Egypt from the First Intermediate Period (ca. 2100 BC) to the Roman era. It consisted of layers of linen or papyrus covered with plaster or resin gum, then often richly decorated. Some of the Fayum mummies had their portraits painted directly on the cartonnage. The linen or papyrus was laid onto the mummy with the sticky resin or plaster in a technique similar to papier-mâché. The cartonnage, which could be moulded to the shape of the body, then hardened to form a shell, which could be painted or gilded. Scholars still debate whether or not the portraits are realistic representations of their subjects. Egyptian ideas about the afterlife dictated that mummies needed to be readily identified. On the other hand, many of the images show healthy-looking youths, with few elderly or ill, and Egyptians did believe that images could influence the forms their souls took in the afterlife.

Researchers have found that many encaustic methods were used, including the use of hot and cold wax and a range of soft or hard tools, used cold or heated. Many of the encaustic portraits incorporate gold leaf. Sometimes the entire background is gilded; in other cases, jewellery and garment decoration are highlighted in this way. Another painting technique is tempera, in which the pigment is mixed with animal glue or some other water-soluble binding agent. Tempera portraits have a matte surface. The faces are usually shown frontally, unlike many of the encaustic ones, which are shown in three-quarter view. The paintings show evidence of firm brush strokes and feature a simpler treatment of light and shade, closer to native Egyptian artistic traditions. Some portraits were created using a mix of encaustic and tempera techniques.

End of a tradition
Research suggests that Fayum mummy portraiture ended in the mid-third century. This may have been due to the economic crisis of the third century, which reduced the spending power of the Egyptian upper classes. It coincides with an increasing neglect of Egyptian temples, as well as the beginning of a general decline in pagan religions.

The first European to discover the existence of the Fayum portraits was Pietro della Valle (1586–1642) on his visit to Egypt in 1616. He transported some portraits to Europe. However, European interest in the portraits only really ignited in 1887 when locals excavated a number of them, which were bought by Theodor Graf, an Austrian businessman. In 1888–9, British archaeologist W.M. Flinders Petrie discovered another hoard of the portraits at Hawara. Today, the Fayum portraits are exhibited in top museums around the world.

SOCIETY IN THE LATE EMPIRE

A style that continues to fascinate

The Fayum mummy portraits have been celebrated for more than a century due to the realism of their faces and expressions, which seem to reach across the millennia to establish an intimate connection with modern viewers.

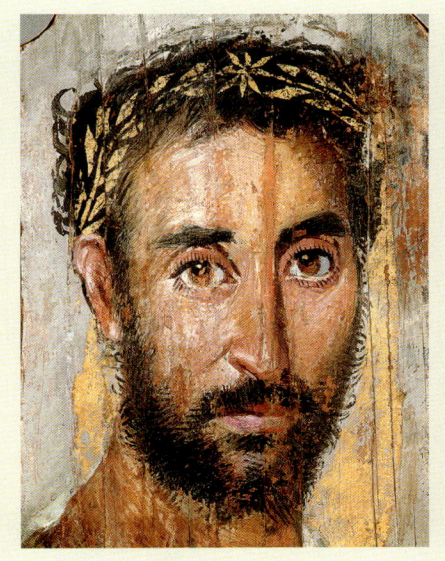

MAN CROWNED WITH LAUREL
The eyes and beard are painted with admirable detail. Ca. 150–180 (John Paul Getty Museum, Los Angeles).

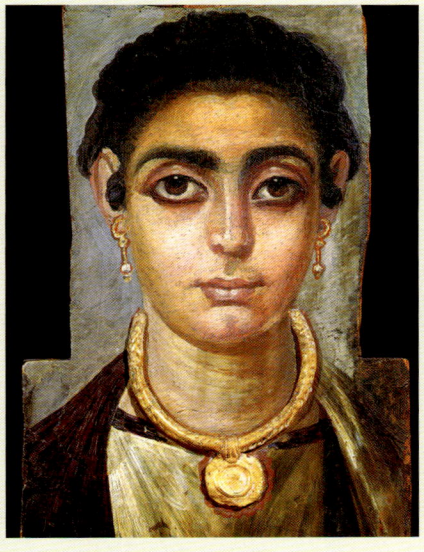

WOMAN OF THE CLASSIC PERIOD
This female subject catches the attention with her bold look and gold necklace. Ca. 150–180 (particular Collection).

'THE EUROPEAN'
Deriving her name from her pale complexion, she has an oblique look and large eyes. Ca. 160 (Louvre Museum, Paris).

MAN OF THE THIRD CENTURY
This bearded man has a penetrating gaze. Ca. 225–250 (John Paul Getty Museum, Los Angeles).

FEMININE HEAD
Her necklace and sophisticated hairstyle are impeccably reproduced. Mid-third century (Metropolitan Museum of Art, New York).

MAN WITH A TUNIC
The man has a sad expression, and wears a Roman tunic of the period. Third century (Musées Royaux d'Art et d'Histoire, Brussels).

THE SCRIBE
A mosaic found in Roman-era Christian cemetery in Tabarka (Roman: Thabraca) in north-western Tunisia (Bardo Museum, Tunisia). Next page: The Baptism of Christ from a fragment of a sarcophagus, 4th century (Museo della Civiltà Romana, Rome).

PHILOSOPHY AND RELIGION IN THE LATE EMPIRE

The spread of Christianity through the Greco-Roman world between the second and fifth centuries led to a period of intellectual upheaval and cross-fertilization as philosophers and theologians attempted to navigate between competing systems of thought. Early Christians were influenced by Gnosticism, a religious movement that emerged in the first century. Classical and Christian thinkers alike found common ground in Neoplatonism, blending Platonism with the Christian belief in salvation.

The dominant Hellenic philosophies in the second century, when Christianity began to make an impact, were Stoicism, Epicureanism and Platonism. The Stoics' belief in the value of hard work, their aversion to excess and their recognition of human weakness in the face of physical desire all chimed with the early Christians. But the Stoics and Christians differed in one important respect: the Stoics did not believe in God, Heaven or any form of afterlife. Epicureans also shared some common attitudes with Christians, especially their belief in compassion, forgiveness, generosity, inclusion, hospitality and love. Yet, like the Stoics, they believed that nothing existed beyond the physical realm that humans can ever know about.

Of the three classical traditions, Platonism came closest to the Christian view of the divine. The Platonists believed that the physical forms we see around us are transitory and imperfect

THE FALL OF ROME

versions of ideal Forms, which are eternal, perfect and unchanging. Physical forms are many and diverse, whereas ideal forms are single and unified.

The Platonists imposed a hierarchy of values on these different qualities, so eternity, unity and immateriality are superior to temporality, division and materiality. They spoke of the 'One', a transcendent, ineffable, divine entity; the source of all that exists. To early Christians, this sounded a lot like God. Even more closely aligned with their beliefs was a philosophy that emerged out of Platonism in the mid-third century, called Neoplatonism.

Neoplatonism and Christianity

The founder of Neoplatonism was an Egyptian philosopher called Plotinus (ca. 205–ca. 270). Plotinus affirmed that the One contains no division or multiplicity and is beyond all categories of being and non-being. Our idea of 'being', he said, is derived from our experience of physical objects, but the infinite, transcendent One is beyond all such concepts. It is not like any existing thing, and is prior to all that we call existence. Plotinus proposed that the One had three aspects. First there is the transcendent and ineffable aspect.

Flowing from this is the second aspect, Intelligence, which consists of the Forms. The third aspect is Soul. This comprises the higher soul, which remains in contemplation of the Forms in the realm of Intelligence, and the lower soul, contained in the world of senses and matter. This threefold concept of divinity fitted well with the Christian doctrine of the Holy Trinity. Plotinus further taught that the human soul, in descending from the immaterial to the material world, forgets part of its divine nature as it becomes one of many. Yet all human souls share in the divinity of the One and will eventually return to the divine realm after they die. This resonated with the Christian belief in the salvation of the soul.

Plotinus's Syrian student Porphyry (ca. 233–ca. 309) further developed his teacher's ideas about the soul. He said that through the exercise of virtue and contemplation of the

STATUE OF A BARBARIAN PRISONER
For the Greeks and Romans, any foreigner was a 'barbarian', and many of them believed barbarians to be intellectually inferior and unable to reason. The Christians made no such distinctions between people of different places, an attitude that helped the spread of their religion beyond the Roman Empire. Porphyry statue, red and marble.

Plotinus and his system

At the age of 27, around the year 232, Plotinus travelled to Alexandria and became a student of Ammonius Saccas. After 11 years in Alexandria, Plotinus joined the Roman army and went to Persia. Later, he settled in Rome and began writing his famous *Enneads*.

Plotinus sought to demonstrate, with his system, why there is evil in the world, and how one might obtain salvation. When humans forget their higher soul and focus on material things, they lose sight of their unity with the One, and this can lead them into evil acts. By leading a virtuous life and contemplating the higher soul, they can have a vision of the One. Plotinus claimed to have had several such mystical experiences. His system was therefore not abstract philosophy but a practical approach to life. Image: Roman sarcophagus showing Plotinus and his pupils, 270 AD (Vatican Museums, Rome).

spirit (which Christians might call prayer), the soul can ascend from the material realm to the divine. There was certainly common ground with Christian philosophy here, yet Porphyry was explicitly anti-Christian and a defender of paganism. In his 15-volume work *Adversus Christianos* ('Against the Christians'), of which only fragments remain, he wrote: 'The gods have proclaimed Christ to have been most pious, but the Christians are a confused and vicious sect.'

The next great figure in Neoplatonism was a Syrian philosopher called Iamblichus (ca. 245–ca. 325), who studied under Porphyry. Iamblichus rejected Porphyry's belief that the soul could ascend to the divine through the practice of virtue and spiritual contemplation alone. Instead he emphasized the need for religious ritual as a means of communing with the divine. Iamblichus accepted that the One is unknowable to us and cannot be communicated with directly, but he introduced the concept of other entities – superhuman beings that we *could* access through prayer and offerings.

He declared that embodied souls could achieve salvation through *theurgy* ('god-work'), by performing religious rituals. Julian the Apostate (331–363), the last non-Christian Roman emperor, was a follower of Iamblichus, and attempted a revival of paganism based on his ideas. Yet Christian philosophers such as Pseudo-Dionysus the Areopagite (late fifth-early sixth century) were also influenced by his work, reinventing Iamblichus's 'superhuman beings' as angels.

The final great Neoplatonist philosopher was Proclus (412–485). He expanded on Iamblichus's ideas by adding a new kind of being to the divine hierarchy, which he called *henads*. Like the One, the *henads* are beyond being, but they stand at the head of chains of causation (*seirai*) and give these chains their particular character. He identified the *henads* with the Greek gods, so one *henad* might be equivalent to Helios, god of the sun, and be the cause of all sunny things. Proclus saw the *henads* as a connecting or intermediate stage between the absolute unity of the One, and the multiplicity of the material world.

While the Christians were greatly influenced by Neoplatonism, they also wished to create an explicitly Christian theology of their own. One of the most influential early Christian theologians was Origen of Alexandria (ca. 184–ca. 253). Origen was a student of Ammonius Saccas, a Platonist who also taught Plotinus. It may be that he was influenced in his thinking by the Platonist idea of the One, for this is very similar to his idea of God – a perfect unity, transcending all things material, and

THE FALL OF ROME

Heresies and pagan cults

In the fourth and fifth centuries, doctrines were defined by Christians, and heresies were born. Initially, these were simply alternative theologies, but their followers were quickly isolated by the Church and recast as rebels. Heretical movements included Arianism (Christ was created by God and so distinct and subordinate to him); Adoptionism (Christ is not the child of God, but a man adopted by him); Docetism (Christ's body was only human in appearance); Nestorianism (Christ's humanity is distinct from his divinity) and Monophysitism (Christ has only one nature, the divine). For most of the fourth century, Christian emperors also worked with the Church to suppress paganism and pagan cults. A brief period of toleration from 361 ended in 375 with the ascension of Emperor Gratian. Under him and his successors Valentinian II and Theodosius the Great, popular cults such as those of Mithras and Cybele were outlawed. In the words of Edward Gibbon, idolatry became a 'crime against the supreme majesty of the creator.' Image: Sanctuary of the cult of Mithras in the Basilica of San Clemente al Laterano, Rome.

therefore inconceivable and unknowable. Yet Origen saw God, in a more Christian sense, as fundamentally good, just and wise.

It is God's goodness that leads him to reveal himself through the Logos, the rational, creative principle that permeates the universe. The Logos, according to Origen, acts on humans through their capacity for logic and rational thought, guiding them to the truth of God's revelation. Origen helped develop the Christian idea of the Trinity, and was among the first to name the Holy Spirit as part of the Godhead. He also believed that souls existed before the creation of the material world and that they fell varying distances, some to become angels, others descending further to become humans, and the most wicked falling furthest to become devils.

Gnosticism and Manichaeism

Growing up alongside Christianity, and very influential in its development, was a system of thought known as Gnosticism. Founded in the first century AD by Jews and early Christians, Gnosticism went on to flourish in the Mediterranean world in the second century. There were many varieties of Gnosticism, but in broad terms the Gnostics believed in a remote, supreme and unknowable godhead, the Monad. Emanating from the Monad are lower divine beings called aeons. One of these aeons, the Demiurge, created the physical world. Gnostics viewed the Demiurge as a malevolent character, weaker than the Monad but opposed to it. The Demiurge creates servants called Archons that preside over the physical realm and sometimes present obstacles to the souls seeking to escape it. Some Gnostics viewed the jealous god of the Hebrew Old Testament as the Demiurge, creator of the corrupt material world.

Souls descend from the *pleroma* ('region of light') into the physical world where they become human beings. They can return to the *pleroma* when they obtain *gnosis* (esoteric or intuitive knowledge of the divine). Many early Christians, including Paul the Apostle, were highly influenced by Gnosticism. Both Christians and Gnostics saw Jesus as a divine mediator (an *aeon*, in Gnostic terminology) sent to help humanity achieve salvation of the soul (*gnosis*). Where early Christians differed from the Gnostics was in their belief that humanity's 'fallen' state is not due to the Demiurge but to Adam and Eve and their original sin.

Gnosticism developed in the late first century and early second century, simultaneous with the writing of the New Testament. It reached its height from the mid-second to early third century, when it spread through the Roman and Persian Empires and among Arian Goths. Different traditions of Gnosticism emerged in each locality. Its fortunes began to wane during the third century in the face of Rome's economic and cultural deterioration and a growing antipathy from mainstream Christians. In the fourth century, the orthodox Church condemned Gnosticism as a heresy and support for it began to decline.

Both Gnosticism and Christianity believed in an omnipotent God. In this they differed from Manichaeism, the third major religious movement that developed in this period.

Manichaeism was founded by Mani (ca. 216–ca. 276), who lived in Persia during the Sasanian Empire. Mani was influenced by a Mesopotamian gnostic called Bardaisan, and as such Manichaeism can be viewed as part of the family of Gnostic religions. Like other forms of Gnosticism, Manichaeism preaches a dualistic vision of the cosmos, divided into realms of light (divinity) and darkness (materiality). Mani taught that there is a constant battle going on between the good, spiritual realm of light, and the evil, material world of darkness. God is not all-powerful in this struggle, for he is opposed by a semi-eternal evil power, Satan. Every one of us is a battleground for these eternally duelling powers, and our souls are under the influence of both light and dark.

Like the Gnostics, the Manicheans believed that God didn't create the world, but it was the result of Satan (or the Demiurge, in Gnostic terms) striking out against God, which is why the world is full of pain and suffering. Souls have fallen and become entangled with evil matter. Salvation is possible through *nous* (the spirit or

PLUTO AND SATAN
The character of Satan in Manichaeism and Christianity bears some similarities to Pluto, ruler of the underworld in Roman mythology, also identified with malevolence and darkness. This mural, from a catacomb beneath a tomb on Via Latina, near Rome, shows the hero Heracles rescuing Alcestis from the underworld, watched by Cerberus the three-headed dog.

THE FALL OF ROME

EDUCATION IN THE EMPIRE: TEACHERS AND SCHOOLCHILDREN

Children normally began formal schooling at the age of seven. They would attend an elementary school (*ludus litterarius*), where they would be taught to read and write by a *litterator*. Students faced no exams or tests, and their progress was measured through exercises that were either corrected or applauded. Between the ages of nine and 12, boys from wealthy families would leave their *litterator* and begin study with a *grammaticus*. Poorer boys would already be working as apprentices, while girls, rich or poor, would be preparing for marriage and motherhood. The *grammaticus* would teach his students writing, speaking skills and poetic analysis. They would be expected to read and speak Greek as well as Latin. Aged 14 or 15, the wealthiest and most talented students would go on to study with a *rhetor*. He would teach them the skill of rhetoric (oratory) – vital to any budding lawyer or politician – and geography, music, philosophy, literature, mythology and geometry. The final level of education was philosophical study. Roman students would go to a school where philosophers taught, usually in Greece. Main image: Fourth-century bas-relief of a teacher and students in class (Capitoline Museums, Rome).

TOOLS OF THE SCHOLAR
Inkwells and styluses from the first century (National Museum of Rome).

PHILOSOPHY AND RELIGION IN THE LATE EMPIRE

LEARNING TO READ AND WRITE

Schoolchildren learned to write by copying out letters and words onto a wax tablet (*tabella cerae*) using a metal or wooden stylus. The wax tablet was convenient as it allowed correction and deletion and could be reused. Writing on papyrus or parchment was too costly for use in schools. Image: Fresco from Pompeii of a woman (allegedly the poet Sappho) with a tablet and stylus (Archaeological Museum, Naples).

Reading was always done aloud. Students were taught using imitation, repetition and memorization. They would progress from reading and writing letters to syllables, to lists of words, and eventually to memorizing and dictating texts. Discipline was harsh. Pupils were often beaten with a wooden rod or leather strap if they got something wrong.

1 READING
The teacher would read a piece of text. The students then repeated it and took notes as the teacher explained what it meant.

2 BOOKS
Students learned Greek language and grammar from the works of Homer, and Latin by studying Virgil and Livy.

3 TEACHERS
Most teachers came from great centres of learning, such as Alexandria, Athens, Rhodes or Pergamum.

4 STUDENTS
Most of the children who went on to study rhetoric were the privileged sons of magistrates, senators and senior officials.

The Vulgate: canon of the church of Rome and the first Latin Bible

In the year 382, Pope Damasus I commissioned Jerome, the leading Biblical scholar of his day, to revise the *Vetus Latina* (the original Latin translation of biblical texts) and create a new Latin version of the four Gospels. Jerome went much further. After completing his translation of the Gospels in 383, he then used the Septuagint Greek version of the Old Testament to translate the Psalms (the so-called Gallican Psalter), the Book of Job and several other books. After that, he decided that the Septuagint was not good enough, and he embarked on a translation of the entire Old Testament from original Hebrew versions, completing the process in about 405. Jerome's translation was not immediately accepted, but it was in common use by the mid-sixth century. This edition contained Jerome's translation of the Old Testament and the Gospels, together with earlier Latin versions of the remainder of the New Testament, which may have been slightly revised by Jerome. Various editors revised parts of it over the following centuries, and by the 13th century it had eclipsed the *Vetus Latina* and become known as the Vulgate ('version commonly used'). In 1546, the Council of Trent decreed that the Vulgate was the exclusive Latin authority for the Bible; 46 years later, Pope Clement VIII made it the authoritative biblical text of the Roman Catholic Church.

intelligence), similar to what Gnostics call *gnosis*. Through *nous*, we can come to know our true selves (previously obscured by being mingled with matter) and see that, despite the wretched nature of the material world, we are connected to the transcendent world and to God. The Manicheans believed in following an ascetic life and putting their energies into prayer, almsgiving, confession, hymn singing and fasting. Those who persisted in a life of pleasure were condemned to rebirth in a succession of bodies. The Manicheans community was divided into the 'elect', who were strict ascetics, and the 'hearers', who supported the elect through alms and prayers.

Manichaeism spread east as far as China, and west into Egypt and North Africa, reaching Rome in the early fourth century. Manichean churches were established in southern Gaul and Hispania, and for a brief time it rivalled Christianity as the successor religion to paganism. However, as the Christian Church strengthened its grip on the Roman State, Manicheans came under sustained attack, and by the end of the fifth century the movement had disappeared almost entirely from Western Europe.

St Augustine of Hippo

Many of the great religious and philosophical movements of the late empire converge in the person of St Augustine of Hippo (340–430). The great Roman African theologian and thinker was, at various times in his life, a Manichean (and therefore a kind of Gnostic), a Neoplatonist and a Christian bishop. Although raised a Christian, Augustine became a Manichean at the age of around 17, while he was studying in Carthage. Manichaeism enabled him to resolve his conflict between spiritual and material desires. As a 'hearer', he could keep his girlfriend, while purging himself of sin by serving the Elect. He could also disclaim responsibility for those sins, blaming them on the power of darkness, or evil, within him. Augustine remained a Manichean for almost ten years, after which he became influenced by Neoplatonist ideas. Neoplatonism shared some common ideas with Manichaeism, namely that matter is evil (or inferior) and it traps the human spirit, and that the human spirit contains some spark of the divine that allows it to transcend the material world and rejoin the light or the One. Augustine was very attracted to the Neoplatonist view of God as something infinite, timeless and unchangeable and the cause of everything that exists. It became, for him, a gateway to Christianity.

Under the influence of Ambrose, Bishop of Milan, Augustine converted to Christianity at the age of 31, and he went on to become one of the great Christian theologians. For him, Neoplatonism contained all the major ideas of Christianity, save one: it did not acknowledge Christ. Yet elements of Neoplatonism remained with him and formed a core part of his philosophy. For example, like the Neoplatonists, he maintained that evil did not exist. Just as darkness is the absence of light, so evil is the absence of good. Things are evil or less evil depending on how far they are from the divine.

In 529, the Eastern Roman emperor Justinian I ordered the closure of the Neoplatonist School of Athens. This marked the end of classical Neoplatonism. By this time, Gnosticism and Manichaeism had also virtually disappeared from Europe. Christianity reigned supreme in the West. Yet the ideas it had displaced would live on as influences within its doctrines and theology.

SAINT MARTIN OF TOURS
Martin of Tours was a fourth-century saint who began life as a soldier, went on to become a monk and hermit and ended up as Bishop of Tours. According to legend, he once cut his cloak in two so he could give half to a beggar clad in rags and shivering with cold. In this sixth-century Byzantine mosaic, from the Basilica of Sant' Apollinare Nuovo in Ravenna, Martin of Tours appears in the company of a group of martyrs.

SANTA MARIA IN TRASTEVERE
This basilica, one of the oldest churches in Rome, was founded in the 220s by Pope Callixtus I. Adorning the apse is this 13th-century mosaic of the Coronation of the Virgin. Opposite: Bronze labarum with the Greek letter rho (P) and, attached to the arms, the alpha and omega, a title of Christ. It comes from Aquilea (Kunsthistorisches Museum, Vienna).

THE CHRISTIANIZATION OF THE EMPIRE

A key development in the history of late antiquity is the birth, expansion and consolidation of Christianity, leading to its establishment as the official religion of the Roman Empire. This process laid the foundations for the medieval society that would follow. The turning point in the Christianization of the empire may have been Constantine's victory at the Milvian Bridge in 312. Yet the roots of Rome's conversion to Christianity can be traced all the way back to the first century.

During the middle decades of the first century, apostles such as Paul travelled around the Roman Empire seeking converts to the nascent religion of Christianity. A key decision was taken at the Council of Jerusalem in around 50 AD, when Church leaders agreed that not being circumcised or not following the Jewish dietary laws should not be a bar to joining the Christian community. By allowing Christianity to move beyond the Jewish community it was able to spread through the empire as a new and distinct religion. Paul preached in cities such as Ephesus, Philippi, Corinth and Athens, where the Christian message of eternal life found a keen audience, especially among the poor.

As Christianity grew, it suffered periodic persecutions, beginning in 64 under Nero. Until the Decian persecution of 250, these tended to be localized, sporadic and mob-led. The exclusive nature of Christian communities,

THE FALL OF ROME

Stages in the conversion of the Roman Empire

Years 249–251
Decius promulgates decree unleashing the persecution of the Christians, who are forced to offer sacrifices and commit apostasy.

Years 253–260
Valerian punishes Christians if they do not perform sacrifices to the old gods.

Years 304–311
Diocletian persecutes Christians, decrees the destruction of churches and holy books, and imprisons and executes bishops.

Years 312–337
Constantine and Licinius sanction religious freedom with the Edict of Milan. Helena, mother of Constantine, travels to Jerusalem in 320 and finds the True Cross, the Holy Nails and other relics.

Years 367–383
Gratian removes the privileges of augurs and vestals, supports Pope Damasus I, and rejects the title of Pontifex Maximus for Emperor of Rome.

Years 379–395
Theodosius I makes Christianity the official religion of the Roman Empire with the Edict of Thessalonica (380). The pope is from then on Pontifex Maximus.

---

their defiant monotheism and unwillingness to participate in the rituals of the State religion made them ready targets for scapegoating.

The suffering of Christians, and the courage shown by martyrs, attracted sympathy and admiration. During the second century, the Church acquired more of a structure, with bishops emerging as overseers of urban Christian populations. Yet there remained no consensus on doctrine, methods of worship or the date of Easter, and most Christians did not at this stage own a copy of the works that would become the Christian Bible.

In 250, Emperor Decius, as part of an attempt to restore stability to the empire during the Military Anarchy, demanded that Roman citizens affirm their loyalty by performing a sacrifice and burning incense to the gods and the well-being of the emperor. The sacrifice had to be witnessed by a Roman magistrate. It was the first time Christians had faced legislation forcing them to choose between their faith and death. Some refused and were executed; many performed the ceremonies; others fled or went into hiding. The edict remained in force for no more than a year, but in 257 the persecution recommenced when Emperor Valerian commanded Christian clergy to perform sacrifices to the Roman gods or face banishment. A further decree in 258 ordered the execution of Christian leaders, and forced Christian senators and equites to perform pagan sacrifices or lose their titles and property and be banished. Members of the imperial household and bureaucracy who would not worship the Roman gods would be reduced to slavery. All this suggests that Christianity was well established by this time, with some Christians in very senior positions. Nevertheless, the effect of these persecutions on the Christian community was traumatic. Many of their leaders, including Pope Fabian, Babylas of Antioch and Alexander of Jerusalem, were killed. Some who performed the sacrifices faced hostility from other Christians.

In 260, Emperor Gallienus issued the first official edict of toleration for Christianity. The edict recognized places of worship and cemeteries as Church property and those that had been confiscated were returned to Christian ownership. There followed an era known as the 'Little Peace of the Church' during which Christianity flourished. Over the next four decades, Christian communities became more integrated into Roman society. Christian apologists used classical Greek techniques of rhetoric to defend and explain their faith to figures in authority, and many more were converted. In 272, Christians even asked a Roman emperor to arbitrate on an internal dispute: Paul of Samosata was convicted of heresy but refused to resign as Bishop of Antioch, so Emperor Aurelian ruled that he should step down. According to some estimates, by the year 300 around ten per cent of the empire's population was Christian, and it had become the dominant faith in some urban centres. In 301, the Kingdom of Armenia

---

The expansion of Christianity: third and fourth centuries

Between the years 150 and 250, a small sect developed into the Christian Church, a major institution in the sociocultural life of the empire. The evangelization of the East occurred earlier than it did in the West. When he was governor of Bithynia-Pontus in 112, Pliny wrote a letter to Emperor Trajan reporting on the rootedness of Christianity in the region with Christians of all ages and social status. Christian evangelism began in the Middle East, Asia Minor, Egypt and North Africa; by the end of the third century, the largest Christian communities were in these areas. The Church was especially strong in Greek cities like Corinth, Thessalonica and Philippi, and in the Anatolian cities of Nicomedia, Pergamum, Ephesus, Smyrna, Ancyra and Nicaea. In the West, Christians existed only in small minorities, mainly in urban centres, until the fourth century.

became the first nation in the world to adopt Christianity as its official religion.

Not everything, however, was going the Christians' way. Diocletian, who became emperor in 284, was a religious traditionalist who had purged the army of Christians and surrounded himself with fierce opponents of the Church, notably his co-emperor Galerius. The Little Peace came to an abrupt end in 303 when Diocletian launched a violent campaign against the Christians. The Great Persecution, as it became known, was the most severe ever inflicted by the Roman Empire against the Christian community, and many were killed, tortured, imprisoned or driven into hiding. Despite this, the majority of Christians avoided punishment, and the persecution failed in its main aim, which was to check the rise of the Church. Ordinary Romans were sympathetic to the sufferings of Christians and awed by the courage of the martyrs, and a few may had been inspired to convert. Thoughts of martyrdom certainly hardened the resolve of Christians during this period. As Tertullian, a Christian author from Carthage, said: 'the blood of martyrs was the seed of the Church'.

The persecution did, however, cause schisms within the community, with many churches split between those who had obeyed the order to perform sacrifices (*traditores*) and those who had remained 'pure'. Some of these schisms persisted for many decades. The Donatists of Africa, for example, began in 311 as a rebellion against a *traditore* bishop of Carthage. They argued that the clergy must remain pure for their prayers and sacraments to be valid. The Donatists were still a strong force a century later when they were condemned as heretical. The Melitians in Egypt left the Church there similarly divided.

The early Church in Ravenna

The city of Ravenna contains a number of significant early Christian churches and monuments, built in the fifth and sixth centuries, that reflect the historical, political and religious events of that period.

Ravenna was the seat of the Western Roman emperors from 402 until 476, when the last of the emperors, Romulus Augustulus, was deposed by Odoacer, who became king of Italy. Odoacer and his successors were Arian Christians, but they coexisted peacefully with the largely Orthodox Christian Italian population. The Arian Baptistery in Ravenna contains mosaics, including one of the baptism of Christ, reflecting the Arian belief in Christ as both human and divine. In 540, Ravenna was conquered by the Byzantine emperor Justinian, who opposed Arian Christianity. After Justinian had completed the conquest of Italy in 554, Ravenna became the seat of the Byzantine government there. The Basilica of San Vitale, built during this period, is one of the greatest examples of Byzantine architecture in Italy. Image: The Lunette of Christ as the Good Shepherd, Mausoleum of Galla Placidia, Ravenna (fifth century).

Turning point

The Great Persecution ended in 311 when Galerius issued an edict permitting Christians to practise their religion so long as they continued to support the state. The following year, Constantine won his famous victory at the Milvian Bridge under the sign of the *labarum*, a Christian symbol, and in 313 he and his co-emperor Licinius issued the Edict of Milan, legalizing Christianity throughout the empire. Constantine may or may not have been a Christian himself by this stage – the evidence is unclear – but he was extremely sympathetic to it. He had to proceed with caution, because most of the imperial court and the army was still pagan, and he continued to show respect to the old gods. Yet this was undoubtedly the turning point in the fortunes of Christianity. The emperor supported the Church with financial donations, he built basilicas, granted tax exemptions to the clergy, promoted Christians to senior positions and returned confiscated property. Constantinople, his new imperial capital on the Bosphorus, was an explicitly Christian city featuring churches and no pagan temples.

Under Constantine, the Church changed from a secretive, underground movement into an officially sanctioned religion within the empire. This alteration in status prompted a necessary reorganization. A formal church hierarchy was set up. At the top were the patriarchs. These were the bishops whose seat of authority, or 'see', was in one of the most important Christian cities. Originally these were Rome, Alexandria, Antioch and Jerusalem, because they were founded by one or more of Jesus's apostles. The patriarchs were regarded as the spiritual successors of their apostolic founders according to the doctrine of apostolic succession. From 381, Constantinople also became an apostolic see, ranked ahead of all the others except Rome. Below the patriarchs were the bishops, each of whom oversaw a diocese, which corresponded with the existing dioceses, or administrative divisions, of the empire. The most senior bishops, called metropolitans, were the bishops of the principal see of an ecclesiastical province, which was composed of several dioceses. Below the bishops were the priests, who oversaw parishes within each diocese, assisted by deacons.

Constantine established a template for Christian emperors of the future. He presided over the Council of Nicaea, acted as judge on Church disputes and supported the Church in every way he could. Constantine did not decide doctrine – that was the role of the bishops – but he considered it his duty to enforce orthodoxy, suppress heresy and uphold ecclesiastical unity. Constantine's decision to leave doctrinal matters to the bishops should have been heeded by his son Constantius II, ruler of the Eastern empire, who met great resistance in 359–360 when he tried to impose his creed of Semi-Arianism (part Nicene Creed, part Arianism) on the Church. In other respects, his reforms met with the Church's approval. In 341, he banned pagan State sacrifices, and in 356 he closed State temples in all cities under his control. The pagan State religion was effectively brought to an end in around 376, when Emperor Gratian renounced the title Pontifex Maximus, or chief high priest, which had been used by all Roman emperors since Augustus.

Before that, Christianity faced another moment of danger with the accession in 360 of the anti-Christian emperor Julian, known to Christians as Julian the Apostate. Julian was a devout pagan, but also a realist. He knew he could not destroy Christianity; neither did he want to. Julian's ambition was to restore the old State religion and to drive Christianity out of the governing classes of the empire. He wished to reinstate Rome's traditional religious eclecticism and tolerance, reopening pagan

THE DONATION OF CONSTANTINE
This fresco by Giulio Romano (1499–1546), in the Hall of Constantine in the Vatican, shows a kneeling Emperor Constantine I handing control of the city of Rome and the entire Western empire to Pope Sylvester I. This never actually happened, and is based on a forgery of an imperial decree, probably dating from the eighth century. It was later used by the papacy to support its claim of political authority.

THE FALL OF ROME

THE SARCOPHAGUS OF JUNIUS BASSUS

After the persecutions of the Christians ended, the art of the new faith came out of the catacombs and private houses to take centre stage in public places, including churches, cemeteries and cathedrals. The sarcophagus of Junius Bassus, prefect of Rome, who died in 359, is one of the most famous pieces of early Christian art. It demonstrates the triumph of the new religion in the heart of the empire, and how the tradition of the classical Roman sarcophagus coexisted at this time with Christian iconography. Carved from a single block of Carrara marble, it measures 234cm long by 142cm high (92 by 56in). Relief carvings cover three of its sides, allowing for its placement against a wall. Its principal face is divided into two rows, each of which features five scenes in high relief from the Old and the New Testaments (Vatican Museums, Rome).

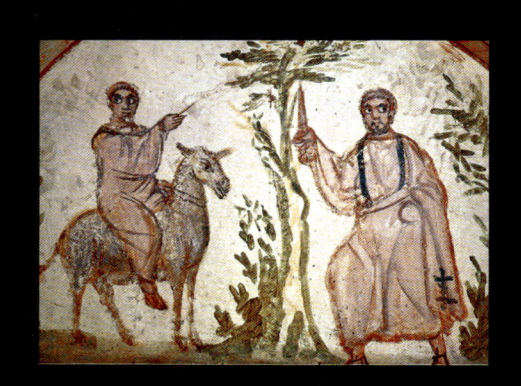

1 SACRIFICE OF ISAAC
Isaac, his hands tied, waits for death, as the angel sent by God stops the hand of Abraham.

2 ARREST OF PETER
Peter, with his hands tied, is escorted by two soldiers to the place where he will be crucified.

3 CHRIST ENTHRONED
With feet supported in the celestial vault, Christ appears between Peter and Paul.

4 ARREST OF JESUS
Jesus between two soldiers. As in the other scenes, he is represented as young and beardless.

5 THE DOUBTS OF PILATE
The procurator, in a curule chair, seems in doubt, while a servant brings him a basin of water to wash his hands.

EARLY CHRISTIAN ART

Sarcophagi from before the fourth century show scenes from Greco-Roman mythology, the life of the deceased, or both. Later sarcophagi feature biblical themes ornamented with flowers and animals and the *chi-rho* or *labarum* of Constantine.

THE CHRISTIANIZATION OF THE EMPIRE

6 JOB ON THE DUNGHILL
This relief illustrates the plight of Job when God removes all his material possessions as a test of faith.

7 ADAM AND EVE IN PARADISE
A representation of the episode in Genesis in which Adam and Eve eat the fruit of the forbidden tree.

8 JESUS IN JERUSALEM
This relief illustrates the episode in which Jesus makes his entrance into Jerusalem on the back of a donkey.

9 DANIEL AND THE LIONS
The prophet Daniel is thrown into a pit of lions and is saved from attack by his faith.

10 ARREST OF PAUL
Like Christ and Peter, Paul is regularly featured in early Christian art. Here he is guided to martyrdom by two soldiers.

THE FALL OF ROME

temples, recalling heretical bishops from exile and promoting Judaism.

Julian's anti-Christian reforms tended to target bishops and senior clergy, removing their privileges, while leaving ordinary worshippers alone. Julian did not reign for long, however. He died from a spear wound while campaigning in the East in 362, and his successors Jovian, Valentinian I and Valens quickly reversed his reforms and restored Christianity to its former status.

The final stages of Rome's Christianization occurred during the reigns of Gratian, Valentinian II and Theodosius I. Under the influence of Ambrose, Bishop of Milan, Gratian repressed pagan worship and prohibited the Arian creed of his late co-emperor Valens. Theodosius continued this work, breaking up pagan associations and removing non-Nicene Christians from the clergy. He abolished whatever remained of the old religion, turning its holidays into work days, closing temples, and banning the old rituals of blood sacrifices, haruspicy (a form of divination by examining the entrails of sacrificed animals) and augury.

In 380, Gratian, Valentinian II and Theodosius I jointly issued the Edict of Thessalonica, which required all subjects to profess the faith of the bishops of Rome and Alexandria. In other words, they made Nicene Christianity the state religion of the Roman Empire. In 381, Theodosius called the Council of Constantinople to further refine the Nicene creed. In 391, he formally forbade all pagan worship and declared all non-Nicene sects heretical and illegal.

Debates and heresies

As Christianity spread, it provoked much theological debate by Christian scholars. They discussed, for example, how Christianity could be reconciled with Hellenistic culture and what books should be contained in the Biblical canon. They wrote and argued about grace, free will and predestination. They also wrote 'apologias', using reason to refute the arguments of those who cast doubt on the truth of Christianity. The most renowned of these theologians became known as the Church Fathers. Early examples are Justin Martyr, Irenaeus, Tertullian, Clement of Alexandria and Origen. Church Fathers of the later fourth and fifth centuries included Augustine of Hippo, Cyril of Jerusalem, Ambrose of Milan, Jerome, John Chrysostom and Athanasius.

At the same time as these debates were happening, the leaders of the Church were concerned to establish orthodoxy, a set of authorized doctrines that everyone should adhere to. Councils of bishops met to agree on such matters and, where a consensus emerged, alternative beliefs were denounced as heresies. The most controversial aspects of doctrine, which produced the greatest number of heresies, were those concerning the nature of the Trinity (trinitarianism) and the nature of Christ (christology). The orthodox teaching on the Trinity, which was finally agreed upon at the Council of Constantinople in 381, was that God the Father, God the Son and the Holy Spirit are all one being in three hypostases. This then raised the christological question of how Jesus could be both divine and human, which was finally resolved by the ecumenical councils of 431 (Ephesus), 451 (Chalcedon) and 680 (Constantinople III).

Many Christians took a different view about the nature of Christ and the Trinity. There were, for example, the Adoptionists, who believed that Jesus was born a man and only became divine later, after he had been adopted as the Son of God. The Apollinarians believed that Jesus had a human body and a lower soul, but a divine mind. The Docetists believed that Jesus's physical body was an illusion, as was his physical death, and that he was in fact a spirit. The Pneumatomachians accepted that Jesus was divine, but said the Holy Spirit was not, being a creation of the Son and therefore a servant of the Father and the Son. The Nestorians believed that Jesus was both human and divine, and these parts were separate within him. Another group, the Monophytes, emerged in reaction to the Nestorians, believing that Jesus had a single nature and that his humanity was absorbed within his divinity.

ANTHONY THE GREAT
This Egyptian anchorite is regarded as the 'Father of all Monks'. Although not the first Christian ascetic, he was the first we know of to go into the wilderness to live as a hermit, which he did in about 270. Marble statue (1588) by Pietro Francavilla, San Marco Monastery, Florence.

SAINT PACHOMIUS (OPPOSITE)
This fourth-century Egyptian monk, founder of cenobitic monasticism, established monastic communities in the Egyptian desert. Mosaic from the Dochiariou Monastery on Mount Athos (16th century).

SCS PA CHOMI

THE FALL OF ROME

The Coptic Church

The Church of Alexandria was founded by St Mark in the first century. The new faith was extremely popular among the native Egyptians (known as Copts). Within half a century, the Church had become firmly established throughout the country, and the scriptures were translated into the local Coptic language. The Coptic Church takes the miaphysite position, believing that Christ's divinity and humanity are mystically united in one nature called the Incarnate Logos. In 451, Emperor Marcian convened the Council of Chalcedon, which ruled that Christ has two natures, which come together into one person and one hypostasis. This was rejected by Pope Dioscorus of Alexandria, resulting in a major schism. Pope Dioscorus was excommunicated, and a new imperial patriarch was appointed to Alexandria. Most of the Egyptian population rejected Chalcedon and remained loyal to their native Church, which became known as the Coptic Orthodox Church of Alexandria. It has remained independent ever since. Left: fourth-century bas-relief of the fish and the cross found in the Coptic necropolis of Ermant, Egypt (Louvre Museum, Paris). Right: Coptic Monastery of San Simeon, Aswan.

The most powerful of the fourth-century heresies, and the one that came closest to being adopted as orthodoxy, was Arianism. The Arians believed that Jesus was the Son of God who was begotten by God the Father at a point in time and was therefore distinct and subordinate to him.

There were many other heretical sects besides these, including the Donatists, who declared that the Church must be a church of saints, not sinners, and that martyrdom was a supreme Christian virtue. The Marcionists rejected the Hebrew Bible and, similar to the Gnostics, believed that the Hebrew God was inferior to the loving God of the New Testament. Debates on all these matters raged on through the fourth century, with emperors often becoming embroiled in the disputes and the Church seemingly ever more divided. The Church found it somewhat easier to act decisively against heresies once orthodoxy had been settled at the Council of Constantinople in 381. Even so, not all attempts at suppressing heresies were successful, and many ultimately died out of their own accord.

Monasticism

From the earliest period of Christianity, there are likely to have been monk-like hermits dedicating themselves to Christ by living an ascetic existence in remote areas. The first records of Christian anchorites date from the second century, beginning with Anthony the Great (251–356), who lived as a hermit in the Egyptian desert. He and others like him were known as the Desert Fathers. The first person to try creating a monastic community was St Macarius, who established several small groups of ascetics in the Egyptian desert in the early fourth century. However, these early worshippers continued to live their lives individually, rather than as a community.

St Pachomius is credited with creating the first cenobitic (communal) monastery on an island in the Nile in 323. Here the devout slept in individual huts, but worked, ate and worshipped together, their lives regulated by a set of religious rules. The head of the monastery came to be known as *abba* ('father' in Syriac), or abbot in English. Pachomius helped to organize other communities, and by the time of his death there are thought to have been 3000 of them in Egypt.

From here, monasticism spread throughout the Middle East and eventually to the Western Roman Empire. One of the first in the West to embrace monasticism was Martin of Tours, who established a hermitage near Milan and then later in Poitiers. After becoming Bishop of Tours in 372, he established a monastery at Marmoutiers, close to Tours. However, this was organized as a colony of hermits rather than as a community with shared spaces. John Cassian studied monastic practice in Egypt and Palestine before moving to Rome. In 410, he established two monasteries near Marseilles, one for men and one for women. He wrote a guide for monastic life that would prove to be very influential. In time, his monasteries would accommodate 5000 monks and nuns.

The transformation of Christianity into the official religion of Rome meant an end to the age of the martyr. For some, a new kind of dedication was required – a new way of expressing their faith. For them, monasticism became a kind of living martyrdom.

THE FALL OF ROME

The basilica, a model for Christian temples

The original Roman basilica had no religious function at all. It was a large public building in the middle of a Roman town, usually next to the main forum.

The Latin word *basilica* comes from the Greek *basilikè stoá*, meaning 'royal stoa' (walkway). Basilicas were used to hold court hearings and other official and public functions. They were the town halls of ancient Rome.

Before the fourth century, Christians were forced to worship in secret places such as caves and private houses. Following Galerius's Edict of Toleration in 311, Christians wished to construct large, purpose-built places of worship. Existing temples seemed unsuitable because of their pagan associations, and because their design, with a large outer area for performing open-air sacrifices, was not appropriate for the new religion. The basilica, however, did seem like a good model for a Christian temple. It was spacious enough inside to accommodate large congregations, and also a reassuringly familiar sight to citizens in every town in the empire.

CONSTANTINE THE GREAT

The first Roman emperor to convert to Christianity, Constantine lived most of his life as a pagan, but joined the Christian faith on his deathbed. Nevertheless, he supported and promoted Christianity throughout his reign, starting with the Edict of Milan in 313.

THE CHRISTIANIZATION OF THE EMPIRE

The model: the Roman basilica

The basilica was the standard design for public buildings repeated in towns across the Roman Empire, due to its versatility, functionality and spaciousness. Basilicas were built on the forum, the focus of civic, legal and commercial life in Roman towns. Above: the Basilica of Constantine in Trier; left: interior of the Christian basilica of St John Lateran in Rome.

There are several variations in the basic design of a basilica, but essentially it is a rectangular building with a central nave and an aisle on each side. The wall supporting the nave roof, called the clerestory, stands above the side aisle roofs and so can be pierced by windows. At one end of the building is the main entrance, while at the other end there is an apse. An apse is a semi-circular or polygonal recess with a domed or sloping roof. Many secular basilicas contained a raised platform at one end upon which a throne could be placed. When adapting the design for their uses, early Christians placed the altar on the platform from where the clergyman would officiate during a mass.

The first great Christian basilica to be built was St John Lateran in Rome, which Constantine I presented to the bishop of Rome in 313, at around the time that the emperor issued the Edict of Milan. The basilica was consecrated in 324. Constantine also built a basilica in Rome on the site that was believed to be the burial place of St Peter. Old St Peter's Basilica, as it came to be known, was built between 319 and 333. The Vatican Hill on the west bank of the Tiber was levelled to make room for the edifice. It had the typical structure of a large basilica, including a wide central nave and two narrower aisles on either side, each separated by 21 marble columns that had been taken from earlier pagan temples. The nave was more than 110m (360ft) long, and the basilica could hold between 3000 and 4000 worshippers at a time. The building was illuminated by eleven windows set into each clerestory wall. A small shrine was built at the place where Peter was supposedly buried. The apse was decorated with a mosaic of Constantine, accompanied by St Peter, presenting a model of the basilica to Jesus. On the clerestory walls were frescoes of the patriarchs, prophets

THE FALL OF ROME

Basilical architecture

The architectural structure of the Roman basilica was perfectly adapted to the liturgical needs of the Christian rite. The congregants in the nave faced towards the apse, where the altar was located and where the priest and other officiants stood.

The first Christian basilicas had a rectangular plan with the apse at one end. The nave was flanked by colonnades, which were structural supports for the building, but also a means of separating the nave from the aisles that ran alongside it. The columns carried either arches or entablature (architrave, frieze and cornice). Although the first churches followed the traditional rectangular Roman basilical plan, a new feature, the transept, was soon added. This was a lateral aisle crossing the nave just before the apse, thus creating the cross-shaped plan that became standard for Western European churches in the Middle Ages. The apse and the nave were connected by an arch called the triumphal arch. If there was a transept, another triumphal arch linked the transept to the nave. In front of the entrance, a large space called the narthex extended the width of the church. A colonnade typically divided the narthex from the nave and aisles.

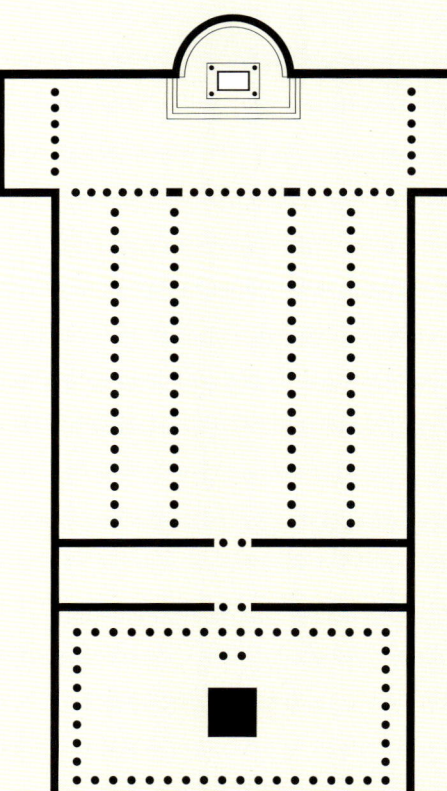

PALAEOCHRISTIAN BASILICA
These drawings show the plan and elevation of a typical early church. Right: Basilica di Santa Maria Maggiore, Rome.

THE CHRISTIANIZATION OF THE EMPIRE

The baptistery

Before the legalization of Christianity, Christians would receive baptism, the sacrament of Christian initiation, in rivers or natural springs, or secretly in the homes of the faithful.

From the time of Constantine, chapels called baptisteries began to be built exclusively for administering baptism. At first these were separate buildings, often large and richly decorated, constructed in the forecourts of basilicas. From the seventh century, they were placed inside churches, as a chapel; later still, they were reduced to the baptismal font alone, located near the church door. The original baptisteries typically had an octagonal plan, the number eight symbolizing 'a new beginning' in Christian numerology. The baptismal font was similarly octagonal, set beneath a domed ciborium or canopy. Byzantine baptisteries encircled the font with columns and an ambulatory. Baptistery roofs were customarily a dome, representing the celestial realm, towards which a Christian progresses after taking the first step of baptism. The most famous baptisteries are those of the Cathedral of Naples (considered the oldest in the West), the great fifth-century baptistery of the Archbasilica of St John Lateran (its octagonal plan is shown on the left), and the Ravenna Baptistery of Neon (above), from the end of the fifth century.

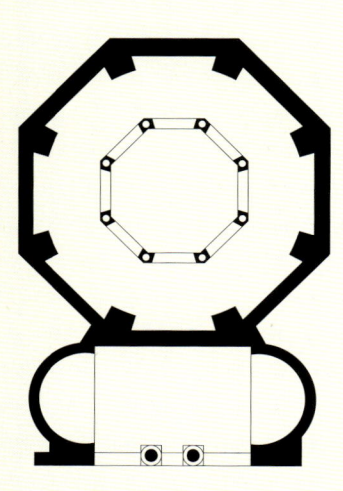

and apostles and scenes from the Old and New Testaments.

The basilica also had a transept – an area set crosswise to the nave – to form a cruciform (cross-shaped) building. Other basilicas with transepts would be built in the fourth century, although oddly their resemblance to the Christian cross did not appear to be realized initially. It was first pointed out in about 380, by the archbishop of Constantinople Gregory Nazianzen when describing the Church of the Holy Apostles in Constantinople.

Old St Peter's Basilica had a plain exterior and a gabled roof that rose more than 30m (98ft) at the centre. The apse was placed at the western end so that the church's façade could be approached from Rome, to the east. The altar featured twisted 'Solomonic' columns, which, according to legend, Constantine took from the Temple of Solomon. The basilica could be entered through any of five doors; these stood behind a large colonnaded atrium with fountains known as the 'Garden of Paradise'. Early basilicas were always preceded by enclosed forecourts surrounded by a colonnade or arcade, like a Greek stoa or a Roman peristyle. This feature would later evolve into the cloister, commonly attached to a church's or cathedral's warm, southern side.

Over the next two centuries, Christian basilicas were built across the Roman Empire, both East and West. There are fine examples of fifth- and sixth-century basilicas in Rome, Ravenna, Bethlehem and Thessalonica. The Basilica of Santa Sabina is the oldest surviving basilica in Rome. Built by Peter of Illyria between 422 and 432, it is located on the Aventine Hill, and still retains its original colonnaded rectangular plan.

THE CHRISTIANIZATION OF THE EMPIRE

ST PAUL'S OUTSIDE THE WALLS
Built by Constantine on the tomb of St Paul, this is one of the five oldest basilicas in Rome and the second biggest after St Peter's.

Architecturally, it represents the transition between the traditional secular Roman basilica and the churches of medieval Christendom. It is named for Sabina, a Roman matron who was beheaded because she had been converted to Christianity by her servant Seraphia, who was then stoned to death.

The interior retains some hints of an early pagan temple to Juno on the same site. (It was common, in antiquity, to build on sites already regarded as sacred.) The high-ceilinged nave contains 24 columns of Proconnesian marble with Corinthian bases and capitals that were reused from the earlier temple. There is also a hole in the floor exposing the base of another column from the earlier temple. In the apse there was a mosaic showing Christ seated on a hill flanked by a good thief and a bad thief while lambs drink from a stream below. This was replaced in 1559 by a fresco showing the same scene. The exterior of the basilica, with its large windows of selenite, is much the same as it was in the fifth century, apart from the bell tower, which was added in the tenth century. The wooden door at the entrance is believed to be the original one. Its panels feature relief carvings of scenes from the Bible.

Another of Rome's early basilicas is Santa Maria Maggiore, located on the Esquiline Hill. It was founded in 432, following the Council of Ephesus in 431 where the doctrine was upheld that the Virgin Mary was the mother of God. Pope Sixtus III built the basilica to commemorate this decision, and this is one of the first churches dedicated to Mary. The magnificent mosaics in the nave and on the triumphal arch show early portrayals of the Virgin. They depict scenes of her life and that of Christ, as well as Old Testament scenes, such as Moses striking a path through the Red Sea.

GOLD PATERA
This splendid embossed piece is part of the Pietroasele Treasure, created by Goths in the late fourth century (National Museum of History of Romania, Bucharest). Opposite: Seventh-century funerary relief of a Frankish warrior (Rheinisches Landesmuseum, Bonn).

THE GERMANIC KINGDOMS

The century and a half between the Visigothic sack of Rome and the Byzantine occupation of Italy witnessed the establishment of several Germanic kingdoms, which filled the political vacuum left by the collapse of the Western Roman Empire in 476. Franks, Goths, Vandals, Saxons and many others spread out across Western Europe and North Africa. From the realms they founded, carved out of former imperial territory, would emerge the powerful kingdoms of medieval Europe.

During the fourth century, many barbarian tribes began settling territory within the empire's frontiers. They became *foederati*, offered money in exchange for military service in the imperial army. As the Western empire grew weaker at the start of the fifth century, the barbarians pushed deeper into its territory. In 406–7, a great mass of Germanic tribes crossed the Rhine. The Franks, Alemanni and Burgundians established themselves in Gaul, while the Visigoths conquered southwestern Gaul and most of Spain. Meanwhile, Angles, Saxons and Jutes crossed to Britain, driving the Romano-British to the western extremities of the isles. In 429, the Vandals crossed to Africa; ten years later, they took Carthage, creating the first Germanic kingdom on imperial soil. And in 493 the Ostrogoths overthrew Odoacer and established their own kingdom in Italy.

By the end of the century, most barbarian peoples had adopted Roman customs, law codes

THE FALL OF ROME

The barbarian kingdoms

Year 406–7
Suevos, Alans and Vandals cross the Rhine and establish themselves in the Iberian Peninsula.

Year 411
Burgundians advance beyond the Rhine border and form the Burgundian kingdom in the Worms region.

Year 418
Theodoric I rules the Visigoth kingdom from Toulouse, Gaul, as a *foederati* of Rome.

Year 429
Genseric leads the Vandals across the straits and founds a Vandal kingdom that will last until 534, when it is destroyed by Byzantium.

Year 481
Clovis I founds the Merovingian dynasty and creates the kingdom of the Franks, centred on Tournai.

Year 493
Theoderic the Great, king of the Ostrogoths, kills Odoacer and founds an Ostrogothic kingdom in Italy.

Year 507
Battle of Vouillé. Victory for the Franks. Clovis expels the Visigoths from most of Gaul and consolidates his kingdom.

and institutions. They embraced Christianity, either Arian or orthodox, and began to turn away from their old languages and speak Latin. Many of them intermarried with Roman families and assumed imperial titles. Leaders such as Clovis the Frank and Theoderic the Ostrogoth established Roman-like kingdoms in their territories.

The Roman influence was at its strongest in southern Europe, where the empire had been in existence for longest. Here, medieval Romance languages emerged from a common Latin heritage. Romanization was reinforced by the brief Byzantine reconquest of North Africa, Italy and parts of Spain in the sixth century. By contrast, the legacy of Roman culture was felt more weakly in Britain and central Europe. Here, the barbarian tribes retained a great deal of their Germanic culture, including their arts and crafts, their oral tradition of epic poetry and the languages they spoke it in.

Kingdom of the Visigoths

Between the fifth and eighth centuries, the Visigoths created a kingdom across much of modern southwest France and the Iberian peninsula. After emerging as a tribe in the late fourth century, they made a devastating debut on the pages of history in 410 when their first king, Alaric, sacked Rome. Under Alaric's successor Ataulf (410–415), the Visigoths established themselves in southwestern Gaul, capturing the city of Toulouse in 413. Ataulf's marriage to Galla Placidia, half-sister of Emperor Honorius, helped seal an alliance with Rome, and the Visigoths became *foederati* of the empire, fighting against Vandals, Alans and Suebi in Iberia. Their nominal aim was to restore Roman order there, but they were really acting in their own interests. In 418, Honorius rewarded the Visigoths, now led by Wallia (415–418), with land in the Garonne Valley of Gallia Aquitania for them to settle and derive tax revenue from. Wallia established his court at Toulouse, which would remain the Visigoth capital for the rest of the fifth century. In 418, Wallia invaded Iberia, decimating the Siling Vandals and Alans.

The barbarian kingdoms – *foederati* of Rome

The empire divided barbarian tribes into two groups: the *dedititii* (surrendered) and the *foederati* (federated). The first kind had confronted Rome and been defeated; the second were at their service. Rome had been making military alliances with the barbarians since the time of the Republic. A *foederatus* was a tribe bound by treaty to provide a contingent of troops, which were integrated into the legions but differentiated from them. At first the Romans would pay the tribes a subsidy in the form of money or food. From the third century, they began offering them land to settle in exchange for military service. The Franks, for example, became *foederati* in 358 when they were offered part of northern Gaul. Image: Seventh-century Visigothic cross from Torredonjimeno (Museum Archaeological, Córdoba).

Under Theodoric (418–451), the Visigoths attempted to expand their Gallic lands, attacking Arles in 425 and 430 and Narbonne in 436, but they were driven back by Flavius Aetius. When the Huns invaded Gaul in 451, Theodoric allied himself with Aetius to oppose them. The Huns were successfully repelled, but Theodoric was killed in battle. In 455, Emperor Avitus authorized the Visigoths, now led by Theodoric II (453–466), to attack the Suebi in Iberia. The Visigoths defeated the Suebi in a battle by the river Orbigo near Astorga in October 456. They went on to sack the Suebian capital, Bracara Augusta (modern Braga), as well as several other Suebian cities, and took over the territories of Hispania Baetica (southern Iberia), Carthaginiensis (east and central) and southern Lusitania (southwest). Although held in the name of the Roman Empire, these were now effectively Visigothic lands. In 461, Emperor Libius Severus offered the Visigoths the city of Narbonne, which led to a revolt by Gallo-Romans under Aegidius. The Visigoths suffered a major defeat against Aegidius in 463, but his rebellion ended with his death in 465.

In 466, King Theodoric II was murdered by his younger brother Euric, who took his crown. Euric (466–484) defeated several other Visigothic chieftains to create the first unified Visigothic kingdom. He attacked the Suebi in Lusitania, bringing most of the region under Visigothic control, and conquered Hispania Tarraconensis (northeastern Iberia), the last bastion of Roman rule in the peninsula. Euric also expanded Visigothic territory in southern Gaul around the Loire and the Rhone rivers, and captured Arles and Marseille in Provence. In 475, Euric forced Emperor Julius Nepos to grant full independence to the new Visigothic Kingdom in exchange for the return of Provence. Following the fall of Romulus Augustulus, the last Roman emperor, Euric quickly recaptured Provence. By the time of Euric's death in 484, the Kingdom of the Visigoths encompassed Gallia Aquitania and Gallia Narbonensis (about a third of modern France), and almost the entire Iberian peninsula, with the exception of the Suebian kingdom of Gallaecia in the northwest.

Of all the barbarian tribes, the Visigoths were arguably the most Romanized, and Euric was one of their more learned rulers. He liked to surround himself at court with Gallo-Roman nobles, and he was the first of the Germanic kings to issue a formal law code, the Code of Euric (471).

The Visigothic Kingdom, which reached its height under Euric, began to struggle during the reign of his successor Alaric II (484–507).

BREVIARY OF ALARIC (OVERLEAF)
Illumination from a collection of Roman laws issued by Visigothic king Alaric II in 506. It applied not to the Visigoths, who lived under their own laws, but to his Gallo-Roman subjects.

THE FALL OF ROME

Code of Euric, the first Germanic law code

The Visigoth king Euric tried to strengthen the administration of his realm by developing a collection of laws, which he issued in around 476. The compilation was the work of his foremost adviser, a Roman jurist called Leo. The code enshrines in law the tribal customs of the Visigoths and reflects the social hierarchy of their society, with the king at the top, followed by a class of lords, freedmen and finally slaves. However, the code is notable also for acknowledging the rights of Euric's Roman subjects. It incorporates existing Roman statutes covering contracts of sale, loans, maritime trade, the use and trade of slaves, and the property rights of women. The palimpsest manuscript of the code is preserved in Paris. Of its 350 laws, only 47 are preserved. Image: page from the Code of Euric (National Library, Madrid).

In the 490s, the Visigoths came into conflict with the Franks under their king, Clovis I. Frankish pressure sent Visigoth refugees into Tarraconensis, sparking a rebellion there. In 507, the Franks and Burgundians defeated the Visigoths at the Battle of Vouillé near Poitiers, and Alaric was killed. Toulouse was sacked, and by 508 the Visigoths had lost most of their Gallic territories, with the exception of Septimania in the south.

Alaric II was succeeded by his illegitimate son Gesalec. His disastrous reign ended quickly when he was defeated by the Ostrogothic king of Italy Theoderic the Great. Theoderic placed his grandson (and the son of Alaric II) Amalaric (511–531) on the Visigoth throne. Amalaric was still a child and the kingdom was effectively ruled by Theudis, Theoderic's general. When Theoderic died in 526, Amalaric took control of his kingdom. Five years later, he was defeated by the Frankish king Childebert I, and then murdered. Theudis (531–548) took the Visigoth throne, despite being an Ostrogoth. He attempted to conquer Mauretania Tingitana in North Africa but was defeated by a Byzantine force. Theudis was murdered in 548, and Theudigisel briefly took power before being assassinated himself a year later. The next ruler, Agila I (549–554), faced numerous revolts, not least for his Arianism, which stirred a rebellion by Roman Catholics in southern Iberia. One of the rebels, Athnagild, defeated and deposed Agila in 554. During Athnagild's reign (554–567), the Byzantine emperor Justinian I invaded Iberia, seizing much of Hispania Baetica.

Kingdom of the Suebi

The Suebi were one of a number of Germanic tribes that crossed the frozen Rhine in 406–7. Their origins are mysterious; however, some scholars believe they may have been the same as the Quadi, a tribe originating in a region north of the middle Danube. By the summer of 409, the Suebi, along with Vandals and Alans, were pushing south towards Iberia, entering the peninsula that autumn. For the next two years, they plundered the cities and countryside, causing widespread famine. In 411, the

excorporediqi theodosianvs
noiollnrein theodo sio
  aug

THE FALL OF ROME

Battle of Vouillé: the end of Arianism in Gaul

This battle was fought between the Franks commanded by Clovis, and the Visigoths led by Alaric II. It took place in the spring of 507 on the plains of Vouillé (*Campus Vogladensis*), near Poitiers, in the far north of the Visigoth kingdom.

Clovis's Salian Franks were reinforced by a force of Ripuarian Franks under their king Chloderic, and also, according to Isidore of Seville, by the Burgundians. Alaric's Visigoths were assisted by a contingent of Roman troops. Theoderic the Great of the Ostrogoths had promised Alaric his support, but had been held up in Italy. Clovis stationed his archers at the rear and sent the rest of his army into the Visigoth ranks to fight hand to hand. During the battle, Clovis allegedly killed Alaric, whereupon the Visigoths broke and fled 'as was their custom' in Gregory of Tours' rather uncharitable words. The battle handed Clovis control of southwestern Gaul and left the Visigoths with just Septimania. Left: Visigothic gold coin with the image of Alaric II; right: *Alaric in the Battle of Vouillé*, oil painting by José Leonardo (1605–1656; Museum of the Army, Madrid).

barbarian groups agreed a division of the lands between them: the Siling Vandals took Hispania Baetica; the Alans settled Lusitania and Hispania Carthaginensis; and the Hasding Vandals and the Suebi shared Gallaecia in the northwest. The Suebi took the west of the province, by the Atlantic coast, and made Bracara Augusta their capital.

The Visigothic invasion of Iberia in 418 devastated the Siling Vandals and the Alans, leaving the Hasding Vandals and the Suebi as the dominant forces on the peninsula. In 419, a conflict arose between the two tribes. The Suebi under their king Hermeric (ca. 406–438), together with allied Roman imperial forces, defeated the Vandals at the Battle of the Nervasos Mountains. In 429, the Vandals departed for Africa, leaving the Suebians as the last barbarian tribe in Iberia. Hermeric spent the rest of his reign extending and consolidating Suebian rule over the whole province of Gallaecia. His son, King Rechila (438–448), managed to expand Suebian rule into Lusitania and then into parts of Baetica and Carthaginensis.

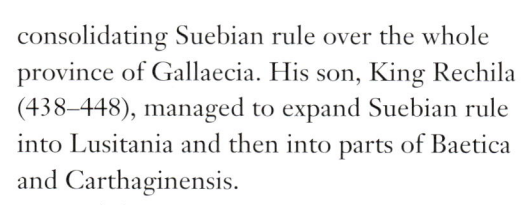

Rechila was succeeded by his son Rechiar (448–456), who was the first Roman Catholic among the Germanic kings. In 455, after Rechiar launched campaigns into Roman Carthaginensis and Tarraconensis, Emperor Avitus sent the Visigoths to attack the Suebians. The consequence was devastating for the Suebians, who were driven back into their Gallaecian heartland. Rechiar was killed, ending Hermeric's dynasty. The Suebians were plunged into a period of turmoil and schism during which a number of rulers briefly took power. In 464, a former ambassador called Remismund became king, managing to unite the various factions of the Suebi under his rule.

THE GERMANIC KINGDOMS

Gunderic was succeeded by his brother Genseric (428–477), who transported his entire people (some 80,000) to Africa in 429. He may have done this at the invitation of Bonifacius, the military ruler of Africa, who perhaps wished to use the Vandals' military strength as leverage in his struggle with the imperial government in Ravenna. If so, Bonifacius miscalculated. The Vandals rampaged across the North African coast, capturing Hippo Regius in 430 and making it their first capital. They defeated Bonifacius's army, then crushed the combined armies of the Eastern and Western empires. In 435, Genseric concluded a treaty with the Romans under which the Vandals became *foederati* of Rome in exchange for Vandal control of coastal Numidia and parts of Mauretania. In 439, Genseric broke the treaty and launched a surprise invasion of Africa Proconsularis, capturing Carthage. Genseric made Carthage the capital of his kingdom, which he set about turning into a major Mediterranean power, capturing the islands of Sicily, Sardinia, Corsica, Malta and the Balearics. The Vandals were Arian and soon came into conflict with their Trinitarian (Catholic and Donatist) subjects. Genseric exiled or killed Catholic bishops, and discriminated against Trinitarian lay people, excluding them from public office and frequently confiscating their property.

Under a new treaty with the Romans in 442, Vandal control of Proconsular Africa was confirmed; they also gained Byzacena and Tripolitania. This did not stop Genseric from regularly raiding the Mediterranean coasts of both Eastern and Western empires. In an effort to appease the Vandals, Emperor Valentinian III offered his daughter Eudocia's hand in marriage to Genseric's son Huneric. But ten years later, in 455, Petronius Maximus seized power, and cancelled the betrothal. An enraged Genseric launched an invasion of Italy. The Vandals captured Rome and carried away many valuables. Eudocia, and her mother Licinia Eudoxia, were taken to North Africa.

In 460, Emperor Majorian assembled a fleet at Carthaginiensis to attack Vandal Africa, but

In 466, Remismund and his people, who had been mostly pagan, were converted to Arianism by a Visigoth missionary called Ajax. They would remain so until their conversion to Catholicism in the 560s.

Kingdom of the Vandals

The Vandals first appeared in history in the second century BC when they migrated from southern Scandinavia to settle lands in Silesia. They were among the tribes that crossed the Rhine in 406–7 and headed south into Iberia in 409. The Vandals were composed of two main groups: the Hasdingi, who settled in Gallaecia, and the Silingi, who took over Baetica. After the devastating attack on Iberia by the Visigoths in 418, the remnants of the Siling Vandals and the Alans were forced to submit to the rule of the Hasding Vandal ruler Gunderic (407–428).

Suebi, Vandals and Alans in Spain

Year 406–407
Crossing the Rhine. Germanic Suebi and Vandals, along with Iranian-speaking nomadic Alans, cross the frozen river.

Year 409
Spain. In August and September they cross the Pyrenees into Spain at the Roncesvalles pass.

Years 410–415
Bagaudae. The Vascones, Cantabrians and Astures, displaced by the invaders, form bands of *bagaudae* (peasant insurgents) dedicated to looting.

Year 411
Foederati. The barbarians federate with Rome. The Suebi receive lands in Gallaecia; the Hasdingian Vandals in Gallaecia and Lusitania, and the Silingian Vandals in Baetica.

Year 422
Gunderic. The Vandals, under Gunderic's command, defeat the imperial army and plunder and occupy Baetica.

Years 438–449
Suebian Kingdom The Suebians expand as far south as the Valley of Guadiana and occupy Baetica and Lusitania.

411

Rise and fall of the Suebian kingdom of Gallaecia

By 430, the Suebians, based in Gallaecia, were the sole remaining barbarian power in Iberia. In the 440s, their king, Rechila, managed to bring the entire Peninsula under his control, save Tarraconensis. In 449, Rechila secured an alliance with the Visigoths by marrying the daughter of their king Theodoric. Four years later, Rechila's son and successor, Rechiar, signed a pact with the Romans and returned the province of Carthaginensis, which his father had occupied. But Rechiar repented this decision and in 456 he invaded Carthaginensis again, as well as Tarraconensis. This prompted the Romans to form an alliance with the Visigoths, who in 456 inflicted a crushing defeat on the Suebians. The Visigoths pursued Rechiar to the Suebian capital, Braga, which they sacked and then cut off the king's head. Rechiar's disastrous reign had brought the kingdom close to collapse and reduced it to its heartland in the northwest of the peninsula. Under Remismundo (464–469), the kingdom was converted to Arianism, and it would remain so until Theodemir (559–570) restored the Suebians to Catholicism. In 575, the Visigothic king Leovigild attacked the Suebians and made King Miro (570–583) his vassal. Five years later, Leovigild destroyed the Suebian kingdom and turned its territory into a new Visigothic province. Image: gold coin featuring the head of one of the Suebian kings of Gallaecia.

it was destroyed by traitors paid by the Vandals. Eight years later, the Western and Eastern empires coordinated another attempt to conquer Africa with a fleet commanded by Basiliscus. Contemporary sources allege the fleet consisted of 1113 ships carrying 100,000 men, though recent scholarship suggests a smaller force of 30,000 to 50,000 soldiers and sailors. At the Battle of Cap Bon, the Vandals, with 500 ships, destroyed the Western fleet and part of the Eastern through the use of fire ships. The Vandals then tried to invade the Peloponnese, but suffered a heavy defeat by the Maniots at Kenipolis. In retaliation, they seized 500 hostages at Zakynthos, chopped them up and threw the pieces overboard. After that, the Romans gave up their struggle against the Vandals, and in the 470s Genseric signed peace treaties with both Ravenna and Constantinople. When he died in 477, aged 88, he left the Vandals in full control of the western Mediterranean from Gibraltar to Tripolitana.

Genseric was succeeded by Huneric (477–484), who abandoned his father's aggressive foreign policy in order to focus on internal matters. Huneric began issuing the first Vandal coinage, although only in low denominations; high-denomination imperial coinage continued to circulate, demonstrating the continuing prestige of Rome, even after its empire's demise. Initially, Huneric eased the persecution of Trinitarians, but then in 483 he began issuing edicts against Catholics, removing bishops from office and banishing them to Corsica. A few were executed after refusing to become Arians. His successor, Gunthamund (484–496), made peace with the Catholics. Under him, Vandal power began to decline: they lost part of Sicily to the Ostrogoths and came under increasing pressure from Berbers to the south.

The fourth Vandal king was Thrasamund (496–523). He made an alliance with Theoderic the Ostrogoth, marrying his sister Amalfrida, and ended the persecution of Catholics, improving Vandal relations with the Byzantine Empire. Yet Vandal power continued to decline during this period, and they suffered two serious defeats by the Berbers, who sacked the port city of Leptis Magna in 523. Thrasamund was succeeded by Huneric's son Hilderic (523–530), who had Catholic sympathies, thanks to the influence of his mother Eudocia. He allowed a Catholic bishop to take office in Carthage, and many Vandals began to convert to Catholicism. In 530, Hilderic was overthrown by his cousin Gelimer, who restored Arianism as the official Vandal religion. This angered the Byzantine emperor Justinian, who sent an army under Belisarius in 533 with the intention of restoring Hilderic to the throne. Belisarius defeated Gelimer at the Battle of Ad Decimum, and took Carthage, but not in time to save Hilderic, who had already been executed. The Vandals were again defeated at Tricarmarum, and Belisarius took Hippo. In 534, Gelimer surrendered to the Byzantines, ending the kingdom of the Vandals.

Kingdom of the Ostrogoths

The Ostrogoths, the eastern branch of the Goths, were settled in Dacia when, during the late fourth century, they were conquered by the Huns. After the collapse of the Hunnic empire in 454, Emperor Marcian resettled the Ostrogoths in Pannonia, part of the Eastern empire, as *foederati*. By 488, they were becoming restless and increasingly difficult for Zeno, the Eastern emperor, to manage. Zeno was also having trouble with Odoacer, king of Italy, who was threatening Byzantine territory and not respecting the rights of Roman citizens in Italy. Therefore, Zeno promised Theoderic, ruler of the Ostrogoths, that he and his people could have the Italian peninsula if they could defeat and remove Odoacer.

Theoderic led his army to Italy in 488 and defeated Odoacer at Isonzo and Verona in 489, and at Adda in 490. In 493, he captured

GREAT BATHS OF MAKTAR
Located 96km (60 miles) from Le Kef, Tunis, Maktar was already important in the Carthaginian era, but it was Trajan who endowed it with its main monuments, including a triumphal arch and forum. The vast bathing complex contains a maze of rooms surrounded by walls more than 10m (33ft) high. Maktar was occupied by Vandals in 439 and formed part of their North African kingdom; in 533, it passed into the hands of the Byzantine Empire.

THE FALL OF ROME

BOETHIUS
A Roman senator, consul and philosopher of the early sixth century, Boethius entered public service under the Ostrogothic king Theoderic the Great. Theoderic later imprisoned and executed him in 524 on charges of treason. While in jail, Boethius wrote his magnum opus, Consolation of Philosophy, *a treatise on fortune, death and other matters, which became a popular and influential work during the Middle Ages. Ivory diptych of Boethius (Christian Civic Museum, Brescia).*

Odoacer's capital at Ravenna. On 25 February, the two leaders signed a treaty, agreeing to divide Italy between them. At a banquet on 15 March to celebrate the treaty, however, Theoderic made a toast, then drew his sword and killed Odoacer. There followed a widespread massacre of Odoacer's soldiers and supporters. Theoderic and his Goths were now masters of Italy.

Like Odoacer, Theoderic was nominally a viceroy, ruling Italy on behalf of the Eastern emperor. In reality, he was an independent ruler, although, unlike Odoacer, he maintained an outward show of subordination to Constantinople. Theoderic kept the Roman institutions of government, including the Senate. As viceroy, Theoderic could not pass laws himself, but this did not stop him issuing edicts. He staffed the civil administration with Romans, while ensuring the army remained dominated by Goths. Romans and Goths lived largely separate lives, with the Goths dwelling mainly in northern Italy. Roman citizens lived under the laws of the empire, and the Goths followed their own traditional laws. The two peoples were also divided by religion, the Goths being mainly Arian, and the Romans mostly Catholic. Unlike many Visigoth and Vandal rulers, Theoderic showed religious toleration towards his Catholic subjects, a policy he also extended to Jews. He styled himself 'King of the Goths and Romans', demonstrating his desire to be leader of both peoples.

In his foreign policy, Theoderic aspired to a dominant position among the fraternity of barbarian kingdoms, as a counterbalance to the Eastern empire. His main tool for achieving this was the marriage alliance: he married his daughters to the Visigothic king Alaric II and the Burgundian prince Sigismund, and his sister Amalfrida to the Vandal king Thrasamund, while he himself married Audofleda, sister of the Frankish king Clovis I. Marriage bonds were not always enough to maintain peace, however. Theoderic was drawn into a war against Clovis in 508, after he had attacked the Visigoths. In the course of this campaign, the Ostrogoths helped save Septimania for the Visigoths, as well as annexing Provence at the expense of the Burgundians. He was able to extend his influence over the Visigothic kingdom by placing the infant Amalaric (son of his daughter and Alaric II) on the throne, with his general Theudis acting as regent.

Theoderic's relations with Constantinople were often fractious, especially in 504–5, when the Ostrogoths captured Pannonia, and in 508, when Emperor Anastasius sent a fleet to raid the coast of Apulia. It didn't help that Clovis portrayed himself as champion of the Catholic Church against the 'heretical' Arian Goths.

Theoderic died in 526 and was succeeded by his 10-year-old grandson Athalaric, whose mother Amalasuntha became regent. With Theoderic gone, the network of alliances he had built up soon broke down. Amalaric asserted his autonomy over the Visigoths, relations with the Vandals declined, and the

Franks became more expansionist in Gaul. Amalasuntha sought support from the Senate in Rome and the newly crowned Eastern emperor Justinian I. Her pro-Roman stance alienated the Gothic nobles, already uneasy about being ruled by a woman. They forced her to sack Athalaric's Roman tutors, insisting he be raised as a warrior. Instead, Athalaric opted for a life of debauchery and excess that would kill him prematurely in October 534. Amalasuntha became queen, but she lived in constant fear of being usurped by a discontented noble. She attempted to strengthen her position by making her cousin, the Gothic nobleman Theodahad, her co-ruler. However, Theodahad imprisoned Amalasuntha on an island in a Tuscan lake, and in May 535 she was murdered.

When Justinian I heard about this, he was outraged and sent an army to reclaim Italy for the empire. The Gothic War between the Byzantine Empire and the Ostrogothic Kingdom lasted from 535 until 554. Although the Byzantines took Ravenna and deposed the Ostrogothic king Witiges in 540, the Goths rallied around a new ruler, Totila, and by 543 had almost managed to retake Italy. It took the Byzantine general Narses a further 11 years to subdue them. The war left Italy devastated and considerably depopulated. Consequently, the Byzantine rulers were unable to resist an invasion by the Lombards in 568, who captured large parts of the Italian peninsula.

Kingdom of the Franks

The Franks emerged in the third century as a group of small Germanic tribes united by a common language and culture. They lived on the lower Rhine, and were one of the many peoples pressing at the borders of the Roman Empire. In 358, one Frankish tribe, the Salians,

VANDAL RIDER
This fifth-century Roman mosaic from Carthage shows a mounted Vandal in the midst of battle near a castle (British Museum, London).

LAMB OF GOD (OVERLEAF)
In this mosaic from the Basilica of San Vitale in Ravenna, the Lamb of God appears in a field of stars, surrounded by a crown of leaves and fruits supported by the four archangels.

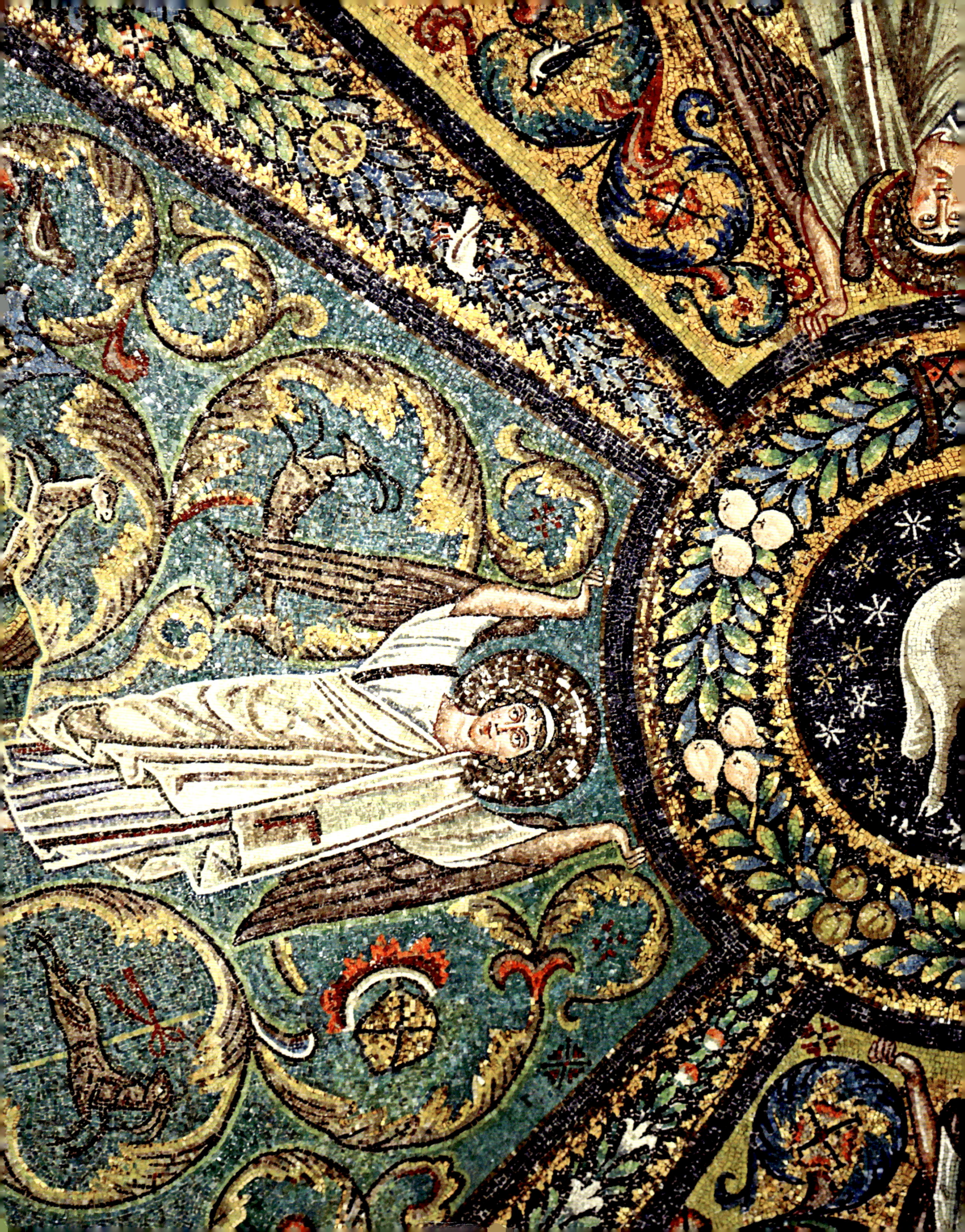

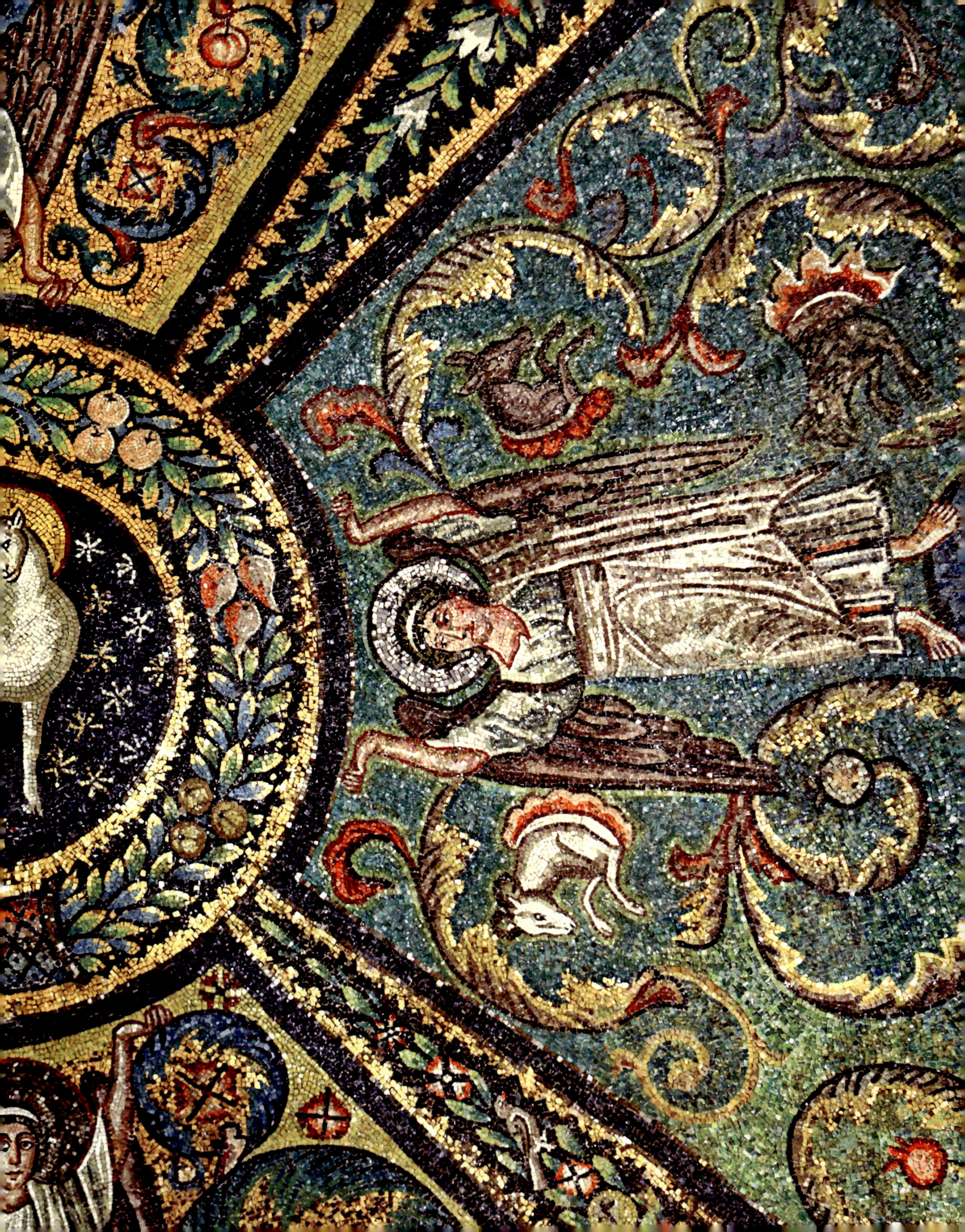

Rise of the Merovingian kings

Years 448–457
Merovech. Founder of the Merovingian dynasty of the Salian Franks.

Years 457–481
Childeric I. Merovech's son and Frankish king in northern part of Roman Gaul.

Years 481–491
Clovis I. First king of the Franks to unite all the Frankish tribes under one ruler.

Years 496–507
Conversion of Clovis to Roman Catholicism. Clovis's victory over the Visigoths at Vouillé brought Aquitania under Frankish rule.

Year 511
Death of Clovis. The kingdom is divided between his four sons, Theuderic, Childebert, Chlodomer and Chlotar.

Year 558
Chlothar I. The king of Neustria reunifies the Kingdom of the Franks.

Year 561
Chilperic I. Inherits the throne of the Franks from his father Chlothar.

Year 558
Dagobert I. After years of division, he reunites the Franks under his rule. The last Merovingian to wield real power.

Year 561
Childeric III. Last of the Merovingian kings, deposed by Pepin the Short, father of Charlemagne, who founded the Carolingian dynasty.

---

was given permission to settle in Gaul between the Meuse and Scheldt rivers (part of modern Belgium). They became *foederati*, with their soldiers serving as auxiliaries in the Roman army. Following the mass crossing of the Rhine by barbarian tribes in 406–7, the Franks took advantage of the collapse of Roman authority to consolidate and expand their territory, seizing lands to the west of the middle Rhine and edging into northeastern Gaul. By 480, the Franks had solidified their hold over the Gallic provinces of Germania and Belgica. The Gallo-Roman minority here became subsumed within the Frankish population, and Latin gradually ceased to be spoken.

In 481, Childeric, ruler of one of the Frankish groups, was succeeded by Clovis I, who united the Franks under his authority. Clovis converted to Roman Catholicism and encouraged the mass adoption of Nicene Christianity by the Franks, which further helped to unite them as a people. By distinguishing himself in this way from the Arian Visigoths, Clovis was able to win the support of the Gallo-Roman population in Gaul, the orthodox clergy and the Byzantine emperor in Constantinople. He led the Franks on a series of military campaigns, conquering the Roman rump state of Soissons, the Bretons and the Alemanni, and by 496 he had brought all of northern Gaul under his rule. Having established a united Frankish kingdom in the north, Clovis advanced southwards in 507 and defeated the Visigoths, conquering most of their Gallic territories. By the end of his 30-year reign, Clovis ruled all of Gaul save Visigothic Septimania in the southwest and the Burgundian kingdom in the southeast.

Clovis founded a dynasty of rulers, the Merovingians (named for his grandfather Merovich). When he died in 511, his kingdom was, according to Frankish custom, divided between his four adult sons: Theuderic I ruled from his capital at Reims; Chlodomer from Orléans; Childebert I from Paris; and Chlothar I from Soissons. During their reigns, Frankish territory continued to expand, with their conquests of the Thuringii (532), the Burgundians (534) and the Saxons and Frisians (ca. 560). The four kings were frequently in conflict with each other. When Chlodomer died in 524, Chlothar had his young sons murdered so he could take a share of his kingdom, which was, as custom dictated, divided between the surviving brothers. Theuderic died in 534, and his son Theudebert had to fight his uncles Childebert and Chlothar to defend his inheritance, which was the largest of the Frankish subkingdoms.

Theudebert was the first Frankish king to mint gold coins with his own image on them, rather than that of the Byzantine emperor, thus formally ending any pretence of fealty to Constantinople. Theudebert died in 548, followed by Childebert in 558, enabling Chlothar to reunite the entire Frankish realm under a single ruler. The Merovingian dynasty would continue to rule over the Frankish

---

The rise of the kingdom of Clovis the Frank

The expansion of the Frankish kingdom was not only due to Clovis's military expertise, but also to his skill as a diplomat. He secured important alliances through the marriage of his relatives, and his conversion to Catholicism won him the loyalty of the Gallo-Roman nobility. Clovis acceded to the throne aged 15 and, as was the custom among the Franks, wished to enlarge his kingdom in order to distribute it between his children. Clovis inherited a relatively small realm in northern Gaul. By the time he died, his kingdom reached from the English Channel to the Pyrenees, and beyond the Rhine as far as the Alps. Image: front of a ninth-century Carolingian ivory chest showing the baptism of Clovis (Musée de la Picardie, Amiens).

Kingdom of the Burgundians

The Burgundians were a tribe of Scandinavian origin that by the late third century had settled on the east bank of the Rhine, and they were part of the mass invasion of Gaul in 406–7. In 411 their king, Gunther, along with the Alan king Goar, proclaimed the usurper Jovinus emperor. With Jovinus's authorization, Gunther settled his people on the western bank of the Rhine between the Lauter and Nahe rivers, capturing the cities of Borbetomagus (which Gunther made his capital), Speyer and Strasbourg. After Jovinus was killed, Emperor Honorius officially granted this territory to the Burgundians as *foederati* of the empire. Despite their new status, the Burgundians continued to launch raids into Gallia Belgica. In 437, Roman general Flavius Aetius retaliated by calling in an army of Hun mercenaries, who devastated the Burgundian kingdom. According to reports, the majority of Burgundians were massacred, including Gunther.

In 443, the survivors, now led by Gunderic, were resettled by Aetius in the Roman province of Maxima Sequanorum in the Sapaudia (Savoy) region of southeastern Gaul, and they established their new capital at Lugdunum (modern Lyon). Again they were made *foederati*, and in 451 Gunderic fought alongside Aetius against Attila the Hun. When Gunderic died in 473, his kingdom was divided between his sons, Gundobad, Chilperic II, Gundomar and Godegisel. Gundobad, who ruled from Lugdunum, was the most powerful and ruthless of the four, and soon set about murdering his brothers – a task he had completed by 500, leaving him as sole ruler of the Burgundians.

THE FALL OF ROME

THE ART OF THE BARBARIANS

The Germanic tribes that invaded the Western empire during its decline were not a homogenous group, but they shared some common cultural features. They had no tradition of monumental art, architecture or large sculpture, prefering 'mobile' art for personal display, usually combined with a practical function, such as weapons, tools, clothing fasteners and horse harnesses. Although human figures were mostly absent from barbarian art, many featured geometric lines and shapes, fierce and beautiful animals and pagan symbols. In the second century, Goths of southern Russia, influenced by Scythian and Sarmatian art, began creating gold objects inlaid with precious stones, as well as polychrome (multicoloured) objects such as swords and belt buckles. They took this style with them on their migrations to Italy, Spain and southern Gaul.

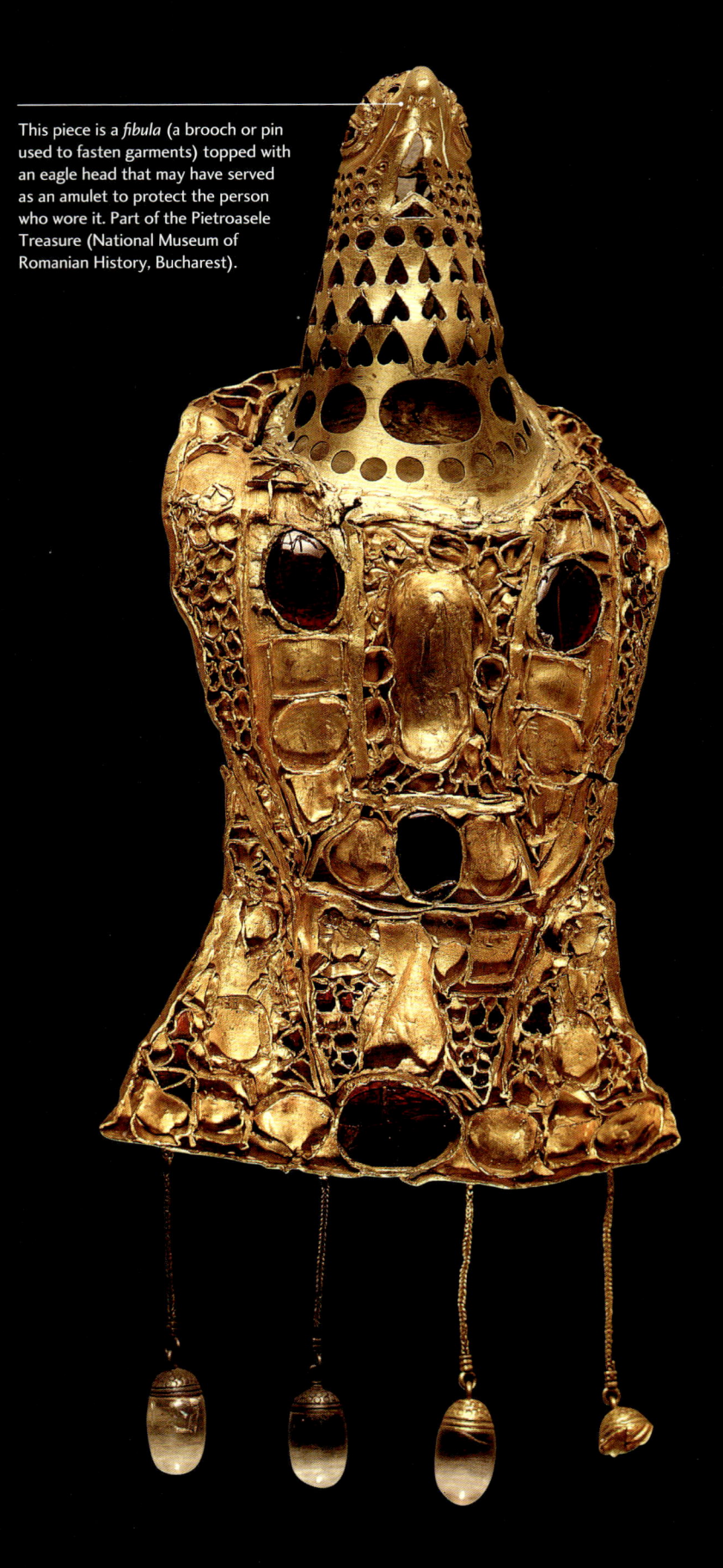

This piece is a *fibula* (a brooch or pin used to fasten garments) topped with an eagle head that may have served as an amulet to protect the person who wore it. Part of the Pietroasele Treasure (National Museum of Romanian History, Bucharest).

WARRIOR'S NECKLACE
A fourth-century Scandinavian gorget made of braided gold fibre (Statens Historiska Museet, Stockholm).

THE GERMANIC KINGDOMS

This gold *fibula* inlaid with semiprecious stones is part of the Pietroasele Treasure, a horde of late fourth-century Gothic treasure, including some 22 gold objects, discovered in 1837 near the Romanian village of Pietroasele (National Museum of Romanian History, Bucharest).

CLOISONNÉ, AN ANCIENT ART

Goths often decorated their metal objects using an ancient technique called *cloisonné*. First they added compartments (*cloisons* in French) to the metal object by soldering silver or gold wires to its surface. These compartments were then filled with precious or semiprecious stones, enamel or small tesserae of iridescent glass shaped to fit the space. Barbarian artists of the migration era often used red garnets, glass or enamel with gold wire in small, thick-walled cloisons. This *cloisonné* gold *fibula* in the shape of an eagle dates to the late fifth century. It came from a grave attributed to a Gothic king called Omharus in the Apahida necropolis, uncovered in Romania in 1968 (National Museum of Romanian History, Bucharest).

THE FALL OF ROME

PEVENSEY CASTLE
This castle, built in the 11th century following the Norman conquest of England, was constructed over the remains of the third-century Roman fortress of Anderida, erected in East Sussex against incursions of Angles and Saxons.

One of the brothers, Chilperic II, had a daughter called Clotilde, who was married to the Frankish king Clovis. After killing her father, Gundobad exiled her. Clotilde would have her revenge in 523 when she sent her sons, the Frankish kings, to attack the Burgundians. The Franks smashed the Burgundians at the Battle of Autun in 532, and the Burgundian king, Godomar, was killed. Two years later, the Burgundian kingdom was swallowed up into the Frankish realm, and the Burgundians then disappeared from history.

Anglo-Saxon kingdoms

The formation of the Anglo-Saxon kingdoms in Britain during the fifth and sixth centuries is shrouded in myth and mystery. What little we know has been pieced together from the very few contemporary accounts, together with archaeological evidence. From the fourth century, Germanic peoples began migrating to Britain. Most of them were Angles, Saxons and Jutes. Many were used as *foederati* to swell the ranks of the Roman army. The Angles came from 'Anglia', believed to be the province of Schleswig-Holstein on the Danish-German border; the Saxons were from Old Saxony in northern Germany, and the Jutes were most probably from the Jutland Peninsula. These migrant peoples would later come to be referred to collectively as Anglo-Saxons.

Following the departure of the Roman army from Britain in around 410, Anglo-Saxon migration increased. There are various theories about the nature of this migration. Traditional histories claim that there was a mass invasion of Anglo-Saxons, driving the Romano-British off their lands and into the extreme western parts of the islands. Most modern historians believe the process was more gradual and largely characterized by coexistence.

According to tradition, it all began when two Germanic warlords called Hengist and Horsa arrived in England with their forces at the invitation of a British king called Vortigern, who needed help defending his country against Pictish and Scottish raiders. Later, Hengist and Horsa turned on Vortigern and seized his kingdom. Certainly there seems to have been a large influx of Anglo-Saxons from around 430 – estimates range from between 20,000 and 100,000 arriving in Britain during this period. Contemporary chronicles suggest that the migrants revolted some time during the 440s and began a campaign of conquest and devastation that spread as far as the western sea. Archaeological evidence indicates that the Anglo-Saxons were established in southern and eastern Britain by 500. By this time the kingdom of Kent had been founded by Jutes, and the kingdom of Sussex by South Saxons, as were several permanent settlements in East Anglia.

It is possible that they had advanced further inland than this: Gildas, a contemporary chronicler, writes that the British, led by a man called Ambrosius Aurelianus, fought back against the Anglo-Saxons, and the conflict

Saint Patrick, Christian missionary and 'apostle of Ireland'

St Patrick is regarded as the founder of Christianity in Ireland. The dates of his birth and death are uncertain, but he was active as a missionary in the second half of the fifth century. Patrick was born in Roman Britain, the son of a deacon, although Patrick was not a believer at that stage. At the age of 16, he was captured by pirates who took him to Ireland, where he was held as a slave for six years. During this period, he converted to Christianity. Later, he was ordained as a priest in Europe, before returning to pagan Ireland as a missionary. He travelled around the country baptizing thousands of people, both the poor and the wealthy, and ordaining priests to lead the newly established Christian communities. Image: reliquary of Saint Patrick in Romanesque style, 11th century (National Museum of Ireland, Dublin).

culminated in about the year 500 with a major British victory at the Battle of Mount Bladen (the site of which has yet to be identified). This seems to have stemmed the Anglo-Saxon advance for a time, with the invaders driven back to the southeastern coastlands. In about 520, the West Saxons, led by Cerdic, founded the kingdom of Wessex in Hampshire. The kingdom of Bernicia was established in about 547. Of the other kingdoms founded in the sixth century – Essex, East Anglia, Mercia, Linsey and Deira – dates of origin are unknown. Chronicles report another major campaign against the Britons in 577, led by Cealin, king of Wessex, who succeeded in capturing Cirencester, Gloucester and Bath. But then internecine fighting halted the Saxon advance. Cealin was replaced by Ceol, possibly his nephew, and Cirencester was captured by another Anglo-Saxon kingdom, Mercia.

Christianity had been introduced to Britain during the Roman occupation, but it is not clear how many Britons were Christian when the pagan Anglo-Saxons arrived. In 597, Pope Gregory sent Augustine to convert the Anglo-Saxons. King Æthelbert of Kent gave Augustine land to build a church, and Augustine founded his see at Canterbury, where he baptized Æthelbert in 601. Missionaries from Christian Ireland helped convert the north and east of England, while Sussex and the Isle of Wight were converted by St Wilfrid in the 680s.

By the early 600s, a new order had emerged in Britain dominated by seven major Anglo-Saxon kingdoms, known as the Heptarchy: East Anglia, Mercia, Northumbria (with its sub-kingdoms, Bernicia and Deira), Wessex, Essex, Kent and Sussex. The Heptarchy would ultimately unite in the tenth century into a centralized kingdom called England.

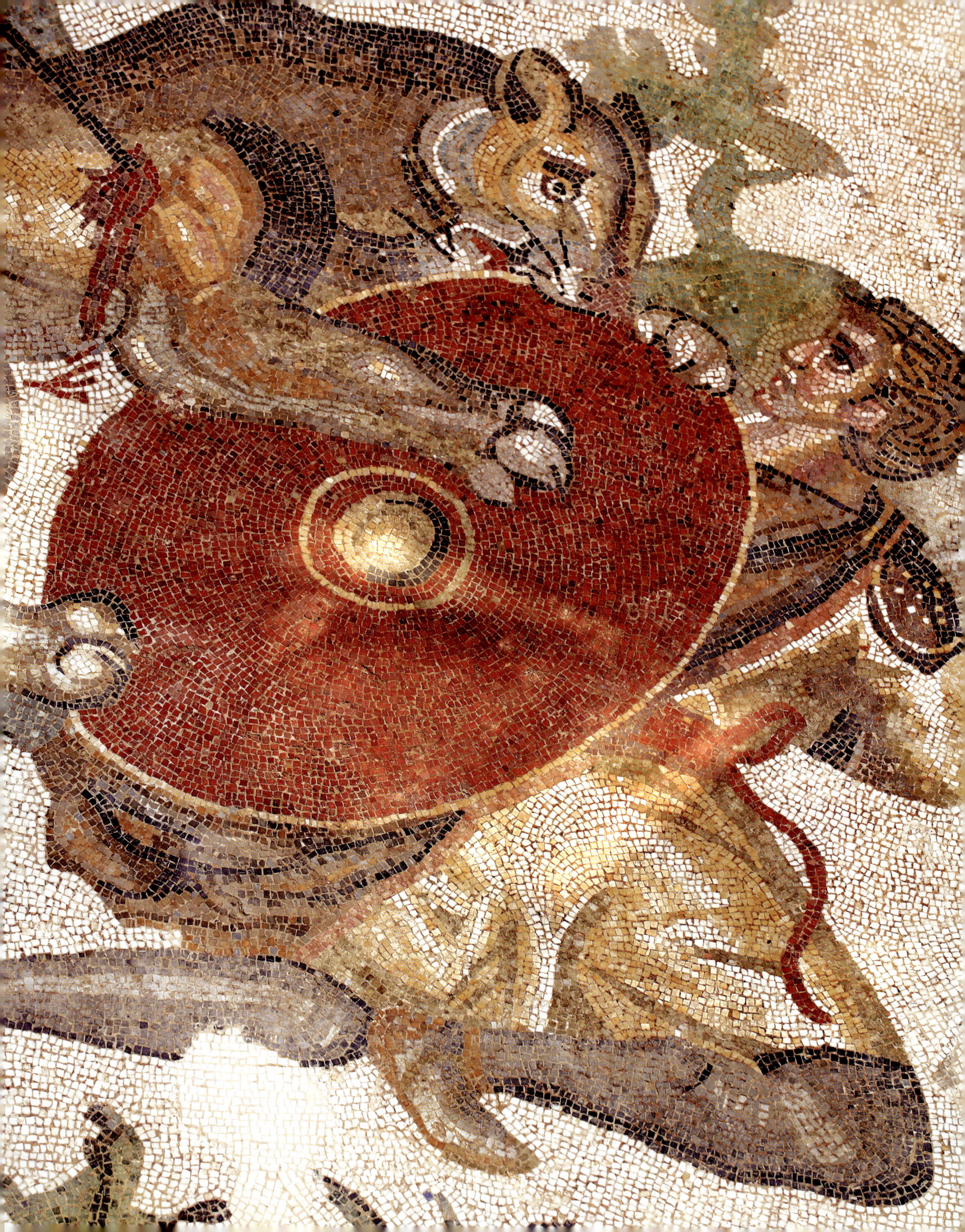

Appendices

Comparative Chronologies:

Rome, kingdoms and empires in the East, states and border territories in the West   426–429

Genealogy of the Julio-Claudian Dynasty   432

Genealogy of the Flavian Dynasty   434

Genealogy of the Antonine Dynasty   435

List of Dynasties   436–437

LEFT:
A wounded lioness pounces on a soldier in a fourth-century mosiac from the Villa del Casale, located in the Sicilian town of Piazza Armerina, Sicily.

Comparative Chronology

ROME

44–27 BC	27 BC–14 AD	14–41
• Gaius Octavius Thurinus, known as Octavian, Julius Caesar's adopted son and heir • Second Triumvirate: Mark Antony, Octavian and Marcus Aemilius Lepidus • Persecution of Julius Caesar's supporters and struggle for power between Mark Antony and Octavian • Creation of a Hellenistic-oriental kingdom by Mark Antony and Cleopatra • Agrippa's victory over Cleopatra's fleet at Actium **CULTURAL FACTS** • Virgil writes the *Eclogues* (Bucolics) and the *Georgics*	• The Senate grants the title of Augustus to Octavian • Reinstatement of the Republic • Augustus receives *Tribunicia potestas* (tribunician power) and *imperium proconsulare maius* • Peace in the empire **CULTURAL FACTS** • *Ara Pacis*, an altar in Rome dedicated to Pax, the Roman goddess of Peace • Poetry by Horace and Ovid. • Virgil's *Aeneid*	• Principate of Tiberius • Death of Germanicus in Syria and trial of Gnaeus Calpurnius Piso • Power in the hands of Lucius Aelius Sejanus, Praetorian prefect • Expansion of the law of treason (*lex maiestatis*) • Transformation of the Principate into a theocratic monarchy by Caligula **CULTURAL FACTS** • Construction of the Domus Tiberiana on the Palatine

KINGDOMS AND EMPIRES IN THE EAST

44–27 BC	27 BC–14 AD
Parthia: • Invasion of Syria, Cilicia and Caria Armenia: • Armenia, goal of Romans and Parthians Judaea: • Pacorus I, Parthian prince, declares war against Judaea • Herod the Great, king of Judaea **CULTURAL FACTS** • Caesarea Maritima founded • Expansion of the Temple of Jerusalem	Parthia: • Conquest of Gandhara (Indus Valley) • Artabanes III fights Rome for the control of Armenia Judaea: • Kingdom divided between Herod Archelaus and Herod Antipas, sons of Herod the Great Kingdom of the Nabataeans: • War of King Aretas against Herod • Antipas, king of Judaea **CULTURAL FACTS** • Tombs and temples of Petra

STATES AND BORDER TERRITORIES IN THE WEST

44–27 BC	27 BC–14 AD	14–41
Mauretania: • Bogud and Bocchus II reign in Mauretania • Rebellion in Tingis • Bocchus II leaves the kingdom of Mauretania in his inheritance to Octavian Numidia: • Marriage of Juba II and Cleopatra Selene II, daughter of Mark Antony and Cleopatra	Germania: • Marcomanni – a confederation of Germanic and Celtic tribes • Rome is defeated at Teutoburg Forest by Arminius, chieftain of the Germanic Cherusci tribe Dalmatia: • Bato I, leader of the Illyrians, rebels against Rome Illyria: • The Scordisci invade Macedonia	Germania: • Maroboduus is defeated by Arminius, chieftain of the Cherusci tribe • Germanicus pillages the land of the Chatti Pannonia: • Drusus, son of Tiberius, organizes the province Mauretania: • Tacfarinas begins an uprising in North Africa against Ptolemy's government • Caligula murders Ptolemy in Rome, the last sovereign of Mauretania

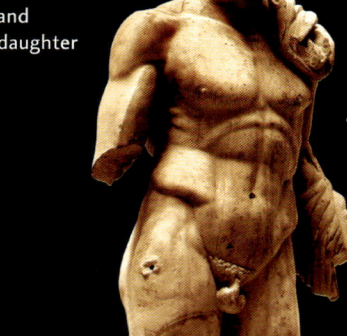

41–54

- Claudius acclaimed as emperor by the Praetorian Guard
- Mauretania divided into Mauretania Caesariensis and Mauretania Tingitana
- Conquest of southern Britannia
- Attempted coup d'etat by Claudius's wife Messalina and Senator Gaius Silius

CULTURAL FACTS
- Construction of the Port of Claudius in Ostia

54–68

- Nero, son of Agrippina the Lesser, ascends the throne
- Tax reform and suppression of indirect taxes
- Resumption of trials for treason (*lex maiestatis*)
- Gaius Calpurnius Piso leads a conspiracy against Nero

CULTURAL FACTS
- Construction of Nero's palace Domus Aurea
- Poetry of Seneca the Younger and Lucan

68–69

- Rebellion of Gaius Julius Vindex, governor of Gallia Lugdunensis
- Insubordination of Servius Sulpicius Galba, governor of Hispania Tarraconensis, and the prefect of the Praetorian Guard, Gaius Nymphidius Sabinus
- Treason of prefects of the Praetorian Guard, Gaius Ophonius Tigellinus and Gaius Nymphidius Sabinus
- Vitellius proclaimed emperor
- Battle of Bedriacum

CULTURAL FACTS
- Capitol destroyed by fire

14–41

Kingdom of the Nabataeans:
- The Nabataean kingdom reaches its greatest splendour under Aretas IV

Armenia
- The Arsacid dynasty of Parthia controls Armenia. Reign of Arsaces I

China:
- Wang Mang, of the Xin Dynasty, tries to end slavery and to impose a revolutionary land redistribution system

CULTURAL FACTS
- Construction of the Temple of Bel, Palmyra

41–54

Parthia:
- Vologases I conquers Armenia for his brother Tiridates

Judaea:
- Herod Agrippa appointed king of Judaea by Claudius

Egypt:
- Jewish revolt in Alexandria

China:
- Liu Xiu (Guang Wu Di), first emperor of the Han Oriental dynasty

54–69

Judaea:
- First Jewish war
- **Vespasian** appointed to suppress the Jewish revolt
- Flavius Josephus, governor of Galilee

Kingdom of the Nabataeans:
- loss of Damascus

Armenia:
- Tigranes VI proclaimed ruler of Armenia after the victory of Gnaeus Domitius Corbulo

---

41–54

- Vannius, of the Germanic tribe the Quadi, rules over the Marcomanni
- Kingdom of the Suebi distributed among the nephews of Vannius, loyal to Rome

Britannia:
- Caligula plans a campaign against the Britons
- Battles of the Medway and Thames. Defeat of the Catuvellauni by the troops of Aulus Plautius
- Guerrilla war of Caratacus, chieftain of the Catuvellauni, against Publius Ostorius Scapula

54–69

- Fight of the Hermunduri against the Chatti, next to the source of the Saale River

Britannia:
- Rebellion of Venutius against Cartimandua, queen of the Brigantes and ally of Rome
- Boudica, queen of the Iceni, revolts with the support of the Trinovantes and Catuvellauni

CULTURAL FACTS
- Canal between the Rhine and Meuse rivers (Fossa Corbulonis)
- Corinth Canal dug across the Isthmus

Comparative Chronology

ROME

69–81
- End of the civil war. Vespasian declared emperor
- *Lex de Imperio Vespasiani* (law regulating Vespasian's authority) establishes the powers of the emperor
- The provinces of Hispania receive the Latin right
- Eruption of Mount Vesuvius buries several settlements, including Pompeii

CULTURAL FACTS
- Construction of the Colosseum (Flavian amphitheatre) in Rome
- Death of Pliny the Elder during the eruption of Vesuvius

81–96
- Domitian's rise to power
- Deterioration in relations between the Senate and the emperor
- Imposition of a regime of terror with executions of suspected conspirators
- Conspiracy of Domitia Longina

CULTURAL FACTS
- Martial's *Epigrams*
- Construction of the Domus Flavia on the Palatine
- Josephus's *Jewish Antiquities*

98–117
- Assassination of Domitian and promotion to the throne of Nerva
- Start of the long reign of optimus princeps Trajan
- Creation of the Food Institute
- Extension of the *colonus* (tenant farmers) to Africa to maintain the supply of grain to the capital

CULTURAL FACTS
- Tacitus writes *Agricola* and *Germania*
- Pliny the Younger's *Panegyricus Traiani*
- Construction of Trajan's Forum
- New port in Ostia

KINGDOMS AND EMPIRES IN THE EAST

69–81
Judaea:
- Conquest of Jerusalem and taking of the fortress at Masada, putting an end to the Jewish uprising against Rome

Armenia:
- Incorporation of the kingdoms of Armenia Minor and Commagene into the Roman Empire

Parthia:
- Attack on the Parthian kingdom by the Alans
- Invasion of the Roman Empire

CULTURAL FACTS
- Destruction of the Temple of Jerusalem

98–117
Arabia:
- End of the Nabataean kingdom, which becomes part of the Roman province of Arabia

Armenia:
- Annexation of the territory to the Roman Empire

Parthia:
- Roman offensive
- Rome conquers Assyria and Mesopotamia

CULTURAL FACTS
- Good-quality paper is invented in Han China

STATES AND BORDER TERRITORIES IN THE WEST

69–81
Britannia:
- Rebellion of Silu... Caledonians

Germania and Gau...
- Insurrection of t... creation of the Em...

Limes of the Danub...
- Invasion of Sarm... Dacians, defeated ... Minucius

81–96
- ...mpaigns in Britannia
- ...e Caledonians at the Battle of ...
- ...hatti
- ...n of the border with the
- ... of the Agri Decumates
- ...f Lucius Antonius Saturninus, ... of the province of Germania ...rior

...es of the Danube:
- ...War against Dacians, ...ommanded by Decebalus

98–117
Britannia:
- Rome retreats from Scotland

Germania
- Foundation of the Colonia Ulpia Traiana in Roman Dacia

Limes of the Danube:
- Roman victory in the First Dacian War
- Roman victory in the Second Dacian War and creation of the province of Dacia

CULTURAL FACTS
- Construction of Timgad

117–138

- Hadrian ascends the throne
- Murder of senators accused of conspiring against Hadrian
- Deterioration in relations between the emperor and the Senate
- Abandonment of campaigns of conquest
- Division of Italy into four regions under imperial legates with consular rank, acting as governors

CULTURAL FACTS
- Reconstruction of the Pantheon in Rome
- Construction of Hadrian's Villa in Tivoli

138–180

- Antoninus Pius ascends the throne
- Succession of Marcus Aurelius – repeated military conflicts
- Good relations between the emperor and Senate
- Lucius Verus at war with the Parthians
- Plague spreads across the empire
- Rebellion of Avidius Cassius in the East

CULTURAL FACTS
- Construction of the Temple of Antoninus and Faustina in the Roman Forum

180–192

- Commodus becomes the first emperor born during his father's reign
- Plague across the empire
- Commodus assumes autocratic power, seeing himself as the reincarnation of Hercules

CULTURAL FACTS
- Early works of the Christian writer Tertullian

117–138

Judaea:
- Foundation of the Aelia Capitolina colony in ancient Jerusalem
- Bar Kokhba revolt

Parthia:
- With the exception of Armenia, Trajan abandons his efforts at conquest

India:
- Pinnacle of the Kushan Empire under the government of Kanishka I
- Indian Embassy present at the court of Hadrian

138–180

Parthia:
- Reign of Antoninus Pius. Maintenance of peace
- Military campaign of Vologases III against Roman possessions in the Near East

India:
- The Kushan Empire holds on to its power under the governments of emperors Vasishka and Huvishka

China:
- Emperors Lui Zhi and Lui Hong maintain the flowering of the Han Dynasty

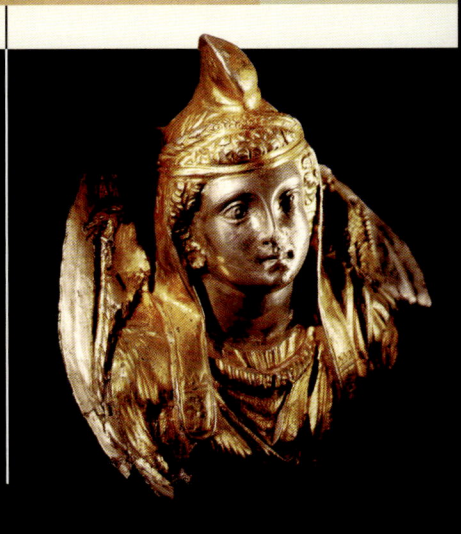

117–138

Britannia:
- Construction of Hadrian's Wall

Germania:
- Fortification of Germanic *limes* as in Britannia

Africa:
- Hadrian addresses the army at Lambaesis
- 13

8–180

Britannia:
- Construction of the Antonine Wall

Germania
- Strengthening defences and eastward expansion of the territories of the empire

Limes of the Danube:
- Sporadic clashes under Antoninus
- The Marcomanni at war with Rome

Africa:
- End of the revolt of the Mauri

180–192

Britannia:
- Attacks by barbarian tribes, who cross Hadrian's Wall
- The future emperor Pertinax suppresses a rebellion of legionaries

Germania:
- Clashes with barbarian tribes
- Creation of new jobs in the fortifications of *limes*

Limes of the Danube:
- Brief continuation of clashes beyond the borders
- Covenants established with the barbarian tribes and withdrawal of Roman forces

Comparative Chronology

ROME

193–235
- Emperor Commodus's assassination leads to civil war
- Rise of the Severan dynasty
- Septimius Severus annexes the northern half of Mesopotamia
- Antonine Constitution
- Murder of Geta and later Caracalla

CULTURAL FACTS
- Tertullian's *Apologeticus*
- Ban on Jews and Christians proselytizing

235–284
- State of military anarchy
- Succession of military emperors
- Increase in the number of imperial usurpations
- Great Plague of Rome
- Invasions of northern Italy

CULTURAL FACTS
- Millennial celebrations in Rome
- First edicts regarding the persecution of Christians
- Emperor Aurelian reforms the Roman cult of Sol, elevating the sun god to one of the premier divinities of the empire

284–305
- Emperor Diocletian
- Establishment of the tetrarchy as a system of government and succession
- Fragmentation of the empire between East and West begins
- Diocletian's monetary reform
- Edict on Maximum Prices
- Administrative restructuring of the empire's provinces

CULTURAL FACTS
- Edict against the Manicheans
- Major persecution of Christians

KINGDOMS AND EMPIRES IN THE EAST

193–235
Persia:
- Civil war breaks out
- Sasanian Empire founded by Ardashir I
- Assimilation of the Parthian Empire into the Sasanian. Persia united

CULTURAL FACTS
- City of Ardashir-Khwarrah founded by Ardashir I as centre of Sasanian power
- Ardashir I uses the title Shahanshah, meaning 'king of kings'

235–284
Persia:
- Sapor I, king of Persia
- Expansion of Persia, conquest of Antioch and Syria, Sasanian victory over Rome at Battle of Edessa

CULTURAL FACTS
- Founding of new Persian cities by Sapor I
- Policy of religious tolerance in Persia
- Expansion of Manichaeism

284–305
Persia:
- Reign of Narses I
- Victorious campaign of Emperor Galerius against the Persians
- Defeat of Narses by Galerius at the Battle of Callinicum
- Withdrawal of the Persians from Armenia and Georgia

Egypt:
- Fiscal reform

CULTURAL FACTS
- Anti-Manichean policies in Persia

STATES AND BORDER TERRITORIES IN THE WEST

193–235
Britannia:
- Septimius Severus dies while campaigning in Britannia

Germania:
- The Alemanni cross the Rhine
- Expansion of Christianity into Mesopotamia and Mauretania

235–284
Germania:
- Constant activity of the Alemanni along the Rhine frontier
- The Goths expand their lands along the Danube
- Threat of Saxons and Frisians in the north of Germania
- Goths cross into province of Raetia, south of the Danube

Gaul:
- The Franks and Alemanni invade Gaul

Illyria:
- Major invasion of the Balkans
- Loss of Roman Dacia

284–305
Germania:
- Maximian defeats the Alemanni, Burgundians and Heruli
- Fortification of the *limes* of the Rhine
- The Alemanni and Saxons increase pressure on Rome's German frontier

306–337
- Battle of the Milvian Bridge
- Constantine defeats Licinius
- Edict of Toleration by Galerius
- The Edict of Milan gives Christianity legal status in the empire
- First Christian symbols on Roman coins

337–395
- Battle of Mursa Major between Constantius II and the usurper Magnentius
- Unification on the empire under Constantius II
- Julian the Apostate attempts to revive polytheistic Roman religious practices at the expense of Christianity
- First official division of the empire between East and West

CULTURAL FACTS
- Hilary, Bishop of Poitiers
- Pope Damasus I
- Martin, Bishop of Tours
- Ambrosius, Bishop of Milan

395–476
- Wave of usurpations in the West
- Rome sacked and looted by Alaric the Visigoth
- Battle of the Catalaunian Plains: Rome and the Visigoths defeat Attila the Hun
- End of the empire in the West

CULTURAL FACTS
- Christianity becomes the empire's only official religion
- Pagan cults are forbidden

306–337
Persia:
- Accession of Sapor II of Persia

Byzantium:
- Foundation of Constantinople

CULTURAL FACTS
- Donatist schism
- Lactantius, early Roman Christian writer
- Council of Nicaea (325), the first ecumenical council of the Christian church, called by Constantine
- Death of Arius, founder of Arianism

337–395
Persia:
- Sapor II continues political expansion
- Peace treaty between Persia and Rome
- Sapor II takes territory in central Asia

Egypt:
- Spread of cenobitism and monasticism

CULTURAL FACTS
- Eusebius of Caesarea, historian of the Church, dies in Judaea
- Pachomius the Great preaches cenobitic monasticism in the East

395–476
Byzantium:
- Reinforcement of the walls of Constantinople by Theodosius II

Egypt:
- Condemnation of Monophysitism

CULTURAL FACTS
- Saint Jerome dies in Palestine
- Ecumenical council at Ephesus
- Council of Chalcedon

306–337
Germania:
- First *foedus* (treaty) between Romans and Goths

CULTURAL FACTS
- Translation of the Bible into the Gothic language promoted by Bishop Ulfilas
- Conversion of the Goths to Arian Christianity
- Condemnation of Arianism at the Council of Nicaea (325)

337–395
Britannia:
- Invasion by Northern hordes
- Rome regains territory in Britannia

Germania:
- Julian defeats the Alemanni at Strasbourg
- Incursions of the Goths into the *limes* of the Rhine
- Treaty agreed between Rome and the Alemanni
- Valens agrees a truce with the Goths
- Expansion of the Huns
- Disaster at Adrianople: Valens is killed in battle and Rome defeated by the Goths

395–476
Britannia:
- Invading waves of Angles, Saxons and Jutes

Germania:
- Eutropius defeats a Hun invasion
- Alaric the Visigoth poses a threat to Italy
- Alaric is defeated at the Battle of Pollentia
- Vandals, Swabians and Burgundians cross the Rhine
- Attila the Hun
- Theodoric the Great, king of the Ostrogoths

Genealogy of the Julio-Claudian Dynasty

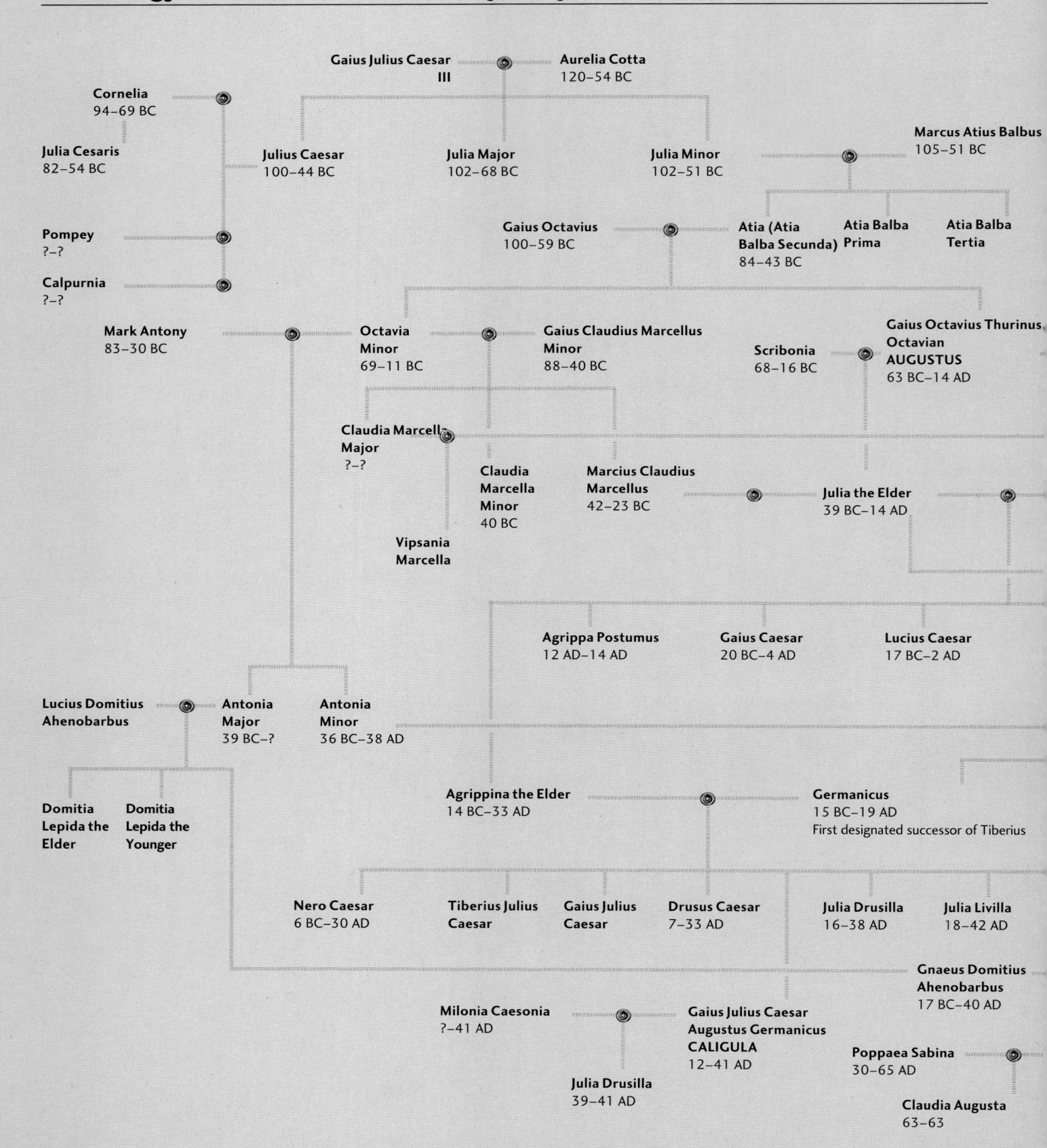

Gaius Julius Caesar III — **Aurelia Cotta** 120–54 BC

Cornelia 94–69 BC

Julia Cesaris 82–54 BC

Julius Caesar 100–44 BC

Julia Major 102–68 BC

Julia Minor 102–51 BC

Marcus Atius Balbus 105–51 BC

Pompey ?–?

Calpurnia ?–?

Gaius Octavius 100–59 BC

Atia (Atia Balba Secunda) 84–43 BC

Atia Balba Prima

Atia Balba Tertia

Mark Antony 83–30 BC

Octavia Minor 69–11 BC

Gaius Claudius Marcellus Minor 88–40 BC

Scribonia 68–16 BC

Gaius Octavius Thurinus Octavian AUGUSTUS 63 BC–14 AD

Claudia Marcella Major ?–?

Claudia Marcella Minor 40 BC

Marcius Claudius Marcellus 42–23 BC

Julia the Elder 39 BC–14 AD

Vipsania Marcella

Agrippa Postumus 12 AD–14 AD

Gaius Caesar 20 BC–4 AD

Lucius Caesar 17 BC–2 AD

Lucius Domitius Ahenobarbus

Antonia Major 39 BC–?

Antonia Minor 36 BC–38 AD

Domitia Lepida the Elder

Domitia Lepida the Younger

Agrippina the Elder 14 BC–33 AD

Germanicus 15 BC–19 AD
First designated successor of Tiberius

Nero Caesar 6 BC–30 AD

Tiberius Julius Caesar

Gaius Julius Caesar

Drusus Caesar 7–33 AD

Julia Drusilla 16–38 AD

Julia Livilla 18–42 AD

Gnaeus Domitius Ahenobarbus 17 BC–40 AD

Milonia Caesonia ?–41 AD

Gaius Julius Caesar Augustus Germanicus CALIGULA 12–41 AD

Poppaea Sabina 30–65 AD

Julia Drusilla 39–41 AD

Claudia Augusta 63–63

APPENDICES

EMPERORS OF THE JULIO-CLAUDIAN DYNASTY

AUGUSTUS
Reigned: 27 BC–14 AD

TIBERIUS
Reigned: 14–37 AD

CALIGULA
Reigned: 37–41 AD

CLAUDIUS
Reigned: 41–54 AD

NERO
Reigned: 54–68 AD

Members of the Julio-Claudian family as represented in the Ara Pacis altar frieze in Rome. Foreground, left to right, Emperor Tiberius, Antonia Minor with her son Germanicus, Drusus the Elder and Antonia the Elder with her daughter Domicia.

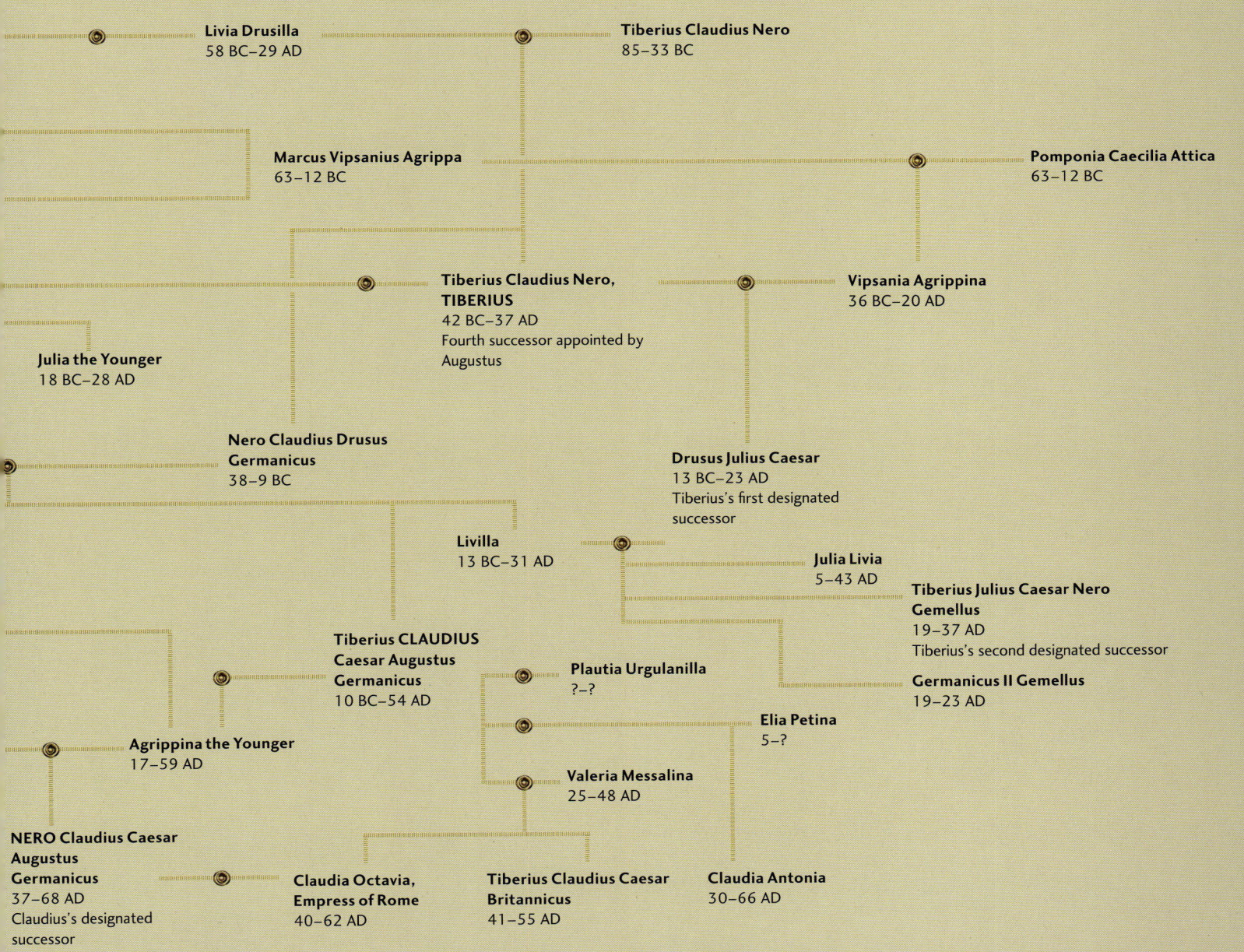

Livia Drusilla
58 BC–29 AD

Tiberius Claudius Nero
85–33 BC

Marcus Vipsanius Agrippa
63–12 BC

Pomponia Caecilia Attica
63–12 BC

Tiberius Claudius Nero, TIBERIUS
42 BC–37 AD
Fourth successor appointed by Augustus

Vipsania Agrippina
36 BC–20 AD

Julia the Younger
18 BC–28 AD

Nero Claudius Drusus Germanicus
38–9 BC

Drusus Julius Caesar
13 BC–23 AD
Tiberius's first designated successor

Livilla
13 BC–31 AD

Julia Livia
5–43 AD

Tiberius Julius Caesar Nero Gemellus
19–37 AD
Tiberius's second designated successor

Tiberius CLAUDIUS Caesar Augustus Germanicus
10 BC–54 AD

Plautia Urgulanilla
?–?

Germanicus II Gemellus
19–23 AD

Agrippina the Younger
17–59 AD

Valeria Messalina
25–48 AD

Elia Petina
5–?

NERO Claudius Caesar Augustus Germanicus
37–68 AD
Claudius's designated successor

Claudia Octavia, Empress of Rome
40–62 AD

Tiberius Claudius Caesar Britannicus
41–55 AD

Claudia Antonia
30–66 AD

APPENDICES

Genealogy of the Flavian Dynasty

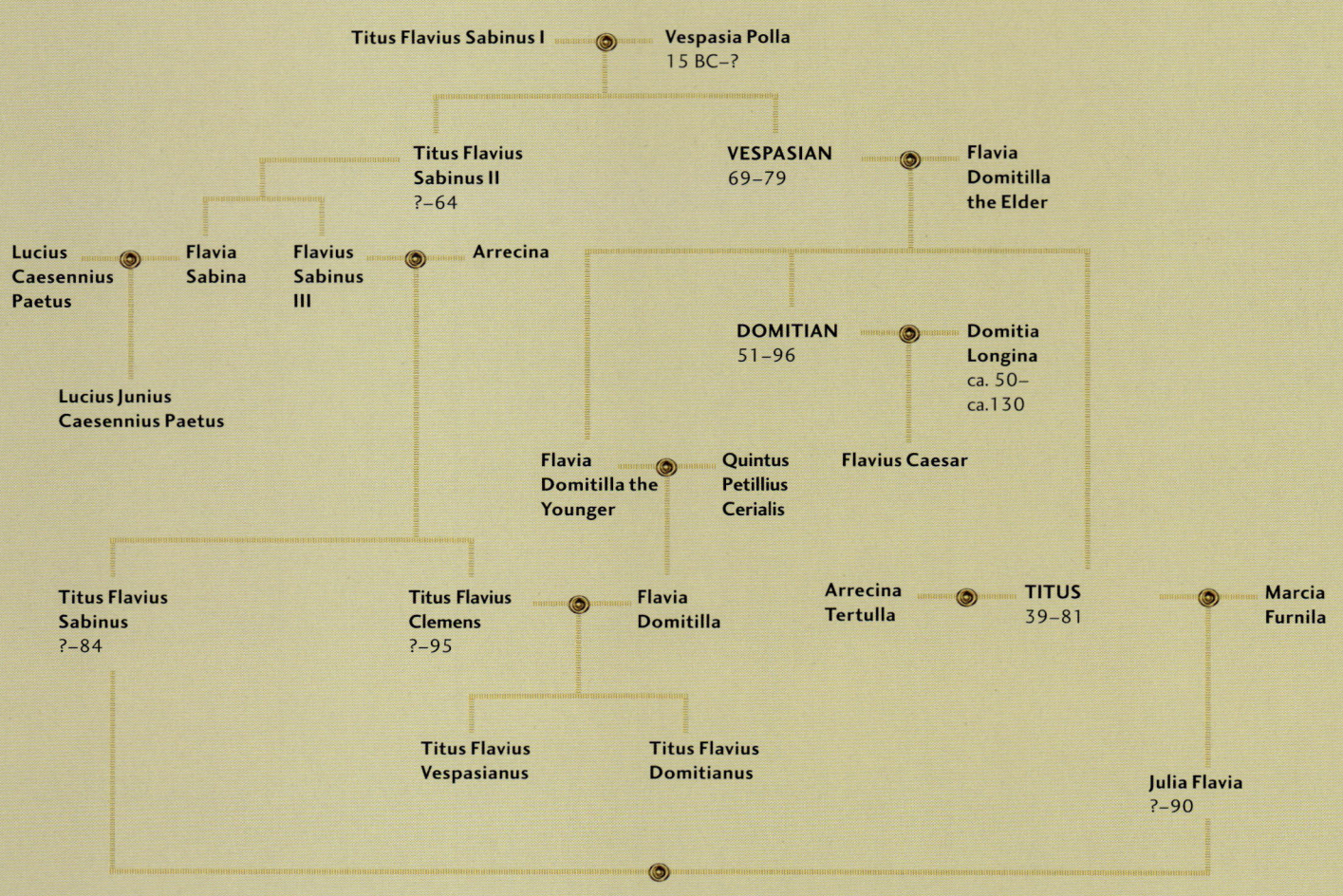

Titus Flavius Sabinus I — Vespasia Polla
15 BC–?

- Titus Flavius Sabinus II ?–64
- VESPASIAN 69–79 — Flavia Domitilla the Elder

- Lucius Caesennius Paetus — Flavia Sabina
- Flavius Sabinus III
- Arrecina

- DOMITIAN 51–96 — Domitia Longina ca. 50–ca.130

- Lucius Junius Caesennius Paetus

- Flavia Domitilla the Younger — Quintus Petillius Cerialis
- Flavius Caesar

- Titus Flavius Sabinus ?–84
- Titus Flavius Clemens ?–95 — Flavia Domitilla
- Arrecina Tertulla — TITUS 39–81 — Marcia Furnila

- Titus Flavius Vespasianus
- Titus Flavius Domitianus

- Julia Flavia ?–90

EMPERORS OF THE FLAVIAN DYNASTY

VESPASIAN
1-7-69 to 23-6-79

DOMITIAN
14-9-81 to 18-9-96

TITUS
24-6-79 to 13-9-81

EMPERORS OF THE ANTONINE DYNASTY

NERVA
18-9-96 to 27-1-98

TRAJAN
28-1-98 to 7-8-117

HADRIAN
11-8-117 to 10-7-138

ANTONINUS PIUS
10-7-138 to 7-3-161

MARCUS AURELIUS
7-3-161 to 17-3-180
161 to 169, with his adoptive brother Lucius Verus
177 to 180 with his son Commodus

COMMODUS
17-3-180 to 31-12-192

DACIAN WARS. *Detail of Trajan's column showing a crowd bidding farewell to the troops leaving for the Dacian front led by Emperor Trajan.*

Genealogy of the Antonine Dynasty

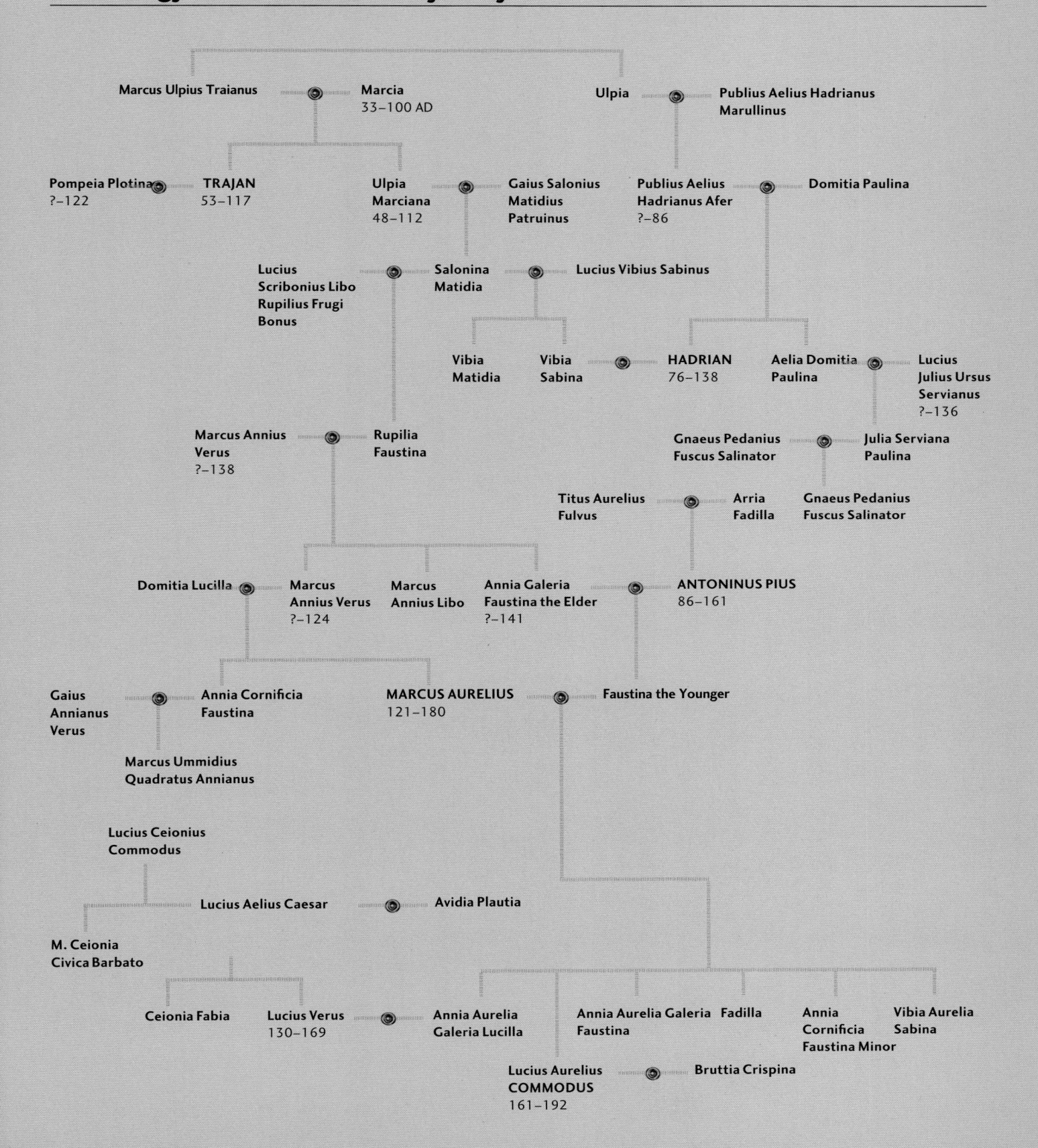

- Marcus Ulpius Traianus — Marcia (33–100 AD)
- Ulpia — Publius Aelius Hadrianus Marullinus

- Pompeia Plotina (?–122) — **TRAJAN** (53–117)
- Ulpia Marciana (48–112) — Gaius Salonius Matidius Patruinus
- Publius Aelius Hadrianus Afer (?–86) — Domitia Paulina

- Lucius Scribonius Libo Rupilius Frugi Bonus — Salonina Matidia — Lucius Vibius Sabinus

- Vibia Matidia
- Vibia Sabina — **HADRIAN** (76–138)
- Aelia Domitia Paulina — Lucius Julius Ursus Servianus (?–136)

- Marcus Annius Verus (?–138) — Rupilia Faustina
- Gnaeus Pedanius Fuscus Salinator — Julia Serviana Paulina

- Titus Aurelius Fulvus — Arria Fadilla — Gnaeus Pedanius Fuscus Salinator

- Domitia Lucilla — Marcus Annius Verus (?–124)
- Marcus Annius Libo
- Annia Galeria Faustina the Elder (?–141) — **ANTONINUS PIUS** (86–161)

- Gaius Annianus Verus — Annia Cornificia Faustina
- **MARCUS AURELIUS** (121–180) — Faustina the Younger
- Marcus Ummidius Quadratus Annianus

- Lucius Ceionius Commodus
- Lucius Aelius Caesar — Avidia Plautia
- M. Ceionia Civica Barbato

- Ceionia Fabia
- Lucius Verus (130–169) — Annia Aurelia Galeria Lucilla
- Annia Aurelia Galeria Faustina
- Fadilla
- Annia Cornificia Faustina Minor
- Vibia Aurelia Sabina

- Lucius Aurelius **COMMODUS** (161–192) — Bruttia Crispina

LIST OF DYNASTIES

SEVERAN DYNASTY

Pertinax	193
Didius Julianus	193
Septimius Severus	193–198
Septimius Severus with Caracalla (co-emperors)	198–209
Septimius Severus with Caracalla and Geta (co-emperors)	209–211
Caracalla and Geta (co-emperors)	211
Caracalla	211–217
Macrinus	217–218
Elagabalus	218–222
Alexander Severus	222–235

MILITARY ANARCHY

Maximinus Thrax	235–238
Gordian I and Gordian II (co-emperors in Africa)	238
Balbinus and Pupienus (co-emperors in Italy)	238
Gordian III	238–244
Philip the Arab	244–247
Philip the Arab and Philip II (co-emperors)	247–249
Decius	249–251
Hostilian (proclaimed by the Senate)	251
Trebonianus Gallus and Volusianus (proclaimed by the legions of the Danube)	251–253
Aemilian (proclaimed by the legions of the Danube)	253
Valerian (proclaimed by the legions of the Rhine) and Gallienus (co-emperors)	253–260
Gallienus	260–268

ILLYRIAN EMPERORS

Claudius II 'Gothicus'	268–270
Quintillus	270
Aurelian	270–275
Tacitus	275–276
Florianus	276
Probus	276–282
Carus	282–283
Carinus and Numerian (co-emperors)	283–284
Carinus	284–285

FROM THE TETRARCHY TO CONSTANTINE

Diocletian (Augustus)	284–305
Maximian (Augustus)	286–305
(self-proclaimed Augustus)	306–308, 310
Constantius I (Caesar)	293–305
(Augustus)	305–306
Galerius (Caesar)	293–305
(Augustus)	305–311
Severus II (Caesar)	305–306
(Augustus)	306–307
Maxentius (Augustus)	306–312
Maximus II (as Caesar in the east, under Galerius)	305–310
(in competition with Licinius)	310–313
Constantine I the Great (Caesar)	306–307
(Augustus)	307–312

(Co-emperor with Licinius)	312–324
(Sole emperor)	324–337
Licinius	
(Augustus)	308–312
(Co-emperor with Constantine)	312–324

CONSTANTINE'S LINEAGE

Constantine II	
(Gaul, Britannia, Hispania)	337–340
Constans	
(Italy, Africa, Illyris)	337–350
(The West)	340–250
Constantius II	
(Constantinople and the East)	337–340
(The East)	340–353
(The East and West)	353–361
Constantius Gallus	
(Caesar of the East)	351–354
Magnentius	
(Usurper in the West)	350–353
Julian the Apostate	
(Caesar in the West)	355–360
(Augustus)	360–361
(Emperor in the East and West)	361–363
Jovian	
(Proclaimed by Julian's troops)	363–364

VALENTINIAN DYNASTY

Valentinian I (West)	364–375
Valens (East)	364–378
Gratian (Augustus under Valentinian I)	367–375
Gratian and Valentinian II	
(Western co-emperors)	375–383
Magnus Maximus	
(Usurper in the West)	383–388
Valentinian II (West)	388–392
Eugenius	
(Usurper in the West)	392–394
Theodosius I the Great	
(Augustus of the East)	379–392
(Emperor of the whole empire)	392–395

THE ROMAN EMPIRE IN THE WEST

Honorius	395–423
Honorius and Constantine III	
(co-emperors)	421
Joannes (Usurper)	423–425
Valentinian III	425–455
Petronius Maximus	455
Avitus	455–456
Majorian (usurper)	457–461
Libius Severus	461–465
Anthemius	467–472
Olybrius	472
Glycerius	473–474
Julius Nepos	474–475
Romulus Augustulus	475–476

THE ROMAN EMPIRE IN THE EAST

Arcadius	395–408
Theodosius II	408–450
Marcian	450–457
Leo I 'the Thracian'	457–474
Leo II	474
Zeno	474–491

INDEX

Page references in **bold** indicate illustrations and captions

Abritus, Battle of (251 AD) 304
Actium, Battle of (31 BC) **14**, **30**, 30–31, **31**
Ad Decimum, Battle of (533 AD) 413
Adoptionism 380, 394
Adrianople, Battle of (324 AD) 324
Adrianople, Battle of (378 AD) 334
Aelia Capitolina **239**
Aetius 349, 350–54
Agri Decumates, the 194, 195
Agricola, Julius 161, 195, 196
agriculture 189, 233, 309, 362, 363–67, 370, **370**
Agrippa, Herod 94
Agrippa, Marcus Vipsanius 17, 18, 22, 25, **26**, 31, **40**, 43, 44–45, 48, **49**, 59, 60
Agrippina the Younger 100–101, 111, 114–15, **119**
Ahenobarbus, Gnaeus Domitius 22, 93
Alans, the 164, 334, 342, 345, 348, 349, 352, 408, 410
Alaric 343, 344–45, **344–45**
Albinus, Clodius 292
Albinus, Decimus Junius Brutus 19
Alcántra Bridge, Spain **209**
Alemanni, the 405, 418
Alexander Severus, Emperor **295**, 295–98
Alexander the Great 16, **91**, 220, 293–94
Alexander, Tiberius Julius 155
Altar to Mithras **241**
Amphictyonic League, the 188
amphitheatres 59, 60–61, **146**, **165**, 173
    Arles **182**
    the Colosseum 55, 57, 61, 125, 166, **168–69**, 173, 190, **279**, 279–81, **280–81**
    a day at the 280–81
    dramatic performances 283
    El Djem **299**, **363**
    Italica **264–65**
    at Petra 316
    at Pompeii 177, 178
    Roman Theatre of Orange, Vacluse, France **10**
    theatre of Mérida **128**

Anglo-Saxon kingdoms 422–23
animal hunts 268, 280–81, **363**, 366
Anthemius, Emperor 356
Anthony the Great **394**, 396
Antinous 227, 230
anti-Semitism 94–96, 329–30 *see also* Jewish revolts
Antonia Minor **70**
Antonine Plague, the 371
Antoninus Column **249**
Antoninus Pius, Emperor 206, **250**
    the apotheosis of **249**
    building projects **230**, **247**, **248**
    charitable works 248
    named as successor 246
    Pax Romana 249–50
    period of prosperity 246–48
    timeline 246
Aphrodisias, Stadium of **189**
Apollinarians 394
Apollodorus of Pergamon 17, 18
Apotheosis of Claudius **89**
apparel *see* clothing
Appian 25
aqueducts 60, 61, 92, 97
    Aqua Claudia **86**
    Aqua Traiana 218
    Aqueduct of Segovia **168**
Aquilia Severa 294
Ara Pacis (Altar of Peace) 40, 59
Arcadius, Emperor 336, 340, **342**
Arch of Constantine 326, **326–27**, **362**
Arch of Titus 166, **168**, 173
Arch of Trajan 215
architecture *see* buildings and architecture
Arianism 329, 380, 396, 411, 412, 413
Aristides, Aelius 210
armies of Rome, the *see* legions
Arrianus, Flavius 236
Asiaticus, Publius Valerius 100
astrology 18
Athenodorus, Claudius 197
Atimetus, Lucius Cornelius 270
Attianus, Acilius 224
Atticus, Curtius 69
Attila the Hun 350, **350–51**, 352–53, **353**, 419
Auctus, Lucius Cocceius 25
Augustine of Hippo 356

Augustus, Emperor 27, **32**, **34**, **36**, **40**, **70**, **71**
    appointed as consul 33
    bans the Eastern cults 84
    Battle of Actium (31 BC) **14**, 30–31
    Battle of Modena (43 BC) 19–20
    Battle of Perusia (40 BC) 22
    Battle of Philippi (42 BC) 22, **23**
    Battle of the Teutoburg Forest (9 AD) 50–52
    becomes Pontifex Maximus 35–36, **36**
    building projects 26, 55–56, 59, 61
    Cassius Dio on 19, 34, 53
    changes name to Augustus 34, 36
    dealing with rebellions 39–42, **43**, 43–44
    death of 52–53, **52–53**
    the death of Agrippa 44–45
    and the defeat of Sextus Pompey 24–25
    early life 15–16
    entertainment at the amphitheatre 280, 281
    and the equestrians 359
    'euergetism' 26
    famine (22 BC) 42–43
    Forum of Augustus 21
    his *Res Gestae* 34, 42–43, 55, 66
    his succession 45–50
    and Julius Caesar 16–17, 18
    and the legions 106, 108, 109
    and the *Lex Titia* pact 20, 21
    likened to Apollo 35
    and Mark Anthony 18, 27, 30
    marriage to Livia Drusilla 24
    naumachia 118
    and the Praetorian Guard 38
    and public morality 38–39
    reforms 33–34, 35–39, 56
    revenge on the Caesaricides 20–22
    Roman Theatre of Orange, Vacluse, France **10**
    the Second Triumvirate 20–21
    start of a public career 16–19
    Suetonius on 16–17, 22, 142
    timeline 16
    votive shield **42**
Augustus, Servius Sulpicius Galba Caesar *see* Galba, Emperor
Aurelian, Emperor 141, 305, 319

INDEX

Aurelian Walls **304**
Aurelius, Marcus 248
Avitus, Emperor 354
and the Visigoths 406, 410

Balbinus, Emperor 300
banquets 116–17
baptism 402
Bar Kokhba revolt 238–39
Barbarian migrations 348, **348–49**
basilicas 398–403
    Basilica di Santa Maria Maggiore, Rome **400–401**, 403
    Basilica of Constantine, Trier **399**
    Basilica of San Vitale, Ravenna 390, **415**
    Basilica of Santa Sabina, Rome 402–3
    Basilica of Trastevere **386**
    Basilica Ulpia 218, **218**
    Old St Peter's Basilica, Rome **399**, 399–402
    St Paul's Basilica, Rome **403**
Basso **364**
Bassus, Junius 392–93, **392–93**
Bassus, Quintus Caecilius 22
Batavian insurrection, the 156–58, **157**
baths 122, **127**
    Baths of Caracalla 296–97
    Baths of Diocletian 370, **370**
    Baths of Trajan 218
    Great Baths of Maktar **413**
    in Pompeii 176, 178
Battles
    Abritus (251 AD) 304
    Actium (31 BC) **14**, **30**, 30–31, **31**
    Ad Decimum (533 AD) 413
    Adrianople (324 AD) 324
    Adrianople (378 AD) 334
    Bedriacum (69 AD) 106, 133–34, **134–35**, 138, 155–56
    Cap Bon (468 AD) 412
    Cibalae (314 AD) 324
    Edessa (260 AD) 300, **300–301**, 304
    Mardia (316-7 AD) 324
    Margus River (285 AD) 306
    Milvian Bridge (312 AD) **322–23**, 323, 390
    Modena (43 BC) 19–20
    Mons Graupius, (84 AD) 195, 196

Mons Seleucus (353 AD) 329
Mount Bladen (500 AD) 423
Mylae (36 BC) 25
Naulochus (36 BC) 25
Nervasos Mountains (419 AD) 410
Perusia (40 BC) 22
Philippi (42 BC) 22, **23**
Resaena (243 AD) 300
Rimini (432 AD) 351
Save (388 AD) 336
Tapae (88 AD) 196
Teutoburg Forest (9 AD) 50–52
Tzirallum (313 AD) 324
Verona (312 AD) 362, **362**
Vouillé (507 AD) 408, 410, **410**
Bedriacum, Battle of (69 AD) 106, 133–34, **134–35**, 138, 155–56
Berenice of Cilicia 169–72
Bible, the 384
Black Death 154, 272
Blaesus, Quintus Junius 67
Boethius 414
Bonifacius 349, 350–51, 411
Boudica 120–21
Britannicus, Claudius Tiberius Germanicus 92, 93, 98, 112
brothels, in Pompeii 176, 178
Bruttia Crispina 269
Brutus, Marcus Junius 18, 20, 22
buildings and architecture 55–61 see also villas and palaces
    Alcántra Bridge, Spain **209**
    Altar to Mithras **241**
    Antoninus Column **249**
    Aqua Claudia **86**
    Aqua Traiana 218
    Aqueduct of Segovia **168**
    aqueducts 60, 61, 92, 97
    Arch of Constantine 326, **326–27**, **362**
    Arch of Titus 166, **168**, 173
    Arch of Trajan 215
    Aurelian Walls 304
    Basilica di Santa Maria Maggiore, Rome **400–401**, 403
    Basilica of Constantine, Trier **399**
    Basilica of Santa Sabina, Rome 402–3
    Basilica of Trastevere **386**
    Basilica Ulpia 218, **218**
    Baths of Caracalla 296, **296–97**

Baths of Diocletian 370, **370**
Baths of Trajan 218
Castel Sant' Angelo 230, **233**
the catacombs 200, 203
Circus Maximus 285, **285**, 366, **366–67**
Colonia Ulpia Traiana Augusta Dacica Sarmizegetusa **214**
Colosseum, Rome **55**, **57**, 61, 166, **168–69**, 173, 190, **279**, 279–81, **280–81**
Column of Marcus Aurelius **250**
Coptic Monastery of San Simeon, Aswan **396–97**
Deva fortress **164–65**
dwellings 92, **93**, 140–44, 176, 179
El Djem Amphitheatre **299**, 363
Forum of Aquileia **139**
Forum of Augustus 21
Forum of Nerva 191
Forums of Rome, the 55, **55**, **57**, 58, **58**
Gate of Antoninus Pius, Sbeitla **248**
Great Baths of Maktar **413**
Hadrian's Wall, Britain **222**, 224–25, **224–25**
House of Augustus, Rome **39**
La Maison Carrée **45**
Leptis Magna, Libya 294, **294–95**
Lugo, the city of 80 towers 360, **361**
Mausoleum of Augustus **52–53**, 53, 79
Mausoleum of Constantina **325**
Mausoleum of Galla Placidia, Ravenna 346, **346–47**, 390
Obelisk of Theosius **335**
Old St Peter's Basilica, Rome **399**, 399–402
Palatine Towers **371**
the Pantheon 45, 59, **59**, 230, **232–33**
Piazza Navona, Rome **186**, 190, 283
Plutei Traiani **216–17**
in Pompeii 176–81
Portus Augusti, Ostia 96–97, **96–97**
Roman Baths **127**
Roman Theatre of Orange, Vacluse, France **10**
St Paul's Basilica, Rome **403**
Stadium of Aphrodisias **189**
Stadium of Domitian 61

INDEX

Temple of Antoninus and Faustina **247**
Temple of Augustus and Livia, Vienne, France **74**
Temple of Hadrian, Ephesus **229**
Temple of Janes, Rome 39
Temple of Jupiter Capitolinus 166, 172
Temple of Peace 166
Temple of the Apollo Palatinus 68
Temple of Venus Genetrix 19, **19**, 55, 218
Templum Pacis 58
theatre of Mérida **128**
Theodosian Wall, Constantinople 340, **341**
Timgad, Algeria **215**
Trajan's Column **211**, 213, 218, **220–21**
Trajan's Market **219**
Transitional Forum 206, **207**
Triclinium, Herculaneum **116**
Burgundians, the 266, 342, 345, **349**, 352, 355, 405, 408, 419–22

Caesar, Drusus Julius **71**
Caesar, Gaius **40**, **70**
Caesar, Julius *see* Julius Caesar, Emperor
Caesar, Lucius Aelius 245–46
Caesar, Lucius Julius 20
Caesar, Nero Julius **70**
Caligula, Emperor **79**
　　accusations of incest 81
　　the annexation of Mauretania 82, **82–83**
　　ascends the throne 79–80
　　the assassination of 85, **85**
　　building projects 61
　　campaign against Germanica 82
　　Cassius Dio on 84
　　the conquest of Brittania 97
　　extortion 84
　　his madness 80–82
　　named as heir to Tiberius 74, 78
　　names Julia Drusilla his heir 81
　　the resurgence of Eastern cults 84
　　Suetonius on 80, 84
　　Tacitus on 80
　　timeline 79
　　travels through the provinces 82–83
　　the tyranny of 83–84
　　and Vespasian 154
Callixtus I, Pope **386**

Camillus, Marcus Furius 104, 107
camps, legions **108–9**
Cap Bon, Battle of (468 AD) 412
Capri, Tiberius's retreat to 68–69, **72–73**
Caracalla, Emperor **293**, 293–94, **297**
caravan trade 314–15, 318
Carinus, Emperor 306
cartonnage 374
Carus, Emperor 305–6
Cassius, Avidius 253, 258–60
Cassius Dio *see* Dio, Cassius
Castel Sant' Angelo 230, **233**
catacombs, the 200, 203
Cato of Utica 17
Celer, Quintus Caecilius Metellus 141
Celso, C. Stazio **365**
Cerialis, Quintus Petillius 157, 161
Chaerea, Cassius 85
chariots **135**, 268, 283, 284, **284**, 285
children
　　education of **382**, 382–83, **385**
　　orphaned children 207, 208–9, 250
Christianity 200–203, 241, 310, 311, 316, 324, 329–30, 331, 332, **332**, 337, **355**, 356, **375**, 377–81, **381**, 385, **385**, **386**, 418, 423
Church Fathers, the 394
Cibalae, Battle of (314 AD) 324
Cicero 20, 55, 141, 145
Circus Maximus 285, **285**, 366, **366–67**
cithara, the 121–22, **122**
cities, society in 367–70
Civilis, Juilius 156–58
Claudia Livia Julia 71, 72, 75, **75–77**
Claudius, Emperor **86**, **89**, **90–91**
　　the adoption of Nero 100, 101
　　the application of justice 92
　　army strength 109
　　becomes Emperor 87–88
　　building projects 60, 92, **93**, 96–97, **96–97**
　　Cassius Dio on 88
　　the division of Mauretania 82, 93–94
　　entertainment at the amphitheatre 281
　　expedition to Britannia 97–98, **98**
　　governing through moderation 88–92

the intelligence of 88
and the kingdom of Palestine 94, **94**
the marriages of 92–93, 100–101
naumachia 118
the poisoning of 101
and public services 92
requests tolerance towards Jews 94–96
revolts of Alexandria 94–96
Seneca on 88, 92
Suetonius on 88, 89, 96, 101
Tacitus on 92, 118
timeline 89
villas and palaces 142
Claudius Gothicus, Emperor 305, 371
Cleander, Marcus Aurelius 268–69
Cleopatra **28**
　　Battle of Actium (31 BC) 30–31
　　and Julius Caesar 16
　　and Mark Anthony 23, 26, 28–29
climate and disease 370–71
　　cloisonné **421**
clothing **34**, 80, **81**, **91**, **92**, **117**, 236
　　armour **210**, **226**, **262**
　　gladiators 282–83
Code of Euric, the 407, 408, **408**
Cogidubnus, Tiberius Claudius 120
collegia (guilds) 368
coloni, the 363, 366, 370
Colonia Ulpia Traiana Augusta Dacica Sarmizegetusa **214**
Colosseum, Rome **55**, **57**, 61, 125, 166, **168–69**, 173, 190, **279**, 279–81, **280–81**
Column of Marcus Aurelius **250**
comets, appearance of 19
commerce, under Nero 114, **114–15**
Commodus, Emperor **262**, **266**, **272**
　　the 20 names of 276
　　Cassius Dio on 264, 265, 268
　　conspiracy against 267, 268
　　a controversial reign 264–65
　　the Danubian problem 263–64, 266
　　death of 274–76, **277**
　　enmity with the Senate 265, 267, 272
　　and the gladiators 264, 268, **269**
　　government of the empire 269–74
　　legislation 264, 272

and the plague 272
succeeds to the throne 263
timeline 264
the War on Deserters 273
conscription, the legions 106
Constans, Emperor 328–29
Constantine II, Emperor 324, 328–29, **360**
Constantine the Great, Emperor **320**
    Arch of Constantine 326, **326–27**, **362**
    and the army 362
    baptism of 324
    Battle of Adrianople (324 AD) 324
    Battle of Cibalae (314 AD) 324
    Battle of Mardia (316–17 AD) 324
    Battle of Milvian Bridge (312 AD) 390
    Battle of the Milvian Bridge (312 AD) **322–23**, 323
    Battle of Verona (312 AD) 362, **362**
    becomes Dacicus Maximus 328
    becomes emperor 321
    building works 325, 326, **326–27**, 328
    and Christianity 322, **322–23**, 325–28, **329**, 390–91, **391**, 398
    death of 324
    the Edict of Milan 323–24
    the heirs of 328–29
    and the tetrarchy 321–23
    timeline 328
Constantinius Chlorus, Emperor **290**, 306, **307**, 308, 311, 321
Constantius II, Emperor 328–30, 329, 391
Constantius III, Emperor 344, 345, 348
Coptic Church, the 396
corruption 362–63
cremation 254
Cult of Cybele 241–42, 380
Cult of Isis 242–43
Cult of the Lares Compitales 16

Dacian Wars 210–14, **220–21**
Damasus I, Pope 384
Decius, Emperor 301, 304, 310, 388
deification 90–91
Delphic Oracle, the 35
Deva fortress **164–65**

Dio, Cassius
    on Augustus 19, 34, 53
    on the Avidius revolt 259
    on the Battle of Actium (31 BC) 31
    on the Battle of Modena (43 BC) 20
    on Caligula 84
    on Claudia Livia Julia 75
    on Claudius 88
    on Commodus 264, 265, 268
    on Domitian 185, 198, 199
    on Faustina 260
    on the fire of Rome 172
    on Gaius Cilinius Maecenas 18
    on Hadrian 224, 227
    on how to be a good emperor 277
    on Lucius Aelius Sejanus 72
    on Lucius Verginius Rufus 130
    on Mark Anthony 30
    on Nero 122
    on Nerva 206
    on the punishment of oblivion 75
    on Seneca 112, 125
    on Tiberius 78
    on Titus 172, 173
    on Trajan 209, 218, 220
    on Vespasian **167**
Diocletian, Emperor **290**, **306**, **307**
    agriculture 366
    and the army 360, 362
    Baths of Diocletian 370, **370**
    building works 308
    creates the tetrarchy 306, 307
    Edict of Maximum Prices 309–10
    establishes a camp at Palmyra 319
    Palace of Diocletian, Split **311**
    the persecution of Christians 310, 311, 389
    reforms 306–11
    reorganizing the empire 308, **308–9**
    and trade 368
Dioscorus, Pope 396
disease 370–71
    plague, the 154, 272, 371
Docetism 380, 394
Dolabella, Publius Cornelius 67
Domitia Longina 198
Domitian, Emperor 167, **185**, **186**, **188**, **194**, **197**
    administration of the Empire 186–90
    the 'Bald Nero' 184–86
    Battle of Tapae (88 AD) 196

becomes Emperor 183–84
building projects 61, **182**, **186**, 190–91, **199**
Cassius Dio on 185, 198, 199
consolidating the borders 191–96
conspiracies against 198–99
death of 199
economic policies 196–98
and Julia Flavia **173**
preparation for leadership 168–69
public charity 189–90
Suetonius on 185, 186, 198
Tacitus on 185–86
timeline 184
and the Vestal Virgins **190**
Domus Aurea 122, **124–25**, 143, **168**
Domus Flavia **192–93**, **199**
Donatists, the 328, 396
Drusus, Nero Claudius *see* Germanicus
dwellings 92, **93** *see also* villas and palaces
in Pompeii 176, 179

eagles, as symbols **50**, 52, **89**, 91
Early Christianity 200–203
Eastern cults, the resurgence of 84, 241–43
Edessa, Battle of (260 AD) 300, **300–301**, 304
Edict of Milan 323–24, 398
Edict of Thessalonica 394
Edict of Toleration 398
education **382**, 382–83, **385**
Egyptian cults 242–43
El Djem Amphitheatre **299**, **363**
Elagabalus, Emperor 294–95
elections 38
Eleusinian Mysteries 237, **238**, 260
Empire, maps of the **12–13**, **150–51**, **212–13**, **288–89**, **336–37**
entertainment 116, 121–22 *see also* amphitheatres; festivals; stadiums
animal hunts 268, 280–81, **363**, 366
chariot racing **135**, 268, 283, 284, **284**, 285
dramatic performances 283
horse racing 283, 285
naumachia 118
panhellic games 127
sporting events 177, 283

INDEX

Epicureanism 377
epidemic diseases 370–71
    plague, the 154, 272, 371
epigraphic texts 364–65
equestrians 188, 230–32, 272, 359–60
equites primipilares 360
'euergetism' 26
Eugenius, Emperor 337
Eurycles, Gaius Julius 236
Eutropius 208, 340–41

famines 42–43, 96–97
Faustina 247, **247**, 258, **258**, 259, 260
Fayum mummy portraits 373–75
Felix 349, 350
festivals 36, 90, 189, 218, 242
    Eastern cults 84
    panhellic games 127
Field of Mars 55, 56, 58–60
fire brigades 36
fires of Rome 172
    Great Fire of Rome 122, **122**, 202
Flaccus, Gaius Norbanus 21
Flavian Amphitheatre *see* Colosseum, Rome
Florianus, Emperor 305
Florus 227
foederati of Rome 405, 406, **406–7**, 418
food and drink 116–17
formations, legions 104
forums 274
    Forum of Aquileia **139**
    Forum of Augustus 21
    Forum of Nerva 191
    Forum of Pompeii 178, **178**
    Forums of Rome, the 55, **55**, **57**, 58, **58**
Franks, the 348, 349, **349**, 350, 352, 366, 405, 406, 408, 410, **410**, 414, 415–19
Frontinus, Sixtus Julius 161
Furia Sabina Tranquilina 300

Galba, Emperor 69, 82, 109, 129–32, **133**, 154
Galenus, Claudius 256, **256**
Galerius, Emperor **290**, 306, **307**, 308, 310, 311, 321–22, 390, 398
Galla Placidia 346, **346–47**, 349–51, 406

Gallienus, Emperor 108, 304–5, 360, 388
Gallus, Gaius Cestius 126
Galo, Gaius Cornelius 38
Gate of Antoninus Pius, Sbeitla **248**
gem carvings 71
Gem of Augustus, the **34**
Gemellus, Tiberius 81
Germanic kingdoms and people, the 266, **266–67**, 405–23
Germanicus 44, 50, 52, 65–66, 67–68, **69**, **70**
Germanicus, Gaius Julius Caesar *see* Caligula, Emperor
Germanicus, Tiberius Claudius Drusus Nero *see* Claudius, Emperor
Geta, Emperor 293, **293**
Geta, Gnaeus Hosidius 94
gladiators 84, 173, 189–90, 218, 264, **269**, 281–83
Glycerius, Emperor 357
Gnosticism 380–84
gods and goddesses, Roman 140
    Apollo 35, **122**, 142
    Ceres **25**, **51**
    Dionysus 35
    Fortuna **128**
    Jupiter **34**, 39
    Mars **21**, **44**
    Minerva **190**, 191
    Pluto **381**
    Roma **34**
    Sol Invictus 305
    Venus **19**, **44**, 179
Goethe, J. W. 174
Gordian I, Emperor 299
Gordian II, Emperor 299, **299**
Gordian III, Emperor 299, 300, **358**
government structure **330**
Gratian, Emperor 334, 335–36
    and Christianity 394
    the outlawing of cults 380
    renounces the tilte Pontifex Maximus 329
Great Baths of Maktar **413**
Great Cameo, France **70–71**
Great Fire of Rome 122, **122**, 202
Great Persecution, the 389
Gregory the Great, Pope 208, 209
guilds 368

Hadrian, Emperor 207, **225**, **228**, **230**, **326**
    and Antinous 90
    army reforms 109
    becomes Emperor 223–24
    in Britannia **222**, 224–25, **224–25**, 227, **228**, **229**
    building projects 59, **229**, 230, **232–33**, 237
    Cassius Dio on 224, 227
    choosing his succession 245–46
    early life 224
    the government of 230–33
    and the Greek world **236–37**, 236–38
    his empire 233–36
    his military life 226
    his travels 226–30
    his villa **146–47**, 227, 236
    the Jewish rebellion 238–39
    the Panhellenion **236–37**, 237–38
    reorganization of the army 226
    timeline 224
Hadrian's Wall, Britain **222**, 224–25, **224–25**
Hadrianus, Publius Aelius *see* Hadrian, Emperor
health of the population 370–71
    the plague 154, 272, 371
Herculaneum 92, 116, 141, 172, 174–75
Herennius Etruscus, Emperor 304
Herodian 107, 265
Honorius, Emperor 336, 337, **342**
    and Alaric 344–45, **344–45**
    and the Burgundians 419
    and Flavius Stilicho 340–44
    the loss of Britannia 348
    the rebellion of Jovinus 345
    and the Visigoths 406
Horace 18, 44, 56
horse racing 283, 285
Hostilian, Emperor 371
House of Augustus, Rome **39**
housing 92, 93 *see also* villas and palaces
    in Pompeii 176, 179
Huns, the 344, 348, 349, 350, 351, 352–53, 406, 413, 419

Iamblichus 378–79
Ides of March, the 18, 19
Illyrian Emperors 305
inscriptions 364–65
insulae (multi-storey apartments) 92
interment 254, **254–55**
Irenaeus 394
Isiac festivities 84

Jerome 384
Jewish revolts 221, 230, 238–39
    Vespasian and the 154, 158–60, **160**
Josephus, Flavius 85, 112, 159, 160, 185
Jovian, Emperor 332, 394
Julia Domna 293
Julia Drusilla 81–82
Julia Flavia **173**, 199
Julia Maesa 294
Julian, Emperor **325**, 330–32, **331**, 379, 391–94
Julianus, Salvius 232
Julius Caesar, Emperor
    assassination of 18, 20–22
    building projects 60–61
    and Cleopatra 16
    the conquest of Britannia **98**
    entertainment at the amphitheatre 280–81
    gladiators 282
    naumachia 118
    and Octavian 16–17, 18
    villas and palaces 141–42
Julius Nepos, Emperor 357, 407
Justin Martyr 394
Justinian, Emperor 247
    closes the Neoplatonist School of Athens 385
    and the Ostrogoths 415
    and the Vandals 413
Justinian I, Emperor 319
Juvenal **99**, 185

La Maison Carrée **45**
Lacer, Caius Julius **209**
Laco, Graecinius 74
Laetus, Quintus Aemilius 274, **277**
Lamia, Lucius Aelius 42
Lares Compitales, the cult of the 16
latifundia 363, 366–67
latrines **167**

legions, the 103–9, 130, **132**, 138, 161, 194, 206, 362
    Valeria Victrix Legion **164–65**
    the War on Deserters 273
Lepidus, Marcus Aemilius 20, 21, 26, 81
Leptis Magna, Libya 294, **294–95**
Lex Titia pact 20, 21
Libius Severus, Emperor 356, 407
Licinius, Emperor 322, 323, 324
Licinius II, Emperor 324, 325
Limes Germanicus **194–95**
'Little Peace of the Church' 388, 389
Livia Drusilla 24, **25**, **32**, 48, 49, 51, 53, 63–64, 65–66, 68, **71**, 73–74, **74**, **81**, 89
Livy, Titus 68, 88, 103
Longinus, Gaius Cassius 18, 20, 22
Lucilla Augusta 267, 268
Ludovisi Battle **301**
Lugo, the city of 80 towers 360, **361**

Macrinus, Emperor 294
Macro, Naevius Sutorius 73, 74
Maecenas, Gaius Cilnius 17, 18
Magna Mater 241–42
Magnentius 329
Magnus, Pompeius 100
Maiuri, Amedeo 175
Majorian, Emperor 354–55, 411–12
Manichaeism 310–11, **381**, 381–85
Marcellinus, Ammianus 360
Marcellus, Marcus Claudius 39, 43, 48
Marcian, Emperor 396
Marcionists, the 396
Marcomannic War 253–58
Marcus Aurelius, Emperor **244**, 246, **252**, **326**
    the Avidius Cassius revolt 258–60
    becomes emperor 250
    the besieged fortress 260–61
    charitable works 250
    Column of Marcus Aurelius **250**
    Marcomannic War 253–58
    and the Mysteries of Eleusis 260
    Parthian War **252**, 252–53
    the plague 154
    and Stoicism 250, 252
    the symbology in his relief **260–61**
    timeline 253
    the writings of 252

Mardia, Battle of (316–17 AD) 324
Margus River, Battle of the (285 AD) 306
Marius, General Gaius 106
Mark Anthony **29**
    Battle of Actium (31 BC) 30–31
    Battle of Modena (43 BC) 19–20
    Battle of Philippi (42 BC) 22, **23**
    Cassius Dio on 30
    and Cleopatra 23, 26, 28–29
    eulogy for Julius Caesar 18
    his will 27, 30
    and the *Lex Titia* pact 20, 21
    marriage to Octavia 23
    semblance to Dionysus 35
markets **219**
Maron, Publius Virgil see Virgil
Martial 185, 199
Martius Martinianus, Emperor 324–25
Masada, the conquest of **162–63**
Maternus 273
Mau, August 180
mausoleums
    Castel Sant' Angelo 230, **233**
    Mausoleum of Augustus **52–53**, 53, 79
    Mausoleum of Constantina **325**
    Mausoleum of Galla Placidia, Ravenna 346, **346–47**, 390
Maxentius, Emperor 322, 323
Maximian, Emperor **290**, 306, **307**, 308, 311, 322, 324
Maximinus Daia, Emperor 321, 322, 323
Maximus Thrax, Emperor 298–300
medicine, the practice of **256–57**
Mérida, theatre of **128**
Merovingian dynasty 418–19
Messalina, Valeria 93, 98–100, **99**, 101
migration, into cities 367
Military Anarchy, the 298–305
Milvian Bridge, Battle of the (312 AD) **322–23**, 323, 390
Mithraism 84, 243, 380
Modena, Battle of (43 BC) 19–20
Monasticism 386–97
Monophysitism 380, 394
Mons Graupius, Battle of (84 AD) 195, 196
Mons Seleucus, Battle of (353 AD) 329
morality 38–39, 81, 294, **357**

INDEX

mosaics
- banquet and spectacle **363**
- the baptism of Christ 390
- Ceres harvesting wheat 272, **273**
- chained dog **174**
- Coronation of the Virgin **386**
- death **180**
- fishing scene **259**
- gladiators **282–83**
- hunting scenes 366, **366–67**, **425**
- the Lamb of God **415**
- musicians **180**
- Opus Sectile **192**
- the scribe **376**
- St Martin of Tours **385**
- St Pachomius **394**
- Vandals in battle **415**

Mount Bladen, Battle of (500 AD) 423
Mucianus, Gaius Licinius 135, 138, 155, 156, 159
mummy portraits 373–75
Mylae, Battle of (36 BC) 25
Mysteries of Eleusis 237, **238**, 260
mythology 18, 56–58, 140, 208, 209, **381** *see also* gods and goddesses, Roman

Nabataens, the 313–18
Namatianus, Claudius Rutilius 56
Narcissus, Tiberius Claudius 96, 98, 100
Naulochus, Battle of (36 BC) 25
naumachia 118
Navy, the 105
Neoplatonism 378–80, 385
Nero, Emperor 61, **110**, **202**
- adopted by Claudius 100, 101
- adultery with Poppaea 115–18
- the Armenian dispute 119–20
- army strength 109
- assassination attempt led by Vinicianus 126–27
- becomes emperor 101, 111
- building projects 61, **93**
- Cassius Dio on 122
- and Christianity 202, 387
- commerce and taxes under 114, **114–15**
- commits suicide 131, **131**
- the conspiracy of Calpurnius Piso 122–24
- currency devaluation 113–14
- education 111–12
- executions 118–19
- and the fate of Britannicus 112
- the fire that devastated Rome 122, **122**, 202
- and Galba's revolt 129, 130
- the Judaean revolt 126
- matricide 114–15, **119**
- *naumachia* 118
- rebellion in Britannia 120–21
- the reconstruction of Rome 122, **124–25**
- reforms 112–14
- Seneca on 112
- and Seneca's suicide 125–26
- social re-education programme 121–22, **122**
- Suetonius on 18, 122
- timeline 112
- the unpopularity of 127
- villas and palaces 141, 143–44

Nerva, Emperor 139, 141, 206, **206**, 206–7
Nerva, Marcus Cocceius 69
Nervasos Mountains, Battle of (419 AD) 410
Nestorianism 380, 394
Nicene Creed, the 328, 329
Niger, Pescennius 292
Numerian, Emperor 306

Obelisk of Theosius **335**
oblivion, the punishment of 74–75
Octavian see Augustus, Emperor
Odenathus, Septimius 304, 319
Old St Peter's Basilica, Rome **399**, 399–402
Olybrius, Emperor 356
oratory **368**
Origen of Alexandria 379–80, 394
Ostrogoths, the 334, 336, 342, 348, 349, 352, **355**, 405, 412, 413–15
Otho, Emperor **133**, 133–34, 154
Ovid 18, 58

paintings
- in Pompeii 180–81
- in Rome 181

Palace of Diocletian, Split **311**
palaces *see* villas and palaces

Palatine Hill, Rome **39**, 53, 61, **75–77**, 140, 141, 142, 143, 191, 192–93, **199**, 285
Palatine Towers **371**
Palmyrenes, the 318–19
Panhellenion, the **236–37**, 237–38
panhellic games 127
Pantheon, the **45**, 59, 59, 230, **232–33**
Parthian War 219–21, **252**, 252–53
Paterculus 72
Paternus, Tarrutenius 268
Paul the Apostle 380
Paulinus, Gaius Suetonius 94
Paullus, Aemilius 20
pay and benefits, legions 107
Perennis, Tigidius 268
Pertinax, Emperor 292
Perusia, Battle of (40 BC) 22
Petra, city of the Nabataeans 313, 314–18, **315**, **316–17**
Petronius Maximus, Emperor 354, 411
Petronius, Titus 126
Philip the Arab, Emperor 300–301
Philippi, Battle of (42 BC) 22, **23**
Piazza Navona, Rome **186**, 190, 283
Pietroasele Treasure **404**, **420**, **421**
Piso, Gaius Calpurnius 122–24, 125
Piso, Gnaeus Calpurnius 68
Plague of Cyprian 371
plague, the
- Antonine Plague 371
- Black Death 154, 272
- Plague of Cyprian 371

Platonism 377–78
Plautus, Rubellius 112, 115, 119
Pliny the Elder 125, 167, 175, 180
Pliny the Younger 91, 175, 185, 186, 202, 208, 214
Plotinus 378, **378–79**
Plutarch 103, 112, 132, 138
Plutei Traiani, the **216–17**
Pneumatomachians 394
poetry 18, 24, **99**, 185, 199, 208
Pompeianus, Tiberius Claudius 268
Pompeii, destruction of (79 AD) 44, **116**, **117**, **141**, 142, **144**, 172, 174–81
Pompey, Sextus 20, 21, 23, 24–26
Poppaea Sabina 115–18
population, decline of 367–68, 370
Porphyra 378

444

Portus Augusti, Ostia 96–97, **96–97**
Postumus, Agrippa 50, 64
Praetorian Guard, the 38, 72, 78, **78**, 156, 160, 194, 198, 206, 292, 294–95, 360
Primus, Marcus Antonius 138, 139, 155, 156, 159
Priscus, Neratius 223
Priscus, Titus Julius 138
Probus, Emperor 305
Proclus 379
Proculus, Lucius Aradius Valerius 366
Proculus, Quintus Popmonius **38**
Propertius 18
prostitution 39, 176, 178
protection rackets 362
Pseudo-Dionysus the Areopagite 379
public latrines **167**
public migration 367
public morality 38–39
Pupienus, Emperor 300

Quietus, Lusius 223, 224
Quintianus, Claudius Pompeianus 267
Quintillus, Emperor 305

Ravenna, the early Church in 390
Regulus, Emilius 85
Regulus, Publius Memmius 74
religions and philosophy *see also* gods and goddesses, Roman; mythology
    Adoptionism 380, 394
    Apollinarians 394
    Arianism 329, 380, 396, 411, 412, 413
    Christianity 200–203, 241, 310, 311, 316, 324, 329–30, 331, 332, **332**, 337, **355**, 356, **375**, 377–81, **381**, 385, **385**, **386**, 387–404, 418, 423
    the Coptic Church 396
    Cult of Cybele 241–42, 380
    Cult of Isis 242–43
    Cult of the Lares Compitales 16
    Docetism 380, 394
    the Donatists 328, 396
    Epicureanism 377
    Gnosticism 380–84
    Judaism 154, 158–60, **160**, 221, 230, 238–39
    Manichaeism 310–11, **381**, 381–85
    the Marcionists 396
    Mithraism 84, 243, 380
    Monasticism 386–97
    Monophysitism 380, 394
    Neoplatonism 378–80, 385
    Nestorianism 380, 394
    Platonism 377–78
    Pneumatomachians 394
    Stoicism 377
religious reform 35–36
Resaena, Battle of (243 AD) 300
Rimini, Battle of (432 AD) 351
Roman army *see* legions, the
Roman Empire, maps of 1**2–13**, **150–51**, **212–13**, **288–89**, **336–37**
Roman Navy 105
Roman Theatre of Orange, Vacluse, France **10**
Roman Tripolitania, the **259**
Rome, the foundation and development of 55–61
Romulus Augustulus, Emperor **354**, 357
Romulus, the legend of 56–58, 140
Rufus, Faenius 119, 124
Rufus, Lucius Verginius 130

Sabinus, Cornelius 85
Sabinus, Nymphidius 131, 132
Sabinus, Titus Flavius 97, 153, 156, 158, **173**, 198
Saccas, Ammonius 378
sack of Rome, the 344, **344–45**, 345, 356
Salinator, Pedanius Fuscus 245
San Vitale, Basilica of 390, 415
Sanctuary of Demeter, Eleusis **238**
Saoterus 268
sarcophagi 378, 378–79
    Portonacchio Sarcophagus 254, **254–55**
    Sarcophagus of Junius Bassus 392–93, **392–93**
Saturninus, Antonius 196, 198, 210
Satyricon, the 126
Save, Battle of the (388 AD) 336
Saxa, Lucius Decidius 21
Scribonianus, Lucius Arruntius Camillus 100
seals 71
Second Triumvirate, the 20–21

Sejanus, Lucius Aelius 65, 66, 69, 72–73, 74, 75
Semi-Arianism Creed, the 329, 391
Seneca, Lucius Annaeus 88, 92, 112, **113**, 124, 125–26
Senecio, Quintus Sosius 207, 324
Septimus Severus, Emperor 109, 269, 292–93, **293**, 294, **294–95**, 296, 321, 322, 360
Servianus, Lucius Julius Ursus 207, 245
Severan Dynasty, timeline 292–98
Severus, Sextus Julius 239
Shapur I 300–301, **300–301**, 304
ships, Roman 105
shops
    in Pompeii 177, **270**
    in Rome 270, **271**
Sicarii, the 162
Siculus, Diodorus 313
Siege of Veii (406 BC) 107
siege towers 106
Silanus, Gaius Appius 98
Silanus, Lucius 100
Sixtus III, Pope 403
social mobility 359–62
society, in cities 367–70
sports facilities
    in Pompeii 177
    in Rome 283
St Augustine of Hippo 384–85
St Macarius 396–97
St Martin of Tours **385**
St Pachomius **394**, 397
St Patrick 423
St Paul's Basilica, Rome **403**
stadiums 283
    Circus Maximus 285, 285, 366, **366–67**
    Stadium of Aphrodisias **189**
    Stadium of Domitian 61
statuary, in villas 145, **236**
Stephanus 198–99
Stilichio, Flavius 340–44
Stoicism 377
stolas 80, **81**
Strabo 58, 60, 96, 315
Suebi, the 44, 348, 349, 352, 406, 407, 408–11, 412
Suetonius
    on Agrippa Postumus 50
    on Augustus 16–17, 22, 142
    on Caligula 80, 84
    on Christianity 202

INDEX

on Claudius 88, 89, 96, 101
on Domitian 185, 186, 198
on Gnaeus Domitus Ahenobarbus 93
on Nero 18, 122
prophesy 15
on Tiberius 63, 73, 78
on Titus 169–72
on Vespasian **156**, **167**
on Vitellius **155**
Sulla, Cornelius 112, 119
Sura, Lucius Licinius 207
surgical instruments **257**
symbols **50**, 52, **89**, **91**, 260, **260–61**

Tacitus 45–48, 138
    on Agrippina the Younger 115
    on the Battle of Bedriacum (69 AD) 106
    on Caligula 80
    on Christianity 202
    on the civil wars 166
    on Claudius 92, 118
    on Domitian 185–86
    on Drusus 73
    on Germanicus 68
    on Lucius Aelius Sejanus 66
    on Nerva 207
    on the rebuilding of Rome 122
    on the rule of emperors 269
    on the state of the army 135
    on Tiberius 64, 66, 78
Tacitus, Emperor 305
Tapae, Battle of (88 AD) 196
Taurus, Titus Statilius 101
temples of the emperors 91
    Temple of Antoninus and Faustina **247**
    Temple of Apollo, Pompeii **175**
    Temple of Augustus and Livia, Vienne, France **74**
    Temple of Hadrian, Ephesus **229**
    Temple of Janes, Rome 39
    Temple of Jupiter Capitolinus 166, 172
    Temple of Jupiter, Pompeii 177
    Temple of Peace 166
    Temple of the Apollo Palatinus 68
    Temple of Venus Genetrix 19, **19**, 55, 218
    Temple of Venus, Pompeii 177, 178
Templum Pacis 58
Tertullian 272, 394

tetrarchy, the **290**, **306**, 306–11, 321–23
    timeline 324
Teutoburg Forest, Battle of the (9 AD) 50–52
theatres see amphitheatres
Theodosian Wall, Constantinople 340, **341**
Theodosius II, Emperor 348, 349
Theodosius the Great, Emperor 332–33, **335**, 336–37
    and Christianity 202, 394
    the outlawing of cults 380
Theogenes 18
Tiberius, Emperor 40, 62, 65, 70
    adopted by Augustus 48–50
    Alpine conflict 44
    becomes Emperor 63
    building projects 61
    Cassius Dio on 78
    the conquer of Palmyra 318
    death of 78
    and the Eastern cults 84
    foreign policy 66–68
    in Germania 50–52
    and Germanicus 66, 67–68
    the murder of Agrippa Postumus 64
    names Caligula his heir 74, 78
    political persecutions under 73
    and the Praetorian Guard 78
    refusal to accept honours 65
    rejection of idolatry 91
    retreat to Capri 68–69, **72–73**
    and Sejanus 72–73, 74
    Suetonius on 63, 73, 78
    supports a civil Principate 64–65
    Tacitus on 64, 66, 78
    timeline 64
    Villa of Tiberius **147**
Tigellinus, Offonius 119
timelines
    Antoninus Pius 246
    Augustus (Octavian) 16
    barbarian kingdoms 406
    Caligula 79
    Claudius 89
    Commodus 264
    Constantine the Great 328
    conversion to Christianity 388
    Domitian 184
    the fall of the Roman Empire 352

    Fayum mummy portraits 373
    Hadrian 224
    the house of Theodosius 337
    the Illyrian emperors 305
    the Kingdom of the Nabataens 313
    the last emperors of the West 340
    the legions 103
    Marcus Aurelius 253
    milestones of the second tetrarchy 324
    Nero 112
    Nerva 206
    Princes of the Military Anarchy 298
    rise of the Merovingian kings 418
    the Severan Dynasty 292–98
    Suebi, Vandals and Alans in Spain 411
    Tiberius 64
    Titus 169
    Valentinian dynasty 333
    Vespasian 154
    the year of the four emperors 130
Timesitheus 300
Timgad, Algeria **215**
Titus, Emperor 118
    appointed consul 139
    becomes emperor 169–72
    and Berenice of Cilicia 169–72
    Cassius Dio on 172, 173
    death of 173
    entertainment at the amphitheatre 281
    the eruption of Vesuvius 172
    fire in Rome 172
    the Jewish Revolt 139, 158, 159, 160, **160**, **161**, **168**
    the Judean revolt 126
    preparation for leadership 168–69
    public works 172–73
    Suetonius on 169–72
    timeline 169
togas **34**, 80, **81**, **92**, **117**, 236
Tolerance Edict, the 331
trade 270–71, 368
    caravan trade 314–15, 318
    Edict of Maximum Prices 309–10
    the Nabataens and 313, 314, **314**, 315
    in Palmyra 318
Traianus, Marcus Uplius 164
Trajan, Emperor 91, 109, 118, 139, **201**, **210**, **326**
    the adoption of Hadrian 223–24

becomes emperor 207–8
building projects **209**, 212, 214, **214**, 215, 218, **219**, 220, **413**
Cassius Dio on 209, 218, 220
charitable services 207, 208–9, 218
and Christianity 202
the Dacian Wars 210–14, **220–21**
death of 221
early life 209–10
entertainment at the amphitheatre 281
his empire **212–13**
his government 214–19
named as successor to Nerva 206–7
named Optimus Princeps 208
the Parthian War 219–21
respect for the Senate 208
Trajan's Column **211**, 213, 218, **220–21**
Trajan's Market **219**
Transitional Forum 206, **207**
Trastevere, Basilica of **386**
Triclinium, Herculaneum **116**
Troy, the legend of 56–58
Tullius, Servius 103
tunics 80, **81**
Turino, Gaius Octavio 15–16
Turino, Gaius Octavio Cepia *see* Augustus, Emperor
Tzirallum, Battle of (313 AD) 324

uniforms, legions 103, 104, **132**
Urbicus, Lollius 250
urine tax 166, **167**

Valens, Emperor 332–35, **333**, 394
Valentinian I, Emperor 332–34, **333**, 394
Valentinian II, Emperor 334, 336, 337, 380, 394
Valentinian III, Emperor
    and Atilla the Hun 350
    becomes emperor 348–49
    death of 354
    Galla Placidia as regent to 349–51
    the rise of Aetius 351–52
    and the Vandals 411
Valeria Victrix Legion **164–65**
Valerian, Emperor 300, **300–301**, 304, 310, 388
Valle, Pietro della 374

Vandals, the 294, 305, 342, 348, 349, 350, 352, 354–55, 356, 367, 405, 408, 410, 411–13, **413**, 414
Varro, Marcus Terentius 39
Vatican, the **391**
Vegetius, Flavius 108
Velleius 50
Verona, Battle of (312 AD) 362, **362**
Verus, Lucius 246, 250, 252–53, 255, 260, **267**
Vespasian, Emperor 69, **133**, 135–39, **152**, **156**
    the Batavian insurrection 156–58, **157**
    the Battle of Bedriacum (69 AD) 155–56
    and Britannia 97, 154, 161
    building projects 58, 166, **168**
    and Caligula 154
    Cassius Dio on **167**
    consolidation of the state 165–66
    early life 153–54
    economic reform 166–67, **167**
    and the Jewish Revolt 154, 158–60, **160**
    legitimization of powers 164–65
    reconstructing the borders 160–64
    rise to power 154–56
    social reform 167–68
    Suetonius on **156**, **167**
    timeline 154
Vespasian, Flavius 126
Vespasianus, Titus Flavius *see* Vespasian, Emperor
Vestal Virgins 40, 100, **190**, 294, 335, 337
Vesuvius, eruption of (79 AD) 172, 174–81
Vibia Sabina 224
Victorious Sixth Legion 130
villas and palaces 140–47, **227**
    Domus Aurea 122, **124–25**, 143, **168**
    Domus Flavia **192–93**, **199**
    El Djem, Tunisia **363**
    Palace of Diocletian, Split **311**
    Villa del Casale, Sicily **425**
    Villa of Tiberius **147**
    Villa Romana del Casale, Sicily 366, **366–67**

Vindex, Gaius Julius 129, 130
Vinicianus, Lucius Annius 85, 100, 126
Vipsanius, Gaius Julius Caesar 43
Virgil 18, 22, 24
Visigoths, the 340, 341, 344, 345, 348, 349, 350, 352, 353–55, 356, 405, 406–8, **407**, 410, **410**, 412, 414
Vitellius, Emperor 69, 132–38, **133**, 154–55, **155**
Vitruvius 180
Vouillé, Battle of (507 AD) 408, 410, **410**

war chariots **135**
War on Deserters, the 273
war veterans **215**
water supply, Rome 60
weapons, legions 104, 106, **107**
wheat, the production and distribution of 272, **273**
wine 116–17

INDEX

Photographs

Age FotoStock: 6 top, 7, 21, 26-27, 36, 38, 46-47, 54, 67, 95, 99 left, 102, 103, 114-115, 124, 128, 136-137, 138, 140-141, 143 top, 146-147, 148, 160, 168, 169, 174, 182, 186, 187, 194 top, 199, 200-201, 200, 203 top, 208, 209, 210, 211 top and middle, 214, 215, 219, 225 top, 229 both images, 231, 94-95, 237, 238, 244, 250, 251, 253, 256-257, 257 all images, 280, 285, 286, 294, 304-305, 311, 318-319, 321, 322, 335, 338, 349, 354-355, 363, 364-365, 364, 368, 369, 370, 371 both images, 372, 375, 378, 384, 386, 400-401, 402, 403, 404, 405, 413, 416-417, 420; **aisa:** 40-41 top, 43, 50 main image, 118, 126, 256, 265, 321, 411, 415; **Alamy/Aci online:** 26, 34, 35, 60 bottom, 68, 75, 80 top right, 81 middle, 86, 91, 110, 117 top and middle, 121, 129, 132 bottom, 133 right, 143 bottom, 207, 422; **Album:** 15, 173, 183, 211 bottom, 220-221, 223, 230, 249, 266, 271 top and bottom, 273, 298, 300-301, 302-303, 307 top, 327 top, 358, 359, 383, 408, 421; **Album/AKG-Images:** 18, 20, 22, 37, 39, 85, 90, 92, 108-109, 111, 120, 124-125, 130-131, 140, 142-143, 156, 158, 159, 159, 162, 163, 176 bottom, 177 top right and bottom, 188, 191, 192, 193, 194 left, 202, 204, 218, 232-233, 260, 261 both images, 263, 272, 277, 280-281, 307 bottom middle and right, 322-323, 326-327, 327 bottom, 339, 362, 381, 392, 394; **Album/Oronoz:** 17, 22-23, 30, 113, 133 left, 164 bottom, 271 middle, 295, 300, 307 top, 309, 329, 330, 409; **Araldo de Luca:** 132 top, 166; **Bridgeman/index:** 14, 28-29, 66, 239, 276, 326, 331, 344-345, 357, 375 top middle, 391, 395, 414; **Corbis:** 6 bottom, 48, 55, 74, 80 left, 88, 93, 144, 155 top, 162, 163, 164 top, 167, 175, 177 top left, 180 left, 189, 222, 240, 242, 246, 247, 248, 258, 259, 262, 279, 282-283, 296, 310, 312, 315, 316-317, 327 middle and second from bottom; **Fototeca 9x12:** 59, 139, 152, 179 top; **Getty Images:** 5, 170-171, 205, 225 bottom, 361; **Gtres/hemis.fr:** 10, 19, 45, 82-83, 174, 175, 178, 179 bottom, 181, 299, 328, 396-397; **Erich Lessing/album:** 24, 25, 33, 42, 44, 70-71, 71, 72, 76-77, 78, 80 top left, 89, 94, 104, 106, 116-117, 127, 157, 158, 180 right, 267, 270-271, 274, 291, 297, 323, 324, 325, 342, 346-347, 346, 356, 380, 385, 387, 396, 423; **iStockphoto:** 232; **James I. Stanfield/NGS:** 62; **Manuel Cohen/The art archive:** 278; **Photo Scala, Florence:** 8, 32, 40, 60 top, 63, 69, 72-73, 87, 90-91, 100, 116, 117 bottom, 123, 147, 176 top, 184-185, 192, 193, 203 bottom, 216-217 both images, 227, 228, 236, 241, 243, 254-255, 269, 275, 284 all images, 290, 292-293, 332, 333, 333, 341, 350, 366-367, 373, 375 top right, bottom left and middle, 376, 377, 379, 382, 382-383, 390, 392-393, 398-399, 419, 420, 421; **RMN (musée d'orsay)/hervé lewandowski:** 64-65; **The art archive:** 28, 29 top, 49, 50, 51 bottom, 52-53, 58, 79, 81 left and right, 82, 99 right, 101, 104, 107, 119, 122, 153, 155 bottom, 172, 176 middle, 197 both pics, 206, 211 left, 212, 213, 220 left, 226, 245, 252, 270, 306, 313, 336, 343, 347, 360, 365 top and bottom, 374, 398; **Werner Forman archive/Gtres:** 29 bottom, 84, 161

Drawings: MB Creativitat: 294-295, 296-297, 318 **Gabriel Martín:** 105b, 164-165; **Archivo White Star:** 40-41 bottom, 56-57

Feathers: Alejandra Villanueva.

Cartography: Víctor Hurtado (documentación), merche hernández, eosgis.